Public Economics

OTHER INTERNATIONAL ECONOMIC ASSOCIATION PUBLICATIONS

Public Economics

An Analysis of Public Production and
Consumption and their Relations
to the Private Sectors

Proceedings of a Conference held by the
International Economic Association

EDITED BY J. MARGOLIS AND H. GUITTON

MACMILLAN · London · Melbourne · Toronto
ST MARTIN'S PRESS · New York
1969

© *The International Economic Association 1969*

Published by
MACMILLAN AND CO LTD
Little Essex Street London WC2
and also at Bombay Calcutta and Madras
Macmillan South Africa (Publishers) Pty Ltd Johannesburg
The Macmillan Company of Australia Pty Ltd Melbourne
The Macmillan Company of Canada Ltd Toronto
St Martin's Press Inc New York
Gill and Macmillan Ltd Dublin

Library of Congress catalog card no. 70-84182

Printed in Great Britain by
R. & R. CLARK LTD
Edinburgh

Contents

274452

Acknowledgements

The Conference of the International Economic Association that is recorded in this volume was held jointly and in collaboration with the French 'Centre National de la Recherche Scientifique'. The Centre made itself responsible for that part of the Conference which was concerned with 'Analysis of the Public Economy'; the Association for 'The Public Economy and its Relation to the Private Sector'.

The principal debt of the Association is, as always, to those who planned the work of the Conference and who have edited its proceedings, and especially to Julius Margolis, as chairman of the programme committee of the International Economic Association, and to Professor Henri Guitton who was responsible for that part of the work which was sponsored by the Centre. Our debt is also great to Michael Posner, who acted as rapporteur and who has produced the record of the discussion, despite a load of work that neither he nor we could foresee at the time of the Conference. In this task he received very valuable help from Henri Tulkens. We are, it need hardly be said, very deeply indebted to those who wrote the papers of the Conference and took a major part in the discussions which we here record. Our readers will be the best judges of the remarkable quality and originality of many of the papers printed here.

We wish, as always, to express our gratitude to the Social Sciences Division of UNESCO and to the Ford Foundation for the financial and moral support which they have given to the Association; without it the work of this conference would have been impossible. The Conference owed much of its success to the attractive conditions in which it was held in the Hotel Regina at Biarritz; to the management and staff of the hotel we would like to record our thanks.

List of Participants

Professor A. Barrère, Université de Paris, France.
Professor P. Bauchet, Ecole Nationale d'Administration, Paris, France.
Professor H. P. Chenery, Center for International Affairs, Cambridge, Massachusetts, U.S.A.
Professor D. Delivanis, University of Thessalonika, Greece.
Professor R. Dorfman, University of Berkeley, California, U.S.A.
Professor L. Fauvel, I.E.A., Paris, France.
Professor V. P. Gloushkov, Association of Soviet Economic Scientific Institutions, Moscow.
Professor H. Guitton, Université de Paris, France.
Mr. P. D. Henderson, Ministry of Aviation, U.K.
Professor F. J. Herschel, University of Buenos Aires, Argentine.
Professor J. R. Houssiaux, Université de Nancy, France.
Professor E. James, Université de Paris, France.
Professor R. Jochimsen, University of Kiel, Germany.
Mr. D. Joesoef, Paris, France.
Mr. S. Ch. Kolm, Paris, France.
Professor E. Lipinski, University of Warsaw, Poland.
Professor E. Lundberg, University of Stockholm, Sweden.
Professor E. Malinvaud, Institut National de la Statistique et des Etudes Economiques, Paris, France.
Professor S. A. Marglin, Harvard University, Cambridge, Massachusetts, U.S.A.
Professor J. Margolis, Institute of Engineering-Economic Systems, Stanford University, California, U.S.A.
Professor R. Mossé, Université de Grenoble, France.
Professor R. A. Musgrave, Harvard University, Cambridge, Massachusetts, U.S.A.
Professor F. Neumark, University of Frankfurt-am-Main, Germany.
Professor G. U. Papi, University of Rome, Italy.
Dr. W. Pendleton, Ford Foundation, New York, U.S.A.
Professor M. H. Peston, Queen Mary College, London, U.K.
Professor K. N. Plotnikov, Association of Soviet Economic Scientific Institutions, Moscow, U.S.S.R.
Professor A. Pokrovski, U.S.S.R. Academy of Sciences, Moscow, U.S.S.R.
Mr. M. V. Posner, Pembroke College, Cambridge, U.K.
Professor W. Prest, University of Melbourne, Australia.
Professor E. A. G. Robinson, University of Cambridge, U.K.
Professor P. A. Samuelson, Massachusetts Institute of Technology, Cambridge, Massachusetts, U.S.A.
Professor J. Sandee, Nederlandse Economische Hogeschool, Rotterdam, Netherlands.
Mr. K. Schmidt-Luders, Directeur de l'Industrie et de l'Energie, OECD, Paris, France.
Professor A. K. Sen, Delhi School of Economics, India.
Professor N. V. Sovani, U.N. Research Institute for Social Development, Geneva, Switzerland.
Mr. L. Stoleru, Commissariat Général du Plan, Paris, France.
Mr. M. Tardos, Institute for Market Research, Budapest, Hungary.
Mr. J. Terny, CEPREL, Arcueil (Seine), France.

Mr. H. Tulkens, Center for Operations Research and Econometrics, Heverlee, Belgium.
Mr. R. Turvey, The Electricity Council, London, U.K.
Mr. Z. H. van de Pas, Netherlands Central Planning Bureau, The Hague, Holland.
Professor L. Westphal, Harvard University, Cambridge, Massachusetts, U.S.A.
Professor S. P. Wickham, Université de Lyon, France.
Professor J. G. Zielinski, Central School of Planning and Statistics, Warsaw, Poland.

Introduction

Julius Margolis

It was fitting that the Conference on the Analysis of the Public Sector be held in France where there existed a tradition of economic analysis for public works planning and a remarkable renaissance of analysis in many branches of the public services. The French experiences are being duplicated in many nations of the world as increasing recognition has been given to the value of economic concepts and models to guide the operations of government. The authors and discussants came from many countries, with widely differing traditions of government, but the common scientific language of economics permitted a meaningful discussion of the problems of public services. Unfortunately, there was no unanimity about appropriate concepts and solutions, but despite the differences in viewpoint among members of the Conference, there were advances in our understanding of the problems at the level of theory and of practice; advances recognised by all.

The central theme of the Conference, the economic analysis of the public sector, is an ancient concern of economists but now going through a transformation. The study of public finance and public regulation of industry has firm roots in the nineteenth century; planning was born in the twentieth century and became a major field before the mid-century mark; but the scientific analysis of the behaviour of governments dates only from World War II. Despite the youth of the field, the work is vigorous. The papers in this volume attest to the high order of analytical rigour and the advances in policy analysis which have been made; they also indicate the great gaps in knowledge which we have.

Though these papers are restricted to a discussion of governments, they illustrate the recent application of economic analysis to the study of all of social behaviour. Economic science was shaped by efforts to explain the production and distribution of marketable goods, but the analytical tools have found additional use in the study of many aspects of social behaviour. The system of economic analysis is one way of viewing any aspect of society; the concepts of economic analysis have value wherever it is appropriate to assume purposive behaviour. It is true that market behaviour is most amenable to the economists' tools, however private consumption and investment outside the market, and public consumption and investment can also be illuminated. The application of economic analysis to social and public policy and programmes is not simple, but then if it were simple it would not be interesting.

1

The papers fell into four major categories. Papers of the first set were distinguished by their successful extension of economic theory to the analysis of the public sector of the economy. The problems they dealt with have plagued the economic theorist, but they have created equal difficulties for the applied analyst as well. The four papers of the second set were concerned with the pricing and investment behaviour of public enterprises, as well as the rules that they could adopt for efficient operations. The third set placed the previously discussed economic issues in the context of public administration, since political, budgetary and administrative controls will constrain the actions of a public enterprise. The final set of papers placed the discussion of public enterprise in the broader context of stabilisation programming, the mix of activities in non-socialist economies, and recent developments in the Soviet economy.

The most successful set of papers dealt with economic theory. Unfortunately, the theorist is still outpacing the applied analyst. Much attention was given to the recent developments in the theory of public goods. Since these goods cannot be individually packaged, it is extremely difficult to establish a procedure by which to value them on the basis of individualistic evaluations, or to design a procedure by which the government could be led to supply the optimal amount of these services. The papers explored the sources of these difficulties and the possibilities of decision-making procedures to overcome them, especially in cases where goods could be characterised as a mixture of public and private. Though our understanding of the problem and possible solutions was extended, it was clear that much more work would be necessary before operational solutions would be available.

The other major topic discussed in several of the papers was the derivation of a rule for optimality for economic organisation. Recognising the inadequacy of the traditional Pareto criteria, several papers explored the addition of other considerations which would enable one to judge distributional aspects and therefore satisfy equity as well as efficiency conditions. Two specific issues were dealt with in detail – the evaluation of risk in optimal resource allocation, and the problems of information and control in a decentralised economy. The former topic has been neglected by theorists, while the latter is of pressing concern to those responsible for planning economic ministries.

The papers on pricing and investment behaviour and criteria provided a very informative, critical survey of both practices and principles. Though many analytical and practical problems persist, it is clear that great advances have been made over the last two decades. The advocacy of simple rules, such as marginal cost pricing, have given place to more sophisticated treatment of the many complexities, among them self-financing constraints, highly variable demands, social goals and so on. Investment criteria which were simple analogies from business have incorporated social criteria, budgetary constraints, informal limitations and so on. The differences about best rules that were revealed by the discussants were small relative to the consensus about the major developments in analysis.

The next series, on government organisation and behaviour of public enterprises, was less satisfactory from the perspective of firm knowledge. Clearly, the peculiar political and administrative conditions of public enterprise seriously affect the patterns of production and the types of optimal rules that could be adopted. The papers were rich in hypotheses and interpretation, and though they contained some analytical models, it was evident that much more theorising was necessary in this area of investigation. The theoretical developments of the first set of papers dealt with rules and with organisational forms, but, unfortunately, the models were not extended to the levels discussed in the third section.

The last series of papers dealt with the relationships among planning, control and the public sector. The particular topics ranged from stability planning to managerial criteria, and the general topics form the appropriate role of the State to comparative models of the behaviour of the public and private sectors. These are issues of enormous complexity, and though they could not be adequately treated in the confines of a part of a programme, the papers and discussion provided a broad frame of reference within which the more narrow considerations of the public sector could be discussed.

2

When we survey the papers and discussion, a division between two types of analytical work becomes apparent: (1) the development of better tools for decision-making by the managers of public enterprises, and (2) the creation of an institutional structure which would constrain the public agencies so that decisions would be better even if managers were not wise or public-spirited. The classification is similar to the division in the private economy between decision-making within the firm and the study of markets and industries. Two papers which represent these two approaches are Stoleru's dealing with pricing and investment criteria and Marglin's analysing optimal decentralisation in the economy. Clearly, it would be an error to draw too sharp a line between rules for an enterprise and the design of an institutional structure since enterprise behaviour is severely constrained by the institutional structure. For instance, an enterprise's actions are limited by the authority given to the top management, the range of alternatives it can consider, its freedom to raise funds and so on. Therefore, in a fundamental sense, a managerial decision is highly dependent on how the government is organised, though it is still useful to separate out the rules for enterprise management from a concern with the organisation of the government.

The interdependency between an agency's decisions and the organisation of the government as a whole points to the impossibility of fully divorcing economic from political analysis. The environment of the agency is set by a host of political considerations which permeate every decision and seriously affect the style of analysis which an agency can adopt. Unfortunately, almost all economic studies of the public sector abstract from political factors, and thereby severely limit the applicability of the studies. This shortcoming is not meant to be a criticism of our authors and their colleagues, after all they are economists and not political scientists. However, the government is a set of politically organised administrative units and therefore market concepts are insufficient to analyse fully government behaviour, but the tools and concepts derived from the study of market behaviour can play a useful role. The shortcomings and the virtues of economic analysis can be seen in the discussions of one topic which is touched upon in many papers – the social objective function or the evaluation of public output.

3

The evaluation of the output of public agencies is discussed in this volume mainly in the guise of the choice of social objective functions – an evaluation rule by which to choose the best set of packages of public outputs. Though it would seem imperative for an agency to have an objective function or to evaluate its outputs, it would be an error to assume that government agencies are active searchers for an objective function. We say this even though every agency must choose among alternative technologies, different mixes of outputs, and different sectors of the public to be served. However, many agencies suppress an explicit consideration of the problem of choice by pretending that their actions are dictated by legislation or executive orders. To economists, the fact that choices are being made is too obvious to be noted, but to administrators it often comes as a surprise. Administrators, once challenged, may be convinced that they can and do seek out alternative ways to perform their functions, but they resist the suggestion that they do choose among outputs. Once an agency overcomes the inertia of tradition and initiates a self-conscious evaluation of what it is doing, it immediately becomes aware of its need for a set of criteria by which to judge its actions. What goals should control their choices? How can these goals be translated to operational measurements? What rules can be set to encourage agencies to optimise or at least to make reasonably satisfactory choices?

The social objective function is a rule to compare the values of varying amounts or qualities of outputs and thereby make likely the choice of the best package of public outputs. The search for operational objective functions has taken two general forms. The approach most common to the literature of economic theory is the aggregation of individual preferences. A less rigorously stated approach, which is found more frequently in practice, is a social ordering expressed by the government.

The distinction between these two approaches can be blurred if one believes that the political process is a mechanism by which individual preferences are aggregated. The distinction becomes strong if one views the political process as a distinctly different form of resource allocation where the motive force is a view of the public interest which may bear little relationship to the aggregation of individual preferences. Dorfman's paper tries to incorporate both views.

The choice of the two views is not solely a scientific issue but is partly dependent upon the attitude one holds of the role of an economist as an adviser to a client and who the client is supposed to be. One group would support the position that the employer, be it a public agency or the political leaders, formulates the goals and the economist assists him in designing an appropriate programme. They would be concerned with values but only to study the best way for the client to formulate his set of objectives so as to achieve his underlying values. In contrast to this view of the economist, as an agent of a decision-maker, an alternative view holds that the appropriate client for the economist is the 'public'.

The economist then seeks his values from scientific principles or from a moral consensus. Implicit in many papers given at the Conference and in the operational techniques invented by economists to evaluate public outputs is the assumption that the economist can formulate the social consensus and it exists as an aggregation of individual valuations as expressed in market or market-like processes. A corollary is the rejection of the legitimacy of an active role of the political process as a formulator of the public interest. The result, which could be anticipated, is a tension between the economic analyst, with his view of the public interest, and the political decision-maker, who does not share the economists' view of the public welfare. The economist, as defender of his view of the public interest, does not only advocate a set of numbers, shadow prices, which he believes should be used to evaluate public outputs, but he also urges changes in the structure of the government so that it is more responsive to the preferences of individuals. Those who accept the authority of administrative officials or political leaders have quite different views of appropriate objective functions, of what numbers should be used to evaluate outputs and of structural changes. We do not mean to imply that the individualistic model has no place for a political decision. All would agree that the government must take a stand on the distribution of income but the individualist model would assign this function to income transfers and then insist that the public output be judged solely on allocational criteria.

The aggregation of individuals' preferences approach can be described in terms which are little more than the extension of the private market. It is assumed that for various technical reasons (spelled out most completely in the Conference papers on the subject of public goods and externalities) that the private market must be supplemented by public production and distribution. The essential character of the government's objective function according to this view is the assignment of value weights which would have been revealed by market behaviour, if there had been some way to overcome the technical limitations which gave rise to public supply and a perfectly competitive market were able to operate. This individualistic view is usually supplemented by a judgement in regard to the distribution of income, a far from trivial departure from individualistic sovereignty. It is this imputation of an imagined market which underlies the measurement procedures adopted in benefits-costs analysis. The measurement rule used to determine the value of a government output is: estimate what the users of the public product would be willing to pay, i.e. the market clearing price. Since the products are distributed at zero prices there are no direct measures by which the prices can be discovered and several indirect processes are relied upon to reveal this price. Let us briefly discuss the two most common approaches.

The most common technique used to evaluate public output is to consider the product as an intermediate good and then to estimate the value of the marginal product of the good in further production. Illustrations are found in natural and human resources development. Some goods are easily and naturally treated in this fashion. For example, most water is used in agriculture, power generation and industrial processing. Productivity studies of irrigated farms provide the information about the value of the product of an incremental acre-foot of water to determine the agricultural value of the water. It is assumed that the farmer would pay this amount as a price for the water and therefore the marginal product is identified as the 'imputed market price', or 'shadow price' of water. There are many problems in properly estimating the value of the marginal product, but these problems are small compared to those which arise when we consider the application of this technique to public outputs like education and health, where the production process is not as easily specified as for water.

For educational outputs, statistical studies have found a correlation between years of schooling and income. Therefore, it is argued that the earning capacity of an individual has been increased by the additional years of schooling. Further, it is said that the individual should be willing to pay that increment of expected income, less his foregone earnings while he is in school, for the educational facilities provided him. In practice, of course, an individual would not be expected to make such a payment, but this is attributed to the immature judgement of a student and his lack of capital. But does this relationship between education and income, even if it could be convincingly established, exhaust the reasons for public education or is it even the dominant factor? Clearly, the government is interested in many consequences beyond the income of the person. For instance, will he be a better and more responsible participant in the political process? Will he be a better neighbour? Will he have developed values and insights which will make him a more effective parent? Many more goals for education have been asserted, but all we want to establish here is that governments will find unsatisfactory a rule for the design of educational facilities, or for the determination of its scale, which is based upon an individual's expected income enhancement.

In the case of health services, a different set of problems develop. Health is much more of a consumer good than education. Health, as an intermediate product, is valued by the additional working time and increased productivity associated with a reduction in disability. A saved life is valued at the present value of the expected income stream it would have earned. (Some would say that it should be net of the consumption of the saved life and therefore it should be the present value of his savings.) Certainly individuals are concerned about the loss of working time, but pain, discomfort and the fear of incapacity and death may be even more of a basis of willingness to pay to avoid illness. If the health programme were designed to maximise benefits measured by income growth, then the diseases of the aged would be ignored and diseases of women would receive relatively little support. Neither individuals nor governments are prepared to accept the enhanced income as a basis for determining the private or social benefits of health.

A second approach to estimate what individuals are willing to pay is based upon the cost savings of the public service, i.e. the costs that individuals would have incurred if the public service were not supplied. This approach is most commonly adopted in the fields of transportation and power. Generally, it is assumed that there is an inelastic demand for the output and therefore the public somehow would have managed to transport the goods or to develop energy though the costs would have been much higher. The major sources of savings are private carrier costs in the case of transportation and private generation of energy in the case of power.

The cost-savings approach to benefits measurement faces two problems : the identification of the alternatives which were saved and the constraints imposed upon policy if user savings are the basis of evaluation. In the case of transportation, the cost savings are realised by shippers and travellers. An improved highway would reduce the travel time and operating costs of travelling between any two points. Presumably the users of the highways would be willing to pay that difference. Similar calculations are not readily available for other public services. The 'savings' in these cases are alternative facilities or programmes which would have been provided by the government. Unfortunately, public agencies are notoriously poor in considering alternatives. For instance, an apprenticeship training programme may be an alternative to vocational training in a school, but the educational ministry is unlikely to consider an inservice programme as an interesting or feasible alternative. Importing goods may be an alternative to agricultural expansion, but this is not likely to be considered. Organisations are not active searchers for information about alternatives they are not likely to pursue. It is also true that many of the most feasible alternatives may be those ruled out by legal or administrative constraints and never even considered. For instance, a change in the tax structure may provide a very different set of incentives for private consumption which would accomplish the same objectives as collective consumption, but it might never be considered by an operating agency. As a consequence, estimates of costs of alternatives which are saved are notoriously bad.

The evaluation of public output in terms of costs-savings by users is based upon an assumption that we are to be guided by the efficiency calculations of the individual beneficiaries of the project. Political and administrative leaders resist the policy conclusions drawn from these studies since they see them as restrictive of their freedom to plan the development of the nation. For instance, the benefits-costs calculations might indicate the most efficient transportation network but efficiency has never been a sufficient criterion for governments in their locational policies. It is possible that governments have erred in trying to support their declining regions, to populate their empty places, or to stem the flow of population to their capitals, but the public support of these programmes has been great. Though economic arguments of external economies and diseconomies have been used to defend these programmes, it is clear that regional objectives have been pursued for their own sakes, with a willingness on the part of the government to sacrifice national income for these benefits.

I have described the individualistic assumptions underlying the benefits-costs evaluations and the objections to them by political leaders. In principle it may be argued that all of the public services are characterised by many widespread externalities so that no simple set of imputed prices can be estimated from observing individual behaviour, but the political process represents a procedure to approximate the summation of individual preferences. (In modern language, the legislative allocations are the revealed preferences of the electorate.) The game of political manœuvre is interpreted as a set of transactions, political bargains, where both parties benefit. Therefore, a statistical analysis of legislative appropriations would solve for those numbers which can be interpreted as the value of public outputs agreed upon by the competing social groups. The attempts to derive such estimates have not met with much success. This is not surprising when we consider how poorly equipped the legislators or top-decision-makers are about the consequences or dimensions of the programmes they control.

There is an alternative formulation of the legislator or administrator as representative of the aggregate of citizens. It is argued that unrestrained political bargaining is not optimal, but that the addition of appropriate information to the decision-making process would lead to Pareto optimal outcomes. The first step of the analyst is to design a quantitative measure of the product of the public output. This is not difficult in the case of most commercial, marketable commodities like food, clothing or machines, but for services like recreation, education or national defence an appropriate unit of output is not obvious. The most common measures refer to use of the service rather than their desired qualities, e.g. years of schooling rather than increased productivity, socialisation and so on. The second step is to estimate the costs of resources necessary to produce the outputs – the costs may be stated in real or financial terms. The above information is equivalent to the marginal rate of transformation between two public services. The decision-maker is then asked to revise the expenditure levels among the public services – the revision, if the authorities are responsive to the public, would be in the direction of equating the marginal rate of substitution in utilities to the marginal rates of transformation in production. The famed systems analysis decision-making process in the U.S. Department of Defense has this structure, but it would be hazardous to associate it with any order of social welfare. A decision-maker who seeks to be most effective will welcome this information-structure, but there is a great gap between the decision-maker's objective function and the social welfare, defined over individual preferences. In practice, this pattern of information for decision-making is more appropriate to the view of a public interest, defined as a social ordering expressed by the government, to which we now turn.

The first seven papers of the Conference accepted the view of the existence of a set of individual preferences relevant to public services. From this perspective the problem of the design of government is to construct a decision-making process which would implement these objectives. The next four papers were not concerned with the source of public objectives, but their analysis of the criteria that should be used in the design of public activities implied the same judgement. The remaining papers dealt with the problems of government from a different perspective; they implied a social view of the public interest, or they treated the government as an independent social body with objectives and rules somewhat independent of evaluations of individuals. This latter approach is common to political scientists, sociologists and applied economists, but rejected by welfare economists. What are the elements of this latter approach, in terms used by the welfare economists who predominate in the first papers?

Two points about individual preference and one about institutions must be made. Many, probably the most important, public services are characterised by a high order of interdependency in the utility functions. I.e. individuals are not indifferent to the amounts of public services consumed by others. Of course, interdependency is not restricted to public services, witness the frequent legislation encouraging or discouraging private consumption of certain goods, but interdependencies are typical of public goods. We care about the use by others of the library, the park, the school and the courts. Unfortunately, there is no straightforward way by which we can aggregate these preferences over individuals. Interdependencies in utilities are nigh impossible to handle in the decentralised private market. Aggregation difficulties worry the theorists but probably they are not the crucial problem.

Individuals are not very knowledgeable about their preference structures for the goods they regularly buy for their own consumption; they are far more ignorant about their preference structures for goods they do not buy and which are consumed by others. Man is an imaginative and charitable animal, but he is limited. It would be more proper to characterise the individual as ignorant of his preference structure in regard to the consumption of others. Under these conditions, widespread interdependencies and ignorance, a government cannot restrict itself to implementing the rudimentary preferences of individuals, instead it will assume the more active role of formulating the public interest. Individual valuations will enter in an imperfect way as the government receives public support or censure.

If we accept the political leadership role of government are we forced to abandon the use of criteria by which to judge the behaviour of government? An economist, who sees no criteria other than individual preferences, would insist that this would be the inevitable consequence – we would be forced to endorse every political act. In his mind, an appeal to 'social goals' is no more than an endorsement of a political legislature or government which has the 'legitimate authority' to impose its will. I am dubious about the narrow conclusion, that we will have no basis to criticise government, but I confess that I share the discomfort of many of our authors who find it difficult to abandon an individualistic base for criteria. But this is the limitation of traditional economic analysis.

The welfare economist has led us to deep understanding (witness the first seven papers); the applied economist has demonstrated the strength of these arguments in evaluating government behaviour (witness the next four papers); but the last papers which grapple with the analysis of government in a less restricted framework are no less significant. Implicit in these papers is a recognition that the government provides leadership, for good or bad, and ensures social stability which may result in subsidies and redistributions at the expense of economic efficiency. Once we concede that this broader framework may be necessary for the analysis of public activities, then it becomes necessary to give rigorous content to these functions. Further, it is necessary to understand better the operating conditions of government, the legislative and administrative processes, which seeks to perform these broader set of functions. Government is not a lifeless institution. It would be too simple to assume that the public personnel seek to maximise objectives identified by a single authority; that there are no internal difficulties of managing the public bodies; that there are no incentives for the personnel to seek diverse and inconsistent objectives. The government is a very complex organisation, and before we assert rules for its adoption we must know far more about the possibilities of its internal management and responsiveness to external influences. In other words, we require a body of theory comparable to the organisation analysis for the private firm and market analysis for industries. The second half of the Conference papers grappled with these problems, but the primitive state of our theory is too apparent. It is hazardous to predict the direction of scientific research, but I will forecast that the next decades of work on public policy analysis will concentrate heavily on the analysis of the structure and behaviour of governments and thereby give more insight to policy formulation and optimal programmes of policy implementation. The economist has begun to assume an important role in top administrative leadership and in time he will begin to conceptualise the operations of government and design innovations to make it more effective and responsive.

1 The Role of the State in Mixed Economies [1]

G. U. Papi

1 CONCEPT OF INDIVIDUAL PLANNING

The compulsion to make a plan and to analyse all the factors it involves is as primeval as the compulsion for man to engage in activities that are guided by reason and projected in time. Whatever the economic regime in force – from the most liberal regime to the collectivist regime, under which the individual still retains a minimum freedom of choice – the plan plays its part as one of the essentials of all action that implicates the future. It is the logical imperative inherent in any undertaking that extends beyond the present, conditioned by the reasoning powers of the individual and the possibilities offered by his milieu.

Every individual has roots embedded in the past and binding him to certain commitments. But he is also constantly attaining a certain liberty which, as it matures, releases him from these past commitments – contracts, controls, obligations of various kinds – while at the same time he finds himself undertaking fresh commitments – fresh contracts, fresh controls, fresh obligations, by virtue of which a more or less considerable portion of the present becomes crystallised and sets the pattern for his future activity. At each instant, each individual, in relation to the milieu in which he operates, disposes of what frees him from the past and of what remains of his current commitments; he allocates these availabilities to consumption or to investments, either present or future (savings), according to the principle of maximum utilisation, aimed at the fullest possible satisfaction of his personal needs.

At the basis of this principle we find the perceptivity of the individual. This at first inclines him towards a position of equilibrium. But immediately afterwards this same perceptivity compels him to examine the possibilities of *prolonging*, or of *improving*, the position he has reached, taking into account changes which may have occurred in his environment, or subjective changes which might upset that position.

The 'plan' can indeed be defined as the projection into a more or less distant future, of a state of maximum satisfaction or of a tendency towards

---

[1] Translated into English by M. C. Lemierre.

maximum satisfaction, in relation to the means that are available. Personal experience, or the experience of other people, can modify the projection according to the forecasts which the individual may make in relation to the milieu in which he lives.

The 'plan' is thus the instrument employed by man's highest faculties in order to attain, consolidate and defend a level of well-being which all kinds of circumstances may tend to enhance or, more frequently, to debase.

2   THE ELEMENTS OF AN INDIVIDUAL PLAN

(A) CONSIDERATION OF MARGINAL UTILITY

From this brief outline it is easy to deduce the constituent elements of a plan. First and foremost comes the consideration of marginal utility. By facilitating the definition of present equilibrium, marginal utility constitutes an essential element in the establishment of a plan, representing the starting point for any concept of equilibrium or trend towards the future achievement of equilibrium.

(B) PROVISION AGAINST THE FUTURE

When the individual frees himself from the commitments binding him to the past and endeavours to foresee the consequences that may ensue from changes in his present position, he is said to be providing against the future which means that he is visualising the future and setting his course so as to attain the goals he has in mind.

(C) DIRECT OR INDIRECT INSURANCE AGAINST FORESEEABLE RISKS

A plan designed to achieve certain aims may eventually become inadequate for this purpose. When we try to look into the future, we perceive it to be full of *risks*. It is these risks which prompt the individual to take measures which will help him to eliminate them. If a plan is to achieve complete fulfilment of its aims, it must keep in very close step with reality and it is therefore necessary to have recourse to a third element which we may call the element of *insurance*. This enables the plan to be adjusted, from the outset and throughout its development, to any changing circumstances.

An estimate of a person's assets – from which his income is derived – at considerably less than their current value, constitutes the most *elementary form of insurance* against these risks at the time of making the forecasts. The plan thereby at once acquires a certain measure of *flexibility*. The risks envisaged are chiefly those of events which can have an adverse effect on income and which can be foreseen when the distribution of the assets is first planned: price increases, currency devaluation, etc.

But, even when a person foresees the future and on certain dates *replaces* the present income, prices, demand and supply by incomes, prices, demand and supply evaluated according to his forecast, the plan still remains vulnerable to the risks of *unfavourable differences* between the reality and his forecasts.

The very limitations of the types of insurance selected serve to emphasise their utility. These types of insurance may be used *once* or a specified *number* of times. They become ineffective once the events they were to cover have occurred. Consequently, when the unfavourable differences between the reality and the forecasts persist for a *longer period* than the insurance measures provided for in the plan, it becomes necessary to adapt the latter to the new conditions of the market and reorganise it on a new basis rather than take out fresh insurances on the old basis.

3 THE FUNCTION OF INDIVIDUAL PLANNING

Without going deeper into the matter it is already possible to make the following observation:

The *consumer* draws up a plan of consumption in order to be more sure of *benefiting* on predetermined dates of the income available to him. This income ultimately consists of consumer goods. The plan serves to protect it against certain possibilities of reduction or to ensure its regular time-phasing.

The *producer* establishes a plan in order to obtain an income with the help of various factors which can combine in different ways as time goes on. It might be possible to do without a consumption plan but not without a production plan, even if it is only a rudimentary one. In order to facilitate examination of the plan it may be split up into two parts – the *cost* plan and the *price* plan. The two plans are linked by marginal considerations and both are designed to achieve the same aim, namely to obtain the maximum income for the planner.

The plans designed to *produce* an income involve consequences of *much vaster scope* than that of the consumption plans. They consequently ensure much greater *regularity* first and foremost for the income of the entrepreneur, secondly for the incomes of all his collaboration and lastly for the consumption of all these individuals. They ensure greater *stability* for the whole economic system, in which each individual has a share of activity projected into the future.

By the insurance it provides against general risks and against risks deriving from those same unfavourable differences between the reality and the forecasts, any consumer or producer plan eliminates the even greater and more objective risk of individual actions being throttled by events that may restrain the inclinations of the individual and finally his *liberty* to satisfy them within the framework of a collectivity. Consequently, the more the complexity of modern life gives rise to events likely to take the individual away from the activity that would correspond most closely to his inclinations and his capabilities, the greater the importance which the plan assumes in its role as defender of the activity, personality and liberty of the individual. Economic planning – rational planning – does not run counter to freedom but on the contrary serves to guarantee it.

4   INFERIORITY, FROM THE ECONOMIC ANGLE, OF STATE OR PUBLIC ADMINISTRATION PLANNING

Not only do the public administrations practise planning on a much vaster scale but they also programme interventions directed at specific categories of individuals.

To obtain a clear picture of the position we must consider whether, in the plan of a public administration – production plan, financing plan, e.g. the budget of a particular State – we find evidence of the principles of marginal utility, provision against the future, insurance, close adherence to the conditions of the market, all of which are logical pre-requisites for the concept of 'economic planning'. The answer is important, since the realities with which the plans of the public administrations have to contend are just as full of surprises as those with which private planning has to reckon; and private planning, it must not be forgotten, always constitutes the *prior condition* for planning by the public authorites. Payment of taxes or subscriptions to loans can only be demanded from individuals who are capable of producing an income and who, more or less consciously, make plans to this end.

Planning by the public authorities is only desirable if, with specific aims in view, it *alleviates* a situation. It is not desirable if it produces a *permanent aggravation* of the position. State action may sometimes be better than private or small-groups action, but it must first be proved that it is guided by rational planning that will be of some real use to the community.

5 THE FUNCTION OF STATE PLANNING

From the economic point of view the producers of the State lie under a disadvantage in relation to those of the private sector – consumers and producers – where planning is becoming increasingly widespread. Numbers of writers have drawn attention to this disadvantage, which appears to be due, in the first place, to the fact that the public administrations, when establishing their plan for intervention, do not abide strictly by the economic principle, do not effect their calculations on the basis of the essential elements of all planning, namely marginal utility, provision against the future, insurance against certain risks, adherence to market conditions.

This inferiority is due more particularly to the obstacles raised by the difficulty of making the necessary practical calculations for the elements of a plan. For instance, there is the difficulty of calculating the risks of a social phenomenon such as a strike or a lock-out of which the extent cannot be known, when the State is drawing up its plan. Another example is the difficulty of calculating the insurance against the risk of the State budget failing to work out as anticipated. This form of insurance has been ignored in the past for the simple reason that, if the State has made a miscalculation, it could always fall back on taxes or on loans. But measures of this kind usually only serve to aggravate the situation. Hence the need to provide beforehand for possible remedies.

A subjective obstacle may consist, for example, in the difficulty of comparing, in terms of marginal utility, actions commanded by aims between which a choice has to be made: increase of armaments, better administration of justice, long-term supplies, intensification of public works in order to valorise the national territory. To which should preference be given? What should the time-phasing be? The choice thus involved is a non-economic one.

The inferiority of State planning may also be attributed to the fact that its interventions are numerous and often prompted by conflicting interests. One intervention may very well *contradict* another and neutralise its effect.

This may give rise to a new element of cost 'deficit' in relation to the result of the intervention. It might even be said that a new element consisting in the introduction of less rational directives – contrary to the *economic* principles – is found to be incorporated in all State activity. In putting one of its plans into effect, the State may, indeed, have to contend with obstacles created by its own activities.

Hence the necessity that not only should the cost of any State interventions compare favourably with its result but also that such intervention should avoid neutralising in any way other simultaneous or
programmed interventions; that is to say, it should avoid counteracting
any other aims which the State is pursuing.

The significance of State planning thus becomes clearer: it emerges as
the instrument available to the statesman bringing his highest faculties to
bear on promoting the development of the total of incomes, of savings and
of the national heritage. It should eliminate not only any contradictions
between the interventions programmed by the public Administrations
but also any contradictions between these interventions and the plans which
producers and consumers in the private sector have drawn up in the hope
that they will not be disrupted by the Administration; and lastly it should
eliminate any contradiction between the plans of the consumers and those
of the producers, endeavouring rather to bring them into harmony.

The more the economic principle can predominate in the preparation
and revision of public plans, the greater the development of the productive
factors, the greater the rise in income and the easier it becomes to correlate State intervention with the economy theory, by means of the
concept of planning and its constituent elements.

6 CONCEPT OF REGIONAL PLANNING

By the term 'region' we may understand either a 'group of countries'
showing similar characteristics as regards climate, soil and, to some
extent, their basic institutions; or else a 'part of a country', clearly defined
from the geographical point of view and having characteristics which show
it to be less developed than other parts of the country. 'Regional' planning, or programming, represents the translation into practical terms,
according to the circumstances and characteristics prevailing in the
particular localities, of the main guiding principles of a national plan,
since it is agreed that there must be no conflict or contradiction between the
directives of national planning and the local directives.

Strictly speaking, the concept of regional planning appears to be highly
suitable for economies which are entirely governed by central planning
and where the responsible authorities empower the local authorities to
translate into practical terms the guiding principles of the national plan,
in all the sectors of economic activity. The concept of regional planning
does not emerge as clearly in the so-called 'mixed economies', where the
action of the public bodies proceeds simultaneously with the action and

initiatives of the private sector. In these mixed economies the only feasible type of planning is that of the public authorities since, though it may be necessary to preserve and respect certain individual rights, the activities and the initiatives of the private sector are directly affected by the general economic policy, i.e. by the interventions of the State in the fields of production, distribution, currency, credit, taxation and public expenditure among many others.

In a 'mixed economy' both *national* and *regional* development plans have their justification in the need, common to both forms of planning, to ensure coherency for interventions in the country's economic policy, in relation to the aims which the collectivity wishes to achieve.

Recent experience in Italy shows that the policy of 'extraordinary' (non-recurring) public expenditures and the policy of economic incentives offered to the private sector, in order to encourage the development of the more backward regions of Southern Italy and the islands, have had the effect of making more and more people take steps to qualify for the special advantages offered by the government. This threatened to burden the public finances with too heavy a load and made it essential to 'co-ordinate' local initiatives and regional planning more and more closely with the general principles of public planning.

Every national economic plan includes as one of its chief aims that of reducing the discrepancies found in the rates of development in different parts of the country. The national plan cannot of course fail to analyse the causes of this regional disequilibrium. For each region, therefore, it becomes necessary to enquire first of all into the efficacy of the 'general' and 'special' public services – health, training and education – and to make sure that there are sufficient public works capable of making the geographical and ecological conditions increasingly attractive for subsequent private investment. For each region a study will have to be made of the present situation, using uniform methods that will enable comparisons to be drawn between the various regions and facilitate the co-ordination of the regional developments in the national economic plan. For each region information must be obtained as to the most outstanding needs and as to the possibilities in relation to the labour available, the scale of the investments and their distribution among the production sectors, and the productivity of each sector. For each region it will be necessary to ascertain what progress has been made in the suppression of illiteracy and in the development of vocational training, through the progressive rationalisation, industrialisation and commercialisation of agricultural activities, so as to achieve a lasting increase in the agricultural income.

The elimination of differences in the regional stages of development calls for a broad national policy firmly based on certain principles, for there can be no question of having a country's economic policy split up into so many independent regional policies. The factors that assist economic development, like those that obstruct it, are always the same whether they relate to a single 'region', to the whole 'country' or to a group of countries comprising a continent. Logically, the autonomy of the regional plans comes to an end as soon as the structure of national public planning has been determined. After a careful study has been made of each region's deficiencies and possibilities of development, the role of the regional plans, without conflicting in any way with the national plan, is to make the fullest possible local use of the factors of production.

7 ESSENTIAL CONDITIONS FOR SETTING UP NATIONAL OR REGIONAL PLANNING OF STATE ACTIVITY

(A) REFERENCE TO A 'THEORY OF ECONOMIC DEVELOPMENT'

What is the significance of national planning in a 'mixed economy'? Planning represents one of the instruments which a government may use to attain its goals. But it is an instrument which should be used with great care.

A government aiming at the balanced economic development of the country, i.e. a rise in both national and *per capita* income, a better distribution of income between members of the collectivity, the elimination of any differences of income between the various 'production sectors' and between the different 'regions' of the country, must not fail to refer to a 'theory' of economic development and fluctuations, in working out the practical measures of such development. In other words, it must inevitably have recourse to an *adequate explanation* of the actual process whereby the country's development can be achieved and which it must always keep in mind when adopting any particular measure of economic policy. Failure to refer to adequate economic theories can produce little but 'wishful thinking', or possibly an orgy of statistics. It is urgent, however, to revert to strictly 'economic' matters and problems, for statistics are only the instrument we use for analysing economic problems. Unfortunately, we are frequently so preoccupied with the instrument that we tend to overlook the precise economic aim that was in view, and instead of studying economic problems we become engrossed in economic statistics.

The economic development of a region or a country cannot be 'automatically' translated into practical terms. Economic development can only be achieved by the untiring efforts of both the private sector and the responsible authorities, working together to create a whole series of 'internal' and 'external economies' for production undertakings. The appropriate combination of these two types of economy can bring about circumstances which are 'favourable' to production activities and will have the effect of increasing the real income, both national and *per capita*, and consequently of increasing the effective demand for goods and services.

Demand does not indeed increase with an increase in population. Effective demand can only increase if there has first been an increase in the country's real income. To achieve this result, it is necessary to understand the processes whereby it is possible to establish the 'internal' and 'external economies' for the production undertakings. In other studies we have analysed these processes of economic development and have tried to outline an appropriate framework. *Diagnostical* framework: trend factors, economic fluctuation factors, factors responsible for the formation and persistence of backward areas. *Remedial* framework: productivity of private or public investment creating conditions more conducive to economic recovery; development of agricultural production by an appropriate policy of rationalisation, industrialisation and commercialisation of agricultural activity, which implies the elimination of all subsistence; agriculture development of the industry of transformation of agricultural products; development of the other branches of industry and of tertiary activities towards which, as a result of technical progress, it may become advisable to divert surplus labour from the land. However, in the different types of models it is impossible to find any reference, explicit or implicit, to a theory or an explanation of economic development. And gradually some light is being thrown on the comment I made some fifteen years ago with regard to the nature of these static models. Under the most favourable hypothesis one might speak of 'comparative statics': ratio between situations of achievement. A set of simultaneous relations between global quantities in the so-called models of 'coherency' provides no indication of the means whereby the economic development of a country can be achieved. This fact makes the models unsuitable for the dynamic research essential when economic development is concerned.

In any particular country, even the regional plans – if they are intended for inclusion in an organic national plan – can only serve to amplify the broad lines of sequence, phasing and action implied by a process of development.

(B) PRIOR STUDY OF THE PROBLEMS PRESENTED BY THE MAIN
    SECTORS OF ECONOMIC ACTIVITY

Since dynamic research is thus required to explain a process of economic
development and, since it is necessary to examine by what private means
the responsible authorities can establish for each production enterprise,
the internal and external economies which will then give rise to certain
favourable circumstances for the production activity, there is no call for the
use of macro-economic instruments, at least in the initial phase of planning. On the other hand it is essential to investigate every possibility for
the creation of economies for each sector of production, or one might
almost say for each enterprise. This will lead to the identification of the
main problems presented by the various production centres and a study
of the solutions for each problem will pave the way for the finalisation of
development.

Unfortunately this kind of information is obtainable neither from the
'national accounts' nor from the 'models of development' which are
inevitably based on assumptions which greatly simplify the facts, nor
from any other 'macro-economic' presentations of real phenomena. Bearing always in mind the explanation of the dynamics of development, it
therefore becomes necessary to make an exhaustive study of the different
sectors of production of goods and services. An analysis is needed to
help us to understand the reasons why, in any process of economic
development, there tend to be incessant changes in the structure, dimensions and relative importance of the various production sectors – agriculture, industry, trade, services. If this prior knowledge of the problems
of each sector of economic activity is lacking, the whole development of
the country may be jeopardised.

*Logical Weakness of Planning based on the Proviso 'Other things being
equal'.* The importance of this prior familiarity with the problems of each
economic sector becomes fully apparent when, starting from what has
occurred in the past, an attempt is made to establish 'forecasts' or more or
less long-term 'planning' based on the proviso 'other things being equal'.

This formula, however, implies a whole set of assumptions which
frequently bear no relation to economic reality: (i) national and international policies strictly identical to those of the past; (ii) stable prices;
(iii) same rate of increase in the country's real income as in previous years;
(iv) the same overall investments and savings as in the past. These are
not very realistic assumptions. And the logical weakness becomes all the

more manifest as they relate to a distant future. It is a weakness which can be partly remedied by prior knowledge of the problems of each production sector and by endeavouring to choose solutions which will prove convergent in the final achievement of development. For – and this seems elementary – it is one thing to make forecasts and prepare programmes without having *previously* considered the problems of national life, i.e. taking as the starting point a past situation or a present one, despite the fact that there may be shortcomings, mistakes and wrong directions which will inevitably be projected for what they are worth into the future; and it is another thing to draw up a development plan after carefully co-ordinating the direct and indirect action of the public authorities, after closely studying the problems of each sector of activity and endeavouring to provide them with solutions which will constitute a basic contribution to the balanced development of the country.

On the other hand, the logical weakness of the forecasts tends to become more acute if the sector problems have not been previously examined or if wrong priorities have been assigned to their solutions; for instance, if priority has been given to the industrialisation of a country before anything has been done to improve the conditions of the human element and to initiate the rational development of the agricultural income. These are mistakes which can be observed in most of the plans and programmes of countries which are undergoing development.

It can thus be noted that when projections and forecasts are not based on prior micro-economic studies, they may well turn out to be little more than flights of fancy concerning the possibilities of increasing overall quantities, and though they may abound in formulae, they bear little relation to the facts of economic development.[1]

[1] A peculiar result is often produced. First, a laboratory hypothesis is established, e.g. that a country's rate of economic development will be 5% in the first ten years. Then it is added that if the gross national product is to increase by 5%, agricultural production, for instance, should increase by at least 4% per annum. These are, of course, working hypotheses. But when they are brought to the attention of the government, it frequently happens that they are transformed into 'goals' to be attained by that government, regardless of the hard facts. The government, only too pleased to announce an appreciable rate of increase in the national income, then endeavours to adopt measures calculated to push development up to the desired rate.

Unfortunately these measures are soon found to be dangerous for the country's economy and in fact the desired goal is not by any means attained. Why? Because, in order to transform a working hypothesis into an actual fact, consideration must first be given to the logical phasing of a development process. A study must be made of the problems arising in each sector of activity, private or public. For all these problems, solutions must be sought which will be suited to the country's economic development; in other words, external and internal economies must be worked out for the production undertakings, in full knowledge of the main problems of the sector; and

B

It would not suffice – in order to dispense with this preliminary analysis of sector problems – to suggest 'breaking down' the global quantities taken from the national accounts. It is logical to proceed from a micro-economic analysis to a macro-economic presentation of the findings; but it is in no way equally logical to proceed from an incidental 'aggregate' in the national accounts to a series of 'breakdowns' possibly pursued even as far as the behaviour of the individual. And the illogicality stems precisely from the 'haphazard' character of the original aggregate which affects all the successive stages of the breakdown.

This brings us to the core of our discussion. Planning can help to promote economic development in that it does away with contraditions and with sporadic action. But the economic development of a country depends on the creation of external and internal economies for all kinds of production undertakings. And this is possible only if an exhaustive study has previously been made of the main problems of each sector and of the appropriate solutions that will contribute to the economic development of the country. It shows the vital importance of the preliminary phases of planning and the dangers of failing to refer to an economic theory and to make an exhaustive study of the problems of each sector.

(c) CONCEPT OF THE MEANS WHEREBY THE STATE CAN PROMOTE A COUNTRY'S ECONOMIC DEVELOPMENT

The third condition to be met is that the government should have a very clear conception of the practical means whereby it can promote the economic development of the country.

These means consist in:

(i) the production of the 'general' public services: defence of the territory, administration of justice, public security, education in all its stages, hygiene and public health ensured throughout the country; the spread of education tends to facilitate the movement of manpower from one production sector to another and to provide, as the country progresses, a supply of increasingly skilled labour; whilst the adequate propagation of hygiene, measures for the prevention of disease, improvement of sanitary conditions in the depressed areas will help to improve the physique of the individual;

(ii) the production of 'special' public services, i.e. those which can be sold by units, for the purpose of promoting the consumption of

---

at the same time there must be a full enquiry into the effectiveness of the investments and of the action of the State or of the responsible public bodies.

'services' such as transport, postal, telegraph and telephone communications;

(iii) the carrying out of 'public works': roads, ports, development and conversion schemes, power stations, all of which will produce radical changes in the structure of the country and help to attract private investment;

(iv) the production, in certain cases, of goods and services in competition with the private sector;

(v) taxation and appropriate utilisation of savings available in institutions such as Banks, Finance Corporations, Insurance Companies and Provident Funds; economic policy in all its many aspects.

A clear conception of the means to which the State can have recourse is essential for working out 'priorities' for the use of one means or the other. For example, if agricultural activity is to be successfully developed in the direction of rationalisation, industrialisation and commercialisation, a whole background of general public services will first have to be provided. Or again, if certain types of inland transport are to be encouraged, there must first be an appropriate development of roads, ports, means of communication.

(D) STRICT CO-ORDINATION OF STATE ACTION

Mechanism of Taxation. A fourth condition to be respected by any government firmly resolved to promote the balanced economic development of the country, is the obligation first to ensure strict co-ordination of its own activities in respect of: (i) taxation of incomes and savings; (ii) public expenditure; (iii) investments in the various sectors.

With regard to the first of these activities, it is well known that the ordinary form of income tax entails *reduced consumption* on the part of those with fixed, low and moderate incomes. It *does little to encourage* new investment. It *sterilises* saving and affects the whole economic structure of the country in ways which cannot be disregarded.

In order to avert all these adverse effects, an attempt is made to define the 'conditions' which a tax system should respect so as to allow the real national income to increase: (i) prevention of *tax evasion*; (ii) *avoidance of double taxation*; (iii) overall cost of taxation *proportionate* to the taxable income; (iv) *flexibility* of the tax system in relation to the varying phases of economic fluctuation; (v) recourse to *exceptional* financial measures – special taxes, loans – according to the country's *available liquidities* or to the *possibilities of credit* which the banks may be prepared to advance on the real anticipated income.

These various conditions set the pattern for 'optimum taxation', whether of income or of savings – they define the concept of 'tax mechanism' whether for ordinary or special taxes. They help to determine the minimum cost of the State's collection of taxes in a given collectivity and hence to determine the *economic limit* of taxation of a country. The more a government is compelled by force of circumstances, to deviate from these principles, the greater the increase in cost to the collectivity of the Government's tax levy.

Mechanism of Public Expenditure. Similar considerations can be applied to the concept of the public expenditure mechanism. Public expenditure may be allocated to the *production* of the 'general' public services – administration of justice, public security, health, education – or to the production of 'special' public works' such as railways, ports, roads, power stations; or, again, to grants and subsidies.

All public expenditure can be said to affect the economic development of the country. Economic development is chiefly affected, however, by expenditure designed to improve the factors of production or to help the producers in one way or another.

The scale of public expenditure can be increased:

—by an increase in the total income;
—by greater efficiency of the financial administration which can obtain more revenue if it is on the look-out for any rise in incomes;
—by the imposition of higher taxes or by allowing fewer exemptions;
—by allocating smaller sums to sectors not directly concerned in economic development;
—by increasing the revenue from national property;
—by increasing State borrowing;
—by reducing the Treasury's liquid assets available to Banks and other institutions.

It is widely thought that the effects of public expenditure tend to offset the effects of taxation which, as we have seen, may diminish the incomes of the tax-payers. In fact, however, public expenditure on general public services, public works, subsidies and support prices may sometimes have the effect of eliminating risk and consequently lowering production costs; in other words they may sometimes result in creating in the budgets of the individual producers or consumers *new* income which will be additional to the income already existing in the country.

When the mechanism is properly organised it should show the greater part of public expenditure to be resulting in the creation of 'new income' in the balance-sheets of the consumers and producers. And as in the case of the 'taxation mechanism', the 'public expenditure mechanism' tends to mark the economic limit of the State's spending activities.

We thus find that a country's income is affected by the interplay of the technique of revenue on the one hand and of the technique of expenditure on the other hand.

Mechanism of State Intervention. Alongside these two large-scale activities of the State, there is another one, no less far-reaching in its scope, namely that of 'interventions', which involve neither taxation nor the issuing of loans nor public expenditure. Nevertheless these State interventions likewise have a considerable effect on national income and very frequently not only on the income of the country concerned but also on the income of all the countries with which the first country does business. Here, too, we must now try to determine the *economic limit* of the activity of State intervention.

The 'mechanism of intervention' is in effect nothing more than a 'series of plans' – public plans – which may provide for only a *single* intervention – producing a favourable ratio between a known present cost and a minimum useful result; or, as is frequently the case for *several interventions, each* of them based on a favourable ratio between a known present cost and a maximum useful result.

When several interventions are to take place simultaneously, the plans of the State and the public bodies must first and foremost *avoid any contradictions* between the goals envisaged and must as far as possible comply with the criteria of *marginal utility, provision against the future,* insurance against certain risks, *flexibility* in relation to market conditions – that is to say exactly the same criteria as those governing the preparation of consumption and production plans in the private sector.

If the plans of the public authorities are drawn up with the necessary care, the concept of 'mechanism of intervention' represents the *maximum effectiveness* of State action; the economic limit of such intervention; the maximum compatibility between different public interventions; the minimum of loss for the private producers and consumers; and consequently the maximum *compatibility* between the plans drawn up by the private producers on the one hand and by the public bodies on the other hand.

It may be wondered whether these concepts of 'mechanism' are really helpful. The fact is that for an *individual,* whose assets are only limited, it is easy to follow a logical line of action and use the minimum of his available assets to achieve certain aims. But for the State, constantly subjected to pressure from all sides, the concept of rational conduct remains somewhat vague. By analysing the results obtained from these broad sectors of public activity – taxation, expenditure, intervention – it becomes easier to determine the conditions of the greatest economic effectiveness, by which the conduct of the State should be guided.

Varying circumstances and multiple considerations may lead the State to deviate from these conditions. But a clear-sighted government will keep them in sight in endeavouring to set up the three 'mechanisms', particularly when in the interest of all the members of the collectivity, it is seeking to develop the real income of the country.

This strict co-ordination of the complex activities of the State should of course extend to the activity of the numerous structures in which, directly or indirectly, the State participates in one way or other.

The co-ordinated activities of the State and of the structures in which it is concerned will thus give rise to a whole series of public and semi-public actions which will carry enough weight and be sufficiently far-reaching to influence the activity even of the individual man. A result of this kind is certainly in the long run more effective than the results that can be looked for from certain incentives or certain 'restrictions of individual liberty' which are proving to be decidedly limited in their effects.

(E) STEADY GROWTH OF REAL SAVINGS IN THE PRIVATE SECTOR

There still remains a fifth condition to be fulfilled if planning is to prove effective: the stability of the purchasing power of the national currency.

First there must be a steady rate of increase in real savings in the private sector. Private 'saving' is what is left of each man's income after the deduction of expenditure on consumption and on income tax or other forms of taxation. This surplus may be used for domestic investment – purchase of a house or of stocks and shares, liquid assets, bank deposits – or for investment abroad.

Company savings consist in non-distributed profits, and funds set aside for amortisation, which is the means of ensuring the continuity of capital. Company savings come under the heading of private savings.

It is not enough to take into consideration the means whereby the monetary availabilities of a country can be increased. If economic development is to be financed on a really permanent basis, there must be a steady growth of real savings and an 'effective accumulation' of fresh capital in the concrete form of establishment of 'stocks'. The mere increase of monetary availabilities can facilitate economic development only in the somewhat rare case where – by a *completely accurate* forecast of the formation of real future income – it precedes the availability of fresh capital.

'Public saving' is the difference between revenue and expenditure; it is a form of saving which has shown considerable increases in the economy of certain countries. It may, however, be queried whether the growth of this type of saving is desirable in countries already bearing a heavy burden of taxation. It must be seen what the position of this form of saving is in relation to the others – private savings and business savings.

The view is widely held that the banking system can promote the creation of savings by the 'establishment of deposits' and the expansion of investment. In fact, however, this is an outstanding example of the necessity of distinguishing between the 'real aspects' and the 'monetary aspects' of the growth of savings. The creation of deposits does not necessarily give rise to an increase in real savings which can subsequently be transformed into the capital essential for the economic development of a country.

A more realistic course is to broaden and increase the efficacy of the 'market' also spoken of as the 'capital market' because of the credit establishments which carry out vast operations there. The possibility of the money market attracting the liquidities existing in the Provident Societies; the level of the rate of interest on loans for the promotion of investment; changes in the financial legislation covering certain credit operations – all are factors closely linked to the formation of real savings. To achieve a better organisation of the money market, there must inevitably be co-ordination of investments – private and public – in order to avoid perturbing the operations of the money market and the working of the banking system.

(F) THE DIRECTIVES OF THE CENTRAL BANK MUST NOT BE
    CONTRAVENED BY THE DIRECTIVES OF THE STATE TREASURY

Here again we find the concept of 'mechanism of intervention', or the requirement that the policy of the Central Bank shall not be contravened by the policy of the State Treasury.

In the past, the extent to which the ordinary credit Banks could grant loans was limited by the proportion of the Banks' deposits with the Central Bank in relation to the circulation of cheques. Observance of this limitation could be further enforced by the open-market operations.

This concept could be applied in practice only up to 1914. The principle was already being questioned in 1931. At the present time it has become less practicable than ever, in view of the short-term indebtedness of the Treasury, through the issuing of loans. The proportion of such bonds in the portfolios of the ordinary credit Banks is now very considerable. Today, if the Banks find their own reserves falling as the result of open-market operations, they buy Bonds and use them as security to borrow from the Central Bank. Control of the basis of credit passes from the Central Bank to the State Treasury. This is confirmed by the fact that the same movements tend to produce offers of Bonds on the market and liquid availabilities from the ordinary credit Banks.

As the placing of Treasury Bonds is a government prerogative, the effectiveness of a country's monetary policy depends on the concordance between the directives of the Central Bank and those of the Treasury, in respect of the extent of the national debt.

Nor could the Treasury deviate from this principle and authorize public expenditure continually *in excess* of revenue. This course of action would likewise interfere with any stabilising measures initiated by the Central Bank.

8 BALANCE BETWEEN PRIVATE AND PUBLIC ACTIVITIES

Having reached this stage of our analysis, we are now in a position to answer the question 'is planning necessary to promote the economic development of a country?' The answer is definitely in the affirmative as regards the co-ordination and planning of the highly complex activity of the State or of the undertakings in which the State plays a part in one way or other. And the need to plan co-ordinated public activities is all the more vital in countries which are only in the *early stages* of their development. But at each of these stages – which correspond in fact to definite increases in real income and real saving – the concept of 'mechanism of taxation', 'mechanism of expenditure' and 'mechanism of intervention', serve to indicate the economic limit of the State's activity.

If a State is assumed to have *exclusively economic* aims, the balance between the private and public spheres of activity tends to be set at the limit of the expansion of public activity that will be compatible with a continuing rate of increase in the global income. If the State also pursues *extra economic* aims, the balance between private and public activity tends to be set at the limit of the expansion of non-economic public activity beyond which the rate of increase of the global income begins to decline. This limit may even be conceived as representing not so much a fixed point as an 'area of equilibrium' between public and private activities. As long as this limit has not been reached, countries may indulge in the luxury of pursuing aims, embarking on expenditures or engaging in interventions which are of no practical use for either the present generations or those to come.

But, should the expansion of the numerous activities of the State exceed this limit, to the extent of gradually encroaching on the various activities of the private sector, then the decline in the rate of growth of the total income should point to the need to reverse the policy and give the private sector more opportunity for development. It will be preferable for the State to recover a more stable equilibrium with the private sector of activity, a more stable equilibrium between what the State can offer the collectivity without causing too great a fall in the standard of living, and what the collectivity can reasonably demand from the public authorities.

If there is a steady rate of increase in real savings and if the concepts of 'taxation', 'expenditure' and 'intervention' mechanisms are adhered to, then the purchasing power of the currency will remain stable; in other words, there will be an equilibrium, at the prevailing market prices, between the flow of goods and services and the flow of liquid assets.

9 THE ROLE OF THE STATE IN THE ECONOMIC DEVELOPMENT OF A COUNTRY

We have tried to show what the action of the State must be in order to ensure the balanced economic development of the country. Nothing else can take the place of this action. But at the same time, the State must not consider itself to be the 'protagonist' of the country's economic development. The 'protagonist' of a country's economic development is always the individual, with all the plenitude of his personality, his power of imagination, his spirit of sacrifice, his fervent idealism. It is the individual who produces his income, endeavours to apportion it between consumption, savings and investments, in proportions which tend to vary according to the circumstances of life in the collectivity and within limitations which may be laid down by law. Within these limits, the individual must be allowed to give free play to all his energy and aspirations. If this opportunity for private individual action is curtailed by a 'regimentation' of collective life, under the delusion that the State can do everything and do it better, we are entitled to ask who will be equal to the task of achieving the country's economic development. Will it be achieved by government decrees? By the threat of penalties for trans-

gressors? By the work of the civil servants? Unfortunately this elementary truth is not always grasped by people who imagine that a different
political regime would facilitate the economic development of a country.

Let us take a concrete example, such as the development of agricultural
activity. We have already drawn attention to the problems involved in
attempting to improve the structures of a country: the need to elevate
the human element by providing more and better schools, the need to
ensure higher standards of hygiene and public health, the need to make the
national territory increasingly attractive to private investment, the need
to make agricultural earnings more competitive with those in other
sectors. The solutions to these problems represent the 'stages' through
which agriculture must be piloted by appropriate public action before it
can become an economic proposition and play its part in the balanced
economic development of the country.

As these are results to be attained only in the long term, a considerable
proportion of the country's agriculture will have to be *preserved* in the
meantime, even if it is not an economic proposition. The State will have
to grant various forms of protection, either to the agricultural *producers* –
e.g. guaranteed prices, purchase of agricultural produce by State agencies
so as to avoid a glut on the market, price support integration of the
incomes from agricultural produce – or in favour of the consumers – e.g.
prohibition of exports, subsidies for imports, credit facilities.

10 TO PROMOTE THE ECONOMIC AND SOCIAL DEVELOPMENT OF A COUNTRY IT IS NEITHER NECESSARY NOR DESIRABLE TO ELIMINATE PERSONAL INITIATIVE

Whether it be a matter of solving 'structural' problems and fostering the
vital evolution of agriculture, or of supportive uneconomic sections of
agriculture and endeavouring to solve the problems of price and market
stabilisation until such time as the entirety of agricultural activity shall
have been reduced to more economic proportions and shall concentrate
solely on producing for the market, it does not appear to be in any way
essential or desirable to 'nationalise' farm land, that is to say to expro-
priate the land owners and institute 'collectivist planning'. We have to
recognise a basic fact. Whether the ownership of the land and of the
means of production remains in private hands or is taken over by the
State, the process of development remains *the same* as regards both the
initial impetus and the successive stages through which it must pass to

attain the concrete results to which we have just referred. A political regime different from that of our Western countries could do *nothing* to change this process, could not avoid passing through *exactly the same* stages as those we have described, could introduce no change in their logical sequence, could not by-pass even a single stage in the hope of accelerating the results. The truth of this is amply borne out by a multitude of data exposing the inadequacy or even total lack of economic interest attaching to the pursuit of agricultural activities under collectivist planning regimes, precisely because these countries have omitted to proceed by the various stages involved in balanced economic development. It can thus be deduced that, whatever the political regime, the action of the State is certainly a *necessary* condition but by no means a *sufficient* one to promote the economic development of a country.

Anyone who, without prejudice and without ideological preferences, sets out to examine the real possibilities of a country's development, will readily agree that it is certainly necessary to plan and to co-ordinate the activities of the State and of the public authorities in attempting to promote:

(i) the balanced economic development of the country, by the production of general and special public services and by the creation of public works; and

(ii) an appropriate structural policy and a policy of price and market stabilisation in the various sectors of production, e.g. in agriculture.

But, within the framework carefully prepared by the State, the 'prime mover' in economic development will be seen to consist in the multiple activities of private citizens and the more freedom they are allowed, the more fruitful these activities become. It is, after all, precisely this combined effort and this concordance between personal initiative and public action which has hitherto been responsible for creating what is best and most lasting in our modern civilisation.

The increasingly conscious collaboration between the public and private sector will lead to even better results in the future if, in the face of such tremendous problems, the citizens of all countries can succeed in tightening the bonds of growing comprehension and solidarity, in the interest of their maximum mutual prosperity. If, on the contrary, they continue to cling to the old prejudices and make it their one idea to bring about each other's downfall, a great many vital problems will fail to be solved and each country's economic development will be gravely compromised.

2 Internal Consistency in the Public Economy
The Plan and the Market [1]

A. Barrère

1 INTRODUCTORY

The theory of the overall balance of production, according to J. R. Hicks, suffers from three main deficiencies, the second of which he defines as follows: 'It abstracts from the economic activity of the State; this is very important, but the State is a very incalculable economic unit, so that the extent to which its actions can be allowed for in economic theory is somewhat limited. (This is, of course, a deficiency of economic theory as such, and as a whole.)' [2]

Needless to say, I am not trying in this paper [3] to make good this deficiency. I shall merely attempt a survey of the problems involved in the overall balance of production in a national economy in which the State has become a specific economic unit operating in such a way that the market is no longer left alone to regulate and steer the economic activity of the country.

As we enter this largely unknown territory, I shall therefore just attempt to pave the way to an understanding of the integration of the State's economic activity into the overall balance of production.

As an example I shall rely on the case of the French economy in which the State now is such a specific economic unit, endowed with its own motivations plus the power to make macro-economic decisions that bring irreversible forces into play. A few significant facts may illustrate the vital role now played by the State:

—a large fraction of the basic factors of production are now included in the 'nationised sector';

—the State collects and spends 25 per cent of the gross national product, pays out 30 per cent of the country's total wages and salaries and directly finances or guarantees some 40 to 50 per cent of total investments;

[1] Translated from the French by Mme Perstein.
[2] J. R. Hicks, *Value and Capital*, pp. 99–100.
[3] I wish to convey my thanks to Mrs J. M. Parly, Assistante à la Faculté de Droit et des Sciences Économiques de Paris, and to M. Jean Cartelier and M. Michel Châtelus, collaborateurs techniques of the C.N.R.S., for their useful co-operation.

—indicative planning endeavours to co-ordinate the respective objectives of public and private activities, hence this problem of how to ensure consistency between planning and market.

In an earlier paper I dealt with the question of whether consistency in public concerns should remain subject to market moves or determined by planning. Approaching now the same question on a wider basis, I must try to determine how 'consistency' and 'compatibility' can be ensured as between the activities which are governed by the decisions of the State and those which depend on the decisions of private concerns and individuals. While in my previous study the two determining factors for consistency were planning and market only, I now have to deal with a third one, the budget.

The question therefore becomes considerably more complex, for in addition to the processes of competition and concerted action (*concertation*), we now have to reckon with a process of coercion due to the budget. The problem might still have been relatively simple if the use of coercion were only a method to deal with market pressures and planning guidelines whenever these conflict; coercion, however, also comes into play because of the special needs of the Public Authority's own economic activities, which make themselves felt both *ad extra* and *ad intra* (outwards and inwards).

Coercion, concerted action and competition are therefore jointly involved in a series of reciprocal relationships and interactions.

The financial budget [1] is a set of compulsory decisions backed by means of enforcement, relating not only to the Administration but also to firms and individuals operating on the market.

The planning targets are indicative by nature but become compulsory for the public economy as soon as they get included in budget appropriations.

The public authority must in any case submit to some of the market demands, especially in the field of prices, salaries and wages and capital earnings.

It is true that the public authority enjoys some leeway regarding the realisation of the plan's instructions and may also intervene on the market. But it must stop short of the point at which such discretionary measures would conflict with the ultimate purposes of concerted action and competition.

---

[1] For the purpose of simplification, the term 'financial budget' is meant to cover both estimated revenue and expenditures and the Appropriation Bill.

Taking into account this coercion aspect of the economy as a third factor of the global prerequisite of consistency, a series of new questions arise which can be solved only by reference to the basic patterns and systems within which the activities concerned take place. Before dealing with the overall consistency of public and private activities, within the framework of the national economy, however, it first remains to ascertain how the public economy can, as a system, ensure its own internal consistency.

2   CONSISTENCY IN THE PUBLIC ECONOMY

This question may be examined from two different viewpoints. From an interpretative viewpoint, we have to ascertain whether it is possible for any public economy to be conceived and interpreted rationally. According to the above comments by J. R. Hicks, we must ascertain to what extent the State's economic activity, when governed by coercion, is effectively organised into a specific system that is theoretically consonant with the system governed by trade and market with which it is in constant contact. From an operational viewpoint, we must ascertain how coercion and planning ensure consistency in the economic activities of the State. These are the two points to be examined in the first section of this paper. To avoid any misunderstanding, we must first define the two terms we are going to use: 'consistency' (*cohérence*) and 'compatibility' (*compatibilité*).

Consistency and Compatibility.   For the purposes of this paper, we define these words as follows: [1]

'Consistency' (*cohérence*) is a condition; economic phenomena may be said to be consistent when they may combine into a whole, on a stable and lasting basis, free from internal discrepancies.

'Compatibility' (*compatibilité*) is a quality or disposition; economic phenomena may be said to be compatible when they adjust to each other; compatibility results from such adjustments.

Consistency involves the idea of a balanced whole, resulting, as would do a series of fluxes formed into a circuit, from a number of interconnections between the various products or assets in circulation.

Any one-way change in this system of interconnections destroys the

---

[1] Professor Barrère refers to the definitions given in the French Language Littré Dictionary. Unfortunately these have no clear-cut equivalent in, for instance, the *Oxford English Dictionary.* [Ed.]

whole balance and therefore destroys consistency. Being dependent on lasting stability, consistency is related to the medium and long-term concepts.

Compatibility involves the idea of temporary adjustment such as that which may be established only for a time, between the volume of anticipated investment and the volume of the actual flow of savings. It is of short-term significance, but whenever ensured, consistency can also be achieved and maintained through a succession of limited periods. Compatibility therefore often represents the first stage towards gradual consistency.

(A) THE PUBLIC ECONOMY AS A THEORETICALLY CONSISTENT SYSTEM

From now on, unfortunately, the very vague terminology which is in use reflects a certain lack of clear thought and a lack of precise knowledge of the question under discussion.

We must therefore be first quite clear about our approach to the question, for it would be useless to seek agreement on our conclusions if there were any misunderstanding on our basic premises.[1]

The State as Public Authority and the State as Economic Agent. A basic distinction must be drawn between the State acting as public authority and the State considered as an economic agent, that is, submitted to the general responsibility of the public economy.

The State as public authority is a decision-making centre regarding ultimate aims and major options relating to the national general policy, including the economic implications of this general policy. The State makes choices which are political in respect of ultimate aims and economic in respect of means of implementation. In order to achieve the goals set through these choices, the State has the exclusive privilege to exercise public coercion.

The State as economic agent is a decision-making centre governing and regulating part of the national economic activities, either because throughout the years it traditionally has been entrusted with the control of a fraction of the production machinery (public property) or because it has now acquired (nationalisation) or become a partner in (mixed economy, co-operatives, etc.), the management or control of this machinery.

---

[1] Our approach is different, for example, from that adopted in the scholarly work by Richard A. Musgrave, *The Theory of Public Finance: a study in public economy*, not because of any scientific difference, but because we do not use the words 'public economy' in the same sense and the subject matter relates to different historical circumstances.

Although there may be a great variety of situations, not only from one country to another, but also within any one country, a number of constants are apparent.

The ultimate aims of the economic activities for which the State as economic agent is responsible are not determined by the market but by the public authority by virtue of its general policy choices. The direction in which public activities are to be steered depends on motivations which are not basically related to the market but to decisions that are political because they relate to ultimate aims. On the other hand, decisions that are economic in terms of means of implementation – the choice of investments for example – are a matter for the economic agent rather than the public authority. Lastly, to ensure acceptance of its choices and effect the necessary adjustments, the State as economic agent may exercise coercion as it is empowered to by its joint character of public authority.

The public economy can therefore be defined as the fraction of the national economy which is under governmental management and subject to public coercion, towards the achievement of certain objectives which are determined according to political policies.

This gives rise to a number of major differences. The public economy does not trade in or sell the goods and services it produces; it distributes them according to statutory procedures, either for free or according to fixed rates. It keeps outside the market in that it does not take part in trade as a principle, and its activities are not dependent on some demand tending to cover needs which could be met by the interplay of competing suppliers and customers.

The characteristics of a public economy are now quite clear: it is an economy of coercion as opposed to a market economy; it is an economy of allocation as opposed to a trade economy; it is a system achieving consistency through collection of taxes, provision of services, operation of a fixed scale of charges, as opposed to a system which achieves some balance through the interplay of supply, demand and prices.

The Analytic Concepts. It follows that the concepts applied to the theory of the market cannot be applied to a study of the public economy. In other words, the operation of the public economy cannot be analysed in terms of supply, demand and prices.

This does not mean that the public economy is completely extraneous to the market; it remains related to the market but is never subjected to the system of supply and demand in that neither its ultimate aims nor its means and resources nor its general trends or level of activity are determined by forces set in motion by the price system.

Although it does not determine the activity of the public economy, the market, however, can bring an indirect and subsidiary influence to bear on certain parts or sectors of that economy.

The Various Sectors of the Public Economy.   The public economy includes three sectors: public services, publicly-operated concerns (*exploitations*), public interventions (or the State interference area).[1]

The public services sector represents the Administration in the broadest sense, i.e. as a producer of utilities of general interest, or of a public nature.   It is generally analysed in terms of political or financial science but we shall see that it is also worthy of an economic analysis.

The publicly-operated concerns sector covers production units which supply utilities of private interest and charge for them.

This second sector is sometimes called the 'productive sector' or 'the public enterprise sector', but neither of these two terms appears to be quite appropriate.   There is the fact that the public services sector also produces goods and services.   Moreover, as the production units in the second sector make their goods and services available at a fixed rate of charge, they come under the heading of 'publicly operated concerns' rather than that of 'public enterprise'.

It should be noted that this sector offers quite a number of different situations.   Some production units, though 'nationalised', do not belong to it: such is the case in France of the Régie Nationale des Usines Renault, which is a government concern selling on the market.

The so-called sector of 'public interventions' or State interference covers an area whose limits are not always clearly defined, as it lies midway between the economy of coercion and the market economy.   It refers to private production units which enjoy some governmental financial support (grants or subsidies).   This assistance is made available either directly to the production unit itself or to the individuals who benefit from its services and who use it to meet their needs.   The purpose of this 'interventions' sector is to have certain needs met at a cost lower than that governed by the market.

Including the Public Services Sector into the Analysis.   The public services sector is too frequently excluded from any economic analysis on the grounds that the Administration is not engaged in production.

[1] On this particular question and about public economy in general, see Alain Barrère, *Économie et institutions financières*, I, 25–83 (Dalloz, Paris, 1965).

This is a wrong approach, to be detected also in national accounting, where the Administration is often denied an 'operating account' (*compte d'exploitation*) on the grounds that since its production is not sold it can hardly be assessed. So, in a country where higher education is the responsibility of the private sector, its services value is included in the national product while in countries where universities are public services, the national accounts only include some of the costs based on corresponding budgetary appropriations. This practice not only invalidates any comparison between various national products but also distorts and vitiates the analysis itself. In fact the Administration does, on one hand, produce goods and services for the benefit of the economic activity as a whole, which, moreover, are extremely valuable to individuals and to enterprise – education, public health, transport, sanitation, etc. – while, on the other hand, it creates external economies which by their very nature cannot be priced but which represent, nevertheless, substantial costs.

Furthermore, from the mere necessity of finding an offset for the fraction of the national product absorbed by the Administration, the public services must be included in the overall economic activities, which means that they cannot be considered from a political and financial viewpoint exclusively.

This gives rise to two problems:

—What is the part played by this sector in the public economy as a whole and how can consistency be achieved between this sector and the other two sectors, the 'publicly-operated concerns' and the 'public interventions'?
—How can consistency be achieved between the economy of coercion and the market economy within the framework of the national economy?

This now brings us to the problem of the operational consistency of a national economy based on two operational principles, coercion and competition, interacting on each other in their respective areas.

(B) THE OPERATIONAL CONSISTENCY OF THE PUBLIC ECONOMY

If the operational principle of the public economy lies, not in the market free interplay, but in governmental or 'public' coercion, it is now necessary to ascertain how coercion can be applied. It is precisely because the State as an economic agent enjoys very wide powers whenever applying coercion, that the use of coercion must be strictly regulated.

The regulating procedures exist at the level of forecasting ('anticipations') (being determined by the Plan, the Financing Budget and the

Economic Budget) and at the level of the means of implementation: they are meant to integrate the contributions of the public economy into the overall growth of the national economy.

Indicative Planning.   The French system of planning constitutes a 'concerted and consistent system of reference for anyone who has to make economic decisions based on forecasting' (Fifth Plan).   For the State itself, for all concerns and business firms, for all households it therefore presents a comprehensive picture of the economic future on the basis of which medium or long-term decisions may be made.   'The function of the Plan is to suggest a common view of future economic development that may provide guidelines for individual behaviour.' [1]

Based on such a concept, French planning presents three main characteristics which make it different from systems in which comprehensive and total programming leaves no room left to the market:

(i) The French Plan is a consistent build-up of medium and long-term trends which complement the short-term trends as derived and defined from the market.

(ii) The French Plan sets out growth and development targets and indicates ways and means of achieving these.   It 'does not merely proclaim probabilities, it also shows what is desirable'.[2]   This plan is drawn up in the form of quantitative technical objectives: rate of growth, volume of investment, patterns of consumption, etc.

(iii) The French Plan reduces uncertainties and conflicts because it formulates programmes which make it a better distribution of the available resources possible.   As the data necessary for forecasting are better known, the areas of uncertainty are limited with the result that there is only a narrow margin of incompatibilities to be adjusted *a posteriori* by the interplay of prices.

This means that the market mechanisms are not entirely eliminated; they still play their typical role in shaping short-term activities but planning supplements their action in the long-term run.   It would, moreover, be desirable for some preventive action to take place where prices and quantities require adjustment, in order to eliminate excessive variations.

Given the above approach, one has to envisage a dual projection, in

---

[1] *Préparation du Ve Plan.*   Rapport sur les principales orientations, Loi no. 64 1265 of 22.12.64.   *Journal officiel*, 23.12.64, p. 40.

[2] *Préparation du Ve Plan*, op. cit.   *Journal officiel*, 23.12.64, p. 44.

terms of volume and value which would throw some light on the long-term conditions necessary for the realisation of the Plan's objectives. These conditions relate to the attitudes of investors and consumers, the rehabilitation of the capital market, any wage increases. They determine the *ex ante* factors of consistency at a given level of planning by government, business and households.

However, although planning remains indicative on the whole, it may become binding for the State as economic agent as soon as the public authority, when endorsing the recommendations found in the Plan, undertakes to implement them in its own sphere of economic activity. This, in turn, raises a new problem as to what the relationship must be between the planned programmes and the formulation of the forecasts and decisions of the public economy.

CONSISTENCY IN FORECASTING

What does the implementation of the Plan mean for the public economy?

The Meaning of the Plan

(i) In the public services sector, the implementation of the Plan's recommendations implies the inclusion in the budget of the appropriations needed to achieve the targets set for that specific sector: school-building programmes, road construction, power networks, for instance.

(ii) In the sector of the government-operated concerns, the Plan's successful implementation depends on two factors. It depends on the one hand on the attitude of the State itself towards these concerns, which may vary considerably, ranging from direct control to simply making good any deficit, or providing financial assistance; according to circumstances, the government may decide to make capital endowments, grant loans, give regular financial support, determine prices, expand activities. . . . On the other hand, it also depends on the way the other economic agents react to the central government's decisions: subscribing to loans issued by the nationalised sector, accepting or rejecting the announced wage rates. . . .

(iii) In the 'government interference area', the State as economic agent tends to give precedence to the State as public authority. This is because the activities in this sector depend primarily on private decisions which, in part at least, result from some impetus provided by the State through fiscal or financial incentives, such as tax relief in respect of investments or financial aid for housing projects. The reactions of individuals to the action of the public authority play a major role in the implementation of the Plan in this sector.

The Financial Budget. The Plan as formulated by the State as economic agent, viewed as a consistent presentation of the basic decisions affecting a specified period, therefore covers several main items: the public services' own financial budget, whatever subsidies and other forms of assistance are granted to publicly operated concerns, and all measures of intervention affecting private activities such as tax relief, fines and penalties, subsidies, loans, etc.

As to how these various types of measures must be taken care of in the accounting statutory framework (formal State budget, special budget, *lois de programme*) is but a technical problem for which various solutions are found according to whatever accounting procedures are in force in each and every country. There is, however, an economic problem to be solved, as these decisions must all be consistent with each other. The financial budget understood in this way is therefore of a dual nature:

—it embodies decisions whose nature is determined by the overall policy of the public authority, and which are compulsory and therefore accompanied by means of coercive enforcement;
—it allocates the financial resources required by the public economy to carry out the medium-term programmes according to yearly targets.

That is the framework within which we have to consider the problem of the internal consistency of the public economy.

The Economic Budget as a Framework for Consistency. Consistency must be ensured between the choice of targets and the general trend of the decisions contained in the Plan on one hand, and the yearly compulsory decisions contained in the financial budget on the other hand.

It is obviously necessary that the investment and consumption expenditures as stated in the budget and deriving from the power of decision of the government must be consistent with the programmes drawn up and co-ordinated under the overall authority of the Commissariat au Plan.

Gaps or discrepancies may, however, still occur frequently, mainly because all three sectors may be competing within the public economy field itself and claiming part of the same resources.

Conflicts may also arise because of the dual character of the State as both an economic agent and a public authority.

Not only must the internal consistency of the public economy be ensured but attention must also be paid to frequent conflicts between the decisions the State makes to carry out its commitments under the Plan in its own three sectors, and the decisions it takes concerning the various markets in order to ensure an overall consistency in public and private planning.

Consistency appears therefore to be necessary in both these fields and in order to achieve consistency more easily, one may make use of the information supplied by the provisional economic budget (estimates); these estimates are used mainly for co-ordinating the financial budget and the Plan.

The economic budget is 'a provisional or forecasting account designed to provide information such as to prevent unbalance or conflicting measures for the purposes of short-term policies. Unlike the financial budget, the economic budget is not some sort of formal and legal act but an instrument designed to help the economic authorities make enlightened decisions.'[1]

As regards the consistency of the public economy itself, the economic budget makes it possible to get a relatively accurate estimate of the expected revenue from taxation, the volume of expenditure which can reasonably be sustained, the amount of resources available to the Treasury, the probable size of the budgetary deficit, etc. The information it provides is particularly helpful when comes the time of the annual compulsory decisions to be made.

As regards consistency between the public economy and the market economy, the economic budget shows how the public financial needs stand in relation to the total national available resources and therefore reveals areas of general agreement or conflict. A method such as this obviously involves substantially changing the traditional procedures of budgetary and financial administration and management. In France, in 1959–65, the volume of taxation, the operating expenditures, the public investments, the reduction of the Treasury deficit were all pre-determined not so much for reasons connected with traditional budgetary and financial policy but because of certain requirements of an economic character, as the public economy was committed to achieve the targets as they had been defined in the Plan. The economic budget also promotes the gradual integration of the activities of the State as economic agent into the implementation measures of the growth targets, and it is no longer a question of how to balance accounts such as in a financial budget

---

[1] See Alain Barrère, *Économie et institutions financières*, vol. II, p. 636, on the economic budget as a whole.

but how to correlate taxes, public consumption and investment and public financial needs on the one hand, with the volume and the pattern of incomes, prices, salaries and wages and external trade on the other. The economic budget regulates the various ways the public economy contributes to the growth of the national economy as a whole; it is the framework within which overall consistency can be achieved and it establishes a necessary link between the forecasts set out in the financial budget of the State and all targets relating to private production, investment and consumption as proposed in the respective programmes.

CONSISTENCY IN IMPLEMENTATION

Once consistency has been ensured in forecasting, it must also be ensured in implementation. As the already-made decisions are binding in respect of resources and incomes, it is at this point that the question of consistency in implementation measures arises; coercion plays a capital role in this field.

The coercion principle. As a principle, the use of coercion may be defined as follows: the way the market distributes the resources and incomes available to the national economy may not always comply with the requirements involved in achieving the Plan's medium-term targets. The public authority must then try and establish a pattern of distribution for these resources and incomes which ensures that they are effectively used towards the realisation of these specific targets.

In other words the contents of the various public and private plans must be adjusted. In this connection, two remarks are called for:

(i) Public coercion constitutes a powerful means of allocation of the resources of the national economy. As these resources are limited, the State can give the public economy *de facto* priority for their use by adjusting taxation, making selective credit available, granting subsidies, etc. But it can also restrict the allocations made to itself so that private concerns and individuals may get their supplies at lower prices. The State is constantly kept informed by the reactions of the market as to scarcities as well as to the private sector's needs, so that, while it is not subjected to any market pressures, it still may use price variations as helpful indicators whenever the introduction of coercive measures becomes necessary.

(ii) As regards incomes, the question is how to correct any basic maladjustment to growth due to the free play of the market. This type of maladjustment may derive from the very pattern of distribution of incomes or from the way these are used for consumption and saving. To effect the necessary adjustments, the public authority can then resort to various series of measures.

Coercion Measures. The State is first of all able to exercise direct control through formally setting wages and salaries rates, profit margins, regulating interest and prices, etc.; but it may also wisely apply somewhat less conspicuous but equally efficient measures borrowed from the techniques of the public economy itself. There are several possibilities.

The size of private incomes can easily be changed through taxation or government loans. By an appropriate reduction of certain categories of incomes, it becomes possible to curb private consumption and bring about a transfer of savings to the State. On the other hand, tax relief can increase the spending capacity of certain sectors of the population, and so increase the opportunities they get to meet their needs.

The varied utilisation of incomes can also be directed in such a way that, while the amount of income itself is not affected, the consumers' and private concerns' plans may be brought into line with the consumption and investment requirements resulting from the Plan.

Lastly, the total demand pattern can be modified even more directly by higher taxation, so as to produce more revenue and finance the development of public consumption. There will then be a greater demand for public consumer goods at the expense of private consumer goods. There are many variations on this particular theme, but they are so widely known that there is no need to dwell on them.

It may only be mentioned that the public authority can, through public interventions, resort to selective taxation and tax incentives to guide the utilisation of resources and incomes in accordance with the prerequisites of consistency in public and private planning.

In France, the system of selective taxation has been applied towards four main objectives:

—creating and expanding activities in areas where development seems desirable (reduction of transfer and licence duties);
—developing scientific and technical research through a reduction of profit taxes, amortisation and transfer duties;
—adjusting the size and organisation of enterprises and concerns to international competitive conditions through financing facilities;
—meeting the financial requirements involved in reaching the Plan's targets through a number of exemptions and privileges in respect of financial operations.

The economic budget, as we have seen, then creates a link between the public economy and the market. Not only does it constitute a useful means of information for the management and administration of the financial budget, but it also facilitates 'compatibility' as between public and private activities. The short-term decisions (financial budget) may be more easily integrated into the medium-term policies (Plan), taking into account, as revealed through the markets, those various requirements to be met if an overall balance is to be ensured.

How can this 'compatibility' be achieved?

3 HOW TO ENSURE CONSISTENCY IN THE PUBLIC AND PRIVATE SECTORS

The question arises as to how consistency in both types of economic activities, coercive and market, can be ensured within long-term planning so that the production may keep on increasing towards the realisation of set targets through common action by the public and private economy.

In order to answer this question, one should regularly check the progress of three rates of growth: the expected rate of growth, the actual rate of growth, and the adjusted rate of growth respectively.

THE PRINCIPLE OF EXPECTED GROWTH

The so-called 'Plan' defines the trends of the medium-term economic policy and provides for consistency to be ensured as to quantitative targets and means to achieve them.

The Rate of Growth. The Plan's quantitative programming, however, only provides end-date targets but not intermediate ones to be realised each and every year within the 4-year Plan. Therefore it might be considered that all the economic units are free to organise their own individual efforts as they see fit within these time-limits so long as the overall objectives are achieved. This, however, would be far too haphazard an approach. Therefore, each economic unit sets for its own benefit a periodical average growth rate, so that the overall plan itself must eventually achieve a steady linear progress every year.

Thus a yearly expected rate of growth is provided; this rate, which generally averages 5 or 5·5 per cent, is supposed to be equal to the production increase rate necessary if the Fourth and Fifth Plans' targets are to be achieved.

This overall rate can naturally be broken down by sectors, as the Plan provides for specialised objectives. This disaggregation, however, cannot be very detailed; rates of growth relate mainly to private and public consumption and investment, total production, and domestic trade – they may also relate to incomes, wages and costs, but rather as a series of forecasts or desirable levels, or simply maxima not to be exceeded.

In this paper we limit ourselves to the determination of total production, investment and consumption rates. These are basic reference rates corresponding to the expected medium-term growth. How is this expected growth to be realised?

Implementation of Expected Growth. As the yearly economic progress towards end-targets is not determined through planning, we must establish the short-term and linked-up stages by which medium-term total targets may be achieved. The various elements of short-term economic policies should be fitted into overall medium-term programmes. Precise operating growth variables must be integrated as far as both the public and the market economies are concerned.

Since private industries, concerns and households are under no obligation to help achieve the planned targets, it may be useful to have incentives so that the private sector is induced to play its part towards the ultimate goals.

Two kinds of very effective incentives immediately come to mind:

(i) The public sector can on its own take care of its share of the Plan's recommendations. In view of the impact made by any macro-economic decision by the government acting in its capacity as an economic unit, any measures taken by both the public services and the publicly-sponsored concerns in the field of public investment (which amounts to 40-50 per cent of the total investment) as well as in the field of public consumption or wage-scaling, will be extremely stimulating.

(ii) Governmental indirect interference by way of grants-in-aid, loans, premiums, special allowances, and tax privileges as part of public action towards co-ordinating public and private programmes is also of great importance.

These principles are in fact illustrated and defined in the economic and financial reports (*rapports économiques et financiers*) and the forecasting accounts (*comptes prévisionnels*) on the basis of which the government shapes the general economic policy which is its responsibility.

As an illustration of how one can evaluate regular progress in this field, we shall study the results recorded at the end of the first year of implementation of the Fourth Plan. The economic report for 1962 stated the following: 'The economic forecasts that are established by the planning modernisation committees do not simply anticipate what might happen between now and 1965. They are established in co-operation with all active economic units and therefore bear witness to a common desire for growth. They further imply that the government fully intends to play its stimulating, regulating, and, in some main sectors, directly interfering part, which in modern societies properly belongs to the public authority.'

How is this multipart role to be assumed? By developing forecasts for the next year. These were defined for 1962 in the following way:

—the rate of growth is set at 5·5 per cent, i.e. constantly equal to the average yearly rate necessary for the realisation of the planned end targets;
—in publicly-sponsored concerns, investment is to be sharply increased;
—the increase in private investment is to be higher than the production rate;
—households' actual income is to increase by 5·5 per cent, which implies a similar increase in consumption and savings;
—more satisfactory foreign trade opportunities are to be looked for.

On that basis, it becomes possible to assess sectorial rates of growth for 1962, that is to determine in quantitative terms under what conditions the targets for that year can be achieved. This entails measuring all the elements of the annual programmes that are included in medium-term programmes.

TABLE ONE
PROJECTED RATES OF YEARLY PROGRAMMES

	Growth rate for 1962	Planned reference rate
Gross domestic production	5·5	5·5
Total imports	7·5	6·1
Consumption by households	5·5	5·2
Government services consumption	3·5	5·0
Gross investment	6·5	7·0
Total exports	6·0	5·5
Private industrial investment	7·0	6·6
Investment by households	1·5	6·1
Government services investment	10·5	10·2

One major difference between short-term planning and the general economic progress according to medium-term programmes must be immediately noted. In the former, consumption patterns favour household consumption at the expense of public consumption whereas household investment is considerably lower with no offsetting increase in investment in publicly-sponsored concerns and government services, even though there is some planned increase there too. In this case, political motivation is a determining factor.

I must next examine the direct part the public economy is supposed to play in implementing growth programmes. The 1962 budget provides for increased expenditure in education, training, scientific and technical research, and capital investment generally. This means including long-term growth requirements into the short-term plans of the public economy.

Furthermore, the short-term programmes include short-term equilibrium policy provisions to ensure balanced growth. These provisions are intended to offset any possible tightness on the labour market and to control foreign trade. The budgetary provisions for these economic intervention procedures are 50 per cent higher than the previous year; the planned measures mainly relate to the agricultural markets. It is on the basis of those annual programmes that the expected growth plans are implemented.

The Significance of the Expected Growth. While the planned targets are expressed in measured rates of growth for every economic sector, plus a total rate of growth, the annual progress on the other hand is gradually determined through the steps taken by the individual economic units (that is, the government, the private concerns, the household) and the short-term policies aimed at maintaining those steps are consistent despite changing conditions over time.

But it would be impossible for the expected rate of growth to keep all successive stages of the economy within the fixed limits of a single linear progression, which would itself be established once and for all on the basis of the planned-end targets. These only provide a reference rate of growth to pave the way and not to lose sight of if the end-targets are to be achieved. As to sectorial rates, they may only be determined for shorter periods, due to the market-changing conditions, which, however, medium-term planning cannot fully assess. What the planned expected rate of growth therefore eventually becomes is a measured target on the basis of which sectorial rates of growth can be determined. These sectorial rates cover an area whose upper and lower boundaries indicate what the consistency and compatibility required levels are, i.e. the minimum consistency required in medium-term growth programmes according to the main Plan, and the minimum compatibility required in the various successive economic stages resulting from changing market conditions. Such is the path of the expected rate of growth, the realisation of which raises quite a few difficult problems.

The Path of Actual Growth.   While the expected rate of growth runs steadily along a linear path, the actual growth, in terms of actual achievements, follows a somewhat different course.   It does not progress like a car keeping to a single narrow lane on a straight highway, but erratically covers a progress area the width of which varies according to various obstacles set up by the sectorial rates when these appear to be incompatible with the market conditions.

Actual growth raises a double question:

—as consistency is predetermined, it cannot be observed whenever the actual path deviates too much from the planned medium-term targets;
—growth targets may be achieved but may also result in various unbalances whenever short-term incompatibilities are created by changing conditions on the market.

The problem can thus be defined in the following way: the short-term policy implemented by the government, as the public authority in charge, must help determine a path:

(i) which meets all consistency requirements in the realisation of sectorial rates of growth: for public and private consumption, government services investment, private concerns and household investment, domestic trade;
(ii) which also must help reduce short-term incompatibilities that might appear within a given set of relative prices as evidence of unbalanced growth.

The problem to be solved, therefore, is how to determine such a path of growth that the sectorial rates of growth, on the one hand, be compatible with the overall rate on the basis of which the planned targets should be achieved, and, on the other hand, also be maintained within certain limits, which, once exceeded, result in certain disequilibrium areas, as to prices, wages, employment, balance of payment, etc.

Incompatibility Factors.   A few incompatibilities may develop through the action of some factors that at least deserve to be mentioned: the unpredictable event, the exogenous condition.

While planning has been defined as greatly reducing the world of uncertainty, it cannot eradicate all of it. Planning can of course greatly reduce it by the use of the law of large numbers, compensatory effects, future positions that are likely to be contradictory. Planning also can of course bring the future down to a near certainty by applying the theory of probability but there is nevertheless one area that escapes all attempts of speculative ascertainment – uncertainty *stricto sensu*, which cannot be reduced to likelihood. As an illustration of this, one may refer, during the period of implementation of the French Fourth Plan, to the economic consequences that followed the return and integration of people of French descent from Algeria. The event as such could have been foreseen for some time, but it carried effects on employment, consumption, capital flow, price increases in some fields, which were too difficult to reduce to a schedule of probability, appropriately dated. It is, however, well-known that the event had quite an impact on the progress of the realisation of the Plan in 1963.

Apart from the unpredictable, one must not discount the heterogeneity factor, as exemplified by the activity of the publicly operated concerns. It has already been mentioned that their ultimate ends depend on governmental trends which are inherently governed by political motivations. The means of implementation, however, are governed by the market conditions, so that their capital investment and operating costs depend on the price system and fluctuations. These ends and means are therefore heterogenous, which may result in incompatibilities between the targets to be achieved, and the available resources. For instance, costs may appear to be too high due to underestimated expenses, or deficiencies in management, or any number of such reasons.

These incompatibilities soon give rise to reactions through what may be called competition effects affecting the budget, and coercion effects affecting the market, with possible inter-actions between the two. This point requires some further elaboration.

The Competition Effect. A competition effect may affect the budget because the latter registers reactions caused by the occasional incompatibilities mentioned earlier and these reactions are such as to impair the consistency which the public economy has tried to maintain for both budgeting and planning. While the trend approved for public activities is not subject to market impulses, it nevertheless reacts to market variations, especially as far as the prices of goods and services are concerned, whose variations in turn affect costs. Experience often shows that an increase in prices is followed by an increase in expenditure higher than the corresponding increase in revenue (which is what happened in 1963) and that an increase in private consumption makes it necessary for the government to offset it by reducing consumption in government services. In a similar way, a wage increase on the labour market due to labour scarcity or to some special union policy, is bound to bring about an increase in public salaries. New capital flows may also result in difficulties – or opportunities – for the treasury to meet its expenses, which in turn may have far-reaching consequences for future budgetary and monetary policies.

The Coercion Effect. A coercion effect may be felt on the market, because of a direct government measure, or because of the government's response to an emerging incompatibility. It may well be that, in the first case, public investment, being stimulated by privileged governmental borrowing on the financial and monetary markets, makes capital more scarce for a number of expanding concerns. The financial governmental needs gaining actual priority because of the special provisions mentioned earlier may affect the way concerns' needs can be met and eventually tighten interest rates. Another example occurs whenever there is an increase in public utilities prices so that the administration of the relevant services may be better balanced – any such increase is likely to affect a number of prices, even sometimes all prices through costs.

Even more important is the coercion effect recorded as a governmental response to market variations, intended to make programmes compatible when the market itself is not able to guarantee this within a given series of relative prices on the basis of which consistent planning has been evolved. Then public intervention, aimed at prices, wages, expenditure, tends to coercively reduce any incompatibilities in the public and the private programmes in regard to each other.

Incompatibilities as revealed by Actual Growth. The competition effects, as felt on the budget and the coercion effects, as felt on the market, may therefore foster cumulative variations that the budgetary policy will somehow have to offset.

The results shown for 1963, i.e. the last year of the Fourth Plan, are a case in point.

Towards the end of 1962, it was already clear that the actual progress would show considerable deviations as compared to the expected growth.

In 1963, those fears were confirmed. A triple-way distortion could thus be found:

—the gross fixed capital formation was lower than expected (5·7 as compared to 7) while total consumption increased sharply;
—public consumption increased more (7·9 as compared to 5·0) than household consumption did (6·1 as compared to 5·2);
—domestic trade reached a higher level than expected, with imports expanding much more than exports did.

Lack of consistency then is particularly apparent. The public economy has exceeded all the rates of growth which had been recommended: public investment reached the 12·5 mark as against the 10·2 target, which is clear evidence of coercion affecting the capital market and also anyone who was interested in financing out of internal funds, as gross fixed capital formation had decreased and household and private concerns investment must have absorbed the consequent reductions (3·3 as against 6·1 and 5·1 as against 6·6 respectively). The earnings distributed by the public economy increased more rapidly (18 per cent in value) than the whole wage range (13·1 per cent). Therefore, in a number of publicly operated concerns (power, transportation), an increase in prices was necessary, as well as for some prices more or less directly subject to government decisions. This emphasises the cumulative character of the coercion effect.

A few consequences make themselves felt on the market: while the overall rate of growth decreased in 1963 (G.D.P.: 4·7 as against a planned rate at 5·5), a distortion in total demand, which first started in 1962, gets more and more pronounced. Household consumption expenses increase and the usual increase in prices soon occurs. The inflationary process itself soon starts too, gradually gaining momentum, and brings out the incompatibilities which had gradually become apparent in the public and private sectors programmes and which could not be smoothed over so as to maintain the balance required if planning was to be consistent. Consistency and compatibility therefore were not achieved. The various effects we have mentioned have resulted in the non-realisation of the proposed targets and in cumulative disequilibriums. What might the solution be? Is it possible to bring the actual growth back to the level of the planned and expected growth?

HOW TO ACHIEVE COMPATIBILITY THROUGH ADJUSTMENTS

Figures 1, 2 and 3 in the Annex (pp. 48–53) show that the progress of expected growth and actual growth over the period 1959–66 was not uniform. A series of deviations may be noted at once, not only in the overall curve of gross domestic production, but also in the various sectorial progress curves.

The Gap between Expected and Actual Growth. What these gaps indicate in the first place is that targets are not achieved and that incompatibilities are emerging. They also point to discrepancies between the content of the Plan and the disequilibrium of the market, as well as between short-term and medium-term policies.

At this juncture the most valuable point is to observe the different behaviours in the public sector and the private concerns and households. This can be summarised as follows:

—the public economy generally tries to conform to the overall national plan in the realisation of its own programmes. Therefore, the gaps between what was planned and what is achieved are often positive, that is, the increase in public investment and consumption is higher than expected. This may be explained by the confirmed intent of the political authorities to live up to their planning and to achieve their own targets. It is repeatedly proclaimed that planned targets must be achieved, at least as far as the share of the government, as an economic unit, is concerned.[1] These declarations may be more political than economic in character but they are nevertheless consistent with the inner motivation of the subject of public economy. To that extent the coercion effects recorded on the market may very well be the determining factor which will help achieving consistency and extenuating incompatibilities:

—on the contrary, private concerns and households, in both the investment and consumption fields, may cut loose from the planned targets, which for them, in any case, are mere guidelines only, and tend to follow the market directions. In that regard, the market plays its usual part in reducing incompatibilities and plays it its own way: when there are more spending opportunities, prices increase, and the consumer goods market expands at the expense of capital investment by households, etc. Inflationary pressures, trade imbalances, wage increases start affecting the public economy through their competition effects.

The government is then confronted with discrepancies appearing

---

[1] It may be appropriate to quote the Act of Finance, 1964, which states: 'In the 1964 budget it is intended above all to maintain expansion rates. The government intends to keep on pursuing its main policy of social progress and economic development according to the goals of the 4th Plan.'

C

between the content of the Plan and the market variations and has therefore a choice of two alternatives:

—to try and achieve the planned targets while mitigating as much as possible all market disequilibria;
—or to try and reduce market disequilibria while giving up consistency, which means giving up every hope of achieving the planned targets.

Should the first alternative be adopted, the motivations of the government as an economic unit responsible for the entire public economy get stronger than its motivations as the authority responsible for equilibrium, because it is then felt that the planned targets represent an ultimate minimum for the nation, taking into account the needs of a modern society whose population is steadily increasing. Should the second alternative be adopted, the government as the public authority must on the contrary feel that the need for short-term balance, either economically, or politically, is the determining factor.

The dilemma does not appear to be a choice to be made between planning and market, or between public and private economies, but between two main ends: either the realisation of a planned rate of growth, even at the price of a few disequilibria, or the maintenance of a certain level of balance, even if the rate of growth must then be lower.

Experience, however, has shown that a solution might be found out of this dilemma, through an adjusted path of growth, which, while extenuating all imbalances, tries to eventually catch up with the total end-targets.

Adjusting the Path of Growth. Whenever the actual growth sharply deviates from the expected growth, many problems arise. It is clear that the realisation of some forecasts is frustrated and that the market behaviour remains somehow uncontrolled, but it also underlines the difficulty of integrating short-term projects into medium-term policies. For the Plan does not provide any integrating procedures that may tone down short-term disequilibriums. Therefore, when short-term disequilibria get large enough to require attending to, only outside initiative can reduce incompatibilities and repair consistency.

These outside interventions may often refer to the Plan but only for the sake of appearances. In fact, when the gap between actual growth and expected growth is of real importance, recourse to the Plan is useless because it only provides information as to what should have been achieved and does not provide any means of adjustment or subsidiary solutions. As it does not include any detailed information about the required annual rate of growth, medium-term policies are still submitted to all the risks of short-term development.

Independent measures aimed at bridging the gaps may both appear as evidence of failure on the part of the actual growth to conform to expectation, and serve as a means of evolving an adjusted path which may meet the deficiencies of the Plan and the market. That was the reason behind the provisional 1958–9 Plan and the stabilisation 1963–4 Plan. These at least offer some valid advantages: they have been developed by the authority responsible for their implementation; they are binding for both coercive economic forces and trade; they can be modified and adjusted according to short-term conditions, so that, during their period of implementation, short-term and medium-term programmes and public and private economy can somehow be integrated, and both consistency and balance requirements can be met.

Corrective Programmes. These come into play only in dangerous circumstances. Under more ordinary circumstances, short-term measures are adopted for the next year on the basis of forecasting accounts which themselves take into account partial achievements as already recorded. Actual growth can then be corrected by yearly forecasts, including a rate of growth which attempts to adjust for the next year the progress achieved up to that date. This is the uneven corrective growth curve shown in Figs. 1 and 2 next to the expected and actual growth curves.

The corrective growth attempts to meet both the need for realising the planned targets and the need for maintaining a sound balance. It therefore brings together, or tries to, short-term and long-term policies within the same co-ordinated prospect. From the main reference plan one may then come down to annual forecasts which can more appropriately be called 'programmes'.

A basic agreement is thus realised between the following propositions:

—the financial budget is the real 'economic programme' of the public economy. Its yearly character lays down the general time-table of the measures which will shape up the public activities and have a momentum effect on the market. The competitive effects due to the market variations which may affect the budget are also recorded within that yearly framework;

—the forecasting programme, being also established on this yearly basis, makes it possible (through the economic budget) to state more accurately what conditions are to be fulfilled to ensure compatibility in the short-term prospect;

—moreover, both 'plans' are streamlined in their *ex ante* character. They may be somewhat less useful as a 'statement of targets' and 'reference plan' but they now certainly constitute a more consistent set of forecasts, which belongs much more to economic planning as such.

4 CONCLUSIONS

Our purpose in this general study of the various problems involved was merely to define them in broad terms. This assessment has shown that wherever the public economy plays a major part, it is necessary to know what the overall growth targets are in order to consistently integrate governmental measures into the national economic efforts.

These measures may derive from two opposite centres of economic decision: one of these two 'poles' is related to the part assigned to the public economy in the realisation of the planned targets, so that the ultimate targets are achieved through direct governmental action which also gives an impulse to the private sector. The other 'pole' is related to any attempt to reduce 'incompatibilities' emerging on the market. The final choice eventually depends on what the government responsible for the general economic policy prefers itself.

The government is, however, an economic unit with a double motivation: it takes care of both the public economic activities and the broad principles of a general economic policy at the same time. Therefore it is quite difficult for the purpose of economic analysis to only take this economic unit into account, because its decisions are to a large extent, sometimes even entirely, governed by its motivations and responsibilities as a public authority. Both the public economy regulating authorities and the political organs responsible for a general economic policy have a strong hold on the government, which results in pressures and strain.

Coercive measures, which are an exclusive feature of the government, represent its means of ensuring consistency in its own specific economic sphere of action, as well as the necessary controlling power over the market which, nevertheless, remains outside its own specific domain. But these two purposes are heterogenous: coercion is enforced through a series of statutory procedures and its use is limited by political and economic considerations; on the other hand the market is submitted to a number of balancing mechanisms which operate according to their own kind of inner logic.

This heterogenous character makes any interpretative analysis difficult: recourse to coercive measures must derive from the very needs of planning, budgeting, or direct intervention, whereas market mechanisms are set into motion spontaneously and automatically by competition interplay. It is impossible to use the same analytical instruments on both levels, but the question nevertheless arises as to how to use them at the same time, in order to take care of all necessary elements in a single integrated scientific analysis.

ANNEX

INTERPRETATION OF THE DIAGRAMS

Figures 1 and 2 have a logarithmic ordinate so that rates of growth can be read from the slopes. Accordingly, the straight lines on the figure show the scale for the rate of growth. Taking as origin, for each period, the logarithm of the volume of domestic gross production achieved during the preceding period, it is possible to notice the impact of the actual rate of growth on the realisation of the Plan targets expressed in volume. It appears on Fig. 1, for instance, that the actual rate of growth of domestic gross production in 1965 [1] was inferior to the main rate forecast by the Plan, which prevented the achievement of the ultimate goals. In other words, the lead which obtained during the first year (since the dashed line is above the solid line up to 1964) was more than offset in 1965.

In Fig. 2 the anticipated rates of growth are related to the provisional results available at the time when the economic prospects were worked out. This scheme is intended to condemn the will (or lack of will or impossibility) to take corrective measures when the actual evolution is not consistent with the Plan goals. Although the results for 1963 clearly demonstrated a deviation of the actual progress of the economy from the steady path towards the objectives of the Fourth Plan, the perspectives for 1964 – whose spontaneous character was stressed by the Government – could only reinforce this tendency.

Figures 3, 4, 5 and 6 are based on an arithmetic scale and the rate of change of the variables can be read on the Y axis.

It is possible to read simultaneously:

1   The consistency or lack of consistency of the behaviour of any particular variable with the Plan targets.
2   The distortions which may occur in the relative rates of growth of different variables (by comparing identically dashed curves).

---

[1] The data referred to are provided by the provisional accounts for 1965.

For instance it can be read directly from Fig. 3 that in 1964 total consumption grew less rapidly than had been anticipated by the Fourth Plan, and that in 1962 and 1963 the relative rates of growth of gross fixed capital formation and total consumption behaved adversely to the Plan goals (mainly because of the rapid expansion of total consumption).

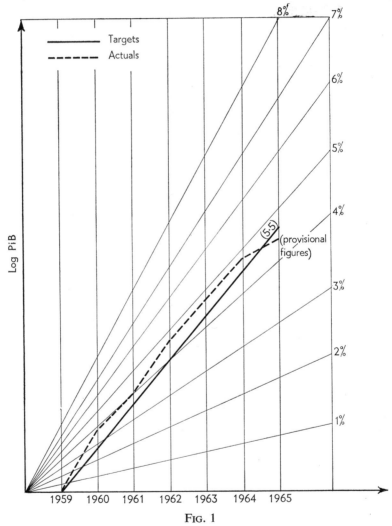

FIG. 1

Targets and Actuals for Gross Domestic Product during the Interim Plan and the Fourth Plan

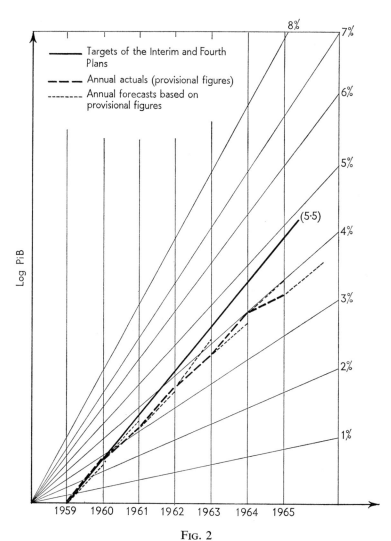

Fig. 2

Short Term "Plans" for Gross Domestic Product during the Interim
and Fourth Plans

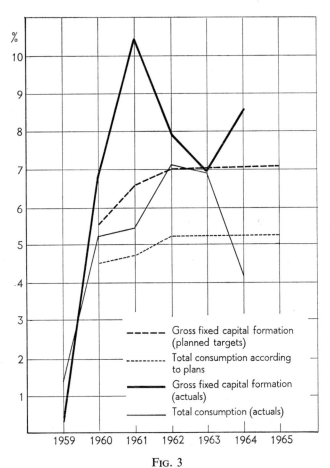

FIG. 3
Annual Rates of Growth as compared with preceding year

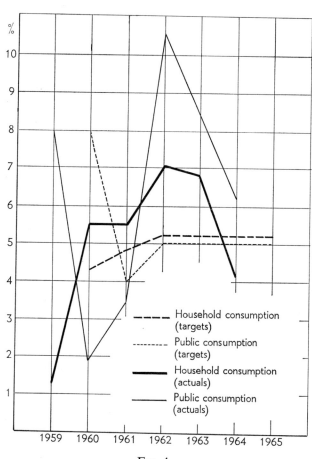

FIG. 4

Annual Rates of Growth of Various Sectors of
Consumption

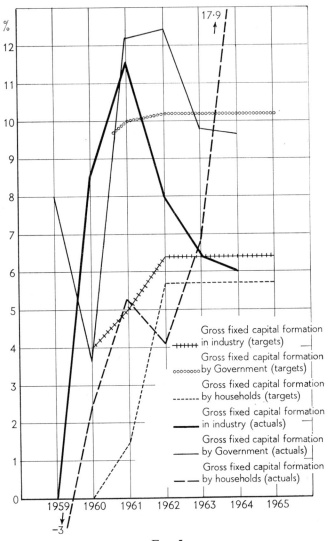

FIG. 5

Annual Rates of Growth of Various Sectors of Capital
Formation

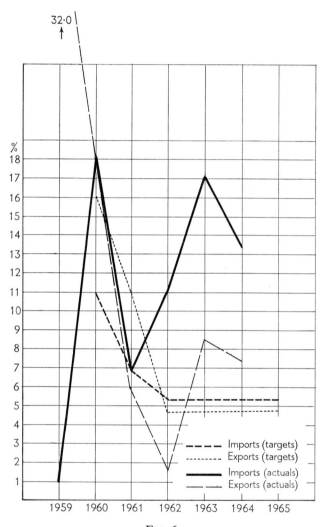

FIG. 6

Annual Rates of Growth of Imports and Exports

3 Information in Price and Command Systems of Planning

S. A. Marglin

1 INTRODUCTION

This essay investigates alternative methods of organising a search for the optimal allocation of resources. 'Decentralisation and centralisation' originally appeared in the title, but I despaired of defining these terms satisfactorily. One possibility for which there is precedent would be to use the term 'centralised' to describe an economy in which 'firms' send all available information about production functions to the 'planning board' or 'ministry of production', and the ministry determines the allocation of resources without further reference to the firms except to inform them of its decision. I think many economists think of centralisation in this way, and Thomas Marschak's pioneering paper so formalises centralisation.[1] Any iterative determination of resource allocation that involves communication between the firms and the ministry in the course of determining the allocation of resources thus becomes 'decentralised', regardless of the nature of communications.

I think this dichotomy is not very useful in setting out the issues involved in choosing among various kinds of economic organisation. Centralisation defined à la Marschak is probably vacuous: Long before the advent of 'Liebermanism' Soviet resource allocation involved iterative 'bargaining' between higher and lower echelons; this give and take is described in a paper by Herbert Levine which bears the title 'The Centralised Planning of Supply in Soviet Industry'.[2] Levine's title is not amiss; Soviet resource allocation was not 'decentralised' in the sense we usually attach to this word.

In any event 'price and command' more accurately reflects the issues I wish to address here. By 'price system' I shall mean a set of rules for iteratively seeking out the optimal resource allocation that has the following properties: (1) firms adjust trial demands for inputs (and supplies of

[1] Thomas Marschak, 'Centralisation and Decentralisation in Economic Organisations', *Econometrica*, vol. 37, 3 (July 1959).
[2] Herbert Levine, 'The Centralised Planning of Supply in Soviet Industry', *Comparisons of the United States and Soviet Economies* (Joint Economic Committee, Washington, D.C.: United States Government Printing Office, 1960) esp. pp. 156–62.

outputs) on the basis of profits evaluated at current prices and inform the ministry of their demands (and supplies) corresponding to prices issued by the ministry; (2) the ministry revises prices myopically, that is, on the basis of current or past information submitted by firms. The Lange–Taylor rule [1] is a well-known example of a price system: firms base trial demands (and supplies) on profit maximisation at trial prices given by the ministry, and the ministry revises prices in proportion to excess demands. 'Command system' will refer to iterative search rules in which the information flows are reversed: (1) each firm submits information to the ministry about its production function in the neighbourhood of a trial allocation of resources assigned by the Ministry; (2) the ministry revises the trial allocation on the basis of the information submitted by the firms. Price and command systems are both examples of controlled *tâtonnement*. The emphasis in both systems is on feedback between the ministry and the firms.

The aim of this essay is more or less destructive: to expose as a myth the conventional idea that price systems economise greatly on calculation and flows of information relative to command systems in searching for an optimal allocation of resources. It will be argued that price systems require essentially the same calculations as command systems, and – perhaps more surprising – that the information flows implicit in the trial demands and offers of firms are sufficient to search for the optimum allocation of resources by means of commands. Not only is there no great economy either of calculation or of information in price systems, but also a virtue widely claimed for price systems – that, by requiring firms to submit only trial demands and offers, they permit firms to maintain secrets about their production functions that command systems require them to divulge – is nonexistent.[2]

2 THE SETTING OF THE PROBLEM

The question of command vs. price appears in the simplest problem of resource allocation: the allocation by the ministry of production of a

---

[1] Oskar Lange and Fred Taylor, *On the Economic Theory of Socialism*, ed. Benjamin Lippincott (Minneapolis, Minnesota: The University of Minnesota Press, 1958).

[2] Leonid Hurwicz, 'Conditions for Economic Efficiency of Centralised and Decentralised Structures', in Gregory Grossman (ed.), *Value and Plan* (Berkeley and Los Angeles: University of California Press, 1960), p. 169 ff. and Kenneth Arrow and Leonid Hurwicz, 'Decentralisation and Computation in Resource Allocation', in *Essays in Economics and Econometrics*, ed. Pfouts (Chapel Hill: University of North Carolina Press, 1960), p. 36.

limited resource among distinct enterprises so as to maximise the total output of the ensemble of firms. Denote the allocation of input per year to the ith of m firms by x_i and the ith firm's production function by $f_i(x_i)$. Each allocation is defined by a vector $x = \langle x_1, \ldots, x_m \rangle$, and the task of the ministry is formally to find the allocation x for which

$$F(x) \equiv \sum_{i=1}^{m} f_i(x_i) = \max_{x}$$

subject to the constraint that total input utilisation per unit time shall not exceed a given amount c:

$$E(x) \equiv \sum_{i=1}^{m} x_i - c \leq 0.$$

To keep matters at their simplest, diminishing returns (strict concavity) as well as differentiability will be assumed. Complications that occur at the boundary $x_i = 0$ will be ignored.[1] The first assumption – strict concavity – is essential to the discussion that follows. The obstacles to price-directed resource allocation presented by constant and increasing returns are well known[2] and planning under increasing returns is, I believe, the subject of a paper presented to this conference by Hollis Chenery. I shall say no more about this problem. The disregard of the complications that take place at boundaries is purely for mathematical convenience. The work of a large number of mathematical economists over the last two decades has made it a relatively straightforward exercise to extend discussions of interior maxima of strictly concave differentiable functions to take care of corner maxima. Moreover, the scalars x_i and c could easily be replaced by n-dimensional vectors of inputs, extension from the one input to the n-input case is not quite automatic, but the essence of the argument remains, n-dimensional

[1] Sufficient to guarantee that a corner solution will never be of interest is the assumption that the marginal productivity at each firm becomes infinite as its allocation of input from the ministry approaches zero:
$$\lim_{x_i \to 0} f_i'(x_i) = \infty.$$

[2] On the problem of price-guided search for the optium in the case of constant returns, see Paul Samuelson, 'Market Mechanisms and Maximization', esp. pp. 436–8 and 470–1, in vol. I of *Collected Scientific Papers of Paul Samuelson*, ed. Joseph Stiglitz (Cambridge: Massachusetts Institute of Technology Press, 1966). On the problems presented by increasing returns, see Paul Samuelson, *Foundations of Economic Analysis* (Cambridge: Harvard University Press, 1947), pp. 131–2; A. Pigou, *The Economics of Welfare* (London: Macmillan, 1932), part II; Francis Bator, 'The Simple Analytics of Welfare Maximisation', *American Economic Review*, vol. 47, 1 (Mar. 1957), pp. 47–53.

vectors of first derivatives and $n \times n$ Hessian matrices of second derivatives play the role of the scalars f'_i and f''_i in the discussion that follows.

Associated with the allocation $x*$ which maximises output subject to the input constraint is a price $p*$ endowing $x*$ with the profit-maximising property

$$F(x*) - p*E(x*) > F(x) - p*E(x), \quad x \neq x* \tag{1}$$

and the rent-minimising property

$$-p*E(x*) \leq -pE(x*), \quad p \geq 0, \tag{2}$$

$-E(x*)$ representing the excess supply associated with the optimal allocation of resources. Since production functions are assumed to be strictly concave and smooth, and corner solutions have been assumed away, (1) and (2) can be reformulated in terms of the following conditions:

$$f'_i(x^*_i) - p* = 0, \quad i = 1, \ldots, m. \tag{3}$$

$$p*E(x*) = 0. \tag{4}$$

Equation (3) says that the marginal profit at all firms must be zero for the input price $p*$; that is, the marginal productivity at all firms must be the same and equal to $p*$. Equation (4) says that either firm demands for inputs must in the aggregate equal supply ($E(x*) = 0$), or the price of input must be zero. In general we shall assume the first of these possibilities holds.

If $p*$ is known, then x^*_i can be found from equation (3). Conversely, if x^*_i is known, then $p*$ can be deduced from equation (3). If both $x*$ and $p*$ are known to the ministry, it hardly matters from the point of view of information whether the ministry implements the optimal allocation by means of prices or commands. That is, the ministry can announce the price $p*$ and instruct each firm to choose x_i to maximise profits

$$f_i(x_i) - p*x_i.$$

Or the ministry can directly allocate x^*_i units of input to firm i and command it to produce $f_i(x^*_i)$. The sole informational economy afforded by the use of $p*$ is that the ministry can make an identical announcement to all firms. Command implementation requires a separate instruction, x^*_i, to each firm.

From the point of view of incentives, as distinct from information, the instruction to maximise profits has the advantage that it can be made self-enforcing. If the reward to each firm manager is made proportional to firm profits, he has a direct and immediate reason to implement the ministry's instruction to maximise profits. Command implementation of the optimal allocation offers no such immediate and natural means of making the firm manager's interest coincide with the ministry's.

The distinction between prices as information and prices as incentives is closely related to the difference between *finding* the optimal allocation and *supporting* the optimum (however the optimum might be found). The contention of this essay is that prices have little to recommend themselves over commands in the role of searching for the optimum. No such assertion is advanced with respect to the problem of implementing the optimal allocation.

Discovering the optimal allocation presents no difficulties if all production functions are known to the ministry. But we assume that the cost of determining input-output relationships in their entirety is so great that finding the optimal allocation by means of direct maximisation of $F(x)$ subject to the constraint $E(x) \leq 0$ can be ruled out. On the other hand the ministry need not be entirely ignorant of production possibilities. If production has a previous history, the ministry will inherit an allocation $x^0 = \langle x_i^0, \ldots, x_m^0 \rangle$ from the preceding time period and know the corresponding output vector of $\langle f_1(x_1^0), \ldots, f_m(x_m^0) \rangle$. A search for the optimum allocation is required only in the event of a change in the total supply of input which makes x^0 no longer optimal.[1]

3 NAÏVE RULES OF SEARCH

One rule typically followed by government agencies in analogous situations is to adjust the operating levels of all subagencies by the same proportion. If this year's budget is 5 per cent less than last year's, the government agency may simply instruct all subagencies to cut expenditures back by 5 per cent. The corresponding rule for our ministry would be to change the input level of each firm according to the formula

(R-1)
$$\Delta x_i = -\frac{x_i^0}{\Sigma x_i^0} E(x^0).$$
(5)

If all firms are originally operating at about the same level, (5) corresponds approximately to the equal cut-back rule

(R-2)
$$\Delta x_i = -\frac{E(x^0)}{m}.$$
(6)

[1] For simplicity we confine our attention here to changes in input supply. In a model with more than one output analogous problems would appear with changes in preference functions.

Such rules as (R-1) and (R-2) are generally abhorred by economists because they take no account of differences among the production functions of different firms. Even if the allocation x^0 were optimal for the previous level of input, so that

$$f_i'(x_1^0) = \ldots = f_m'(x_m^0),$$

it would be only by accident that (R-1) or (R-2) would preserve this necessary condition of optimality for the new level of aggregate input utilisation c. Only by the purest coincidence would marginal productivities at all firms change by the same proportion of their respective percentage or absolute change in input.

4 THE ZOUTENDIJK–DORFMAN RULE OF SEARCH: THE LINEAR CONSTRAINED GRADIENT

One adjustment rule that does take account of differences in marginal productivities is to move towards a feasible solution in several steps, each time changing the allocation in a manner which maximises industry output subject to the distance moved in each step. If we employ linear approximations to our production functions at the origin of each move, this procedure of searching for the optimum becomes the linear 'constrained gradient' process developed by G. Zoutendijk [1] and independently by Robert Dorfman.[2] Formally, the iteration beginning from the allocation $x^k = \langle x_1^k, \ldots, x_m^k \rangle$ chooses a vector of changes [3]

$$\Delta x^{k+1} = \langle \Delta x_1^{k+1}, \ldots, x_m^{k+1} \rangle$$

for which

$$\max_{\Delta x} = \Sigma \{ f_i(x_i^k) + f_i'(x_i^k) \Delta x_i^{k+1} \}$$

subject to a constraint upon reduction of excess demand or supply

$$\Sigma \Delta x_i^{k+1} = - \frac{\sigma}{\sigma_0} E(x^k) \tag{8}$$

and subject to a constraint on the distance moved

$$\{ \Sigma (\Delta x^{k+1})^2 \} = \sigma \tag{9}$$

[1] G. Zoutendijk, *Methods of Feasible Directions, A Study in Linear and Non-Linear Programming* (Amsterdam: Elsevier Publishing Co., 1960), Part III.
[2] Robert Dorfman, 'Steepest Ascent Under Constraint', paper presented to the symposium on simulation held at the Western Data Processing Center, U.C.L.A., Los Angeles, California, September, 1961.   [3] By definition $\Delta x^{k+1} \equiv x^{k+1} - x^k$.

In (8) the parameter σ_0 is arbitrary, save that it be sufficiently large $\left[> \dfrac{\{E(x^k)\}^2}{m} \right]$ to permit the existence of a feasible move.

The adjustment rule emerging from following the constrained gradient is the familiar one of changing the input allocation to each firm in proportion to the marginal profitability of production; that is

(R-3P)
$$\Delta x_i^{k+1} = \frac{\sigma}{\lambda^{k+1}} \{f_i'(x_i^k) - p^{k+1}\}, \tag{10}$$

p^{k+1} is the price of input associated with the move from x^k; that is, the Lagrangian multiplier associated with the constraint requiring reduction of excess demand. λ^{k+1} is the Lagrangian multiplier associated with the constraint on the size of the move. The rule for price formation is to take a weighted sum of the (1) excess demand and (2) the average over all firms of the marginal productivity of input:

(R-3P)
$$p^{k+1} = \frac{\lambda^{k+1}}{\sigma} \frac{E(x^k)}{m} + \frac{\Sigma f_i'(x_i^k)}{m}. \tag{11}$$

The Lagrangian multiplier associated with the distance constraint is given by the formula

(R-3P)
$$\lambda^{k+1} = \frac{\sqrt{(m[\text{var}\{f_i'(x_i^k)\}])}}{\sqrt{\left[\dfrac{1 - \{E(x^k)\}^2}{\sigma_0 m} \right]}} \tag{12}$$

where
$$m\{\text{var}(f_i')\} = \Sigma(f_i')^2 - \frac{(\Sigma f_i')^2}{m}.$$

Equation (10) can be rewritten as

(R-3C)
$$\Delta x_i^{k+1} = \sigma \left\{ -\frac{1}{\sigma_0} \frac{E(x^k)}{m} + \sqrt{\left[\dfrac{1 - \dfrac{[E(x^k)]^2}{\sigma_0 m}}{m[\text{var}(f_i')]} \right]} \left(f_i' - \frac{\Sigma f_i'}{m} \right) \right\} \tag{13}$$

The relationship between the constrained gradient method of search and the naïve adjustment rule (R-2) emerges clearly from examination of (R-3C). Like (R-2) the constrained gradient begins by dividing the excess demand equally among projects; the first term in parentheses in (13) includes the factor $-\dfrac{E(x^k)}{m}$. But the constrained gradient does not try to eliminate the excess demand at one stroke; instead, a proportion of excess demand $\dfrac{\sigma}{\sigma_0}$ is eliminated at each move. Moreover, the constrained gradient supplements the arbitrary rule of equal division among firms of the required change in excess demand by changing the allocation to each firm in proportion to the amount by which the firm's marginal productivity differs from the average of marginal productivities over all firms. Firms with marginal productivities higher than average receive a greater allocation of input, firms whose marginal productivities are below average a smaller allocation of input than that dictated by a change proportional to $\dfrac{E(x^k)}{m}$.[1]

Is the adjustment rule which emerges from the following the constrained gradient based on prices or commands? The answer is both; it depends on which form is employed. (R-3C) corresponds to command adjustment of inputs. At each step the firm communicates to the ministry its marginal productivity of input. The ministry then changes the allocation to each firm in accordance with (13), and the process is repeated.

(R-3P) corresponds to a market-like adjustment process. The ministry sets the price of input p^{k+1} and the speed-of-adjustment constant $\dfrac{\lambda^{k+1}}{\sigma}$, and each firm changes its demand for input in proportion to its marginal profitability of production at the given input price. The only problem in concerting the procedure is that the price-formation rule requires the ministry to have information on marginal productivities at x^k in order to determine p^{k+1}. And this conflicts with the elementary requirement of price guided search that firms be required to communicate only their respective input demands to the ministry. Except for the first iteration, it is possible to modify the price formation rule to make it compatible with the market. At x^0, the ministry determines price according to (11):

$$p^1 = \frac{\lambda^1}{\sigma} \frac{E(x^0)}{m} + \frac{\Sigma f_i'(x_i^0)}{m}$$

with λ^1 given by (12). But at each successive iteration, the ministry

---

[1] If the origin of the search x^0 was previously optimal, then
$$f_i' = \ldots f'_m$$
at x^0. Hence the second term within parenthesis of (13) will vanish, and the constrained gradient will reduce to (R-2) for the first iteration – except for the size of the move. But differences among marginal productivities can be expected to emerge in subsequent iterations, for only by the most unlikely coincidence would equal changes in the allocation of inputs to all firms result in equal changes in marginal productivities.

employs the marginal productivities associated with the *previous* (rather than the current) allocation:

$$p^{k+1} = \frac{\lambda^{k+1}}{\sigma} \frac{E(x^k)}{m} + \frac{Ef_i'(x_i^{k-1})}{m}. \quad k = 1, \ldots \quad (14)$$

where

$$\lambda^{k+1} = \frac{\sqrt{(m[\text{var}\{f_i'(x^{k-1})\}])}}{\left[1 - \dfrac{\{E(x^k)\}^2}{\sigma_0 m}\right]}. \quad (15)$$

If the size of each move σ is small, the difference between employing current marginal productivities and penultimate marginal productivities is negligible.

How can the ministry know even penultimate marginal productivities without requiring divulgence of information by firms about their production functions? The answer is that firms cannot avoid divulging the requisite information when they submit changes in demands in accordance with (R-3P):

(R-3P) $$\Delta x_i^{k+1} = \frac{\sigma}{\lambda^{k+1}}\{f_i'(x_i^k) - p^{k+1}\}. \quad (10)$$

When firm i relays Δx_i^{k+1} to the ministry, it transforms (10) into an equation with but one unknown: $f_i'(x_i^k)$. Thus the ministry need only solve (10) for $f_i'(x_i^k)$ to have the information it requires to determine p^{k+2} and λ^{k+2} according to (14) and (15).

Clearly, the secrecy requirement is incompatible with price-guided search for the optimum. The use of prices merely changes the *form* in which firms transmit information about their production functions. Rather than *explicitly* communicating their respective marginal productivities to the ministry as in the command version of the constrained gradient, the firms *implicitly* communicate this information in the guise of changing their demands for inputs.

The equivalence between the two forms of the adjustment rule, (R-3P) and (R-3C), ought to contribute to the clarification of a frequent misunderstanding of the relationship between gradients and price-guided methods of search for the optimal allocation of resources. By concentrating one's attention on (R-3P) it is easy – but incorrect – to conclude that the constrained gradient necessarily implies a market-like process. Price-guided adjustment is consistent with the constrained gradient, but so is a command adjustment. The main difference between the two is the *form* in which firms transmit their information about their production functions. The *substance* is essentially the same in both cases. Hence the frequent claim that the use of prices economises significantly on calculation and information is clearly bogus. The calculations are the same whether adjustment by means of prices or commands. The sole economy afforded by prices is that the information transmitted by the ministry – p – is the same for all firms; by contrast command adjustment requires a separate instruction – Δx_i – for each firm.

5 THE ARROW–HURWICZ–UZAWA RULE OF SEARCH: THE LAGRANGIAN GRADIENT

These remarks apply equally to an algorithm more in the spirit of Kenneth Arrow, Leonid Hurwicz and Hirofumi Uzawa:[1] this algorithm is based on finding the saddle point of the linear approximation to the Lagrangian form

$$\max_{\Delta x} \min_{\Delta p} = \Sigma\{f_i(x_i^k) + f_i'(x_i^k)\,\Delta x_i^{k+1}\} - \{p^k + \Delta p^{k+1}\}\{E(x^k) + \Sigma\Delta x_i^{k+1}\}$$

that is, maximising with respect to Δx_i's and minimising with respect to Δp, subject to the constraint on the size of the move

$$\sqrt{\{\Sigma(\Delta x_i^{k+1})^2 + (\Delta p^{k+1})^2\}} = \sigma.$$

This leads to a rule for changing outputs that is identical to that produced by the linear constrained gradient,

$$\Delta x_i^{k+1} = \frac{\sigma}{\lambda^{k+1}}\{f_i'(x_i^k) - p^{k+1}\}, \tag{10}$$

but to a different rule for determining prices. Instead of setting price equal to a weighted sum of excess demand and the average of marginal products, the Arrow–Hurwicz–Uzawa Lagrangian gradient sets the $k+1^{st}$ price equal to a weighted average of the $k+1st$ excess demand and the kth price:

$$\Delta p^{k+1} = \frac{\sigma}{\lambda^{k+1}}E(x^{k+1}). \tag{16}$$

To find price and quantity changes, (10) and (16) must be solved simultaneously since p^{k+1} enters into (10) and x^{k+1} into (16). In matrix form

[1] Kenneth Arrow, Leonid Hurwicz and Hirofumi Uzawa, *Studies in Linear and Non-Linear Programming* (Stanford, California: Stanford University Press, 1958) part II.

the system of equations can be written

$$
\begin{bmatrix}
\lambda^{k+1} & 0\ldots & 0 & & \sigma \\
0 & \lambda^{k+1} & & & \cdot \\
\cdot & \cdot & & & \cdot \\
\cdot & \cdot & & & \cdot \\
0\ldots & \cdot & \lambda^{k+1} & & \sigma \\
\sigma\ldots & & \sigma & & \lambda^{k+1}
\end{bmatrix}
\begin{bmatrix}
\Delta x_i^{k+1} \\
\cdot \\
\cdot \\
\cdot \\
\Delta x_m^{k+1} \\
\Delta p^{k+1}
\end{bmatrix}
= \sigma
\begin{bmatrix}
f_i'(x_i^k) - p^k \\
\cdot \\
\cdot \\
\cdot \\
f_m'(x_m^k) - p^k \\
E(x^k)
\end{bmatrix}
\qquad (17)
$$

The equation for λ^{k+1} is

$$
\lambda^{k+1} = \sqrt{[\Sigma\{f_i'(x_i^k) - p^{k+1}\}^2 + \{E(x^{k+1})\}^2]} \qquad (18)
$$

(17) supplemented by (18) is the system of equations the ministry would solve at each iteration for command implementation of the Lagrangian gradient. The right-hand side of (17) is filled in with the marginal products reported by firm managers at the previous trial allocation x^k, the excess demand, $E(x^k)$, and the previous trial price p^k.

For price-guided operations the suggested procedure is infeasible because it requires information that is not available to the firms, namely, the marginal products of other firms. The easiest way of rendering the Lagrangian gradient fit for the market is to adopt a modification to the one suggested for the linear constrained gradient: substitution of $E(x^k)$ for $E(x^{k+1})$ in (16) makes the current iteration's price independent of the current iteration's demand changes. In addition, the formula for the parameter λ^{k+1} has to be modified to avoid the need for current information on marginal products and excess demand. In place of (18) we could use

$$
\lambda^{k+1} = \sqrt{[\Sigma\{f_i'(x^{k-1}) - p^k\}^2 + \{E(x^k)\}^2]}.
$$

With these changes, market-like operation of the Arrow–Hurwicz–Uzawa algorithm is feasible. The information flows, price from the ministry to the firms, demands from the firms to the ministry, parallel the flows of the linear constrained gradient.

6   THE LANGE–TAYLOR RULE OF SEARCH: THE QUADRATIC CONSTRAINED GRADIENT

The near-equivalence of price and command versions of adjustment might be an accident of linear approximation. Other procedures might not be so easily amenable to price and command interpretation. Consider for example the now classic rule implicit over thirty years ago in the work of Fred Taylor and Oskar Lange.[1] The ministry announces a price p^k, and each firm maximises profit with input evaluated at the given price:

(R-4P)
$$x_i^k = x_i: \quad f_i(x_i) - p^k x_i = \frac{\max}{x_i} \qquad (19)$$

The ministry then changes the price in proportion to the excess demand corresponding to the kth round demands generated by (19):

(R-4P)
$$\Delta p^{k+1} = \theta E(x^k), \qquad (20)$$

where θ is a positive constant of proportionality.

As stated, the Lange–Taylor rule for search is clearly a price-guided one; indeed, it was proposed to illustrate the compatibility of price guidance and socialism. But this is not the end of the matter. (R-4P) can be transformed into a command rule almost as easily as the linear constrained gradient rule (R-3P) was transformed into (R-3C).

As we have already observed, the marginal condition derived from the expression

$$f_i(x_i) - px_i = \frac{\max}{x_i}$$

for fixed p is

$$f_i' - p = 0. \qquad (21)$$

Differentiation of (21) with respect to price gives

$$\frac{dx_i}{dp} = f_i''^{-1}. \qquad (22)$$

Hence combining (20) with (22) we have, to a linear approximation,

$$\Delta x^{k+1} = \frac{dx_i}{dp} \Delta p^{k+1} = \{f_i''(x_i^k)\}^{-1} \theta E(x^k). \qquad (23)$$

The interpretation of (23) is obvious: the ministry asks the ith firm to inform it of the rate of change of marginal productivity, $f_i''(x_i^k)$, associated with the trial allocation x_i^k. It then changes the ith firm's allocation of input in proportion to the inverse of this rate of change, the constant of proportionality being θ-times the excess demand associated with x^k.[2]

---

[1] Oskar Lange and Fred Taylor, *On the Economic Theory of Socialism*, ed. Benjamin Lippincott (Minneapolis, Minnesota: The University of Minn. Press, 1958).

[2] In the n-input case the scenario is slightly altered: in place of the scalar $E(x^k)$, there is now a vector of excess demands associated with the kth trial allocation:

$$E^k \equiv \langle E_1(x^k), \ldots, E_n(x^k) \rangle.$$

(E_j represents the excess demand for the jth input: x^k is now a matrix, x_{ij}^k representing

The common sense of this rule is that maintenance of firm profits at a maximum maintains equality among marginal products; the price to which each firm equates marginal productivity is the same for all firms. And maintenance of equality among marginal products requires the input allocated to each firm to vary inversely with the rate of change of the firm's marginal product. If the search for the optimum is command-guided, price can be dispensed with, and the change in firm i's input can be explicitly determined by the rate at which its marginal product declines and the excess demand rather than implicitly *via* (1) profit maximisation by the firm and (2) price changes proportional to excess demand by the ministry.

Actually, the equivalence between the command process described by (23) and the price process described by (19) and (20) holds only in the limit as the step size goes to zero so that adjustment becomes continuous rather than discrete, and furthermore, only if at the origin x^0 marginal products are equal. That is, if we replace x_i by x^0 in (23), the resulting path described by

$$\dot{x}_i = \{f''_i(x_i)\}^{-1}\theta E(x)$$

---

the amount of the jth input allocated to the ith firm.) And a matrix of second derivatives of the production function

$$\|f_{i,\,jh}\| \equiv \begin{bmatrix} f_{i,11} & \cdots & f_{i,1n} \\ \cdot & & \cdot \\ \cdot & & \cdot \\ \cdot & & \cdot \\ f_{i,n1} & \cdots & f_{i,nn} \end{bmatrix}$$

replaces the scalar f''_i. The elements of the inverse of $\|f_{i,\,jh}\|$ will be denoted $\hat{f}_{i,\,j}$. That is,

$$\|f_i I_{\,jh}\|^{-1} \equiv \begin{bmatrix} \hat{f}_{i,11} & \cdots & \hat{f}_{i,1n} \\ \cdot & & \cdot \\ \cdot & & \cdot \\ \hat{f}_{i,n1} & \cdots & \hat{f}_{i,nn} \end{bmatrix}.$$

The ministry informs the firm of the vector of excess demands E^k as well of the kth trial allocation. That is, the message to the firm i is a $2n$-vector.

$$\langle x_{i1}^k, \ldots, x_{in}^k; . E_1(x^k), \ldots, E_n(x^k) \rangle.$$

In reply, the firm sends the ministry an n-vector of products of rows of $\|f_{i,\,jh}\|^{-1}$ and E^k,

$$\langle \sum_h \hat{f}_{i,\,1h} E_h(x^k), \ldots, \sum_h \hat{f}_{i,\,nh} E_h(x^k) \rangle$$

the $\hat{f}_{i,jh}$ being computed at the trial allocation $\langle x_{i1}^k, \ldots, x_{in}^k \rangle$. The ministry computes the new trial allocation according to the formula

$$\Delta x_{ij}^{k+1} = \theta \sum_h \hat{f}_{i,jh} E_h(x^k).$$

is exactly the same as the path traced out by the Lange–Taylor algorithm

$$\frac{\max}{x_i} = f_i(x_i) - px_i \tag{24}$$

$$\dot{p} = \theta E(x), \tag{25}$$

provided that at x^0,

$$f_1'(x_1^0) = \ldots = f_m'(x_m^0).$$

Why does equivalance between price and command hold only in the limit as the step size goes to zero? The problem in the discrete case is that the command rule (23) – unlike the price rule (19) – allows marginal products to become different at different firms. Hence in the non-continuous case, (23) must be supplemented by a rule for checking the tendency of marginal products to move apart if the command version of the Lange–Taylor process is to converge to x^*. One possibility is to alternate application of (22) with application of (R-3C) to transfer input among enterprises in a fashion which reduces the discrepancy among marginal productivities without changing excess demands. That is, odd-numbered iterations might obey the rule

$$\Delta x_i^{2k+1} = \{f_i''(x_i^{2k})\}^{-1} \theta E(x^{2k}) \quad k = 0, \ldots$$

and even-numbered moves might take place in accordance with the system

$$\frac{\max}{\Delta x} = \Sigma \{f_i(x_i^{2k+1}) + f_i'(x_i^{2k+1}) \Delta x_i^{2(k+1)}\}$$

$$\Sigma \Delta x_i^2({k+1}) = 0$$

$$\sqrt{\{\Sigma(\Delta x^{2(k+1)})^2\}} = \sigma$$

which leads to the rule

$$\Delta x_i^{2(k+1)} = \rho \left\{ f_i'(x_i^{2k+1}) - \frac{\Sigma f_i'(x_i^{2k1+})}{m} \right\} \quad k = 0, \ldots$$

where

$$\rho = \frac{\sigma}{\sqrt{(m[\mathrm{var}\{f_i'(x^{2k+1})\}])}}.$$

Since the two rules are complementary, improvement might be obtained by combining them at every step instead of applying them sequentially. The resulting algorithm is

$$\Delta x_i^{k+1} = [f_i''(x_i^k)]^{-1} \theta E(x^k) + \rho \left\{ f_i'(x_i^k) - \frac{f_i'(x_i^k)}{m} \right\} \tag{26}$$

(except for the obvious substitution of k for $2k+1$ in the definition of ρ). The rule embodied in equation (26) is clearly a modified version of the constrained gradient rule, (R-3C). Chiefly the modification consists of changing the first term, which determines the division of the excess demand among firms. Instead of allocating the excess demand equally among all firms, as the first term of (R-3C) does, (26) allocates excess demand to firms in inverse proportion to the rate at which marginal productivity changes. The second term of (26) and (R-3C) are identical, except for the parameter outside the brackets which applies equally to all firms. Both rules change the input allocation to firm i in proportion to the amount by which its marginal productivity differs from the average marginal productivity of all firms.

The only difficulty with rule (26) is that it wastes information: evaluation of second derivatives of the production functions is required for operation of the algorithm, but this information is utilised only in the first term, not in the (second) term designed to control departures from the mean marginal productivity. This waste of information suggests the utility of substituting in (26) a *weighted* average of marginal productivities for the unweighted average, $f_i(x_i^k)/m$. The natural weights are the inverses of the rates at which marginal productivities change; instead of the average in which weights are $1/m$, we use

$$\frac{\Sigma [f_i''(x_i^k)]^{-1} f_i'(x_i^k)}{\Sigma [f_i''(x_i^k)]^{-1}}.$$

This substitution leads to

$$\Delta x_i^{k+1} = [f_i''(x_i^k)]^{-1} \theta E(x^k) + \rho \left[f_i'(x_i^k) - \frac{\Sigma \{f_i''(x_i^k)\}^{-1} f_i'(x_i^k)}{\Sigma \{f_i''(x_i^k)\}^{-1}} \right] \qquad (27)$$

in place of (26).

It is natural at this point to look for the 'integral' of (27), that is, the system of objective function and constraints which generates (27) as its first-order condition of maximisation in the way that (7) together with (8) and (9) generated the rules (R-3C) and (R-3P). In other words, it is natural to ask what – if anything – (27) maximises. The answer is that if in searching for the optimum by means of gradients we replace the *linear* approximation to the production function (7) by a *quadratic* approximation

$$\max_{\Delta x} = \Sigma \{ f_i(x_i^k) + f_i'(x_i^k) \Delta x_i^{k+1} + \tfrac{1}{2} f_i''(x_i^k) (\Delta x_i^{k+1})^2 \} \qquad (28)$$

and retain the constraint

$$\Sigma \Delta x_i^{k+1} = -\frac{\sigma}{\sigma_0} E(x^k), \tag{8}$$

we generate as the condition of constrained maximisation

(R-4P′) $\quad\quad \Delta x_i^k + 1 = \{f_i''(x_i^k)\}^{-1}\{f_i'(x_i^k) - p^{k+1}\}$ (29)

with the companion price-formation rule

(R-4P) $\quad\quad p^{k+1} = \dfrac{-\dfrac{\sigma}{\sigma_0}E(x^k)}{\Sigma[f_i''(x_i^k)]^{-1}} + \dfrac{\Sigma\{f_i''(x_i^k)\}^{-1}f_i'(x_i^k)}{\Sigma\{f_i''(x_i^k)\}^{-1}}.$ (30)

Combining (29) with (30), we have

(R-4C) $\quad\quad \Delta x_i^{k+1} = [f_i''(x_i^k)^{-1}]\left[-\dfrac{\sigma}{\sigma_0}\Sigma\{f_i''(x_i^k)\}^{-1}\right]E(x^k)$

$$-f_i''(x_i^k)^{-1}\left[f_i'(x_i^k) - \frac{\Sigma\{f_i''(x_i^k)\}^{-1}f_i'(x_i^k)}{\Sigma\{f_i''(x_i^k)\}^{-1}}\right]. \tag{31}$$

With the substitution for θ of the expression $-\dfrac{\sigma_0}{\sigma}\Sigma\{f_i''(x_i^k)\}^{-1}$ and with the substitution for ρ of $-\{f_i''(x_i^k)\}^{-1}$, (R-4C) becomes identical to (27).

Our equations suggest that the adjustment role inspired by quadratic approximation to the objective function can be implemented by prices, (R-4P′), as well as commands, (R-4C). But the price-guided version is feasible only in the limit as the step size goes to zero and the rule derived from the quadratic approximation to the objective function becomes the original Lange–Taylor process. The problem is that in the discrete case price formation requires knowledge of both f_i' and f_i'', but the ministry cannot infer both from changes in firm demands determined according to (29). There are, unfortunately, two unknowns in our equation. As the step size goes to zero, however, equality of marginal products is preserved throughout the adjustment process, and (R-4P′) collapses into the continuous Lange–Taylor rule (24) and (25). In this case the firm cannot avoid revealing f_i'' and f_i' to the ministry when it responds to price changes. Revelation of f_i'' is implicit in the rate at which x_i changes,[1] and

---

[1] In the n-input case, it is the vector

$$\langle \Sigma_h f_{i,\,1h} E_h(x^k), \ldots, \Sigma_h f_{i,\,nh} E_h(x^k)\rangle$$

that is implicitly revealed by the vector of rates of change of demand

$$\langle \dot{x}_{i1}, \ldots, \dot{x}_{in}\rangle.$$

(See footnote 2, p. 65, for the notation employed here.)

revelation of f'_i is implicit in profit maximisation, which dictates that f'_i be equal to p.

The speed-of-adjustment constraint

$$\sqrt{\{\Sigma(\Delta x^{k+1})^2\}} = \sigma \tag{9}$$

is omitted from the system (28)–(8) because it is not needed in the present instance to guarantee the existence of a solution. With a *linear* approximation like (7)–(8), optimising without the imposition of a ceiling on the size of the move will suggest infinite values for the x_i's (either $+\infty$ or $-\infty$), but the curvature introduced by the quadratic term in (28) bounds the optimal Δx's, and obviates the need for a speed-of-adjustment constraint. Nevertheless, the augmented quadratic system

$$\max_{\Delta x} = \Sigma\{f'_i(x_i^i)\,\Delta x_i^{k+1} + \tfrac{1}{2}f''_i(x_i^k)\,(\Delta x_i^{k+1})^2\} \tag{28}$$

$$\Sigma\Delta x_i^{k+1} = -\frac{\sigma}{\sigma_0}E(x^k) \tag{8}$$

$$\sqrt{\{\Sigma(\Delta x_i^{k+1})^2\}} = \sigma \tag{9}$$

is of interest, for it is natural to attempt to compare the quadratic constrained gradient with the linear constrained gradient (7)–(8)–(9), and to do this the size of the move must be the same in the two systems. The adjustment rules associated with (28)–(8)–(9) are identical with (R-4C) and (R-4P′) except that $f''_i(x_i^k)^{-1}$ is replaced by $\left\{f''_i(x_i^k) - \dfrac{\mu^{k+1}}{\sigma}\right\}^{-1}$ where μ^{k+1} is the Lagrangian multiplier associated with (9). (R-4P) thus becomes

(R-4P″) $$\Delta x_i^{k+1} = -\left\{f''_i(x_i^k) - \frac{\mu^{k+1}}{\sigma}\right\}^{-1}\{f'_i(x_i^k) - p^{k+1}\}.$$

The price-formation rule becomes

(R-4P″) $$p^{k+1} = \frac{\dfrac{\sigma}{\sigma_0}E(x^k)}{\Sigma\left\{f''_i(x_i^k) - \dfrac{\mu^{k+1}}{\sigma}\right\}^{-1}} + \frac{\Sigma\left\{f''_i(x_i^k) - \dfrac{\mu^{k+1}}{\sigma}\right\}^{-1}f'_i(x_i^k)}{\Sigma\left\{f''_i(x_i^k) - \dfrac{\mu^{k+1}}{\sigma}\right\}^{-1}}.$$

The centralised version of the rule becomes

(R-4C″) $$\Delta x_i^{k+1} = \left\{f''_i(x_i^k) - \frac{\mu^{k+1}}{\sigma}\right\}\left[-\frac{\sigma}{\sigma_0}\Sigma\left\{f''_i(x_i^k) - \frac{\mu^{k+1}}{\sigma}\right\}^{-1}\right]E(x^k)$$

$$-\left\{f_i''(x_i^k)-\frac{\mu^{k+1}}{\sigma}\right\}^{-1}\left[f_i'(x_i^k)-\frac{\sum\left\{f_i''(x_i^k)-\frac{\mu^{k+1}}{\sigma}\right\}^{-1}f_i'(x_i^k)}{\sum\left\{f_i''(x_i^k)-\frac{\mu^{k+1}}{\sigma}\right\}^{-1}}\right].$$

The Lagrangian multiplier μ^{k+1} is found by adding the equation

$$\sum\{f_i'(x_i^k)\Delta x_i^{k+1}+f_i''(x_i^k)(\Delta x_i^{k+1})^2\}+p^{k+1}\frac{\sigma}{\sigma_0}E(x^k)-\mu^{k+1}\sigma=0$$

to the system.

With step size equal, 'cost effectiveness' comparisons can readily be made between the linear constrained gradient and the quadratic constrained gradient. The most natural procedure is to identify the cost of adjustment with the number of observations of $f_i(x_i)$ required to estimate its derivatives: two for f_i' and three for f_i''. Then the quadratic gradient is clearly more costly, but equally clearly it gives a better approximation to the production function, at least locally. But comparisons of benefits and costs of different algorithms really have nothing to do with the issue of prices vs. command, and further discussion can be properly put off to another occasion.

What do all these manipulations accomplish? First, it has been shown that the adjustment rule proposed by Lange and Taylor for equating supply and demand can be given a command interpretation. Command operation requires generalisation of the adjustment rule proposed by Lange and Taylor, but only because of the discreteness of the step. (The second term of (R-4C) vanishes if, despite discreteness, all firms happen to maintain equal marginal productivities as they do perforce in the continuous version; the adjustment required by discreteness then becomes superfluous.) Second, the Lange–Taylor rule, generalised or not, is a member of the family of constrained gradient methods of search. It differs from the linear constrained gradient only in that it employs a quadratic approximation to the objective function rather than a linear approximation. Replacement of the linear approximation by the quadratic approximation is tantamount to introduction of local foresight in the rule to vary the allocation of resources directly with marginal profits. In both (R-3P) and (R-4P') sgn x is equal to sgn $(f_i'-p)$; (27) differs from (8) only in the proportionality factor, replacement of the linear approximation by the quadratic approximation leading to replacement of the constant σ/λ^{k+1} by a factor reflecting local foresight about changes in marginal productivity, $-f_i''^{-1}$. The quadratic price formation rule (28) also differs from the linear rule (11): the quadratic price rule, unlike the linear price rule, reflects anticipated changes in marginal products as well as current marginal products.[1]

7 THE PROBLEM OF INCENTIVES

We have up to now simply assumed that firm managers would respond honestly to requests for information by the ministry, whether the requests were for changes in demands caused by changes in trial prices or for changes in marginal productivities resulting from changes in trial allocations. But how do we justify our faith in the honesty of firm managers? Why should they be interested in playing the price game? Or the command game?

In cursory remarks on implementing the optimum (p. 57 above), it was suggested that the enlightened self-interest of the firm leads it to play the price game according to the rules, and that the lack of a corresponding self-interest is an obstacle to the implementation of the command game. However, it was emphasised that price brings the self-interest of the firm into line with the interest of the ministry only when the firm is actually rewarded proportionately to the profits it earns at the price p^*,

$$f_i(x_i) - p^* x_i \qquad i = 1, \ldots, m.$$

Otherwise, the manager of firm i has no incentive to respond to the price p^* with the demand for x_i^*. In the presence of increasing returns or external economies, rewards proportionate to profits do not ensure that the firm's interest coincides with the ministry's. The existence of increasing returns, for example, may cause the ministry's interest in maximum output to require one firm to produce at a point of minimum profits and others to shut down altogether despite the possibility that zero output provides only locally maximal, not globally maximal, profits. The situation is even more complicated in the n-input case.

Equally important, the problem of supporting or implementing the optimal allocation once known is logically distinct from the problem of

---

[1] Mathematically, the Lange–Taylor rule is simply Newton's method for finding the root of an equation. Why? First, finding the root of the equation system $f_i' - p \equiv 0$ is equivalent to finding the saddle point of $F(x) - pE(x)$, given our assumptions of strict concavity and the existence of an interior solution. Second, using a linear approximation to the equation of the first order condition, *à la* Newton, is identical to using a quadratic approximation to the objective function, *à la* Lange and Taylor. I am indebted to Paul Samuelson for pointing out that using Newton's method to solve an equation system is equivalent to using successive quadratic approximations to find the extremals of the equation system's 'integral'.

finding the optimum. One can imagine support of the optimal plan by the profit motive coupled with a command system of search. Suppose firm managers are told in advance of the search (1) that rewards will vary directly with profits once production gets under way; (2) that the allocation of input must satisfy the supply constraint $E(x) \leq 0$ before production can begin; (3) that the price employed by the ministry to compute the value of input, and hence profits, will be set equal to the average of marginal productivities at all firms. Suppose further that the number of firms is large, and that there is no collusion among firms. Then it is in each firm manager's interest, as well as in the ministry's, to find the allocation of input that maximises total output, x^*. For in this model no single firm has a perceptible influence on the price that will ultimately be fixed by the ministry, and it is therefore in the firm's interest that its own allocation of input equate marginal product with price. Consequently the manager has every reason not to misrepresent his production function to the ministry.[1]

Conversely, price systems do not invariably provide firms with incentives that reflect the ministry's interest in output maximisation even when rewards are proportionate to profits. Firms are rarely totally ignorant of other firms' production possibilities, and unless the number of firms is large, each manager can attempt to utilise his knowledge about other firms to influence the price of input in a manner favourable to his own profits. For example,[2] suppose there are two firms and that firm 1 knows firm 2's production function. Suppose that firm 2 naïvely plays the profit-maximising game on the assumption that the price of input is fixed and that firm 1 utilises its knowledge of firm 2's production function and behaviour to maximise its own profits. During the search for the optimum, firm 1's goal is to find x_1, x_2 and p for which

$$\max_{x_1 p} = f_1(x_1) - px_1$$

[1] However, a 'prisoners' dilemma' – see R. Duncan Luce and Howard Raiffa, *Games and Decisions* (New York: Wiley, 1957) ch. 5 – faces the manager. Precisely because he has an imperceptible influence on the price, his desire for a leisurely, quiet life may lead him to pay little attention to the accuracy of the reports of marginal productivities that he files with the ministry, at least in the early stages of search. This is the case whether or not other managers play the game carefully. Hence there is the possibility that each will decide to leave the burden of finding the optima to the others and that the command game will be thwarted. The uncertainty of the manager as to when a halt will be called to the search for the optimum would seem to be his only reason for playing the game carefully. Note that the same problem exists in price games.

[2] I am grateful to Edmond Malinvaud for this example, as well as for the advice to emphasise the need for the number of firms to be large if the profit motive is to couple the firm's with the ministry's interest.

subject to the constraint that the total output utilisation not exceed the available supply,

$$E(x) \equiv x_1 + x_2 - c \leq 0, \tag{32}$$

and the constraint resulting from firm 2's profit-maximising behaviour

$$f'_2(x_2) = p. \tag{33}$$

The usual Lagrangian techniques lead to the profit-maximising condition

$$f'_1(x_1) + x_1 f''_2(x_2) = p \tag{34}$$

which, along with (32) and (33), determines the triple $\langle \bar{x}_1, \bar{x}_2, \bar{p} \rangle$ that maximises firm 1's profits. Since $f''_2(x_2)$ is negative, profit maximisation leads firm 1 to seek an allocation for which its own marginal productivity exceeds the price. The gain from the reduction in price that this allocation permits relative to the allocation $\langle x_1^*, x_2^*, p^* \rangle$ for which

$$f'_1(x_1) = p$$

exceeds the loss from not equating marginal productivity with price. It follows that in responding to various trial prices announced by the ministry it is in the interest of firm 1 to understate demands relative to the demands that with trial prices regarded as fixed would (1) accurately reflect marginal profits in the linear constrained and Lagrangian gradients, or (2) maximise profits in the Lange–Taylor version of the quadratic constrained gradient.

However, as the number of firms, m, becomes large, the value to firm 1 of knowledge of all other firms' productive opportunities becomes small, and in the limit firm 1's self-interest leads it to play the game in the manner Lange intended. The allocation-price vector optimal for firm 1, when firm 1 knows the other firms' production function and knows as well that other firms will play the price game on the assumption of a fixed price, approaches the allocation-price vector that maximises total output. Mathematically, the $(m+1)$-tuple $\langle x, p \rangle$ approaches $\langle x^*, p^* \rangle$ as m increases without bound.

The proof of this assertion requires only an examination of the profit-maximising condition for firm 1 in the presence of $m-1$ other firms that equate marginal productivity to price, under the assumption that all m production functions are known to firm 1. As before, firm 1 seeks the vector $\langle x, p \rangle$ for which

$$\max_{x_1, p} = f_1(x_1) - px_1$$

subject to

$$E(x) \leq 0$$

and subject to $m-1$ additional constraints

$$f'_i(x_i) = p \qquad i = 2, \ldots, m.$$

The profit-maximising condition – compare equation (34) – is

$$f'_1(x_1) + \frac{x_1}{\sum\limits_{i=2}^{m} \{f''_i(x_i)\}^{-1}} = p.$$

Since the second term on the left-hand side approaches zero as m increases without bound, the condition of profit maximisation for firm 1 approaches the condition of total output maximisation. Firm 1's superior knowledge of the evironment gives it an incentive for 'cheating' in the price game only when it is one of few firms. Thus, whether the search for the optimum is conducted by prices or commands, the competitive assumption of a large number of firms is required to make the profit motive an effective instrument of the ministry's will.

These brief remarks are intended to emphasise the usefulness of prices and profits in uniting the interest of the firm (and by extension the individual) to the interest of the ministry (read society). Provided the environment is decomposable (external economies are absent), diminishing returns reign, and the number of agents is large, the profit motive leads each agent to behave in the manner Adam Smith and Oskar Lange intended. But the role of prices is crucial in supporting the optimum, not in finding the optimum; command systems of search as well as price systems can be coupled with implementation of the optimal plan by means of the profit motive.

8 CONCLUSIONS

The goal of this paper has been to shift the spotlight in the command vs. price debate from the organising and processing of information about production functions to other problems like incentives, uncertainty and the cost of economic transition. Calculation and the flow of information appear to be a secondary issue because for each of the popular price-guided rules of search for the optimum examined here, there exists an informationally equivalent command rule;[1] the difference between the

[1] For the Lange–Taylor rule, the assertion is true only in the limit as the step size goes to zero.

D

rules lies in the form in which information is communicated rather than in the substantive information requirements. A corollary of the identity of informational requirements is that price-guided as well as commanded search for the optimum is inconsistent with the preservation of secrecy about production functions, a 'virtue' widely acclaimed for price-guided research. When firms demand inputs according to prescribed rules like 'change demand for inputs in proportion to marginal profits' or 'change demand to maximise profits', it requires no more than secondary school algebra to discover as much information about the firm's marginal products as is needed to search for the optimum by means of commands. The firms implicitly signal this information when they change input demands. The equations generated by the gradient processes studied here are susceptible to the interpretation that changes in resource allocations be determined by excess demand and averages of marginal products or by excess demands and previous prices. But the same equations are equally susceptible to the interpretation that each firm's resource allocation be determined by commands based on excess demand and the difference between its own marginal product and the average – weighted or unweighted – of marginal products; in the command interpretation prices never explicitly enter the picture. An observer aware only of the sequence of vectors $\{x^k\}$ would be unable to decide whether he is watching a price- or command-guided search for the optimum.

The sole informational economy afforded by the prices relative to commands is that price-guided search can get along with but a single, common message from the ministry to the firms at each iteration: the current trial price of input. By contrast command-guided search requires a separate message for each firm: the current trial allocation of input. This economy of information is roughly equivalent to the saving from being able to insert a single advertisement in a newspaper rather than being obliged to insert a separate advertisement for each firm. This seems a thin reed on which to attempt to support claims for informational superiority of price-guided search.

This is not to suggest that prices are irrelevant. On the contrary: a properly functioning price system couples the individual's interest to society's, and no economy has attempted for long to function without prices, at least in markets for consumers' goods. But the crucial role of prices in providing incentives to economic agents should not be confused with their role in providing information. It is the problem of incentives, I believe, that gives rise to the new prominence attached to prices in the Soviet Union by the reforms known collectively as 'Liebermanism'.

The time has surely come for the emphasis to shift back to incentives from the informational sidetrack whither Oskar Lange's brilliant essay [1] led – an essay, which for all its virtues, never even considered the problem of how to interest economic agents in playing the shadow price game it advocated.

[1] 'On the Economic Theory of Socialism', reprinted in a volume of the same name edited by Benjamin Lippincott, op. cit.

4 The Mechanism for Management of Socialist Industry

J. G. Zielinski

1 THE SOCIALIST ENTERPRISE AS A CYBERNETIC SYSTEM

For the purpose of management theory it is convenient to consider the socialist enterprise as a cybernetic system consisting of:

> (a) feeding system;
> (b) information system;
> (c) stimulation system; and
> (d) steering system.

Graphically this is presented in Fig. 1.

(i) THE FEEDING SYSTEM

The enterprise is endowed with a certain volume of fixed and variable capital. With the help of this capital the production process of the enterprise is organised. The results of this production process – goods or services – are sold at *buying prices* and a certain total revenue is realised. Before these receipts can enter again the feeding system of the enterprise they are subjected to two regulatory processes:

(a) the first determines the total amount of financial resources which will remain at the enterprise's disposal;

(b) the second determines – within limits – the use of resources which remain within the enterprise. The circulation of this part of total revenue which remains within the enterprise we call the *dependent* feeding system.

Because the socialist enterprise is a fraction of the total of state ownership, we have to distinguish also a so-called *independent* feeding system. On the basis of macro-economic considerations, the Central Planning Board (C.P.B.) can decide that the resources of a given enterprise shall be enlarged beyond the volume determined by the dependent feeding system. For example, it may be decided that the enterprise shall be substantially expanded. Such steps are financed from the centralised investment fund and this flow of resources we label the independent feeding system.

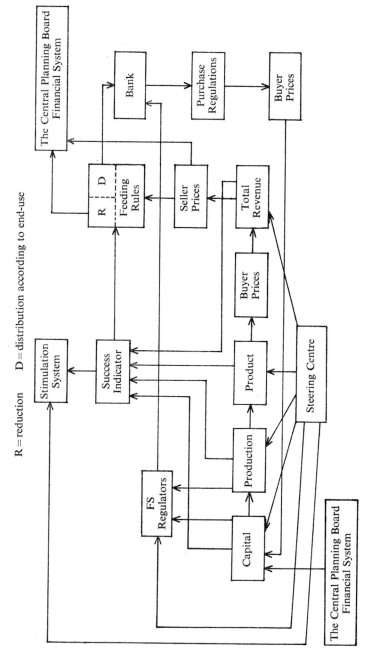

FIG. 1. THE SOCIALIST ENTERPRISE AS A CYBERNETIC SYSTEM
(Simplified Diagram)

R = reduction   D = distribution according to end-use

(ii) THE INFORMATION SYSTEM

The activity of the enterprise can be subdivided into a multiplicity of *economic events*: the use of raw materials and manpower, production of certain goods and services, etc. These economic events or their certain features are registered according to existing *transformation rules* (methods of accounting) which determine what is to be registered and how. There are, for example, rules of registering the use of electric energy, manpower, volume of output, level of costs, etc. Economic events or their features aggregated according to transformation rules and usually compared to certain bases or norms we shall call *analysers*. By analysers we understand all kinds of performance indicators pertaining to the whole or some part of enterprise activity, e.g. unit use of raw materials, level of costs, level of stock, quality of product, etc. As a rule, analysers are equipped with standards, bases of comparison, e.g. input norms, planned level of unit costs, planned volume of output, profit and the like.

In every enterprise there is a multiplicity of analysers serving different tasks. These tasks can be divided into general – fulfilled by all analysers – and specific – by some of them.

The general task of all analysers is to 'watch' economic events and supply the enterprise steering centre (the management) with information necessary for operative decisions. The general character of this task reveals itself by the fact that all analysers are connected with the steering centre.

In addition to this general task, some groups of analysers serve specific goals. Using as a criterion the system with which given analysers are connected, we can subdivide them into three main groups:

(a) *Success indicators* which are connected with the stimulation system. Within given constraints they are the main determinants of enterprise strategy and tactics. Dozens of different success indicators have been used simultaneously or consecutively in socialist countries.

(b) *Regulators of the feeding system* (FS regulators). They are connected with the feeding system and regulate and control the flow of resources or of specific types of resources. The most important FS regulators are so-called 'output indices' which are the basis of planning and controlling the employment and the wage fund of enterprises and industrial associations.

(c) *Technico-economic analysers* which are the instruments for controlling specific processes within the enterprise, e.g. use of inputs, quality of output, etc. They are connected with the steering centre through the information-system only, and, sometimes also, through the stimulation system with the lower echelons of managerial hierarchy.

We have to remember that frequently the same analyser, for example profit, fulfils more than one specific function. E.g. profit is usually both success indicator and one of the FS regulators. We shall return to this problem later.

(iii) THE STIMULATION SYSTEM

One or more analysers are connected with the stimulation system of the enterprise. Construction of the stimulation system may vary greatly. The most simple stimulation system consists of three parts: (a) a success indicator (MP) which at the same time is the source of the bonus fund (FP), (b) a bonus coefficient (W) which determines the relationship between MP and FP and (c) the distribution coefficient (P) which determines how the bonus fund is to be divided between the members of the management. So:

$$FP = MP \times W$$

and individual bonus (FPi):

$$FPi = MP \times W \times P.$$

In the actual practice of socialist countries the stimulation system is much more complicated and, as a rule, consists of the following:
- (a) the rules as to how the volume of the bonus fund is to be determined;
- (b) the sources of its financing;
- (c) the conditions which entitle the enterprise to establish the bonus fund (usually a certain level of the success indicator has to be achieved);
- (d) the conditions for paying the bonuses out of the bonus fund;
- (e) the rules of the bonus fund distribution between members of the management.

(iv) THE STEERING SYSTEM

Under *ceteris paribus* assumption, the steering system, i.e. the strategy and tactics of the enterprise, is determined by the construction of the feeding, information and stimulation systems. It means that the steering system can be meaningfully analysed only when the remaining systems are given. At the same time, the steering system can be used as a test of how effectively the other systems are constructed and functioning. If the behaviour of the enterprise does not conform to the C.P.B. objectives, it means that there is a fault somewhere in one or several of the other systems. It is an important task of economic analysis to find out where in the remaining systems lie the causes of the undesirable behaviour of the enterprise and to indicate the proper remedies.

2 THE MANAGEMENT MECHANISM

For effective management of plan fulfilment, the C.P.B. needs a properly constructed management mechanism. The management mechanism can be defined as a system of interrelated tools of economic policy used for directing the economic activities of economic units, within the framework of the same form of ownership.[1] The tasks of the management mechanism consist of:

(a) inducing the economic units to plan fulfilment;
(b) inducing the economic units to adopt an economic behaviour within the process of plan fulfilment and outside of it.

(i) THE ELEMENTS OF THE MANAGEMENT MECHANISM

The management mechanism consists of three parts:

(a) The information transmitting system from and to the C.P.B.[2] In socialist countries there are four basic *information carriers* presently in use: (1) prices, (2) plan indices: obligatory (administrative orders) and informational, (3) rates of bonuses and (4) operational changes in the information and/or stimulation systems.
(b) The principles of enterprise functioning, which we shall call the *management formula*.
(c) The macro-economic feeding system which consists of the financial-credit system and the rules concerning the purchases of inputs and the selling of outputs. The management mechanism is presented graphically in Fig. 2.

---

[1] My thinking along the lines presented in this paper was greatly influenced by the work of O. Lange and other colleagues (see References [2] and [6] on p. 97), to whom I make grateful acknowledgements.

[2] The households and private farmers are influenced by the C.P.B. with the help of the *steering mechanism*. The main difference between management and steering mechanisms lies in the fact that the latter consists of two elements only: an information transmitting system and a macro-economic feeding system. The principles of the functioning of the household or of the individual farmer are not determined by the C.P.B. but by the nature of an economic unit involved.

Fig. 2 indicates that the enterprise is influenced by transmitted information and/or by a macro-feeding system through its management formula. This simple thesis is of great practical importance, because it stresses the fact that *how* the enterprise reacts to a given stimulus or constraint depends on how its management formula is constructed. It can be generalised into the thesis of the *integral* character of a management mechanism. The fact that all elements of a management mechanism are closely interrelated within and between themselves is one of the basic causes of theoretical and practical difficulties in constructing an efficient, internally consistent management mechanism.

FIG. 2. THE MANAGEMENT MECHANISM

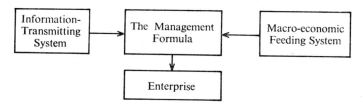

(ii) THE MANAGEMENT FORMULA

Let us now consider in some detail the central part of the management mechanism – the management formula. Every management formula consists of the following elements:

  (a) methods of accounting which transform certain features of economic events into success indicators and FS regulators;
  (b) a success indicator or indicators and FS regulator or regulators;

FIG. 3. SIMPLE MANAGEMENT FORMULA

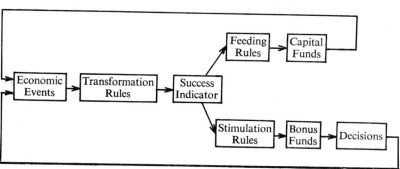

FIG. 4. COMPLEX MANAGEMENT FORMULA

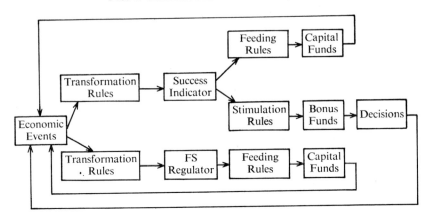

FIG. 5. EXCEEDINGLY COMPLEX MANAGEMENT FORMULA

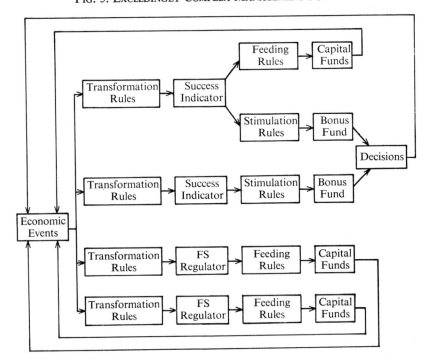

(c) stimulation rules (bonus regulations) which determine the inter-relations between success indicators, bonus funds and management bonuses actually paid;

(d) a bonus fund or funds;

(e) feeding rules which determine the relationship between the FS regulators and enterprise capital funds (investment and operative);

(f) capital funds.

Depending on the construction of the second element of the management formula, we can distinguish their three basic types:

Type 1: A simple management formula, which consists of one success indicator which at the same time serves as the only FS regulator. (See Fig. 3.)

Type 2: A complex management formula, which consists of one success-indicator/FS-regulator plus one extra FS regulator. (See Fig. 4.)

Type 3: An exceedingly complex management formula in which the number of success-indicators/FS-regulators is greater than three. (See Fig. 5.)

It is easy to supply actual and/or theoretical examples of all three types of management formula. Of Type 1: capitalist enterprise generally, Yugoslav practice and Czechoslovak proposed reforms; of Type 2: some Polish proposals; Type 3: the current practice of Poland and most socialist countries.

3 DIFFERENT MODELS FOR MANAGEMENT OF SOCIALIST INDUSTRY

Depending on the type of information carrier used by the C.P.B. for managing the socialist industry, we can distinguish two management models:

(a) parametric, when prices and/or rates of bonuses are used;

(b) non-parametric, when administrative orders and/or changes in management formulae are used.

Model (a) uses *cipher* information, which has to be deciphered by the information-stimulation systems of the enterprise. Model (b) uses *open* information.

(i) PURE AND MIXED MANAGEMENT MODELS

Pure models assume – *ex definitione* – that only one type of information is used: cipher or open. The actual practice of socialist countries represents a mixed model, in which both types of information are used simultaneously. This means that the management formula is constructed in such a way that it can receive cipher information. At the same time,

FIG. 6. PARAMETRIC MANAGEMENT

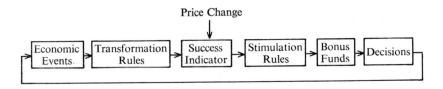

FIG. 7. THE FALSE PRESENTATION OF NON-PARAMETRIC MANAGEMENT

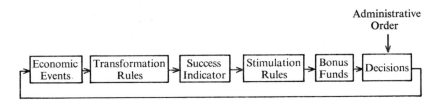

FIG. 8. THE CORRECT PRESENTATION OF NON-PARAMETRIC MANAGEMENT

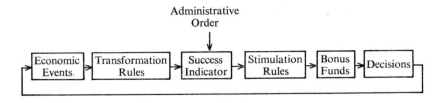

however, open information is also used. Let us consider this problem in some detail.

The price information enters the enterprise management formula in the way depicted in Fig. 6. How does open information enter management formula? It would be false to visualise it as it is presented in Fig. 7. We cannot ignore that the actual management formula consists of information and stimulation systems which influence the enterprise reaction to open information. It is well known that many administrative orders are not fulfilled in practice and this cannot be explained by external circumstances only. On the contrary, to a great extent it is the result of contradictions between the economic interest of the enterprise (determined by the construction of information-stimulation systems and the cipher information entering them) and open information. The actual path of open information is presented in Fig. 8. It means that actual behaviour of the enterprise is the compromise between the action dictated by cipher information and open information. There is ample evidence to support this thesis.[1] Needless to say, such a compromise would be unnecessary if both types of information contained exactly the same information. As we shall indicate later, this is impossible, however, for technical reasons.

(ii) OPERATIONAL PRICES ARE USED IN MANAGEMENT MODELS

As we have indicated elsewhere,[2] there are four types of prices used in present-day socialist countries:

(a) programming prices used for construction of an internally consistent plan; these prices are used for aggregation only and prevail in most of actual planning exercises;

(b) shadow or accounting prices are used for partial optimisation in the process of plan construction; at present these prices are used in investment and foreign trade effectiveness calculations only;

(c) operational prices used in the process of plan fulfilment, as one of the information carriers used in managing the socialist industry, and

(d) consumer goods prices, which are – in principle – market-clearing prices for consumer goods.

Whenever we speak about prices in this paper we mean operational prices.

---

[1] The former Polish Minister of Internal Trade, Dr M. Lesz, recently quoted a number of examples of not fulfilling the assortment plan and commented [3]: 'We have here a certain regularity, a certain law; the level of plan fulfilment of a given good is directly proportional to the value of production per hour of labour'. He traced it to the use of gross value of output as a main success indicator.

[2] The problem of prices is more fully discussed in [4], [5] and [7].

4   THE CONSTRUCTION OF MANAGEMENT FORMULAE AND THE POSSIBILITY OF PARAMETRIC MANAGEMENT

The possibility of using cipher information depends – to a great extent – on the construction of management formula and especially its information system.

(i) THE RECEPTION SPHERE OF SUCCESS INDICATORS

Every success indicator has a certain reception sphere. By the reception sphere of a success indicator we understand how many and what features of economic events are registered in a success indicator and influence its magnitude. Needless to say, the range of the reception sphere of different success indicators shows marked differences.

We can use the range of the reception sphere as a criterion for dividing all success indicators into two groups:

(a) Those success indicators with the broadest reception sphere we shall call *synthetic* success indicators. The broadest reception spheres have success indicators which are *reductors* of costs and revenues. Only success indicators based on profit are such reductors.

(b) All other success indicators we shall call specialised success indicators. Their characteristic feature is that their reception sphere registers economic events from the input *or* output side, never from both. No specialised success indicator is a cost-revenue reductor *ex definitione*.

The features of economic events are determined by:

(a) the activity of the enterprise itself; e.g. diminishing the steel input per unit of output;

(b) information transmitted from the C.P.B.; e.g. price increase of steel will change the cost effect of a given steel input;

(c) information sent from the customers; e.g. lack of orders may force the enterprise to change its product mix.

The success indicator can be considered as a receiver-transmitter, which receives different information and transmits it to the enterprise steering centre and the C.P.B. This is presented in Fig. 9.

The proper construction of the enterprise information system requires

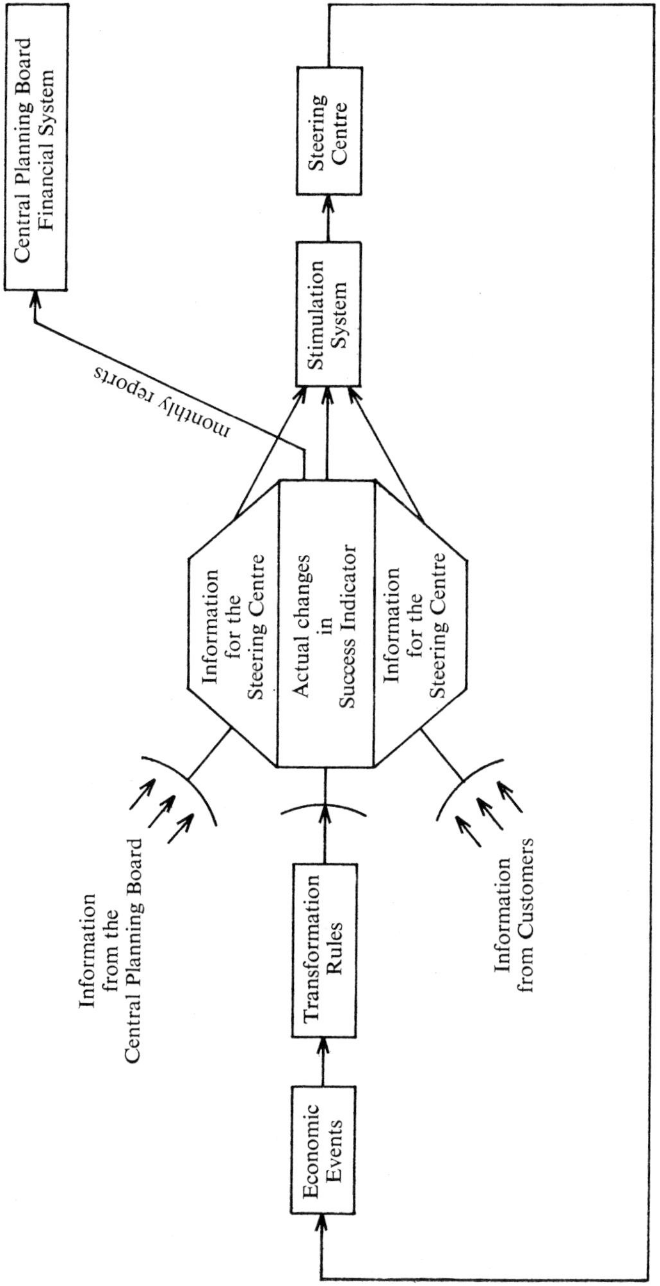

FIG. 9. THE SUCCESS INDICATOR AS A RECEIVER-TRANSMITTER

that the sensitivity of the proposed (or actual) success indicator to these three sources of information is carefully analysed. This is the problem of how broad or narrow is the reception sphere of a given success indicator. Another important problem in constructing the information system of the enterprise is to ensure the *proper reaction* of the success indicator to economic events. A change in economic events considered desirable by the C.P.B. should induce desirable changes, from the enterprise point of view, in the success indicator.

For the sake of brevity we present the determinants of the reception sphere and type of reaction of success indicator in a table form (see Table 1, p. 96) without presenting proofs and illustrations.

(ii) THE RECEPTION SPHERE AND PARAMETRIC MANAGEMENT

For the purpose of management theory it is useful to distinguish the following concepts:

  (a) the sphere of enterprise activity (activity sphere), which covers all economic events within the enterprise.
  (b) the sphere of enterprise authority (authority sphere), which covers these economic events over which the enterprise has the power or the right to command;
  (c) the reception sphere of the success indicator or indicators, which, as has already been defined, cover those economic events which are registered in the success indicator.

In all multi-level economic structures, from capitalist business corporations to socialist industrial associations, the activity sphere is broader than the authority sphere. This part of enterprise activity (activity sphere minus authority sphere) must *ex definitione* be governed by open information. The use of parametric management cannot go beyond the range of the reception sphere and the authority sphere. With properly constructed management formulae, the reception sphere is equal to the activity sphere and parametric management is confined to the authority sphere. This leads us to an obvious thesis that the necessary prerequisite for wider use of prices requires:

  (a) broadening the reception sphere of the success indicator or indicators;
  (b) broadening the sphere of enterprise authority.

The above relationships are presented in Fig. 10. In actual practice we frequently encounter the violations of these relationships. The reception sphere of success indicators is often narrower than the authority sphere, which leaves – for a time being – some activities not steered by the C.P.B. This leads to efforts to broaden the reception sphere or – if they are unsuccessful – to extend the sphere of open information and – as a result – diminishing the authority sphere.

FIG. 10. THE RECEPTION SPHERE AND PARAMETRIC MANAGEMENT

Activity Sphere = Reception Sphere

Authority Sphere The Sphere Governed by Cipher Information	The Sphere of Central Planning Board Decisions The Sphere Governed by Open Information

5 CHANGES IN MANAGEMENT FORMULA AS A STEERING DEVICE

Thus far we have discussed the situation where the management formula is given and constant and the C.P.B. influence the enterprise behaviour by changing prices and/or administrative orders. However, in actual practice of socialist countries changing the management formula is frequently used as a semi-operational steering device. These changes in management formula usually occur in information and/or stimulation systems.

(i) CHANGES IN THE INFORMATION SYSTEM AS A SEMI-OPERATIONAL STEERING DEVICE

The introduction of new success indicators was a frequently used device for influencing the enterprise behaviour. It was the result of two phenomena:

First of all, the basic success indicator used – gross value of output – had a very narrow reception sphere. It resulted – as is well known – in very uneconomic behaviour on the part of enterprise management. By introducing new, specialised success indicators – quality, cost reduction and the like – the C.P.B. sought to influence the enterprise behaviour in a desirable direction.

The second reason was the policy of practically constant operational prices. With constant prices, the C.P.B. was left with four remaining types of information carriers: administrative orders, rates of bonuses, bonus conditions and new success indicators. The last was used rather indiscriminately and resulted in approximately 50 success indicators being used in Polish industry in 1960.

The use of success indicators as a semi-operational steering device has a number of disadvantages. First of all it leads to their inflation. It is relatively easy to introduce new success indicators, but it is very difficult to eliminate success indicators once introduced. Every success indicator is a source of income to some managerial group and resistance to any effort to eliminate it is very powerful indeed as the Polish experience clearly shows.[1] From the management theory point of view, the use of narrow specialised success indicators means also that it becomes impossible to create the system of specialised success indicators which covers the whole activity sphere of the enterprise. It can be achieved with the help of two broad specialised success indicators; costs and output. The moment, however, we enter the path of narrow specialised success indicators – the task becomes impossible: there are hundreds of economic events within the activity sphere of any enterprise.

Secondly, the use of specialised success indicators creates an exceedingly complex information system within the enterprise, with half a dozen or even a dozen of success indicators, each having a different reception sphere, specific transformation rules, bonus system, etc. With such complex information-stimulation systems, the prediction of actual enterprise behaviour becomes practically impossible.

A good example of a variable information system is the actual solution (introduced in 1964) of information-stimulation systems in Polish industrial enterprises. It is depicted in Fig. 11. I shall postpone my comments on it to the next section.

(ii) CHANGES IN STIMULATION SYSTEM AS A SEMI-OPERATIONAL STEERING DEVICE

The bonus system functioning in Poland in 1960–3 can serve as an illustration of flexible stimulation system used as a semi-operational steering device. It is presented in Fig. 12.

---

[1] The introduction of new bonus system in Poland in 1960 (it was terminated in 1963) was accompanied by efforts to eliminate specialised success indicators and bonuses belonging to them. Only two specialised success indicators – out of over 50 – were actually eliminated, however, because of managers' resistance. See [1], p. 97.

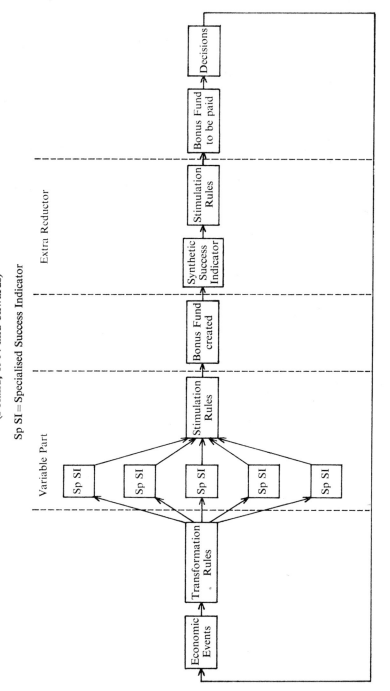

FIG. 11. AN EXAMPLE OF A VARIABLE INFORMATION SYSTEM
(Poland, 1964 and onwards)

Sp SI = Specialised Success Indicator

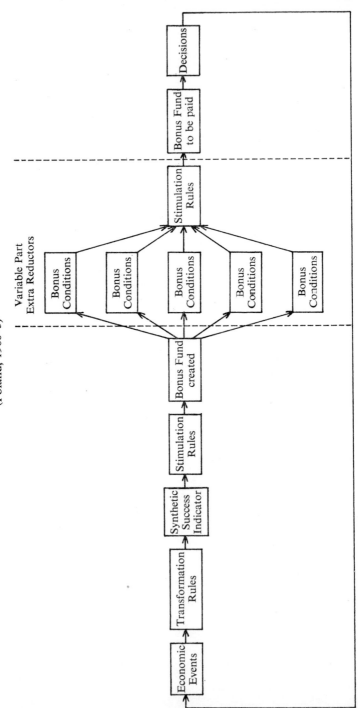

Fig. 12. An Example of a Variable Stimulation System
(Poland, 1960–3)

In both systems (Figs 11 and 12), industrial associations are given the right to change specialised success indicators or bonus conditions each year, as a tool for influencing the economic behaviour of enterprises. In both systems, a synthetic success indicator acts as a necessary but not sufficient condition for obtaining bonuses. If a certain level of profit is not achieved, no bonuses are paid out to management; but even high profits do not entitle the enterprise management to bonuses if certain defined objectives are not fulfilled.

6 THE SIMULTANEOUS USE OF DIFFERENT INFORMATION CARRIERS FOR TRANSMITTING THE SAME INFORMATION AND THE RELIABILITY OF THE MANAGEMENT MECHANISM

The current economic policy of socialist countries uses simultaneously different information carriers for transmitting the same information to the enterprise. For example, presently in Poland the information on the desirable product mix is sent to the enterprise with the simultaneous help of three information carriers: (1) an administrative order about required assortment; (2) the price ratio for different products; (3) the bonus ratio for assortment and other defined objectives.

Today it is technically impossible to be sure that these different carriers transmit exactly the same information. As a result, the product mix as determined by administrative orders differs from the product mix which would result from profit maximising behaviour with given prices, and differs also from the relative bonus attractiveness of fulfilling the assortment plan, rather than, let us say, introducing new products, to which also certain bonus value is assigned. In this situation, by using different information carriers for transmitting the same information we do not increase the *reliability* of the management mechanism. Rather we diminish the effectiveness of each type of information.

The situation would be different if we use additional information carriers, when the existing one does not work. For example, with the linear horizontal cost function, the price of output is not sufficient information to determine the proper volume of output. In such a case open information from the C.P.B. would be valuable. But this open information is not repeating the same information which is already transmitted by the price system: it supplies additional information. The reliability of the system can be increased when there are additional information carriers ready for use when functioning information carriers do not work.

As long, however, as they do function properly, additional information carriers should have zero value.

7 SOME CONCLUDING REMARKS

Both practical experience and theoretical considerations lead one to the conclusion that the way to improve the functioning of socialist economies lies in the direction of using success indicators with the broadest possible reception sphere (synthetic success indicators), strictly limiting the use of open information and using prices as the main information carrier. Such system, however, requires that a number of conditions must be fulfilled – most of them not easy to achieve – for its proper functioning. Thus far, it seems, economists have been more successful in criticising the non-parametric system than in drawing *feasible* blueprints, including the problems of transition, for the parametric one. The present author is himself no exception to this verdict.

ANNEX

TABLE ONE

DETERMINANTS OF RECEPTION SPHERE AND OF TYPE OF REACTION OF VALUE SUCCESS INDICATORS

Determinants *Reception Sphere* *Type of Reaction*	*Construction of Success Indicator*	*Trans- formation Rules*	*Completeness of Price System*	*Principles of Price Fixing*
Sensitivity to the activity of the enterprise itself	X		X	X
Sensitivity to the information transmitted from the C.P.B.	X	X		X
Sensitivity to the information transmitted by customers	X		X	
Type of Reaction to economic events and/or external information	X	X		X

REFERENCES

[1] B. Fick, *Bodzce ekonomiczne w przemysle* (*Economic Incentives in Industry*), Warsaw 1965.
[2] O. Lange, *Wstep do cybernetyki ekonomicznej* (*Introduction to Economic Cybernetics*), Warsaw 1965.
[3] M. Lesz, *Bodzce i mierniki przedsiebiorstwa przemyskowego a potrzeby rynku* (*Incentives and Success Indicators of Industrial Enterprise and Requirements of the Market*). Konferencja o miernikach oceny dzialalnosci przedsiebiorstwa. Materialy przedkonferencyjne. (Materials for Conference on Success Indicators. In mimeographed form.)
[4] *Studies on the Theory of Reproduction and Prices*, Warsaw 1964.
[5] A. Wakar and J. G. Zielinski, 'Socialist Operational Price Systems', *American Economic Review*, Mar. 1963, 1, pp. 109–27.
[6] J. G. Zielinski, 'The Consumption Model and the Tools of its Implementation', in *On Political Economy and Econometrics. Essays in Honour of Professor O. Lange*. Warsaw 1964.
[7] J. Wieckowski, *Rola zysku w kierowaniu produkcja* (*The Role of Profit in the Management of Production*). Warsaw 1965.

5 Pure Theory of Public Expenditure and Taxation [1]

P. A. Samuelson

1 INTRODUCTION

About a decade ago, I set out in three brief papers [2] a unifying theory of optimal resource allocation to public or social goods and optimal distribution of tax burdens. This theory proved to be, although I did not know as much about its history as I should have, a culmination of a century of writing on public expenditure, by such authors as Pantaleoni (1883), Sax (1883), Mazzola (1890), Wicksell (1896), and above all Lindahl (1919).[3] On the problem of optimal taxation, I had behind me the writings of all the great neo-classical writers: Walras, Marshall, Pareto, Edgeworth, Wicksell and Pigou, culminating in the classic 1938 synthesis of modern welfare economics by Abram Bergson.

The time was ripe for a grand theoretical synthesis of 'benefit' and 'optimal burden' theories of taxation. The building blocks were all there, and what only was needed was for a chimpanzee to come along with the motivation to put them together. My motivation came from dim remembrance of the basic Lindahl diagram in a pre-war article by Richard Musgrave. I perceived it was not quite right for the general case, and when a challenge came, in another connection, to show the worth of mathematics in economics, I used the pure theory of public expenditure as an instance to show how fruitful symbolic methods could be.

In one way, this was fortunate. From the beginning the theory was formulated in definitive general terms: three pages provided the nucleus

[1] I am grateful to Felicity Skidmore for research assistance and to the Carnegie Corporation for a reflective 1965–6 year.

[2] P. A. Samuelson, 'The Pure Theory of Public Expenditure', *Review of Economics and Statistics*, XXXVI (1954) 387–9; ibid. XXXVII (1955), 'Diagramatic Exposition of a Theory of Public Expenditure', 350–6; ibid. XL (1958), 'Aspects of Public Expenditure Theories', 332–8. These are reproduced in P. A. Samuelson, *Collected Scientific Papers*, vol. II, ch. 92, pp. 1223–5; ch. 93, pp. 1226–32; ch. 94, pp. 1233–9. Special acknowledgements are made there to the contemporaneous researches of Richard A. Musgrave and Howard R. Bowen, and to criticisms by S. Enke, J. Margolis and G. Colm.

[3] R. A. Musgrave and A. T. Peacock (eds.), *Classics in the Theory of Public Finance* (London, Macmillan for International Economic Association, 1958) give valuable English translations, and also related works by Adolph Wagner, Barone and many others.

from which all the corollaries could be drawn. In another way, the mathematical garb was unfortunate. Only a few people interested in public finance handle mathematical economics easily, and a number of the theory's essential points have, I think, been misunderstood by writers in the field.[1] A subsequent diagrammatic and literary exposition apparently did not suffice to elucidate sufficiently the theory's essential properties, perhaps not a surprising fact in view of the intrinsic complexities of the subject and the historical misconceptions that have become fossilised in the literature.

I propose here to give a brief review of the analysis, both in its expenditure and tax sides, trying to relate it to modern economic theory and to previous public finance writings. In the alloted space, probably more can be accomplished in trying to clear up misunderstandings than in making new applications.[2] Although the model is primarily concerned with normative, optimality conditions, some attention will be paid to actual behaviour patterns and to the deviations from optimality to be expected from various proposed mechanisms.

2 HISTORICAL DICHOTOMIES

Public finance treatises tended to separate the discussion of expenditure from that of taxation. Most words were devoted to taxes: expenditure somehow got decided and had to be paid for. Two main theories of who should bear the taxes were distinguished: those with greater ability to pay – somehow defined and measured – should pay more; those who received greater 'benefit' from the expenditure should pay more. Eclectric writers, like Smith, hoped that both arguments could be used to reinforce the notion that people with more wealth or income (or 'faculty') should pay more taxes.

By and large, conservative writers liked to stress benefit theories, as a way of holding down the role of government;[3] radical writers liked to

[1] Leif Johansen, *Public Economics* (Amsterdam, North Holland, 1965) ch. 6, is a notable exception. Except with respect to two issues that will be later mentioned, his work and mine run parallel.

[2] Because Musgrave's *The Principles of Public Finance* (New York, McGraw-Hill, 1958) has displaced Pigou's treatise as the classical work on the subject, I devote some attention to its exposition of these matters. Many of my criticisms are met by the reformulations of Musgrave in his paper for this conference; and from neighbourly conversations I know that we are in basic agreement on most issues. Nevertheless, the 1958 text does reflect, and shape, views of many other scholars and therefore does deserve notice.

[3] Wicksell was a partial exception: though not a conservative, he was almost an anarchist in his fear of unresponsive government.

stress ability-to-pay, as a wedge toward reducing inequality of incomes and property.

Legalistic modes of thought dominated. Had governmentless men once come together in a social compact which kept limits on the coercive power government might use against free men?[1] Such views conduced to a benefit point of view, culminating in the Wicksell–Lindahl voluntary-exchange theory of public finance. Did not men have a property right to their property, and therefore was government free to implement ability-to-pay notions by significantly redistributing incomes among the citizenry? Proudhon's saying, 'all property is theft', was a *tu quoque riposte* to the view, 'all interference with property is theft'.

It is silly in 1966 to brood over legality notions of earlier centuries (but folly to read earlier writers without realising that this is germane to understanding their words). Yet disputes over legalisms do give some reflections of the hazy value judgements and sketchy social welfare functions that various people have below the surface.

At least from the time of Bentham, a new notion gained in prominence. Would this public expenditure programme coupled with that tax structure lead to a greater sum total of human happiness than some other one? Which pattern is socially optimal? Even if we strip this utilitarian formulation of its crude and materialistic calculus of hedonism, replacing it by some ordinal notion of a modern social welfare function, it tends to subvert the older notions of 'legitimacy' – that things are done as they are because they have always been so done; that people have a contractual right to no changes; that it is 'unjust' to do certain things to people, even under the purpose of maximising the social welfare.

Bentham and his successors were individualists. At least, individuals provided the parts out of which they formed the whole. But it was the whole on which they concentrated – the maximisation of social welfare. Two quite different notions of 'justice' or 'equity' have lived on in unpeaceful coexistence within western men these last two centuries: a thinker like Stuart Mill was quite torn between them.

On the one hand, a just or equitable society is one in which incomes are properly allocated to produce the greatest bliss for the whole universe

---

[1] If one assumes that a man has no alternative on this or any other planet to being a citizen, or that the loss of consumers' surplus he would experience if he opted to 'quit civilisation' were great, then society by an all-or-none offer could 'coax' him into acquiescence to almost any tax burden. So even if one accepted the dubious premises of a social compact theory, little would follow therefrom. If one allows any group of citizens to form a coalition and opt out, more interesting consequences follow but we end up in the morass of indeterminate *n*-person game theory.

– even if that means sacrificing something of one man's well-being in the good cause of adding more to the rest of mankind's well-being. Against this is the notion that each man, by virtue of being a man, has an inviolable core of rights that cannot be infringed even to secure some net increment to the social good,[1] or at least cannot be infringed in his case unless all others (who are somehow comparable!) are being similarly treated.

This second notion of justice, an analytic philosopher would notice, is somehow tied up with a 'symmetry principle', in which other traits than being a man are posited to be irrelevant. Whether women, minor children, lunatics, neurotics, drunks, chimpanzees, ants, amoebae, carrots, and DNA molecules are to be excluded or included in the universe of discourse becomes a nice question. Furthermore, men may be alike in being men but unlike in other respects: how do you dole out equal treatment to unequals? In the twentieth century, this second notion of justice is appealed to, not very successfully, to exercise veto power in extension of activities of government.[2]

I suspect that a persevering scholar could work up a social welfare function that incorporated into itself *both* notions of justice. I shall not assay such an ambitious task here, but shall concentrate on the ordinary case of a social welfare function – pleading as possible justification that, if we address ourselves to the problem of optimal public finance for a society *far* in the future, there will be plenty of time to make changes without thwarting people's expectations or trampling on their legal rights

[1] Wicksell illustrates the confusion. His just theory of taxation is designed to protect each man from injustice in the second sense; but his famous sentences underlying application of his theory, 'It is clear that justice in taxation tacitly presupposes justice in the existing distribution of property and income' (Musgrave and Peacock, op. cit. p. 108), points in the Bentham-welfare direction – as does Lindahl's quotation from him 'it would obviously be nonsense to speak of "a just proportion of an unjust whole"' (Musgrave and Peacock, op. cit. p. 227). Neither Wicksell nor Lindahl – nor for that matter a host of discredited worshippers of Pareto-optimality – face up to the consequences of non-tacit failure of the presupposition about optimal interpersonal distribution of dollars. Moreover, a failure of Pareto-optimality could be identified as a regrettable and pitiable inefficiency, without implying an identifiable unjustly treated party.

[2] Not surprisingly, its spokesmen like to appeal to unanimity – or, to use an Irish Bull – to near-unanimity in social decision making. However, a unanimity requirement can, and usually does, lead to no way of deciding between two alternatives (and leads, at best, to a non-transitive ordering); and they hope either that this will be resolved by favouring the *status quo*, putting the burden of proof upon *all* change, or – and this will become an increasingly important strain in libertarian thinking, the farther away recedes the laissez faire conditions of Victorian capitalism – putting the burden of proof upon any departure from their defined condition of inviolable natural rights and individual liberties (inclusive of property rights).

(human and property). Furthermore, as part of optimal feasibility theory, if we wish we can embody some of these second notions of justice as side-constraints on the maximum social welfare problem.

3 PSEUDO-DEMAND ALGORITHM TO COMPUTE EQUILIBRIUM

Although my analysis is in the tradition of the voluntary-exchange tax theories of Wicksell and Lindahl, one of my main findings has been the falsity of that theory's relying upon voluntarism.[1] Another has been the impossibility of truly separating benefit-allocation and redistribution-equity considerations, since these intrinsically overlap and must be simultaneously resolved. Neither of these views seem to have been embraced by public finance experts with complete joy. A third source of criticism of my analysis concerns itself with the alleged assumption in my model of 'equal consumption' by all.

This last confusion can be simply disposed of. A public good – call it x or x_2 or x_{n+m} – is simply one with the property of involving a 'consumption externality', in the sense of entering into two or more persons' preference functions simultaneously. Thus, public good x_2 might be liked by Man 1, disliked by Man 2, and be quite indifferent to all other men; or it might be 'much' liked by Man 1 and 'little' liked by Man 2, and be disregarded by all others. This was made clear to any careful reader of my papers: when I equated $x_2^1 = x_2^2 = \ldots = x_2^s = x_2$, that did not imply any equality in the relevant marginal rate of substitutions $(\partial u^i/\partial x_2)/\partial u^i/\partial x_1^i$, or even that they have the same sign.

I shall now present [2] a pseduo-demand analysis that would provide an *omniscient* planner with one method of solving the optimality equations of the original model:

$$\text{I} \quad F\left(\sum_{i=1}^{s} x_1^i, \ldots, \sum_{i=1}^{s} x_n^i, x_{n+1}, \ldots, x_{n+m} \right) = 0$$

---

[1] R. A. Musgrave, op. cit. p. 86 n. gives the opposite impression, failing to mention that more than one-third of my original exposition was given to the game-theoretic reasons why people will not reveal their preferences for public goods as they do in the case of private goods.

[2] This mathematical version can be skipped by those content to read the special case of the Graphical Appendix. The Johansen interpretation of Lindahl, which Musgrave's current paper develops, can be generalised to the pseudo-demand model. I received Robert Dorfman's paper for the conference, 'General Equilibrium with Public Goods', too late to relate it to this discussion.

$$\text{II} \quad \frac{u^i_j}{u^i_1} = -\frac{F_j}{F_1}, \qquad (j=2,\ldots,n; \ i=1,\ldots,s)$$

$$\text{III} \quad \sum_{i=1}^{s} \frac{u^i_{n+k}}{u^i_1} = -\frac{F_{n+k}}{F_1}, \qquad (k=1,\ldots,m)$$

$$\text{IV} \quad \frac{U_i u^i_1}{U_1 u^1_1} = 1 \qquad (i=2,\ldots,s)$$

where $F[.]$ is the social production-possibility frontier relating public and private goods (including private factors of production as negative goods); where $u^i(x^i_1,\ldots, x^i_n, x_{n+1},\ldots, x_{n+m})$ is the ith man's ordinal preference function for public and private goods; where $U(u^1,\ldots, u^s)$ is the (individualistic) social welfare function of Bergson type that provides an ethical evaluation of the well-beings of different persons; and where numerical subscripts to a function denote such partial derivatives as $\partial F/\partial x_r$, $\partial u^i/\partial x_r$, $\partial U/\partial u_r$.

If there were only private goods, we could rely on each man to calculate and present his demand functions once we gave him his budget income and market prices at which he could trade freely. *With public goods, he has every reason not to provide us with revelatory demand functions.* So I imagine a referee, who is appointed by the planning authority and who somehow knows man i's indifference function u^i. This referee calculates for him what I call his pseudo-demand functions, for both private and public goods, on the assumption that his utility is maximised subject to a budget equation involving a fixed lump-sum algebraic net income L^i, provided for him by the State (and aside from his incomes from owned factors, which are already included in some of the private variables $-x^i_j$); and subject to fixed (uniform) prices, $(P_1,\ldots, P_n)$, at which he can freely buy (or sell) private goods; and subject to fixed (non-uniform between people) *pseudo*-tax-prices $(P^i_{n+1},\ldots, P^i_{n+m})$ at which the referee *pretends* the man can buy as much or as little of the public goods as he pleases. (What kinds of exclusion devices would be needed to make this pretence less bizarre, I shall not go into since this is all merely a computing algorithm, which an electronic computer could use, dispensing with the dramatic device of a referee and market terminology.)

The referee solves for each man the maximum problem

$$\max_{(x^i_j,\, x_{n+k})} u^i(x^i_1,\ldots, x^i_n; \ x_{n+1},\ldots, x_{n+m})$$

subject to the pseudo-budget equation

$$(P_1 x^i_1 + \ldots + P_n x^i_n) + (P^i_{n+1} x_{n+1} + \ldots + P^i_{n+m} x_{n+m}) = L^i \gtreqless 0,$$

to get the pseudo-demand functions:

$$x_j^i = D_j^i(P_1, \ldots, P_n; \; P_{n+1}^i, \ldots, P_{n+m}^i; \; L^i), \qquad (j = 1, \ldots, n)$$
$$x_{n+k} = D_{n+k}^i(P_1, \ldots, P_n; \; P_{n+1}^i, \ldots, P_{n+m}^i; \; L^i), \qquad (k = 1, \ldots, m)$$

The co-ordinator of all the referees now solves the pseudo-general-equilibrium problem in which all markets are cleared in terms of supply and demand, but taking into account the necessary equality of all public good variables, $D_{n+k}^1 = D_{n+k}^2 = \ldots = D_{n+k}^s.$[1] The full conditions of pseudo-market equilibrium are:

(a) $\quad F\left(\ldots, \; \sum_{i=1}^{s} x_j^i, \ldots, \; \ldots, x_{n+k}, \ldots\right) = 0$

(b) $\quad \dfrac{P_j}{P_1} = -\dfrac{F_j}{F_1} \qquad (j = 2, \ldots, n)$

(c) $\quad \sum_{i=1}^{s} \dfrac{P_{n+k}^i}{P_1} = -\dfrac{F_{n+k}}{F_1} \qquad (k = 1, \ldots, m)$

(d) $\quad x_j^i = D_j^i(\ldots, P_j, \ldots; \; \ldots, P_{n+k}^i, \ldots; L^i) \qquad (i = 1, \ldots, s; \; j = 1, \ldots, n)$

(e) $\quad x_{n+k} = D_{n+k}^i(\ldots, P_j, \ldots; \; \ldots, P_{n+k}^i, \ldots; L^i) \quad (i = 1, \ldots, s)$

(f) $\quad \dfrac{U_i u_1^i}{U_1 u_1^1} = 1 \qquad (i = 2, \ldots, s)$

Careful examination of (a)–(f) shows we can eliminate from them the pecuniary variables $(P_1, \ldots, P_m; \; \ldots, P_{n+1}^i, \ldots, P_{n+m}^i, \ldots; \; L^1, \ldots, L^s)$ and be left with the solution to I–IV above. So we do have a possible (but not necessarily practical or most-efficient, and certainly not a spontaneous) computing algorithm for achieving the desired optimum.

Similar careful examination of (a)–(e) will show that by manipulating the pattern of lump-sum (L^i), we can trace out *all* the Pareto-optimal solutions to I–III: i.e. by giving Man 1 relatively much L^1 at the expense of Man 2's L^2, we can increase the ordinal utility u^1 at the expense of u^2 along society's utility-possibility frontier.[2]

---

[1] This has no implications of equal satisfaction from the public good. Moreover, if Man *i* hates a good, x_{n+k}, its pseudo-price to him may have to be negative, namely $P_{n+k}^i < 0$.

[2] This is Chart 4 in my second paper; it is also Fig. 4–6 of Musgrave, op. cit. p. 83, despite the author's belief that only two of his points are on it. The author is confused in thinking that he can validly derive a different utility frontier from mine by 'a difference in the treatment of income distribution' (p. 81). When he subjects his men to

Finally, let us consider a pseudo *laissez-faire* solution of the equations in which all lump-sum redistributions are set equal to zero. With $L^i \equiv 0$, and returns conditions suitable for viable competitive *laissez-faire*, one particular solution will be found for (a)–(e), but, of course, with (f) not honoured. It is a theorem that pseudo *laissez-faire* does lead to Pareto-optimality,[1] but generally not to ethically-optimal maximum welfare.

---

different benefit-tax payments, he washes out his own assumption of predetermined income distribution (or effectively offsets it). This may be a convenient place to note, for the interested reader, the few places where a close reading of Musgrave leads to disagreement between us. The possibility or impossibility to apply an 'exclusion principle' is less crucial than consumption externality, since often exclusion would be wrong where possible (8–9). 'Joint consumption' is not an apt name for consumption externality (10 n. 1). The Benefit vs. Ability-To-Pay Dichotomy of the whole book needs careful qualification along with the Allocation vs. Distribution Dichotomy. The partial equilibrium analysis of Lindahl and Bowen (74–80) is not something different from my general equilibrium analysis (81–86); as the present Appendix makes clear it can be rigorously treated as a special case of my analysis. The p. 86 footnote and relevant text discussion does not do justice to my game-theoretic objections to the voluntary-exchange theory, and the income distribution assumptions underlying Fig. 4 come to the same theory as mine if the Fig. 4–6 frontier is validly derived. On p. 84, paragraph 2, the author seems to be saying that Pareto-optimality is unique for private goods but not for public: in fact, neither is uniqe and the same distributional problem arises.

An important final point should be recognised. Suppose we ignore Musgrave's Stabilisation Branch, as we ought to be able to do in a timeless Say's Law world. Should his Allocation Budget 'balance', and his Distribution Budget balance out algebraically to zero? Only if constant-returns-to-scale holds for the production functon $F(\cdot)$ can there be a balance of $\Sigma_k \Sigma_i P^i_{n+k} X_k$ pseudo-receipts and cost to government of public goods. Under increasing returns ΣL^i must be negative to subsidise losses from MC pricing. Even if ΣL^i can be zero under constant returns, it need not: lump-sum divergences from P^i_{n+m} can be offset by divergences from the (L^i) solution of (a)–(e) or (a)–(f) *without harming the optimal solution*!

[1] Leif Johansen, op. cit., has proved this theorem for his version of the Lindahl mechanism, pp. 134–5. In his following pages, particularly at pp. 136–8, Johansen misses perceiving the theorem of my previous paragraph – that with *proper* choice of (L^i), the Lindahl pseudo-market algorithm will provide a maximum to a specified social welfare function – and he is therefore too hard on the mechanism in the sense of criticising it for the wrong reason. Musgrave's paper at this current I.E.A. September 1966 Meeting, in his paragraph 21 commenting on Lindahl and Johansen does seem to perceive the essential theorem, recognising tacitly that the proper reallocation of income is not *prior* to public good determination but must be done *simultaneously* with it. (This is also the case in a Good Society involving only private goods and optimal income distribution.) But in the following paragraphs, Musgrave is too easy on the Pseudo-Demand mechanism; in his desire to be 'parochial', attributable perhaps to an underlying desire to be 'practical', he overlooks the *necessarily* 'pseudo' character of the pseduo-demand analysis of (a)–(e). Moreover, he tacitly lapses into the cardinal sin of the narrow 'new welfare' economists: 'If you can't get (or even define!) the maximum of a social welfare function, settle for Pareto-optimality', as if *that* were second-best or even 99th best.

I believe that those conservative economists who have been most doubt-ful about or antagonistic toward ability-to-pay redistributional theories of taxation have been groping toward some notion like that of my pseudo *laissez-faire* equilibrium. Another group, less conservative, have been groping toward the notion of my pseudo general-equilibrium with what-ever degree of redistribution (of the lumpsum L^i, or more feasible progressive taxation involving some dead-weight losses) is considered currently optimal or feasible. Within this pseduo analysis, the partial separation of Benefit-Allocation and Equity-Redistribution elements can be given some analytical meaning.

4 AFFIRMATION OF DOUBTS

Whatever the relevance of the pseudo-equilibrium algorithm to a computer omniscient with respect to the F, u^i and U functions, we must not forget that it has *no* relevance to motivated market behaviour. Moreover, it is striking how Wicksell and Lindahl, and even Musgrave and Johansen (and now Dorfman's name can perhaps be added), after getting a glimpse of pseudo-equilibrium descend to the swampland of mathematical politics, ending up with inconclusive behaviour patterns by legislatures, factions and parties, running inevitably afoul of Arrow's Impossibility Theorem. Game theory, except in trivial cases, propounds paradoxes rather than solves problems.

It is possible that Professors Harsanyi or Bishop could apply advanced game theory – Nash threat points, etc. – to the problem of how two or more consumers of public goods will actually interact; even if one has doubts about the axioms of such models, the fruit of such an exercise might be of some interest. But I am not aware that those fascinated by the benefit notion have done much in this area. I find naive the belief of Wicksell that simultaneous voting on expenditure and taxes will promote an optimum. His requirement for 'unanimity', which pitifully degenerates into a requirement for 'approximate (!) unanimity', comes as an anti-climax. (What does a three-quarters majority have that a four-quarter doesn't have? Less unlikelihood. By that criterion, we edge back toward a simple majority, with its paradoxes.)

A corrosive nihilism seems needed to puncture the bubble of vague and wishful thinking in these matters. Let me select an example from one of the most acute of the modern writers, Leif Johansen. He seems to believe that Pareto optimality will be arrived at by voting [perhaps by unani-mity?] concluding, 'If all questions which in one way or another are interrelated are dealt with simultaneously, one should in principle arrive at Pareto-optimality' (op. cit. p. 52). I find no warrant in game theory for this. 'Simultaneity' is a red herring. If there were only one Pareto-optimal configuration, a valid theorem might be demonstrated that it would be selected by unanimous vote. In that Utopia no problems would arise, and *every* social welfare function, $U(u^1, u^2, \ldots)$, would lead to the same outcome. But in the economic cases under consideration, why should one man not refuse to go to a particular Pareto-optimal point in the hope of being able to better himself by refusing to make the vote unanimous? The Prisoner's Dilemma – in which it is Pareto-optimal for neither of two accomplices to confess secretly, but in which it is safer for either to confess if the other might – is merely the philosopher's reminder, of what economists studying break-down of cartel behaviour have always known, that Pareto-optimality is a definition not an inevitable destination.

My doubts do not assert that passably good organisation of the public household is impossible or unlikely,[1] but merely that theorists have not yet provided us with much analysis of these matters that has validity or plausibility. If I stimulate someone to resolve my doubts, that will make two people happy.[2]

5 SEMANTICS OF SOCIAL OR PUBLIC GOODS

I should like to close with a final regret. In my papers I often spoke of 'polar' cases: e.g. the polar case of a 'pure private good', like $x_1 = x_1^1 + x_1^2 + \ldots$, whose x_1^i 'entered' in a single person's utility function. At

---

[1] If someone did demonstrate such an assertion, its corollary would not necessarily be 'Spend less on government' or 'Spend more on government'.

[2] After reading my first draft, Professor James Buchanan of the University of Virginia wrote me that in my earlier papers I had been almost too easy on Wicksell, but in this paper I am very hard on him. I agree. Since 1954, I have had a chance to read him in English and not just German. Professor Kolm has also expressed the view that I am too critical of Wicksell. Since Knut Wicksell is my scientific hero, I should explicate. I agree that Wicksell should not be confused with Lindahl, even though his mathematical help to Lindahl made precise what Lindahl meant; and Wicksell deserves credit for exposing the nonsense of voluntarism in pseudo-tax and other formulations. In this sense Wicksell is a devastating critic of Lindahl. But where I must fault Wicksell, and here my opinion differs from that of Kolm and Johansen, is in connection with his unsubstantiated faith that somehow within Parliament or political democracy an efficacious unanimous move to Pareto-optimality (and the ethically right point of this set) can be found. Professor Kolm seems to share Wicksell's belief that n men in a room or a universe will end up on the Pareto frontier. I do not. If they were right, there would be never any practical problem of welfare efficiency. Society would spontaneously get itself efficiently organised always.

E

the other pole was what I called a 'pure public good', which 'entered' into everybody's utility: thus, with $x_2 = x_2^1 = x_2^2 = \ldots$, we have $u^i(x_1^i, x_2)$ in each case. I did not demur when critics claimed that most of reality fell between these extreme poles or stools, but instead suggested that these realistic cases could probably be analysed fruitfully as a 'blend' of the two polar cases.

I now wonder whether this was optimal semantics. Since, as I have already pointed out and insisted upon, a public good may have zero or negative influence on some person(s), most of the cases brought forward as allegedly not involving either pole can in fact be regarded formally as belonging to the public-good pole rather than having to be regarded as a blend between the two poles.

Thus, consider what I have given in this paper as the definition of a public good, and what I might better have insisted upon as a definition in my first and subsequent papers: 'A public good is one that enters two or more persons' utility.'[1] What are we left with? Two poles and a continuum in between? No. With a knife-edge pole of the private-good case, and with *all* the rest of the world in the public-good domain by virtue of involving some 'consumption externality'.[2]

[1] Perhaps the word 'enters' should be replaced by 'enters irreducibly' to take account of a subtle semantic difficulty. Whether the same good appears in two utility functions can be affected by the definitions and symbolisms used to represent variables. Thus, we may have fireworks in your function and mine; but, without changing the substance of the case, suppose we redefine as distinct variables, fireworks exploded in the sky, y; fireworks observed (or observable) by you, z; fireworks observed by me, v. Then it might be misleadingly said that there are no variables entering literally into more than one utility function and we have here 'purely private' goods. However, by such a change in symbolism all public good phenomena could be defined out of existence. This shows the need for some such word as 'irreducibly' in any formal definition. In the last analysis, we can diagnose the existence of the private good phenomena which can be optimally handled by the market only by a simultaneous scrutiny of the variables and of how they enter in both the utility functions and the technological side constraints. This warning is all the more necessary in the case where there could conceivably be found an 'exclusion' device that would enable the joint-supply nature of the problem to be dramatised; the point is that we need the theory of public goods to decide just when such devices ought to be used. Later in the Appendix I work with various dummy variables that give point to these remarks.

For the $(n+1)$th time, let me repeat the warning that a *public good* should not *necessarily* be run by public rather than private enterprise.

[2] Consider the last half of the current Musgrave paper, which is supposed to be concerned with non-polar cases of social goods. In particular, consider the taxonomic table in paragraph 30. The most general case there can be written in my terminology as

$$u^1(\ldots, x_2, x_3, \ldots) = f^1(\ldots, \lambda^1 x_2 + \gamma^1 x_3, \ldots)$$
$$u^2(\ldots, x_2, x_3, \ldots) = f^2(\ldots, \lambda^2 x_2 + \gamma^2 x_3, \ldots)$$

instead of as $U_A(Y_A + \beta Y_B)$ and $U_B(Y_B + \gamma Y_A)$. But please note the vital point: formally the above u^i fit *perfectly* into my original analysis and if it be called a polar

It is like the problem of pure competition and monopoly. Once people thought of these as two poles: pure (or perfect?) competition vs. pure (or perfect) monopoly, with real-world phenomena mostly an inbetween blend called 'imperfect' or 'monopolistic' competition. After decades of debate, it is now pretty much agreed, I think, that it is more fruitful to abandon the pole of 'perfect monopoly', and consider the real world as being a good or bad approximation to the pure competition role, with various new phenomena coming in as we depart in different directions from pure competition.

So I now think the useful terminology in this field should be: pure private goods in which the market mechanism works optimally, and possibly close approximations to them, versus the whole field of consumption-externalities or public goods.

This does, however, lead to an uncomfortable situation. If the experts remain nihilistic about algorithms to allocate public goods, and if all but a knife-edge of reality falls in that domain,[1] nihilism about most of economics, rather than merely public finance, seems to be implied.

What is the reply to this grave query? I am not sure. But here are some considerations I believe to be relevant.

First, if worst came to worst and there were found to be no way out of

---

case *then the second half of Musgrave's paper is formally as much concerned with the polar case as is the first.*

[1] Those who build social norms out of individual norms, so that social $U = U(u^1, u^2, \ldots)$ rather than belonging to some external group mind, must note that little is left of the 'tree property' of private goods in U, if people through altruism or envy have in their u^i the bread consumption of other people, namely x_1^2 in u^2. Against critics who believe in an organic theory of the state or in a patriotic code of good conduct, individualists win a hollow victory if *every* good now becomes a public good Formally, my equations (II'–III') now become

$$\frac{\Sigma_i U_i u^i_{n+k}}{\Sigma_i U_i u^i_{n+1}} = -\frac{F_{n+k}}{F_{n+1}}, \qquad (n=0; \ k=2,\ldots,m).$$

These m – 1 conditions can be split up into a Pareto-optimality set II' and an interpersonal-equity set III' in the regular case where $s < m-1$ and the rank of $[u^i_{o+j}]$ is always s. We can then, by renumbering of goods if necessary, write down the $m - s$ and the $s - 1$ conditions

II' (u^j_{o+i}, f_i) is to be of rank s

III' $$\frac{\Sigma_i U_i u^i_{o+k}}{\Sigma_i U_i u^i_{o+1}} = -\frac{F_{o+k}}{F_{o+1}}, \qquad (k=2,\ldots,s).$$

Now the pseudo-market equilibrium conditions (a)–(e) become completely pseudo. To the degree that a near-tree property prevails for some variables, it may pay to keep a $U(u^1, u^2, \ldots)$ formulation rather than work directly with a general $U(x_{o+1}, x_{o+2}, \ldots)$. I wish to thank Professor S. Kolm for pointing out an error in my first-draft formulation.

the indictment, we should have to face up to the disappointing truth. It would be ostrich-like to do otherwise.

Second, much of reality may be found *near* to the pole of private goods, and to this degree the problem becomes less acute.

Third, and this is much the most constructive and comforting point, nihilism or doubt about the solution for the general case of any public good might be out of order in connection with many particular forms of public goods. It is here that many of my critics will turn out to have a valid point (but not, I hope in the end, a point against me or my analysis).

Let me illustrate by some possible examples. Consider cinemas in a large town. Because of deviations from constant-returns-to-scale ('indivisibilities', if you like), my well-being depends on your being willing to watch movies and in fact I might get a greater thrill out of a film if I watch it in the same room with hundreds of other people. Doubtless, film watching will enter more than one u^i function as a public good variable x_{n+k}. But, if the town is populous and distances are small, free enterprise might well result in optimal replication of cinema theatres, each operating at capacity audiences, with fares set competitively at short and long-run marginal and average costs. This is a case where an exclusion principle can, and should, operate.[1]

What is much needed, I believe, are serious analytical studies of cases where public good situations can be solved by algorithms immune to bilateral-monopoly or game-theoretic objections.

Until such cogent analyses are forthcoming, an attitude of sympathetic scepticism seems justified. For the theory of public goods is not simply an extension of Mangoldt–Marshall joint supply or of joint demand. In general, they involve 'consumption externality'[2] with a game-theoretic or bi-lateral monopoly element of indeterminacy of the sort that may not be removable by use of an 'exclusion' device or that cannot *optimally* be handled by such a device.[3]

The Appendix, which is not less important than the paper, relates my general equilibrium analysis to traditional analyses of partial equilibrium.

---

[1] I believe that Herbert Mohring has adduced cases of public road financing where replication provides optimal solutions. See my paper 'The Monopolistic Competition Revolution', in R. E. Kuenne (ed.), *Monopolistic Competition Theory: Essays in Honor of Edward H. Chamberlain* (Wiley, New York, 1967) pp. 105–38, particularly pp. 128–37 where replication and 'asymptotic homogeneity' is rigorously analysed.

[2] In his current paper Musgrave uses the somewhat doubtful term 'non-rivalness in consumption' for what I call 'consumption externality'.

[3] At the end of my Graphical Appendix I illustrate with examples of electricity and roads some of the varieties of experience that enter into the case of public goods.

APPENDIX: PSEUDO MARKET EQUILIBRIUM

(A) THE LINDAHL–JOHANSEN CASE

Since the 1880s it has been known that partial equilibrium is a rigorously legitimately special case of general equilibrium if the marginal utility of money is *strictly constant* for each person, and it is in this case that the concepts of consumers' surplus become unambiguously simple. Wicksell (pp. 101–3 of Musgrave and Peacock), Lindahl (pp. 171–2 and 223–4 of Musgrave and Peacock), and Johansen (pp. 163–75 of *Public Economics*), and Dorfman (I believe, implicitly, in using his numerical measure of benefit) have considered this strong case. If we couple with constancy of the marginal utility of money, the assumption of constant opportunity cost, an assumption much more special than that of constant returns to scale, the pseudo equilibrium of my text becomes identical to the equilibrium of the famous Lindahl diagram (Musgrave and Peacock, p. 170 and Musgrave, Fig. 4-2).

Specifically, for $(i = 1, 2)$, let

$$u^i(x_1^i, x_2) = 1 \cdot x_1^i + f_i(x_2), f_i'' < 0$$
$$F(x_1^1 + x_1^2, x_2) = 1 \cdot (x_1^1 + x_2^1) + Mx_2 - \overline{V}^1 - \overline{V}^2 = 0$$

where $\overline{V}^i$ represents the fixed labour supply of Man i that will always be employed and without disutility.

Set $P_1 = 1$ as numeraire, and face each man with respective pseudo tax-prices P_2^1 and P_2^2. Each man's referee will maximise his u^i by setting

$$f_i'(x_2) = P_2^i \qquad (i = 1, 2); \tag{1}$$

adding all P_2^i vertically and equating to marginal cost, M, we have the equilibrium condition

$$f_1'(x_2) + f_2'(x_2) = M, \tag{2}$$

which can be solved for the optimum level of public good, x_2^*.

Because of the independence of utility of the good and constancy of marginal utility of the private good (which serves as numeraire or money), there is only *one* pseudo-demand curve for each man (independently of considerable variations in income and taxes).

To convert the pseudo-demand analysis into the Lindahl–Johansen diagram, as can be done without reinterpretations only in the constant-cost case, call $P_2^1/M = h = x$, the percentage of cost of the public good charged to Man 1. The condition

$$\frac{P_2^1}{M} + \frac{P_2^2}{M} = 1 \tag{3}$$

becomes their $h+(1-h)=1$. So we can plot $h=f_1'(x_2)/M$ against x_2 and $1-h=f_2'(x_2)/M$ against x_2, to get the Lindahl diagram.

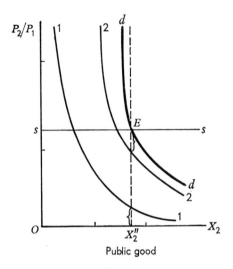

FIG. 1

In this Bowen form of the Lindahl diagram, 11 represents pseudo-demand for Man 1; 22 that for Man 2; their vertical sum, *dd*, intersects the *ss* supply curve to give pseudo-tax equilibrium

We can superimpose on this diagram the contours of equal

$$u^1(x_1^1, x_2) = u^1(\overline{V}^1 + L^1 - P_2^1 x_2, x_2) = 1 \cdot (\overline{V}^1 + L^1 - hMx_2) + f_1(x_2)$$
$$u^2(x_1^2, x_2) = u^2(\overline{V}^2 + L^2 - P_2^2 x_2, x_2) = 1 \, (\overline{V}^2 + L^2 - (1-h) Mx_2) + f_2(x_2). \quad (4)$$

The generalised contract curve of mutually tangent u^i contours is seen to be vertical in this case of constant marginal utility of the private good, going through E and confirming the Pareto-optimality of the Lindahl case of pseudo equilibrium. The Bowen and Lindahl curves, and their intersections, are in this case unchanged by a redistribution of income.

It also happens to be true, what should not have impressed Lindahl as being important, that the total of *money* utilities summed over people,

$$\{\overline{V}^1 + L^1 - P_2^1 x_2 + f_1(x_2)\} + \{\overline{V}^2 + L^2 - P_2^2 x_2 + f_2(x_2)\}$$
$$= \sum_i \overline{V}^i + \sum_i L^i - Mx_2 + \sum_i f_i(x_2) \quad (5)$$

is in this case at a maximum at the pseudo equilibrium of Lindahl x_2^*. But who thinks social welfare can be measured in terms of money independently of the distribution of incomes? Thus, the social welfare function might be

$$U = W_1(u^1) + W_2(u^2), \quad W_i'' < 0 \tag{6}$$

and only at one particular $(x_1^{1*}, x_1^{2*}, x_2^*)$ configuration will true U be at a maximum. Yet at all possible $(x_1^{1*} + A, x_1^{2*} - A, x_2^*)$ will Lindahl's E equilibrium be found to maximise the sum of *money* utilities.

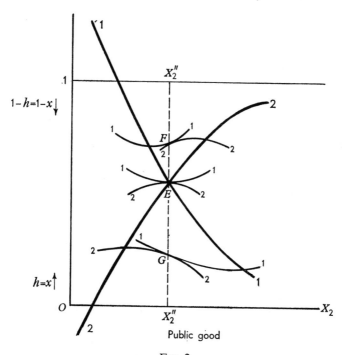

Fig. 2

Here Man 2's pseudo-demand is turned upside down and measured downward from the cost level shown earlier as *ss*. The pseudo-demands intersect at E level, that point of mutual *horizontal* tangency of the men's indifference contours. The special assumption of constant marginal utility of the private good is what makes the contract curve of mutual tangencies, *FEG*, happen to be vertical so that redistributions of income will not affect the optimum X_2^* – an unrealistic result

How can the maximum U of (6) be achieved? It can be achieved by charging each man the P_2^{i*} (i.e. $h^* = x^*$) that can be read off the diagrams, and by giving men the proper $(L^{1*}, L^{2*}) = (B^*, -B^*)$ lump-sum transfers, This should delight Musgrave or anyone who wishes to keep separate the benefit Allocation and ability-to-pay Distribution components.

However, the primacy of such a taxing pattern is negated once we see that there are an *infinity* of other tax patterns that lead to exactly the same thing. Thus, set x^* as above but with

$$P_2^1 = P_2^{1*} + C$$
$$P_2^2 = P_2^{2*} - C$$
$$L^1 = B^* - Cx_2^*$$
$$L^2 = - B^* + Cx_2^*. \tag{7}$$

Then for *any* C, not only $C = 0$ as the Lindahl theory formally requires, we end up with Pareto-optimal configuration that maximises true social welfare U!

It may be argued that setting tax-prices at $P_2^{i*} \pm C$ will produce false pseudo-prices and lead to the wrong determination of x_2. But remember these are *pseudo* tax prices, not *actual* ones at which people are non-excluded from using the public good. The referee for Man i is a fiction, used for exposition of the computation. Once x_2^* is optimally determined, it is there regardless of stated tax-prices. All anyone cares about in the end is his total (algebraic) tax, $P_2^i x_2 - L^i$, and not how Musgrave or anyone else cares to compartmentalise it.

Suppose by a clever 'excluder device', one could make *pseudo-tax* prices genuine prices. Thus, set x_2 so large that after one uses the excluder on Man i, his x_2 – now called x_2^i – can agree with his no-longer-pseudo demand function, $D_2^i(P_1; P_2^i; L^i)$. (Such an experiment involves social waste, but never mind: charge it as a temporary cost of learning enough to achieve optimal organisation.) Will an actual citizen, man in the street i and not an imaginary omniscient referee, act out his demand function $D_2^i(\ldots)$? Certainly he will not. If all but one man is foolish enough to act as the Lindahl theory requires, it pays that last man to dissemble and hide his true liking for x_2.[1]

---

[1] I agree with Johansen's characterisation of the problem as one of indeterminate bilateral-monopoly. Marshallian joint supply is *not* a true analogy. Suppose wool, Y_1, and mutton, Y_2, are produced by sheep, Y_3, in equal amounts, with $Y_1 = Y_2 = Y_3 = Y$ by choice of units and $P_3 = S(Y_3)$ is the supply curve of sheep, while $P_1 = D_1(Y_1)$ and $P_2 = D_2(Y_2)$ are the demand curves for wool and mutton. Then equilibrium can be written as

$$P_1 + P_2 = P_3, \qquad P_1(Y) + P_2(Y) = S(Y),$$

which looks like the Bowen demand diagram. But note that the Bowen curves are pseudo and not genuinely motivated observable relations. Increasing the number of men, s, only makes things worse; by contrast, in ordinary private markets, increasing the number of sellers and numbers of buyers increases the relevance of the supply-demand relations. The true analogy is with joint supply of sheep, where each of mutton, wool and other products are in the hands of *separate* complete *monopolists*!

Hence, as Wicksell sensed when he threw the problem out of the market-place and into the legislature, it pays no one to behave according to the voluntary-exchange theory. So they will not. All of Lindahl's prattling about 'equality of bargaining power' as leading to his solution, with the implication that unbalanced power situations will spread around his solution the way errors spread around a mean value, is gratuitous assertion. Who believes it? Why should anyone?

In point of fact, Wicksell (and I suppose Lindahl himself), Musgrave and Johansen (and Dorfman) all throw the matter into the game-theoretic wilderness of Parliament. Does Wicksell's discussion of voting lead anywhere? And if the chapters of Musgrave and Johansen dealing with mathematical politics do lead anywhere, what possible connections do such chapters have with their Lindahl sections? I ask to be informed, not to criticise.

Take for example the Galbraith view that the public sector is too small compared to the private sector. It may be true that x_2 (or x_{n+k}) is too small and x_1^i (or x_j^i) too large. But how convincing is Johansen's attempt to deduce this bias from the Lindahl apparatus? Actually, other economists have argued that public good x_{n+k} tend to be too large because each legislator thinks he might as well get public works for his region, since others are getting some for theirs and since the cost of his region's projects will tend to get spread over all – and yet, these economists argue, if all legislators together could act by agreement, they would all admit the nation would be better off with a sizeable cut in public expenditures. This is a possibility but, to me, just as inconclusive a generalisation as an alleged game-theoretic corroboration of the Galbraith thesis.

I hope this Appendix shows that whatever are the demerits of my general equilibrium formulations, they are shared by the special Lindahl version of them.

(B) THE DEFINITIONAL PROBLEM

A warning should be registered in connection with my present jettisoning of the concept of a polar public good. Even if, semantically, a variable can be put into more than one individual utility function, we shall not have a *standard* public good case unless it enters in the production-possibility frontier and industry production functions in the standard way (as an earlier footnote mentioned). Moreover, the variable in question may not have the returns and other properties of an ordinary good, private or public.

Here are some examples. Suppose two (or more) families have summer

E 2

homes out on a peninsula. The cost of bringing electricity to them has a separable-cost and joint-cost aspect. Thus, each can properly be charged the separate marginal cost of the electricity that he draws from outside the system. But the common cost of the line is a public good. Suppose x_1^1 and x_1^2 are the respective powers drawn. Suppose x_2 is the (annual) common-cost variable, arranged to take on only the two values: zero if the line is not useable, one if it has been made useable. The utility to Man i of the power *consumed* can be written as the formal product $x_2 x_1^i$; and, with x_0^i an ordinary private good, the maximum problem can be written with proper choice of units

$$\max \; U\{u^1(x_0^1, x_2 x_1^1), \; u^2(x_0^2, x_2 x_1^2)\} \tag{8}$$

subject to

$$x_0^1 + x_0^2 + (x_1^1 + x_1^2) + Mx_2 = 0$$

and x_2 restricted to 0 or 1.

Because the dummy variable x_2 has the discrete (0, 1) property, the tangency conditions of my equations have no applicability and must be replaced by finite-difference maximum conditions. Even if x_2 could be regarded as a continuous real-variable function, the resulting tangency conditions might be boundary inequalities of the type familiar in modern non-linear programming. Even here, because the product $x_2 x_1^i$ is involved, one would not have the quasi-concavity conditions on the u^i functions that make necessary and sufficient conditions identical and rule out multiple local maxima. As is well known in non-concave programming, the resulting 'search' problem can be a formidable combinatorial task. Moreover, turning that task over to a hypothetical perfectly discriminating monopolist, who is supposed to find out people's tastes by a great variety of all-or-none offers is simply to fob off the computational problem on a middleman; to make things worse, the perfect discriminator would face the game-theoretic problem of bilateral monopoly, a fact that the ordinary theoretical discussion conveniently and blissfully forgets.

(C) ROAD USE AS PUBLIC GOODS

The use of dummy variables, like x_2 with the (0, 1) property, is a convenient way of handling some problems where exclusion is possible (albeit not always socially desirable). Another example that illustrates the all-pervasiveness of the consumption externality property of public goods is provided by optimal car road or rail road pricing and allocation. Suppose marginal cost of using a road by car or truck is zero (being the negligible amount of induced wear and tear). Let there be an annual cost of building (and replacing) the road of A. If the road is uncrowded, once built, it should charge no use tolls. If we call x_2, a zero-one variable that indicates absence or presence of the road, our maximum problem is

$$\max U[u^1(x_1^1, x_2), u^2(x_1^2, x_2)] \text{ subject to } x_1^1 + x_1^2 = C - Ax_2, \qquad (9)$$

with Pareto-optimality defined by

$$\max u^1(x_1^1, x_2) \text{ subject to above constraint and } u^2(x_1^2, x_2) \geq \bar{u}^2 \qquad (10)$$

Benefit theorists attracted to the Lindahl approach would be tempted to raise the cost A as the sum of two pseudo tax-prices $P_2^1 + P_2^2$, which would also have to pass the test

$$u^1(\overline{V}^1 + L^1 - P_2^1, 1) \geq u^1(\overline{V}^1 + L^1, 0)$$
$$u^2(\overline{V}^2 + L^2 - P_2^2, 1) \geq u^2(\overline{V}^2 + L^2, 0). \qquad (11)$$

There is absolutely no reason why the $[L^i]$ expressions should be assignable prior to the decision whether or not to build the roads. Indeed, it is quite possible that the above inequalities would be met for one set of $[L^i]$, at the same time that another set of $[L^i]$ satisfy the opposite criteria for *not* building the road:

$$u^i(\overline{V}^i + L^i - P_2^i, 1) < u^i(\overline{V}^i + L^i, 0). \qquad (12)$$

This means, 'Along one part of the Pareto-optimality frontier, the road should not be built; but along another part, it should be built.' There is nothing paradoxical about this: hospitals for the poor are good things with one income-distribution goal and bad things with another. Given a $U(u^1, u^2, \ldots)$ social welfare function, the proper place on the Pareto frontier is selected, along with its implied public-good decisions.

Again, there is no need to use pseudo-tax-pricing with $A = P_2^1 + P_2^2$. I cannot agree with Musgrave that 'Each tub should stand on *its* own bottom'. The purpose of benefit-pricing is not to secure justice for each man, but rather to ensure that we do not end up (i) with everybody worse off, (ii) and where 'society' doesn't want to be. The true problem is to determine 'how big the bottoms shall be' *and* 'what shall be over them'.

Specifically, as a perfectly-good alternative to Lindahl-Musgrave pricing:

(i) Decide to produce the road (if they so decide).
(ii) Set benefit pseudo-tax prices at zero: $P_2^1 = 0 = P_2^2$.
(iii) Allocate remaining private income by optimal (L^1, L^2) lump-sum items that add up to a negative (rather than a zero) total.

Moral: If you know enough to use the Lindahl pseudo prices, you don't have to use them.

Finally, here is a further example of consumption externalities of the public good – or rather, 'public bad', type.

Let the road get crowded. Now Man i's pleasure in using it depends on how many others are using it. As before, let x_1^i be an ordinary private good such as bread, x_2 be a $(0, 1)$ variable depending on whether the road is there or not. Let x_{2+i} be the amount of riding on the road than Man i does. Now we write

$$u^i = u^i(x_1^i, x_2 x_{2+i}, x_2 \sum_{q \neq i} x_{2+q}), \quad u_1^i > 0, \quad u_2^i > 0, \quad u_3^i < 0. \tag{13}$$

Our production-budget constraint for society is

$$1(\sum_i x_1^i) + Ax_2 = C \tag{14}$$

since increasing x_{2+i} use adds nothing to *physical* resource cost.

If we decide to build the road, and set $x_2^* = 1$ the proper programme involves the equation (III')

$$\text{(III')} \qquad \frac{u_2^i}{u_1^i} = 0 - \sum_{q \neq i} \frac{u_3^q}{u_1^q} = \sum_{q \neq i} \left| \frac{u_3^q}{u_1^q} \right| = \mu_i > 0.$$

Clearly there should be a toll or tax price that is *not* a pseudo price. It *should exclude* us from using a bit more of x_{2+i} if we cannot meet the 'psychological marginal cost', μ_i. If all people are 'alike', with all u_3^q/u_1^q alike, we would get *uniform* toll tax prices, $\mu \equiv \mu_i$. Their purpose is to hold down use in order to benefit us all. The revenues they collect have nought to do with A, unless the road can be replicated with each new road costing A. Then it can be shown – and I suppose this is what Mohring's result involves – as the number of people $\to \infty$, there is an optimal density of traffic for each road, an optimal number of roads (asymptotically proportional to s), and for which use-tolls u^* exactly cover long-run costs A. But it is this large-number replicability that has taken us out of government enterprise and back to private-good market optimality. (Note: the private good is then the single road with all *its* joint users, x_{2+q}.)[1]

(D) DECREASING COSTS PHENOMENA AS PUBLIC GOODS

Where marginal cost pricing will not cover full costs, we encounter a version of the public-good problem. There is a popular but fallacious notion that this calls for uniform percentage markups over MC, a result

---

[1] See my cited essay on the Chamberlin monopolistic competition revolution for statement and proof of a theorem that replicability of indivisible units leads asymptotically to the constant-returns-to-scale homogeneity relations of viable perfect competition. R. E. Kuenne (ed.), op. cit.

that happens to be true when such a pattern is equivalent to putting a tax on a factor inelastic in supply. In the general case, if a subsidy financed by ideal lump-sum taxes is not feasible, the feasible optimum involves greater P/MC discrepancies where demand is inelastic. Suppose the government operates a network of uncrowded roads. Let the demands for roads $1, 2, \ldots, k, \ldots, K$ be given by independent functions $B_k(q_k)$, where $B_k(q_k)$ can be taken because of optimal lump-sum L_i redistribution to represent the social money value of total utility from the indicated amount of road use. Let the total cost of road k, measured in money of constant social marginal utility, be $C_k(q_k)$. Then the social magnitude to be maximised is of the consumer-producer surplus form

$$\max_{q_k} \sum_1^K \{B_k(q_k) - C_k(q_k)\}. \tag{15}$$

This leads to $P = MC$ conditions of the form

$$B_k'(q_k) = P_k = C_k'(q_k), \qquad (k = 1, \ldots, K) \tag{16}$$

with solution $(q_1^*, \ldots, q_K^*)$. If average costs are falling, the government will run the roads at an algebraic loss given by

$$\sum_1^K \{C_k(q_k^*) - q_k^* B_k'(q_k^*)\}. \tag{17}$$

This loss should ideally be made up out of lump-sum taxes (L^i) optimally distributed among the populace. (If the loss is a gain it should be optimally distributed as a negative tax.)

The above conditions (16) are only local marginal conditions and must be supplemented by the 'total' or 'global' test-conditions

$$B_k(q_k^*) - C_k(q_k^*) \geq B_k(0) - C_k(0), \qquad (k = 1, \ldots, K). \tag{18}$$

The case of interdependent utilities and costs provide an example of the formidable problem of total or global conditions associated with public goods, a problem in principle like the Chamberlinian one of finding the optimal regime of differentiated products. When one compares a situation with one or more q_k zero rather than positive q_k^*, any 'prior' rectification of the social marginal utility of money will become upset. So, generally, a consumer-surplus money magnitude cannot be found as a surrogate or social utility (or for Pareto-optimum problems). None the less, as an illustration of the formidable difficulties involved in getting any usefulness out of total conditions, consider the case where we are to maximise such a consumer-producer money surplus sum

$$B(q_1,\ldots,q_k,\ldots) - C(q_1,\ldots,q_k,\ldots)$$
$$= N(Q) \text{ for short}$$

The number, K, of potential goods can be indefinitely large, many being alternatives and only a small subset being optimally positive at any one time. Even though it is more realistic to consider discontinuities (due to 'indivisibilities') at the origin, where a $q_k=0$, let us for simplicity assume B and C have smooth partial derivatives. Then, according to modern Kuhn–Tucker non-linear programming

$$\max_{q_k} N(q_1, q_2,\ldots)$$

requires

$$\frac{\partial N}{\partial q_k} = 0 \qquad \text{if } q_k > 0$$

$$\frac{\partial N}{\partial q_k} \leq 0 \qquad \text{if } q_k = 0$$

Consider all the points that satisfy these conditions. They could be infinite in number. They could even be a non-denumerable infinity. But suppose they are finite in number, being $Q^1, Q^2,\ldots, Q^M$, where M can easily be in the millions. Then to *find* this set and verify that the *optimum optimorum*, which may be denoted by Q^1, does satisfy the 'total' tests

$$N(Q^1) \geq N(Q^j) \qquad (j=2,\ldots,M)$$

might well involve trillions of hours of computing-machine time. No practical market algorithm for solving such a search problem has ever been found.

(E) THE OPTIMAL MARKUP THEOREM

Now let us consider the 'feasibility' problem. Given that some specified (algebraic) subsidy, S, is available to help meet the loss, we solve the problem

$$\max_{q_k} \sum_1^K \{B_k(q_k) - C_k(q_k)\} \text{ subject to}$$

$$\sum_1^K \{q_k B_k'(q_k) - C_k(q_k)\} = -S$$

By Lagrangean multiplier technique, we set up

$$L(q_1, \ldots, q_K; \ \lambda) = \sum_1^K \{B_k(q_k) - C_k(q_k)\} + \lambda \left[\sum_1^K \{q_k B_k'(q_k) - C_k(q_k)\} + S \right]$$

and require for a maximum that L be at a stationary point defined by

$$\frac{\partial L}{\partial q_k} = 0 = \{B_k'(q_k) - C_k'(q_k)\}(1 + \lambda) + \lambda q_k B_k''(q_k) \tag{20}$$

$$\frac{\partial L}{\partial \lambda} = 0 = \sum_1^K \{q_k B_k'(q_k) - C_k'(q_k)\} + S$$

The first K equations can be rearranged to become

$$\frac{B_k' - C_k'}{B_k'} = \frac{P_k - MC_k}{P_k} = \frac{+\lambda}{1 + \lambda} \frac{1}{E_k} \qquad (k = 1, \ldots, K) \tag{21}$$

where E_k is the usual absolute Marshallian elasticity of demand

$$E_k = -\frac{dq_k}{dP_k} \frac{P_k}{q_k} = -\frac{B'(q_k)}{q_k B''(q_k)} \tag{22}$$

Calling $(1 + \lambda)/\lambda = 1 + \beta$, which will normally be greater than one, we end up with the discriminating-welfare markup rule

$$\frac{P_k - MC_k}{P_k} = \frac{1}{(1 + \beta)E_k}. \tag{23}$$

This rule, which is a straightforward extension of the feasibility analysis of Frank Ramsey and M. Boiteux, and which has also been independently derived by J. Drèze, has the following interpretation:

> To maximise feasible welfare, do not use a uniform markup rule. Instead act like a discriminating monopolist (not a 'perfectly discriminating one' but one who can charge different prices in the K independent markets, in the Yntema–Robinson fashion) – but, blow up the true elasticity of demand, E_k, of every market by the same proportion, pretending that it is $(1 + \beta)E_k$, where the coefficient $1 + \beta$ depends on the plentitude of S, the available subsidy.

Thus, if S is fully plentiful, $\beta = 0$ and we have ideal $P = MC$ pricing. Should S be so small that a discriminating monopolist could only break even, β would become 0. (This shows that, although all monopoly is a bad or non-optimal thing, in a sense discriminating monopoly pricing is 'better' than uniform pricing.) Even if an Yntema–Robinson discriminator could not break even by any pricing, which means *a fortiori* that a simple monopolist could not, it may still pay in terms of consumer-producer surplus to operate the roads. The total conditions, for each feasible S, involves testing each road's right to exist and that of every possible subset. If the decision is between the whole road network or none, the total condition is

$$\sum_1^K \{B_k(q_k^*) - C_k(q_k^*)\} - S \geq \sum_1^K B_k(0) - C_k(0) \tag{24}$$

where the right-hand side may have a different interpretation in the short run than in the long.

All of the above analysis applies with small modification if costs or demands are not independent. Thus, if we replace additive costs, $\Sigma C_k(q_k)$, by $C(q_1, \ldots, q_K)$, we merely have to replace marginal costs, $C_k'(q_k)$, by the partial derivative, $\partial C(q_1, \ldots, q_K)/\partial C_k$; and similarly for non-independent utilities. In particular, the usual Yntema–Robinson discussion of discriminating monopoly replaces $\Sigma C_k(q_k)$ by $C(\Sigma q_k)$, it being assumed that the products sold to different markets are exactly alike physically.

This has an important application to our road problem. Two separate demands, say $B_1'(q_1)$ and $B_2'(q_2)$, could be for rides on the same road but by different users. The theory says, 'Don't charge different men the same price for the same service, charge the one with more inelastic demand the higher price – and this in the interest of minimising the deadweight loss due to unfeasibility of financing social losses by ideal lump-sum tax.' Is this not 'unjust', in the second sense described earlier? (Does it not violate the Churchmen notion of 'commutative justice'?) One can answer: 'It does maximise the total of social utility expressed in money (and presumably reflecting the fact that in the background proper redistributions and compensations are being made to keep social $U(u^1, u^2, \ldots)$ at its feasible maximum).' But one should also note that there is a partial self-inconsistency in the problem. If you have to rely on $P - MC$ markups, that must be because ideal lump-sum L^i are not feasible. Then how can they be counted on to be operating in the background to keep incomes distributed equitably and ensure equality of social marginal utility of every person's dollar? As mentioned in my third paper, the proper optimum under these feasibility conditions involves pricing that favours people with dollars of greater ethical weight and involves a compromise between deadweight-loss-minimisation and interpersonal 'Robin-Hood' pricings.

(F) RAMSEY'S FEASIBILITY OR SECOND-BEST OPTIMALITY

Not only is the above a theory of subsidy, it is also a theory of optimal goods-and-services taxing of the Ramsey–Pigou type. Suppose $C_k(q_k)$ represents integrated marginal costs of a competitive industry. And suppose that S is now a negative subsidy, namely the amount of revenue that has to be raised from *ad valorem* or *specific* taxes on $(q_1, \ldots, q_K)$. (This can include taxes on factors of the income-tax type if we vary our convention and let some q_k represent inputs with algebraic signs changed; but this extension I ignore here.)

Then the optimality conditions of (20) define for us the ideal Ramsey–Pigou pattern of (differentiated!) excises.

If (percentage) tax rates are defined by

$$t_k = \frac{P_k - MC_k}{P_k} \tag{25}$$

then conditions (20) and (21) give us directly the optimally-differentiated pattern

t_k inversely proportional to elasticity of demand, E_k, or

$$t_k = \frac{1}{(1 + \beta)E_k} \tag{26}$$

where β depends on the size of the revenue to be raised, $-S$. This accords with the modern notion: Taxes on things in inelastic demand tend to do the least harm.[1]

It is easy to show that, for *small* $|S|$, we get the Ramsey rule: 'Select $P_k - MC_k$ tax discrepancies so as to change every q_k in the same proportion away from the ideal $P_k = MC_k$ configuration.' So long as R'_k and C'_k remain strictly linear, such a rule is exact for large, finite changes.

[1] Note: my assumption of constancy of the marginal utility of money banishes the income effects that separate ordinary price elasticities of demand and the more relevant Slutsky–Hicks compensated-elasticities-of-demand.

6 Provision for Social Goods

R. A. Musgrave

1 THE THEORY OF SOCIAL GOODS

The theory of social goods deals with the features which distinguish social from private goods, and the problems encountered in making public provisions for the former. This theory has been developed rather fully with reference to the polar case of a pure social good, but its application to the important range of mixed goods remains to be explored. We begin with a review of the polar case and then proceed to the more complex situation of mixed goods. Emphasis will be on the nature of social goods and the characteristics of optimal provision. The equally important problem of how to implement this solution is dealt with only incidentally. The discussion will be in terms of current consumer goods, but essentially the same applies to that of durable consumer and intermediate goods.

PUBLIC PROVISION VS. PUBLIC PRODUCTION

To begin with, we must distinguish between 'public provision' as we use the term, and public production. Public provision refers to a situation where certain goods are furnished to the consumer not in response to individual market purchases, but free of direct charge and through the budgetary process. Such public provision may take the form of public purchases from private firms, or public production. Similarly, public production may involve goods which are sold to individual consumers in the market. The issue of resource allocation between social or private goods (whether produced publicly or privately) is the central theoretical issue of public finance or public economy as here understood. It is quite distinct from and largely unrelated to that of private vs. public management of production (whether of private or of social goods), i.e. to the traditional distinction between socialism and capitalism.

The problem of social goods as here conceived, thus, exists in both the socialist and the capitalist context. In the latter, certain characteristics of social goods require public provision through the budgetary process. In the former, these very characteristics make it impossible to use the market (or queue) type of allocation applicable in a socialism with consumer choice.[1]   Rather, such goods must again be allocated through a political system of preference determination quite analogous to that needed in the capitalist system.[2]

SUBJECTIVE PREFERENCE HYPOTHESIS

Next, one must choose between two approaches to the theory of social wants or social goods, involving two alternative premises regarding the underlying preference system.   One approach is to argue that all allocation, whether to private or to social goods is to bo be made in line with individual consumer preferences.   The utility of defence along with that of door locks and ice cream is included in the individual's preference function, and both goods should be provided in relation thereto.   The social utility function relates to the ordering of welfare positions among individuals, but leaves the choice between particular goods to them. This excludes neither some degree of delegation of decision making (be it to legislators or civil servants), nor implementation through a more or less imperfect mechanism of decision by voting.   Nor does it presume extreme 'egotism' in individual behaviour.   Some allowance may be made in the utility function A for utility derived by B.   But it differs fundamentally from an alternative that postulates some elite or central authority (benevolent or not) which knows best, and imposes its preferences on the individual. A may be asked to consume Q_x even though he would prefer Q_y produced with the same resource input.   The student of fiscal affairs who wishes to build a predictive model will investigate whether the existing set of institutions corresponds more closely to the one or the other system.   But for purposes of a normative theory, which defines optimal fiscal behaviour, the choice between the two approaches is essentially ideological.   It will not be discussed here and unless otherwise noted (see paragraphs 43–5, where the case of merit wants is dealt with), we will proceed on the premise of individual choice.

This leaves us with an individualistic or subjective as distinct from an imposed or collective view of the preference system.   At the same time, certain goods have characteristics which require group action to secure their provision, in line with individual preference.   Such goods are here

---

[1] See for instance O. Lange and F. M. Taylor, *On the Economics of Socialism*, ed. B. E. Lippincot (University of Minnesota Press, 1938).

[2] At the same time, other aspects of the fiscal system (including the stabilisation and distribution functions, the specific function of taxes, and the extent to which merit wants are recognised) differ sharply under socialist and capitalist conditions.   See my forthcoming *Fiscal Systems* (Yale University Press, 1967) part I.

referred to as social goods. To emphasise that the distinguishing characteristic derives from the nature of the good, rather than the utility function,
I now prefer the term social good to my earlier terminology of social
want.[1] By the same token, the term imposed want is preferable where
the alternative system is considered.

2 THE POLAR CASE

Our first task is to determine the characteristics which must apply if a
good is to be provided for publicly, i.e. to qualify as a social good. Much
has been said about this in the literature, some helpful and some not.
From this discussion there emerge two features which are most relevant
and interesting. The first is the characteristic of non-rivalness in consumption, i.e. the existence of a beneficial consumption externality. The second
is the characteristic of non-excludability from consumption. The two
are distinct features and need not coincide. Each plays a different role.

NON-RIVALNESS IN CONSUMPTION

Social goods are defined as goods, the benefits from which are such that
A's partaking therein does not interfere with the benefits derived by B.
They differ from private goods, whose benefits are enjoyed by either A
or B. The two goods enter the utility functions of A and B as U_A
$= U_A(X_A, Y)$ and $U_B = U_B(X_B, Y)$ where X_A and X_B are the amounts of
the private good X which are purchased by the two respectively, while Y
is the total supply of the social good. The total output, subject to the
transformation function, is given by $O = X_A + X_B + Y$.

The condition of non-rivalness in consumption (or, which is the same,
the existence of beneficial consumption externalities) means that the same
physical output (the fruits of the same factor input) is enjoyed by both
A and B. This does not mean that the same subjective benefit must be
derived, or even that precisely the same product quality is available to
both. Consumer A who lives close to the police station has better protection than B who lives far away. Yet, the two consumption acts are
non-rival, and we deal with a social good.

Due to the non-rivalness of consumption, individual demand curves
are added vertically,[2] rather than horizontally as in the case of private
goods. Or A's demand curve may be considered a supply curve from

---

[1] See part I of my *The Theory of Public Finance* (McGraw-Hill, 1958).
[2] See H. R. Bowen, *Toward Social Economy* (New York: Rinehart & Co., 1948)
p. 177.

B's point of view and vice versa.[1] The cost share payable by *A* will be the less, the more is paid by *B*, and the more additional consumers participate. Contrary to the case of private goods, a consumer will find it to his advantage to have tastes which are similar to those of others.

As Samuelson has shown, Pareto optimality for the supply of social goods requires that marginal cost equal the sum of the marginal rates of substitution of *A* and *B*, whereas for the private good it is equal to each of these two rates.[2] Assuming preferences to be known, what does this imply for the pricing of social goods, and the possibility of separating allocational and distributional considerations in the public household? This will be considered further on page 127.

NON-EXCLUDABILITY FROM CONSUMPTION

Let us turn first to another characteristic difficulty of social goods, which relates to the process of preference determination. For the case of private goods, the market mechanism may be likened to an auction system, where the product goes to the highest bidder. Consumers must reveal their preferences, since otherwise they will be excluded from the enjoyment of the goods which they wish to purchase. But now consider the case of a social good, such as national defence, which is virtually such that no one can be excluded. As a result, consumers will be hesitant or unwilling to reveal true preferences. Being one among many, a consumer will argue that the total supply and hence the benefit which accrues to him will not be affected significantly by his contribution. If the government invites declaration of preferences and bills accordingly, he will respond by understating his preference. Since preference revelation is not secured automatically by the auction function of the market, another mechanism (e.g. voting procedures) must be substituted to determine preferences. This second difference stems from non-excludability and relates to the revelation of preferences.

While the case of defence combines non-rivalness in consumption with non-excludability, this is not a necessary situation. The existence of non-rivalness in consumption does not necessarily mean that exclusion is impossible; and the existence of rival consumption does not always mean that exclusion is possible. The first case is illustrated by an existing

---

[1] See E. Lindahl, *Die Gerechtigkeit der Besteurung* (London, 1910) p. 89. Reprinted in Musgrave and Peacock (ed.), *Classics in the Theory of Public Finance* (Int. Ec. Association).

[1] See P. A. Samuelson, 'The Pure Theory of Public Expenditure', *Rev. Econ. and Statistics*, xxxvi (1954) and 'Diagrammatic Exposition of a Theory of Public Expenditure', ibid. xxxvii (1955).

bridge which is not crowded, but which readily permits the charging of tolls. In this situation, charging of tolls is inefficient because it does not meet the Pareto condition for social goods. The second case is illustrated by *A*'s apple orchard, the nectar of which is consumed by the bees of either *B or C*. In this case, market failure occurs because of non-excludability, even though we are dealing with rival consumption. Social (non-rival) goods need not be non-excludable goods and vice versa. The occurence of either feature calls for group action to secure proper provision, but for different reasons.[1]

There are some situations where excludability is impossible (defence) and others where it is available at little or no cost (ice cream or use of bridge). In the former case, we have no choice in the matter. In the latter case, exclusion may be desirable but need not always be so. It should be applied only with regard to goods, the benefits of which are rival, but not with regard to goods whose benefits are non-rival. The non-crowded bridge should not be subject to tolls even if the gatekeeper is cheap or would be otherwise unemployable and hence involved no resource cost. The currently popular drive to 'internalise externalities' is thus subject to qualification. It should be added, however, that the situation with regard to external costs is asymmetrical. Such costs should be internalised even if non-rival. Whereas exclusion of additional consumers from the enjoyment of benefits is a loss, preventing the imposition of a burden on all is a gain.

The two preceding situations (excludability is impossible or available at zero cost) are not all inclusive. In many cases excludability may be possible but at a significant cost. If the situation is such that exclusion should be applied if available at zero cost, the problem is then one of weighing the gains from exclusion (which forces revelation of preferences and obviates the need for a political mechanism of preference determination) against the costs. Thus, the cost of traffic congestion in New York City streets should be internalised, provided that the mechanism of so doing is not too costly. Exclusion technology is thus a factor in deciding what costs should be internalised. At the margin, the cost of internalising should be equated with the gain in consumer surplus which results therefrom.[2]

Let us return to the double-polar case of a good which is both non-rival and non-excludable, such as defence. We have noted that the

---

[1] For a discussion of various forms of market failure, see F. M. Bator, 'The Anatomy of Market Failure', *Quarterly Journal of Economics*, Aug 1958.

[2] This rule has been suggested to me by R. Turvey.

individual consumer, being one among many, will not reveal his true preference without the pressure of a voting system which imposes a mandatory decision. Such a voting system, though necessary to induce preference revelation, has its efficiency cost. For one thing, voting takes time and equipment; for another, the outcome will not please all participants. The economist's assignment for the political scientist is to solve the dilemma of devising a voting system which permits the best expression of preference (a system similar to point rather than majority voting) while giving least play to strategy (which might be most dominant under point voting).

This cost is avoidable in a situation where numbers are small. In this case, individual bargaining will be feasible, and non-excludability loses much of its significance. A market in externalities can be created.[1] This, however, is not a pure gain, as the existence of small numbers creates a new set of imperfections. We have here another distinction between social and private goods. As I have noted earlier, the increase in numbers improves the market allocation of private goods, but only moves the social good from one trouble (small-number imperfection) to another (non-revelation).[2]

OPTIMAL ALLOCATION WITH PREFERENCES GIVEN, AND THE DISTRIBUTION ISSUE

Let us now disregard the exclusion issue and its implications for revelation and assume that individual preferences are known to the planner. What then constitutes an optimal solution for the purely non-rival good?

The now classical formulation of the problem, as given by Samuelson,[3] determines a set of feasible solutions, involving (1) different divisions of total output between the public good and the private good, and (2) different divisions of the total supply of private goods between A and B. All these solutions are Pareto optimal in that any departure from the set involves a loss to either A or B. The optimum optimorum is then chosen on the basis of a social utility function which weighs the relative welfare positions of A and B. The solution of the social goods problem is thus

---

[1] See R. H. Coase, 'The Problem of Social Cost', *Journal of Law and Economics*, III (October 1960); J. Buchanan, 'Policy and the Pigouvian Margins', *Economica*, XXIX (1962); S. Wellisz, 'On External Diseconomics and the Government Assisted Invisible Hand', *Economica*, November 1964; R. Turvey, 'On Divergences between Social Cost and Private Cost', *Economica*, Aug. 1963.

[2] Musgrave, *Theory of Public Finance*, op. cit. p. 80.

[3] P. A. Samuelson, op. cit.

made part of the general problem of welfare maximisation including the *entire* issue of distribution and production choice of private goods.

This formulation meets the test of theoretical rigour and sweeping elegance and ranks among the great contributions to the theory of welfare economics as applies to public finance. Yet, it leaves the more parochially inclined fiscal theorist somewhat dissatisfied. The extreme generality of the formulation renders it difficult to focus on the specifically fiscal problem and to relate the theoretical model to implementational schemes.

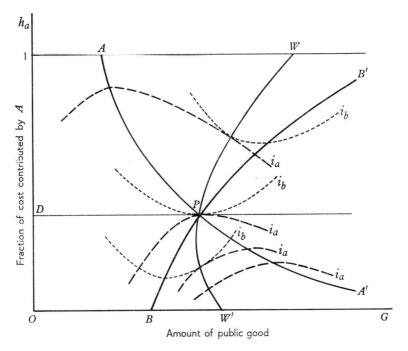

FIG. 1   JOHANSEN'S EXPOSITION OF LINDAHL DIAGRAM [1]

(for explanation see p. 131 n. 2)

More attractive, from his point of view, is the spirit of the Lindahl formulation,[1] especially as revised in a recent article by Leif Johansen,[2] and of my earlier attempt at restatement.[3] In these models, the concern

[1] E. Lindahl, op. cit.

[2] L. Johansen, 'Some Notes on the Lindahl Theory of Public Expenditures', *Intern. Economic Review*, IV (1963).   [3] R. A. Musgrave, op. cit. p. 81.

is directly with tax-expenditure determination on the basis of a given initial state of distribution, following Wicksell's proposition that the 'proper' distribution of the tax burden cannot be determined unless a 'proper' distribution of income is assumed to exist at the outset.[1]

Johansen's analysis begins with a given state of distribution in terms of factor endowments. With the help of certain simplifying assumptions he derives an offer schedule for A, showing the preferred amount of social goods for various divisions of cost shares between A and B. A similar curve is derived for B, and their intersection corresponds to the P point in the well-known Lindahl diagram. (See AA' and BB' in Fig. 1)[2] As Johansen shows, this P point is one but not the only Pareto optimal solution, as it is only one among other points on the contract curve, WW' corresponding to different divisions of the welfare gain from the introduction of social goods between A and B. Since Johansen attaches no particular merit to the P point, he is still left with a distributional issue and need for a social utility function. However, the scope of the distributional problem is reduced, due to the initial assumption of a given distribution of resource endowment.

This formulation may be considered a special case of Samuelson's broader framework, but it is more attractive for purposes of fiscal theory as it permits us to focus explicitly on the crucial policy problem of tax shares. At the same time, it leaves open the question of why the initial state of resource endowment was considered proper. As long as the distribution of the gain from the introduction of social goods remains to be distributed, how is it possible to predetermine the 'proper' resource endowment? The social utility function, which determines the state of distribution cannot relate merely to the distribution which would result in the absence of social goods, but must cover the entire resource use, including social goods. We are still left with an inconsistency which is successfully removed in Samuelson's general formulation.

---

[1] K. Wicksell, *Finanztheoretische Untersuchungen* (Jena, 1896). Excerpts reprinted in Musgrave and Peacock, op. cit.

[2] The dashed indifference curves show combinations of public goods output (G) and cost shares contributed by A_a (h) among which taxpayer A is indifferent. They are derived from the taxpayers' basic preference patterns between a private good X and a public good G, and a given initial resource endowment in terms of X. The dotted indifference lines for B are concave to the abscissa, since $h_B = 1 - h_A$. The lines AA' and BB' show the most preferred values for various cost shares. The line WW', or contract curve, is the locus of the points on which the two sets of indifference curves are tangent. Only at point P do the most preferred positions coincide. Since the indifference curves in Fig. 1 refer to a given resource endowment, they will shift if the endowment is changed, and the WW' curve will shift accordingly.

But this is not the only possible solution. Instead of substituting this general formulation, the point P may be re-established (or established) as the optimal solution by hypothesising that the initial distribution of resource endowment has been derived from the social welfare function on the assumption that cost shares in the budget will be allocated according to a pricing rule which yields this result. Given my primary interest in developing a useful theory of public finance (the purpose of a theoretical tool being after all its applicability to relevant issues), I find this helpful for various reasons.

First, it suggests a method of pricing for social goods which is analogous to that of pricing for private goods in the sense that for each consumer there must be an equality of the marginal rates of substitution between social and private goods on the one side, and the ratio of *his* price for social goods and the *uniform* price for private goods on the other. The difference indicated by the italics denotes that the price of the social good to the individual (unlike that of the private good) is not equal to the marginal cost for the economy, but to the individual consumer's share therein.

Given this information, the provision of social goods may be considered an efficiency problem in resource use, analogous to the traditional practice with regard to private goods, where it is concluded that, in the absence of externalities and on the basis of a given distribution of resource endowment, the competitive solution is to be preferred. The allocation of both social and private goods follows a pricing rule and (contrary to the view which identifies economic issues with private goods [1]), one is as 'economic' as the other. There remains, to be sure, the difference that implementation of the pricing rule for private goods is achieved more readily than that for public goods, where non-excludability requires a political mechanism to secure preference revelation. But this is a problem of implementation, not different in kind from public controls to secure competition in private markets. Indeed, our pricing rule (choice of the P point) has the further advantage that it offers an operational reference point in evaluating the quality of alternative voting systems (e.g. qualified majority, plurality, etc.) as well as of parliamentary procedures (piecemeal vs. overall legislation in appropriating funds, ear-marking, combining tax and expenditure decisions, etc.) in approximating an optimal solution to the social goods problem. This is necessary if our theory is to be useful at a more applied level.

Above all, it is evident to the most casual observer that real world

[1] See, for instance, Howard Ellis, 'The Economic Way of Thinking', *American Economic Review*, Mar 1950.

decisions are frequently rendered inefficient because (as a matter of fiscal politics) allocation objectives are mixed with distributional objectives. Usually, these objectives can be implemented more economically through direct tax-transfer measures, leaving the choice between social and private goods to be made on consumer-preference grounds.[1]

ADDENDUM ON SEPARATION OF ISSUES [2]

I remain convinced that the separation between allocation and distribution aspects offers a more useful approach to public finance theory, notwithstanding re-emphasis of their interdependence in Professor Samuelson's preceding paper. Unless a basis for separation is established, we are left with a theory of public expenditures or, better, resource use in which the tax problem has no conceptual place. But without this, the theory gives little aid to the analysis of fiscal problems as they actually arise. Hence the public finance theorist's need for a somewhat more parochial approach.

I grant that it is not possible to define the distribution goal merely in terms of resource endowment; and that it is not possible, by use of the Pareto rule, to determine *the* optimal allocation pattern. But suppose that the utility frontier has been determined and that a point theron has been chosen as optimal. We may then work back to a distribution of resource endowments which corresponds to this point, provided that a specific pricing rule (e.g. marginal cost pricing) is followed. Having done so, allocation according to marginal cost pricing will be optimal.

I see no objection to this construction as an analytical device.[3] The

---

[1] This is not to deny that subsidies in kind may be appropriate in the merit good context (see p. 143).

[2] This section has been added, subsequent to the Conference, to complement Professor Samuelson's cross-references in his preceding paper.

[3] Professor Samuelson is correct, however, in criticising certain aspects of my earlier presentation. (See my *The Theory of Public Finance*, pp. 80–5.) In particular: (1) There is an inconsistency between the argument of p. 81 where the resource endowment is taken as given, and of p. 84, where the government is given the task of choosing among points on the utility frontier. If the given endowment distribution is accepted as 'correct', one must also stipulate a specific pricing rule as done on p. 85; and in this case one arrives at a specific point on the utility frontier. (2) Professor Samuelson is correct in pointing out that my utility frontier over range XY (p. 83) is a part of his frontier, each intermediate point reflecting a different pricing rule. (3) It was somewhat misleading to argue (p. 84) that indeterminancy arises in the case of public goods only. This is correct only if the prevailing distribution of endowments is assumed to stipulate marginal cost pricing for private goods, while making no such stipulation for social goods. The difference disappears if pricing rules are stipulated for both cases. (4) Professor Samuelson suggests that I am mistaken in requiring the budget of the 'Allocation Branch' to be balanced, since a subsidy is required for decreasing cost industries. I accept the principle that subsidy is needed in a truly decreasing cost case, but wonder

question, rather, is whether it is a useful tool. The issue applies to both a world of private and of public goods. In the private good context, a move from a situation of average cost pricing to marginal cost pricing can be said unequivocally to involve a gain to society only if the relative welfare positions which result from marginal cost policy are considered desirable. Otherwise, the loss from worsened distribution may outweigh the gain in Pareto efficiency. Unless this condition is met (i.e. the distribution of resource endowment, given marginal cost pricing, is assumed to be correct), nothing can be said about the comparative merits of one or another market structure. There would be no basis (with regard to allocation objectives at least) for antitrust policy, and the case against such measures as price-maintenance legislation. I submit that this is not a reasonable judgement. One need not be a 'slave to Pareto optimicity' to believe that more will be accomplished by retaining the fiction of 'proper' distribution when dealing with market structures, while applying distributional correctives directly with regard to income.

Much the same argument applies with regard to social goods. To be sure, the basic issue of distribution (how would one distribute income in a world of private goods which involve no externalities) must be admitted as a problem of budget policy because, as just noted, it is accomplished better through direct redistribution (tax-transfer measures) than through price adjustments. But there is much to be said for separating it from the additional problem of providing for social goods. By adopting our pricing rule, the latter may again be seen as an allocation issue, thereby expediting the provision of such goods in response to individual preferences and reducing the extent to which it is distorted by purely distributive considerations. While the implementation of the pricing rule is more difficult in the case of social goods, due to non-excludability and its consequences for revelation, this also renders the availability of a yardstick for efficient behaviour the more important. While Professor Samuelson is correct in pointing out that too little has been done regarding the evaluation of alternative rules of decision making, I do not take quite as nihilistic a view regarding the possibility of work in this area.

3 MIXED CASES

The preceding discussion has dealt with the case of a pure social good, i.e. a good the benefits of which are wholly non-rival. This approach has

how significant a factor this is for the broad range of social goods. (See pp. 136–40 of my *The Theory of Public Finance*.)

been subject to the criticism that this case does not exist, or, if at all, applies to defence only; and that in fact most goods which give rise to private benefits also involve externalities in varying degrees and hence combine both social and private good characteristics. Granted that such is the case, it hardly renders the theoretical discussion of the polar case useless. Economic categories (not even the proverbial distinction between consumer and capital goods) rarely apply in pure form. We can do better, however, and show that the above analysis may be applied to at least some important types of mixed cases.

CASE I. SOCIAL GOODS WITH LIMITED SPILLOVER

The utility function for the social-good case was defined as $U_A = U_A(X_A, Y)$ and $U_B = U_B(X_B, Y)$ where Y is the social good. This may also be written as $U_A = U_A(X_A, Y_{PA} + Y_{PB})$ and $U_B = U_B(X_B, Y_{PA} + Y_{PB})$ where Y_{PA} are units of Y paid for by A and Y_{PB} are units of Y paid for by B. Since the benefits derived by A from Y_{PB} are the same as those derived from Y_{PA}, and vice versa for B, the distinction between Y_{PA} and Y_{PB} is only a 'payment' matter. Both being fully beneficial to both A and B, the question of who pays and the 'location' of the direct consumption input may be disregarded. But suppose now that the situation is asymmetrical. The utility functions read $U_A = U_A(X_A, Y_A + Y_B)$ and $U_B = U_B(X_B, Y_B)$. X is again a purely private good. Consumption of X by A is useful to A but of no concern to B, and vice versa. Consumption of Y by B, however, is beneficial to A, and indeed a perfect substitute of own-consumption inputs by A. In other words, Y_B is a pure social good to A but a private good to B. The social good quality of of Y is non-reciprocal. Anti-pollution measures undertaken by B who lives upstream are helpful to A who lives downstream, but not vice versa. The meaning of the subscript is now not merely one of finance but of 'initial consumption input'. The initial location of this consumption input, which was irrelevant in the case of the pure social good, is now of crucial importance. Since A does not care whether the consumption input is with A or with B, A will be prepared to subsidise B's consumption.

This type of limited spillover is of particular interest with regard to the interrelationship between fiscal units, be they localities or nations. If such unit is treated as a person, it being assumed that the respective community preferences are internally determined, the problem of benefit spillovers between fiscal units is indeed the same as that between individuals.

Before dealing with any particular situation, it is useful to develop a taxonomy of partial spillovers, which provides a bridge between purely private goods and purely social goods.

$U_A =$	$U_B =$			
	$U(Y_B)$	$U(Y_B + \beta Y_A)$	$U(Y_B + \gamma Y_A)$	$U(Y_B + Y_A)$
$U(Y_A)$	1	2	2	5
$U(Y_A + \beta Y_B)$	2	3	4	6
$U(Y_A + \gamma Y_B)$	2	4	3	6
$U(Y_A + Y_B)$	5	6	6	7

The subscripts A and B indicate in which community (or on behalf of which individual) the consumption input occurs. The β and γ coefficients indicate the benefit discounts or premiums attached to the foreign, relative to the own-input. If β in A's utility function is equal to 1, A is indifferent whether the consumption input occurs (one gallon of insect spray is released) in A or in B. If β equals ·5, one input unit in B is worth one-half as much to A as one input unit in A and so forth. The essential point is that insect spraying in B reduces pests not only in B but also in A, but that the input per gallon in B may well be less productive (in terms of reduction of pests in A) than would the input of the same gallon in A. The distribution of striking force between the members of an alliance is another illustration.[1] The values of γ and β are here assumed to be non-negative and not to exceed 1, but this is not a necessary assumption.

Case 1 will be recognised as the polar case of the private good, where there are no externalities at all, and Case 7 as that of the pure social good, where there is full and reciprocal spillover. Situations 2 and 5 are situations of non-reciprocal spillover, with the spillover being partial in Case 2 and full in 5. Cases 3, 4 and 6 involve reciprocal spillovers. In Case 3 the reciprocal spillover is symmetrical, while in 4 and 6 it is not. In Cases 5 and 6 at least one party benefits from spill-ins on a 1:1 basis, whereas in 2, 3 and 4 benefits from spill-ins are subject to a 'discount'.

To avoid confusion, let it be noted again that we are dealing here with consumption externalities. Own-consumption by (spraying in) A helps pest reduction in B. This is the case whether the spray is produced by A, B, or whether it is imported from C. The location of production remains a matter of trade theory in the traditional sense. A corresponding set of cases can be developed which deals with production externalities. Thus, the production of chemicals may generate unpleasant odours,

[1] See M. Olson, 'An Economic Theory of Alliances', *Review of Economics and Statistics*, 1966.

which may or may not drift across the border. No one likes to live next to a smoke stack. This poses analogous problems, but they are not dealt with here.

Nor can we attempt to develop the consumption cases in detail, but a brief comment on Case 2 may be useful to illustrate the nature of the problem. We compare an initial situation (1) where A and B each adjust their own purchases to that of the other party, but no side payments can be made, with a new situation (2) which comes about if side payments and negotiations are permitted. Adding a purely private good X to the picture (where both β and γ equal zero), it can be shown that the consumption of Y is increased when moving from (1) to (2). This is the case because income as well as substitution effects for both A and B favour increased consumption of Y.[1] At the same time, it does *not* follow that factor inputs into Y will be increased. In fact, it is quite possible that factor inputs will be decreased because consumption is shifted to the more efficient site, i.e. from A to B.[2] In Case 3 where the spillover situation is symmetrical, such gain from relocation of factor input is not possible, and the introduction of side payments may be expected to increase total inputs as well as consumption.

How does a situation of type 2 or 5 relate to the pure social good case of type 7? In Case 5 for instance, Y is a fully private good for B but a fully social good for A. As a result, A will subsidise consumption by B, and resort to own-consumption only if the total supply which he desires at a price equal to cost or own-input, exceeds the amount for which B's marginal evaluation becomes zero. In the small number case, such a result might be approximated by bargaining. In the large number case, the A's will be called upon to pay taxes which are used to subsidise (though at less than 100 per cent) the purchases of own-inputs by the B's. We are left with a selective tax-subsidy scheme, with a transfer from inefficient own-consumers or recipients of spill-ins to efficient own-consumers or originators of spill-outs.

---

[1] Alan Williams – 'The Optimal Provision of Public Goods in a System of Local Government', *Journal of Political Economy*, vol. LXXIV, no. 1 (February 1966) – reaches the conclusion that consumption may arise or fall. This difference in result arises because Williams compares our initial situation (1) where A and B adjust themselves to the other's consumption of Y but *no* compensation is paid, with one (2) where consumption *must* be paid. With compensation mandatory, one party may come to be worse off. For him the income effect is negative and consumption may fall. Our comparison assumes moving from (1) to a situation (3) where compensation *may* be paid.

[2] This very useful distinction between change in consumption and change in factor input has been advanced by J. Buchanan. See, for instance, J. M. Buchanan and M. Z. Kafoglis, 'A Note on Public Goods Supply', *American Economic Review*, June 1963.

CASE II.   NON-SUBSTITUTE EXTERNALITIES

In Case I we have dealt with situations where B's own-consumption of Y is a substitute for A's own-consumption of Y, even though the productivity per unit of input into B may be less, from A's point of view, than

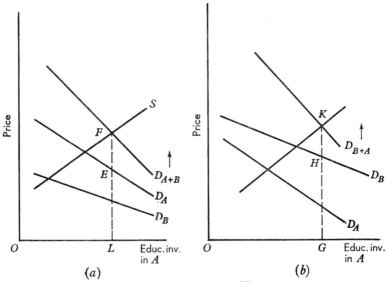

(a)   (b)

FIG. 2   INTERDEPENDENT UTILITY

a similar input into A.   Consider now a somewhat different situation. The utility functions are $U_A = U_A(X_A, Y_A, Y_B)$ and $U_B = U_B(X_B, Y_B, Y_A)$. This is a situation where A derives a benefit from B's consumption of Y, but this benefit is entirely different from (no direct substitute for) his own consumption of Y.[1]   For instance, A may invest in his own education to raise his income, or to be better able to enjoy literature; and he may have an interest in B's education, either for 'altruistic' reasons, or because this increases his safety or the pleasantness of his social environment.   In this situation A will again be willing to subsidise B and vice versa, but A's own demand for Y_A will not be related directly to the level of Y_B. Y_A and Y_B are rival rather than substitute commodities.

The situation regarding Y_A and Y_B is shown in Fig. 2, where diagram (a) shows the demand for Y_A (education investment in A). D_A is A's demand, D_B is B's demand, and the two are added vertically into D_{A+B} or market demand.   If S is the supply schedule (the cost of pencils which

---

[1] The two demands are related only in the sense of general consumer equilibrium where, to some degree, the demand for *all* commodities is interdependent.

A needs for his studies), total input into *A* will equal *OL*. Adopting a solution analogous to Lindahl's *P* point, *A* will pay *EL* and *B* will pay *EF*. The subsidy rate received by *A* and paid by *B* equals *EF/FL*. Fig. 2(b) gives the same picture for education investment in *B*, with a subsidy rate equal to *HK/GK* and input equal to *OG*. Total education input (allowing compensation to be paid) equals *OL + OG*. Transferring the argument to the large number case, we arrive at a situation where everyone's own education becomes a social good for everyone else; but unlike the polar case, the solution is not provision through the budget with 100 per cent tax finance. Rather, we end up with a general tax-subsidy scheme, where the rate of subsidy depends upon the relative weights of the private and social goods components of *Y*. The polar case of 100 per cent tax finance is but a limiting solution of the general theory of subsidy. It arises where the entire benefit is in social form, while private benefit is equal to zero.

CASE III. MIXED BENEFIT GOODS

Finally, consider a situation where the utility functions read $U_A = U_A(X_A, Y_A, Y_A + Y_B)$ and $U_B = U_B(X_B, Y_B, Y_B + Y_A)$. We are now dealing with a good which generates two types of benefits, one which is purely private and applies to own-consumption only; and another, which is wholly social and which is enjoyed equally independent of the locus of consumption input. This case bears similarities to and differs from both the preceding sets of situations. It is similar to the situations under Case I in that Y_B and Y_A appear in additive form, but differs in that outside consumption is a substitute for only one, not all aspects of own-consumption. Discount coefficients may again be added as in Case I. Also, this situation is similar to that of Case II in that there are some aspects of own-consumption which cannot be substituted for by outside consumption; but it differs from it in that such benefits as are derived from outside consumption do serve as substitutes for some aspects of own consumption.

The education case may again be drawn upon to illustrate this situation, it being as reasonable to interpret it in the Case III as in the Case II sense. *A* derives benefits from his own education such as higher earnings, but also values the environment of a close cultural society to which everyone's education (including his own) contributes. The attraction of the present formulation is that it neatly transforms the all-or-nothing case of the pure social good into a generalised theory of public subsidy. To simplify matters, we assume again that the proper solution of the pure

F

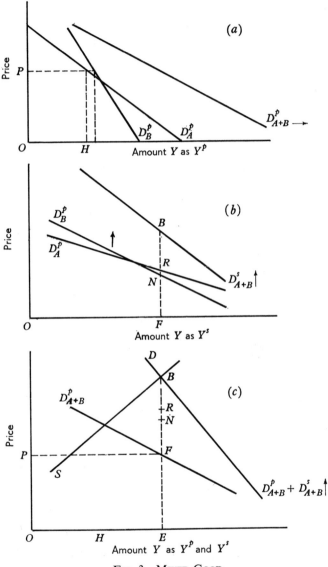

FIG. 3   MIXED GOOD

social good case is given by the intersection of offer curves, i.e. the Lindahl–Johansen P point. Now let D_A^p and D_B^p in Fig. 6.3 (a) be A's and B's demand curves for Y as a private good. Adding horizontally, we obtain the market demand schedule D_{A+B}^p. Similarly, let D_A^s and D_B^s in Fig. 3 (b) be the respective marginal evaluation (offer) curves for Y as a social good. Adding vertically, we obtain the 'market' demand schedule D_{A+B}^s. Similarly, let D_A^s and D_B^s in Fig. 3 (b) be the respective marginal evaluation (offer) curves for Y as a social good. Adding vertically, we obtain the 'market' demand schedule D_{A+B}^s. Finally, in Fig. 3 (c) we add the two market schedules vertically to obtain a total 'market' demand, including both features of Y.[1] We also enter D_{A+B}^p the market demand curve for Y as a private good. S is the industry supply schedule, showing the average cost per physical unit of Y. The horizontal axis in all three figures is drawn in the same scale.

Output is determined at OE with A purchasing OH and B purchasing HE. The market price, accounting for private benefit paid by each, is $OP = EF$; and FB is the unit subsidy, accounting for the social benefit. Of this, FN (see Fig. 3[b]) is contributed by B and $FR = NB$ by A. Again, the traditional theory in terms of a 100 per cent tax and expenditure type of budgetary provision is converted into a general theory of subsidy. For a purely social good, D_{A+B}^p in Fig. 3 (c) coincides with the horizontal axis, and the subsidy equals 100 per cent. For a purely private good, (D_{A+B}^p) coincides with $(D_{A+B}^p) + (D_{A+B}^s)$ and the subsidy is zero. We again have a general tax-subsidy scheme, where all purchasers of the good receive the same subsidy rate. Even the smoke nuisance case can be incorporated into the argument by assuming D^s to be negative, in which case $(D_{A+B}^p) + (D_{A+B}^s)$ lies below (D_{A+B}^p), and a compensatory tax (the proceeds from which can be returned by lump-sum subsidy) is called for.

The analysis of cases B and C, as considered in the preceding sections, may be incorporated into the modern theory. Samuelson's derivation of the optimality condition may be adapted accordingly, the subsidy part of the cost being equated with the sum of the rates of substitution of A and B and the remainder with market price.

The fact that governments typically provide social goods where a 100 per cent subsidy is called for, but rarely where a lesser rate is indicated, shows a rigidity in social behaviour which leads to inefficient results. If

---

[1] The reader may be puzzled why $D_A^p + D_B^p$, which has been added horizontally originally, is now included in a vertical addition. The reason is that the same physical output is available for both (joint) social use and (divided) private use.

many goods are indeed of the mixed type, an extensive set of subsidies at varying rates would be called for.

Determination of the proper subsidy rate is undertaken through the budget process and poses precisely the same difficulties (including non-revelation of preferences, choice of point on Johansen's WW' curve, etc.) already familiar from the polar case of social goods.

ADDENDUM ON SEMANTICS[1]

Professor Samuelson, in his preceding paper, rejects the taxonomy of pages 136-7, and proposes that one should draw only a single line between the knife-edge concept of the purely private good (my Case 1) and all the rest. He has no use for my concept of a polar social good as defined by my Case 7. The abandonment of monopoly as a counterpole to competition in the theory of market structure is drawn upon as an analogy.

It seems to me that this analogy does not apply. Pure competition, presumably, is chosen as a point of departure because it is of particular interest (at least to the slaves of Pareto optimality) due to its welfare implications. Pure monopoly is but one among a wide range of 'imperfections' which may arise, reduction in numbers being but one of many ways in which reality may depart from the norm. Thus it does not provide an alternative pole. The situation differs with my Cases 1 and 7. In the first case we deal with private benefit only, without externalities. In the second case, we deal with external benefits only, without private aspects. Thus, the first case involves a situation where (subject to the necessary distributional assumptions) the competitive market mechanism leads to an optimal result. The second case involves a situation where (given large numbers) nothing can be left to the guidance of voluntary market payments. In between these poles lies a situation where varying degrees of subsidy are called for. Case 7, therefore, constitutes a polar situation in a meaningful sense.

All this, of course, is quite compatible with Professor Samuelson's claim that his general formulation covers all these cases in a formal fashion. Indeed, it was my very purpose to point out that similar analysis can be applied to mixed situations. But semantics, as the history of economic thought so well shows, is not a trivial matter; and I remain persuaded that systematic explanation of non-polar situations will be helpful, as they may point to different policy solution.

---

[1] This section has been added, subsequent to the conference, to complement Professor Samuelson's cross-references in his preceding paper.

4 MERIT WANTS

In concluding, a word should be added regarding the role of merit wants. As noted in Section 4, this entire discussion has been based on the assumption that social goods should be supplied in line with individual preferences. This may be objected to, because the critic feels that preferences should be imposed with certain limits by a chosen elite, be it because its members are better educated, possess greater innate wisdom, or belong to a particular party or sect. Or, it may be objected to simply as unrealistic since, in fact, a considerable part of budget expenditures go to provide goods (e.g. low cost housing or milk for babies) which are rival in consumption and readily subject to exclusion). From this it may be concluded that society in fact wishes to impose a substantial degree of interference with consumer preference; and that therefore a theory of imposed choice should be incorporated into the fiscal model. Wants with regard to which consumer choice is abandoned and the satisfaction of which is imposed I have referred to as merit wants, and have argued that they remain outside the normative model.[1]

A possible reconciliation may be obtained by granting that rational individual choice requires acquaintance with alternatives and that experimentation (even though it may involve imposed choice on a temporary basis) may be needed to obtain the necessary information. Temporary use of imposed choice may also be justified as an aid to the learning process. Thus, what appears to be imposed choice may be compatible, in the longer run, with the objective of intelligent free choice. This, however, is a somewhat uneasy position to one who may deplore the poor taste of the 'public', but would rather persuade than force them to choose otherwise. Yet, it is not without some validity in the realities of the social framework.

An alternative possibility of reconciliation emerges along these lines: Many of the phenomena which appear to be of the merit good type can actually be explained by interdependence of utilities. The situation is similar to that described in our Case II, where A's utility function was given by $U_A = U_A(X_A, Y_A, Y_B)$. In other words, A derives a utility from his own consumption of Y, but he also derives a utility (though of a different kind) from B's consumption of Y. This, in fact, is a quite widespread attitude regarding the consumption of basic commodities, e.g. minimum requirements of food, shelter, health and so forth. The social philosophy of Western society appears to be such that the freedom to

---

[1] See my *Theory of Public Finance*, pp. 13 ff.

tolerate inequality in the distribution of luxury consumption and saving is purchased at the cost of earmarked (specific) subsidies which assure equality in the consumption of necessities. Looked at in terms of this double standard, subsidies in kind, especially to low income groups, make sense; and what appeared to be the wholly different phenomena of merit wants may be incorporated into a subjective preference theory.

In *this* context, the position of section (7), which views the problem in terms of social goods, rather than wants, also need be revised. However this may be, the case for reconciling merit wants with personal choice should not be carried too far: the possibility remains that choice is to be imposed *per se*, and here our basic analysis of social goods does not apply.

7 The Optimal Production of Social Justice

S. Ch. Kolm

1 GENERAL INTENT

(A) A USEFUL STUDY OF PUBLIC ECONOMICS REQUIRES THE EXPLICIT ANALYSIS OF SOCIAL JUSTICE

The distribution of welfare is one of the *raisons d'être* and fundamental social functions of the public economy. It is closely intermingled with the other one – the efficiency of the productive process in collaboration with the market – in all public economic problems: distribution of ownership and income, production of public goods and services, taxation, pricing of public utilities, market regulation, monetary measures; this tie appears both in the means and in the deep ends of growth, employment and price stabilisation policies.

For this reason, the help that economic policy may expect to receive from economics is limited by a serious shortcoming of the latter: descriptive economics has analysed at length both productive efficiency and income distribution, normative economics has many recommendations on how to achieve efficiency, but economics, in its present state, has almost nothing to say about the normative aspects of welfare distribution, i.e. about social justice. Worse, welfare economists used to devote a great part of their endeavours to attempts to get rid of this problem, instead of trying to solve it as we shall do here.[1]

Several devices have been invented in order to achieve this ablation of social justice problems. They consist in introducing in choice analysis a separation which does not describe a constraint of actual choices, in

[1] It is difficult to argue that efficiency is more important than justice. Therefore one could say, loosely speaking, that more than nine-tenths of all economist-hours are devoted to the study of only half of the problem. Also, we hope we prove further that the marginal productivity of social justice analysis is not low. One of the possible reasons for this resource misallocation may be that the United States is presently the leading country in economics, and it also happens to be the country in the world where for clear historical and economic reasons, the population cares the least about distributive justice. Elsewhere, to teach economics is very much to transform justice-minded students into efficiency-minded economists. Furthermore, the British economic tradition, which the United States follows, has been less interested in this problem than most others, the Italian one in particular (see my comments on Professor Sen's paper in this volume).

order to study only a part of these ones. Therefore, these analyses are sub-optimisations and their effective practical usefulness is imperatively conditioned by the optimality of the neglected domains. They deserve exactly the same criticism as those that economists use to address to partial equilibrium analyses.

One of these devices is to suppose that a social welfare function is *a priori* and exogenously given to the economist; but it is often not so, and, above all, the maximum of this function is the optimum only if the political and/or administrative process which defines the function, or chooses the public officials whose opinions it represents, is itself optimal. Another device is to suppose that social justice is always achieved *par ailleurs* thanks to income transfers; but this hypothesis may not hold, and by definition it does not help in determining what transfers are required by distributive justice considerations.[1]

It is interesting to notice that these two devices are both currently used in choices of public expenditure projects with the same justification that technicians of public allocation are neither able nor entitled to take distribution decisions, and that they generally *lead to different choices* for the following reason. The users of a social welfare function (as well as the others) interpret this argument in a way which makes it exclude direct income transfers from the variables of the choice under consideration. Hence, they generally have to weight the marginal monetary equivalents for various individuals, whereas these weights are equal for the other school.

(B) ECONOMICS, POLITICAL ECONOMY OR POLITICAL PHILOSOPHY?

But some supporters of these conceptual dichotomies will agree that they are necessary in order to distinguish the field of political economy (which, when scientific, we call economics), on the one hand, and that of political philosophy on the other. Border claims between fields of study are generally useless and sterile discussions. However, let us just mention the four main reasons which should convince economists to consider social justice analysis as a branch of economics and, more precisely, of public economics.

To begin with, problems of both compensatory and distributive justice

---

[1] To the economists who refuse to consider anything more specific than the so-called 'Pareto-optimality' (with given tastes and technology), let us recall that this is legitimate for Pareto only because he devotes two thousand pages of a treatise of 'Sociology' to the study of 'the remainder'!

are generally thoroughly intermixed with efficiency aspects, and these ties are especially conspicuous in the public economy. Very often, the decisions which must be taken are such that a one-sided view of the problem is useless.

Moreover, political philosophy has by and large failed to propose scientific criteria, i.e. criteria presenting the double character of precise definition and wide applicability which would have made them operational and therefore useful for policy choices. It must now be the turn of social justice analysis to leave philosophy and join science.

Furthermore, one may wonder whether most contemporary economists do not say anything about social justice because they consider it as out of their field, or whether they consider it as out of their field because they do not know what to say about it. In the latter case, they would be wrong since, as we shall see further, social justice analysis may be studied with the traditional tools of efficiency analysis. Besides, the best distinction between economics and other social sciences may turn out to be more a question of method than a question of object.

Finally, interest in social justice is certainly in the intellectual tradition of political economy. Most great economists could not avoid considering this field, even if they relegate it in a category called 'social' situated beyond the 'properly economic' sphere or prior to it (and sometimes dealt with in a separate book). Furthermore, this question is very close to the basic point of contemporary economists' discussions about 'social rationality' and voting procedures. Finally, the various traditions stemming from Ricardo, who points out income distribution as the 'principal problem' of political economy, either emphasises social justice and its violation by exploitation, or should not be able to omit to take it into account since, nowadays, its consideration influences notably the distribution of real disposable incomes.

(c) THEORETICAL AND PRACTICAL DETERMINATION OF THE SOCIAL OPTIMUM

Since our complete definition of the social optimum will use the tools of classical economic analysis, it may be considered either as a generalisation of this one, or as the correction of its biggest mistake. Then, the above-mentioned devices become useless, or, at least, they shift from the domain of the definition and of the proof of existence and uniqueness of the optimum to the field of its practical determination (where they rejoin other tools which are not less useful).

More precisely, this mistake of classical economics is the one which

F 2

permits the multiplicity   of the so-called 'Pareto-optimal' situations. This degeneracy of the optimum conditions is due either to the omission of the existence of opinions on wealth distribution, or to a failure to see that these opinions in general determine the optimum even if they are 'uncommensurable' to material needs.

Therefore, the definition of the optimal distribution of welfare does not result from any value judgement made by the economist.   He is an observer of citizens' value judgements and opinions, as he is an observer of their tastes on consumer's goods.   From these data he may deduce, in the same manner, the optimal production of goods and the optimal distribution of wealth.   Useful normative economics is therefore a positive science since its basis is the *objective* observation of subjective opinions.

But the knowledge of these opinions presents exactly the same 'revelation' difficulties as that of the tastes for public goods.[1]   As for any knowledge problem, the efficient method is the scientific one which consists in the interaction between observation procedures and an explicit theoretical construction.   For our problem, the former are opinion polls, analysis of political phenomena (votes, selection of elites, etc.), studies of descriptive ethics, etc.   We must propose bases for the latter, i.e. we must begin the construction of a theory of social justice.   To compare with a neighbouring field, this theory will be to these observations what the theory of consumer's choice is to demand analysis.

A theory of social justice must begin by discovering the objective properties of the concepts under consideration.   Speaking of *noumena*,[2] a property is said to be objective if it is subjective for everybody; it may then be included in a definition of the vocable.[3]   Now, as is well known by election candidates, consensus is the wider the less precisely defined the property is: collective will is 'the clearer the vaguer'.   But, as they verify when elected, a property is the more useful to guide choices the more precise it is.   Hence the first task of the science of social justice is to seek properties which both stand a good chance to be considered as 'natural' and are defined with precision.

---

[1] And, similarly too, but less than for some public goods, to the problem of the knowledge of opinions by the observer is added that of their own opinions by the individuals themselves.   Paul Valéry said about this point, 'Politics has long been the art to prevent people from taking care of their own concern; it now consists in asking them questions on issues about which they have no idea'.

[2] I.e. intelligible objects, as opposed to phenomena or sensible objects.   Our previous argument is that somebody's noumenal conceptions are phenomena for an observer.

[3] The word 'property' needs, of course, to be made more precise ; on this point, see the difference between 'moderate egalitarianism' and 'satiation' which is mentioned in Part 7.

The result of this research is that, in social justice problems, informed opinions happen to present much wider domains of coincidence than is *a priori* believed. Among these is compensatory justice which is distinguished from distributive justice partly for this reason. But, chiefly, even about distributive justice people agree more than they themselves think. The reason is that the logical equivalence of some properties is not visible without using a rather advanced mathematical apparatus in demonstrations which are sometimes far from elementary. As a result, some persons admit some properties and find no justification to others, other persons have the reverse opinion, whereas all these properties may turn out to be logically equivalent.[1]

(D) SAMPLE OF PROBLEMS SOLVED OR IN THE SOLUTION OF WHICH THIS STUDY PARTICIPATES

The definition of the optimum enables us to solve the famous problem of the optimal distribution of a given homogenous wealth. This is done in Part 3, where, moreover, the effect of limitative constraints is considered. This is tantamount to the distribution of a given heterogenous wealth with constant prices. In Part 5, price effects and the effect of distribution on production are taken into account.

The ties between production and distribution originate in incentives to produce and in the distribution of capital (which may be tangible, human or social, on the one hand, received, innate or earned, on the other). They create the problems of choice between justice and efficiency, which are discussed in Parts 5 and 6 (and to the solution of which Part 7 contributes). These choices, which are in general compromises, constitute the traditionally missing or suspect link of the benefit-cost analyses to which every public decision should be submitted. Indeed, these costs and benefits are always composed of three parts: implementation costs, effects on the efficiency of the economic system, effects on social justice; the choices under consideration arbitrate between the latter and the other two. But since the relative importances of these three parts vary much according to the kinds of actions, the proposed theory adds the more to traditional analysis the more important social justice effects are. Therefore, income transfers and the choice of the optimal progressivity of income taxes will be among the favourite fields of application. But problems of distributive and compensatory justices appear in a non-negligible way in almost all questions of taxation, public expenditures, regulation, etc.

---

[1] An important instance is given by the various ways of expressing that the Lorenz curve of a distribution is thoroughly 'above' that of another. Cf. Parts 6 and 7.

The distributions under consideration may be among the individuals of a given society, among societies, and among generations.

The resulting optimum is not in general a situation of maximum social income (exhaustively reckoned, including leisure consumption: cf. the 'leisurely equivalent' of Part 5). Indeed, societies often sacrifice production in order to achieve some justice.[1] Therefore, the usual measure of the welfare of a society *per capita* social income, is not a good measure since it omits the consumption of social justice. It is suggested in Part 6 that the good measure for a distribution of incomes out of which the compensatory justice effects have been taken care of (cf. Part 5) is its 'equal equivalent', i.e. the individual income which, if everybody had the same income, would yield a situation as good as the one under consideration; it is generally equal to the 'economic equivalent' of the distribution, which is the smallest *per capita* income of the situations equivalent to the one under consideration. The injustice of the allotment is measured by the difference between the *per capita* income and this equivalent; its justice is measured by the ratio of the latter to the former: it is the welfare productivity of social income (a production of dollars of welfare per dollar of social income). The fundamental concepts and properties of distributive justice opinions are exposed in Part 6 and their logical relations are shown in Part 7 which we believe to be very important.[2]

Besides, several other pieces of analysis which we had to devise in the course of this study are thought to have an interest *per se*, such as the 'social individual values' and the synthesis of the 'metaclassical' cases of optimal public allocation of Part 2, the 'technical social welfare functions' and the political processes of revelation of Part 3, and some others.

2 FUNDAMENTAL CONCEPTS OF SOCIAL ECONOMY

(A) PROBLEM AND VARIABLES

The mere existence of an optimality problem implies many properties of its constitutive elements.

First, the useful notion of an optimum is relative to a given choice problem. The optimum is simply what exists when the best choice is made. The constraints are all those which effectively exist in the situation under consideration, and only these. No *a priori* discrimination is made

---

[1] In some societies, though, social income would increase if ownership and income were less unequally distributed.
[2] Parts 6 and 7 altogether may be read independently from the others.

according to the nature of these constraints, and therefore all 'second best' problems are included in the analysis.[1,2]

Second, the query for an optimum arises because an action must be chosen ('inaction' is a particular action). Now, when states are defined so as to be mutually exclusive and jointly exhaustive of the possible, one cannot avoid to choose one and only one action. Hence, a state can both usefully and logically be called an optimum only if it exists, if it is possible and if it is unique. Conversely, if an optimality condition is accepted and happens to belong to only one possible state, then this one is the optimum.

A state of society is described by the levels z_h of the characteristic variable h. Such a representation seems to be always possible. Let $z = [z_h]$ be the vector of the z_h's.

Since the subject of this note is not technical indivisibilities, we suppose, in this part and in the next, that the z_h's may vary continuously (but they may be constrained by inequalities). Let us notice that this assumption may be much less restrictive than one may think, since many of the phenomena labelled by economists as 'indivisibilities' or 'causes of increasing returns to scale' can be analysed as mere collective consumptions of inputs by the various units of the output.

(B) INDIVIDUAL VALUES AND SOCIAL INDIVIDUAL VALUES

In this Part and in the next one, the word 'value' is only defined as *marginal* and *measured in money*: the value of a variable h is a 'monetary equivalent per unit of a small variation of z_h.[3] We distinguish the *individual value* v_h^i and the *social individual value* s_h^i of the variable h to citizen i. The difference between them is that in s_h^i i takes into account that h has a value for other citizens, whereas this effect is not considered in v_h^i.

These values depend upon the state, i.e. they are function of z. Furthermore, for given z and h v_h^i and s_h^i may be different when $z_h + dz_h$ tends to z_h by higher and by lower levels; we shall neglect this refinement for the

---

[1] Alternatives may be distinguished according to their date and their eventuality. Therefore, the evolution and the uncertainty of the constraints are taken into account.

[2] Some of these constraints are due to the agents' behaviours. Of course, the knowledge and the technical skills of producers define the production function. But we also take into account, if necessary, behaviours in imperfect markets. This means that we adopt a '*second best policy*' as opposed to a *Kantian policy* which orders to act as if everybody acted in the best way, and which justifies, for instance, the *a priori* recommendation of marginal cost pricing of public utilities.

[3] Therefore, if there exists a corresponding utility, the value is the ratio of h's marginal utility to the marginal utility of money.

sake of simplicity: all further results can be straightforwardly extended to this case by replacing the equalities by the relevant inequalities.

(C) RESPECT OF VALUATIONS

Given v_h^j, the direct monetary equivalent to j of the infinitesimal variation dz_h, i.e. $(v_h^j.dz_h)$, is a variable of the social state described by $z + dz$. If the individual value of this variable to citizen i is the same for all the h's of a certain set, it is said that *i respects j's valuation for all the variables of this set in the state described by z.* If all the variables which can be defined constitute such a set, it is said that *i respects j's valuation in the state described by z*; in this case, let us call v_j^i this value.[1] If this condition is verified for every pair i, j, it is said that there is *general respect of valuations in the state described by z.* Loosely speaking, v_j^i is the individual value to i of the fact that something is worth one dollar to j; i's respect of j's valuation says that this value to i does not depend on the nature of the cause of this dollar's worth to j. Each citizen in integrated psychic state respects his own valuation and $v_i = 1$. v_j^i is the individual value to i of j's income or wealth measured in money.

(D) INDIVIDUAL VALUES OF OTHERS' WEALTH

There is no exclusion as for the reasons why v_j^i is, say, larger than v_k^i. It just means that, other things remaining the same, i prefers that an extra dollar (i.e. a small amount of money wealth) is given to j rather to k, and that, *ceteris paribus*, i favours a transfer of wealth from k to j (at least in small quantities). This might be, for instance, because i thinks that j deserves more than k an increase in wealth because of j's own merits, or because j is poorer than k and i is an egalitarian, or just because i likes j and does not care for k, or for any other reason.

(E) EGOISMS

v_j^i depends on i's 'tastes' or opinions, on j's objective situation, and on the degree and nature of i's awareness of the existence of the specific individual j. v_j^i may be positive, negative, or null. It may be quite different from zero; in particular, it is generally high for members of the same family; it may even be greater than one.[2] However, v_j^i has more generally a low absolute value. But it is extremely important to distinguish the case where v_j^i is identically zero from the case where it is only

---

[1] In all the following, indexes i, j, k are affected to citizens and indexes g, h to variables.

[2] Such a value is revealed in the case of a gift (intrafamilial, charity, etc.) in which the giver does not take into account others' opinions.

infinitely small. Indeed, in the latter case the ratios $\dfrac{v_j^i}{v_k^i}$ may have a definite value even if both their numerators and their denominators are infinitely small; these ratios measure i's opinions on the distribution of wealth, from which we shall deduce the optimal distribution. Therefore v_j^i may take share in the theoretical determination of the optimum even if there is no sum of money that i would 'practically' be disposed to yield for j's wealth to be increased of one dollar. Furthermore, let us not forget that the number of citizens in a society, several millions for instance, is itself 'practically infinitely large', and this may counterbalance, in a sense made explicit further on, the 'practically infinite smallness' of the v_j^i's so as to give non-infinitely small numbers.

The following vocabulary will naturally be used. $v_j^i < 1$: i's *egoism* toward j; v_j^i is infinitely small: i's *strong egoism* toward j; in this case, i thinks that j's welfare is *incommensurable* to his own. $\sum\limits_{j \neq i} v_j^i \chi_j$ is infinitely small for any set of numbers χ_j: i's *lexicographic egoism*; this term is used since j's opinions are, then, partly lexicographically ordered: first of all, he wants his own wealth to be as high as possible, but, given his own wealth, he has an opinion about wealth distribution among the other citizens.[1] When a characteristic holds for all citizens, we say that it is *general*. Of course, those characterisations refer to a specific state of society.

(F) RELATION BETWEEN INDIVIDUAL VALUES AND SOCIAL INDIVIDUAL VALUES

Let s_j^i be the *social* individual value to citizen i of citizen j's income or wealth. Let us compute the relation between the s_j^i's and the v_j^i's when general respect of valuations prevails. Incomes and wealths are, of course, measured in money.

A small variation of j's wealth is valued by i as a sum of first, this variation if j happens to be i, and second, a sum of terms each of them showing how much i *directly* values the fact that each citizen k values this variation directly and indirectly. Therefore, δ_{ij} being the Kroneker numbers,[2] $s_j^i = \delta_{ij} + \sum\limits_{k \neq i} v_k^i s_j^k$. Using matrix notation, call I a unity matrix

---

[1] Of course, i's lexicographic egoism implies his strong egoism for every $j \neq i$; the reverse is not true if citizens are in a 'practically infinite' number. Incommensurabilities with infinitely large v_j^i's or $\sum\limits_{j} v_j^i \chi_j$'s, positive or negative, describe i's total sacrifices for j's or society' good or evil; these cases, although they have a huge social and historical importance, are not studied here.   [2] I.e. $\delta_{ij} = 0$ if $i..j$ and $\delta_{ij} = 1$ if $i = j$.

of the required rank, $S = [s^i_j]$, $V = [v^i_j] - I$, where the upper index is the row index and the lower one the column index. Then, the above relation is $S = I + V S$ or, if $I - V$ is regular, $S = (I \quad V)^{-1}$.

The reader can check this result by proving it in another way which is longer but more heuristic and perhaps more revealing of the deep nature of the relation between the v^i_j's and the s^i_j's: to increase j's wealth of a small quantity taken as unit of value increases i's 'psychic wealth' first directly of v^i_j, second indirectly because it increases k's 'psychic wealth' for all k neither i nor j, third more indirectly because l's 'psychic wealth' is increased because k's is increased because j's is increased for all l neither i nor k and k not j, and so on to infinity. The sum of the effects of all these 'rounds' of valuation is

$$v^i_j + \sum_{k \neq i,j} v^i_k \, v^k_j + \sum_{\substack{l \neq i,k \\ k \neq l,j}} v^i_l \, v^l_k \, v^k_j + \dots,$$

which is an entry of the matrix $I + V + V^2 + V^3 + \dots$. If this infinite sum converges, its value, which is s^i_j, is an entry of the matrix $(I - V)^{-1}$.

Consider a case of general strong egoism: all v^i_j's are infinitely small. Each term of this sum is composed of 'secondary' terms which generally have an order of smallness one degree higher than those of the preceding one, but which are more numerous by an order of magnitude which is the number of individuals. Therefore, these terms may be of the same order of magnitude if the size of the population makes for the smallness of the v^i_j's. However, if there is general lexicographical egoism, each term of the entries of $I + V + V^2 + \dots$ is infinitely small relative to the preceding one.

Social individual values of the variable h are, of course, obtained from its individual values by the relation $s^i_h = \sum_j s^i_j \, v^j_h$, or, calling S_h the column-vector of s^i_h's and V_h the column-vector of v^i_h's, $S_h = S \, V_h$.

It is always easy, and only slightly longer, to write the corresponding relations when some specified valuations are not respected. In particular, this may happen for the various 'rounds' of valuation previously described. For instance, if the value to i of the fact that j's wealth has a value to k is zero for all, i, j, k with $i \neq k \neq j$, then $S = I + V$.

(G) THE OPTIMUM

The property of the optimum which will be used to characterise it, is the following: *when wealth and income distribution is optimal* and, *a priori*, in this case only, the values (*monetary*, *marginal*) of a variable to various citizens may be meaningfully added. Therefore, the optimum is defined by the property that (1) it is a possible state, and (2) $\sum_{i,h} s_h^i \cdot dz_h \leq 0$ for all possible $z + dz$. Let us call $z^* = z_h^*$ the optimum's z.

If h is an independent variable not constrained by an inequality at the optimum, the states respectively described by $z_h^* + dz_h$ and $z_h^* - dz_h$ with the other variables at the optimum's levels, are possible. The optimality condition is then $\sum_i s_h^i = 0$ or, calling e a n-dimensional column-vector of 1's $e'\, S_h = 0$.

In a case of general lexicographical egoism, the condition $e'\, S_h = 0$ is tantamount to the condition $e'\, V_h = 0$ except when V_h is such that $e'\, V_h \equiv 0$. This happens if h is a transfer from j to i since then $v_h^i = v_i^i = l$, $v_h^j = -v_j^j = -l$ and $v_h^k = 0$ for $k \neq i, j$. . . . More generally, this happens for every effect which is a redistribution of wealth among members of the society (for instance, the redistribution effect found in the determination of the optimal rate of inflation). In other words, in order to solve the *distribution* problem in this case, we shall have to consider terms one degree of smallness higher than those which determine social *efficiency* optimality conditions.

(H) CLASSICAL AND META-CLASSICAL PARTICULAR CASES

When one presents a generalisation, the first thing to do is to check that the already known cases are effectively peculiar cases of the new one. Let us indicate briefly the principles of this verification and some other consequences.

Classical and meta-classical optimality conditions are peculiar cases of the general above-stated conditions, obtained when: (1) there is general lexicographical egoism, and (2) the variables under consideration have the following properties.

(1) *Classical Cases*
   (a) *Individual Choices.* The only non-zero individual values of h and h' are v_h^i and $v_h^{i'}$ for a specified i, it is possible that only these two variables vary, and they are only tied by i's production function or budgetary constraint; the optimality condition comes down to the classical relations between marginal utilities, marginal productivities, marginal costs, marginal revenues and prices.
   (b) *Bilateral Exchange.* z_h and $z_{h'}$ are quantities of the same good at the disposal of, respectively, i and j, the only non-zero values of these variables are v_h^i and $v_{h'}^i$, it is possible that only these two variables vary, and they are only tied by $z_h + z_{h'} = \text{constant}$; the optimality condition comes down to the classical $v_h^i = v_{h'}^i$.

(2)   *Meta-classical Cases*

   (a) *Kinked constraints and discontinuous values.*   Extension in in-
       equalities of the classical and following equalities.

   (b) *Collective consumptions and public goods.*[1]   The quantity z_h of such
       a good being taken as the independent free variable, and reckoning
       the costs as negative v_h^i's, the optimality conditions gives $\sum v_h^i = 0$.

   (c) *External effects.*   Same formula for independent free variables;
       all the v_h^i's can have any sign.

   (d) *'Intermediary cases between purely private and purely public good.'*
       Consider as many different parameters as are necessary to describe
       the 'good' (some of them may be called 'quantities') and apply the
       general formula to these z_h's.   For each independent free parameter,
       any of the preceding cases can apply.

   (e) *Qualities.*   The same optimality formula applies for the parameters
       describing the quality of any kind of good consumed in any way by
       any number of persons.

   (f) *Merit wants.* h is a consumption (possibly leisure) of j.   But some
       $i \neq j$ are such that $v_h^i \neq 0$ for another reason than a physical external
       effect.   If c_h is the marginal cost of the production of h, this good
       must be sold to j at the price $p_h^j = c_h - \sum_{i \neq j} v_h^i$ which may be larger or
       smaller than (fortuitously equal to) c_h.   Or if h is rationed to j, p_h^j
       must be the dual variable of this constraint.   It is, of course, a true
       merit want only if j's valuations are not respected; if they were,
       one would have $v_h^i = v_j^i\, v_h^j$ and, calling $v_j = \sum_{i \neq j} v_j^i$, $p_h^j = v_h^j = \dfrac{c_h}{1 + v_j}$, and
       it is only a multiplication by $1 + v_j$ of j's real income.

   (g) *The social contract theory of public finance.*   If z and $z + dz$ are two
       possible states such that $\sum_{i,h} v_h^i \cdot dz_h > 0$, there exists a set of variations
       of taxes and monetary compensations in which i receives globally
       dt_i (positive, negative, or null), such that $\sum dt_i = 0$ and $\sum_h v_h^i \cdot dz_h$
       $+ dt_i > 0$ for all i's.   Since general lexicographical egoism prevails,
       this means that all citizens prefer unanimously the state described
       by $z + dz$ accompanied by this set of dt_i's to the state described by z.

---

[1] Historically, this condition has been enunciated before the above-mentioned
'classical' conditions (with, of course, some awkwardness as far as marginalism is
concerned), since it is the subject of Dupuit's studies in 1844.   (Mind that in his diagram
the index of users – and not the quantity of the good – is a variable, which some famous
authors forgot.)

Such variations of taxes and compensations do not exist if and only if $\sum_{i,h} v_h^i \cdot dz_h \leq 0$, which is the optimality condition for z.

(h) *Second best.* This problem is settled by the definition of the constraints (see above).

(i) *Education, advertising and propaganda,* as modifying *tastes and opinions.* Consider the v_h^i's as some variables z_h. (The effect of these sections on *knowledge* or belief is a 'classical' efficiency problem).

(j) *Collective concerns.* Generally, we suggest to call 'collective concerns' all parameters h such that several $v_h^i \neq 0$ in a way different from that of bilateral exchange. Cases (b), (c), (d), (e), (f) and (i) above and social justice give instances of collective concerns. The general optimality formula applies.

(I) 'PARETO-OPTIMALITY'

$\sum_{i,h} s_h^i \cdot dz_h \leq 0$ may be written $\sum_i (\sum_h s_h^i \cdot dz_h) \leq 0$. Therefore, at the optimum, there does not exist any possible variation dz such that $\sum_h s_h^i \cdot dz_h \geq 0$ for all i, with the inequality holding for at least one i; i.e. there is no possible point $z^* + dz$ preferred or equivalent to z^* for every citizen, and preferred for at least one of them. Therefore, the optimum is one of the so-called 'Pareto optimums'.

(J) TRUE OPTIMALITY, OR STABILITY

Let us write $s_h^i(z)$ for the level of s_h^i at z, and $s_h(z) = \sum_i s_h^i(z)$.

The optimum is 'true' or 'stable' if $\sum_h s_h(z^* + dz) \cdot (-dz) \geq 0$ for all possible $z^* + dz$. Let us call $s_{gh} = \dfrac{\delta s_g}{\delta z_h}$ if this derivative exists. Then, z^* describes a true optimum if and only if, at this point, $\sum_{g,h} s_{gh} \cdot dz_g \cdot dz_h \leq 0$ for all possible $z^* + dz$. That is, the quadratic form built on $[s_{gh} + s_{hg}]$ and subject to the constraints of the problem at z^* must be negative semi-definite at this point.

(K) EXISTENCE AND UNIQUENESS OF THE OPTIMUM

If the optimum defined by the stated condition were not unique or did not exist, this would mean that some variable(s) and/or some constraint(s) have been forgotten. Moreover, let us mention the two following sufficient conditions.

1) *Local Uniqueness*

There does not exist any continuum of points verifying the optimality conditions and such that $z*$ is one of them if there is no possible dz from $z*$ such that the above-mentioned quadratic form is zero for this direction.

(2) *Existence*

A result of Part 4 below will prove that the optimum exists if the domain of possible points is compact and convex and if citizens have strictly quasi-concave utility functions for the relevant variables.

3 OPTIMAL DISTRIBUTION

(A) THE PROBLEM OF THE OPTIMAL DISTRIBUTION OF A GIVEN HOMOGENOUS WEALTH

(1) *Variables*

In order to show that the optimum is well defined, let us focus our attention on the problem which economists believe to be the cause of indeterminacy: the distribution of wealth. Let us begin to solve the problem in its barest form: the distribution of a homogenous given wealth.

Homogenous only means that all the elements of wealth are meaningfully commensurable for the problem under consideration. In a problem of distributive justice, the measure implied by this term is the money value of the elements, with given prices. Therefore, 'homogenous' is a synonym of 'with constant prices' (and free exchange). This problem of the optimal distribution of wealth with given prices is the exact complement of the problem of classical economics which is the investigation of the optimal price system with given distribution. The 'fixed point' of the aggregate of those two problems is the social optimum. In Part 5, we shall consider explicitely the effects of the distribution on prices on the one hand, and on the quantity of distributable wealth on the other. This latter effect raises important problems about the definition of what must be distributed. In the present Part, the problem may simply be considered as the distribution of a given quantity of a divisible good, a sum of money for instance.

(2) *Previous Proposals*

Therefore, the problem is to distribute optimally a given quantity X to n individuals, each one i receiving x_i, such that $\sum x_i = X$. Several 'solutions' have already been proposed to this problem,[1] but we find them thoroughly arbitrary. This arbitrariness is either shared complementarily between the choice of a 'starting point' and assumptions of similarity of individual utilities,[2] or it draws more heavily on the latter. The least similarity which is always assumed is that all individuals have cardinal utilities: now, even if they had such indexes for risky choices, there would be no reason to use them for a normative definition of the optimum; on the contrary, the solution presented here uses only purely ordinal considerations. (Also, some of the criticised proposals are defined for two persons only.)

(3) *Constraints*

We shall notice the consequence of the fact that if a part of the wealth may be costlessly destroyed or disappropriated, the constraint is in fact $\sum x_i \leq X$. The constraint $\sum x_i = X$ or $\sum x_i \leq X$ is called the *wealth constraint*. We shall also study the effect of *limitative constraints* of the form $x_i \geq \bar{x}_i$. If $\bar{x}_i = 0$, it is a *non-negativity constraint*. The existence of non-negativity constraints depends on the definition of the variables of the specific problem studied. For instance, a negative x_i may represent a debt of i's without specification of the creditor ('to the bearer'); when some x_i may be negative, X may as well be zero (creation of claims) or negative (debt sharing), as positive (distribution of wealth *stricto sensu*). But there may also be other kinds of limitative constraints than non-negativity: for instance, $\bar{x}_i > 0$ may be a subsistence minimum income, or $\bar{x}_i < 0$ a maximum indebtedness, etc.

When the wealth constraint is an inequality, it may happen that it is not binding at the optimum. We shall not forget these cases although they seem rather unlikely to happen in direct applications of the simple model studied, because they represent a more interesting phenomenon when the whole socio-economic system is considered.

[1] Cf. J. F. Nash, 'The Bargaining Problem', *Econometrica*, 18 (1950) pp. 155–62, and 'Two-Person Cooperative Games', *Econometrica*, 21, pp. 128–40; N. Raiffa, 'Arbitration schemes for Generalized Two Person Games', in *Contribution to the Theory of Games*, ed. Kuhn and Tucker, II pp. 361–87, *Annals of Mathematical Studies*, 24 (Princeton University Press, 1953); D. Luce and N. Raiffa, '*Games and Decisions*' (Wiley), ch. 6, for the 'Shapley solution' and a critical exposition of the others. See also R. Strotz, 'How Income Ought to be Distributed: a Paradox in Distributive Ethics', *Journal of Political Economy*, June 1958.

[2] These similarities have nothing to do with Harsanyi's and Tinbergen's, presented in Part 5 below, who obtain it by considering parameters as variables, i.e. by increasing the number of the arguments of utility functions, which remain ordinal (there is only one argument in the theories under criticism).

Finally, we could easily have shown the effects of the implementation costs of transfers due to the consumption of resources by administration, information and coercion processes.

(4) *Values*

For the sake of simplicity of exposition, we shall suppose that general respect of valuations prevails. If the value to i of the fact that j's wealth has a value to k were zero for all i, j, k with $i \neq k \neq j$, $S = (I - V)^{-1}$ would be replaced by $S = I + V$. Moreover, one may easily check that $S = (I - V)^{-1}$ is equivalent to $I + V$ in the problem studied here if general lexicographical egoism prevails.

(5) *The Optimum*

Let x be the vector of the x_i's and $x^* = [x_i^*]$ the one which describes the optimum.

From paragraph G of Part 2, the optimum is defined by the fact that $\sum_{i,j} s_j^i(x^*) . dx_j \leq 0$ for all possible $x^* + dx$.

(B) ONLY THE WEALTH CONSTRAINT IS BINDING

(1) *First Order Conditions*

(a) *Equality.* The constraint $\Sigma x_j = X$ imposes $\Sigma dx_j = 0$ and only this. Therefore, at the optimum, $s_j = \sum_i s_j^i$ is independent of j.[1] Let s be this value.

Since the matrix S is constant-sum, the matrix V such that $S = I + VS$ has the same property. Let v be this common value of the $v_j = \sum_{i \neq j} v_j^i$'s. Then, $s = 1 + vs$. $s_j = s$, or $v_j = v$, constitute a set of $n - 1$ generally independent conditions which, with $\Sigma x_i^* = X$, give n equations which in general the n unknowns x_i^*.

(b) *Inequality.* The binding constraint $\Sigma x_j \leq X$ imposes $\Sigma dx_j \leq 0$. Therefore, the condition is the same as the preceding one with, furthermore, $s \geq 0$ and therefore $v < 1$.

(c) *Transfer Determination.* Let us notice that the equations $\sum_{i \neq j} v_j^i = v$ are effective even if v is infinitely small and, *a fortiori*, even if all v_j^i's$(i \neq j)$ are infinitely small.

The reason of this fact is that in the optimality condition for a transfer

---

[1] This is tantamount to applying to income (or wealth) transfers the marginalised Dupuit's principle.

between j and k, $s_j = s_k$, the terms stemming from the values of their own wealth to j and k, $v_j^j = v_k^k = 1$, which are of a higher order of magnitude, cancel each other.

The equation $v_j = v_k$ may be written $\Sigma v_j^i + v_j^k = \Sigma v_k^i + v_k^j$. If n is large,

$$\underset{i \neq j, k}{} \qquad \underset{i \neq j, k}{}$$

the terms v_j^k and v_k^j and their derivatives will most often be negligible with respect to the sum of the other terms and of their derivatives. In this case, one may say that in society's comparison of j's and k's wealths, j's and k's own opinions do not matter: the community of the others acts toward them as a judge imposing his will. This is in fact what generally happens for income and wealth redistributions.

(d) *Example of the case of two citizens.* This phenomenon cannot appear if there is only two citizens. The only interest of this case is that it may be represented graphically (Fig. 7.1). As may be readily verified, the optimality condition $v_2^1 = v_1^2$ says that the wealth line $x_1 + x_2 = X$ is, at the optimum, a bisector of the angle of the tangents to the citizens' indifference curves which pass by this point.

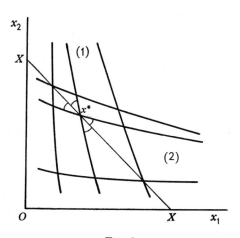

Fɪɢ. 1

(2) *Second Order Conditions*

(a) *True optimality.* Call $s_{ij} = \dfrac{\delta s_i}{x_j}$. x^* is a true optimum if and only if the

signs of the principal minors of $\begin{vmatrix} 0 & e' \\ e & [s_{ij} + s_{ji}] \end{vmatrix}$ alternate at this point.

(b) *Uniqueness.* (i) *Sufficient condition for local uniqueness.* There does not exist a continuum of points such that x^* is one of them and every one fulfills the optimality conditions, if, at x^*,

$$\begin{vmatrix} 0 & e' \\ e & [s_{ij}] \end{vmatrix} \neq 0, \text{ or, calling } v_{jk}^i = \frac{\delta v_j^i}{\delta x_k} \text{ and } v_{ij} = \frac{\delta v_i}{\delta x_j}$$

$$\begin{vmatrix} 0 & e' \\ e & [v_{ij}] \end{vmatrix} \neq 0. \text{ Might this condition not be fulfilled?}$$

(ii) *Cases of degeneracy.* The most plausible case in which it would happen seems, *a priori*, to be that of the existence of a set $\mathscr{I}$ of i's having at least two elements and of a set of n real numbers λ_j, such that for all $i \in \mathscr{I}$, all j, and at x^*, either $v_{ij} = \lambda_j$, or $v_{ji} = \lambda_j$. In the first case, it may be that all equations $v_j = v$ for $i \in \mathscr{I}$ may be replaced by only one; in the second case, it may be that only $\sum_{i \in \mathscr{I}} x_i^*$ is determined instead of each x^* for $i \in \mathscr{I}$. These two cases may happen, for instance, if there exists such a set $\mathscr{I}$ and a set of n^2 real numbers λ_j^k such that for all $i \in \mathscr{I}$ and all j, k, at x^*, either $v_{ij}^k = \lambda_j^k$, or $v_{ji}^k = \lambda_j^k$ (notice that, $\lambda_j^k = 0$ if $k \in \mathscr{I}$ in the first case, and $\lambda_j^j = 0$ whatever $\mathscr{I}$ in the second case); this means that either the values to any citizen of i's' wealths for all $i \in \mathscr{I}$ are equally affected by the variations of any citizen's wealth, or that the value to any citizen of the wealth of any citizen is equally affected by variations in i's' wealths for $i \in \mathscr{I}$; in other words, i's' wealths for $i \in \mathscr{I}$ are not distinguished by anybody either for the effect of wealths on their values, or for their effects on the values of wealths.

If any of these conditions holds not only for x^* but also for all the points of a continuum containing x^*, then it is sufficient for the indeterminacy of the optimum.

The first of the mentioned cases happens in this manner when for all k the functions v_i^k are the same for all $i \in \mathscr{I}$, and the second one when for all k and j the functions v_j^k depend on the x_i's for $i \in \mathscr{I}$ only by the intermediary of $\sum_{i \in \mathscr{I}} x_i$. To the extreme, the classical degeneracy is found when $v_j^i \equiv 0$ for all different i and j's; the optimum is then indeterminate on $\sum x_i = X$.

(iii) *Sociological determination of the optimum.* Those degeneracies of the optimality conditions seem to be very unlikely. Practically, these conditions fail to determine the optimal distribution of wealth between two persons only if nobody sees any reason to discriminate between them for this purpose, (and if, more-over, cross opinions of these two persons on each other's wealth cancel out (for instance if the corresponding values are zero). Notice that in this case one could argue that this indeterminacy does not matter, since, then, nobody thinks that there is an optimal distribution problem there: in some sense the mere existence of such a problem gives, *ipso facto*, the theoretical tool needed to solve it. But, furthermore, such a case is very unlikely to happen since, if it does, this means that these two individuals belong to the same groups for every classification of people felt by any person as relevant for distribution.

Conversely, somebody's opinions take part in the determination of the optimal distribution between two persons only if he discriminates between them for this purpose. If he sees no reason to establish such a discrimination among several people, his opinions only participate in the determination of the sum of their wealths.

Moreover, of course, the relative magnitudes of the v_j^i's and of their derivatives is of primary importance (for instance, intra-familial distribution is mainly determined by intrafamilial opinions).

Let us also emphasise the crucial point that everybody is *within* the society: all opinions, from whomever they come, are sub-mitted to the same process, and therefore there is no exterior ethical observer. Everybody is both judge and judged; this seems to be a mere matter of fact.

(c) *Existence.* Cf. paragraph K-2 of Part 2. The set of possible points under consideration is convex.

(C) THE WEALTH CONSTRAINT AND SOME LIMITATIVE CONSTRAINTS ARE BINDING

(1) *First Order Conditions*

The consequences of the optimality condition ($\Sigma s_j.dx_j \leq 0$ for all possible $x^* + dx$) in the various cases are the following.

(a) *Equality.* $\Sigma x_i = X$, $x_j \geq \bar{x}_j$ for all $j \in \mathcal{J}$, $\Sigma x_i^* = X$ and $x_j^* = \bar{x}_j$ for all $j \in \mathcal{J}$ imply that for all possible $x^* + dx$, $\Sigma dx_i = 0$ and $dx_j \geq 0$ for all $j \in \mathcal{J}$. Therefore, the optimality condition is $s_j = s$ for all $j \notin \mathcal{J}$ and $s_j \leq s$ for all $j \in \mathcal{J}$. This gives, with the binding constraints, n generally independent equations to determine the n unknowns x_i^*.

(b) *Inequality.* $\Sigma x_i \leq X$, $x_j \geq \bar{x}_j$ for all $j \in \mathcal{J}$, $\Sigma x_j^* = X$ and $x_j^* = \bar{x}_j$ for all $j \in \mathcal{J}$ imply that for all possible $x^* + dx$, $\Sigma dx_i \leq 0$ and $dx_j \geq 0$ for all

$j \in \mathscr{J}$. Therefore, the condition is the same as the preceding one with, furthermore, $s \geq 0$.

(2) *True Optimality, Uniqueness, Existence*

If x^* is a true optimum, the signs of the principal minors of

$$\begin{vmatrix} 0 & e' \\ e & [s_{ij} + s_{ji}] \end{vmatrix}$$ where i and $j \notin \mathscr{J}$ alternate at this point.

If $\begin{vmatrix} 0 & e' \\ e & [s_{ij}] \end{vmatrix}$ where i and $j \notin \mathscr{J}$ is not zero at x^*, then there does not exist a continuum of points such that x^* is one of them, $x_k = \bar{x}_k$ for all $k \in \mathscr{J}$, and everyone verifies the optimality conditions.

The remark of paragraph B-2 (c) is also true here.

(D) CHARACTERISTICS OF SOCIAL DISTRIBUTION OPINIONS

(1) *Loci of Optimal Distributions*

(a) The set of points x defined by $s_j = s$ or $v_j = v$ for all j, s and v being variable parameters, is called the *locus of optimal distributions*. It is generally one-dimensional. Its intersection with the hyperplane (or plane) $\Sigma x_i = X$, when it is the only binding constraint, is the optimum.

(b) The set of points x defined by $s_j = s$ for all $j \in \mathscr{I}$, s being a variable parameter, is the *locus of the optimal distributions for $\mathscr{I}$*. Its intersection with the intersection of the hyperplane (or planes) $\Sigma x_i = X$ and $x_j = \bar{x}_j$ for $j \notin \mathscr{I}$ is the optimum when they are the only binding constraints.

(2) *Social Altruism or Jealousy*

At the optimum, one may say that s_j is the 'social value' of x_j. s may therefore be called the *social value of distributed wealth*. $s > 1$, or $s < 1$, means that 'society as a whole' is willing to pay more than one dollar, or less than one dollar, for one dollar to be distributed to one of its members. Therefore, the names of *social altruism* if $s > 1$ and of *social jealousy* if $s < 1$ should be adopted. When only the wealth constraint is binding, $s \geq 1$ is equivalent to $v \geq 0$. In this case, s and v are respectively eigenvalues of S and V.

By varying the wealth constraint and supposing it to be the only binding one, social altruism when $s > 1$ and $v > 0$, and social jealousy when $s < 1$ and $v < 0$, are defined for all points of the locus of optimal distributions.

It might be extended to the other x's by calling, then, s and v the eigenvalues of, respectively, S and V which tend to the column-sums when x tends to a point of this locus. These definitions are consistent since $s = 1 + vs$ holds for any corresponding eigen-values of S and V.

(3) *Exercise for the Reader*

   (a) *Statement.* Find the locus of optimal distributions and the social value of distributed wealth (when only the wealth constraint is binding), when citizens i have ordinal maximands a specification of which is $u^i = \sum_j \alpha^i_j x_j^{\beta_j}$ where the α^i_j's and β_j's are constants. Analyse the special sub-case when specifications are $u^i = \prod_j x_j^{\alpha_j^i}$.

   (b) *Solution.* Let A be the matrix $\left[\dfrac{\alpha^i_j \beta_j}{\alpha^i_i \beta_i} - \delta_{ij} \right]$ in the general case and $[\alpha^i_j - \delta_{ij}]$ with $\alpha^i_i = 1$ in the special sub-case, j being the row index^i and i the column index. Then v is an eigen-value of A. Let $x^0_i{}^{1-\beta}$ in the general case and x^0_i in the special sub-case be a corresponding eigen-vector. Then, λ being a variable parameter, the equations of the locus of optimal distributions are $x_i = \lambda^{\frac{1}{1-\beta_i}} x^0_i$ in the general case and $x_i = \lambda\, x^0_i$ in the special sub-case. v is a constant on this locus. For $n = 2$ in the special sub-case, the equation of the locus of optimal distributions is $\dfrac{x_1}{x_2} = \sqrt{\left(\dfrac{\alpha_1^2}{\alpha_2^1} \right)}$.

(4) *Unconstrained 'Pareto' Optima and Contract Locus*

By definition, at an unconstrained optimum there does not exist any direction of dx such that $S.dx \geq 0$.[1] Therefore there exists a direction of dx such that $S.dx = 0$, and $|S| = 0$. Indeed, if this did not hold, the row vectors of S would be independent, a direction perpendicular to $n - 1$ of them would not be perpendicular to the remaining one, and there would exist a dx on this direction that $\sum_j s^i_j.dx_j = 0$ for the $n - 1$ vectors and $\sum_j s^i_j.dx > 0$ for the remaining one, which is contrary to the hypothesis.

The direction of dx such that $S.dx = 0$ (which is in general almost everywhere unique) is that of a common tangent to all indifference loci, if they exist, which pass by this point. The locus of equation $|S| = 0$ is the *contract locus*.

---

[1] Vectorial inequality.

5   Singular Points

The points such that $|I - V| = 0$ are singular points where S is not defined.

(E) SOCIAL SATIETY

(1)   *Generalities*

If the wealth constraint is not binding at the optimum, there is *social satiety*. Of course, this does not imply individual satieties. Those cases, which we mention for the sake of completeness, may not be as uninteresting as one may *a priori* think. They happen in two kinds of situations which are respectively represented by intersections of a locus of optimal distributions with the contract locus and with the locus of singular points. In the first case, $s = 0$ and $v = \pm \infty$; in the second case, $v = 1$ and $s = \pm \infty$. In the first case, the 'social value' of one more dollar *distributed* is zero: social wealth is, in a sense, 'bound by civil jealousies'. We shall call these two cases 'contract optimum' and 'singular optimum'.

(2)   *Contract Optimum*

(a) *Unconstrained contract optimum.*   (i) *Definition*: $\Sigma s_j . dx_j \leq 0$ whatever dx if and only if $s_j = 0$ for all j. This gives n generally independent conditions to determine the n unknowns x_i^*. These conditions imply that row-vectors, as well as column-vectors, of S are not linearly independent, i.e. that $|S| = 0$. More precisely, this point is an unconstrained 'Pareto' optimum since every optimum is a 'Pareto optimum' (cf. Part 2; if there existed a direction of dx such that $S . dx \geq 0$, it would violate the optimality condition). Therefore, as already mentioned, this optimum is a point of the locus of optimal distributions where $s = 0$, and it is an intersection of this locus with the contract locus.

(ii) *True optimality and local uniqueness.* This point is a true optimum if and only if the quadratic form constructed on the matrix $[s_{ij} + s_{ji}]$ is negative semi-definite. There does not exist a continuum of points such that x^* is one of them and everyone verifies the optimality conditions, if $|[s_{ij}]| \neq 0$.

(b) *Constrained contract optimum.*   (i) *Definition*: If limitative constraints $x_i \geq \bar{x}_i$ for $i \in \mathscr{J}$ are binding, the optimum is defined by the condition $\Sigma s_j . dx_j \leq 0$ for all dx such that $dx_i \geq 0$ for all $i \in \mathscr{J}$, i.e. $s_j = 0$ for all $j \notin \mathscr{J}$ and $s_j \leq 0$ for all $j \in \mathscr{J}$. This condition and the binding constraints give n generally independent conditions to determine the n unknowns x_i^*. This point is, of course, a 'Pareto' optimum bound by these constraints. It is also a point where $s=0$ of the locus of optimal distributions for citizens not in $\mathscr{J}$.

(ii) *True optimality and local uniqueness.* If this point is a true optimum, the signs of the principal minors of $|[s_{ij}+s_{ji}]|$ where i and $j \notin \mathscr{J}$ alternate. There exists no continuum of points such that x^* is one of them, each one verifies the optimality conditions, and $x_k = \bar{x}_k$ for all $k \in \mathscr{J}$, if $|[s_{ij}]|$ where i and $j \notin \mathscr{J}$ is not zero.

3 Singular Optimum

S and therefore the s_j's are not defined at a singular point. However, the conditions of true optimality may characterise such a point as an optimum: a possible singular point x^* is an optimum if and only if $\Sigma s_j(x^*+dx).dx_j \leq 0$ for every possible x^*+dx. It may be that at x^*, no constraint is binding or limitative constraints are binding, or even the wealth constraint is binding, alone or with limitative constraints. Those points are intersections of the locus of singular points with the corresponding constraints and loci of optimal distributions. It is easy to specify the general optimality condition in each case.

4 SOCIAL RATIONALITY?

(A) IRRELEVANT MAXIMISATIONS

Let us come back to the general definition of the optimum. The fashion among economists is, when they are shown an optimum, to ask what it implicitly maximises. This question reveals a belief that every optimisation is the manifestation of a maximisation. Now, the optimum is the object and the most basic concept of Normative Economics. The maximisation, if any, is only a derived and not fundamental device: it is just an often useful but not necessary tool.

Hence, the above-mentioned question is trivial: the optimum being defined, any function which takes its maximum in this state (or, more refined, its maximum subject to the constraints of the problem) is a suitable answer.

Yet, the differential used in the definition of the optimum, $\Sigma_{i,h} s_h^i.dz_h$, is generally not integrable. More precisely, its integrability cannot be deduced from that of the $\Sigma_h s_h.dz_h$ for every i, i.e. from every individual's rationality.

But, it will be argued, maximisation, whether explicit or implicit, is a consequence of choice rationality, and this property seems to force conviction. However, the most convincing definition of rationality is the one which refers to transitivity of choices between pairs of alternatives. Now, pair-wise choices are irrelevant to the problem under consideration since if a set of alternatives contains two elements, an infinity of other elements linking them continuously is also possible from the assumption on the possibility set. Therefore, the relevant rationality is that of 'revealed preferences'. The axiom of independence of irrelevant alternatives,[1] also called, in another form, the weak axiom of revealed preferences, holds for the defined optimum if it does for every citizen. Therefore, the crux of the question seems to be the strong axiom of revealed preferences. One may suggest that it is *a priori* less bound to force conviction than the previously mentioned 'direct' transitivity. But, anyway, all these axioms (direct transitivity, and weak and strong axioms of revealed preferences) require the consideration of several sets of constraints. This raises the fundamental point of the difference between normative analysis and demand or behavioural analysis in economics: they do not have the same aims nor the same *raison d'être*, and there is no reason *a priori* why the concepts of the one should be valid for the other. Now, demand theory aims at predicting agents' decisions in various possible conditions, and for that purpose it needs hypotheses about their behaviour; rationality is one of them. On the other hand, the object of a normative theory is to define and to determine the optimum (i.e. to point out the right public action) under the given, and unique, set of constraints (which may be uncertain, dated for the future, etc.); what should be done *if* there were other constraints is simply irrelevant to the problem. Therefore, there is no ground to assert that rationality is *necessary* in the latter problem; however, maximising techniques may be interesting for other reasons.

Since the Social Welfare Function is the object of one of the most provoking misunderstandings in economics, let us note clearly the logics of the point. One often hears: 'you *need*, or you *must have*, some Social Welfare Function'. Is this right or wrong? The answer is: it depends on what is meant by 'function' and, with the usual interpretation, it is just wrong. Call m the number of dimensions of z, R^m the m-dimensional Euclidian space, R^1 the set of real numbers, $\mathscr{P}(R^m)$ the set of the parts

---

[1] We mean here this axiom *stricto sensu*: the optimum is not changed if non-optimal possible alternatives become impossible: and if some alternatives become possible, the optimum either is the same or is one of the new alternatives, but it cannot be a formerly possible and non-optimal alternative. Arrow's axiom of the same name (for social preferences) implies moreover that the social optimum is independent from any characteristic of individual values but orderings. Obviously, the above defined optimum verifies all these conditions.

of R^m and P the set of possible z's (hence $P \epsilon P(R^m)$). Then consider the four following functions:

(1) $W(z)$ from $z \epsilon R^m$ to $W \epsilon R^1$,
(2) $W(z)$ from $z \epsilon P$ to $W \epsilon R^1$,
(3) $z^*(S)$ from $S \epsilon \mathscr{P}(R^m)$ to $z^* \epsilon S$,
(4) $z^*(P)$ from P to $z^* \epsilon P$.

What is usually meant is a function of type (1) such that its value $W(z^*)$ at the optimal $z^* \epsilon P$ is the maximum of $W(z)$ for all $z \epsilon P$. Sometimes, it is a function of type (2), which is better for the present reasoning since it requires less: $W(z)$ need to be defined only on P. Now, if z^* which maximises $W(z)$ on P exists and is unique, then the existence of W solves the problem. But one cannot say that such a device is indispensable: it is *sufficient but not necessary*. What is needed and required is a function of *type* (4) and only this. Note that types (3) and (4) are vector-valued functions with sets of vectors as arguments; moreover, the range of type (4) functions contain only one element (there is no 'variable').

(B) THE THREE CONCEPTS OF A SOCIAL WELFARE FUNCTION

Even restricting Social Welfare Functions to their usual logical meaning, their social meaning remains ambiguous. In fact, there exists three thoroughly different concepts of such a Social Welfare Function. They are conveniently distinguished by the Kantian labels of Categorical, Pragmatical and Technical.[1]

(1) *A Categorical Social Welfare Function*
This aims at describing 'Society's preferences'. It bears some similarity to Rousseau's 'General Will' or to the 'People's Will'. This function is the object of Arrow's study *Social Choices and Individual Values*.[2]

(2) *A pragmatical Social Welfare Function*
This describes social and ethical opinions of a rational individual who may be, for instance, the economist, a public official, etc. It is the object of Bergson's [3] and Samuelson's [4] studies, among others.

---

[2] One could also say, by translating appropriately Saint Thomas's classification, that this function is respectively given to the economist as *principium*, as *modus*, or as *exercicium*.

[2] Cowles Commission Monograph, Wiley.

[3] 'A Reformulation of Certain Aspects of Welfare Economics', *Quarterly Journal of Economics*, Feb 1938.

[4] *Foundations of Economic Analysis* (Harvard University Press) ch. viii.

Let us recall that Arrow shows that there does not exist in general any Categorical Social Welfare Function satisfying some reasonably requirable properties. On the other hand, the maximum of a Pragmatical Social Welfare Function is the optimum only if the process which chooses the individual whose opinions it describes is itself optimal, but this function says nothing about this 'representation' (in Arrow's analysis it would correspond to the 'dictator' case [1]). Roughly, a Categorical Social Welfare Function would solve the right problem but it does not exist, whereas a Pragmatical Social Welfare Function exists but it shuns the basic problem.

(3)   *The Technical Social Welfare Function*

There exists a third concept of Social Welfare Function: the *Technical Social Welfare Function*. From this standpoint, this function is but one of the economist's computation and implementation tools. It may help him to specify an optimum which may generally be defined without it. The interest of this function is purely operational: it enables him to use maximisation computation techniques, it may help decentralising the work of a team or of a hierarchy, or even it may help in distinguishing the analysis of tastes and opinions from that of possibilities when this is meaningful.

(C) VILFREDO PARETO'S IDEAS

It is relevant, at this point, to recall Vilfredo Pareto's true ideas. This author is certainly a classic if by this is meant 'widely referred to and seldom read'; but he is not if this suggests that he limits his science to 'Pareto-optimality'. It may even be thought that the use of this expression without further qualification is a calumny: Pareto was more clever, complete and deep than is implied by it. He uses his famous pre-ordering for mainly semantic reasons, to distinguish between the three notions of 'maximum of *ophelimity for* a collectivity' ('Pareto' optimum with 'direct' individual values), 'maximum of *utility for* a collectivity' ('Pareto' optimum with social individual values taking into account all three categories of effects: direct, indirect and interdependence of utilities), and 'maximum of *utility of* a collectivity' (maximum of a Pragmatical Social Welfare Function), and also to distinguish between the domains of 'Political Economy' and of 'Sociology'. See on this point the chapter

---

[1] And in Rousseau's to the 'Legislator'. However, this latter's role is more subtle since he must not force and cannot convince; but he may transform individuals' values and he may lie by invoking God's Will! (Cf. *Du Contrat Social*, ch. vii.)

xii of the *Treatise of General Sociology*. As may be read in this text and in the article 'Il massimo di utilità per una collettività in Sociologia',[1] Pareto's optimum is defined by a process which is mid-way between the method presented in Part 2 above and a Pragmatical Social Welfare Function.

There, Pareto successively considers the variations of citizens' ophelimities $\delta\varphi_i$, which cause a variation $\Sigma_j a_j^i . \delta\varphi_j$ in each citizen i's Social Welfare Function, the terms of which are aggregated for all citizens by the 'Government' in the variation $\Sigma_{i,j} b_j^i . a_j^i . \delta\varphi_j$ of its Social Welfare Function (with perhaps $b_j^i = b_k^i$ for all i, j, k). This latter variation is zero at the optimum.

(D) APPROXIMATE UNANIMITY

Not only from a historical but also from a semantical point of view, it would be advantageous to replace the traditional expressions using Pareto's name by what they actually mean, and in particular by expressions using the words *unanimity and unanimous*.[2]

It is of some interest to notice that, whereas the *unanimity* pre-ordering yields the famous classical indeterminacy of the optimum among its maximal states ('Pareto optima'), the above-given definition of the *unique* optimum shows that it is the state reached by a *unanimity minus one* decision rule applied to each small variation of the vector of parameters. This rule includes complete unanimity, which is sufficient to give the optimality conditions of the 'Classical and Meta-Classical' cases (paragraph II-H). But the determination of the optimal distribution requires the 'minus one'; indeed, the analyses of paragraph III show that in any point which is not the optimum there exist marginal transfers between two persons accompanied by compensations yielded or received by all citizens, such that the whole operation is favoured by all citizens except, generally, the one who yields the (small) transferred sum under consideration. A sequence of such operations can stop only at the optimum.

This process can be justified for its own sake and this justification must be considered along with the other properties of the optimum. Complete unanimity of all the n citizens at each move is thought to be an ethically good criterion; it is itself accepted at unanimity. But it generally does

---

[1] *Giornale degli economisti*, Apr 1913, pp. 337–40.

[2] Using the vocabulary of ordering relations, 'unanimity-maximal' and 'unanimity-maximality' would replace 'Pareto-optimum' and 'Pareto-optimality', 'unanimously preferred' would replace the sometimes used 'Pareto-better'.

G

not yield and define a unique state. As the optimum must be unique, it is a useless criterion. The requirement to have everybody agree is logically too strong (equivalently, the conditions it gives are too weak). The least weakening of this requirement is to have only $n - 1$ citizens agree at least (i.e. unanimity of the n citizens is still possible). This being for infinitely small moves, the question of changing being raised an infinitely great number of times, and the dissenting citizen being left undefined (and being generally not the same one in the various moves), we obtain the process which we have shown to be sufficient to yield and define a unique state, which we characterised as the optimum.

But the determination of the optimum by such a process requires in theory an infinity of decisions bearing on infinitely small modifications. Practically, the costs of all kinds (material, time, effort, etc. . . .) of the exchanges of information and compensations between citizens, contrive to reduce the number of operations and to make them concern non-infinitely small quantities. This may lead to use a majority rule less stringent than the '$n - 1$ majority'.

These remarks validate Wicksell's analysis for the choice of the budget by a Parliament: let us recall that, according to this author, *approximate unanimity* of the members yields a uniquely determined optimum provided all the parameters of expenditures and receipts are questioned and decided upon simultaneously.[1]

(E) TECHNICAL SOCIAL WELFARE FUNCTIONS

The optimum being theoretically defined, it is interesting to investigate how maximands can be constructed and whether there exist particularly operational and meaningful similar tools.

(1) *Discriminating Integrating Factors*
Although there does not exist in general any integrating factor for the optimum's differential $\sum\limits_{i,h} s_h^i . dz_h$, if citizens are rational there exist discriminating integrating factors $\lambda^i(z)$ such that $\lambda^i(z^*) = \lambda > 0$ for all i, and

---

[1] Cf. Knut Wicksell: 'Ein neues Prinzip der gerechten Besteuerung', *Finanzteoretische Untersuchungen*, Jena 1896: partial English translation: 'A new Principle of Just Taxation', in *Classics in the Theory of Public Finance*, ed. Musgrave and Peacock. However, one may reproach Wicksell for not being sufficiently explicit on the fundamental point of the determinacy of undeterminacy of the optimum. Moreover, his remarks on the effect of the initial distribution of wealth are out of place if the budget also has a distribution function. Finally, Wicksell does not consider a sequence of decisions. Nevertheless, our analysis gives an explanation of the letter of his text and permits to consider it as being very deep.

such that $\Sigma\lambda^i(z).\Sigma s_h^i.dz_h$ be a total differential. Indeed, call $u^i(z)$ a
specification of i's ordinal utility index, u_0^i the marginal utility for i of his
money income,[1] $U([u^i])$ a Social Welfare Function respecting valuations
and such that, at $z=z^*$, $u_0^i.\dfrac{dU}{du^i}$ be the same for all i. Then, taking

$\lambda^i(z)=u_0^i(z).\dfrac{\delta U([u^i(z)])}{\delta u^i}$, one has $\Sigma\lambda^i.\Sigma s_h^i.dz_h \equiv dU$ and, at the optimum,

$\lambda\Sigma s_h^i(z^*).dz = dU \leq 0$ for all possible z^*+dz. Therefore, U has a maximum
at z^*.

(2) The Relativist Social Welfare Function

People's opinions on a possible state of society depend on the state of
society in which people are when they have these opinions. In other words,
the value of a possible social state for each individual is relative to the
viewpoint social state. Let us measure this value by the quantity of
money m_i which must be given to ($m_i>0$) or taken from ($m_i<0$) this individual i in the viewpoint state in order to make the resulting state equivalent to the judged state. Calling 1 the viewpoint state and 2 the judged state,
$m_i=m_i(z^1, z^2)$ is, for short, the money equivalent of state 2 from state 1.

In general, $m_i(z^1, z^2) \neq -m_i(z^2, z^1)$.[2] However, when z^1 and z^2 are
infinitely close to each other and neglecting terms of higher order,
$m_i(z, z+dz) = -m_i(z+dz, z) = \Sigma s_h^i.dz_h$.

P being the set of possible z and $V(z)$ a neighbourhood of z, the definition
of the optimum may be written $\Sigma m_i(z^*, z) \leq 0$ for all $z\epsilon P\cap V(z)$. Call
$m=\Sigma m_i$; this summation is legitimate and meaningful since the m_i's
are quantities of the same good. From the precedent remark and from
$m_i(z, z) = m(z, z) = 0$ for all z, the optimum's definition may be written

$$\underset{z\epsilon P\cap V(z^*)}{\max}\ m(z^*, z) = m(z^*, z^*) = \underset{z\epsilon P\cap V(z^*)}{\min}\ m(z, z^*).$$

Therefore, the point $z^1=z^2=z^*$ is a saddle point of the function $m(z^1, z^2)$
subject to the problem's constraints. Conversely, if this function has
only one saddle point under these conditions, it is z^*. This property gives
a way of computing the optimum by the operation $\underset{z^1\epsilon P}{\min}\ \underset{z^2\epsilon P}{\max}\ m(z^1, z^2)$.

---

[1] u_0^i is the *direct* marginal utility, i.e. it does not take into account other citizens'
valuation of i's wealth.
[2] This is the famous 'Scitovsky's Paradox' – see 'A Note on Welfare Propositions in
Economics', *Review of Economic Studies*, Nov 1941.

Of course, although m_i and m depend on the chosen *numéraire*, the result does not depend on it as long as the choice is among goods which have the same relative price for each citizen at the optimum.

It is well known that the operation $\min\limits_{z^1 \epsilon P} \max\limits_{z^2 \epsilon P} m(z^1, z^2)$ has a solution if P is compact and convex and if m is continuous and quasi-concave in z^2 and continuous and quasi-convex in z^1. It is straightforward to show that all these properties of m result from the continuity and the quasi-concavity of all individual ordinal utilities.

Finally, let us notice that $m(z, z+dz) = \Sigma s_h(z).dz_h$, and therefore $\min\limits_{z} \max\limits_{z+dz} .m(z, z+dz)$ is equivalent to $\min\limits_{[s_h(z)]} \max\limits_{dz} \Sigma s_h(z).dz_h$, which is a marginally Von Neumann-like primal-dual form.

(F) PERFECT BIPARTISM AND MAJORITY BIPARTISM

Economists using pragmatical Social Welfare Functions often suppose that they represent the tastes of some 'benevolent dictator'. The Relativist Social Welfare Function enables us to link the definition of the optimum to a political situation which is much more relevant to Western democracies: the two-party system. But it also does much more than that: it gives an instance of how the quality of actual political processes can be appraised by their closeness to similar but ideal processes which we know yield the optimum. Note that we already know another possibility of such a comparison between an actual and a perfect, optimum-yielding process, namely the 'approximate unanimity' studied in paragraph D: according to what was said there, a social choice process is likely to be good if it consists of many independent decisions on small variations of all the variables, each with the requirement of a very high majority.

Let z^1 and z^2 be the states which result or would result from the implementation of the programmes of each of the two parties 1 and 2. $m(z^1, z^2)$ is the sum of citizens' money equivalent of party 2 being in charge instead of party 1. *Perfect bipartism* is the zero-sum two-person game played by the two parties on P with variables z^1 and z^2, and with pay-off the algebraic transfer of $m(z^1, z^2)$ from 1 to 2. We have proven that *this political process implements the social optimum* and that, in this state, the two programmes come to the same and the transfer is zero.

Therefore, it is interesting to know how closely does real-world bipartism approximate perfect bipartism. The two differ because what parties in fact seek is the majority of votes. That is to say, the function $m(z^1, z^2) = \Sigma m_i(z^1, z^2)$ is replaced by the function $\Sigma sgn\, m_i(z^1, z^2)$, meaning that m_i is replaced by $+1$ if it is positive and by -1 if it is negative. Hence, the quality of this *majority bipartism* as a system of social choice can be appraised from the distribution of the m_i's in the society. It is perfect if this distribution is symmetrical, and in a large and diversified country with many problems involved in the vote the law of large numbers may provide this property. Then, the only imperfection that remains comes from the combination of imperfect knowledge of both the citizens on the meaning of the programmes and the parties on citizen's preferences with the cost of voting and of changing the policy: the former prevents a one-play game from being optimal where as the latter attaches costs to the multiplicity of plays.

(G) HEURISTIC OPTIMISATIONS

(1) *Minimaximisations*

From the preceding paragraph, the optimum may be computed by using, with some obvious precautions, sequences of z^n such that, for instance, z^{n+1} is the solution of $\max\limits_{z \epsilon P} m(z^n, z)$, or of $\min\limits_{z \epsilon P} m(z, z^n)$, or, else, that z^n is the solution of $\max\limits_{z \epsilon P} m(z^{n-1}, z)$ and z^{n+1} the solution of $\min\limits_{z \epsilon P} m(z, z^n)$.

(2) *The Marginal Surplus Method*

The marginal surplus method consists in moving from each z of a possible small variation dz such that $\Sigma s_h . dz_h > 0$. When the optimum is reached, this operation is no longer possible. The *maximum marginal surplus method* consists in moving in the possible direction which makes the smallest possible angle with the vector $[s_h]$. When the direction of $[s_h]$ is itself possible, it comes to the method of orthogonal trajectories.

5 SOCIAL JUSTICE AND EFFICIENCY

We shall now relax the restrictive hypothesis of the somewhat sketchy model of Part 3. On the one hand, a variable generally influences both distribution and the wealth to be distributed. On the other hand, a redistribution influences prices which in turn influence real distribution. These latter effects introduce to the distinction between distributive and compensatory justice; generalisation and deepening of his distinction prove to be fruitful. When the compensation for work supply is properly taken into account, the reasons why distribution and production, and also justice and efficiency, are interlocked, may be reduced to problems of distribution of capital if this term is exhaustively understood.

(A) DISTINCTION BETWEEN PRODUCTION EFFECT AND DISTRIBUTION EFFECT

(1) *General Case*

The optimality condition is $\Sigma s_h^i . dz_h \leq 0$ or $\Sigma s_j^i . v_h^j . dz_h \leq 0$, that is to say,
$ {}_{i,h} {}_{i,j,h}$
calling $[v_h^j] = W$, $e'\, S\, W . dz \leq 0$, or, finally, $e'\, W . dz + e'\, S\, V\, W . dz \leq 0$. The first term is the production effect and the second one is the distribution effect.[1]

If there is no constraint on income and wealth transfers, at the optimum $e'\, S = e's$ with generally $s > 0$ (cf. Part 3). Then, the optimality condition comes to $e'\, W . dz \leq 0$: only the production effect exists.

(2) *Effects of an Independent Variable*

Let $z_h = \zeta$ be an independent variable unconstrained at the optimum. For applications ζ may be a parameter of any public economic action.

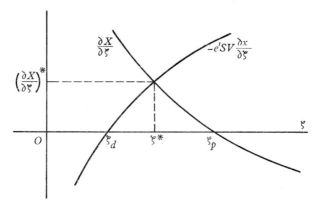

FIG. 2   PRICE EFFECTS, AND INCOME EFFECTS COMPENSATED FOR
PRICE EFFECTS

Let x_i be i's income exhaustively reckoned (for instance, the value to i of public services is included, taxes are excluded, etc.); $X = \Sigma x_i$ is the social
$ {}_{i}$
income, and $v_h^i = \dfrac{\delta x_i}{\delta \zeta}$. Always, $x = [x_i]$. The optimality condition is then, distinguishing both terms, $\dfrac{\delta X}{\delta \zeta} + e'\, S\, V \dfrac{\delta x}{\delta \zeta} = 0$. Social income maximisa-

---

[1] Note that $S - I = V\, S = S\, V = V(I - V)^{-1} = (I - V)^{-1}\, V$. We still suppose, just to keep the exposition in a short space, that general respect of valuations prevails.

tion would give the condition $\dfrac{\delta X}{\delta \zeta} = 0$, from which $\zeta = \zeta_p$ (cf. Fig. 2). If only distributive justice were considered, the condition would be $e' \, S \, V \dfrac{\delta x}{\delta \zeta}$ $= 0$, from which $\zeta = \zeta_d$. The optimum ζ^* is *a priori* a compromise between both of them. The two extreme cases are: a purely productive action where $\dfrac{\delta X}{\delta \zeta} \equiv 0$ and $\zeta^* = \zeta_d$ and a purely redistributive action where $e' \, S \, V \dfrac{\delta x}{\delta \zeta}$ $\equiv 0$ and $\zeta^* = \zeta_p$.

(B) PRICE EFFECTS AND INCOME EFFECTS COMPENSATED FOR PRICE EFFECTS

(1) *Price Effects*

Since individuals consume and own several kinds of goods and since they work, a modification in their incomes and wealths causes shifts in supplies and demands and therefore modifies prices, which, in turn, causes a variation in real incomes and wealths which is added to the initial modification. For brevity's sake, let us restrict the exposition to the case of competitive equilibrium; other types of markets, collective consumptions, various types of taxes, etc., could easily be introduced in the analysis.

Let p_h be the price of good h, q_h^a the quantity of h consumed (>0) or produced (<0) by agent a. $a = i$ is a household, $a = k$ is a firm. Therefore, $q_h^i < 0$ is a quantity of production factor (work or capital) yielded. Δ represents differences, sufficiently small to be considered as differentials, between two concurrential *equilibria*. Calling $x_i = \sum_h p_h \, q_h^i$, Δx_i is a variation in i's income stemming from redistributive actions (transfers, taxes, etc.).

Let us create variations Δx_i. When all adjustments have been completed prices have changed by Δp_h; this causes a reverse change in i's real income of $\Delta_c x_i \triangleq \sum_h q_h^j . \Delta p_h$. Therefore, the actual total variation of i's real income is $\Delta x_i - \Delta_c x_i = \Delta \sum_h p_h \, q_h^i - \sum_h q_h^i . \Delta p_h = \sum_h p_h . \Delta q_h^i \triangleq \Delta_d x_i$. This variation is the relevant one for distributive justice problems. It is the constant-price income variation. $\Delta_c x_i$ is the price effect on income. Therefore, the differential variables of optimal income distribution theory are income effects compensated for price effects, just as the differential variables of price and individual choice theory are price effects compensated for income effects.

(2) *The Compensation is Pure*

From $\Delta x_i = \Delta_d x_i + \Delta_c x_i$, one may say that the total income effect is the sum of a distribution effect and of a compensation effect. Under perfect competition, the latter is the price effect. It is purely compensatory if $\Sigma \Delta_c x_i = 0$. This, in fact, holds for the following reason. Since firms always maximise profits with given prices and, to begin with, produce efficiently, $\underset{h}{\Sigma} p_h . \Delta q_h^k = 0$ for all k. But since competition always forces these profits to zero, $\underset{h}{\Sigma} (p_h . \Delta q_h^k + q_h^k . \Delta p_h) = 0$ for all k. Hence, $\underset{h}{\Sigma} q_h^k . \Delta p_h = 0$ for all k, and therefore $\underset{h \ k}{\Sigma} (\Sigma q_h^k) . \Delta p_h = 0$. But, since markets are cleared, $\underset{k}{\Sigma} q_h^k = -\underset{i}{\Sigma} q_h^i$ for all h. Finally, $\underset{i,h}{\Sigma} q_h^i . \Delta p_h = 0$, that is $\Sigma \Delta_c x_i = 0$.

Therefore, $\Sigma \Delta_d x_i = \Sigma \Delta x_i$; in particular, $\Sigma \Delta_d x_i = 0$ if $\Sigma \Delta x_i = 0$, i.e. if the action is a purely redistributive one.

(3) *Individual Values of Nominal Incomes*

Distributive justice opinions refer to variations of real incomes $\Delta_d x_i$, but distributive justice instruments are variations of nominal incomes Δx_i. The v_j^i's of Part 2 refer, of course, to real incomes. To determine optimal distributions, one may directly consider the value v_{jn}^i of j's nominal income for i, taking into account induced price variations. These two values are tied by $v_j^i . \Delta_d x_j = v_{jn}^i . \Delta x_j$, that is $v_{jn}^i = v_j^i \left(1 - \dfrac{\Delta_c x_j}{\Delta x_j} \right)$, or $\dfrac{v_{jn}^i}{v_j^i} = \underset{h}{\Sigma} \dfrac{\delta q_h^i}{\delta x_j} . p_h$, where $\dfrac{\delta q_h^j}{\delta x_i}$ is the slope of i's Engel curve for the good h.

Since $\Delta_c x_i$ is what must be given to or taken from i in order to *compensate* the losses or gains he incurs from price changes, the justice the differential variables of which are these $\Delta_c x_i$, may be conveniently labelled '*compensatory justice*'.

(c) COMPENSATORY JUSTICE AND DISTRIBUTIVE JUSTICE

The precedent example illustrates with precision the difference between *distributive justice* on the one hand, and on the other *compensatory justice* which is *Aristotle's rectificative justice,*[1] and *Saint Thomas's* (and *Henri Simon's*) *commutative justice.*[2, 3, 4]

(1) *Compensatory Justice*

Most generally, an action of compensatory justice aims at 'compensating' a person for his being in a situation instead of in another one; it is a 'rectification' of the first state with respect to the second one. When the compensation is fully achieved, the first situation accompanied by this compensation is equivalent to the second one for this person. When the compensation is incomplete, the first situation accompanied by the compensation is thought by this person to be better than one of the two situations and worst than the other one. Therefore, the basic tools of compensatory justice are indifference and ordering relations, i.e. ordinal utility, for this person.

The difference between the two states under consideration may be caused by a variety of phenomena. The problem may be to keep a *statu quo* in utility level: the two states are then before and after the occurrence of some event. Compensatory justice also defines the *just* price of a service (to be distinguished, *ex ante*, from its utility to the beneficiaries): the two states are with and without this service. It may also aim at compensating some objective differences between individuals' situations such as family liabilities, health situations, incurred risks, work penibility, inconveniences of residence, inherited wealth, opportunities received from society and nature, some aspects of their tastes, etc.: the two states are then two individual situations dissimilar from this viewpoint.

[1] *Nicomachean Ethics*, Book v. Note that our two categories constitute altogether only Aristotle's *partial justice* which corresponds to the modern meanings of the word justice. His *complete justice* is 'good acting in Society', or 'virtue toward others' and is far beyond our present understanding of this term.

[2] *Theological Sum*, 2. 2ae. 9. 61, De partibus justiciae, art. 1 and 2. The author owes this reference to Professor H. Guitton.

[3] *Economic Policy for a Free Society*, Introduction: A Political Credo (University of Chicago Press).

[4] For lack of space, we cannot present here the comparative analysis of the various dichotomies of justice which men found useful to consider, although this study is extremely rewarding to understand what they meant. One would find, besides compensatory and distributive justices, and partial and complete justices, the Greek concepts of dikaiosynē and ison-isotes, and the oppositions between meritarian and egalitarian justices, between the principles 'to each according to his work' and 'to each according to his needs', between equality of opportunity and equality of wealth, and in the fiscal field, between 'horizontal equity' and 'vertical equity', between benefit and capacity taxation principles, between 'purely fiscal' and 'socio-political' taxations (Wegner), which leads to Professor Musgrave's distinctions between 'Distribution' and 'Allocation branches', and which all the Law's concepts and distinctions must be added.

(2)   *A Proposal from Professors Harsanyi and Tinbergen*

From this enumeration, one may think that all justice may be reduced to compensatory justice. This idea has been brilliantly exposed by Professor Tinbergen,[1] as Professor Harsanyi had previously done;[2] he suggests that all parameters of individual's ordinal utility functions be considered as variables. Then all individuals have the same ordinal utility function ('human nature'?), and justice may be defined as the fact that the point, the co-ordinates of which are the parameters of the existing state, is on the same indifference locus for every individual.[3]

However, although extremely interesting, this theory does not consider closely enough the effects of the constraints. Call 'just' a state so defined and 'unjust' the other states. The constraints may be such that there exists a possible unjust situation which would be preferred by every individual to the best possible just situation.[4] Nay, no possible just situation may even exist. Most generally, the constraints impose substitutions between individual ordinal utility indexes and there is no reason why the best of possible states would be a just one. Hence, justice opinions must be more refined than a just-unjust manicheism in order to judge the distributions of these indexes. This is the role of distributive justice.

(3)   *Variables of Distributive Justice*

Since compensatory justice deals with differences in the shape of indifference loci, distributive justice may reduce its variables to one utility index for each individual. Many specifications of these ordinal utility indexes could be chosen;[5] to pass from one to another is a problem of compensatory justice. However, one of these specifications is more operational and practically meaningful than the others: that is a money income. But the definition of the relevant income must free it from the effects taken care of by compensatory justice.

[1] Proceedings of the American Economic Association 1956 meeting, *American Economic Review*, May 1957.

[2] 'Cardinal Welfare, Individualistic Ethics, and Interpersonal Comparison of Utility', *Journal of Political Economy*, Aug. 1955.

[3] With the permutations of co-ordinates required for each of these surfaces to represent the same variables *from the point of view of the individual under consideration* (for instance, if figure 1 told the whole story, one income vector or one set of indifference curves would have to incur a symmetry around the first bisector).

[4] Compare: '*Summum jus summa injuria*'.

[5] When all variables are defined '*à la* Harsanyi–Tinbergen', the same specification of the common ordinal utility index can be chosen for all individuals. Then, Tinbergen's justice is the equality of these indexes.

Now, the income of a given period, which is used in present and future consumption and in gifts and legacies,[1, 2] stems from work and capital, these two terms being understood in their broadest sense. In order to make income a variable of distributive justice, the first task of compensatory justice is to subtract from it the just compensation for work.

(D) WORK COMPENSATION: THE LEISURELY EQUIVALENT

(1) *Definition*

Consider an individual. Let c be the vector of the quantities of goods he consumes or acquires. Let t be the vector of the parameters of his work: durations, intensities, conditions, etc., of the various types of work he performs. The parameter t_0 is always the total duration of his work and $t_0 = 0$ means that he does not work. Let $u(c, t)$ be an ordinal utility index for this individual. When $t_0 = 0$, u is not sensitive to the others t_i's. The individual's physical and intellectual capacities are described by $t \in T(c)$. It may be that T depends little on c in wide ranges.[3] Let $r = f(t)$ be the individual's income. f reckons altogether incomes from all origins, including material capital (itself defined so as to include financial assets). This notation is used because some 'tangible' assets yield an income by co-operating with some elements of t, and although the income yielded by other such assets is independent of t. Finally, let $c \epsilon b(r)$ be the individual's budgetary constraint. b depends on prices or on supply curves, and on non-negativities, discontinuities, and other physical constraints on c.[4]

Then, the *leisurely equivalent income* x is defined by the equation

$$\text{maximum of } \left. u(c, t) \right. = \text{maximum of } \left. u(c, t) \right.$$
$$\text{subject to } \left| \begin{array}{l} c \epsilon b(r) \\ r = f(t) \\ t \in T(c) \end{array} \right. \qquad \text{subject to } \left| \begin{array}{l} t_0 = 0 \\ c \epsilon b(x) \end{array} \right.$$

[1] Of course, taxes are deducted and the money value to the individual of collective services are included (they cancel each other in case of 'benefit' taxes or tolls with perfect and complete discrimination, both by consumer and by unit of the service).

[2] One of the reasons why distributive justice cares about disposable incomes and not about utility functions is the argument that 'each one is responsible for his own tastes', and therefore that the way in which people choose to lay out their income is their own concern; distributive justice cares only about the distribution of undifferentiated purchasing power, quite apart from its use. In fact, what is basically distributed is freedom of economic choice.

[3] Among possible reasons for this dependence: nutrition, housing, transportation and information services, etc.

[4] The *marketing work* necessary to buy c could also easily be taken into account.

x is income compensated for work disutility (and, eventually, pleasantness).[1]

2 Graphical Representation and Example

x may be represented graphically (Fig. 3) by $v(\bar{r}, \bar{t}_0) \stackrel{\Delta}{=} \max u(c, t)$ subject to $c \epsilon b(\bar{r})$, $\bar{r} = f(\bar{t})$, $t \epsilon T(c)$, $t_0 = \bar{t}$:, and by calling $\bar{r} = \varphi(\bar{t}_0)$ the solution of $\bar{r} = f[t^*(\bar{t}_0, \bar{r}]$ where t^* is the t which results from the maximisation. Then, the remaining problem has only two variables, $\bar{r}$ and t_0, and the maximisation of $v(\bar{r}, \bar{t}_0)$ subject to the constraint $\bar{r} = \varphi(\bar{t}_0)$ yields the optimum $\bar{r}$, $\bar{t}_0$.

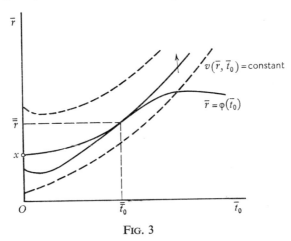

FIG. 3

For instance, if work income is independent from owned material capital and if the wage-rate s is fixed, $\varphi(\bar{t}_0) = r_K + s\bar{t}_0$ where r_K is the income yielded by this capital. If, moreover, $v(\bar{r}, \bar{t}_0) = \bar{r} - \alpha\bar{t}_0^2 - \beta$, then $x = r_K + \frac{1}{2} s\, \bar{t}_0 = r - \frac{1}{2} s\, t_0$: leisurely equivalent income is capital income plus half work income (or total income less half the work income).

(E) PROBLEMS OF CAPITAL OWNERSHIP [2]

When the supply of labour is taken care of in this manner, relations between distribution and production come down to questions of capital

---

[1] An 'n-hour equivalent' with $t_0 = n$ instead of $t_0 = 0$ could have been chosen (for instance, $n = 8$ for Oscar Lange in *On the Economic Theory of Socialism*), but in this case u would depend on t in the right-hand maximisation and the problem would be more complicated, whether the other components of t remain free or whether they are fixed too.

[2] For brevity's sake, the following remarks are reduced to a *memento*. Their consideration is indispensable to the study of the relations between production and distribution.

ownership. Taking these terms in their most extensive sense, there are three forms of capital and three forms of capital appropriation.

(1) *Material, Human and Social Capital*

Material capital is made of claims and of goods owned by title or directly. *Human capital* is physical (strength, health), and intellectual and in this case it contains *abilities* such as intelligence and memory on the one hand and knowledge on the other hand; needs and tastes could be reckoned with it. *Social capital* includes connections,[1] family notoriety and also residence, race, culture, etc., because of the opinions other individuals have on them; social capital yields an income both through markets and through political influence on public expenditures, revenues, transfers and regulations.

(2) *Received, Innate and Acquired Property*

Capital possessed by an individual may have been *given* by society, notably: by heritage, by education, training, and health paid by parents or government, by family social situation. Human capital, both for productive aptitudes and for characteristics appreciated by other people, may be *innate* in the individual. Finally, the three forms of capital may have been *accumulated* by the individual thanks to his work and to the capital he owned in the past.

(3) *Appropriation and Compensation*

A situation resulting from a capital distribution can be modified in two ways. First, *ownership* can be redistributed; but this is not possible for those elements of capital which are embodied in the individual. However, second, the distribution of any kind of capital can be *compensated* in various ways. To analyse the relation between justice and efficiency, one has to study both the justice effects and the efficiency effects of each of these parameters of the overall distribution.

(4) *Variables of Social Justice Opinions*

Some *justice opinions* do not want to question the distribution of capital of any kind received by gifts and legacies; however, for many people these variables are self-contradictory from a justice point of view since they think that free disposal of his wealth by the giver may be justice whereas the same action may create an unjust inequality among receivers.

---

[1] For instance, nepotism ('to each one according to his uncle') is a social capital for the nephew.

Some opinions, also, do not want to question innate capital distribution by correcting compensations, except for pathologic handicaps.   Finally, many opinions refuse to question earned property, at least as long as it has been earned by own work, and also, for some opinions, by capital acquired by own work (generally, those opinions confuse work income and work compensation).[1]

(5) *Production Effects of Distribution*
What classical (and Marxist) economics study under the name of 'distribution' is the effect of the production process on the distribution of incomes to the various factor owners.   Here, we must also take consideration of the reverse effect: that of distribution on production.   One may distinguish three ways through which this effect acts.   The first one comes from the productive efficiency of the poolings of the various elements of material, human and social capital into what is at the disposal of each individual; of course, this efficiency effect is due to the fact that several of these elements cannot be hired nor sold, or that this cannot be without cost.   The second way is the effect on factor supplies of the incentive to earn due to needs; tastes and prices influence by this way, but the most studied effect is that of disposable income on the supply of work and capital (and notably savings).   The third way, also often studied, is the incentive to produce due to the expected effective yields of efforts and sacrifices (i.e. Pigou's 'announcement effect'[2]).

(6) *Restricted and Generalised Efficiencies*
The use of the word 'efficient' is ambiguous.   When the actual constraints are taken into account, this word may have two meanings.   Restricted efficiency only considers production as usually understood, including the consumption of factors by their owners (leisure in particular); it may then be said, for instance, that an inefficient situation is preferred because of justice reasons.   In generalised efficiency, on the opposite, justice production is considered among society's outputs, and it is described by all the many parameters which allow its characterisation; in this case, the optimum is always one of the 'efficient' situations.   Its choice among them requires the consideration of justice opinions.

---

[1] It is difficult to understand what the present American creed of 'Equality of Opportunities' exactly accepts to question.   The case seems clear for social capital. It is doubtful for human capital and it may lead to a contradiction with other basic ethical beliefs for material capital.   The present Soviet creed of 'to each one according to his work' is certainly better defined.

[2] *A Study in Public Finance* (Part 2, chs. v, vi).

6 PROPERTIES OF DISTRIBUTIVE JUSTICE OPINIONS

(A) PROBLEM, DEFINITIONS, NOTATIONS

(1) *Problem*

Traditional economics deals with efficiency analysis and gives, with utility theory, the tool of compensatory justice analysis. Hence, there remains to build distributive justice analysis. The general method of Part 2 is valid for this purpose. But there remains to know citizens' opinions about the justice of distribution. A systematic approach to this huge problem must be based on an *a priori* analysis of the structures of distributive justice opinions. It has been remarked in Part 1 that a property which belongs to every citizen's opinion may be called 'objective', i.e. that it may be included in a definition of the terms 'justice' and 'just'. Hence, much hope and interest is derived from the results of the next Part which show many unexpected ties, implications and equivalences between very natural but seemingly unrelated properties. This Part is devoted to the exposition of these properties.

(2) *Distributive Justice Opinions and Variables*

Two precautions are necessary in order to deal with a distributive justice opinion free from other effects. First, the opinion considered is not the one which would be expressed for tactical reasons in order to improve the situation of he who expresses it or to modify the situations of people he personally likes or dislikes; in brief, it is an impartial opinion. Such an opinion is expressed by a rational individual when indeed this expression does not influence these situations: in a mere investigation, by a vote in a political poll with a great number of voters,[1] when he does not belong to the society for which distribution is judged, etc. Second, the variables must be individual incomes x_i of each individual i, corrected for compensatory justice effects, as defined in the previous part.

(3) *Preferences and Equal Equivalent*

Let n be the number of individuals, x the vector of the x_i's, $x = \Sigma x_i$ the 'social income', $\bar{x} = \dfrac{\Sigma x_i}{n}$ the '*per capita*' or 'average' income. Following the usual terminology, let $\dfrac{x_i - \bar{x}}{\sigma}$, where σ is the standard deviation of the

---

[1] Compare with perfectly competitive markets, where the acts of individually unimportant agents reveal the true values of the goods to them. Cf. also the remark in par. B, 1, c of Part 3 above.

distribution of the x_i's, be the 'reduced income'. The distribution is *equal* if $x = e\bar{x}$ [1] and *unequal* in the opposite case. Let us represent the described opinion by rational preferences,[2] and let $\xi(x)$ be any specification of the corresponding ordinal index. Call $\xi_i = \dfrac{\delta\xi}{\delta x_i}$.

The *equal equivalent* of x is the scalar $\bar{\bar{x}}$ such that $e\bar{\bar{x}} \sim x$, that is, $\xi(e\bar{\bar{x}}) = \xi(x)$. Therefore $\bar{\bar{x}}$ is a ξ if ξ is an increasing function of $\bar{\bar{x}}$ at $e\bar{\bar{x}}$ (it is sufficient for this that, at this point, $\xi_i \geq 0$ for all i, with the inequality holding for at least one i).

Figures 4 and 5 show the problem in the case $n = 2$. $\in = \max [\bar{x} : x = e\bar{x}]$ for possible x's, is the equal maximum.

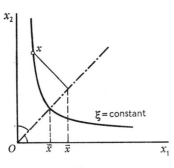

FIG. 4

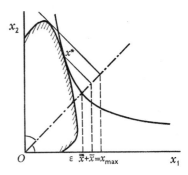

FIG. 5

(4) *Justice and Injustices of the Distributions*

If $x = e\bar{x}$, $\bar{x} = \bar{\bar{x}}$. Hence, $i = \bar{x} - \bar{\bar{x}}$ is a monetary measure of the injustice of the distribution. Call it *injustice* and call $\hat{\imath} = \dfrac{i}{\bar{x}} = 1 - \dfrac{\bar{\bar{x}}}{\bar{x}}$ the *relative injustice*. i is injustice per person and $\hat{\imath}$ is injustice per dollar of social income. Then, $j = 1 - \hat{\imath} = \dfrac{\bar{\bar{x}}}{\bar{x}}$ will naturally be called *justice*. It is the productivity of social income, i.e. the efficiency of each dollar of social income, in welfare measured in money. $\dfrac{\bar{\bar{x}} - \bar{x}}{\sigma} = -\dfrac{i}{\sigma}$ will, of course, be called the *reduced equal equivalent*.

[1] e is, again, a n-dimensional column-vector of 1's.
[2] For which we shall use the usual ordering notations $>$, $\sim$ and $\succsim$.

(5) *Economic Equivalent, Relative Cost and Yield of the Distribution*
Other meaningful measures are the *economic equivalent* of the distribution:
$\bar{x} = \dfrac{\min}{x} \; [\tilde{x} : x \sim x]$ where x is a variable distribution vector, the cost of

the distribution $c = \bar{x} - \tilde{x}$, the relative cost of the distribution $\hat{c} = \dfrac{c}{\bar{x}} = 1 - \dfrac{\tilde{x}}{\bar{x}}$,

and the yield of the distribution $d = 1 - \hat{c} = \dfrac{\tilde{x}}{\bar{x}}$. However, with the most
interesting of the properties studied below, $\tilde{x} = \bar{x}$, $c = \hat{\imath}$, $\hat{c} = \hat{\imath}$, $d = j$.

(6) *Choice between Justice and Efficiency*
To single out the choice between justice and efficiency, let us first perform
an efficiency sub-optimisation maximising ξ on the set of possible distributions, given $\bar{x}$. The equal equivalent of the outcome is a function
$\bar{\bar{x}}(\bar{x})$. The choice (generally a compromise) between justice and efficiency
is then shown by Figs. 6 and 7.

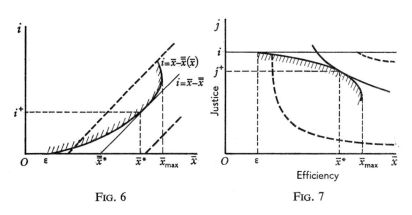

FIG. 6   FIG. 7

(7) *Comparison of redistributions*
A transformation $x \to \phi(x)$ preserving X is an income *redistribution*. Given
two redistributions ϕ^1 and ϕ^2, the latter is said to be uniformly preferred
(alternatively, strictly uniformly preferred) to the former if, for all x,
$\phi^2(x) \gtrless \phi^1(x)$ (alternatively, $\phi^2(x) > \phi^1(x)$).

(B) PROPERTIES

The properties which appear to be natural and meaningful under analysis
are the following. They all are ordinal.

benevolence

$$benevolence: \quad x^2 \geq x^1 \Rightarrow x^2 > x^1.$$
$$non\text{-}malevolence: \quad x^2 \geq x^1 \Rightarrow x^2 > x^1.$$

impartiality or non-discrimination: x^π being the vectors obtained from x by permutations of its co-ordinates ($\pi = 1, \ldots n!$), $x^\pi \sim x$.[1]

rectifiance

$$rectifiance: \quad (x_i - x_j)(\xi_i - \xi_j) \leq 0.$$
$$strict\ rectifiance: \quad x_i < x_j \Rightarrow \xi_i > \xi_j.$$

Therefore, an opinion is rectifiant if, *ceteris paribus*, a dollar more to society is thought to be better if it goes to the richer than to the poorer of any two individuals, and a transfer of a dollar from the former to the latter is thought to be a good thing.[2]

isophily

Call $y_i = \min_{\pi} \sum_{j=1}^{i} x_j^\pi$ and $y = [y_i]$. Roughly speaking (since some x_j's may be equal) y_i is the sum of the i smallest x_j's. Note that $y_n = X$, $x^2 = x^1 \Leftrightarrow y^2 = y^1$, $x^2 \geq x^1 \Rightarrow y^2 \geq y^1$. The curve $\left(\dfrac{\nu}{n}, \dfrac{y_\nu}{y_n}\right)$ is the Lorenz curve of the distribution x.[3] The following properties are then defined:

---

[1] If the i's are different generations, a reconciliation between Ramsey's and the Soviets' time-preference on the one hand, and the other economists' on the other, is to say that preference is impartial but that capital productivity causes that, at the optimum, x_1 and x_2 being incomes at dates t_1 and t_2 such that $t_2 > t_1$, $\xi_2 < \xi_1$ and therefore the discount rate is positive (see Fig. 5).

[2] For instance, opinions expressed by Pigou (*Wealth and Welfare*, p. 24) and Dalton ('The Measurement of the Inequality of Incomes', *Economic Journal*, September 1920, p. 351) are strictly rectifiant; the latter calls rectifiance the 'principle of transfers'.

[3] ξ is a functional of the curve (ν, y_ν). $\bar{x}$ is the slope of the straight line equivalent to this curve. For some problems it is useful to consider the characteristic numbers $\dfrac{\nu}{n}$ where ν is respectively defined by $x_\nu = \bar{x}$, $x_\nu = \bar{\bar{x}}$, $y_\nu = \nu\bar{x}$ (cf. Fig. 8). Note that for the first of these ν's, $\nu\bar{x} - y_\nu = \frac{1}{2}\Sigma|x_i - x|$

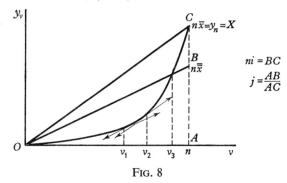

$$n i = BC$$
$$j = \frac{AB}{AC}$$

FIG. 8

> *constant-sum isophily*: $X^2 = X^1$ and $y^2 \geq y^1 \Rightarrow x^2 \gtrsim x^1$.
> *strict constant-sum isophily*: $X^2 = X^1$ and $y^2 \geq y^1 \Rightarrow x^2 \gtrsim x^1$.

In these two properties, x^2's Lorenz curve is 'never under' x^1's.

> *super-isophily*: $X^2 > X^1$ and $y^2 \geq y^1 \Rightarrow x^2 > x^1$.
> *isophily*: $y^2 \geq y^1 \Rightarrow x^2 \gtrsim x^1$.
> *strict isophily*: $y^2 \geq y^1 \Rightarrow x^2 > x^1$.

averages preference

An opinion is said to prefer averages when it favours an income distribution which, without changing the total sum, replaces each income by a linear average (linear convex combination) of the former ones because this somewhat attenuates the injustice due to the inequality of the initial distribution. This redistribution transforms x^1 into x^2 such that $x_i^2 = \Sigma_j b_{ij} x_j^1$ where $b_{ij} \geq 0$ and $\Sigma_j b_{ij} = 1$. Moreover, $X^2 = X^1$ implies $\Sigma_j (1 - \Sigma_i b_{ij}) x_j^1 = 0$, and since there exists at least n independent vectors x^1, $\Sigma_i b_{ij} = 1$. Therefore, the matrix $B = [b_{ij}]$ is bistochastic.

Note that if x^1 is an equal distribution, $x^2 = x^1$. Conversely, the reader should verify that Bx where B is bistochastic is the only linear transformation which (i) transforms every non-negative vector into a non-negative vector, (ii) preserves the total sum X, and (iii) transforms at least one equal distribution into an equal distribution.

Then, the following properties are defined:

> *averages preference*: $Bx \gtrsim x$.
> *strict averages preference*: $Bx > x$ if $Bx \neq x^\pi$.

Call Bx a *linear vectorial average* and call the transformation $x \rightarrow Bx$ an *equalising redistribution*.

mixtures preference

For an impartial opinion, $x\pi \sim x$. A mixture by linear convex combination of the vectors x^π is in some sense more equally distributed without this changing the total sum of incomes. It may be preferred to x for this reason. Hence the following properties are defined for every set of non-negative numbers λ_π such that $\Sigma \lambda_n = 1$:

> *mixtures preference*: $\Sigma \lambda_\pi x^\pi \gtrsim x$.
> *strict mixtures preference*: $\Sigma \lambda_\pi x^\pi > x$ if $\lambda_\pi \neq 1$.[1]

---

[1] Mixtures preference suggests a redistribution method: to transform x into $\Sigma \lambda_\pi x$ one may share all incomes in same proportions (the λ_π's), and then permute each of the

Fig. 9 shows the plan $X = $ constant for the case $n = 3$.

satiation

  satiation: the preference is quasi-concave, i.e. $\{x : x \gtrsim x^0\}$ is convex.

  strict satiation: the preference is strictly quasi-concave, i.e. $\{x : x \gtrsim x^0\}$ is strictly convex.

  constant-sum satiation: $\{x : x \gtrsim x^0, X = X^0\}$ is convex.

  concavity or convexity of injustice

  i and $\bar{x}$ are functions of x; when one is concave or strictly concave, the other is convex or strictly convex, in the same domain.

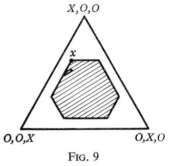

FIG. 9

intensive, increasing, decreasing justice

  The justice of a distribution is often felt as depending only on relative incomes $\dfrac{x_i}{x_j}$, i.e. as an intensive property; then, λ being a scalar, $j(\lambda x)$ $= j(x)$; this is equivalent to $\bar{x}$ and i being homogenous of degree 1 functions of x and to indifference loci being homothetic with each other from the origin. Justice is said to be, respectively, increasing or decreasing according to, for $\lambda > 1$, either $j(\lambda x) > j(x)$ or $j(\lambda x) < j(x)$ hold, which is equivalent to either $x(\lambda \bar{x}) > \lambda . \bar{x}(x)$ or $\bar{x}(\lambda x) < \lambda . \bar{x}(x)$, and to either $i(\lambda x) < \lambda . i(x)$ or $i(\lambda x) > \lambda . i(x)$.

absolute, increasing, decreasing injustice

  The injustice of a distribution is absolute if it does not change when all incomes vary by the same quantity, positive or negative, μ, i.e. when $i(x + e\mu) = i(x)$; this is equivalent to $x(x + e\mu) = x(x) + \mu$ and to the fact that indifference loci correspond to each other by translations parallel to e. Injustice is said to be, respectively, increasing or decreasing according to, for $\mu > 0$, either $i(x + e\mu) > i(x)$ or $i(x + e\mu) < i(x)$, which is equivalent to either $\bar{x}(x + e\mu) < \bar{x}(x) + \mu$ or $\bar{x}(x + e\mu) > \bar{x}(x) + \mu$.

so-defined 'brackets' among individuals. This operation can be realised by exchanges between individuals taken two by two of their corresponding 'brackets', which is equivalent to an income transfer from the richest to the poorest of the two. Therefore, a mixture obeys to Dalton's principle of successive transfers (op. cit. p. 351). The reciprocal results from theorem 1 below.

  If transfers are costly, one may want to minimise their number. To begin with one may try to minimise the number of permutations, i.e. that of proportional 'brackets', i.e. that of $\lambda_\pi \neq 0$ (although this is not equivalent since in a permutation some individuals may correspond to themselves). From *Caratheodory*'s theorem this number can always be reduced to n at most. It may often be reduced more.

Decreasing justice and increasing injustice are two (non-equivalent) ways of saying that justice per person is a luxury.[1]

justice sensitivity

Given two opinions for which the justice of a distribution x is, respectively, $j^1(x)$ and $j^2(x)$, it is said: that the former is more sensitive to justice than the latter for distribution x if $j^1(x) < j^2(x)$, that the former is uniformly more sensitive to justice than the latter if $j^1(x) \leq j^2(x)$ for all x, that the former is strictly uniformly more sensitive than the latter if $j^1(x) < j^2(x)$ for all unequal distributions.

independence

Independence means that the opinion on income distributions to the individuals of a group does not depend on income distribution in the remainder of the society. More precisely, call $x_{\mathscr{I}}$ the vector of the x_i's for $i \in \mathscr{I}$ and $x_{-\mathscr{I}}$ the vector of the x_i's for $i \notin \mathscr{I}$, write $x = (x_{\mathscr{I}}, x_{-\mathscr{I}})$, and specify by indexes 1 and 2 some of those vectors. Then, the opinion is said to be independent when (with corresponding preferences and indifferences),

$$\left(x_{\mathscr{I}}^1, x_{-\mathscr{I}}^1\right) \overset{>}{\underset{<}{\sim}} \left(x_{\mathscr{I}}^2, x_{-\mathscr{I}}^1\right) \Leftrightarrow \left(x_{\mathscr{I}}^1, x_{-\mathscr{I}}^2\right) \overset{>}{\underset{<}{\sim}} \left(x_{\mathscr{I}}^2, x_{-\mathscr{I}}^2\right),$$

for all such x's and all $\mathscr{I}$.[2]

It is easily shown that a necessary and sufficient condition of independence is that, for all i, j and $k \neq i, j$, the opinion on income distribution between i and j does not depend on k's income, i.e. that

$$\frac{\delta}{\delta x_k} \frac{\xi_i}{\xi_j} = 0.$$

Obviously, (1) the opinion is independent if there exists a specification of the ordinal index ξ of the form $\Sigma f_i(x_i)$ where f_i is a function of x_i, and (2) any linear function of this specification has the same form, i.e. this form is a cardinal property. Conversely, the reader may easily verify that, if the opinion is independent, then, (1) there exist such specifications, and (2) they all constitute a unique cardinal specification, i.e. they all

---

[1] Authors generally express their opinion by saying that '*ceteris paribus*, such type of modification of incomes increases or diminishes inequality', being understood that a decrease in inequality is a good thing and an increase in it a bad one. But they fail to make precise whether they are concerned with relative or absolute inequality. However, here is how we understand the following authors. For Taussig (*Principles of Economics*, II 485), justice is intensive. For Dalton (op. cit), justice is decreasing. For Cannan (*Elementary Political Economy*, p. 137), Loria (*La sintesi economica*, p. 369) and Dalton (op. cit), injustice is decreasing.

[2] There exists more restrictive sufficient conditions for this to hold, which require that the relation is verified for some specified sets of at least $n-1$ sets $\mathscr{I}$.

are transformed from each other by increasing linear transformations. If, moreover, the opinion is impartial, this form is $\Sigma f(x_i)$. Then, obviously, f is any function of a unique family each member of which is transformed into any other by an increasing linear transformation.[1] Therefore, such an opinion is thoroughly characterised by the function $\dfrac{f''}{f'}$ or $\check{\imath} = -\dfrac{1}{2}\dfrac{f''}{f'}$ since the *real* integration of the differential equation $f'' + 2\,\check{\imath}f' = 0$ yields such a family. The reader may easily verify that $\check{\imath} = \lim\limits_{\sigma \to 0} \dfrac{i}{\sigma^2}$: it is, for low-dispersion distributions, the marginal injustice per person per unit of variance of incomes. Hence we call it *marginal injustice*. The marginal injustice per dollar per unit of variance of distributed dollars, or, for short, the *marginal relative injustice*, is then $\lim\limits_{\sigma \to 0} \dfrac{\hat{\imath}}{\sigma^2/\bar{x}^2}$, i.e. w being the variable, $w.\check{\imath}(w)$.

7 FUNDAMENTAL STRUCTURE OF DISTRIBUTIVE JUSTICE

We present in this Part the main theorems of distributive justice. For lack of space, we do not give the demonstrations. From a mathematical point of view, some of these relations are new; others are well known from mathematicians but the grouping of properties we present often enables one to give demonstrations much simpler than those which already exist.[2]

(A) MODERATE EGALITARIANISM

(1) *Fundamental Theorems*
   Theorem 1. The four following properties are equivalent: (i) recifiance and impartiality altogether, (ii) constant-sum isophily, (iii) averages preference, (iv) mixtures preference.

---

[1] That is the reason why we reproach Dalton (op. cit.) for choosing measures of the inequality of welfare distribution of the form $\dfrac{f(\bar{x})}{f(\bar{x})}$ which depends on the addition of a constant to f.

Besides, let us notice that $\bar{x}$, $\check{\imath}$ and j verify this author's 'principle of proportionate additions to persons' since, calling n_k the number of individuals who have the same income x_k, $\bar{x}$ defined by $f(\bar{x}) = \Sigma \dfrac{n_k}{n} f(x_k)$, and $\bar{x} = \Sigma \dfrac{n_k}{n} x_k$, do not change when all n_k's (the sum of which is n) vary in the same proportion.

[2] That is in particular the case for the Birkhoff–von Neumann, Ostrowski, Hardy–Littlewood–Pólya and Schur theorems.

Theorem 2. The three following properties are equivalent: (i) strict constant-sum isophily, (ii) strict averages preference, (iii) strict mixtures preference.

Theorem 3. Strict rectifiance and impartiality altogether imply the properties of theorem 2.

Remark. The reciprocal of theorem 3 is not true.

Theorem 4. The properties of theorem 1 and benevolence altogether are equivalent to super-isophily.

Theorem 5. The properties of theorem 2 and benevolence altogether are equivalent to strict isophily.

Theorem 6. The properties of theorem 1 and non-malevolence altogether are equivalent to isophily.

(2) *Comparison of Redistributions*

Theorem 7. Given two equalising redistributions the matrices of which are respectively B^1 and B^2, either if the latter is uniformly preferred to the former for all opinions having theorem 1 properties, or, alternatively, if the latter is strictly uniformly preferred to the former for all opinions having theorem 2 properties, and if B^1 is regular, then there exists a bistochastic matrix B such that $B^2 = B\,B^1$.

Remark. Theorem 7 states, of course, that B does not depend on x.[1] The latter redistribution is then said to be *more equalising* than the former. The obtained relation expresses that each row-vector of B^2 is a linear convex combination of the row-vectors of B.

(3) *Independence*

Theorem 8. For a benevolent, impartial and independent opinion, the properties of each of the two following groups are equivalent.

(1) isophily, rectifiance, satiation, $i \geq 0$, $i \geq 0$, concavity of f, (2) strict isophily, strict rectifiance, strict satiation, $i > 0$ out of the locus of equal distributions, $i > 0$ except on a set measure zero, strict concavity of f.

Theorem 9. (1) A distribution is not worse than another for all isophile opinions if and only if it is not worse for all independent, impartial, non-malevolent and rectifiant opinions.

(2) A distribution is better than another for all strictly isophile opinions if and only if it is better for all independent, impartial, benevolent and strictly rectifiant opinions.

---

[1] The demonstration of this theorem requires some negative x_i's to be considered, which, according to remarks of Parts 3 and 5, are acceptable and represent debt for taxes on work income.

Remark. Of course, what is interesting is the sufficiency with independent opinions only.

(B) INTENSIVE JUSTICE AND ABSOLUTE INJUSTICE

(1) *Intensive Justice and Absolute Injustice altogether*

Theorem 10. An opinion feels altogether justice to be intensive and injustice to be absolute if and only if the reduced equal equivalent depends upon reduced incomes only.

Remark. Equivalently, injustice is the product of the standard deviation of the distribution by a function of reduced incomes only.

Theorem 11. If an opinion having the properties of theorem 10 either is independent or judges only two incomes, the ordinal preference index has a linear specification and the equal equivalent and injustice are linear combinations of incomes.

Remark. The equal equivalent is a convex linear combination if, moreover, the opinion is non-malevolent.

Theorem 12. If an opinion having the properties of theorem 11 is impartial, injustice is null and the equal equivalent is the *per capita* income.

(2) *Independence and Intensive Justice or Absolute Injustice*

Theorem 13. Justice is intensive for an independent opinion if and only if the ordinal preference index has a specification of the form $\Sigma \alpha_i x_i^\beta$ or $\Pi x_i^{\alpha_i}$ where β and the α_i's are constants.

Theorem 14. Injustice is absolute for an independent opinion if and only if the ordinal preference index has a specification of the form $\Sigma \alpha_i \, e\beta x_i$ where β and the α_i's are constants.

Note. Theorem 15 and 16 are corollaries of theorems 13 and 14 obtained when the opinion is impartial and hence when the ordinal preference index has a specification of the form $\Sigma f(x_i)$.

Theorem 15. Justice is intensive for an impartial independent opinion if and only if f has a power or logarithmic specification.[1]

---

[1] In this latter case, a specification of the ordinal index is $\Sigma \log x_i$. Therefore, this case may result from the conjunction of independence, impartiality, and an hypothesis similar to Bernoulli's on 'moral wealth' or to Weber-Fechner's on 'sensation.' It suggests that a Nation's welfare would be better measured by the *geometric mean* of incomes rather than by their arithmetic mean, or *per capita* income, which is usually chosen: this would make allowance for inequalities in distribution. Note incidentally that if income distribution is Log-normal, as has often been suggested (Gibrat, Champernowne, Brown and Aitchison, etc.), this suggestion comes to use the median of incomes rather than their (arithmetic) mean; (in this case, the Lorenz curve is symmetric).

Theorem 16. Injustice is absolute for an impartial independent opinion if and only if f has an exponential specification.

Remark. Theorems 11 and 12 may be obtained, respectively, from the conjunction of the properties of theorems 13 and 14 and of theorems 15 and 16.

Theorem 17. Non-malevolence and isophily hold if and only if

(1) for the properties of theorem 13, (a) for $\Sigma \alpha_i x_i^\beta$ either $\beta \leq 0$ and $\alpha_i \leq 0$ for all i, or $0 \leq \beta \leq 1$ and $\alpha_i \geq 0$ for all i, and (b) for $\Pi x_i^{\alpha_i}$, $\alpha_i \geq 0$ for all i.

(2) for the properties of theorem 14, $\beta \leq 0$ and $\alpha_i \leq 0$ for all i.

(C) MARGINAL INJUSTICES FOR IMPARTIAL INDEPENDENT OPINIONS

Theorem 18. Properties of theorems 15 and 16 are respectively equivalent to the constancy of relative marginal injustice and of marginal injustice.

Theorem 19. (1) For a benevolent, impartial, independent and isophile opinion, marginal injustice is convex (vs. strictly convex) if injustice is convex (vs. strictly convex out of the locus of equal distributions).

(2) For a benevolent, impartial, independent opinion, injustice is concave (vs. strictly concave out of the locus of equal distributions) if $\dfrac{1}{i}$ is convex (vs. strictly convex).

Theorem 20. Given two benevolent, impartial and independent opinions marked by indexes 1 and 2, and for an interval of variation of incomes,

(1) 1 is uniformly more sensitive to justice than 2 if and only if $i_i \geq i_2$ (or the function $f_2 f_1^{-1}$ is convex) in this interval.

(2) 1 is strictly uniformly more sensitive to justice than 2 if and only if $i_2 > i_1$ with the possible exception of a set of measure zero (or the function $f_2 f_1^{-1}$ is strictly convex) in this interval.

Remark. Some properties of theorem 8 are corollaries of theorem 20 obtained when f_2 is linear and $i_2 = 0$.

(D) AGGREGATIONS OF SOCIETIES, DISTRIBUTIONS AND OPINIONS

(1) *Aggregation of Societies*

Theorem 21. Consider the gathering of several societies into a single one. Populations, social incomes, equal equivalents, justices, injustices, and relative injustices for the constituent societies represented by index k and for the aggregate society are respectively n_k and $n = \Sigma n_k$, X_k and $X = \Sigma X_k$, $\bar{x}_k$ and $\bar{x}$, j_k and j, i_k and i, $\hat{i}_k$ and $\hat{i}$. then, for an independent, impartial, benevolent and rectifiant opinion,

$$\bar{x} \leq \sum \frac{n_k}{n} \bar{x}_k, \; j \leq \sum \frac{X_k}{X} j_k, \; i \geq \sum \frac{n_k}{n} i_k, \; \hat{i} \geq \sum \frac{X_k}{X} \hat{i}_k.$$

If, moreover, rectifiance is strict, the first and third inequalities are strict if and only if all x_k's are not equal and the second and fourth inequalities are strict if and only if all j_k's are not equal.

(2) *Composition of Distributions*

Theorem 22. If intensive justice and satiation hold, then, for distributions x^k,

$$\bar{x}(\Sigma x^k) \geq \Sigma \bar{x}(x^k), \; i(\Sigma x^k) \leq \Sigma i(x^k),$$

$$j(\Sigma x^k) \geq \Sigma \frac{\bar{x}^k}{\Sigma \bar{x}^k} j(x^k), \; \hat{i}(\Sigma x^k) \leq \Sigma \frac{\bar{x}^k}{\Sigma \bar{x}^k} \hat{i}(x^k).$$

If, moreover, satiation is strict, all inequalities are strict if and only if all x^k's are not colinear.

3 *Aggregation of Opinions*

Liminary note. Following Pareto, let us aggregate citizens' opinions represented by ordinal indexes $\xi^h(x)$ into a social opinion represented by the ordinal index $\xi(x)$ thanks to a function F such that $\xi(x) \equiv ([\xi^h])$. The aggregation is said to be benevolent toward h if $F'_h > 0$. It is said to be non-malevolent if $F'_h \geq 0$ for all h.

Theorem 23. (1) If all citizens are isophile and if the aggregation is non-malevolent, society is isophile.

(2) If, moreover, there exists at least one strictly isophile citizen for whom the aggregation is benevolent, society is strictly isophile.

Remark. Hence one can say, roughly, that the properties of moderate egalitarianism are conserved by a benevolent aggregation. It is not so for the usually considered property, namely satiation; for it, the more general conservation theorem is *a priori* rather arbitrary: $\xi(x)$ is quasi-concave if there exists a set of convex specifications of the ordinal indexes $\xi^h(x)$ such that $F([\xi^h])$ be non-decreasing quasi-concave. In brief, moderate egalitarianism possesses altogether two complementary characteristics: people agree more than they think about it, and when they agree it must be a property of social preferences.

ANNEX

SEPARABILITY BETWEEN PUBLIC ALLOCATION AND THE DISTRIBUTION OF DISPOSABLE INCOME

The most realistic of the simplest descriptions of the public economy is to distinguish a function of choosing tax rates and transfers which re-allocate private disposable incomes, on the one hand, and a function of allocating the budget between several public goods, on the other. These two functions are tied in two ways. First, they are interlocked by the budget constraint; there is no risk that this be overlooked by policy-makers since it is represented by the accounting relations. But, second, the ethically right objective variables, of both distribution and allocation, are individuals' welfares which depend on both own private disposable incomes and public goods. The public economic process creates welfare losses if it fails to take these latter links into account.

Now, in all countries, the political and administrative performances of these two functions are widely dissociated. Neither the parliaments, nor the governments, nor the administrations, usually take the structure of the income tax, for instance, into account when choosing between public goods; nor do they ordinarily take the structure of the public good basket content into account when they choose income tax rates. We propose here to question the validity of these habits. Their reason can clearly be attributed to the information, transaction and collective and individual decision costs and impediments which would be incurred by taking everything in consideration all at once '*à la* Wicksell'. But no optimum is to be reached without any idea of how bad or how innocuous these habits are. In so far as they are good, the knowledge of this fact would be of great interest since, then, for instance, parliaments would be right to adopt tax structures without caring for the content of future expenditure budgets, and technical civil servants would be right to use the surplus rules as if distribution were optimal, without caring for the optimality of political processes.

Of course, the separation is always valid for decisions implying only small variations of the variables and around the optimum. Unfortunately this is not the case for many public decisions, and in particular for most of those which are taken at the central politico-administrative levels. Hence, we must find the conditions for validity 'in the large'. We restrict our attention to the welfare link since the budget accounting link (which, at full employment, represents the physical scarcity, but which may take stabilisation aims into account) cannot be overlooked.

Formally, the link by individual welfares will be represented in the usual way by individual ordinal utility indexes depending each on the quantities of individual's private consumption goods which are x_j^i and constitute a vector x^i for each individual i, and depending all on a vector of quantities of public goods, y. Write them $u^i(x^i, y)$. The x^i's are the right variables for the distribution of individuals' disposable incomes if this distribution takes the price situation into account; if prices were supposed to be fixed, x^i would be reduced to a scalar: i's disposable money income. Call: x the set of all the x_j^i's, $S([u^i])$ a social welfare function respecting consumers' sovereignty, $S_i = \dfrac{\delta S}{\delta u^i}$.

The choice between public goods can be performed without regard to the distribution of private disposable incomes when $S([u^i(x^i, y)])$ can be written in the form $U(x, G(y))$ where U and G are functions. Then, obviously, U also 'respects' consumers' sovereignty in the sense that it can be written as $\mathcal{U}([v^i(x^i)], G(y))$ where the v^i's are functions. The conditions required from the u^i's and S in order that this holds are given by theorem 24 below.

The distribution between private disposable incomes can be chosen without regard to the choice of public goods when $S([u^i(x^i, y)])$ can be written in the form $V(F(x), y)$, where V and F are functions. Then, obviously, F also 'respects' consumers' sovereignty in the sense that it can be written $\mathcal{F}([v^i(x^i)])$ where $\mathcal{F}$ and the v^i's are functions. The problem of finding what is implied by this form for S and the u^i's turns out to be unexpectedly difficult. In fact, even in the simplest case of only one private good, one public good and two individuals, it is mathematically a yet unsolved problem of the Theory of Functional Equations. However, we can give a solution in a special case. That is when there exist: (1) a y (call it $\bar{y}$) such that $u^i(x^i, \bar{y})$ does not depend on x^i, for all i's, and (2) a y for each private good j (call it y^j) such that, if u^i depends at all on x^i in the relevant domain, $u^i(x^i, y^j)$ is uniquely inversable for x_j^i, for all i's. This latter assumption is widely acceptable. The former is susceptible of two alternative economic meanings corresponding respectively to an extreme substitutability and an extreme complementarity between private and public goods. The first interpretation is that for sufficiently high abundance of public goods, people would be satiated in private goods.[1]

---

[1] Remark that the domain considered is not bound by physical and budgetary constraints; hence, it is possible to use functions identical to the u^i's in the relevant domain and which have this property for the x^i's of the relevant domain and a great abundance of public goods.

The second interpretation is more satisfactory, although it is far from being thoroughly so: it is that when public goods are provided at an extremely low level, people cannot benefit from private goods (think, for instance, of the public good security). Anyhow, whatever extreme these assumptions may be, the solution they enable to give provides a hint as to what the general solution could be; it is given in theorem 24 below.

Finally, the choices between private disposable incomes on the one hand and between public goods on the other can be made independently from each other when $S([u^i(x_i, y)])$ can be written in the form $W(F(x), G(y))$. Still as noted above, F 'respects' consumers' sovereignty.

The following theorem [1] shows what is required from the u^i's and S in order that these three conditions be fulfilled, or, equivalently, what is implied by the belief that the most usual procedures of the public economy are satisfactory. e, f^i, g, h^i are functions. The symbols o, c, m over a function mean respectively that it is ordinal (i.e. defined up to an increasing function), cardinal, (i.e. defined up to an increasing linear transformation), or multiplicative (i.e. defined up to a multiplication by a positive scalar); when these symbols are written with indexes i over a non-indexed function, this means that these functions for all individuals are transformed from this function, and can be transformed into each other, by the indicated transformation.

Theorem 24

$S([u^i(x^i, y)])$ can be written as,

(i) $U(x, G(y))$ if and only if $\overset{o_i}{\underset{u_i}{}} = \overset{(o_i)}{\underset{e}{}}(y) . v^i(x^i) + f^i(x^i)$

(ii) $V(F(x), y)$ if and only if $\overset{c}{u^i} = \overset{m_i}{g}(y) . \overset{c}{v^i}(x^i) + h^i(y)$,

$$g(\bar{y}) = 0 \text{ and } \overset{c}{S} = \sum \overset{c}{u^i}$$

(iii) $W(F(x), G(y))$ if and only if (ii) holds and moreover $g(y)$ and $\Sigma h^i(y)$ are univoque functions of each other, under the conditions that in all the domain of definition,

for (i): S and u^i are differentiable and $S_i \neq 0$

for (ii) and (iii): there exist $\bar{y}$ and y^j's such that

—S and u^i have continuous partial derivatives and $S_i \neq 0$ for $y \neq \bar{y}$,
—$u^i(x^i, \bar{y})$ are constant,

[1] Still given without demonstration, for lack of space.

—$u^i(x^j, y^j)$ is a uniquely inversable function of x^i_j if u^i depends at all on x^i_j,

(and, hence, obvious corresponding conditions on v, e, f^i, g, h^i for the reciprocal).

These forms are rather restrictive. But one or the other may hold for some public goods (the relation of which with the others must be considered) and hence justify some of the current and/or convenient processes.[1] If not, this calls for an examination of the trade-offs between this welfare loss and the information-decision costs in the budgetary process.

[1] (i) implies that people have the same tastes for public goods; considering localised public goods, residential mobility is a factor which tends to achieve this uniformity.

8 Planners' Preferences: Optimality, Distribution and Social Welfare [1]

A. K. Sen

1 INTRODUCTION

Much of the discussion in the recent years on the operation of public enterprises has concentrated on the goal of achieving 'economic efficiency'. This amounts to the objective of securing Pareto optimality. There is now an extensive literature on the achievement of economic efficiency through decentralised planning. The limitation of this goal is, however, widely recognised. It may be recalled that the Paretian criterion yields only an incomplete ordering, and that the ordering is incomplete not only between any two Pareto optimal points, but possibly between a Pareto optimal point on the one hand and a non-Pareto optimal point on the other. While it is true that every point that is not Pareto optimal is Pareto-wise inferior to *some* Pareto-optimal point (this follows directly from the definition), if two points P and N are arbitrarily chosen, P being Pareto-optimal and N being not so, N need not necessarily be Pareto-wise worse than P. Indeed, when the Paretian incomplete criterion is supplemented by some other criterion consistent with the Pareto rule, it is possible for N to be superior to P. Thus the achievement of Pareto optimality as such guarantees relatively little.[2]

This limitation of the Pareto criterion was, of course, fully appreciated by the pioneers in the field of resource allocation for public enterprises. Indeed both Lange [12] and Lerner [13] showed themselves to be much concerned about the problem of income distribution underlying the operation of public enterprises, and Lerner in particular has extensively discussed the problem of optimal income distribution. Unfortunately, however, the later discussions on the operation of the enterprises have concentrated almost exclusively on the efficiency aspects of the Lange–

---

[1] Thanks are due to Frank Hahn, Stephen Marglin and Ashok Rudra for helpful discussions.

[2] It is on this ground that Graaff [7] (see references on p. 221) recommended the use of what he called 'a just price' for public enterprises, i.e. '*a price which is set with some regard for its effect on the distribution of wealth as well as for its effect on the allocation of resources*' (Graaff [7], p. 155). However, to weave in the distributional judgements into planner's preferences involves sizeable problems, some of which are discussed in this paper.

Lerner economic model. In contrast the focus of this note is on the distributional questions, i.e. on those aspects of the planners' preferences that lie beyond the tests of economic efficiency.

2 SOCIAL WELFARE FUNCTION AND RATIONAL PLANNING

To go beyond the Paretian incomplete ordering has been the main concern of the literature on the social welfare functions. This field is, for obvious reasons, of particular importance for a study of the planners' preferences. However, the discussion has been somewhat obscured by possibilities of confusion between different interpretations of the social welfare function as well as by an inadequate distinction between the *necessary* and *sufficient* conditions for rational planning.

Bergson [3] and Arrow [2] use the expression 'social welfare function' in two very different senses. For Bergson the social welfare function is a real-valued welfare function, W, 'the value of which is understood to depend on all the variables that might be considered as affecting welfare'.[1]

$$W = W(z_1, z_2, \ldots z_n) \tag{1}$$

where the z's stand for the relevant variables, not necessarily economic in character. Given the values of all the z's, the value of W is immediately determined. Armed with this function, the economist's job is simply to choose policies such that W is maximised.

Arrow's use of the expression social welfare function is different. By a social welfare function Arrow means 'a process or rule which, for each set of individual orderings . . . for alternative social states (one ordering for each individual), states a corresponding social ordering of alternative social states'.[2] Unlike the Bergson definition in which a social welfare function is simply a welfare function corresponding to a social ordering, in the case of Arrow it is a *method* of going from individual orderings to a social ordering. The distinction is simple enough but it seems to have been sometimes overlooked.

In his General Possibility Theorem, Arrow demonstrates that no social welfare function exists satisfying a set of four conditions about the method of going from individual preferences to a social ordering.[3] But even when

---

[1] Bergson [4], p. 417.   [2] Arrow [2], p. 23.

[3] The reference here is to the later version of the Theorem, first put forward in French by Arrow [1] in 1952, and then in English in the second edition of Arrow [2], ch. viii. The version of the theorem in the first edition of [2] contained an error from which the second is free.

no social welfare function in general exists in this sense, any individual who has a complete ordering over the alternative social states, which can be represented by a real-valued function, has a social welfare function in the sense of Bergson. To avoid confusion and for brevity, we shall refer to the Bergson social welfare function as *swf*, and the Arrow social welfare function as *SWF*.

Can we say, as Arrow suggests, that the Arrow *SWF* is a method of arriving at a Bergson *swf*?[1] Strictly speaking not. From a Bergson *swf* we can certainly obtain a complete social ordering, but the converse is not true. We may have a complete social ordering but there may not exist any real valued *W* function which can be fitted to it. For example, a complete 'lexicographic ordering' over a two-dimensional real space cannot be represented by any real-valued function.[2] If a *SWF* exists in the sense of Arrow, then we have a complete social ordering based on individual values satisfying some conditions, but this social ordering may or may not correspond to any *swf* in the way defined by Bergson. To summarise we are concerned with three different concepts: (i) a complete social ordering (*cso*), (ii) a real-valued welfare function (*swf*) that corresponds to a complete social ordering, and (iii) a method of going from every set of complete individual orderings to a corresponding complete social ordering (*SWF*). For rational decision making we need no more than a *cso*. The Bergson *swf* is unduly restrictive, and the Arrow *SWF* comes in only as a method of arriving at a *cso*.

In fact, we can go further. Rational decision making does not really require even a *cso*. A *cso* is certainly *sufficient* for being able to choose rationally between any two alternatives, or to choose one (or a set of) alternative(s) among the feasible alternatives. But it is not strictly *necessary*. Essentially what is needed is the existence of a 'choice set'. Let *E* be the set of all the available alternatives ('environment'), and let *R* be the weak social preference relation, i.e. the relation 'socially at least as good as'.[3] Then the definition of the 'choice set' is the following.

The Choice Set: The choice set $C(E)$ is the set of all alternatives x in E such that $(x \, R \, y)$ for every y in E.

If a complete social ordering exists, a choice set certainly exists for that environment. But a *cso* may not exist, and still a choice set may exist.

---

[1] 'In effect, the social welfare function described here is a method of choosing which social welfare function of the Bergson type will be applicable, though, of course, I do not exclude the possibility that the social choice actually arrived at will not be consistent with the particular value judgments formulated by Bergson' (Arrow [2], p. 23).

[2] Debreu [5].

[3] Let *P* stand for the *strict* social preference relation. With the subscript *i*, let R_i and P_i stand for the corresponding weak and strict preference relation of individual *i*.

H

Consider the following simple example. Let x be socially strictly preferred to y, i.e. $(x \, R \, y)$ and *not* $(y \, R \, x)$ and to z, i.e. $(x \, R \, z)$ and *not* $(z \, R \, x)$. However, y and z may not be comparable by the criterion used, i.e. *not* $(y \, R \, z)$, and *not* $(z \, R \, y)$. The ordering is obviously incomplete, and the property of 'connectedness' is violated, but a choice set certainly exists for the three alternatives. Indeed $C[(x, y, z)]$ consists of the single element x.

To conclude, for rational decision making in a given environment the existence of a choice set is sufficient. For this a sufficient but not a necessary condition is the existence of a complete social ordering, and for the latter, in its turn, a sufficient but not a necessary condition is the existence of a Bergson social welfare function.

3 THE GENERAL POSSIBILITY THEOREM AND RESTRICTED PREFERENCES

While the existence of a choice set is sufficient and this does not require the existence of a complete social ordering, it is easy to check that the Paretian incomplete ordering does not, in general, guarantee even the existence of a choice set. There may exist no point such that it is Pareto-wise as good as every other point. The Pareto rule, however, is appealing enough to most of us to be used whenever applicable. In the later version of Arrow's 'General Possibility Theorem',[1] a weaker version of the Pareto rule is used. This says that if all individuals prefer x to y, then the society too prefers x to y. The General Possibility Theorem states that no *SWF* exists that will give us a *cso* for every logically possible set of individual orderings and which will, at the same time, satisfy the weak Pareto Rule, the condition of 'non-dictatorship', and the condition of 'the Independence of Irrelevant Alternatives'. This remarkable result is too well known now to need further discussion here.

Since the Pareto Rule (particularly its weaker version) is highly appealing and so is the condition of non-dictatorship, attempts at escape from the Arrow dilemma have concentrated especially on (a) the condition of the 'Independence of Irrelevant Alternatives', and on (b) the requirement that a complete social ordering exists starting from every logically possible set of individual orderings. Regarding the latter it can be shown that if some 'similarity' exists between the preference pattern of the individuals, then the method of majority decisions will yield a complete social ordering

---

[1] Arrow [1], and Arrow [2], second edition, ch. viii.

satisfying the Pareto Rule and the condition of the Independence of Irrelevant Alternatives. Arrow [2] himself suggested one such condition, viz., 'single-peakedness'.[1] This can be shown to be logically equivalent to the existence of one alternative in every triple that is accepted by everyone to be 'not worst' among the three.[2] This condition can be substantially generalised (Inada [11], Sen [21]). 'Value restricted preferences' require only that in every triple one alternative is generally accepted as either 'not worst', or 'not best', or 'not medium',[3] but the nature of the restriction may vary from triple to triple, i.e. one alternative may be accepted as 'not best' in one triple, and another one as 'not worst' in another, and so on. Value-restricted preference patterns guarantee a *cso* based on majority decisions.[4]

It is certainly too demanding to require that the *SWF* will yield a complete social ordering starting from every logically possible set of individual orderings. Human beings live in societies where there are certain established patterns of values and it is not really very helpful to identify logical possibility with actual likelihood. So the General Possibility Theorem undoubtedly demands too much,[5] and in actual planning we may be quite happy with a *SWF* that is incomplete but does yield a social ordering with the type of individual orderings that are in fact likely.

It is not, however, clear that in the type of distributive situations with which we are concerned the assumption of value-restriction will be in fact satisfied. It will undoubtedly work in many situations, e.g. in one-dimensional left-right voting cases,[6] in situations of overwhelming class conflicts between two classes,[7] in communities where people are extremists

---

[1] Arrow [2], ch. vii. A slightly weaker version is to be found in Inada [11].

[2] Arrow defines single-peakedness of preferences over (x, y, z) in terms of there being an arrangement of (x, y, z), say the one above (with y 'between' x and z), such that for all i, $(x \, R_i \, y)$ implies $(y \, P_i \, z)$. This means that for all i, *Not* $[(x \, R_i \, y), \, Not \, (y \, P_i \, z)]$, i.e. *Not* $[(x \, R_i \, y)$ and $(z \, R_i \, y)]$. Here y is 'not worst' for any individual. The other two cases correspond to x not being worst, and z not being worst.

[3] More formally, y is 'not best' when for all i, *Not* $[(y \, R_i \, z)$ and $(y \, R_i \, x)]$, and 'not medium' when for all i, *Not* $[(x \, R_i \, y)$ and $(y \, R_i \, z)]$, and *Not* $[(z \, R_i \, y)$ and $(y \, R_i \, x)]$. Similarly for x and z.

[4] See Theorem 1 in Sen [21].

[5] An alternative version of the theorem, due to Murakami [17], requires all logically possible orderings being admissible for only one triple. This is a weaker requirement, but the new theorem also requires a strengthening of the Non-dictatorship condition, ruling out not only a general dictator but also a local dictator over such a triple. See also Arrow [2], ch. viii.

[6] This is the standard case of single-peakedness. See Arrow [2], ch. vii.

[7] If all individuals fall into two classes and have opposite preferences, as in a zero-sum game, their preferences will obviously be value restricted. With more than two groups there are problems; see Margolis [15].

around one issue,[1] in societies where a limited amount of leadership is universally accepted to the extent of agreeing with a leader about the relative position of one alternative in any triple.[2] But it is unlikely that we have found in the condition of 'value-restriction' a sure-fire method of getting out of the problem of collective decisions that we actually face in the setting of the preferences for planners.

4 THE INDEPENDENCE OF IRRELEVANT ALTERNATIVES

An alternative method of getting out of the Arrow dilemma is to relax the condition of the 'Independence of Irrelevant Alternatives'. In what follows we shall mostly explore the consequences of this approach. We may first state the condition rigorously:

Condition of the Independence of Irrelevant Alternatives
Let $R_1, R_2, \ldots R_n$ and $R'_1, R'_2 \ldots R'_n$ be two sets of individual orderings and let $C(S)$ and $C'(S)$ be the corresponding choice set functions. If for all pairs of alternatives (x, y) in a set S we have $(x \, R_i \, y)$ if and only if $(x \, R'_i \, y)$, for all i, then $C(S)$ and $C'(S)$ are the same.

This means that if everyone's preference orderings have remained the same for every pair of alternatives in a certain set S, then the choice set $C(S)$ corresponding to that set of alternatives S must remain the same. Note that this rules out two things among others. First, it rules out the influence of the individuals' views on other (irrelevant) alternatives in the social choice between the relevant alternatives. This we shall call the 'irrelevance aspect' of the Condition. Second, it rules out the influence of the intensities of preference between every pair of alternatives of every individual. Not only are the individuals' views on irrelevant alternatives ruled out, so are the individuals' views on anything other than the simple ordering of the *relevant* alternatives. This we may refer to as the 'ordering aspect' of the Condition. It is the last that directly rules out any use of *cardinal* utility indicators.[3]

---

[1] If, the less extreme the position of an alternative around one issue, the less the appeal of it, the preference pattern is single-caved (See Inada [11]), which is a special case of value restriction (Sen [21]).

[2] When individuals belong to classes or groups with symmetrical preference pattern within each class or group, value restriction is more likely to be satisfied than when no such grouping exists.

[3] Note also that if cardinal utility indicators are to be used, Condition 1 will have to be redefined. Instead of defining the social choice as a function of the individual orderings, it will have to be redefined as a function of the individuals' cardinal utility numbers.

It is fair to say that Arrow [2] has himself emphasised mostly the 'irrelevance aspect' of the Condition of the Independence of Irrelevant Alternatives, rather than its 'ordering aspect'. Indeed the name of the Condition also does this, and Arrow's illustrations have been in that line. This is partly quite appropriate, because all cases of experimental determination of utilities get the utility numbers unique only up to a linear transformation separately for each individual, and in this case the 'irrelevance aspect' and the 'ordering aspect' cannot be separated.[1] Such a utility scale is arbitrary until two points on it are fixed. As is usually done with Neumann–Morgenstern utility, this can be fixed, by taking the best alternative for the given individual as 1 and the worst alternative for the given individual as 0. This means that when the relative position of the extreme alternatives change, that affects the entire scale for that individual, and in consequence the measure of utility gaps between the non-extreme alternatives may change also. Thus the placing of 'irrelevant' alternatives affect the measure of preference intensities between the relevant alternatives. The same coincidence of the 'ordering aspect' and the 'irrelevance aspect' takes place with all other methods of making the utility numbers determinate starting from numbers that are measurable only up to a linear transformation. Thus with cardinalisation based on the axioms of von Neumann and Morgenstern [23], or those of Marschak [16], no separation can be made of the 'ordering aspect' and the 'irrelevance aspect' of the Condition. But this is not *generally* true.

An illustration will perhaps clarify the logical difference between the two aspects that Arrow identifies. Suppose each individual has a cardinal scale of utility in interpersonally comparable natural units, and this for everyone is available in a gigantic book placed in a public library. On any week-day we can look up everyone's utility difference between two alternatives x and y, sum them up, and decide whether x is socially preferable to y, or not. We do not have to look at any irrelevant alternatives to fix a scale, for a natural scale exists in this case. Imagine now that after some changes in people's attitudes, a second edition of the book is released, and while the ordering of every alternative by every individual has remained the same, the utility gap between x and y has changed for some individuals. Now the social choice between x and y may be different, and this will indeed violate Arrow's Condition of the Independence of

---

[1] In fact even if utility numbers are unique up to a proportional transformation (i.e. a homogeneous linear transformation), provided no natural correspondence exists between one individual's utility numbers and those of another, the same difficulty is present.

Irrelevant Alternatives.   However, no irrelevant alternative ever entered the picture and the rankings of all such alternatives have remained the same.   What is violated here is strictly the 'ordering aspect' of the Condition.   Furthermore, if the make-belief story were true, it would indeed be very sensible to change the social choice between x and y even though the Condition is violated.   It can be argued, therefore, that this Condition is, in general, unreasonable, and while the 'irrelevance aspect' of the Condition is indeed highly appealing, not so the 'ordering aspect'.

The make-belief story outlined above is, of course, quite unreal.   But its essential feature lies in the existence of some natural scale for each individual's utility.   This unhappily is not provided in a public library as assumed above, and the experimental determinations do not provide a unique natural scale for the individuals.   To be consistent, interpersonal aggregations demand relative uniqueness of these scales, and whatever procedure we select for making it unique for each individual makes the 'ordering aspect' and 'irrelevance aspect' quite inseparable.   On the other hand, the use of cardinal utility need not be based on experimental determination only.   In any case a fairly strong value judgement is involved in regarding, say, the Neumann–Morgenstern utility indicators (or the Goodman–Markowitz indicators) as having ethical significance. A planner has to supplement his experimental information, if any, with other judgements, and depending on the nature of his judgements he may or may not get a unique relative scale for the relevant individuals.[1]

Income redistribution towards greater equality tends to be an important objective in actual planning in many societies.   This is often justified on utilitarian grounds.   Now, this justification is usually based not on experiments of the Neumann–Morgenstern type, or any of the other methods of cardinalisation through experimentation, but usually on a strong personal judgement involving evaluation of the marginal suffering and

---

[1] By a unique *relative* scale we mean that if a certain linear transformation is applied to one individual's numbers, it would have to be correspondingly applied to those of the others.   The utility numbers will not be unique for any individual, but the numbers of different individuals will have a one-to-one correspondence of the type described above. It is easy to check that such a uniform linear transformation preserves all social orderings based on aggregate individual welfare.

If
$$\sum_{i=1}^{m} U_i(x) - \sum_{i=1}^{m} U_i(y) \geq 0,$$

then
$$\sum_{i=1}^{m} U_i'(x) - \sum_{i=1}^{m} U_i'(y) \geq 0, \text{ when } U_i' = a + b \cdot U_i,$$

with a and b as constants.

marginal happiness of individuals at different levels of income. Factual information is, of course, used, but they go beyond the Neumann–Morgenstern experiments into such things as whether an individual 'looks' as if he is much happier or not, how much positive 'signs' of suffering one actually sees on some person, and so on. Bastilles are not usually stormed on the basis of arbitrarily fixed origins and units of experimental utility!

This not to claim that there are not enormous difficulties in the use of cardinal welfare of individuals in social choices. The difficulties are formidable. But the ethical appeal of Arrow's Condition of Independence of Irrelevant Alternatives, which rules out the use of such cardinalisation totally, seems to be derived from an identification of the 'ordering aspect' and the 'irrelevance aspect' of this Condition, which is valid only with a limited class of utility measures.

5 IMPERSONALITY AND THE SOCIAL WELFARE FUNCTION

Once the Condition of the Independence of Irrelevant Alternatives is dropped, it becomes possible to use cardinal utility indicators of the individuals. Perhaps the simplest use of these indicators is in aggregating them to arrive at a *total* social welfare. The following remarkable theorem due to Harsanyi [10] indicates that not only is it simple, it is also highly appealing.

Harsanyi's Aggregation Theorem
If the individual preferences and social preferences all satisfy the Marschak postulates for cardinalisation [16], and if two prospects being indifferent in every individual's preference ordering implies that they are indifferent also in terms of social preference, then social welfare must be a weighted sum of individual cardinal utilities.[1]

For this purpose the postulates of Marschak [16] and those of von Neumann and Morgenstern [23] are equivalent. And these postulates, which are sufficient for cardinalisation of experimental utility, are shown to be sufficient to guarantee that any Bergson *swf* must be a linear aggregate of individual utilities, provided a highly appealing assumption is made about individual and social indifference.

This important theorem can be used in a variety of ways. Harsanyi

[1] The reference is to Postulates I, II, III′ and IV of Marschak [16].

himself links it up with his notion of 'impersonality' as a necessary condition for an individual's 'ethical' preferences:

> ...an individual's preferences satisfy this requirement of impersonality if they indicate what social situation he would choose if he did not know what his personal position would be in the new situation chosen (and in any of its alternatives) but rather had an equal *chance* of obtaining any of the social positions existing in this situation, from the highest down to the lowest.[1]

Harsanyi thus distinguishes between an individual's 'subjective' preferences, and his 'ethical' preferences. The former are his preferences as they actually are, and the latter are those that he would hold if the condition of impersonality is to be satisfied. The latter is 'an expression of what sort of society one would prefer if one had an equal chance of being "put in the place of" any particular member of the society'.[2] Harsanyi defines an individual's social welfare function as that Bergson *swf* which corresponds to his *ethical* preferences. The aggregation theorem interpreted in this light, states that any individual's notion of 'social welfare' must be a linear aggregate of all individuals' utilities.

Harsanyi's notion of 'impersonality' is indeed highly appealing as a basis of making judgements of social welfare.[3] There is, however, the necessity of examining a further problem of aggregation of preferences. How does a planner proceed to take decisions given the Bergson *swf* of each individual? How do we get the *swf* from the ethical preferences of all individuals? Whether or not it makes more sense to aggregate the individuals' social welfare functions rather than their utility functions,[4] the difficulty of aggregation posed by Arrow seems to be present in either case.

Harsanyi does not go much into this question, but his answer to this problem may perhaps be derivable from his statement:

> . . . the more complete our factual information and the more completely individualistic our ethics, the more the different individuals' social welfare functions will converge toward the same objective quantity, namely, the unweighted sum (or rather the unweighted arithmetic mean) of all individual utilities.[5]

---

[1] Harsanyi [10], p. 316.   [2] Harsanyi [9], p. 435.

[3] Cf. Hare [8], Rawls [18], Runciman and Sen [19].

[4] Cf. Marglin's discussion [14] of the 'schizophrenic' argument for deviating from the market rate of saving.

[5] Harsanyi [10], p. 320.

With full information and the full use of the individualistic ethical framework outlined here, if the social welfare function of each individual coincides, there remains no further problem of aggregation of any significance. In an *m*-member community, every person would attach $1/m$ weight to the utility of each individual. It would appear that the value of social welfare thus aggregated impersonally by anyone must coincide with that aggregated by another.

This result is, however, not strictly correct. Much depends on what we mean by complete information. If the reference is to each individual's utility difference between any two alternatives in *unique* units that are interpersonally comparable, then the aggregation procedure will indeed yield the same result. But it might be debatable whether an individual can be assumed to be necessarily maximising the *mathematical expectation* of utility. If, however, the reference is to the Neumann–Morgenstern utility numbers, the mathematical expectation of this will, of course, be the correct thing to maximise, and this corresponds to the reference to the Marschak postulates in the aggregation theorem of Harsanyi. But with these utility indicators, no unique method of aggregation exists. Indeed the following result can be easily proved.

> *Theorem I (non-uniqueness of Impersonal Social Welfare Function):* A social ordering based on a complete knowledge of the Neumann–Morgenstern utility functions of all individuals and obtained with Harsanyi's assumption of impersonality, need not be unique.

The proof is extremely simple, and is unnecessary to give here. The Neumann–Morgenstern utility indicators are unique only up to a linear transformation, and depending on our method of fixing the units of the different individuals' scales we can get different arithmetic means of individual utilities. We provide below a counter-example to the hypothesis that such a *swf* is unique.[1]

For this purpose we choose two methods of the choice of unit, both of which are, in fact, ethically appealing. The first method is the one usually employed, viz., attaching the value 0 to the worst alternative and the value 1 to the best alternative of each individual. The second is to attach the value 0 to the worst alternative and the value 1 to the *sum* of the utility differences between each alternative and the worst one. In possible defence of the second it may be said that the first method attaches too much importance to the placing of two extreme alternatives, while

---

[1] Since the theorem is a negative one, this as it happens also amounts to a proof of it, though not a very efficient one. Our object is to explain the relevance of the result.

H 2

the second takes into account the intermediate alternatives also.

Suppose to the contrary such a social ordering is unique. Consider now a 3-man community with individuals 1 and 2 preferring x to y and that to z, with individual 3 preferring y to x and that to z. Let the Neumann–Morgenstern utility indicators, combined with putting the value of the worst alternative as 0 and the best as 1 yield utility of 1 for x, ·5 for y, and 0 for z for individuals 1 and 2, while it yields utility 1 for y, ·1 for x and 0 for z for individual 3. With 'impersonality' the social welfare from x is ·70, and that from y is ·67. So $(x\,P\,y)$. Consider now a second method of fixing the scale, viz., the sum of the utility difference between each alternative and the worst alternative being equal to 1. With this linear transformation of the original numbers we get utility ·67 from x, ·33 from y, and 0 from z for individuals 1 and 2, and utility ·91 from y, ·09 from x, and 0 from z for individual 3. The social welfare from x with impersonality is ·48, and since we must have, by hypothesis of uniqueness of social ordering, $(x\,P\,y)$, the social welfare from y must be less. But 'impersonality' implies a social welfare of ·52 from y. This is a contradiction, indicating the incorrectness of the contrary supposition.

This means that the rule of 'impersonality' does not yield a unique social ordering even with complete information of the Neumann–Morgenstern utility scale for each individual. In practice, of course, such complete information will not obtain, but even if it did, we do not get an unambiguous social ordering from this. To conclude, Harsanyi's model provides a very appealing background for the Bergson *swf*, but needs some supplementation beyond the information of the Neumann–Morgenstern utility scale for each individual.

While it is seen that it may be too much to expect that every individual's Bergson *swf* will coincide even with complete knowledge and with Harsanyi's model of 'impersonality', the ethical framework outlined there provides an appropriate structure for the formulation of a planner's preferences. A planner has to choose between social alternatives, but the choices are supposed to reflect not his own preferences but that of the society. There are obvious difficulties in aggregating the preferences of the members of the society satisfying a set of conditions of reasonable procedure for aggregations; the set of conditions proposed by Arrow being an obvious example. In practice no planning body in fact refers all (or even a substantial proportion of) the social choices to the entire community on behalf of which it operates.[1] This fact is not regarded as a

---

[1] With long-term investment this is of course unavoidable, since some beneficiaries are yet to be borne. Regarding problems raised by this, see Sen [22], and Marglin [14].

shocking abuse of power, and at most what is expected is that the planner will take into account the preferences of the individuals on whose behalf he plans. This last obligation is best fulfilled by an attempt on the part of the planner to view each social alternative in terms of having an equal chance of being in the shoes of each individual. The obligation, as it were, of the planner is to base his decisions on his 'ethical' preferences (in the sense of Harsanyi) with the characteristic of impersonality, and not on his 'subjective' preferences.

6 LERNER AND PROBABILISTIC EGALITARIANISM

We now turn to one specific aspect of the planner's choice, viz., the pure problem of distribution. The traditional utilitarian argument for equality was based on assuming the same 'capacity for satisfaction' of different individuals. For the purpose of comparison and contrast the assumptions underlying it can be stated.

Assumption 1 (*Income Fixity*): There is a fixed amount of homogeneous income to be distributed among a given number of persons.

Assumption 2 (*Concavity of Identical Utility Functions*): Each individual's utility is a given concave function of his personal income.

Assumption 3 (*Additive Welfare*): Social welfare is the unweighted sum of individual utilities.

With these assumptions, it is easy to prove the classical theorem: *Social welfare is maximised by distributing income equally.*

The difficulties of this approach are well known, and indeed at one stage this theorem provided the main focus of anti-utilitarianism in welfare economics. Later it was in this context that Lerner [13] put forward his celebrated proposition about the 'optimum division of income' as a prelude to the operational rules of public enterprises. Lerner rejected Assumption 2 because of the unacceptability of the condition that all individuals have the *same* utility function. Instead he assumed that we can never discover really how much *exact* satisfaction a given individual has *vis-à-vis* another, and suggested instead that we should concentrate on the value of the mathematical expectation of total satisfaction. And on the basis of this Lerner obtained an argument for equal division that was utilitarian except in the form of being a probabilistic argument. 'If it is impossible, on any division of income, to discover which of any two individuals has a higher marginal utility of income, the probable value of total satisfaction is maximised by dividing income *evenly*.' [1]

This proposition has been the subject of considerable controversy in welfare economics. Samuelson [20] has recently provided an illuminating elaboration of this argument, with a somewhat non-commital evaluation. Friedman [6] had earlier provided a reformulation of the Lerner proposition where the assumption of 'equal ignorance' of people's capacity for satisfaction was replaced by the assumption that 'if individuals were classified by capacity to enjoy income, the probability distribution of income would be the same for all such classes'.[2]

This condition is somewhat opaque. Whether or not we agree with the picturesque view of Samuelson that Friedman's 'rigour has produced a mouse, and not Lerner's mouse', (p. 175), it is certainly difficult to talk of Lerner's problem in terms of probability distributions of income after classifying people by capacity to enjoy income. Lerner's problem arises from the inability of the planner to identify these classes. In that problem incomes of individuals are the policy variables, and their pleasure capacities are given in terms of probability distribution. Samuelson has rightly distinguished between 'the conditional probability distribution of incomes for fixed pleasure capacities' and 'the conditional probability distribution of pleasure capacities for fixed income prospects'.[3]

We present below a reformulation of the Lerner proposition in terms of the conditional probability distributions of pleasure capacities of the individuals.[4] This seems to be a close approximation to the Lerner argument, but even if this is not the case, the theorem seems to be of a certain amount of interest of its own. We retain Assumption 1, and state three other assumptions.

Assumption 2' (Concavity of Utility Functions): All individual utility functions are concave functions of individual income and form a set V.

[1] Lerner [13], p. 29.   [2] Friedman [6], p. 308.   [3] Samuelson [20], p. 176.
[4] Samuelson's own reformulation [20] of the Lerner problem is somewhat akin to Harsanyi's discussion of 'impersonality'. If an individual imagines an equal chance of being put in anyone's shoes, he will prefer an egalitarian distribution. Samuelson does not go into the ethical aspects of this assumption and dismisses it as one which individuals may not in fact make for their *actual* preferences. Note, however, that for Harsanyi's criterion of 'impersonality', an individual has to imagine 'an equal chance of being "put in the place of" any individual member of society, with regard not only to his objective social (and economic) conditions, *but also to his subjective attitudes and tastes*' (Harsanyi [10], p. 316; my italics). Not so in Samuelson's problem, which is how he avoids interpersonal comparisons of utility functions. However, this reduces the ethical relevance of Samuelson's result.

Assumption 4 (*Equi-probability*): The probability distribution of the individual utility functions in V is taken by the planner to be the same for all individuals.

Assumption 3′ (*Additive Probable Welfare*): Probable social welfare is the unweighted sum of the planner's mathematical expectation of individual utilities.

Theorem II (*Probabilistic Egalitarianism*): Given Assumptions 1, 2′, 3′ and 4, probable social welfare is maximised with an equal division of income.

The theorem states that when the probable social welfare is the basis of social ordering, then the result of equal division must be a member of the 'choice set'.

Proof: We use the following notation:

X = aggregate income to be divided;

x_i = income of individual i, $i = 1, 2, \ldots, m$;

U^j = utility function j;

U_i^j = utility of individual i when he has utility function j;

p_i^j = probability of individual i having utility function j;

and $\quad P$ = 'probable social welfare'.

By Assumption 3′, we have the following expression for 'probable welfare':

$$P = \sum_{i=1}^{m} \sum_{j=1}^{n} p_i^j \cdot U^j(x_i) \tag{2}$$

With equal division we have: $x_i = \dfrac{X}{m} = \tilde{x}$ \hfill (3)

Let us define r_i as the difference between individual i's income under any distribution D and his share under equal distribution E. That is:

$$r_i = x_i - \tilde{x} \tag{4}$$

$$\sum_{i=1}^{m} r_i = 0 \tag{5}$$

By Assumption 4, $p_i^j = p^j$, for all i. \hfill (6)

Writing $P(D)$ and $P(E)$ as the value of probable social welfare under distribution D and E respectively, we get from Assumptions 3′ and 4:

$$P(D) - P(E) = \sum_{j=1}^{n} p^j \left\{ \sum_{i=1}^{m} U^j(\tilde{x} + r_i) - m \cdot U^j(\tilde{x}) \right\} \tag{7}$$

From (5) and the concavity of the utility functions, it follows that for each j, the expression within the curly brackets in (7) is non-positive. Hence, from (7):

$$P(D) - P(E) \leqq 0 \tag{8}$$

Since this is true for all D, this completes the proof of the theorem.

7 MAXIMIN POLICY AND EQUAL DISTRIBUTION

There are two difficulties with the theorem of Probabilistic Egalitarianism (Theorem II). First, maximisation of mathematical expectation of utilities (probable social welfare) is not the only possible objective under uncertainty. While other decision rules are not necessarily more appealing, it would be interesting to try out some other ones. In particular, a maximin policy, of maximising the 'security level', is worth examining. Second, Assumption 4 of equi-probability is a very strong assumption. While a planner may be 'ignorant' and uncertain as to who exactly has which utility function, he still may not make the assumption of exactly the same probability distribution of utility functions for everyone. A much weaker assumption is given by Assumption 4'.

> *Assumption* 4' (*Shared Utility Set*): It is not possible for the planner to specify a proper subset S of the set V of utility functions that can be enjoyed only by a proper subset of the individuals.

Note that nothing is assumed about the probability distribution of the utility functions for the different individuals, except that if a utility function can possibly be attributed by the planner to one individual, it can be to another also (though may be with different probabilities).

We have to have a lower bound to aggregate welfare for being able to think in terms of the 'security level'. This is ascertained by assuming that each utility function is bounded from below.

> *Assumption* 5 (*Bounded Utility Functions*): Each utility function in the set V is bounded from below.[1]

An income distribution of the given total is referred to as D. This is an m-vector, and the special vector of equal distribution is referred to as E, where each individual gets $\tilde{x}$. Let C be an m-vector in V with the convention that the i-th element is the utility function assigned to individual i. It thus represents a correspondence between the m individuals and the

---

[1] This assumption is unnecessarily strong, and can be somewhat relaxed.

utility functions in V. $W(C, D)$ represents social welfare from distribution D with utility correspondence C.

> *Theorem III* (*Maximin Egalitarianism*): Given Assumptions 1, 2', 3, 4' and 5, an equal division of income maximises the greatest lower bound of aggregate welfare over all possible utility correspondences, i.e.
> $$\max_{D} \inf_{C} W(C, D) = \inf_{C} W(C, E)$$

Proof. First, suppose that $W(C, E)$ has a minimum for variation in C.[1] In particular: $\min_{C} W(C, E) = W(C^0, E)$. It is obvious that C^0 must be a correspondence where one utility function U^k is attributed to all individuals, where $U^k(\tilde{x}) = \min_{j} U^j(\tilde{x})$. Since U^k is a concave function, for any distribution D where individual i gets $(\tilde{x} + r_i)$ with $\sum_{i=1}^{m} r_i = 0$, we must have:

$$\sum_{k=1}^{m} U(\tilde{x} + r_i) \leq m \cdot U^k(\tilde{x})$$

Hence $\min_{C} W(C, E) = W(C^0, E) \leq W(C^0, D)$ for all D.

This proves the theorem for the special case assumed.

Even if $\min_{C} W(C, E)$ does not exist, $W(C, E)$ must be bounded from below due to Assumption 5. Also, note that for any $W(C^1, E)$ where C^1 represents an assignment of more than one utility function altogether to the group of individuals, there exists an assignment C^2 where only one utility function is attributed to all individuals such that $W(C^2, E) \leq W(C^1, E)$. And since for any such C^2, we have $W(C^2, E) \geq W(C^2, D)$, for all D, the theorem follows immediately.

The theorem will be more interesting if it can be shown to be true even when the same utility function cannot be attributed to all. Two alternative restrictions are considered.

Restriction 1: In any assignment C, no two individuals should have the same utility function.

Restriction 2: In any assignment C, the same utility function is not assigned to every individual.

---

[1] Strictly for proving the theorem we need not, of course, go into this case at all. While the more general case is taken up below, this special case seems worth discussing to make the theorem less opaque.

Restriction 2 is obviously less demanding than 1.

Is Theorem III valid with either of these restrictions? If (WC, E) has a minimum, it will not obviously be with more than one utility function being attributed to the individuals altogether. It does no longer follow immediately that an unequal distribution cannot raise the value of aggregate welfare. We have now more complicated, but more interesting, theorem.

> *Theorem III**: Given Assumptions 1, 2′, 3, 4′ and 5, subject to Restriction 1 or 2, we have:

$$\max_{D} \inf_{C} W(C, D) = \inf_{C} W(C, E)$$

Proof. Let U^j be the utility function assigned to individual i in some assignment C. Consider, now, the two dimensional real space with income of individual i and his utility U_i. Let $U^{j\prime}(\tilde{x})$ be the slope of a line separating the convex region H bordered by the concave function U^j, and the convex region J, where

$$J = \{(U_i, x_i) : U_i \geqq U^j(\tilde{x}), x_i \geqq \tilde{x}\}.$$

If U^j is differentiable at $x_i = \tilde{x}$, then $U^{j\prime}(\tilde{x})$ is simply the derivative of it at that point.

Consider now a C^i, an m-vector in V. Let $C^{i\prime}$ be a m-vector of corresponding $U^{j\prime}(\tilde{x})$. It follows from the concavity of the utility functions that:

$$r . C^{i\prime} \geqq \{C^i(\tilde{x} + r) - C^i(\tilde{x})\} . e, \qquad (9)$$

where r is an m-vector comprising of r_i for each individual as defined in (4) for any distribution of income D, and e is the unit vector.

If $\min_{C} W(C, E)$ exists, let assignment

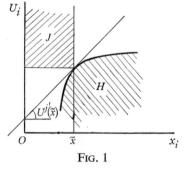

Fig. 1

C^0 yield this minimum.[1] C^0 must, of course, satisfy Restriction 1, or 2, whichever is specified. Let C^0 be the set of all possible assignments of the components of C^0 amongst the individuals. Since $r . e = 0$, there exists

---

[1] See p. 217 n. 1. Once again this analysis of a special case is not strictly necessary for the proof of the theorem, but seems to be helpful to comprehend its content.

C^*, an element of C^0, such that

$$r.C^{*\prime} \leqq 0 \qquad (10)$$

From (9) and (10), a possible utility correspondence exists such that

$$C^*(\tilde{x}+r).e \leqq C^*(\tilde{x}).e \qquad (11)$$

Thus for any distribution D, a utility correspondence C^* exists such that

$$W(C^*, D) \leqq W(C^*, E) = W(C^0, E) \qquad (12)$$

It is thus shown that

$$\min_{C} W(C, E) = W(C^0, E) = \max_{D} \min_{C} W(C, D) \qquad (13)$$

This proves the theorem for the special case when a minimum W exists. Note, however, that even if C^0 is not the minimising utility correspondence but any arbitrarily chosen utility correspondence, (12) still holds. That is for *any* given distribution of income D and *any* utility correspondence C^0, there is a permutation of C^0, viz. C^*, such that the social welfare with distribution D and correspondence C^* is less than or equal to that with distribution E and correspondence C^0. Clearly, therefore, for any distribution D:

$$\inf_{C} W(C, D) \leqq \inf_{C} W(C, E) \qquad (14)$$

This proves the theorem.

Theorems III and III* are valid without the need for making the much-debated equi-probability assumption of Lerner. Further, it is seen that the same policy that maximises the mathematical expectation of social welfare under Lerner's assumptions, also yields a maximin strategy under even weaker assumptions. Since maximin is known to be a conservative policy, it is rather amusing to note that in the pure problem of distribution a conservative should be an egalitarian.

8 CONCLUSIONS

The main conclusions of the paper can now be put together.

1 For rational social choice a Bergson social welfare function is sufficient but unnecessary; a complete social ordering is sufficient and is weaker. In fact, even the existence of a complete social ordering is unnecessary; the existence of a 'choice set' in the given environment is sufficient.

2   The Condition of the Independence of Irrelevant Alternatives has two different aspects, which we have called the 'irrelevance aspect' and the 'ordering aspect'.   The former is highly appealing, but the latter not at all so, and Arrow's Condition rules out violations of the latter even when the former is not violated.   While this makes Arrow's framework less attractive, the two aspects are inseparable with 'experimental' determination of cardinal utility as in the utility system of von Neumann and Morgenstern [23], or of Marschak [16].   The acceptability of the Condition thus depends on our measure of utility.

3   If the Condition of the Independence of Irrelevant Alternatives is dropped, Harsanyi's Aggregation Theorem provides a useful background to deriving a Bergson *swf* from individual preferences.   Harsanyi's requirement of basing such a *swf* on the condition of 'impersonality' is highly appealing.   Unfortunately, however, even with complete knowledge of every individuals' Neumann–Morgenstern utility indicators, the Bergson *swf* derived with the assumption of 'impersonality' need not be unique.   This result (Theorem 1), while easy to prove (given the uniqueness of the Neumann–Morgenstern utility numbers only up to a linear transformation), is important in the context of getting at *the swf* from the different individuals' judgements of social welfare.   The Harsanyi framework is, however, still relevant for a planner's decisions.

4   Lerner's proposition about egalitarianism in a situation of uncertainty regarding the individuals' capacities for satisfaction, can be formulated rigorously in terms of the same probability distribution of utility functions being shared by all individuals (Theorem 2).   The theorem follows simply from the properties of a linear combination of a set of concave functions.

5   Egalitarian distribution is shown to maximise not only the mathematical expectation of social welfare (as claimed by Lerner); it is also a 'maximin' policy (Theorem 3).   This latter result in fact requires *weaker* assumptions than the former; in particular the much-criticised 'equiprobability' assumption of Lerner can be dropped.   Equal division maximises the mathematical expectation of social welfare only with Lerner's equi-probability assumptions, but it is in any case the maximin policy for the planner to follow in a situation of uncertainty.

REFERENCES

[1] K. J. Arrow, 'Le Principe de rationalité dans les décisions collectives', *Économie appliquée*, v (Oct 1952).
[2] K. J. Arrow, *Social Choice and Individual Values* (New York: John Wiley & Sons, 1951; second edition, 1963).
[3] A. Bergson, 'A Reformulation of Certain Aspects of Welfare Economics', *Quarterly Journal of Economics*, LII (Feb 1938).
[4] A. Bergson, 'Socialist Economies', in H. S. Ellis (ed.), *A Survey of Contemporary Economics* (Philadelphia, 1949).
[5] G. Debreu, *Theory of Value* (New York: John Wiley & Sons, 1959).
[6] M. Friedman, *Essays in Positive Economics* (Chicago: The University of Chicago Press, 1953).
[7] J. de V. Graaf, *Theoretical Welfare Economics* (Cambridge: Cambridge University Press, 1957).
[8] R. M. Hare, *The Language of Morals* (Oxford: Clarendon Press, 1953).
[9] J. C. Harsanyi, 'Cardinal Utility in Welfare Economics and in the Theory of Risk-taking', *Journal of Political Economy*, LXI (Oct 1953).
[10] J. C. Harsanyi, 'Cardinal Welfare, Individualistic Ethics, and Interpersonal Comparisons of Utility', *Journal of Political Economy*, LXIII (Aug 1955).
[11] K. Inada, 'A Note on the Simple Majority Decision Rule', *Econometrica*, XXXII (1964).
[12] O. Lange and F. M. Taylor, *On the Economic Theory of Socialism* (Minneapolis: The University of Minnesota Press, 1952).
[13] A. P. Lerner, *Economics of Control* (New York: The Macmillan Co. 1964).
[14] S. A. Marglin, 'The Social Rate of Discount and the Optimum Rate of Investment', *Quarterly Journal of Economics*, LXXVII (Feb 1963).
[15] J. Margolis, 'Metropolitan Finance Problems: Territories, Functions and Growth', in J. M. Buchanan et al., *Public Finances; Needs Sources and Utilization* (Princeton: Princeton University Press, 1961).
[16] J. Marschak, 'Rational Behaviour, Uncertain Prospects, and Measurable Utility', *Econometrica*, XVIII (Apr 1950).
[17] Y. Murakami, 'A Note on the General Possibility Theorem of the Social Welfare Function', *Econometrica*, XXIX (Apr 1961).
[18] J. Rawls, 'Justice as Fairness', *Philosophical Quarterly*, LXVII (1958).
[19] W. G. Runciman and A. K. Sen, 'Games, Justice and the General Will', *Mind*, LXXIV (Oct 1965).
[20] P. A. Samuelson, 'A. P. Lerner at Sixty', *Review of Economic Studies*, XXXI (1964).
[21] A. K. Sen, 'A Possibility Theorem on Majority Decisions', *Econometrica*, XXXIV (Apr 1966).
[22] A. K. Sen, 'On Optimizing the Rate of Saving', *Economic Journal*, LXXI (Sep 1961).
[23] J. von Neumann, and O. Morgenstern, *The Theory of Games and Economic Behaviour* (Princeton: Princeton University Press, 1947).

9 Risk-taking and Resource Allocation

E. Malinvaud

1 INTRODUCTORY

How should public decisions take account of risks and uncertainties that bear on future production and future wants? Such is, if I am not mistaken, the question about which I must open a discussion at this Conference.

My paper will not reach conclusions that would be directly applicable; it aims rather at listing the various problems raised by the question and at proposing an approach to their study. Only such a limited purpose appears to me to be feasible, considering the vagueness of my thoughts and perhaps also the present state of the economic science of our topic. Indeed, the question is particularly complex and stands at the frontier of our knowledge. To give it categorical answers would be premature at this time.

There are three main aspects, which will be considered successively here. First, the presence of uncertainty affects the objective to be assigned to the allocation of resources. Second, rules must be adopted for taking account of random elements in the cost and benefit evaluations that enlighten decisions on public projects. Third, some public intervention in the private economy may aim at improving the efficiency of risk-taking in production and distribution.

This paper will adopt the distinction that has become classical since the fundamental work of F. H. Knight (1921). The results of actions taken by consumers and producers often depend on events that are beyond human control. We shall say that this is a '*risk*' if the relevant events obey probability distributions that are objectively known, usually after a sufficient number of observations. We shall on the other hand speak of '*uncertainty*' if no such objective probability distributions exist. It does not really matter below whether, in the latter case, individuals are willing or not to assign subjective probabilities to the events.

We shall consider here mainly the case of risk. However, part of our discussion will not assume the existence of objective probabilities and will therefore apply to so-called uncertainty. Risk will then be a particular case of uncertainty.

2 CHOICE OF SOCIAL OBJECTIVE

(A) A NEW BUT CLASSICAL APPROACH

As is well known, the theory of resource allocation was built on the principle that the choice among various bundles of final consumptions must be left to the consumers. This principle *a priori* seems to apply whether or not the results of production and the individual preferences depend on unknown events.

However, in an uncertain economy, consumers will really control the choices only if they may reveal their preferences among all the possible 'consumption plans', each plan no longer being a given bundle of goods, but specifying which bundle would be obtained in each of the possible occurrences. To determine such a plan, the consumer must decide on the behaviour he would follow in each of the situations that may happen in the future.

Arrow (1953) and Debreu (1959) have indeed shown that introducing this concept of consumption plan permits a generalisation of the classical theory of welfare economics.[1] A brief account of the theory so generalised will be useful here and serve as a frame of reference in the following parts.

In order to deal with uncertainty, one must obviously start by listing all possible events that are relevant for the case under study; a particular system of outcomes of these events is now called a 'state of the world', or more simply a 'state'. Arrow and Debreu replace the usual concept of good by that of 'contingent good'. If h designates a commodity with given specifications and e a particular state, the contingent good (h, e) will be commodity h under the condition that state e obtains. A contract stipulating the sale of the quantity x_{he} of the contingent good (h, e) implies the delivery of this quantity of commodity h if e obtains, but implies nothing if e does not obtain.

A consumption plan x for a given individual defines the quantities x_{he} that this individual will receive of the various commodities under the various states. We may easily admit that the individual knows how to choose among two consumption plans x^1 and x^2 which would be proposed to him: he takes into account the probabilities he assigns to the various states and the utilities for him of the various commodities. We shall then say that the individual has a system of preferences over the set of consumption plans.[2]

---

[1] The same generalisation was proposed independently by E. Baudier (1954) in a less well-known article that I shall not quote again below.

[2] J. Hirshleifer (1965) has given a particularly clear presentation of this model of consumer choices under uncertainty.

In the same fashion, the outputs that a firm will produce from given quantities of inputs depend on the state that will obtain. The 'production plan' of this firm specifies which net production it will make in each of the states of the world; in other words, such a plan defines a net production y_{he} for every contingent good, i.e. for every couple (h, e). Technical constraints limiting the firm's activity imply that some production plans are feasible while others are not. Thus, we see that the introduction of contingent goods permits us to maintain the same formal representation of a producer as in the certainty case: he will choose a production plan from a set of technically feasible plans.

We may easily understand how the classical theories of equilibrium and welfare economics are transposed. Thus, in a competitive economy, there should exist a market for each contingent good. On the market for good (h, e) would appear already all supplies and demands that will concern commodity h if state e obtains. A price p_{he} would be formed for transactions in the contingent good (h, e) so as to bring about equality between aggregate supply and aggregate demand. This price would be due, immediately and no matter what state will obtain, by the buyer of a claim on a contingent delivery of commodity h. A competitive equilibrium would be characterised by the overall consistency of consumption and production plans of the various agents. We note here that this equilibrium – and in particular the equilibrium prices – is defined with respect to the uncertain situation that the economy experiences and before anyone knows which state will obtain.[1]

By application of the definition due to Pareto, a given system S^0 of plans made by the various agents (one consumption plan for each consumer, one production plan for each firm) is an optimum if it is feasible in all states of the world and if no other feasible System S^1 exists that would be preferred to S^0 by at least one consumer and would not be considered worse by any other consumer.

Under conditions that will not be repeated here, a competitive equilibrium is a Pareto optimum; conversely, any Pareto optimum may be realised as a competitive equilibrium provided an appropriate distribution of initial resources among consumers is enforced.[2]

---

[1] From the prices p_{he} for contingent goods, we may compute various other elements of the value system, notably 'conditional prices' that apply to contracts whose fulfilment is conditional, for both the buyer and seller, on the occurrence of an uncertain event. See in this respect J. Drèze (1965).

[2] We know that, one of the conditions used in the proof of this second result stipulates the convexity of individual preferences, which implies risk-aversion. This condition may, however, be omitted when consumers are infinitely many.

(B) THE RELEVANCE OF THIS APPROACH

According to the theory that has just been outlined,[1] we could then rely on individual tastes and behaviour for the determination of a system of plans that would possess an optimal character. No social attitude towards risk would be required.

It is, however, well known that we cannot stick to this viewpoint. The theory does not prove that the competitive equilibrium provides the 'optimum optimorum', but only one among many Pareto optima. It neglects the existence of social goods and of activities that necessarily belong to public authorities. Taken alone it therefore does not suffice for the theoretical foundation of public management.[2] The existence of risks has even some importance in this respect.

In the first place, the notion of market for contingent goods appears as hardly made concrete in reality. Arrow (1953) finds it in the stock exchange market. A share is indeed a right on a fraction of the future profits of the corporation. These profits being contingent, could be computed from prices for contingent commodities, and therefore also the quotation of the share. Conversely, from the quotations of shares that would be sufficiently numerous and diversified, one could compute competitive prices for contingent goods, at least if the exchange market were perfect.

The facts, however, do not precisely meet the conditions required for the validity of the above ideas. Thus we may hardly imagine how one could choose among various investment projects involving different degrees of risk by using in cost-benefit calculations contingent prices established from the observed quotations of some shares. The present institutions do not permit that the appreciation of risks be left to consumers and transmitted through the market. (I shall come back to this point in the last part of the paper.) In the second place, decisions concerning the risks that society takes often have direct impact on the distribution among consumers, since the eventual losses will often fall on others than those benefiting from eventual profits. Experience shows that compensations, although possible in principle, are seldom made. Since it neglects such consequences on distribution, the market may unduly favour some decisions.[3]

---

[1] I shall not stress here the simplifications made in the Arrow–Debreu model. It assumes in particular that all individuals have identical information. R. Radner (1965) showed how to generalise it in this respect and pointed to new problems that appear when the various agents have not got the same information.

[2] See for instance what R. Musgrave (1959) says of the 'allocation branch'.

[3] F. H. Knight (1921) had already noticed that most measures intended to reduce uncertainty have impact on distribution (see the beginning of ch. xii).

Finally, according to the terminology of R. Musgrave (1959), risk-taking has the aspect of a 'merit-want', since social preferences often seem to depart in this respect from individual preferences. Thus, laws have made insurance compulsory in a number of circumstances, social security for illness and labour accidents being the most notable example. It seems that, on the one hand, men taken individually under-estimate the probability of certain risks to which they are subject, even when an objective evaluation of this probability exists, and that, on the other hand, some people have a dangerous taste for risks, a taste against which society wants to protect them.

For risk-taking as well as for other questions, the classical theory of resource allocation provides a very useful conceptual framework. We shall refer to it again below. But it does not do away with the need for a conscious attitude at the social level. Thus, for a theoretical discussion of public decisions under uncertainty, we must refer to models that explicitly represent the social attitude towards risks.

(C) A MACRO-ECONOMIC APPROACH

We shall do so here using for simplicity a social utility function that will be defined on the aggregate consumption of the contingent goods and be linear with respect to probabilities. Hence we shall not consider the distribution of goods among consumers and we shall accept the axioms allowing for the definition of a linear utility.

From now on, x_{he} will designate the aggregate consumption of commodity h in state e, while q_e will be the probability of this state (commodities and states will be finite in number: $h = 1, 2 \ldots m$; $e = 1, 2 \ldots n$). We shall denote by x_e the vector, with the m components x_{he}, defining the consumption bundle under state e. The symbol x will represent the entire consumption plan as defined by the mn numbers x_{he}.

The utility of consumption plan x will be considered as defined by:

$$\mathcal{U}(x) = \sum_{e=1}^{n} q_e \, U(x_e), \tag{1}$$

U designating a given numerical function with m arguments x_{he} ($h = 1, 2 \ldots m$), called 'utility function'.[1] The number attached to the consumption plan x, also written as $E(U)$, is thus the mathematical expectation of the utility of x_e.

---

[1] This formulation neglects the uncertainties about wants since the utility function does not depend on the state e. At the macro-economic level such uncertainties must have little importance in comparison with those affecting production.

We shall not recall here the limitations to which social utility functions defined directly on aggregate consumption are subject. We also know that the expected utility criterion has given rise to heated debates among economists.[1] Personally I am among those who, without claiming for it an absolute validity, consider it as sufficiently likely, adequate and flexible for providing a useful basis in a serious study of the problems raised by risk-taking. The postulates justifying this criterion do not appear to me as notably restricting the validity of the conclusions we could reach concerning the public management of the economy. They have the advantage of allowing a synthetic view of choices in random situations.

This simplified representation supposes that the social objective consists in the maximation of $\mathcal{U}(x)$ over the set of *a priori* feasible consumption plans. The discussion of social norms then boils down to that of the properties of the function U.

(D) RISK-AVERSION

From our point of view, the most important property is undoubtedly 'risk-aversion'. As was shown by several authors, this is equivalent to the 'concavity' of the function U, i.e. to the classical property of diminishing marginal utility. I shall briefly repeat this here.

Risk-aversion is defined as the preference given to a sure consumption plan $\bar{x}$ over any random plan x such that, for all h, x_{he} has the same expected value in x as in $\bar{x}$. In other words, a random plan x being given, we can associate to it a sure plan in which the consumption $\bar{x}_{he}$ is equal to the quantity:

$$\bar{x}_h = \sum_{e=1}^{n} q_e \, x_{he}, \tag{2}$$

and this whatever the state e. Risk-aversion is expressed by $\mathcal{U}(\bar{x}) \geq \mathcal{U}(x)$, or equivalently by:

$$U\left(\sum_{e=1}^{n} q_e \, x_e\right) \geq \sum_{e=1}^{n} q_e \, U(x_e). \tag{3}$$

Inequality (3) is precisely that defining concavity of the function U (indeed, q_e being the probability of state e, $\Sigma_e q_e$ is equal to 1). Moreover, we know that this property itself implies that the matrix of the second

---

[1] The best reference here is probably to the proceedings of the C.N.R.S. colloquium held in 1952 and to the opposing views expressed notably by M. Allais (1953, a) and P. A. Samuelson (1953).

derivatives U''_{hk} of U with respect to x_{he} and x_{ke} is negative-definite or negative-semi-definite.[1]

In the particular case when all consumption goods would be represented by a single commodity ($m = 1$), U would be a function of a single variable and risk-aversion would be expressed by the fact that its second derivative U'' is negative.

Should collective choices exhibit risk-aversion? Even though I do not know of any discussion on this question that would be perfectly explicit, the affirmative answer is clearly implied by a number of writings. For instance, at the beginning of his last chapter, F. H. Knight (1921) raises as a fundamental question the importance of sacrifices that we must accept in order to *reduce* uncertainties. P. Massé (1959) examines the expected value criterion and concludes: 'We cannot, without running into serious misfortune, replace purely a sum of eventual elements by its expected value. To go without imprudence from uncertainty to certainty, we must take margins with respect to expected values (see p. 207). O. Eckstein (1961) starts from the principle that 'it would be folly' not to prefer, in public decisions, relatively sure operations to those that are more risky (cf. p. 81). His following text shows that this statement must be understood as implying risk-aversion.

3 RISK IN THE ECONOMIC CALCULATIONS OF THE PUBLIC[2]

(A) THE CURRENT DOCTRINE

Supposing then that the social ethic implies some risk-aversion, we must study how this affects the management of public firms. How should risk be taken into account in the economic calculations that precede and lead to decisions concerning the realisation of a project or the choice among competing projects?

We know the present doctrine: risk constitutes an extra cost that must be taken into account in one way or another, either by the evaluation of a special item deducted from the net expected profit of each period, or by the application of a systematic increase in the expenses according to some

---

[1] One easily proves this, for any concave function f of the vector x, by developing to the second order in the neighbourhood of x both members of the following inequality $f(x + t\,du) \geq t f(x + du) + (1 - t)f(x)$, du being any infinitely small vector and t a number between 0 and 1.

[2] J. Hirschleifer (1965) recently discussed the questions we are going to deal with. I shall not undertake here to compare his analysis and results with mine.

'safety coefficient', or still again by an increase of the interest rate used for the computation of present values.[1]

According to this doctrine it is, of course, not enough to take account of the unfortunate events that may occur; one must assign to them a weight greater than their probability. In other words, we should first compute the mathematical expectations of expenses and receipts, then introduce an additional cost by one of the means mentioned above.

At first sight this doctrine seems to follow from risk-aversion. But it looks to me to be less solidly justified than one would believe. I am going to try to show the difficulties it raises by considering a very simple-minded model.

It is indeed true that we may associate a 'risk premium' to any consumption plan, and that this premium is positive in case of risk-aversion. If, as we usually admit, the function U is continuous and increasing, there exists, in view of inequality (3), a number α smaller than 1 such that:

$$U\left(\alpha \sum_{e=1}^{n} q_e x_e\right) = \sum_{e=1}^{n} q_e U(x_e). \tag{4}$$

(This assumes that no component of the vector $\bar{x}$ defined by (2) is negative, or else α should be taken as a multiplier of only the positive components of $\bar{x}$; it also implies the mildly restrictive assumption that the random plan x is preferred to the sure plan in which $x_{he} = 0$ for all h and e.) The random plan is thus equivalent to the sure plan obtained after application of a proportional deduction of $1 - \alpha$ from the expected values of the consumption of the various commodities. The value of the vector $(1 - \alpha)\bar{x}$ is the risk premium.[2]

This positive premium bears, however, on the consumption plan itself. The current doctrine attributes to it a wider application and claims that, in the choice among various productive processes, we must penalise those that are risky. The risk premium should then be introduced in decentralised economic calculations in the same way as the interest rate is introduced. The analogy is suggestive, but might be misleading. The computation of present values according to a unique interest rate applied uniformly to all decentralised calculations draws its justification from the theory of welfare economics, and this thanks to an argument that will not be repeated

---

[1] See P. Massé (1959) in the text quoted on the preceding page and still more precisely on pages 364–7. See also O. Eckstein (1961) p. 82–3.

[2] Other definitions for the risk premium are of course possible, for instance that given by J. W. Pratt (1964).

here. No such justification exists for the introduction of a system of risk premiums. The generalisation of the optimum theory to an uncertain economy along the lines presented above has no direct implication concerning such premiums. In other words, the risk premium defined on the consumption plan is not reflected in a simple way on the cost-benefit evaluation of productive operations.

(B) OPTIMAL ALLOCATION IN A SIMPLE MODEL

In order to study this question more closely, let us consider a very simple model containing only two consumable commodities made from a single primary resource available in a fixed quantity ω (this resource will be called 'labour'). Let us suppose that productivity is uncertain in the production of the first commodity but not in the production of the second. Let z be the quantity of labour used for the first commodity, $\omega - z$ that used for the second. The outputs x_{1e} and x_2 of the two commodities are produced by two firms according to the following production functions:

$$x_{1e} = f_e(z) \qquad x_2 = g(\omega - z). \tag{5}$$

(It is clear from the formulation that the allocation of labour among the two firms must be decided before the state e is known.)

In this model the first order condition for a maximum of $\mathcal{U}$ is easily established and determines the optimal value for z. In view of equation (5), this condition may be written as:

$$\sum_e q_e f'_e \, U'_{1e} - \sum_e q_e \, g' \, U'_{2e} = 0, \tag{6}$$

where f'_e and g' are the derivatives of f_e and g while the first derivatives U'_{1e} and U'_{2e} of U with respect to x_{1e} and x_2 may be considered as functions of z through equalities (5). Equation (6) may also be written:

$$E(f' \, U'_1) - g' \, E(U'_2) = 0. \tag{7}$$

We easily check that (6) or (7) is not only necessary but also sufficient if U exhibits risk-aversion and if the marginal productivities f'_e and g' are decreasing, as we shall assume.

Before discussing the rules of economic calculation that are appropriate for the management of the two firms, we shall inquire whether risk-aversion implies that the labour allocated to the first firm be smaller as the uncertainty on production of the first commodity is larger. We might think so *a priori* since an increase in the risk affecting labour productivity in the first firm seems to make production in the second firm relatively more favourable. This conclusion does not, however, immediately follow from equations (6) or (7).

For the study of this question, let us suppose that $f_e(z)$ depends on e only through a multiplicative factor and write:

$$f_e(z) = (1 + a_e)f(z), \tag{8}$$

with numbers a_e such that:

$$E(a) = \sum_e q_e \, a_e = 0. \tag{9}$$

Let us define:

$$\sigma^2 = E(a^2) = \sum_e q_e \, a_e^2, \tag{10}$$

and suppose that σ^2 is small relative to 1. We must inquire whether the optimal allocation leads to a value of z that is necessarily a decreasing function of σ^2 when there is risk-aversion.

Let $\bar{z}$ be the solution of equation (6) in the case when all a_e are zero ($\sigma^2 = 0$), and let $\bar{x}_1$ be the value of $f(\bar{z})$. Analytic transformations that are too laborious to be repeated here allow equation (6) to be written as follows, to the first order in $(z - \bar{z})$ and σ^2:

$$\{(U_{11}'' f'^2 - 2U_{12}'' f'g' + U_{22}'' g'^2) + (U_1' f'' + U_2' g'')\}(z - \bar{z}) =$$
$$\frac{-\sigma^2}{2}\{2\bar{x}_1 \, U_{11}'' f' + \bar{x}_1^2(U_{111}''' f' - U_{211}''' g')\}, \tag{11}$$

the derivatives being all valued for $z = \bar{z}$, $x_{1e} = \bar{x}_1$ and $x_2 = g(\omega - \bar{z})$.

The curly bracket multiplying $(z - \bar{z})$ is negative as a consequence of risk-aversion (first parenthesis) and of the property of diminishing marginal productivity for functions f and g (second parenthesis). The optimal value for z then decreases with σ^2 if

$$2U_{11}'' f' + \bar{x}_1(U_{111}''' f' - U_{211}''' g') \tag{12}$$

is negative. Note that $f' U_1' - g' U_2' = 0$, since this is precisely equation (6) in the certainty case; expression (12) has therefore the same sign as the following one:

$$2U_{11}'' \, U_2' + \bar{x}_1 \, (U_{111}''' \, U_2' - U_{211}''' \, U_1'). \tag{13}$$

The first term in this sum is negative, but the second has not a definite sign, and the whole expression may very well be positive. Here is an example where it is so.

Let us suppose the utility function is:

$$U = (x_1 - u_1)^\alpha \, (x_2 - u_2)^\beta, \tag{14}$$

u_1, u_2, α and β being given numbers; α and β are positive, their sum is smaller than 1 if there is risk-aversion. Expression (13) then has the form:

$$\frac{\alpha\,\beta(1-\alpha)U}{y_1^3\,y_2^2}\{(2-\alpha)u_1\,y_2 + \alpha u_1\,y_1 + \alpha y_1^2 - \alpha y_1\,y_2\}, \tag{15}$$

y_1 and y_2 designating $x_1 - u_1$ and $x_2 - u_2$ respectively, and all variables being valued at the certainty optimum ($\sigma^2 = 0$). In expression (15) the multiplier is positive and the term between curly brackets is also positive when u_1 is positive and the optimal value of x_1 is sufficiently close to u_1.

Such an example corresponds to the case in which the two commodities are not easily substitutable for one another and in which the first commodity would be a necessity. When the risk affecting the production of the latter increases, a greater quantity of labour must be allocated to it so that the probability of the occurrence of a serious shortage of this commodity is kept low.[1]

Let us note that, if both firms produce the same commodity and risk-aversion holds, then labour is necessarily displaced from the first firm to the second when uncertainty increases. Indeed, in such a case, the utility function has the form $U(x_{1e} + x_2)$ so that $U_1' = U_z'$ and $U_{111}''' = U_{211}'''$; expression (13) is then always negative.

To sum up, the introduction of risk has the result that uncertain

---

[1] This result is substantiated by the one obtained by J. A. Mirrlees (1965) who studied how uncertainty on technical progress modifies the optimal growth path in a macroeconomic model. He found that this uncertainty stimulates capital accumulation at the expense of immediate consumption.

Within our model we may also find simpler examples than that of the utility examples within which the labour allocated to the random process increases with the degree of uncertainty. J. Sandee proposed the following one at the meeting.

Let $f(z) = z + a$ and $g(\omega - z) = \omega - z$, a being a random variable with a rectangular distribution on the interval $[-b, b]$. Let:

$$U = \begin{cases} \beta x_1 + x_2 & \text{if} \quad x_1 \leq \dfrac{\omega}{2} \\ \beta\omega/2 + x_2 & \text{if} \quad x_1 > \dfrac{\omega}{2} \end{cases}$$

β being a number greater than 1. We could prove that the optimal allocation is given by:

$$z = \frac{\omega}{2} + b\left(1 - \frac{2}{\beta}\right)$$

It increases with b, and hence with the uncertainty affecting production of x_1, if β is greater than 2. This again corresponds to a case where commodity 1 would be a necessity since its marginal utility would be high relatively to that of commodity 2 as long as the saturation level $\omega/2$ would not be reached.

operations must be reduced in favour of sure operations if both produce the same commodities, but not necessarily if they have different outputs.

(C) PRICES AND RISK PREMIUM IN A SIMPLE MODEL

Let us examine now which rules could hold for economic calculations in our particular model.

We shall first consider the price vector resulting from the Arrow–Debreu theory. This vector has, in our case, 3 n components (2 consumption commodities plus labour and n states, therefore 3 n contingent goods). Let p_{1e}, p_{2e} and s_e be the components of this vector respectively for the three commodities under state e. Optimum theory asserts that such prices can be validly used for economic calculations. The optimum would be sustained if each firm would maximise the net value of its production and if a planner would choose the consumption plan so as to maximise the social utility $\mathcal{U}$ under an appropriate budget constraint.

Marginal equalities following from these rules would be:

$$\sum_e p_{1e} f'_e = \sum_e s_e,$$
(16)

$$\sum_e p_{2e} g' = \sum_e s_e,$$
(17)

$$\frac{q_e U'_{1e}}{p_{1e}} = \frac{q_e U'_{2e}}{p_{2e}} = \frac{q_\epsilon U'_{1\epsilon}}{p_{1\epsilon}},$$
(18)

from any e and ϵ from 1 to n. Equalities (16) and (17) imply $\sum p_{1e} f'_e - \sum p_{2e} g' = 0$, and equalities (18) then imply fulfilment of condition (6) for an optimum.

Prices p_{1e}, p_{2e} and s_e refer to contracts stipulating that the delivery of the commodity or the furnishing of the labour will be due only if state e obtains. Since the labour allocation comes in fact before the true state can be known, labour contracts are necessarily unconditional; they involve a wage rate s defined from s_e by:

$$s = \sum_{e=1}^{n} s_e,$$
(19)

since the labour is to be furnished in any of the n possible states. Similarly the prices holding for unconditional delivery are:

$$p_1 = \sum_e p_{1e} \qquad p_2 = \sum_e p_{2e}.$$
(20)

Which rules should the firms apply if there exist no prices for contingent goods but only the prices for sure commodities, p_1, p_2 and s? The answer is easy for the second firm since maximisation of the net value of its sure production implies.

$$p_2 \, g' = s, \tag{21}$$

which is precisely equality (17). The classical rule therefore applies to the firm whose production is not subject to any uncertainty.

According to the current doctrine, the first firm should maximise a function of the following form:

$$p_1 \, E(x_1) - sz - R(z), \tag{22}$$

$E(x_1)$ representing the quanity $\sum_e q_e \, x_{1e}$ and $R(z)$ the risk premium.

According to the Arrow–Debreu theory, it should maximise:

$$\sum_e p_{1e} \, x_{1e} - sz. \tag{23}$$

Expressions (22) and (23) coincide, and therefore the current doctrine can be made consistent with sustainment of the optimum, provided the risk premium is:

$$R(z) = \sum_e (p_1 \, q_e - p_{1e}) x_{1e}. \tag{24}$$

For a study of this condition, let us consider the case in which the production function assumes form (8); $R(z)$ then can be written:

$$R(z) = \sum_e (p_1 \, q_e - p_{1e}) \, (1 + a_e) f(z),$$

or, in view of equations (9), (20) and $\sum_e q_e = 1$:

$$R(z) = - \sum_e p_{1e} \, a_e . f(z) \tag{25}$$

This risk premium is necessarily positive, since $\sum_e p_{1e} \, a_e$ is negative when the a_e are not all zero.[1]

---

[1] Indeed, condition (18) on the p_{1e} implies:

$$\frac{p_{1\epsilon}}{q_\epsilon} \bigg/ \frac{p_{1e}}{q_e} = \frac{U_1'[(1 + a_\epsilon)f(z), \, g(\omega - z)]}{U_1'[(1 + a_e)f(z), \, g(\omega - z)]}.$$

Since U_1' is a decreasing function of x_{1e}, $a_e > a_\epsilon$ implies that the right hand side of this equality is greater than 1; hence

$$\frac{p_{1e}}{q_e} < \frac{p_{1\epsilon}}{q_\epsilon}.$$

Consider now two values a_e and a_ϵ such that $a_e > 0$ and $a_\epsilon < 0$. The preceding result implies:

$$a_e p_{1e} < a_e q_e . \frac{a_\epsilon p_{1\epsilon}}{a_\epsilon q_\epsilon}.$$

Thus, at least in our model, the risk premium would indeed be always positive, although the occurrence of uncertainties might lead to an increase in the quantity of labour allocated to the firm that experiences them.[1]

We must, however, point to the difficulties raised by the application of the rule when no market exists for contingent goods. How could an equilibrium price p_1 for unconditional delivery be formed when the supply of commodity 1 is subject to uncertainties? How could the firm have a proper idea of the importance of the risk premium to impute to its production? These questions obviously remain unanswered; the relevance of the current doctrine is therefore notably weakened.[2]

(D) SIZE OF THE RISK PREMIUM FOR THE DECISIONS OF PUBLIC FIRMS

Using an approach similar in principle to the one presented above, K. Arrow (1965) has, however, claimed that, for most public investments, economic decisions should aim at maximising the expected net value of production without any deduction for risk premium. In other words, the appropriate premium, our $R(z)$, would be negligible.

Let P^+ and 0^+ be the sums of the $a_e p_{1e}$ and the $a_e q_e$ over all states e such that $a_e > 0$. We may write:

$$P^+ < Q^+ \frac{a_\epsilon p_{1\epsilon}}{a_\epsilon q_\epsilon}$$

or equivalently $a_\epsilon q_\epsilon . P^+ > a_\epsilon p_{1\epsilon} Q^+$; hence $Q^- P^+ > P^- Q^+$, P^- and Q^- designating the sums of the $a_\epsilon p_{1\epsilon}$ and the $a_\epsilon q_\epsilon$ over all states ϵ such that $a_\epsilon < 0$. The inequality we just arrived at implies the result we wanted to prove, namely $P^+ + P^- < 0$; indeed, suppose $P^+ + P^- \geq 0$ and therefore $Q^+ P^+ + Q^+ P^- \geq 0$; the inequality arrived at would imply $Q^+ P^+ + Q^- P^+ > 0$, which is incompatible with equation (9), namely $Q^+ + Q^- = 0$.

[1] This circumstance is not paradoxical, but results from the fact that the appearance of uncertainties induces a rise on the price p_1 for unconditional delivery of commodity 1. To see this, let p_1 be the value corresponding to certainty $(z = \bar{z})$ and keep the wage rate s constant, which is permissible prices being arbitrary up to a multiplicative constant. Then:

$$\left\{ \sum_e p_{1e}(1 + a_e) \right\} f'(\hat{z}) = \bar{p}_1 f'(\bar{z}) = s,$$

$\hat{z}$ being the optimal value of z under uncertainty. Since $\sum_e p_{1e} a_e < 0$, then $p_1 f'(\hat{z}) > p_1 f'(\bar{z})$ If $\hat{z} > \bar{z}$, then $f'(\hat{z}) < f'(\bar{z})$, and therefore $p_1 > \bar{p}_1$.

[2] We may wonder in particular whether the current practice is well represented by the sequence of operations we assumed above: (i) determination of the unconditional equilibrium price p_1, (ii) determination of the risk premium $R(z)$, (iii) maximisation of the net value of production, i.e. expression (22). For the determination of p_1, uncertainties have a good chance to be neglected, so that the price used might very well be more comparable to our $\bar{p}_1$ than to the true equilibrium price. This would, in most cases, induce a too small allocation of labour to uncertain operations. Could this not be the reason why results of economic calculations for projects involving large risks have sometimes appeared to be in contradiction with common sense?

I

His point follows from the idea that random elements concerning most of public projects are not significantly correlated with random elements affecting the overall national product. (With reference to our model, we could say that the first random elements are similar to our a_e, while the second ones affect the utility U of the consumption programme; the adequate premium $R(z)$ is indeed null if there is no correlation between the a_e and the marginal utilities U'_{1e}, i.e. if $\Sigma a_e p_{1e}$ is null.)

Arrow thinks that most projects are subject to specific risks that have a negligible impact on global production. The current doctrine, which recommends that substantial premiums be taken into account, is unduly influenced by behavioural rules applying to private firms and giving, of course, a high weight to specific risks.[1]

Arrow goes even farther and observes that some public projects, such as those concerning flood control, have the effect of reducing the uncertainties on national production and should therefore be imputed an additional benefit, i.e. a negative premium.

These remarks, about which I shall, however, make a reservation in Section 4 (c) below, suggest the conclusion that the current doctrine probably over-estimates the importance of risk premiums, which are really justified only when very large investments are considered and when the prices used in the evaluation of costs and benefits accurately correspond to equilibrium prices.

(E) RISK PREMIUMS AND DISCOUNTING

At the beginning of his chapter iv, O. Eckstein (1961) discusses the relative merits of the three main methods for taking account of uncertainty in economic calculations. The first one consists in the choice of a horizon that is shorter than the useful life of the equipment included in the project, while the second one is an increase in the discount rate. Eckstein easily shows that the first method can lead to unwise decisions and that it is certainly inferior to the second one.[2]

The third method consists in the application of a security margin that is added to expected costs or subtracted from expected benefits. Eckstein considers, and rightly so it seems, that the choice between the second and third methods must depend on whether uncertainties are related or not to the passing of time. A security margin applied to the expected cost of an

---

[1] In this respect see also the discussion between J. Hirshleifer, W. Vickrey and P. A. Samuelson in the *American Economic Review*, May 1964, pp. 84, 89–90 and 95–6.

[2] The discussion bears a strong analogy to the more classical one dealing with 'break-even time' for investments involving no uncertainty (see, for instance, P. Massé (1959) pp. 33–6).

investment could be justified if its construction involves large risks. Most often, however, an increase of the discount rate would be more appropriate, given the nature of the risks commonly encountered.

In order to judge the validity of this method, we should be precise as to how the discount rate, to which an increase is applied, is first determined. It may be by reference to the capital market or after an econometric study of production functions ruling the growth of the economy. In both cases, the model considered above may help our discussion. We may indeed consider that commodity 2 represents the final goods whose production is immediate, and commodity 1 those whose production involves long time-spans between inputs and outputs. The discount factor for riskless loans is then represented by the ratio p_1/p_2; the 'pure discount rate' is the smaller as this ratio is larger.

To determine the pure rate from the capital market is not easy. This market is rather narrow; the cost for the borrower often does not exactly match the return for the lender. On another occasion I, moreover, argued that, when there exist no market for future commodities, the capital market would hardly bring about consistency among the decisions bearing on the future (see E. Malinvaud (1965)).

Dealing here with uncertainty, we must note that the equilibrium actually reached differs from the one that would be observed if there existed a perfect market for contingent goods. Indeed, the former is affected by the risk on private business, risks that disappear to a large extent for the society as a whole, and also by the behaviour of private firms, notably by their risk-aversion. If a bold transposition is allowed, our model suggests that private risks and risk-aversion from the firms must induce an equilibrium value of p_1/p_2 that is too high, hence a value for the pure discount rate that is too low, relatively to the physical equilibrium actually reached. The marginal rate of substitution between present and future consumption would then correspond to a discount rate that would be greater than the one observed on the capital market. The choice of a higher discount rate in public economic calculations dealing with projects involving risks would then be justified on two accounts: because of the inadequacy of the observed pure rate and because of the risk premium.[1]

One favours today estimation of the discount rate from a production

---

[1] I must make it clear that, at this point, we aim at determining a price system that would be appropriate for the physical equilibrium actually realised, but not at changing this equilibrium so as to make it more satisfactory from the viewpoint of a social criterion (see what S. Marglin said in this respect during the discussion).

function, all the more so as the reference to the capital market appears obscure and doubtful. In principle such a function can be fitted to aggregate time series, so that actual prices matter only in so far as they determine weights for the construction of series in constant prices. The fitted function then defines marginal productivities, i.e. dual prices and interest rates that ought to be adopted for the economic calculations.[1]

This way of proceeding, however, ignores uncertainty, or more precisely it deals directly with average values. Dual prices so determined correspond to our $\bar{p}_1$ and $\bar{p}_2$, not to p_1 and p_2. Since we must expect $\bar{p}_1/\bar{p}_2$ to be smaller than p_1/p_2, the discount rate so determined must exceed the true pure rate of the uncertain economy for which the computation was made.

The preceding remarks do not claim to provide a satisfactory treatment of the difficulties. They rather aim at stating questions that may have been too little considered up to now.

4 PUBLIC POLICIES FOR BETTER RISK-TAKING IN THE PRIVATE ECONOMY

(A) DISTRIBUTION OF RISKS AMONG CONSUMERS

Lacking markets for contingent goods, our institutions guarantee efficiency in risk-taking neither for production nor for distribution. The State must seek to improve economic organisation in this respect.

In the abstract Arrow–Debreu world, markets for contingent goods perform two functions. On the one hand, they result in an efficient distribution of risks among consumers; the most cautious individuals may contract with those liking gambles so as to transfer to them the hazards to which they are naturally subject; consumers may mutually insure themselves against individual risks. On the other hand, the existence of prices for all contingent goods eliminates randomness in the returns from productive operations; any firm can indeed make contracts involving contingent goods and immediately get the sure net value $\sum_{e,h} p_{he} y_{he}$ of a programme that will result in the production of the net quantity y_{he} of commodity h if state e obtains. After some comments on the first function performed by the Arrow–Debreu markets, the following discussion will concentrate on the second function.

---

[1] We know that estimation is not always performed according to such a simple method. Marginal productivities are often estimated directly from the actual factor shares, the reference to time series being necessary only for an evaluation of the rate of technical progress. The following comments of course do not apply in these latter cases.

F. H. Knight (1921) had already pointed out the role of insurance in the distribution of risks. Not long ago, M. Allais (1953. b) made the most thorough study of optimality for this distribution, using, however, a somewhat special model.

The advantageous aspects of a diversified insurance system are seldom challenged. If a dispute may arise it is rather on the advisability of lotteries thanks to which individuals may take chances that are not naturally offered to them (a small probability of a large gain as against a high probability of a small loss). Public morality often disapproves of lotteries, either because it considers that taking such chances conflicts with the psychological health of the individuals and of society as a whole, or, perhaps still more, because it assumes that most citizens are insufficiently trained in probability and do not clearly understand the terms of the contract that a lottery ticket represents.

Whatever the position taken on the above point, a complete system of insurance, and perhaps also of lotteries, is appropriate for dealing with individual risks. But it will leave unfilled an important role that would be played by a system of markets for contingent goods: consumers will not be able to express on the market their preferences concerning the industrial risks that the community may consider taking. K. Arrow (1953) thought that the stock exchange would answer this need: anyone buying a share would reveal himself as ready to accept the industrial risks assumed by the issuing corporation. We may, nevertheless, wonder whether the public is sufficiently well informed to reveal valuable choices in this fashion. Only a few large operators have a clear understanding of the choices involved; can we agree that they represent the consumers better than would, for instance, the political power?

(B) TOWARDS MORE UNIFORMITY IN THE FIRMS' ATTITUDES
ABOUT UNCERTAINTY

In the production sphere, the lack of markets for contingent goods has the effect that firms must adopt a conscious attitude towards risks. It seems that, in this respect, public intervention should assign itself three purposes: (i) to eliminate, as fully as it is feasible, the individual risks, which affect the management of a firm but do not exist for the community as a whole, (ii) to reduce the discrepancies among the evaluations made of the same risk by various firms, (iii) to make sure that the prevailing private attitude agrees well enough with the social attitude.

We may call 'financial risks' those that affect a firm without being real for the community. Indeed they result essentially from the temporary insolvency that a firm, whose management is sound in the long run, could experience. To eliminate such risks should be one of the roles of the financial system. I shall refrain from saying more about it here, being afraid to go too far afield and to show my incompetence.

We easily understand that discrepancies among the firms' evaluations of uncertainties may result in social losses. Indeed a similar phenomenon is well known, namely that following from discrepancies between the firms marginal productivities in the use of a given factor. A simple example will show the analogy.

Let us suppose there are two states, two identical firms producing the same commodity and applying the same technology, and finally a primary resource (labour) available in a fixed quantity ω. Let z and $\omega - z$ be the quantities of labour used by the two firms. In a co-ordinate system $z\,0\,x_1$ let us represent by the curves Γ_{11} and Γ_{12} the variations of the first firm's production, respectively when state 1 and state 2 obtain. In the co-ordinate system $z\,\omega\,x_2$, similar curves Γ_{21} and Γ_{22} for the second firm are symmetrical to the two preceding ones about the line perpendicular to $0\,\omega$ in its middle point z in Fig. 1.

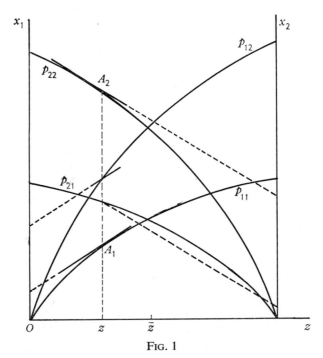

FIG. 1

Let us, moreover, suppose that the first firm acts considering only the unfavourable state 1, either because it considers it as the more likely or because it has a strong risk-aversion. On the other hand, the second firm acts considering only the favourable state 2. (If the discrepancy between the firms' behaviour follows from their assigning different probabilities to state 1, then we have a case of uncertainty rather than risk.)

Equilibrium implies that the marginal productivity of labour takes the same value in firm 1 under state 1 as in firm 2 under state 2; therefore, on the vertical line through z the slopes in A_1 to Γ_{11} and in A_2 to Γ_{22} must be equal in absolute value, but have opposite signs. If the curves are concave downwards, this requirement uniquely determines the equilibrium labour quantity $\hat{z}$. We immediately see that this quantity differs from the optimal one $\bar{z} = \dfrac{\omega}{2}$ and that aggregate production is smaller with $\hat{z}$ than with $\bar{z}$ whether state 1 or state 2 obtains.

Reaching a higher degree of uniformity in the firms' behaviour with respect to uncertain events seems to require two kinds of actions, thanks to which a better agreement between private and social attitudes could also be promoted.

On the one hand, the State should seek to gather and to transmit to the firms the information concerning the various chance events that may affect production and its growth, so that firms accept similar, and preferably correct, estimates of the probabilities of these events. This aim of course belongs to planning, but it seems to be insufficiently achieved now whether or not the country presents itself as planned.

On the other hand, education must give some importance to decisions under uncertainty, and particularly so when it is addressed to those who will assume responsibilities within firms. Training people to clear understanding of the consequences of these decisions will probably have the effect of making attitudes towards risk more uniform, eliminating shy conservatism as well as reckless gambling.

(C) OPTIMAL DEGREE OF RISK-AVERSION IN FIRMS

Neglecting now the diversity of firm behaviour, we must still enquire whether the prevailing attitude may be made to agree with the social norm. This question looks to me to require important research effort in three different directions.

In the first place, we should know which level of risk-aversion would

be implied for the firms by the social utility function. The argument of
K. Arrow (1965), which was quoted above for public enterprises, seems
to apply as well to private firms and to recommend that their decisions
be risk-neutral. This conclusion would probably be too extreme, because
some uncertainties such as those concerning the speed of technical progress or the rate of increase of labour productivity, seem likely to affect
similarly all firms.[1] A low risk-aversion on their part would then appear
to be desirable.

In the second place, we should try to determine whether firms are
really risk-averse and to what extent. The prevailing thesis assumes such
an aversion: the return on capital engaged in production would be on the
average larger, the more the business *a priori* appeared subject to greater
uncertainties. The pure profit, which would remain to the entrepreneur
after the capital has been imputed, its income according to the market
interest rate, would be on average positive and particularly important
for venturesome undertakings.

However, F. H. Knight (1921) has taken the opposite view according
to which businessmen would usually give too little weight to large risks
and would act as if they liked gambling more than security (see ch. xii).
Knight argued his point stating that the then available statistical studies
did not show mean pure profits to be positive but rather the contrary.
Recently, G. J. Stigler (1963) made an analysis of the rates of return on
capital in U.S. manufacturing industries between 1938 and 1954; he
found no significant correlation between the mean rate of return in an
industry and the dispersion of this rate either from one year to another,
or from one firm to another (see pp. 62 and 63).

The question then remains open. It plays such a role for our understanding of economic phenomena that we should devote to it a good deal
of econometric research.

In the third place, we ought to study how firm behaviour could be
brought in line with the social norm, notably through taxation or through
stabilisation policies, which are used for some industries such as agriculture. This requires a theoretical analysis of the equilibrium that is

---

[1] If a_{je} designates the value taken by a parameter of firm j's production function
when state e obtains, it might seem admissible as a first approximation to write a_{je} as the
sum of two terms, one of which b_e common to all firms, the other c_{je} particular to j and
independent of the c_{ke} concerning other firms. As soon as we think over this hypothesis, we see that the relative importance of b_e compared with c_{je} must vary from one
state to another. This makes it impossible to reach a complete agreement between the
firms behaviour and the social utility function: indeed the degree of risk-aversion of the
firms ought to vary from one state to another.

likely to obtain given the firms' behaviour and the institutions ruling them.

Here is as an example a very simple model on which a discussion might be open about the effect of taxation of positive profits.[1]

Let us assume that a firm uses inputs N of labour and K of capital to obtain, after one period, a net production $Q = f(N, K)$; suppose moreover that a risk of obsolescence gives the probability ϕ to the event that capital loses all value at the end of the period (with probability $1 - \phi$, capital remains in use keeping the same value for subsequent production). Let us assume that the prices of the output and capital are both equal to p, while the wage rate is s and the interest rate ρ.

Consider the case in which the social optimum would imply that the firm maximises the expected net value of its production, namely $pf(N, K) - sN - \rho p\, K - \phi p\, K$. Optimal quantities of N and K are given by:

$$\begin{cases} f'_N(N, K) = \dfrac{s}{p}, \\ f'_K(N, K) = \rho + \phi, \end{cases} \tag{26}$$

f'_N and f'_K being the derivatives of f with respect to N and K respectively.

Let a tax be imposed at the rate τ on the profits resulting from production, after deduction of the interest on capital, but only when these

---

[1] The following analysis is reminiscent of the now classical one proposed by E. D. Domar and R. A. Musgrave (1944), which applies to the effect of a similar taxation on the composition of a portfolio made of unequally risky assets, rather than to its effect on the choice of production techniques in random situations (see also R. A. Musgrave (1959), pp. 313–28, to which I shall refer below).

The positive component of the expected profit, g in Musgrave's notation, is here equal to ϕ multiplied by expression (27); the negative component $-r$ is equal to $1 - \mathbf{8}$ multiplied by (28); the expected profit y is of course equal to $g - r$. We may, from the present model, draw a graph similar to figure 14–2 on page 317 in Musgrave (1959). On the yOr plan, the curve OB will limit below the set of points that are feasible for the firm when p, s, ρ, τ and ϕ are fixed. This curve is concave from above in case of diminishing marginal returns ($[f'']$ negative definite). Let i_1, i_2, $i_3 \ldots$ be the indifference curves of the firm, any one of which has the equation:

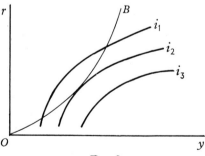

Fig. 2

$$(1 - \phi)V\left(\frac{y + r}{1 - \phi}\right) + \phi V\left(-\frac{r}{\phi}\right) = A,$$

with an appropriate constant A. These curves are concave from below in case of risk-aversion.

profits are positive. Let us finally suppose that the firm's behaviour amounts to maximisation of the expected value of some function ($V(\pi)$, in which π is the disposable profit after tax. (This list of assumptions, although impressive, probably fits the problem under study as a first approximation.)

The disposable profit is equal to

$$(1-\tau)\{pf(N, K) - sN - \rho\, p\, K\} \tag{27}$$

with probability $1-\phi$ and to

$$\{pf(N, K) - sN - (1+\rho)\, p\, K\} \tag{28}$$

with probability ϕ if, as is likely, the first curly bracket is positive but the second negative. Maximisation of the expected value of $V(\pi)$ then implies that N and K be solutions of:

$$\begin{cases} f_N'(N, K) = \dfrac{s}{p}, \\[2mm] f_K'(N, K) = \rho + \phi\ \dfrac{V_2'}{(1-\phi)\,(1-\tau)\,V_1' + \phi V_2'}, \end{cases} \tag{29}$$

V_1' and V_2' being the values taken by the derivative of V respectively in the favourable and unfavourable case. (The derivation of system (29) is direct.)

Comparison between systems (26) and (29) shows that some taxation is favourable to the achievement of the social optimum if the ratio:

$$\frac{V_2'}{(1-\phi)V_1' + \phi V_2'} \tag{30}$$

is smaller than 1; because some positive value of τ then makes equal to 1 the ratio appearing on the right-hand side of the second equation (29), and system (27) then becomes equivalent to system (26). Ratio (30) is smaller than 1 when V_1' exceeds V_2', i.e. when the firm likes gambling, the marginal valuation of profit being larger, the larger is this profit. As we might have expected, taxation of the profit then counteracts the undesirable attitude of the firm. On the other hand, in case of risk-aversion, taxation will induce the firm to choose a quantity of capital that will be still smaller than the already too small quantity chosen in the absence of a tax (too high value of the marginal productivity of capital).

If we believe in this model and in the prevailing thesis asserting risk-aversion in private firms, a taxation of profits that does not imply a public participation in losses has an unfavourable impact on resource allocation under uncertainty.

5 A FINAL COMMENT

While I have considered the social utility function, the economic calculations in the public sector and the policy towards the private sector, I have not ventured to take strong positions. My article has presented a programme for future research much more often than accepted results. I am the first to wish that it may soon appear outdated through the future progress of our science.

REFERENCES

M. Allais (1953, a), 'Fondements d'une théorie positive des choix comportant un risque et critique des postulats et axiomes de l'école américaine', *Économétrie* (C.N.R.S., Paris).

M. Allais (1953, b), 'L'Extension des théories de l'équilibre économique général et du rendement social au cas du risque', *Econometrica*, Apr 1953.

K. Arrow (1953), 'Rôle des valeurs boursières pour la répartition la meilleure des risques', *Économétrie* (C.N.R.S., Paris) 1953. An English translation was published in *Review of Economic Studies*, Apr 1964.

K. Arrow (1965), 'Discounting and Public Investment Criteria', paper written for the Western Resources Conference, 6 Jul 1965.

E. Baudier (1954), 'L'Introduction du temps dans la théorie de l'équilibre général', *Les Cahiers économiques*, Dec 1954.

G. Debreu (1959), *Theory of Value*, J. Wiley & Sons, New York.

E. D. Domar and R. A. Musgrave (1944), 'Proportional Income Taxation and Risk-Taking', *Quarterly Journal of Economics*, May 1944.

J. Drèze (1965), 'Market allocation under uncertainty', paper presented at the Rome Congress of the Econometric Society.

O. Eckstein (1961), *Water-Resource Development – The Economics of Project Evaluation* (Harvard University Press).

J. Hirshleifer (1965), 'Investment Decision Under Uncertainty: Choice-Theoretic Approaches', *Quarterly Journal of Economics*, Nov 1965.

J. Hirshleifer (1966), 'Investment Decision Under Uncertainty: Applications of the State-Preference Approach', *Quarterly Journal of Economics*, May 1966.

F. H. Knight (1921), *Risk, Uncertainty and Profit* (Sentray Press, New York); Reprints of Economic Classics (A. M. Kelley, New York, 1964).

E. Malinvaud (1965), 'Interest Rates in the Allocation of Resources', in F. H. Hahn and F. P. R. Brechling (eds.), *The Theory of Interest Rates* (Macmillan, London).

P. Massé (1959), *Le Choix des investissements* (Dunod, Paris).

J. A. Mirrlees (1965), 'Optimum accumulation under uncertainty', mimeograph note, Trinity College, Cambridge).

P. Musgrave (1959), *The Theory of Public Finance* (McGraw-Hill, New York).

J. W. Pratt (1964), 'Risk aversion in the small and in the large', *Econometrica*, Jan 1964.

R. Radner (1965), 'Competitive Equilibrium under Uncertainty', mimeographed (Center for Research in Management Science, University of California).

P. A. Samuelson (1953), 'Utilité, préférence et probabilité', *Économétrie* (C.N.R.S., Paris).

G. J. Stigler (1963), *Capital and Rates of Return in Manufacturing Industries* (National Bureau of Economic Research, Princeton University Press).

10 General Equilibrium with Public Goods [1]

R. Dorfman

1 INTRODUCTORY

It is becoming fashionable nowadays for economists to dabble in political theory. Partly, we are forced into it; the principal application of economics is to political decisions. Partly we are enticed into it, when we perceive that the tools we have fashioned for our own purposes can be applied with profit to the problems of politics. I am responding here to both motivations.

The current wave of interest began with the writings of Kenneth Arrow [1] and Duncan Black [5], who applied a set-theoretic approach to some problems of political decision-making. It was continued by Anthony Downs [8], who took a very economic point of view. He reasoned that a rational decision in any field is a 'best' decision, which can always be regarded as a decision that maximises something. In the case of politics that something is political support. Once that is recognised, the usual economics of maximising decisions applies. More currently, Charles Lindblom [15] is reacting against the ultra-rationalistic approach and is reminding us that politics is the art of compromise among the conflicting interests of incommensurable groups. Though none of these deal specifically with the problems of public goods, their insights are pertinent and I have borrowed from all of them. In the same strain, I have made use of the point of view expounded by Chester Barnard [2] in the context of maintaining the effectiveness and integrity of an organisation, the approach that emphasises the importance of maintaining a favourable balance of the inducements extended to participants in an organisation over the contributions exacted from them, even when no monetised values are at issue.

The welfare economics of public goods has been set forth, probably definitively, by Paul Samuelson in three influential papers [16, 17, 18] on which I lean heavily. Samuelson's argument was amplified by Strotz [19], with special emphasis on the distributional implications of the provision of public goods. But these contributions had to do with welfare

[1] This research was undertaken during tenure of the Ford Faculty Rotating Research Professorship at the University of California, Berkeley.

optima and paid no attention to the peculiarities of decision-making about public goods.

The best bridge between the ideals established in the framework of welfare economics and the pulls and pushes recognised by the institutional-political approaches is provided by a paper by Howard Bowen [6], which proposes a voting procedure intended to perform the same functions in the political sphere that competitive markets perform in the economic one. I shall discuss Bowen's proposal more extensively below.

All of these streams of writing, and some others that I haven't noted, bear on the problem that I wish to confront: how to formalise the considerations that enter into decisions about public goods. I shall take the time to discuss the concept of public goods in the very next section, but the upshot will be simply that public goods are ordinary economic goods except that their use cannot be rationed nor can their benefits be allocated. In the nature of the case, therefore, decisions about public goods transcend the competence of markets and decentralised decision making. Those decisions stand squarely on the boundary between economics and politics, and we shall so regard them.

How these decisions are made in practice depends on the structure of the government that makes them, and governments are very varied. In a federalised government, such as that of the United States, these decisions are arrived at very differently from the way they are in a centralised government, such as that of France. My formalisation is intended to be non-committal enough to cover all such variations, but in thinking about the problem I have usually had in mind the procedures prevalent in America. According to these procedures, decisions about public goods are part-and-parcel of the regularly recurrent budget-making process. It is then that the levels of expenditure on police and fire protection, public health, national defence, highway maintenance, education and all the rest are proposed, debated and settled. It is the considerations that are debated in this budgeting process that we have to formalise.

In the next section I shall, mostly for the record, discuss the concept of public goods. Section 3 will set forth an abstract, descriptive model of public goods decisions, in the spirit of stationary general equilibrium analysis. In the final section some of the concepts invoked in this model will be mulled over and evaluated.

2 THE CONCEPT OF PUBLIC GOODS

There are certain goods that have the peculiarity that once they are available no one can be precluded from enjoying them whether he contributed to their provision or no. These are the public goods. Law and order is an example, and there are many others too familiar to make further exemplification worth while. Their essential characteristic is that they are enjoyed but not consumed, or that benefit can be derived from them without any act of appropriation. In fact the enjoyment of public goods is often unconscious and even involuntary. For example, if a community fluoridates its water supply even those who object most strenuously to tampering with the natural purity of water will find that their children have fewer cavities. There is then, often in the case of a public good, no definable act of consumption and therefore no way of measuring or defining the amount of it consumed or the marginal cost of providing a small amount of it to a single beneficiary or an individual's private demand curve for its services to him. All this very useful apparatus of economics is irrelevant to public goods.

It was Baumol [3] who, to my knowledge, most clearly enunciated this attitude toward the nature of public goods. Since none can be precluded from enjoying them it is in the interests of each to avoid contributing to them if he can. Therefore the coercive power of the state must be enlisted to compel contributions. And when this is done, wisely, all benefit, for then goods desired by all (or virtually all) can be provided which would otherwise be unavailable to any. Goods of this nature, then, can be provided only by the state, by philanthropists, and as by-products of certain private goods.

The extreme or pure category of public goods are those to which I have already called attention: where the usufruct cannot be denied and where the receipt of benefit is not associated with any deliberate choice or act. There are many such goods but they are a bit hard to list because, like the air, they tend to be invisible. But there are other categories, too. One goes under the heading of 'externalities'. There are some public goods that are produced as joint products with private goods. Leading instances occur in the fields of education and public health.[1] I, myself, have never bothered to be inoculated against infantile paralysis. Nevertheless, I am immune because there are virtually no carriers left in my community. The private good of those who submitted to innoculation has become my public good.

There is a similar side to education. It is brought out in an inverse sort of way by the fact that in the good old days of the American South it was

---

[1] Recognition of the importance of mixed public–private goods goes back to Adolph Wagner at least. See the passage from *Finanzwissenschaft* cited by Wicksell [21, p. 98]. More recently, Leif Johansen appealed to these very same examples [13, p. 180].

illegal to teach a slave to read or write. I submit that the reason for government interest in education, public health, postal services and airways control, to mention only a few instances, is that in each of these cases the
use of private service carries as a joint product a widely diffused communal
benefit. The State therefore takes steps to assure that the private good
is consumed in amounts deemed adequate. But the gains to the direct,
private beneficiaries are distinct from the public benefits derived.

Still another kind of public good exists when the derivation of benefit
is associated with an explicit act of consumption but where it is unduly
inconvenient or expensive to exact a user charge. In such cases, particularly if there is a joint product side to the matter, the commodity may
be treated as if it were a pure public good. Typical examples are roads
and outdoor recreational facilities. Often no charge is made for their use,
though in principle there could be user charges. Curbside parking is an
interesting example. It is treated as an unappropriable public good until
the supply becomes nearly exhausted, then it is found convenient to levy
a user charge.

Finally, we have to consider whether appropriable commodities produced under conditions of low or negligible marginal cost ought to be
considered public goods. Often they are so considered, and sometimes
negligible marginal cost has been used as the definiendum of public goods,
but I shall exclude them. Urban transit and sewage disposal may be
public goods (under the joint product interpretation) but they are not so
by virtue of the strongly decreasing costs of producing their services.
That characteristic makes them 'public utilities' and, though the public
at large has a legitimate interest in having them provided in adequate
amounts, the principles that determine what is adequate provision are
different from the questions that I am confronting.

In short, public goods are those that are consumed jointly rather than
severally. They are goods that place us all in the same boat willy-nilly.
They have no marginal cost that can be assessed, even conceptually,
against an individual occasion of use. Therefore they cannot have
declining marginal costs.

There is a fine distinction to be made, which I am afraid I shall not
always respect. It concerns the notion of the quantity of a public good.
Consider a park as a public good. Is the amount of it the number of acres
of parkland, or the number of 'visitor-days' of use, or what? All that
the government can decide is the number of acres of parkland and the
facilities provided in them, and I am forced to use these magnitudes to
measure the amount of the public good provided. A public good so

defined and measured is an intermediate product, analogous to a productive facility. The benefits, both public and private, yielded by such a good depend on the use that is made of it and this is often a matter for private decision, as in the case of parks.

For public goods, as I have said, there can be no individual choice of quantity and no individual expression of preference in the market-place. All decisions have to be made socially, which is to say politically. Our central task is the formalisation of these political decisions.

3 A DESCRIPTIVE MODEL

I am about to propose a descriptive model of decision making concerning public goods. I do so with a great deal of diffidence. These decisions are political as well as economic, and my acquaintance with the literature of political science is very spotty. So I am a 'primitive' in this field, a man who has to rediscover the first principles for himself and who is likely to drop into the pitfalls that the professionals have avoided for generations. On top of that an economist suffers from a special disability when dealing with political problems: his deeply ingrained habits of mind practically compel him to view everything as an economic problem in which each of the participants is striving to maximise something and the social institutions co-ordinate their efforts toward the maximisation of something else. There is no guarantee that the political world is like that. My amateurishness and my mental set will be amply reflected in what follows.

My approach will be to conceive of a standard stationary general equilibrium model to which a government sector has been added, and to determine some properties of the general equilibrium of this government plus private sector model. For the private sector I borrow heavily from Debreu [7], including even his notation. For the government sector I find it necessary to proceed on my own.

Since my concern is with public goods I shall conceive of a government that does nothing except provide public goods and levy the taxes necessary to finance them. It does not, in particular, make transfer payments or concern itself with economic policy.

I assume that this government is sensitive to the needs and wishes of its body politic. It may have a will of is own, but its first concern is to find some resolution of the conflicting desires and utilities of its citizenry so as to enlist and maintain their loyal support. The citizenry, of course, consists of individuals, but it seems important to me that they form themselves into interest groups, formed largely along socio-economic lines.

These interest groups are, in fact, very complicated phenomena: they overlap (there must be some people who are members of both the Junior Chamber of Commerce and the N.A.A.C.P.), their edges are blurred, from time to time they split, consolidate, and reform. But I shall abstract from all that and assume that there are given interest groups the members of each of which share a common set of preferences as regards public goods. The government, whose officials are themselves members of some of these interest groups, must consult the preferences of each of these groups in arriving at its decisions. How this is done constitutes the heart of my model of the government sector.

As a further simplification I shall assume that decisions concerning tax policy can be separated from decisions concerning public goods. This is not unrealistic. Decisions about public goods are normally made annually as part of the routine of preparing the government's budget. The total burden of taxes must be consistent with these decisions. But the distribution of taxes, or tax policy, is reconsidered much more infrequently and with primary attention to distributive and aggregative considerations. For the purpose of studying public goods decisions we shall take the tax policy as given.

Now I can present my model. The structure of the private sector will be discussed only cursorily so that proper emphasis can be placed on the government and its decisions. A fuller statement of the overall model will be found in the appendix.[1]

The economy cum body-politic, then, consists of a finite number of consumer-voters, a finite number of firms and a government. The government, as we shall see more fully below, provides a vector of public goods, g. In the presence of these public goods, the typical consumer, Mr α, selects a vector of private good consumptions, x^α (negative components signifying contributions), from a closed, convex set X^α, g available to him in the circumstances. The public goods vector, g, is itself a member of a closed, compact set, G, available to the government. The consumer's choice is made in the light of a preference ordering over the elements of X^α, G which has the usual convenient convexity and continuity properties. This choice is constrained by a budget limitation: given any set of prices of private goods, Mr α's net value of consumption cannot exceed the value of his initial resources (if any) plus the value of his shares in the profits of firms less his tax liability. Mr α is assumed to own a share $\theta_{\alpha j}$ of firm j

---

[1] A mathematical appendix is to be prepared and will be available from the author. Reference to it is unnecessary, however, because the principal theorems have been derived independently by Duncan K. Foley [9].

(usually zero) and to be liable for a share $\theta_{\alpha 0}$ (rarely zero) of the expenses of the government.

The typical firm, firm j, produces a vector y^j of private goods (negative components denote net inputs). Its range of choice is restricted to a closed, convex production set Y^j, G, but it does not select the g elements of its choice vector. Instead, taking them as given and taking the prices of private goods as given, it chooses y^j so as to maximise its profit. Its profit is then distributed, with proportion $\theta_{\alpha j}$ going to Mr α.

The government, which will be denoted by subscript 0, is formally very like a firm except that it and it alone can choose the vector of public goods, g, which enters into the available sets of all participants in the economy. The role of the government in this model at least, is to provide public goods. It does this by selecting a vector y^0, g from the closed, convex set Y^0, G available to it. When it makes this choice, it provides the vector g of public goods to the community and a vector y^0 of private goods, most of whose components will presumably be negative. Given a price vector p for private goods, the government also levies a tax of $-\theta_{\alpha 0} p . y^0$ on consumer α.

The coefficients $\theta_{\alpha 0}$ express the tax policy of the government. We shall regard them as given data not subject to decision. The institutional assumption here is that whereas the actual level of taxation is part and parcel of decisions concerning public goods the general tax policy is not, and is not very frequently revised. We shall see below that the separation of tax policy from public goods decisions entails some social inefficiency. But, in fact, these decisions tend to be separated in practice, in the interest of reducing the complexity of the alternatives confronted by government officials and legislators.

Superficially, our assumption seems to specify a very simple tax policy: it is a simple head tax; there are no excises, income taxes, taxes on firms, or tariffs. But it can be interpreted more generously. It can be taken to mean that Mr α knows that in the end, after all the shiftings and complications, he will be assessed about the proportion $\theta_{\alpha 0}$ of the expenses of the government. This formulation does ignore, however, the distortions introduced into the price structure by indirect taxes and, to a lesser extent, by direct taxes.

This describes our economy-polity except for its most crucial feature for our purposes: the principles on which y^0, g is to be selected from the government's available set. It is at this stage that we must break our own ground. Up to this point our concepts and assumptions have had the authority of generations of close thought and scrutiny behind them. Now we are entering a territory in which I have not been able to discover any compelling concensus. We must therefore construct our own principles out of the bits and pieces of doctrine that I have been able to find. What I am about to say, now, has no particular authority behind it.

Decisions about the provision of public goods are conveyed in the government's annual budget. They are reached through a political process in which it is useful to distinguish three groups of participants: government officials, other political leaders and ordinary citizens. The proposals for the budget originate with the government officials, for only they have the staff and information needed to prepare them in the required detail. These proposals, however, cannot be implemented without widespread public understanding and support. Formally, this public assent is conveyed by legislative enactment of the budget, and for this reason I include legislators among the 'other political leaders'. But in fact, and in this model, the process of gaining public acceptance includes much more than pushing a budget bill through the legislature. It involves convincing the great bulk of the members of the public, minorities along with majorities, that their needs and interests have been dealt with fairly.

This process of gaining widespread public acceptance is the most elaborate and noisy step of the whole procedure. The trial balloons, the political breakfasts, legislative hearings and debates, speeches, leaks, editorials, press conferences are all part of it. The key actors are the 'other political leaders': the congeries of politicians, in and out of office, prominent citizens, political commentators, interest-group leaders and others who devote a major portion of their time and efforts to political affairs. The political leaders are the main channel of communication between the government officials and the general public, largely because the general public, being uninformed about political matters, and knowing that it is, relies heavily on *ad hominem* arguments.[1] A member of the public will tend to approve the government's proposals if they come with the endorsement of leaders in whom he has confidence. The leaders therefore play a double role; they are the targets of the government's persuasive efforts and almost simultaneously the conveyors of the government's programme to their followings.

A political leader's authority and influence stems from his constituency: the ordinary people who have confidence in him and who regard his endorsement of a proposal as a powerful argument in its favour. A

---

[1] The rational state of ignorance of the general public is one of the main themes of Anthony Downs's *An Economic Theory of Democracy*.

leader's following consists of people who have come to believe, on the basis of past experience and pronouncements, that the conclusions he comes to on political matters are close to the ones that they would reach if they took the trouble to become informed and to think things through. Expressed somewhat differently, each political leader has a following that consists of people who believe that he thinks and acts on the basis of their broad preconceptions about right, justice and the objectives of political policy. Such a following is likely to be drawn from a fairly homogeneous socio-economic group of citizens, and we shall consider each political leader to be a representative of some definable socio-economic group. In my opinion, it is unrealistic to assume that the ordinary citizen has clearly defined preferences about political decisions and policies, but he accepts the appraisals of political leaders who do have such preferences. Thus, in my economic-political model I conceive that individual consumers have preference maps over bundles of private goods, but that only socio-economic groups (via the leaders in whom they have confidence) have preference maps for public goods.

I have described thus far one direction of the flow of information in the political process, the flow from government officials to political leaders to ordinary citizens. There is also a significant reverse flow. It is obvious that a political leader cannot choose his positions entirely in accordance with his personal whims and preferences. His influence depends upon his followers' confidence in him, and this is constantly being reassessed in the light of his current stands and accumulating evidence. The leader can therefore endorse only proposals that he can 'sell', and that he believes will turn out to enhance, rather than impair, the confidence on which his position depends. He is constantly appraising the fairly vague opinions of his constituents to determine what he can sell, and is simultaneously conveying the results of these appraisals to the government officials to persuade them to frame proposals that he can endorse.

Out of this two-way flow of information emerges a government programme, or budget, that virtually every significant political leader finds acceptable. Some of the leaders may not like it very well, but at the very least they will be able to present it to their constituents as the best compromise attainable in the circumstances. For politics is not a game of 'winner take all'. I am not at all sure why this is, but quite obviously a great deal of effort is expended on providing to each leader and the group he represents at least a fair minimum recognition of their demands. Wicksell [21] recognised this characteristic of public decisions long ago, and asserted it as a moral demand: that taxes should not be levied

against any citizen unless he felt that he was receiving adequate government services and benefits in return.   I do not wish to rest my case on
moral grounds, but merely on the empirical recognition that stable
governments appear to act this way.   New revolutionary regimes, of
course, do not; they run roughshod over the interests of the recently
ousted group.   But a stable government does not discredit any political
leaders or alienate any significant minority.   Perhaps my empirical
observation is not much more than a definition of a responsible, legitimate government.   If so, there are such governments, and my theory
is restricted to them.

   In summary, then, we imagine a body politic to be made up of a number
of socio-economic groups.[1]   A typical member of one of these groups has
only very general ideas about what he would like his government to do,
but each group is represented in the political decision process by one or
more spokesmen who have quite definite preferences and quite definite
ideas about costs and benefits and trade-offs, and whose ideas are consistent with the vague notions of their constituents.   The government
officials strive to formulate a programme of government activities that will
be at least acceptable to all these leaders.   That is the first, and most
demanding, task of the government officials.   It may be that there are
several programmes that are acceptable all around.   If so the government
has some latitude for choosing among them, and we must now conjecture
how this latitude is exercised.

   In terms of our formal model, when the government has found a vector
y^0, g that satisfies all the groups that comprise its body politic, i.e. all
their spokesmen, it has done most of its work.   But there may be numerous
vectors that meet this requirement, and some basis is needed for selecting
among them.

   Should we be content with the doctrine of 'satisficing', saying only
that the government will select some element from the set of universally
acceptable vectors? Should we adopt some version of search and scanning
theory, saying that the government will choose the acceptable vector that
is closest, in some sense, to the vector accepted last year or in some average
of past years? Both of those, I think, are acceptable approaches, the
second not far from Lindblom's [15], but they seem to me to imply an
excessively bloodless government without any purposes of its own or
interest in leadership.   It is trite that 'power corrupts', and I am not sure

   [1] These socio-economic groups should not be confused with the interest groups that
play a central role in the thinking of David Truman [20] and his school.   Their model
of political decisions is substantially different from this one.

that I believe it, but at least power does evoke an interest in getting things done. An aspirant government seeks political power in order to accomplish some objectives, and it attains the power by mobilising public support for those objectives and disarming resistance to them. So I say, but without undue conviction, that we ought to conceive of the government of our model economy-polity as having definite goals that it wishes to attain to the maximum extent possible within the limitations of the political and economic constraints already described.

Furthermore, these goals do not come out of the air. They are the goals of one or more of the socio-economic groups that constitute the body politic. The leaders of the government are themselves members of these groups, and are interested in the welfare of their own and other groups, they have acceded to power by enlisting the support of a sufficient preponderance of those groups, and they can remain in power only by meriting the loyalty of many of the groups while not incurring the excessive hostility of the others. So we shall not impose a separate set of goals for the government, though that would be a defensible, and even interesting, alternative to the formulation being presented. Instead, we shall assume that the goals of the government are the goals of the socio-economic groups that comprise its body-politic with, however, varying degrees of attention to the interests of the different groups. From this point of view, different political parties would be distinguished not by differences in their objectives or programmes but by differences in their degrees of attentiveness to the interests of the various socio-economic groups. What a government so motivated seeks to maximise is some function of the welfares of these socio-economic groups, as perceived by themselves.

I am being subtle here, even to the point of deviousness. De Viti de Marco insists, and rightly, that there is some room for altruism in individual consumers' decisions and substantially more in political decisions. There is room for altruism in this formulation. The discussion of public goods in Section 2 made it clear that the external effects of consumption are public goods. It often happens that the members of group A feel that the members of group B ought to have something for which the latter have no felt need. Bath-tubs for slum-dwellers are often advanced as a notorious example (usually by members of group C, who don't see the point of it). In that case, bath-tubs in rehabilitated slums will enter group A's welfare function, but not group B's (and may enter group C's deleteriously). The individual groups' welfare functions as here conceived do not measure the benefits directly received by the members of that group, but rather benefits to the whole community as perceived by that group. That is how altruism enters the government's objective function, though it is based exclusively on the welfare functions of the constituent groups. Presumably, benefits received directly by members of a group will bulk especially large in the welfare function of that group, but there is room for other considerations.

The government's objectives, then, are an amalgam of the objectives of the groups it governs. The government's leadership is leadership in the direction of the goals of the groups that have predominant influence in it. But, we should reiterate, this leadership is tempered by the need to conciliate all the groups.

In order to express these ideas with adequate precision we must some-how quantify the benefits of public goods as seen by members of citizen group α, and moreover must do so in monetary terms so that the benefits from the provision of public goods can be compared with those of private consumption. The idea of monetary equivalent of a benefit in kind is inherently artificial. Furthermore, the procedure for constructing one is necessarily somewhat arbitrary, as the number of variorum 'compensating variations' attests. The particular method that will be followed is recommended by its conventionality and its convenience.

Our approach is in the willingness-to-pay tradition. Suppose that the government proposes to provide levels of public goods g and to do so by utilizing private goods in quantities y^0. At prices p, which will be regarded as being preassigned until further notice, this will impose on a member of group α a tax burden amounting to $-\theta_{\alpha 0} p y^0$ (remember that $p y^0$ is normally negative). A member of group α will be at least acquiescent if this tax burden does not exceed the most that he is willing to pay for the proposed provision of public goods. But how much is that? To answer this question we conceive of some minimum, basal level of public goods, $\bar{g}$, to which corresponds a low tax burden $-\theta_{\alpha 0} p \bar{y}^0$. There also corresponds a consumption good vector $\bar{x}^\alpha$ which is the best that the consumer can afford at the low level of taxation. (In considering alternative government programmes, the citizen-taxpayer is assumed to ignore the aggregative effects of the government budget, and so shall we.) This combination $\bar{x}^\alpha, \bar{g}$ places the consumer-citizen on some one of his indifference curves or, stated more elaborately, on the boundary of one of his preferred consumption sets. We may now associate with the proposed government output g (as I shall sometimes, rather inaccurately, call the provision of public goods) a private consumption vector x^α chosen as the cheapest consumption vector at the assigned prices such that x^α, g is indifferent to

$\bar{x}^\alpha$, $\bar{g}$. The value of the proposed programme as seen by this citizen may then be taken to be

$$F^\alpha(g, p) = p(\bar{x}^\alpha - x^\alpha),$$

since this is the maximum tax he could afford to pay over and above the inevitable tax $-\theta_{\alpha 0}p\bar{y}^0$ without being forced below the level of welfare corresponding to $\bar{x}^\alpha$, $\bar{g}$. (We do not preclude that this expression may be negative, for an ill-chosen programme.) This is the citizen's gross benefit from the programme. His net benefit, or citizen's surplus, is the excess of his gross benefit over the increase in taxation necessitated by the government's consuming $-y^0$ instead of $-\bar{y}^0$, or

$$\phi^\alpha(y^0, g, p) = F^\alpha(g, p) + \theta_{\alpha 0}p(y^0 - \bar{y}^0).$$

In effect $\phi^\alpha(y^0, g, p)$ compares the tax that a member of group α would be willing to pay to have government output g instead of $\bar{g}$ with the tax that he would actually have to pay. It is necessarily a concave function of y^0, g. For consider any two government programmes $(y^{0'}, g')$ and $(y^{0''}, g'')$, and their corresponding levels of private consumption x'^α and x''^α chosen so that

$$(x'^\alpha, g') \sim (x''^\alpha, g'') \sim (\bar{x}^\alpha, \bar{g}),$$

where $\sim$ symbolises indifference to a member of group α. Consider also any linearly intermediate government programme

$$(y^{0\lambda}, g^\lambda) = \lambda(y^{0'}, g') + (1 - \lambda)(y^{0''}, g''), \qquad 0 < \lambda < 1.$$

Because of the assumed convexity of consumer's preferences:

$$(\lambda x'^\alpha + (1 - \lambda)x''^\alpha, g^\lambda) > (x'^\alpha, g') \sim (x''^\alpha, g'')$$

where $>$ denotes strict preference. Hence, surely

$$px^{\alpha\lambda} \leq \lambda px'^\alpha + (1 - \lambda)px''^\alpha,$$

where

$$(x^{\alpha\lambda}, g^\lambda) \sim (x'^\alpha, g'). \quad \text{Now}$$

$$\phi^\alpha(y^{0\lambda}, g^\lambda, p) = p(\bar{x}^\alpha - x^{\alpha\lambda}) + \theta_{\alpha 0}p(y^{0\lambda} - \bar{y}^0).$$

Subtracting these two expressions and applying the definitions of $\phi^\alpha(y^{0'}, g', p)$ and $\phi^\alpha(y^{0''}, g'', p)$ we obtain

$$\phi^\alpha(y^{0\lambda}, g^\lambda, p) \geq \lambda\phi^\alpha(y^{0'}, g', p) + (1 - \lambda)\phi^\alpha(y^{0''}, g'', p)$$

or concaveness.

We can now pose the problem of choosing the government's programme in the following form: For a given set of prices of private goods, p, find an element in the government's production set Y^0, G so as to maximise

$$\sum_{\alpha} w_{\alpha}\{F^{\alpha}(g, p) + \theta_{\alpha 0} p(y^0 - \bar{y}^0)\}$$

subject to

$$F^{\alpha}(g, p) + \theta_{\alpha 0} p(y^0 - \bar{y}^0) \geq 0, \text{ all } \alpha.$$

The maximand merits a word or two. The weights w_{α} in it measure the government's relative concern for the different socio-economic groups indexed by α. They are a compound of the political influence of these groups and of attention paid to their welfares for more disinterested motives. Altogether it is the kind of social welfare function employed by Samuelson, in [16] and elsewhere, and by Strotz [19] in their studies of the ideal output of public goods.

Thus stated, the problem is seen to be almost a standard concave programming problem, the only unconventional feature being that the optimal point must be selected in a specified closed, convex set, in addition to satisfying the usual concave inequalities. It is close enough to concave programming so that the following theorem applies:

Lemma. Suppose that $f^0(z)$ is a concave function, $f(z)$ is a concave vector-valued function, both defined for $z \in Z$, and that S is a closed, convex subset of Z with an interior. Suppose also that for every non-trivial vector $u \geq 0$ there exists a $z \in S$ such that $uf(z) > 0$. (Inner products will be written in the same way as products of scalars.)

Then, if $f^0(z^*)$ is a maximum of $f^0(z)$ for $z \in S$ satisfying $f(z) \geq 0$, there exist vectors u, v satisfying:

(a) $u \geq 0$, $uf(z^*) = 0$,
(b) $v(z - z^*) \geq 0$ for all $z \in S$, and
(c) $f^0(z) + uf(z) + vz \leq f^0(z^*) + vz^*$ for all $z \in Z$.

The proof, which will not be presented, is a straightforward application of the method used by Karlin [14, p. 200 ff.] to demonstrate the Kuhn–Tucker Theorem.

In applying this theorem to the choice of a government programme, the couple y^0, g plays the role of z and a valuation couple, r, q has to be introduced to play the role of v. Whereupon, if y^{0*}, g^* is an optimal government programme, there exist vectors u, r, q satisfying:

$$u \geq 0, \qquad \sum_{\alpha} u_{\alpha}\{F^{\alpha}(g^*, p) + \theta_{\alpha 0} p(y^{0*} - \bar{y}^0)\} = 0,$$

$$r(y^0 - y^{0*}) + q(g - g^*) \geq 0 \text{ for all } y^0, g \in Y^0, G$$

and

$$\sum_\alpha (w_\alpha + u_\alpha)\{F^\alpha(g, p) + \theta_{\alpha 0}p(y^0 - \bar{y}^0)\} + ry^0 + qg$$

$$\leq \sum_\alpha w_\alpha\{F^\alpha(g^*, p) + \theta_{\alpha 0}p(y^{0*} - \bar{y}^0)\} + ry^{0*} + qg^*$$

for all y^0, g for which the functions are defined.

To interpret this, first let $g = g^*$ and $y^0 = y^{0*} + \Delta y^0$. Most of the terms then cancel, leaving:

$$\sum_\alpha u_\alpha\{F^\alpha(g^*, p) + \theta_{\alpha 0}p(y^{0*} + \Delta y^0 - \bar{y}^0)\} + \sum_\alpha w_\alpha \theta_{\alpha 0}p\Delta y^0 + r\Delta y^0 \leq 0.$$

Most of the first summation drops out because of the second condition on the vector u, so that

$$\{\sum_\alpha (u_\alpha + w_\alpha)\theta_{\alpha 0}p + r\}\Delta y^0 \leq 0$$

for all Δy^0 for which $y^{0*} + \Delta y^0$ lies in the domain of definition of the functions. Consider the ith component of y^0. If y_i^{0*} is in the interior of its domain, Δy_i^0 can be either positive or negative and the last inequality requires

$$r_i = -p_i\sum_\alpha (u_\alpha + w_\alpha)\theta_{\alpha 0}.$$

It is convenient to write $u_0 = \sum_\alpha (u_\alpha + w_\alpha)\theta_{\alpha 0}$, so that if Δy_i^0 can vary freely

$r_i = -u_0 p_i$. If Δy_i^0 cannot vary freely we have to be content with an inequality, but this will happen only in rare and uninteresting cases, essentially only when y_i^0 is restricted to be non-positive and $y_i^{0*} = 0$. I have tried to think of a significant commodity for which a government's net input is likely to be zero, and have come to the conclusion that governments use practically everything, even lipsticks. So, for all intents and purposes we may take $r = -u_0 p$.

Next, to interpret the auxiliary vector q it helps to suppose that the citizens' surplus functions $F^\alpha(g, p)$ are differentiable at g^* at least. Then we can choose $y^0 = y^{0*}, g = g^* + \Delta g$ and obtain

$$\sum_\alpha (u_\alpha + w_\alpha)\{F^{\alpha*} + \Delta g\nabla F^{\alpha*} + \theta_{\alpha 0}p(y^{0*} - \bar{y}^0)\} - u_0 py^{0*} + q(g^* + \Delta g)$$

$$\leq \sum_\alpha w_\alpha\{F^{\alpha*} + \theta_{\alpha 0}p(y^{0*} - \bar{y}^0)\} - u_0 py^{0*} + qg^*$$

for all $g^* + \Delta g$ in the domain of definition, apart from an approximation error of order higher than that of Δg, which can be ignored, using the notation

$$F^{\alpha *} = F^{\alpha}(g^*, p), \text{ and}$$

$$\nabla F^{\alpha *} = \text{gradient of } F^{\alpha}(g, p) \text{ at } (g^*, p).$$

By the same operations as before this reduces to

$$\Delta g\{\sum_{\alpha}(u_{\alpha} + w_{\alpha})\nabla F^{\alpha *} + q\} \leq 0.$$

For single-component variation, then

$$\Delta g_k\{\sum_{\alpha}(u_{\alpha} + w_{\alpha})F_k^{\alpha *} + q_k\} \leq 0,$$

the subscript denoting partial differentiation. It seems sensible to restrict g, the output of government goods, to be non-negative. Then if g_k^* is positive Δg_k can vary freely and the inequality requires

$$q_k = -\sum_{\alpha}(u_{\alpha} + w_{\alpha})F_k^{\alpha *}.$$

That is, the component q_k of q is the negative of a politically weighted sum of the marginal valuations placed by the members of the different socio-economic groups on g_k. If that particular public good is not provided, the variation cannot be negative and the inequality demands only that q_k does not exceed the negative of this weighted sum.

Furthermore, $(-u_0 p, q)$ are the coefficients of the support plane of Y^0, G at y^{0*}, g^* so that

$$q\Delta g - u_0 p\Delta y \geq 0$$

for all $y^{0*} + \Delta y$, $g^* + \Delta g$ belonging to Y^0, G. Then if only one component of g changes from g^* and that change is positive

$$q_k \geq u_0 \frac{p\Delta y}{\Delta g_k}.$$

The fraction on the right is easily interpreted. For any $\Delta g_k \neq 0$ the product $p\Delta y$ has a maximum in the government's production set. The negative of the ratio of this maximum value to Δg_k is the incremental cost per unit of Δg_k, i.e.

$$IC(\Delta g_k) = -\max_{\Delta y} \frac{p\Delta y}{\Delta g_k}$$

$$\text{for } y^{0*} + \Delta y, g^* + \Delta g \in Y^0, G.$$

If the boundary of the production set is differentiable, $IC(\Delta g_k)$ will approach a well-defined limit as $\Delta g_k \to 0$. This limit is the marginal cost of g_k, to be denoted by $MC(g_k)$. Then we have found

$$q_k \geq -u_0 MC(g_k)$$

if $g_k > g_k^*$ is technically possible. For negative values of Δg_k the sense of the inequality is reversed. If Δg_k can vary freely the inequality becomes an equality.

Now we can combine our two results on q_k. If g_k can be varied upward from g_k^* we have found

$$-\sum_\alpha (u_\alpha + w_\alpha) F_k^{\alpha*} \geq q_k \geq -u_0 MC(g_k)$$

or

$$\sum_\alpha (u_\alpha + w_\alpha) F_k^{\alpha*} \leq MC(g_k) \sum_\alpha (u_\alpha + w_\alpha) \theta_{\alpha 0}.$$

In words, the weighted sum of the marginal valuations placed upon the kth public good by the socio-economic groups cannot exceed the marginal cost of that good multiplied by a factor of proportionality. If g_k can be varied downward from g_k^* the inequalities are reversed. An equality results if free variation is possible. That is, in the case of free variation

$$\sum_\alpha (u_\alpha + w_\alpha) F_k^{\alpha*} = MC(g_k) \sum_\alpha (u_\alpha + w_\alpha) \theta_{\alpha 0},$$

or the politically weighted sums of the marginal valuations placed upon the public goods by the different groups are proportional to their marginal costs.

Finally, the u_α are the shadow prices associated with the constraints that no group shall have a negative citizens' surplus. If any group has a positive citizens' surplus the corresponding u_α will be zero. The u_α may be positive for groups with zero citizens' surplus at y^{0*}, g^*. In fact, this vector may be taken as measuring the social cost, as viewed by the government, of meeting the minimum demands of the several socio-economic groups. This can be seen most easily by looking back at the statement of the lemma on concave programming. From conclusions (b) and (c) of that lemma it follows that

$$f^0(z) - f^0(z^*) + uf(z) \leq 0 \text{ for all } z \in Z.$$

If, then, we consider a value of z for which $f^i(z) = f^i(z^*) - 1$ and $f^j(z) = f^j(z^*)$ for all $j \neq i$, then, using conclusion (a),

$$f^0(z) - f^0(z^*) \leq u_i.$$

The coefficient u_i is therefore an upper limit to the amount that the objective function could be increased by permitting a unit violation of the ith constraint. If the functions are sufficiently smooth at z^* this limit is approached by infinitesimal variations.

This throws a little light on one of the ground-rules of our formulation. If some u_α should be very large the indication would be that society could benefit substantially, from the government's viewpoint, from a small infraction of the constraint with respect to that group. The government might therefore be tempted to override the protests of that group in the larger interest. This suggests that we might wish to contemplate negative lower limits to the citizens' surpluses accorded the different groups within the society, and it seems probably that governments do sometimes impose negative citizens' surpluses on politically weak or morally undeserving groups. But we shall not follow this lead.

This is all very fine as a matter of conceptualisation, but in fact the government has to solve its problem by the exercise of judgement, by appeal to previous and analogous experience, and by trial-and-error, just as does the businessman in his attempt to maximise profit. Indeed, regarded as a descriptive formulation, which is what I wish, this apparatus is methodologically identical with the familiar doctrine of business decision making. It proposes an impracticable calculation which, if it could be carried out, would approximate the results obtained by practical decision makers using other means. Some question must surely arise as to the descriptive significance of this model. Such considerations as the stern test of the market and economic Darwinism can be enlisted in support of the descriptive relevance of the received theory of production, but what forces can I summon to enforce the optimal solution of the public goods problem? As far as the constraints go there is the stern test of the voting booth or, in other contexts, of the need to hold a supporting coalition together. For the rest I feel, as I have said before, on even weaker ground. My justification is simply the conventional one: in government affairs as in business if there is an evident opportunity for cutting costs or improving output it will be taken eventually.

In government as in business affairs one of the advantages of decentralisation is that there are many units that can try experiments and that successful innovations can be emulated. This makes the behaviour of local governmental bodies somewhat more analogous to that of independent businessmen. The central government may, perhaps, be slower in exploring its production set but even there there is strong pressure for economical operation.

But I do not wish to claim too much, only to make it plausible that the solution to this programming problem approximates the behaviour of a government in the presence of given pressures, preferences and prices. Let us take it to be so. Then the government decides on an output g of public goods and a net consumption $-y^0$ of private goods. These are connected to what goes on in the private sphere by the fact that the government places the same relative valuations on private goods (our $-u^0p$) that the private sector does. Now the private sector takes over. In the presence of the public goods g and the net drain of $-y^0$ exerted by the government on the private sector, it possesses a general equilibrium position in which $\Sigma y - \Sigma x = -y^0$, where the first summation is taken over all firms and the second over all consumers. This equilibrium will of course be a technically efficient and Pareto-optimal configuration of the private sector. This is discussed in more detail below. This equilibrium includes an equilibrium set of prices for private goods, which will not necessarily be the same as the p on which the government decision was predicated. If the output-p resulting from the general equilibrium differs from the input-p used as a basis for the government's decisions, the government-plus-private economy will not be in full equilibrium and the government would reassess its programme in the light of these market prices. But, it is argued below on the usual fixed-point grounds, there does exist a price vector which if used by the government in formulating its programme will induce a general equilibrium configuration of the economy in which that same set of prices will reappear as the equilibrating price vector.

The set of levels of public goods predicated on this fixed-point price vector has some claim to be considered the equilibrium levels of public goods outputs, with all the efficiency properties appertaining thereto. In particular, it will be technically efficient. The marginal cost of each public good produced will be proportional to a politically weighted sum of the incremental tax burdens that the populace would be willing to assume to obtain a small increment in the level of that good. Some potential public goods may not be provided. If so, the politically weighted sum of the tax burdens that the populace is willing to assume to obtain them will not exceed their marginal costs at zero output multiplied by the same factor of proportionality. It will be impossible to improve the level of the government's objective function either by transfers of resources between the government and private sectors or by reallocation of resources within the government sector.

If the citizens' surplus should be positive for every group at the solution point, then $u = 0$ and the output level of good k would satisfy

$$\sum_\alpha w_\alpha F_k^{\alpha *} = MC(g_k) \sum_\alpha w_\alpha \theta_{\alpha 0}.$$

That is, the sum of the marginal desirabilities of the good to all the groups, weighted in accordance with the government's concern for them, would equal the sum of the tax burdens required for a small increase in output, weighted in the same way. If, for example, the government weights the groups in proportion to the numbers of people in them, say n_α, and if the tax burden is equally shared so $\theta_{\alpha 0} = 1/\Sigma n_\alpha$, then $\Sigma w_\alpha \theta_{\alpha 0} = 1$ and the condition becomes $\Sigma n_\alpha F_k^{\alpha *} = MC(g_k)$, a formula for which there are precedents. But if some of the citizens' surpluses are zero the u will not vanish and this appealing formula will not apply. No more can be claimed for our solution than that. Income transfer could still improve the lot of some socio-economic groups at the expense of others and could increase the value of the government's objective function. Relaxation of the political constraints could also increase the value of the objective function. If a different government should come to power with a different political influence vector w a different equilibrium would emerge, with all the same justifications.

The conclusions reached by this analysis should be compared with the results of previous studies of the public goods problem. I know of three comparable studies, those of Bowen [6], Samuelson [16] and Strotz [19]. All three, in contrast to the present one, take a normative point of view; they seek to specify the ideal output of public goods, in some sense. Samuelson and Strotz lay great emphasis on the importance of tax policy and income transfers as part of the problem of attaining ideal output; Bowen and I exclude those expedients. Bowen works within a partial equilibrium framework, the rest of us are general equilibrators. Still there remains enough similarity to make comparisons worth while.

Bowen, as I said, considers the ideal output of a single public good in a partial equilibrium framework. He does not divide the body politic into socio-economic classes with divergent interests but does admit that individuals will have different preferences with respect to the level of provision of the public good. Each individual's preferences are expressed by his marginal rate of substitution between disposable income and the public good, regarded as a function of the level of output of the public good. In other words, the basic psychological datum is the amount that each individual would be willing to be taxed per unit increase in the output of the public good, for a small increase in its level. The sum of these marginal rates of substitution is the amount that the community in the aggregate would be willing to pay per unit for a small increase in the level of the good. At the ideal level of provision this total willing marginal contribution should be just equal to the marginal cost of the good.

For comparison with this ideal, our model political-economic system would produce the level g_1 for which

$$\sum_\alpha (u_\alpha + w_\alpha) F_1^\alpha = u_0 MC(g_1)$$

where the summation is taken over all individuals and $u_0 = \sum_\alpha (u_\alpha + w_\alpha)\theta_{\alpha 0}$. Our F_1^α is the same concept as Bowen's marginal rate of substitution. Bowen assumes that all individuals are given equal weight in political decisions, so that $w_\alpha = \dfrac{1}{n}$ for all α. $\Sigma\theta_{\alpha 0} = 1$. With these simplifications our formula becomes

$$\sum_\alpha u_\alpha F_1^\alpha + \frac{1}{n}\sum_\alpha F_1^\alpha = MC(g_1)\left(\sum_\alpha u_\alpha \theta_{\alpha 0} + \frac{1}{n}\right).$$

This shows that if $u_\alpha = 0$ for all α, or if the political constraints are disregarded, our optimum is the same as Bowen's. But this is not a likely result. Recall the political constraints:

$$F^\alpha(g, p) + \theta_{\alpha 0} p(y^0 - \bar{y}^0) \geq 0$$

for all groups α or, taken literally in Bowen's case, for all individuals α. For any single public good, there are likely to be groups that have a very low desire for it from the very outset. These constraints require that the output of the good stop expanding when the citizen's surplus of the least enthusiastic group falls to zero, which is likely to be well below Bowen's ideal level. Fluoridation of water supplies and education in family planning are two extreme examples. With respect to them there are politically effective groups such that $F^\alpha(g, p) \leq 0$ for all $g \geq 0$. And in point of fact, there are many jurisdictions in which these public goods are not provided. There are, of course, many less extreme instances. So it appears that the political constraints operate in the direction of under-provision of public goods.

This downward bias results from the rigidity of tax policy and the exclusion of income transfers from our model, but these are not unrealistic exclusions. Its effect is exaggerated when the model is applied to a single good. An important part of the art of politics is skill in holding a coalition

K

together by offering a package of public goods that is satisfactory to each of the groups in the coalition, taken all in all, though some groups may regard some components in the package as being irrelevant or even noxious to their interests. A blatant example is the National Seashore Act in the United States, which mobilised widespread support by proposing the preservation of four widely separated areas, one on each of the sea-coasts. Thus, packaging public goods together moderates the bias toward underprovision by depriving individual groups of item-by-item vetoes, but it probably does not obliterate it. Galbraith [10], for one, has complained about this tendency. On the other hand, it is not possible for our model to yield more than ideal output, in the single good case. For if $u_\alpha = 0$ at the ideal level of output Bowen's criterion and our optimality condition are identical.

The studies by Samuelson and Strotz are so closely related that they can be discussed together. Both are set in general equilibrium frameworks, and both seek the vector of public goods levels that maximises the value of a social welfare function. Samuelson's social welfare indicator is an increasing function of individuals' utilities; Strotz' is linear in individual utilities. Both assume that the output of public and private goods together is constrained by some aggregate social transformation function. As regards the ideal output of public goods they arrive at the same criterion, which Samuelson expresses thus:

$$\sum_\alpha \frac{u^\alpha_{n+j}}{u^\alpha_r} = \frac{F_{n+j}}{F_r}$$

where u^α_{n+j} is the marginal utility of public good j to consumer α,

      u^α_r is the marginal utility of private good r to him, and

      F_{n+j}/F_r is the marginal rate of transformation of private good r into public good j according to the social transformation function.

These concepts do not appear explicitly in our model, and so must be translated. In our notation the marginal utility of public good j to consumer α is proportional to F^*_j, that of private good r is proportional to its price, so Samuelson's left-hand side becomes

$$\sum_\alpha \frac{u^\alpha_{n+j}}{u^\alpha_r} = \sum_\alpha \frac{F^{\alpha*}_{n+j}}{p_r}.$$

The aggregate social transformation function does not come up explicitly in our model but our assumptions on the firms' and the government's production sets are sufficient to assure that there is a social production set and that it has proper convexity. Furthermore, at the private plus government general equilibrium point the supporting plane of the social production set has coefficients proportional to $(p, -q/u_0) = (p, MC(g)_1, \ldots, MC(g_m))$, i.e. the same as the supporting plane of the government's production set. The marginal rates of transformation being simply the ratios of coefficients of the supporting plane, we have $F_{n+j}/F_r = MC(g_j)/p_r$. Accordingly, Samuelson's criterion reduces to

$$\sum_\alpha F_{n+j}^{\alpha*} = MC(g_j),$$

that is, each public good should be produced at the level at which its marginal cost equals the sum of the marginal willingnesses to pay for it on the part of all the citizen-consumers. This is the same as Bowen's criterion, as Samuelson remarked. Both Samuelson and, particularly, Strotz laid great emphasis on the importance of income redistribution, i.e flexible tax policy, in the attainment of this optimum. Since income redistribution is precluded in our model and since there are political constraints besides, such a government as we are imagining could not attain this ideal. All the remarks we made in comparing our model with Bowen's apply with equal force to the comparison with Samuelson's (Strotz concurring).

4 SOME IMPLICATIONS

It will be recalled that when Dupuit wrote his famous paper on the utility of public works he introduced the notion of consumer's surplus but despaired that the demand curves on which it depended could ever be measured. He argued that his concept was useful in spite of the fact that quantification appeared to be impossible. We now know that his pessimism was not altogether justified, although demand curves have remained very difficult to estimate to this very day.

I find myself in a very similar situation, seeing little or no reason to hope that the citizen's surpluses that I have described can be ascertained numerically. Dupuit was wrong; so may I be, but I regard the outlook as bleak.

I know of only one really serious effort to grapple with this problem, and it merits discussion here. In 1943, Howard Bowen proposed a voting procedure for determining the socially ideal level of output of a public good [6].

Bowen's proposal is to put the level of expenditure on a public good to a referendum. Before the referendum the voters are to be made as well informed as possible about the consequences of different levels of expenditure and, in particular, that the cost is to be shared equally among them. At the referendum each voter indicates the level of expenditure that he prefers. The mode of these voters' preferences is then adopted.

It is assumed explicitly that each voter will indicate the level that he, individually, prefers. This level is, of course, the one at which the marginal contribution of a dollar spent on the public good to that voter's welfare, as he sees it, is equal to the marginal worth to him of his tax contribution or of one-*nth* of a dollar. Then, assuming that the individual voters' marginal utilities for the public good are symmetrically distributed, Bowen argues that the mode of the voters' preferences 'may be presumed to indicate the point of intersection between the curve of marginal cost per person and the modal or average curve of marginal substitution [between the public good and disposable income]' [6, p. 37]. This level, moreover, is shown to be the ideal level of the public good in most cases.

Now there are some technical difficulties with this proposal, which are not very instructive to pursue, but, more pertinent to our interest, there is a nasty, game-theoretic side to it, which Bowen would not have passed over as lightly as he did if he had been writing a few years later. For, to keep things simple suppose that two voters, Mr A and Mr B are the whole electorate and that Mr A would like a higher level of the public good than Mr B. This is the sort of information that would be known, at least vaguely, to both of them. If Mr A and Mr B both vote for the levels that they desire, Mr A would get less of the public good than he wants (taking, crudely, the mode of two votes to be the midpoint between them). Mr A can remedy this situation easily by voting for somewhat more than he actually wants. He would be foolish not to do so, just as Mr B would be foolish not to vote for somewhat less than he really wants. This is an especially easy game. The Nash equilibrium point is for Mr A to vote for twice the level that he really wants, and for Mr B to vote for zero. Mr A wins. The assymetry results from the fact that Mr A can vote for as large a scale as he chooses, but Mr B cannot vote for less than zero.

This is a defect to worry about but not necessarily decisive. To add a little realism, suppose there are a number of Mr A's and a number of Mr B's, e.g. some families and some elderly couples all of whom want schools, but do not feel their urgency with equal keenness. The difficulty of co-ordinating even the slight amount of duplicity required to win the game would make Bowen's voting procedure work somewhat better than in the case where all group consultations could be conducted within a single head.

When there are several social groups with divergent interests, then, as Bowen recognised, another difficulty in principle arises. An unweighted mean, median, or mode can be used to average the preferences of symmetrically distributed individuals, but how are the votes of contending interest groups to be averaged? A small cabal from the A group could distort either the arithmetic average or the mode; a small cabal from the B group could capture the mode; even without any connivance the numerically larger group would control the median. Bowen's suggestion is to use a sequence of referenda administered to the groups separately and to adjust the allocation of cost between the groups after each referendum until both groups vote for the same level. But then the proposal looses its intriguing simplicity.

I conclude, then, that Bowen's procedure could not work and, at any rate, is not descriptive of any extant political procedure. In the light of these and other difficulties, which he recognised, Bowen urged strongly the use of public opinion polls for ascertaining citizens' preferences [6, p. 43]. Hotelling has made the same suggestion in a similar connection [12]. More recently Holt recommended the use of questionnaire methods for assistance in determining welfare objectives [11]. My own opinion is that no matter how informative public opinion polls may be for many purposes, they cannot be relied on to disclose the willingness-to-be-taxed functions $F^\alpha(g, p)$.

A great deal is known about the structure and determinants of voters' preferences but I cannot pretend to knowledge of this subject. These preferences appear to be a complex mixture of firmly held convictions and lightly held opinions. The man in the street is swayed easily by arguments about matters remote from his daily concerns and fundamental beliefs. Should the United States be spending $50 billion on national defence? The average citizen is willing to hope that someone in Washington has figured it out about right, or else to accept the authority of his party's spokesmen. What else can he or I do? So it seems that these $F^\alpha(g, p)$ reflect the preferences of group leaders, professional and volunteer, more nearly than they do the preferences of the great rank-and-file. The leaders, who have occasion to become informed and to think things through, know better than the followers where all will stand when the chips are down.

Thus the $F^\alpha(g, p)$ are quite different from demand curves, to which

they have a formal resemblance.   Demand curves pertain to individuals.
Citizens' preferences pertain to groups: they are formed, articulated,
and changed by group leaders (with due respect for deep-seated preconceptions beyond their reach) and are accepted, as long as current, by all
the members of the group.   The citizens' surplus functions, and the
preference maps from which they are derived, reflect the limit to the
exercise of sovereignty by individual citizens.   The $F^\alpha(g, p)$ on the basis
of which a citizen's spokesman makes his decisions is only one of a great
number of such functions consistent with the citizen's desires, as sharply
as he cares to formulate them.   A political leader can, under the pressure
of expediency or changed convictions, change his preference map substantially and carry most of his constituency with him.   Herein lies the
'leadership' of political leaders and their scope for constructive initiative.
They do more than reflect the wishes of their constituents; they define,
articulate and apply them to practical problems.

I am not saying that voters have no preferences worth considering with
respect to public goods.   I am saying that we voters don't know our
preferences; that we have to be told what they are by people who accept
our prejudices and premises and who also understand the consequences
and implications of particular political decisions.   In consequence, surveying voters' preferences is like surveying castles in the sand.   Firm
bedrock is somewhere else.

For an essay that began with an attempt to insert a government sector
into a quantitative model of economic equilibrium, we have come to a
strange result.   We have been led to base our approach on a concept –
citizen's surplus – whose quantifiability is very doubtful.   But we should
not be under any illusions about how quantitative the theory of general
equilibrium is.   It contains no numbers, and its significant theorems are
all qualitative in nature.   So we do no violence to the spirit of the theory
by adding still another concept that defies empirical measurement.   In
so far as the formulation just proposed has merit, it permits the apparatus
of general equilibrium theory to be used to provide guidance for decisions
about public goods.   It indicates the social losses that arise from not
integrating decisions about public goods with tax and income policy.
It helps explain that the discrepancies that have been noted between the
marginal social benefits of public expenditures on different programmes
may be due, not to inattention or maladministration, but to the built-in
protections that the political process provides to minorities in a world
where the delicateent adjustm of tax policy and income distribution is not
always feasible.   Above all, it provides a conceptual framework that may

help bridge the gap between professional economists and practising politicians.

If the economist could free himself of his lofty disdain for the considerations foremost in the mind of the practising government official, he might enhance the sympathetic understanding between himself and officials. With the best will in the world, there is only one way for him to do that. He must accept that a government can no more violate its political constraints than it can transgress its production possibility set, and he must build these constraints into the core of his thinking, as we have done, instead of grudgingly admitting that in the end his recommendations have to be warped in the interests of political feasibility.

It is conventional, and almost obligatory, at the end of a theoretical essay to remind the reader that it is only a crude, first, tentative approximation and that a great deal more work remains to be done. I follow this convention with special enthusiasm in the present instance because the shortcomings of the political model I have proposed are so numerous and significant. Yet I do not believe that they entirely smother the germ of truth that it contains.

In the first place, the 'government' in this model is so simplified that it is practically emasculated. It does nothing but levy taxes and produce public goods. The social waste that we detected stems largely from the failure of this government to co-ordinate its tax policy with its public goods decisions and from its inability to make compensating income transfers. The reader should recall that we excluded these ameliorative fiscal devices by assumption. This assumption seems justified, however: governments in fact do not co-ordinate their tax policies very finely with their expenditure programmes, and it probably would be impractical for them to try to do so. Income transfers would certainly mitigate some of the social waste, but it should be recognised that they introduce distortions of their own and can provide only a limited offset to the costs of meeting what I have called 'political constraints'. Still, a more adequate treatment of the taxation side of governmental decisions would be highly desirable, particularly one that took account of the price structure distortions that taxes inevitably cause.

No attention has been paid to public goods provided by entities other than the government, or to externalities of any kind. Yet these are closely akin to the phenomena we have studied and should be included in any complete treatment.

I am not well satisfied with my characterisation of socio-economic groups or with my treatment of their relationship to their leaders.

Particularly I am aware that the preference maps of government officials, other political leaders, and the general public all are altered in the course of the give-and-take of the political process. I see no objection to conceiving of them as being concrete and definite at any one time (apart from the vagueness of the preferences felt by ordinary citizens), but I am sorry to have to treat them as immutable, which they surely are not. The laws of change of preference maps are a subject for a separate investigation that I could not undertake. In regard to these matters of political theory, I feel that I have gone about as far as my competence and duty as an economist can justify.

I am aware also of some technical defects in the formulation. The most bothersome is that the definition of citizens' surplus, on which so much depends, is ambiguous. The surplus functions of the different socio-economic groups will be affected by the basal level of government activity with which proposed programmes are compared. There is no reason why all groups should compare a proposed programme to the same base. The concept of citizens' surplus seems fundamentally sound, but the formulation permits improvement. I do not know how to improve it.

I have reservations also about the requirement that *no* group receive a negative citizens' surplus. It is a great mathematical convenience and it has Wicksell's blessing, but still I wish I had been able to construct my argument without it.

Finally, this model is subject to all the strong limitations of general equilibrium analysis. It is thoroughly static. It ignores the risks and the uncertainties that are so important an aspect of political as well as economic affairs. It excludes the possibilities of increasing returns in production and of non-convexity of consumers' and citizens' preferences.

The model is, in short, only a beginning which I hope is on the right track.

REFERENCES

[1] Kenneth J. Arrow, *Social Choice and Individual Values* (New York, 1951).
[2] Chester I. Barnard, *The Functions of the Executive* (Cambridge, Mass., 1954).
[3] William J. Baumol, *Welfare Economics and the Theory of the State* (Cambridge, Mass., 1952).
[4] Abram Bergson, 'A reformulation of certain aspects of welfare economics', *Quarterly Journal of Economics*, LII (Feb 1938) 310–34.
[5] Duncan Black, 'On the rationale of group decision-making', *Journal of Political Economy*, LVI (Feb 1948) 23–34.

[6] Howard R. Bowen, 'The interpretation of voting in the allocation of economic resources', *Quarterly Journal of Economics*, LVIII (Nov 1943) 27–48.

[7] Gerard Debreu, *Theory of Value* (New York, 1959).

[8] Anthony Downs, *An Economic Theory of Democracy* (New York, 1957).

[9] Duncan K. Foley, 'Resource allocation and the public sector', *Yale Economic Essays*, forthcoming.

[10] J. Kenneth Galbraith, *The Affluent Society* (Boston, 1958).

[11] Charles C. Holt, 'Quantitative decision analysis and national policy', in Bert G. Hickman (ed.), *Quantitative Planning of Economic Policy* (Washington, 1965) 252–66.

[12] Harold Hotelling, 'The general welfare in relation to problems of taxation and of railway and utility rates', *Econometrica*, VI (Jul 1938) 242–69.

[13] Leif Johansen, *Public Economics* (Amsterdam and Chicago, 1965).

[14] Samuel Karlin, *Mathematical Methods and Theory in Games, Programming, and Economics*, vol. I (Reading, Mass., 1959).

[15] Charles E. Lindblom, *The Intelligence of Democracy* (New York, 1965).

[16] Paul A. Samuelson, 'The pure theory of public expenditure', *Review of Economics and Statistics*, XXXVI (Nov 1954) 387–9.

[17] Paul A. Samuelson, 'Diagrammatic exposition of a theory of public expenditure', *Review of Economics and Statistics*, XXXVII (Nov 1955) 350–6.

[18] Paul A. Samuelson, 'Aspects of public expenditure theories', *Review of Economics and Statistics*, XL (Nov 1958) 332–8.

[19] Robert H. Strotz, 'Two propositions related to public goods', *Review of Economics and Statistics*, XL (Nov 1958) 329–31.

[20] David B. Truman, *The Governmental Process: political interests and Public opinion* (New York, 1960).

[21] Knut Wicksell, 'A new principle of just taxation', in R. A. Musgrave and A. T. Peacock (eds.), *Classics in the Theory of Public Finance* (London and New York, 1964) pp. 72–118.

11 Investment Behaviour Rules and Practices of Public Enterprises

L. Stoleru

(COMMISSARIAT GÉNÉRAL DU PLAN, PARIS)

INTRODUCTION

In many countries, the State has taken over the management of various sectors of the economy. Whatever the technical, political or simply historical reasons for this change from private management, it is important to know what difference it makes. This paper attempts to outline the behavioural differences between government and private management in the specific case of *investment* problems.

With this in mind, the following points will be examined in turn:

1 The scale of public investment compared with the total national investment.
2 Selective investment patterns in the power sector of the economy (the case of Électricité de France).
3 Investment patterns in the transport sector.
4 Investment patterns in the tele-communications sector.
5 Governmental arbitration among sectors and the constraints specific to public enterprises.

1 THE SCALE OF PUBLIC INVESTMENT IN RELATION TO TOTAL NATIONAL INVESTMENT IN FRANCE

(1) DEFINITION OF THE PUBLIC SECTOR

The State is involved in many areas of a modern economy and is engaged in everything from coal production to setting up Maisons de la Culture, not to mention building highways, constructing schools, modernising the telephone system, etc. In fact, the role of the State includes such disparate activities that it is essential to make a distinction between several kinds of public enterprise. One manner of dividing them is into productive and collective undertakings.

A. *Productive Undertakings*

It is customary to include the following public enterprises in this category:

Power sector: Charbonnages de France (coal), Électricité de France (electricity), Gaz de France (gas).

Transport sector: S.N.C.F. (railways), Régie Autonome des Transports Parisiens (Paris bus and underground), Air France and Aéroport de Paris (national airline and Paris airport authority).

Communications sector: Postal service and tele-communications, radio and television.

Services sector: hospitals.

Other sectors: Commissariat à l'Énergie Atomique (Atomic Energy Commission), Office National de l'Azote (nitrogen), Renault (automobiles), other nationalised enterprises in competitive sectors of the economy, tobacco and matches.

In general, the enterprises mentioned above are monopolies in the sense that each is virtually the only enterprise in France supplying a given product: coal, electricity, telephone services, rail transport, etc. This monopoly is more or less strict depending on whether a substitute can be found for a product; there is competition between coal, fuel oil and electricity, but it is not really possible to imagine any domestic competition for tobacco, or the telephone or postal service. International competition exists, of course (e.g. for air traffic). On the other hand, some state-run enterprises are in direct competition with private companies: Renault and Chimie des Charbonnages de France (Chemicals Division of the coal-mining industry) are cases in point. Obviously, their overall management and, in particular, their investment policies will be very closely bound up with the nature of the position they hold on the market.

B. *Collective Undertakings*

As used in the national budget, this title covers all undertakings providing services which are non-productive, in that they are 'not accounted for in the gross domestic product'. However, these services do figure in the national product (where they are evaluated at their cost price). This category includes:

(i) The agricultural infrastructure: irrigation, slaughter-houses, re-distribution of land, regional development.

(ii) Transport infrastructure: roads, ports, canals, civil aviation.
(iii) Urban infrastructure: urban transport, town-planning.
(iv) Schools: secondary schools, universities, research.
(v) Cultural programmes.
(vi) Government building.

These activities constitute what is traditionally called 'public services', and this sector is not accounted as having any calculable productive value.

In fact, if the analysis is taken slightly further, it immediately becomes apparent that the separation between the collective sphere and the productive sphere is very blurred: certain collective goods tend to become merchandise; the creation of 'Agences de Bassin' (water authorities) shows that water will increasingly be considered as a marketable commodity, the appearance of toll-paying motor-ways and of public and privately-owned parking lots has transformed certain aspects of transport so that some 'collective' economic activities could rapidly move into the area of 'productive' activity.

(2) PUBLIC INVESTMENT IN 1964

A. *The Place of Public Investment in National Investment*
Investment in the public sector represented approximately one-third of total national investment.

(In Fr. 000 million in 1964)	Investment in 1964	Percentage
Private enterprise	35·9	40·4
Public sector	28·2	31·8
Housing	24·7	27·8
National investment	88·8	100

In the above table 'public' investment is limited to investment by state-owned enterprises or by government agencies. The State also participates in investment by private enterprises and in housing by means of the loans it grants.

B. *Distribution of Public Investment between Productive and Collective Activities*
Breaking down the figures in terms of the categories defined above, the following sums are obtained:

In Fr. 000 million 1964

Productive investment

Charbonnages de France	1·01
Électricité de France	4·58
Compagnie Nationale du Rhône	0·31
Gaz de France	0·62
Atomic Energy Commission	3·00
S.N.C.F.	3·16
R.A.T.P.	0·30
Post and Telecommunications	1·70
Air France and Paris airport	0·27
Radio and Television Authority	0·25
Hospitals	0·81
Others	1·18
Total	17·19

Collective investment

Agriculture	1·64
Roads	1·83
Ports	0·34
Canals	0·26
Civil Aviation	0·14
Urban infrastructure	1·68
Schools	3·53
Cultural activities	0·26
Sanitation	0·35
Government building	0·97
Total	11·00

Total for public sector   28·19

In this paper, only the productive sector of government economic activity will be considered and, within this category, special attention will be paid to those activities which can be usefully and immediately compared to private enterprises. On the basis of these two criteria, the following public sectors seem most likely to repay close examination:

	Investment
Power sector: coal mines, electricity, Rhône power, gas	6·34
Transport sector: railways, Paris transport, aviation, roads, ports, canals	6·30
Communications sector: Post and Telecommunications Authority	1·70
Competitive sector: (Renault, Nitrogen Office)	1·00
	15·34

In other public sectors (e.g. the Atomic Energy Authority, Radio-Television Authority, Education, Cultural investment, etc.), investment programmes are worked out on the basis of criteria and priorities which are too far removed from those of private enterprise for any useful comparisons to be possible. Roads, ports and canals have been included in the productive sector because 'transport' is increasingly a marketable commodity.

The public sector constituted in this way has a special characteristic: it tends to be extremely capitalistic. In private enterprise, it is extremely rare to invest more than 20 per cent of profits (11 per cent on an average); public enterprises have much higher rates of re-investment: electricity investment: 76 per cent of value added; coal mines investment: 26 per cent of value added; post and tele-communications: 35 per cent of value added.

The consequences of the highly capitalistic nature of some public enterprises will be explored more fully below, following a study of the investment behaviour of the principal public sectors of the economy, namely power, transport and communications.

2 INVESTMENT BEHAVIOUR IN PUBLIC POWER COMPANIES: A CASE STUDY OF ÉLECTRICITÉ DE FRANCE

Among the state-owned enterprises engaged in the production of power are les Charbonnages (coal mines), Électricité de France, Gaz de France and a number of oil companies.

A systematic policy of cut-back has been imposed on the Charbonnages; the declining rate of production is largely dictated by social priorities. Investment policy therefore does not include any programme for expanded capacity but only for replacement or for more productive equipment.

The state-owned oil companies face rather keen competition from the other companies in the same field (both French and foreign companies) and management does not, therefore, differ fundamentally from private management in this case.

Undoubtedly the most interesting case for study is provided by E.D.F. (Électricité de France); it is a very capitalistic enterprise which is expanding rapidly and which enjoys the monopoly of electric power production.

(1) THE CHOICE OF PRODUCTION TARGETS

Demand growth patterns. The process begins with an estimate of future demand based on past behaviour (demand has tended to double every nine or ten years) and on the general prospects for the economy.

The accepted econometric assumption is:

Annual growth rate of electricity demand	=	3·5 per cent plus annual rate of increase for G.D.P.

This overall demand forecast must be supplemented by another estimate of future demand showing:

—distribution throughout the year (winter peaks),
—variations in regional distribution,
—distribution according to sectors of the economy.

Flexibility of demand. The forecasts accordingly obtained are used as the production targets. In fact, these forecasts implicitly entail a certain 'regularity' in the pattern as far as the price of power is concerned. It is always possible to increase or cut back consumption at a given moment by changing the overall price level or by remodelling the rate structure but this would give rise to a dual problem:

Rate-fixing policy. E.D.F. can choose from among a number of policies: a monopoly policy aimed at maximum profits with allowance for flexibility of demand, a policy of the balanced budget in which power is sold at the average cost, a 'true price' policy of selling at marginal cost, i.e. having each customer pay the cost of the last KWh which had to be produced to satisfy his demand.

Since it is not the purpose of this paper to discuss pricing problems, the matter need not be gone into any further. We should merely point out that the three policies are, generally speaking, incompatible (for instance, selling at marginal cost does not guarantee a balanced budget) and that E.D.F. has opted for a rating policy very close to the *marginal cost*.

Rate forecasting. Once a figure has been obtained for the demand for electricity in 1970 or 1975, this production target then becomes the basis for an optimised capital investment programme designed to meet this demand and, often, it only becomes possible to reckon the marginal cost and the corresponding selling rate of power *after* all the figures have been worked out. It is possible that this rate is not consistent with the demand forecast. In these circumstances, the only solution is to prepare for a series of converging iterations. A production target is chosen, the capital equipment required is deduced and the marginal cost of the expanded production calculated; if the price based on this marginal cost does not enable the output to be disposed of, the production target will have to be amended accordingly so as to take into account the flexibility of demand.

Formulating production targets. Setting a total, annual production target is obviously not enough. Electricity cannot be stored and load curves have therefore to be plotted throughout the year. Here again the problem of iterations crops up, even more acutely than in the earlier situation, for the distribution of demand in the course of a day, a month or a year can be influenced to a marked extent by the rate structure.

In practice, the problem is slightly simplified by reducing the load curve to a few key figures, i.e. the level of the peak demand and the length of the high-demand period.

(2) A FIRST STEP: OUTLINING THE CAPITAL INVESTMENT PROGRAMME

A. *Determining the Long-Term Structure of the Capital Equipment*

It might be thought that in evaluating the advisability of building a thermal or hydraulic power station, it would be enough to weigh capital outlay against predicted earnings. In fact, the problem is insoluble because the management policy of the power station – i.e. whether it would operate at the base throughout the year or only for peaking – would have to be known. This, in turn, involves familiarity with the strains on the electric power production system and these are linked with the nature of the capital equipment already in use. The present thermal/hydraulic distribution in France involves strains connected with the *total* peak demand (demand on the entire system in winter time). A different equipment structure – entirely thermal or entirely hydraulic – would shift the strains (to peak hours in the day or to low-water periods, for instance).

Under these conditions, the relative values of a thermal and a hydraulic station providing the *same service* cannot be compared in absolute terms because the value of the service depends essentially on the composition of the entire installation of heavy equipment: the service provided by a given hydraulic station varies, depending on the time of year at which the entire productive system reaches the limits of its capacity.

For this reason, an overall programme must be outlined before any particular power station scheme can be analysed in detail.

B. *The 3-Plan Model*

This overall programme is based on a model of investment behaviour called the '3-plan model' because it covers a fifteen-year period. Using the model, it is possible to work out the optimal capital equipment structure; for this, as we have seen, it is necessary both to define the types of equipment and to *decide on the operating policy which will govern their use.*

(a) *The unknowns in the model.* The possible kinds of equipment are broken down into the main categories (conventional thermal plant; nuclear thermal, gas turbines, various kinds of hydraulic plant) which create – for the three five-year periods – a total of 86 unknowns.

Parameters are then introduced representing the various possible policies (e.g. amount of power produced during the year, during peak periods, etc.); these involve 167 unknowns.

The model thus contains 253 unknowns.

(b) *Constraints.* The conditions the plan is required to comply with are of several kinds:

   (i) *30 Demand constraints*: For each period
          Production⩾Predicted consumption
  (ii) *170 capacity constraints*: For each period
          Production⩽Capacity
  (iii) *15 constraints involving the number of available sites*: For hydraulic power-stations, sites are limited geographically and
          Capacity⩽Geographic limitations on installation.
  (iv) *9 service guarantee constraints*

Production and consumption are both uncertain factors: on the production side there is the random factor of hydraulic power generation and, on the demand side, there are the uncertainties associated with any forecasting. Demand constraints are therefore established on the basis of the *mean* predictable production and consumption but, if the matter were left there, the risk of power shortages would be too great (nearly 50 per cent). Hence the need for additional constraints which reduce the *probability of shortages* to an acceptable figure.

This entails 224 constraints in all.

(c) *Objective target.* The aim is to keep the total cost of equipment to a minimum, total cost here including both actualised investment costs and operating costs.

(d) *Solution.* The linear programme obtained in this way is rather cumbersome to process (253 unknowns, 224 constraints) and it can be streamlined by replacing 'stepped' constraints by 'continuous' constraints, i.e. by departing from linear programming and introducing non-linear functions. This gives a virtually equivalent model containing only 68 unknowns and 48 constraints. The problem can then be solved on an electronic computer.

C. *Interpreting the Capital Equipment Plan*

Once the model has been solved, it provides the structure for the plant required. Naturally, the structure is based on the assumptions made, i.e. chiefly on the forecasts of demand and of the technical possibilities at the production end (for example, the characteristics of nuclear power). If the marginal costs associated with the programme turned out to represent a sharp rise or fall in relation to past trends, the programme would have to be reviewed by adapting the demand to the corresponding variations in rate.

In addition, results are influenced by a number of factors outside the control of E.D.F.: the cost of equipment and supplies, for instance, and especially the rates of discount used in calculations. These figures should be supplied by the central planning agency, the Commissariat du Plan.

Deciding on as *rate of discount* raises many problems which are discussed below. The problems are important and the solution of the programme can be significantly affected if this rate is modified. For example, the decision on whether or not to construct nuclear power plant depends essentially on the rate of interest.

Another external assumption is related to the *service guarantee*. This figure is set rather arbitrarily (the power shortage risk is set at 2 per cent for instance) but solving the programme makes it possible to obtain the relevant *power shortage cost*, i.e. to estimate the saving represented by accepting a 3 per cent risk of a power shortage instead of a 2 per cent risk. This cost can then be compared with the cost of a power failure, certain aspects of which can be reckoned accurately (e.g. the direct loss of earnings for E.D.F., the cost of production losses for customers affected) while other aspects are harder to assess (e.g. the increase in stand-by equipment installed by customers).

(3) OVERALL DETERMINATION OF AN INVESTMENT PROGRAMME

When an overall outline has been worked out in this way, it becomes possible to analyse each project in detail. At this point, it is possible to compare equipment on the basis of *equal service* rendered since the optimal operating policy for each type of equipment is known.

A. *Calculating Profitability*

The basis for the comparison is a thermal power station, a type of installation whose characteristics are well known and which is already in operation.

By comparing it with a hydraulic power station, it is possible to obtain a differential actualised balance-sheet (in comparison with the thermal power station) of earnings; investment costs and operating costs.

Whenever the balance sheet becomes positive, hydraulic equipment should be substituted for thermal; the difficulties with such an approach stem from the fact that the balance-sheet depends essentially on the rate of actualisation adopted. The Commissariat du Plan has recommended that the national rate be considered as 7 per cent, and E.D.F. should be able to install hydraulic or nuclear equipment whenever the balance-sheet described above becomes positive with a rate of 7 per cent. In point of fact, however, the investment credits allocated to E.D.F. by the government will not cover the financing of all such projects.

E.D.F. therefore has to rank its projects in order of priority so as to implement only the most profitable ones. The ranking is based on the 'co-efficient of marginal profitability', which is equal to the ratio of the discounted profit of the previously described balance sheet to the additional amount of investment which would be required to replace thermal with hydraulic plant. By only carrying out the projects which offer the highest profitability co-efficients, the company derives the highest discounted profit which is possible in view of the financing constraints.

However, it would undoubtedly be more logical to use a higher rate of discount than 7 per cent so as to be able to finance effectively all projects whose discounted balance sheets are positive at this rate.

B. *Complementary Nature of Overall and Analytical Methods*

The overall programme provides, as we have seen, for determining the 'mass plan' of the capital equipment, i.e. its general structure and the costs associated with optimal operating policies.

Analytical studies are based on these costs and on the physical characteristics of the capital investment programme; they are used to study, case by case, the thermal, hydraulic and nuclear power station projects.

This approach remains coherent so long as it is possible to assemble all the projects selected and obtain an overall picture which coincides approximately with the overall programme of the 3-plan model. Otherwise, the costs taken into consideration in the profitability calculations for each power station are incorrect and the calculations must be started over again from scratch.

Similar difficulties arise regarding the rate of discount. If the different projects are classified and the list selected in the light of the budgetary constraints, this will give a marginal profitability rate which should, in theory, be the rate of discount used in the 3-plan model. This is, however, not always the case in that the rate used is 7 per cent whereas certain projects, for which the profitability rate is 9 per cent, cannot be financed because of credit restrictions.

An iterative process has, therefore, to be used at each stage, bringing the structure of the 3-plan model closer to the structure of the set of projects chosen after each one has been investigated.

3   INVESTMENT BEHAVIOUR IN THE TRANSPORT SECTOR

1   APPROACHING THE PROBLEM

The Ministry of Transport has tried to tackle the *overall problem* of transport, i.e. to fashion an approach to the problem which can be applied to all means of transport: railways, highways, waterways, air transport, etc.

It has become increasingly apparent that a coherent overall transport scheme is needed if each of the various means of transport is to be expanded in the direction offering the greatest increase in national utility at the lowest additional cost. A major difficulty is that 'transport demand' is, in certain respects, less well defined than 'electricity demand'. The demand for transporting cement by railway can perhaps be reckoned and predicted fairly accurately but it is extremely difficult to speak of the 'demand for use of a motorway'. In other words, it is fairly easy to locate the moment at which too much electricity is being produced, but it is much more difficult to say precisely when too many miles of motorway are being constructed.

In this situation, the only possibility is to learn to predict the benefits to be gained from creating a particular transport link so as to ascertain whether they are sufficient to justify the cost of the infrastructure.

A. *Determining the Benefits*

If a motorway is not built, traffic will continue to use the existing routes and the benefits of a motorway are therefore equivalent to the difference between users' expenses on the new and on the old systems. Both current users and the new 'consumers' who would appear with the creation of a new highway must be included in the calculation. Expenses are fundamentally of three kinds:

> Operating costs: petrol, depreciation, etc.
> Time spent.
> The risk of accidents and the resulting expenditure.

Obviously it is not possible to assess the benefits of a better road accurately without taking into account the time saved and the enhanced safety: as far as petrol alone is concerned, it is often more expensive to travel on a motorway than on an ordinary road. Clearly, therefore, there is more to the question than fuel alone.

The problem remains of how to assess the concrete values of the *time-saving* and *increased safety* provided by highways, trains, aeroplanes and other means of transport.

Behaviour studies and comparisons with methods used abroad (in the U.S.A. in particular) have been adopted to determine values for the time associated with each of several modes of transportation (e.g. 6 frs. per hour per person on highways); safety has been evaluated in terms of the cost of accidents (using insurance statistics). These figures are then used as a basis for economic calculations of the efficiency of investments in the transport sector.

B. *Impossibility of Defining an Overall Programme*

E.D.F. knows that it must satisfy a certain overall demand for electricity. The electricity itself can be produced anywhere and brought to the consumer through an interconnected grid. The situation is very different as far as transport is concerned since, for instance, the construction of a motorway from Paris to Lille is of no use to anyone who needs means of transport elsewhere. Consequently, there can be no overall transport programme except in the sense in which the sum of independent projects constitutes a whole. Of course, for each stretch AB, all the various possible ways of linking A and B need to be examined. Put in another way: it is impossible in this field to study a project 'marginally', in terms of an overall programme, in the way in which an electric power station can be studied marginally to an equipment programme.

C. *Analysis: the Rate of Immediate Profitability*

If we accept the fact that only *independent* projects are possible it becomes necessary, in theory, to compare the actualised benefits with the cost of the investment (plus the actualised costs of maintenance, etc.). But, in view of the special characteristics of transport equipment, the calculation can be simplified by using the *immediate profitability rate* method.

To do this, it must be possible to assume that the curve of accumulated benefits as a function of time is independent of the date of entry into service: the resulting new traffic is small in comparison to the existing traffic. From that date onwards, since the benefits continue to increase and the infrastructure is long-lived, the balance sheet realised at rate i is sure to be positive if the benefit B of the *first year of service* is greater than:

$$B \geqslant iD$$

where D represents the cost of the scheme. The discounted balance S is then:

$$S = D + \sum_n \frac{Bn}{(1+i)n} > -D + \frac{B}{\Sigma(1+i)n} = -D + \frac{B}{i} \geqslant 0.$$

At this point it becomes necessary to work out the year when it would be most profitable to bring the scheme into service; this should be the year in which it is no longer profitable to defer the project further in time; postponing the project one year involves the loss of the benefit B of the first year and results in a saving of iD. In optimum conditions, the situation should therefore be:

$$B = iD$$

We can define the immediate profitability rate as the ratio of the first year's benefit to the cost of the installation:

$$r = \frac{B}{D}$$

The previous condition can be expressed:

$$r \qquad = \qquad i$$
Rate of immediate profitability = Rate of discount

In short, if the assumptions set forth above are correct, before installing a transportation infrastructure it is necessary to wait until the rate of immediate profitability (which increases, like B, with time) attains equality with the rate of discount: the new installation is then not only profitable but a maximum profitability.

2 The Overall Choice of Projects for Implementation

According to what has just been said, the best mode of transport for a given length is the first variable to be determined (by calculation of present values), and the optimum date of entry into service the next. The only thing left to be done in a given year is then to implement all those projects for which the immediate profitability rates have become equal to the actualisation rates.

In practice the problem is complicated by the fact that there are generally not enough credits available to carry out the programme defined in this way: some 'skimming off' is therefore necessary. It can be shown that if all projects have benefits which increase with time (even at different rates provided these rates are more or less regular), this 'skimming off' can be done by *ranking the projects in the order of their rates of immediate profitability*. The point can be shown graphically as follows:

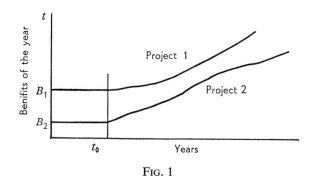

FIG. 1

Let us consider two projects, 1 and 2, with costs $D1$ and $D2$. If they have to be ranked at a given moment t_0, the one which will be less costly to postpone has to be ascertained:

Postponing 1 for a year represents a loss of $B_1 - iD_1 = D_1(r_1 - i)$
Postponing 2 for a year represents a loss of $B_2 - id_2 = D_2(r_2 - i)$

If $r_1 \; r_2$, the smaller loss will result from postponing project 2; *if credits are lacking it will therefore be more advisable to give priority to the schemes which have the highest rates of immediate profitability.*

Influence of the choice of rate of discount. If there were no budgetary constraints, the optimal programme would involve all the projects whose rates of immediate profitability were higher than their rates of discount.

In so far as the assumptions underlying this method are borne out in practice, it follows that the rate of discount should be such that all the projects of the optimal programme *at that rate* can be financed. The experience of the Fifth Plan has shown that this is not at all the case since the rate of discount proposed by the Commissariat du Plan was 7 to 8 per cent, whereas the final decisions as to the sizes of various 'packages' entailed shelving a certain number of highway equipment programmes whose rates of immediate profitability were higher (even distinctly higher) than 8 per cent. We shall have occasion to come back to this problem.

4 INVESTMENT BEHAVIOUR IN THE COMMUNICATIONS SECTOR

(1) THE STRUCTURAL PROBLEMS

In contrast to the case of E.D.F. there is no industrial-type 'telephone' company but rather a Ministry of Telecommunications. An unfortunate consequence of this structure is that all income and expenditure fall under an 'Ancillary Budget' which is approved at the same time as the national budget and which lumps together the postal service, postal cheque accounts and the telephone system. Even at the regional level, the resulting administrative structure is scarcely conducive to economic staff management and accounting.

(2) TEMPORARY PROBLEMS STEMMING FROM THE PRESENT SITUATION

The present state of relative scarcity of funds also poses problems: the number of new authorisations foreseen in the Fifth Plan – 9,000 million francs between 1965 and 1970 – is high in comparison with the past but seems less satisfactory when viewed in the light of the fact that 96,000 million will be required in the course of the next twenty years if, by 1985, we are to reach the degree of advancement in this field which the U.S.A. *now* enjoys.

It is therefore necessary to define priorities without knowing whether they ought to be based on technical criteria or worked out in terms of 'public service'. Is it justifiable to deny telephones to people in a given category when they have no way of obtaining the same service from a competitor to the Ministry? Yet, if profitability is to be taken as the criterion, telephones would surely have to be allocated to commercial establishments and to industry, not to private dwellings. In practice, what happens is that, on the one hand, almost all investments making for increased productivity (e.g. automatic exchanges), no matter how profitable, will be rejected because they do not help relieve the problem of a system which has reached saturation point and, on the other hand, a certain percentage of new lines will be allocated to every type of subscriber.

(3) TECHNICAL PROBLEMS

Even if profitability is taken as the only criterion, the problem is still complicated because profitability is hard to calculate in this field. The marginal cost of installing a new line obviously includes the equipment put at the subscriber's disposal but it should also include part of the cost of the progressive saturation of the system. But the subscribers' responsibility for saturation varies in accordance with different factors, among others the time of day at which the telephone is used: a subscriber who does his phoning outside peak hours does not cost the community much.

The telephone system is fairly rigid and becomes physically saturated when there is a subscriber for every line in a cable, whereas an electricity grid is saturated more progressively.

As far as demand is concerned, predictions are mediocre at best since precise statistics are not available on such aspects of the problem as the areas of heaviest loads, variations in loads during the day, length of calls, etc. In this state of affairs, it is difficult to work out the operating costs for each of the various kinds of calls and subscribers.

An instance of this complexity is provided by the study carried out by the C.E.G.O.S. on the changeover from manual to automatic exchanges: an entire year of research was needed to work out the concept of profitability in this field and to draw up estimates; profitability was shown to be of the order of 15 per cent but it is difficult to draw practical conclusions from this figure until the profitability of other investments has been assessed. The Economics Department is currently working on estimates which should make it possible to compare the profitability of various rival projects.

5 GOVERNMENT ARBITRATION AMONG DIFFERENT SECTORS OF THE ECONOMY AND SPECIAL CONSTRAINTS INFLUENCING PUBLIC ENTERPRISES

GOVERNMENT ARBITRATION BETWEEN SECTORS

A. *Structural Differences in Financing*

It is virtually impossible to find points of comparison between ways in which the state manages, for example, Renault, E.D.F. and the telephone system. Depending on the kind of control, there are very marked differences in government arbitration. Choices are governed fundamentally by the financing constraint and this constraint affects the situation differently, depending on whether or not the enterprise in question is financed entirely out of the budget.

Renault has access to the money market, E.D.F. has access to the bond market and to the funds of the F.D.E.S., while the telephone system has access primarily to the budget.

B. *The Choices of the Fifth Plan*
As a result, the choices have tended particularly to limit enterprises and areas of activity which are essentially dependent on the state; a case in point is the arbitration between the 'transport' investment package and the 'postal service and telephones' package. The general context of this arbitration was that of choosing collective equipment investments. The following table gives the main programme allocation blocks adopted for the Fifth Plan (in thousand millions of 1965 francs).

	Programme Allocations
Highway schemes	14·80
Other transport schemes	4·50
Post Office and Telephone System	10·70
Urban programmes	2·30
Rural collective programmes	5·10
Health, social and cultural programmes	4·65
Education and Research	25·02
	67·07

The arbitration takes place within each total investment package and involves all the participating parties; as a result, highways are more directly in competition with education than with the railways since the latter are not included in the package just as E.D.F. investment is not included in this total sum.

The distribution shown in the table above is effected in two stages. As explained in the report on the Fifth Plan:

(1) During the first phase of their activities (from January to July 1964), the commissions drew up as complete a balance-sheet as possible of the present situation with respect to existing equipment and, working with the basic data which they had assembled, they formulated proposals for programmes which would be satisfactory according to various standards of expectation. The main findings from their analyses appeared in the report on the main options (Chapter III of Part II). On the basis of these studies and of the conclusions which emerged from discussions in the Conseil Économique et Social and in Parliament,

the government assigned preliminary operating volumes to the various sectors.

(2) In the second phase, the commissions' work confirmed the broad outlines of the conclusions of the report on the chief options. Their work made it possible to specify the various possible breakdown patterns within each sector and to shed light on the problems of all kinds (administrative, economic, technical, financial, etc.) involved in implementing the programmes. In addition, as requested, the reports submitted by the regional economic development commissions listed in order of importance the collective schemes needed in the various regions. While their findings confirmed the magnitude of the effort to be made in this respect, they particularly stressed the need for investment in highways and urban programmes and, to a lesser extent, in telecommunications, research and technical and professional training, the latter being an indispensable prerequisite for expanding productive activity in a given area.

The preferences expressed in the context of this first experiment with decentralised consultation reflect the dominant theme of the Fifth Plan, namely to provide our economy, especially by means of increased produtivity, with the ability to face international competition. The investments described above can contribute effectively to this aim by facilitating trade and communications, by creating a propitious climate for innovation and by increasing the numbers and skills of the labour force. These considerations have shaped a policy characterised by satisfactory equilibrium between the requirements of education (with large financial problems posed by the reform of schooling), culture and public health, on the one hand and, on the other, the requirements of national development – while still giving high priority to public expenditure on research.

The programmes thus defined had ultimately to be compatible with the economic and financial targets of the Fifth Plan. These considerations formed the subject of very detailed studies carried out by the 'Commission de l'économie générale et du financement', and resulted in a slight downward revision of the total amount of collective schemes to be carried out by 1970. The growth index covering these projects for the period 1965–1970 none the less remains the highest, by far, of all the indices relating to allocation of production. But the studies mentioned above showed that it would be dangerous to exceed a reasonable ceiling as far as the budgetary contribution and the local communities' opportunities for self-financing and borrowing were concerned. Yet the target is still an ambitious one since it calls for contributions from the national budget to increase over the 1965 to 1970 period twice as rapidly as production.

In these circumstances it is essential, as the present report stresses repeatedly, to seek to expand other sources of finance including, in particular, the contributions from those who benefit from the services rendered by collective schemes.

If better possibilities than those currently envisaged have appeared by the end of the research now being undertaken, two complementary programmes could be launched in two key sectors for national development:

Highways, to the sum of 700 million francs;

Communications, within the limit of one thousand million francs.

C. *Is Technical Arbitration Possible?*

The choice-making methods that have just been cited are based essentially on analyses of needs and of aspirations, on consultations with regional experts and economists (e.g. at the Conseil Économique et Social) and politicians (members of the government and of Parliament). Would it be possible to envisage more technical arbitrations based on estimates of collective profitability?

To make this possible, two conditions would have to be complied with: in the first place it would have to be possible to assess the profitability of investment projects in each sector and, secondly, the different sectors would have to be compared.

The first condition would exclude all the 'non-productive' sectors from the scope of this method: at the present moment, for instance, there is still no way of assigning precise values to investments in education, social programmes, etc. 'Technical' arbitration would therefore have to be restricted to the productive sectors. But it might be possible to improve the methods of estimating the profitability of E.D.F., the railways, the post office, etc., so as to be able to apply uniform methods for classifying investments.

The second condition raises the tricky problem of the discount rate that was discussed under previous headings. It is difficult to see any solution other than comparing the discount rate for each sector to a set interest rate. The first problem is whether to make this rate uniform for the entire economy: is it necessary to be less demanding for durable schemes (such as roads) than for more ephemeral programmes? This is exactly the course of action advocated by M. Desrousseaux [1] when an annual investment constraint exists. However, it would seem more in keeping with the principle of the optimal allocation of resources to set a single rate for the whole economy. But at what level? If the budget is considered to constitute an entity within the economy, the discount rate to be used for calculating state investment must be such that every project which is profitable at that rate can be financed: the maximum rate fixed in this way would be rather high, probably higher than the rate in the financial market, which means that it would be possible to finance other profitable projects for the community by authorising nationalised enterprises to make more use of the money market. Whether or not the rates on the money market would go up as a result remains to be seen. In these circumstances, the only rate with any economic significance would be the rate at which the supply and demand of investment capital are equal. Preliminary drafts of the Plan showed a distribution of the final demand between consumption and investment postulating some arbitration between the present and the future, i.e. in short, an assumed discount rate. After studying the growth rates of the enterprises and of the prevailing interest rates, the Commission proposed a rate of 7 per cent which is slightly higher than the issue rates for medium-term loans. The fact that government arbitrations have resulted in the rejection of marginal projects which were profitable at 7 per cent suggests that this rate is still a little low; it would be difficult to go any higher, however, because the investment calculations would then be based on a rate of discount which was different from the interest rate currently paid by public enterprises. There is a methodological problem here which has not yet been solved.

Analysis of the two conditions thus seems to show that there is still a long way to go before it becomes possible to arbitrate on the basis of technical criteria alone, even in the productive sectors. It might not even be desirable to switch over to them suddenly, at one blow, on account of the public service constraints.

(2) THE INFLUENCE OF PUBLIC SERVICE CONSTRAINTS

A. *The Different Types of Constraints*
These constraints fall into several categories depending on whether public service constraints impinge on enterprises at the level of operating costs, sale prices or management policy.

[1] Desrousseaux, *L'Évolution économique et le comportement industriel* (Dunod, 1966).

(i) *Constraints at the Operating Costs Level.* Wages constitute the most important factor here: the basis on which staff are employed, the status of the personnel and wage increases are almost imposed on the undertaking concerned by government policy. As far as the cost of capital is concerned, fairly strict limitations on access to capital are generally 'compensated' by its low cost. With regard to raw materials, the example of the cost of coal to E.D.F. shows that economic obligations incumbent on the State can restrict freedom of action.

(ii) *Constraints at the rates level.* In addition to special temporary situations such as rate freezes, there are instances of regional constraints which involve setting rates at levels which do not correspond to actual operating costs and of social constraints which require the lowering of rates for some categories of consumers.

(iii) *Constraints at the management policy level.* In one sense these constraints are the most severe of all in so far as the enterprise is 'obliged to supply': there are obligations to supply railway services for certain small localities, obligations to maintain roads and streets, obligations to avoid discriminating against any category of applicants for telephones, etc. Since no increase in pricing flexibility accompanies these obligations, the result is sometimes to create unprofitable lines of activity.

(iv) *Constraints at the equipment programme level.* In addition to the permanent pressure to buy equipment made in France, other constraints connected with the 'National Development' programme must also be given more weight by public enterprises than by others: the attempt to decentralise, the need to industrialise areas which are still predominantly agricultural, etc., are instances of the considerations involved.

B. *Influence on Investment Behaviour*
Needless to say, these constraints exert an influence on an enterprise's decisions and, in particular, on its investment policy. We have already had occasion to mention, for instance, that the tight-money situation has caused the Post Office and Telephones to sacrifice very profitable investments designed to increase productivity in favour of others which will increase capacity so as to be in a position to accept as many applications for subscriptions as possible. The Railways find themselves obliged to provide rolling stock for unprofitable lines or for vacation departures during the peak periods, but are not allowed to refuse service or to change

their rates in any significant way. These constraints, which are natural enough for public service enterprises, shift their behaviour away from a strictly maximum profit orientation and sometimes result in a degree of 'over-investment' in comparison to the policy which would be followed by private enterprise. In fact, this tendency is seldom borne out because of the extremely strong pressures exerted on state financing which must arbitrate very strictly between different sectors.

Perhaps it is financing constraints more than any other which explain why the threshold of profitability for productive equipment has been made rather high and difficult to attain, as if the collection of a franc by taxation were equivalent to collecting more than a franc through the banks or the money market.

12 Aspects of the Pricing Policy of the Nationalised Industries

M. H. Peston

1 THE OBJECTIVES OF THEORY

The purpose of this paper is to consider critically certain aspects of the pricing policies of nationalised industries. The institutional context will be that of the United Kingdom solely on the grounds of convenience, but it is hoped that some of what follows will be relevant to other countries. In considering the U.K. situation, policy, at least in its superficial aspects, is undergoing a definite process of change so that care should be taken in interpreting any particular factual proposition in case it has been overtaken by events.[1]

In preparing this paper for the past year it had been hoped to make some new theoretical contribution which might enable us to make some progress from the admittedly unsatisfactory state of affairs in which economists find this subject. Like so many others, however, I have failed in that attempt, and so must content myself with the consideration of the existing state of theory and with actual policy making.

Concerning the tasks for the theorists in this field, it is obviously reasonable, but quite vacuous, to argue that the value of the resources used up by any activity should be met by the beneficiaries, unless, independently, it has been decided to redistribute towards them or away from them. It is also clear that if marginal benefits exceed marginal costs to some group, the expansion of the activity will, *ceteris paribus*, raise welfare. None of this, however, is helpful since it does not give rise to a practical method for determining and assessing actual policies in terms of their allocative and distributional efficiency. This requires a means of predicting the consequences of policies, a method of testing to see what actually happens, and the construction of appropriate criteria of evaluation. (Graaf suggests that the economist should concentrate on the former task, but this only means either that the study of criteria will go by default to others less well suited to deal with it, or will be dealt with by an economist with

---

[1] A new White Paper on the financial and economic behaviour of the nationalised industries has been expected for some time. When it does eventually appear it may well chart an entirely new course for those industries.

a different name – moral philosopher or evaluation theorist.) [1]

The analysis of the pricing problem has usually started with the familiar revenue and cost curves of the theory of the firm. If marginal benefit is measured by the demand curve, it has been asserted that welfare is maximised by a price and output policy at which demand equals marginal cost.[2] The case of the uncongested bridge with no user cost is usually sufficient to make the point clear.

Given this initial step the debate has then proceeded along a number of different lines. Firstly, there is the clarification of the proposition in terms of the correct specification of revenue and costs. Secondly, there is the consideration of all the variants of the original simple model which give rise to counter examples. Thirdly, there is the issue of the financing of deficits and surpluses. Fourthly, there is a much less academic stream of thought relating to the actual operations of public enterprises, especially to what is sometimes referred to as their commercial behaviour.

The more careful analysis of revenue and costs has been directed to determining such issues as whether particular factors of production are to be taken as fixed or variable, what is the marginal unit of output, what is the correct length of the time horizon for decision purposes, and what is the product actually sold. (All of these are, of course, strongly interrelated.) [3] It has been noticed that it is possible for the average cost curve to be discontinuous at a finite number of points, and for marginal cost to be undefined at those points, and much has been made of that despite the fact that it only takes an infinitesimal perturbation of the average revenue curve, if it were to go through such a point, to overcome the difficulty. Some weight has also been given to the paradoxes of decision making over time with a finite planning horizon. What were opportunity costs yesterday may cease to be opportunity costs today because of yesterday's decisions or because of today's decisions being based on an horizon one day further into the future. Although it is premature to say that most of the problems here have been solved, it is fairly clear that many of those within the public utility field have arisen from misformulation rather than anything else. Thus, in the case of the bridge, a decision to build it can

---

[1] J. de V. Graaf, *Theoretical Welfare Economics* (1957) pp. 170–1.

[2] It is not clear who was the first economist to perceive this extremely important result. Perhaps Launhardt was the first to show a full understanding of it in his *Mathematische Begründung der Volkswirtschaftslehre* (1885).

[3] A discussion of some of these matters can be found in E. H. Phelps Brown and J. Wiseman, *A Course of Applied Economics*, 2nd ed. (1964), ch. vi, pp. 167–209. Note, in particular, their view, 'when indivisibilities are present marginal cost is arbitrary' (p. 178).

L

be taken on a financial basis independent of positive day-to-day user charges (although the financing may be interpreted as an overall user charge for the life of the bridge) and equally independent of its eventual replacement cost. Similarly, it is now seen that the emergence of an un-expected user, so to speak, can give rise to financial problems of equity and income distribution, but not, in the absence of congestion, to user charges.

The investigation more exactly of the products has involved essentially the disaggregation of a seemingly homogeneous product into a variety of products. Electricity at one time or season is not the same as electricity at another; railway lines at one place are not the same as those at another, and so on.[1] One serious consequence of this has been the need to formu-late a theory of price structure rather than one price; a second has been the even greater emphasis that has needed to be placed on joint costs and the difficulty of allocating overheads. While neither of these consequences invalidates (say) the marginal cost pricing rule, they do serve to bring out its limitations.[2]

2 SOME COMPLICATIONS

Turning now to the complications arising from the need to modify the simple competitive model, an incomplete list is as follows:

(1) Second-best arising from government tax and expenditure policies.
(2) Second-best arising from market imperfections.
(3) External effects.
(4) Dynamics and disequilibrium.
(5) Changing tastes.

If we assume that the calculation of revenues and costs by a public utility were such that putting average revenue equal to marginal cost would be a necessary condition for Pareto optimality, the effect of these complications is to make that condition cease to be a necessary one. Moreover, there is the particularly telling second-best theorem that the new necessary conditions may be quite different from the first-best ones. The partial derivative of social benefit (or social cost) with respect to the scale of any activity may not be related in any simple way to private demand or the marginal cost of the activity to the public utility. In

[1] Of course, the costs of recognising this or doing something about it may easily overcome the benefits.

[2] E. J. Mishan expresses the opinion, 'Allocative decisions alone, as it happens, have little to contribute'. See 'A Survey of Welfare Economics 1934–39', *Economic Journal*, June 1960, p. 213.

particular, marginal cost pricing in any industry may move us further from Pareto optimality than average cost pricing.[1]

It is important to remember that these criticisms of the marginal cost pricing rule have nothing to do with its marginality, and it can be expected that, whatever first order maximum rules emerge from more relevant models of the economic system, they will be of the 'marginal type'. As far as changing tastes are concerned, they may, of course, lend support to the view that it is impossible to define satisfactorily social welfare (let alone its maximum) anyway. They are mentioned here simply because in the U.K. context it would be wrong to assume that preference patterns for the products of public utilities can be regarded as fixed, or at least outside the control of the managers of those enterprises. Non-price selling techniques seem to be just as welcome to the nationalised industries as to private industry.

One difficulty in seeking partial or sub-optimal pricing rules for public utilities which would enable them to proceed independently or semi-independently is that some of the actual nationalised industries have an extremely broad impact on the economy. (That is one of the reasons why they were nationalised.) It is extremely unlikely that the economy could be decomposed into sectors in such a way that most of them could be regarded as unaffected by the pricing policy of the electricity industry. A similar point applies to rail, road transport, the post office and the remaining fuel industries. It seems a reasonable guess to suggest that relative prices and output structures throughout the economy will be sensitive to decision making in these sectors.[2]

[1] There is a literature which tries to minimise the seriousness of the second-best problem, but, as far as I know, none of this has been able to show a practical demonstration or test of how to overcome the problem. Thus, the issue is not one (or has not yet been shown to be one) of searching for strong divergences of social costs and benefits from private costs and benefits and then simply of adjusting for them. What is more, except in very special cases the second-best conditions cannot be known without full optimisation of the second-best model; partial analysis has not yet been shown to be of any use at all.

[2] Whilst rehearsing all these negative criticisms, it is perhaps worth mentioning that general considerations of overall optimisation give rise to the view that marginal conditions of any kind (including second order conditions) are in great danger of leading us to a local maximum rather than a global one. See W. J. Baumol, *Welfare Economics and the Theory of the State*, 2nd ed. (1965) pp. 3 ff. On second-best itself the following statement is relevant, 'It follows from this that the task of the policy maker in applying the results of welfare analysis is even less simple than had sometimes been supposed. Changes which, when looked at by themselves, appear to move in the right direction, may well make things worse. Sometimes only the most painstaking of general equilibrium analyses or the most subtle of judgements can avoid the dangers which beset a partial approach to the solution of welfare problems' (p. 19). The view of the present

One last point to be made here, which may be peculiar to the U.K. situation, is that there are strong relationships between them of substitutability and complementarity. Coal, gas and electricity all compete in the market for household heating and cooking and in the market for firm heating. Coal and nuclear fuel compete in electricity generation while coal is used for gas production. (In addition, oil, which is largely in private hands, competes with all these.) Rail and road transport are both complementary and competitive. In addition, rail uses coal, electricity and diesel engines, and transports coal and some oil. Similarly, nationalised air corporations compete with rail and road both for passengers and freight. Even the post office is interrelated with the transport system. In terms of an input-output table, the elements in the intersection of the rows and columns corresponding to these industries are neither mostly zero nor can they be arranged in a triangular pattern.

The existence of these interrelationships suggests that a beginning to finding some rules might be made with an anlaysis of optimisation within this group of industries. There do seem to be signs of interest in this matter in the United Kingdom with the publication recently of two White Papers, one on fuel and the other on transport.[1] It would be wrong to suggest, however, especially as regards fuel policy that the government is yet fully alive to the issues of allocative optimisation within this narrow sector, let alone within the public sector as a whole.

At this point we may leave the welfare aspects of pricing policy to others. While its value as a critical tool cannot be gainsaid, it does seem to have one major drawback, namely that our ability to conjure up and analyse complex cases has progressed much further than our ability to do anything about them in practice. It is all very well to argue that realistic models should be constructed and that we should do empirical work; the trouble is that welfare theory does not lead us to any particular line of investigation that we should concentrate on.

3 THE MEANING OF COMMERCIAL BEHAVIOUR

It is now of interest to turn to another approach to pricing (and to public utility policy, in general) which makes strong claims to be of practical relevance. This is the view that nationalised industries should behave in

---

writer is that even that is over optimistic – we do not know with any confidence how to carry out in practical terms any general equilibrium analysis on this scale.

[1] Ministry of Power, *Fuel Policy*, Cmnd 2798, Oct 1965. Ministry of Transport, *Transport Policy*, Cmnd 3057, Jul 1966.

a commercial manner. In examining this view little or no attempt will be made to place it within a rigorous welfare economics framework since it has been argued already that that is unlikely to be very helpful. Instead the case for commercial behaviour will be examined at an elementary level and in its own terms.

Perhaps the best way to approach this subject is via the relevant White Paper of five years ago.[1] The original nationalisation statutes constrained the industries to break even over several financial years taken together; the White Paper essentially tries to direct them towards making a surplus. The following quotations are worth noting:

> although the industries have obligations of a national and non-commercial kind, they are not, and ought not, to be regarded as social services absolved from economic and commercial justification.[2]

> If the profitability of capital development is assessed on different (and easier) financial criteria from those adopted in industry generally, there is a risk that too much of the nation's savings will be diverted into the nationalised industries. Again, if the prices of the goods and services which the nationalised industries provide are uneconomically low, demand for them (and for investment to produce more of them) may be artificially stimulated.[3]

In case these statements are taken to be the policy only of the previous government, comparison may be made with a more recent White Paper.

> Allowance must be made for the social and non-economic obligations which most nationalised industries are required to undertake. But having done this, it is essential, in order to ensure the most efficient deployment of the national resources, that the minimum return on new capital in the nationalised industries should be comparable with that obtainable elsewhere in the economy. . . . The financial objectives which are agreed from time to time between these industries and the Government define the returns to be sought in the industries' capital assets as a whole and are the guide-lines for the industries' commercial policies.[4]

For these statements to make sense some meaning must be attached to 'commercial'. The meaning within these White Papers is clearly intended to be a financial one, but even here there are a great many possible alternatives. A commercial return may refer to the return on total assets or to

---

[1] *The Financial and Economic Obligations of the Nationalised Industries*, Cmnd 1337, Apr 1961.   [2] Ibid. p. 3.   [3] Ibid. p. 6.
[4] *Public Expenditure: Planning and Control*, Cmnd 2915, Feb 1966. pp. 10–11.

the return on new investments. If it refers to the former, the question must be asked how the assets are valued, and, in particular, whether there is a commercial basis for valuation. If new investment is involved, presumably, the idea would be the internal rate of return, and one may ask whether this means the average internal rate of return on new investment, or the internal rate of the marginal project. It is possible that the government has in mind the rate of interest to be used in discounted cash flow. If that is so, strict financial criteria can be imposed with a low rate of interest by postulating a high shadow price for capital. There are similar difficulties, of course, on the private industry side, namely with the comparison with the average rate of return, or the rate on new investment, or the rate for discounted cash flow. There are also the questions whether commercial refers to private industry as a whole, or the best private industry, or comparable private industry.

Before pursuing these last questions, there is one special aspect of the surplus of nationalised industries that needs to be examined, and that concerns whether it is the same sort of thing as the return to private industry anyway. The best way to consider this question is to compare a tax placed on the products of the nationalised industries with the policy of aiming at a financial surplus. Obviously, there are differences between the two; the tax has to be paid whereas the financial objectives are only targets, and the tax might well be levied on sales rather than as return on capital. Although the first of these differences, in particular, may have administrative consequences within the industries, it is clear that basically the tax and the surplus are pretty well the same. Indeed, as the following quotation shows, this is recognised by the government:

> Thus, the operation of the nationalised industries with an unduly low rate of return on capital is sooner or later damaging to the economy as a whole. It must result either in higher taxation or in greater borrowing by the Exchequer in order to provide for the replacement of their assets and for new development.[1]

If surpluses are interpreted in this way one has moved a long way from a simple analysis of pricing policy and is involved in all the usual issues of incidence and income distribution. Such propositions as 'the electricity consumer ought to pay the full cost of electricity' or 'the traveller on British Railways ought not to be subsidised' are seen to be even more *simpliste*, so to speak, since they fail to place these activities within the

[1] Cmnd 1337, p. 6.

context of government tax and subsidy policy. In other words, whatever running these industries commercially can mean, it can hardly be the same thing as being able to pay taxes or never receiving subsidies.

It has, of course, long been recognised by the advocates of marginal cost pricing in conditions of falling average cost that income distribution considerations must be brought into the analysis of the financing of public utilities. Oddly enough it is less immediately recognised that these same considerations apply in conditions of rising average cost, i.e. when there is a surplus. There is no difference in principle between the distribution of the surplus and the financing of the deficit. In particular, if there were general reasons for arguing that the latter burden must be met by the consumers of the product, it would follow that the former benefit must belong to those consumers too. Whatever difficulties arise in determining who should pay for the deficit also arise in determining who owns the surplus.[1] The object of the argument in the previous paragraph is to take this point further and argue that income distribution questions arise with average cost pricing as well, so that, whether or not they are regarded as the concern of the nationalised industries themselves, they are certainly the concern of the relevant government departments and the Treasury.[2] One would reject the following view, therefore, as on the face of it it is self contradictory, 'Commercial operation does mean, however, that nationalised industries should not be employed as economic, social or political instruments to the detriment of some or all of their customers'.[3]

What then might be meant by commercial operation in this context? Consider first of all the following two points of view:

> If a firm in a highly competitive industry succeeds in selling its products, makes profits which satisfy its shareholders, continues to attract such capital as it requires, gives conditions to its staff which makes them contented, and has a management which commands the respect of all

---

[1] Concerning the symmetry of surpluses and deficits, in practice they are treated assymmetrically. Thus, the deficit of British Railways is treated as government expenditure to be added up with all forms of other public disbursements, but the surpluses of other public utilities are not deducted as negative expenditure or treated as tax revenues. See *Public Expenditure in 1963–64 and 1967–68*, Cmnd 2235. Dec 1963, pp. 7–8, and *Public Expenditure: Planning and Control*, Cmnd 2915, Feb 1966, p. 2.

[2] An extremely interesting aspect of the Treasury in the U.K. is the way it avoids as far as possible the explicit recognition of the problem of the distribution of income between classes. None of the White Papers quoted above consider the financing of nationalised industries in terms of the substitution of regressive taxation for progressive taxation. (They also do not consider their capital investment programmes in relation to the distribution of wealth between classes.)

[3] R. S. Edwards and H. Townsend, *Business Enterprise* (1958) p. 512.

parties, that firm may be said to be efficient. In monopolistic under-takings some of these major benchmarks are missing but the meaning of efficiency remains the same. It is open to those nationalising an industry to give it an organisation consistent with efficiency in this sense, without being inconsistent with their objectives.[1]

The existence of such a surplus as, for example, the spectacular profits of the Prussian State Railways, may be a shining testimony to the efficiency of the administration and to the propriety of the industrial and commercial life of the country; but at the same time the surplus also indicates that the enterprise is far from its optimum degree of utilisation both in national and in individual terms.[2]

Although there is disagreement about what kind of policy increases national welfare, the ability to earn a surplus represents a common factor in defining commercial. Edwards and Townsend in describing their paragon of a firm see, of course, the two crucial difficulties; (a) they want com-mercial to be a good thing, but note the problem of monopoly profit; (b) they are aware that nationalised industries have other objectives which must be made compatible with commercial obligations. Needless to say, in any practical sense they are unable to overcome either of these diffi-culties.

A partial list of what might be meant by commercial is the following:

    (i) The average behaviour of private industry.
   (ii) The best behaviour of private industry.
  (iii) Profit maximisation, short or long run; policy in pursuit of maximum profits.
  (iv) Sales maximisation.
   (v) Risk minimisation or survival maximisation.
  (vi) Cost minimisation.
 (vii) Use of a high interest rate for discounted cash flow, or a short pay-off period for cruder methods of investment appraisal.
(viii) Full cost pricing.
  (ix) High return on capital.
   (x) Any of the above success indicators in conditions of competition rather than monopoly.

A particular distinction to be borne in mind concerns whether commer-cial is to be regarded as an *ex ante* or *ex post* characteristic or even both.

[1] R. S. Edwards and H. Townsend, *Business Enterprise* (1958) p. 483.
[2] K. Wicksell, 'A New Principle of Just Taxation' (1896) in R. A. Musgrave and A. T. Peacock, *Classics in the Theory of Public Finance* (1962) p. 103.

It is important, indeed, that whatever the objectives imposed on the nationalised industries some method of assessment is introduced which does not confuse *ex post* failure (especially in the short run and in individual cases) with wrong *ex ante* decision making. Even in private firms it is recognised that inability to make mistakes may be a bad sign rather than a good sign; this is *a fortiori* true in public utilities where the organisation corresponds to the industry which if it had been split up into a number of competing units would have shown a wide variety of performances.

Apart from this the chief difficulty for the economist in advocating commercial behaviour is not simply that he cannot specify what it is; he is also required to quantify it. Public utilities in the United Kingdom do as a rule possess some monopoly power, and they also have social obligations. Whatever commercial may mean the industries must be constrained not to make monopoly profits (unless these are interpreted as taxes), and must be obliged to take a wider account of their activities than is represented by money revenues and costs. So far no satisfactory way has been discovered of how to do this. The various White Papers refer to taking social obligations into account, and it is even possible to cite specific examples of this (British Railways' under-used lines, uneconomic coal mines, purchase of uneconomic aircraft by B.O.A.C., etc.), but it can scarcely be doubted that the financial targets fixed also in practice reflect different degrees of monopoly power.

If it is true that we do not have any agreement on what 'commercial' means, or on how much 'commercial' behaviour is relevant, it is, of course, impossible to assess satisfactorily the welfare implications of such a policy. It is, perhaps, not unfair to state that in practice policy-making has tended to leave economics and is based on administrative convenience, ease of tax collection (and its political advantages), and the tautology 'if only nationalised industry were like successful private industry it too would be successful'.

Given this it might be futile to ask how might welfare considerations be brought back into the picture. There are, however, a few minor points that are worth mentioning. The first relates to the organisation of the public utilities. It has been mentioned above that the public utilities in the United Kingdom use each other's products, and also compete with one another. It has also been suggested that future research and policy-making might concern itself with optimisation within the public utilities sector itself. If the characteristics of such an optimisation are guessed at, however, it will be seen that they may be in conflict with present policies. Consider, first of all, the pricing of coal if it were owned by the electricity

L 2

industry. The cost of coal for use in power stations would be its value elsewhere; so that if the joint industries were set a financial target, it would not necessarily be the case that 'profits' would be earned on that coal since it might be more suitable to earn them on the resulting electricity. It is by no means clear that with the present organisation of the two industries pricing policy is worked out in that way. Next consider what might happen if the gas and electricity industries were organised jointly. In as far as for heating and cooking they produced services which were extremely close substitutes, optimisation would require the assessment of both gas and electrical facilities together in the merit order, pricing and investment programmes being determined simultaneously. Moreover, for any given set of facilities, and a specific financial target, it would not necessarily be the case that the derived financial performances (if these could ever be got at) would bear any simple relation to the overall performance. To put the point differently, separate financial targets are not worked out for individual power stations. Furthermore, suppose there were four separate generating boards, one for nuclear, one for hydro, one for oil-fired and one for coal-fired stations. Could they by competition reach the overall optimum both as regards merit order in the short run, and investment decisions in the long run, and would it help to give them separate targets?

Similar points could be quoted for other nationalised industries. They give rise to the two generalisations:

(i) Separate organisation of the industry may lead to pricing policies which are inefficient in determining the industries' use of each other's products.
(ii) Separate organisation of the industry may lead to competitive selling policies on a distorted cost and revenue basis.

As opposed to this it seems sensible to argue that the organisation of public utilities should be irrelevant to the principles of the formulation and assessment of optimum policy.

4 SOCIAL RESPONSIBILITIES

Apart from the organisation of the nationalised industries themselves there is the related matter of how they fit into government machine. This is of special significance in connection with their so-called social responsibilities as opposed to their commercial ones. There is no doubt at all that these social responsibilities exist; they are admitted by the government, by the industries themselves, and by economists, even those who belong to the 'commercial' school of thought. Differences exist as to how they are to be taken into account, the chief disagreement being whether the nationalised industries can decide about them themselves, whether this is a matter for the Treasury and the relevant department, or whether this is a joint operation. It is argued that if the nationalised industries look further than their own revenue and costs, this will detract from the efficiency of their operations. They are, anyway, no different from private industry, and it is up to the government to discover particular social obligations and pay the industries to take them into account. The difficulty with this point of view is that the government is not organised to examine each decision in detail to determine its social costs and benefits, and, if it were to do so, this would involve such a close examination and control of the industries that they would lose their independence altogether. At the other extreme merely to insist on the adoption of some broad principles, such as a social rate of discount and correct opportunity costs between different industries, would lead to the neglect of a large number of individual cases.

From the administrative standpoint alone, therefore, it is surely necessary for the nationalised industries themselves to do cost-benefit analysis, possibly in association with the central government and to be able to justify their decision on that basis. If management finds this uncongenial or feel that they are being inefficient, the fault must be seen to lie with the management rather than elsewhere.[1] In this sense, the fact that private industry does not take decisions on a social cost benefit basis, and it is difficult, if not impossible, for central government to do such analyses itself, becomes the strongest reason for nationalisation of industries which are likely to have an important social impact.

[1] It is important not to confuse cost-benefit analysis with the excuse given by poor management in the past that they were merely meeting their social responsibilities. Efficiency must be related to objectives, and if commercial considerations lead to the neglect of social objectives, no matter how happy the management are, they are inefficient.

13 Political and Budgetary Constraints: Some Characteristics and Implications

P. D. Henderson

1 INTRODUCTION

The title of this paper was suggested by the Chairman of the Programme Committee of this Conference, but the sub-title is my own choice. The sub-title originally suggested was: 'Second-best rules and sub-optimisations', to be considered in relation to the management and direction of public enterprises. This form of words seems to imply that political and budgetary constraints must be regarded as external and largely negative factors, which will in principle conflict with the objective of reaching an economic optimum that can be reasonably clearly defined: hence the need to resort to second-best rules and strategies. There is a lot to be said for this way of treating the subject, particularly in relation to public enterprises that are producing goods and services for sale. The problem of devising for these enterprises rules and criteria which take account of specific constraints has recently been the subject of some very fruitful analysis,[1] in which moreover it has been recognised that such constraints may have the positive function of furthering social or economic objectives. But there may be a case for looking at constraints in relation to other aspects of the public economy, and to a wider range of policy issues than directly arise from the management of public enterprises.

If we do this, it seems to me that three things are apparent. First, a neat and tidy classification of constraints is not easy (though distinctions are none the less useful and necessary): thus for example budgetary and political constraints may not be distinct, and each may be imposed partly or wholly in the interests of realising economic objectives. Second, constraints may serve a positive purpose, and even where it is not obvious that this is the case they may be impossible to dispense with. Third, there are considerable problems in devising rules and criteria which will ensure that harmful constraints are not imposed, and that unavoidable or useful constraints are well devised for their purpose.

---

[1] Most notably, to my knowledge, in Marglin, [1] and [2]. (See list of references, p. 325).

Each of these propositions – for which no element of originality is claimed – is illustrated below in relation to three main topics which will be considered in turn: the political constraints that may bear on policies for economic growth; the determination of total public expenditure; and the allocation of public expenditure within categories and programmes.

2 POLITICAL CONSTRAINTS AND ECONOMIC GROWTH POLICIES

It is convenient to start here by referring to a problem which falls outside the terms of reference not only of this paper but of almost all economic writings, namely that of economic growth in the world as a whole, as distinct from an aggregate of countries. In treating the subject of growth, economists and others naturally take as given the existence of a set of sovereign states, in each of which a central authority determines policy with reference to a social welfare function in which only the welfare of its own nationals is given significant weight. This is clearly a realistic and necessary assumption. Yet in accepting it, we are conceding the necessity for what from a world point of view is a very serious degree of suboptimisation. In particular, given the policies that are almost universally followed by national governments, we are ruling out what would probably be the most effective single means to raising the level and rate of growth of world income, while simultaneously improving its distribution: a big increase in the extent of migration from poorer to richer countries. The goal of higher world income must be pursued subject to the constraint that the existing powers of individual states, and thus the extent to which international migration is permitted, must be taken for granted.

Two features of this situation are worth noting. First, the constraints in question, despite the probable scale of their effect on world income, are not the subject of serious controversy: the principle that each government has the right to decide who shall qualify for citizenship, and to impose severe restrictions on entry, is virtually unquestioned.[1] This suggests that, however much one may regret the ways in which particular governments may choose to act on it, it is not an unreasonable principle. Thus we may suppose that even a world authority, with the power to prohibit national restrictions, might be concerned about the possibility that heavy or unlimited migration would generate social tensions of a destructive kind, and

[1] Though there are of course disputes about the form and the precise degree of severity of the restrictions that are imposed in particular cases.

would therefore be prepared to forego some potential improvements in world economic efficiency in the interests of reducing these.

Second, it should be noted that not only is the optimal strategy for world economic efficiency precluded, but there are also good and widely accepted grounds for rejecting the second-best rules. These would presumably enjoin the maximisation of the expected present value of future world consumption (or consumption per head), subject to the constraints imposed by the existence and accepted powers of sovereign states. One might also advocate and hope for a more equitable distribution of consumption between rich and poor; but in order to realise this consistently with second-best rules, the redistribution would have to be effected through cash transfers. It would be inconsistent with allocative efficiency to help the poorer countries by (for example) giving trade preferences to their products, or by causing investment to be undertaken in them when higher-yielding projects could be found in richer countries. It is obvious that such a strategy is inadmissible. Quite apart from the tactical argument that the poorer countries may succeed in getting a greater total amount of aid if it comes to them in a variety of ways, there is the more basic point that to raise the level of consumption in these countries cannot and should not be treated as a matter of organising an effective international system of poor relief. As Marglin has put it, 'the size of the economic pie and its division may not be the only factors of concern to the community – the method of slicing the pie may also be relevant'.[1] There is then a clear case for promoting what one may call balanced growth as between countries and regions.

Thus when the problems of growth are considered in an international setting, economists are often willing – though in varying degrees – to acknowledge that certain constraints may be inevitable or even useful. This readiness to make concessions is not always so apparent when growth is considered in a purely national context. Admittedly the situation is different in one very important respect, since there is normally (though not necessarily)[2] free movement of goods and people within national boundaries. But the case for balanced growth (in our sense of the term) is often, perhaps usually, very strong; and this again implies the need for accepting certain political and distributional constraints. Although the form and extent of such constraints cannot be laid down in any simple way, a number of general points can be made in connection with them.

---

[1] Marglin [1], p. 63.
[2] For instance, restrictions on the movement of labour in Italy were removed only in 1961.

(a) The need to be concerned with balance, and the reasons for this concern, clearly vary a great deal as between different countries. The need is most acute where there are obvious and deeply-felt divisions within the community, and the sense of common nationality and purpose has had relatively little time to develop. Nigeria and Pakistan are leading examples. The problem may be serious in rich and well-established countries, as can be seen from the present situation of Canada and Belgium.

(b) Political constraints of this kind need not be imposed to ensure that poorer regions or groups get a reasonable share in development. They may also be designed to preclude too rapid an increase in this share. Thus, for example, Lewis has argued that in West African societies a federal form of government may be necessary if different tribal groups are to remain together in the same nation, since this will prevent the richer areas from being too heavily taxed in order to subsidise the poorer.[1] Such an arrangement is likely to be consistent with the goal of economic efficiency, but can also be defended on grounds of equity and the need to maintain social cohesion. In this situation the constraints are themselves constrained, for reasons which are political as well as economic.[2]

(c) So far as possible, constraints should be formalised and made explicit. This makes for greater awareness of what is being attempted, and helps in the task of quantifying the implications of alternative policies, and of translating broad policies into specific projects and expenditure programmes.

(d) For consistency and hence economic efficiency, the choice of objectives, and the form of the constraints which are logically implied by this choice, should be determined at a high political level. It should not be the outcome of piecemeal decisions on individual programmes or projects, nor should it be left without effective guidance to the discretion of public enterprises. Violations of this principle are easy to find. Thus in relation to navigation and flood-control expenditures in the United States, Maass has observed that 'there is little discussion of general objectives and little action based explicitly on them. Nor is there translation of legislative objectives into design criteria. Rather, the planning process begins with the design of systems or projects, and this with few useful policy guides to the planner'.[3] Again, some choice instances of unreflecting suboptimisation

[1] Lewis [3], p. 50.
[2] In some situations, it may be that on any but a short-term view the interests of the poorer regions will be best served by concentrating investment in the areas where prospective yields are highest. This is argued in relation to India by Balogh [4].
[3] Maass [5], p. 583.

can be found in the evidence submitted by British nationalised industries to the relevant House of Commons Select Committee.[1]

(e) Finally, the need for constraints raises some interesting questions about the role and functions of economists. Their primary role is clear enough. It is to state alternatives in a clear and logical way, to throw light on the prospective costs and gains that may be associated with different policy choices, and to help in the job of translating broad objectives into more specific decision rules. What is more debatable is whether they should go further than this. In particular, should they be ready to form their own views about the effectiveness of political constraints in achieving the non-economic purposes they are designed to serve, and to give advice on the basis of these views?

The apparently simplest course is to rule out such presumptuous conduct. A more modest interpretation of the role of economists can be justified by reference to a number of factors: a decent intellectual humility, concern for the integrity of the subject,[2] awareness that even a limited role is difficult to carry out well, and regard for administrative tidiness and the division of labour. More worldly considerations may also be involved. By demonstrating that they know their place, economists may hope to ensure that it is not filled by others.

There are, however, several arguments which can be advanced on the other side.

(i) The relation between political constraints and economic efficiency may not be entirely negative and in one direction, since failure to impose constraints that are needed may indirectly affect economic performance.

(ii) In some situations, economists cannot avoid forming views about the wider effects of policy if they are to be of any use at all. The design of foreign aid programmes is an instance of this. Again, it may be important for governments to assess the internal political effects of the economic policies of foreign countries. If economists refuse to bother about such questions, the effects on policy may be unfortunate.[3]

[1] In the gas industry for example, the Welsh Area Board justified its policy in maintaining supplies at a considerable loss in the sparsely populated mid-Wales area partly on the grounds that 'it is in the national interest to keep these communities alive . . . The Board feels that it has a duty to the existing consumer wherever he may be' (Select Committee [6], p. 22).

[2] As Eckstein has remarked, the subject of political constraints is one in which 'the line between realism and bad economics is particularly hard to draw' ([7], p. 451).

[3] This point is illustrated briefly in Henderson [8], pp. 21–2.

(iii) Keeping to a restricted role may encourage a tendency to over-estimate the importance of the factors which economists can claim as falling within their own province.[1] In particular, insufficient consideration may be given to alternative forms of constraints to the ones initially proposed or taken for granted.

(iv) The policy makers, with whom economists are assumed – perhaps rather optimistically – to carry on a reasonably continuous dialogue, may understandably prefer to listen to advisers who are prepared to take a broad view of policy decisions, instead of confining themselves to particular aspects.

(v) There is admittedly no clear dividing line between readiness to judge the total effects of a given policy and advising politicians on how best to pick up some votes. Yet even in the narrow interests of economic efficiency, it may seem important for the right party to form the next government.

There is no simple code of professional conduct which can decide these issues for us.[2]

In concluding this section, we may refer to political constraints of a different kind, which are not related to questions of distribution. Some writers have argued that in the advanced industrial countries the rate of growth is strongly dependent on expectations about the future course of demand, which in turn are considerably influenced by export prospects, and thus by the degree of competitiveness of the economy in international markets. In the British case, it has recently been argued by Beckerman that

> some of the needed response on the supply side in the way of greater investment, more dynamic management, more adaptable labour, faster technical innovation, etc., would be almost automatically forthcoming given an initial rise in competitiveness. This points to concentration on measures such as those in the field of exchange rate adjustment, or in the field of incomes policy, which operate on competitiveness via relative prices rather than relative costs in the first instance.[3]

On this analysis, constraints which restrict the use of exchange rate adjustments or incomes policies are likely to conflict with the objective of economic growth.

---

[1] Cf. the section on the limitations of economic analysis in Heymann [9].
[2] There is an excellent analysis of the problem in Seers [10].
[3] Beckerman [11], p. 81.

The example of exchange rate policy is an interesting one. It is clear that a commitment to maintain a given fixed exchange rate cannot be regarded as a purely political constraint: the choice here is partly one of the best means of realising economic objectives. At the same time, it is equally clear that political considerations may be relevant. A government may reasonably hold that it is bound by earlier commitments, or that even apart from these a devaluation, or resort to a floating rate, would damage its own prestige at home and the country's reputation abroad. And in considering these political repercussions, their possible economic consequences have to be taken into account.[1] This again is a case where political constraints may be justified in part with reference to the indirect economic consequences of failing to impose them. It also illustrates the point that the distinction between different forms of constraint is not always easy to draw.

3 THE DETERMINATION OF TOTAL PUBLIC EXPENDITURE

A discussion of constraints on public expenditure as a whole has to be related to some definition of the total. In the case of the United Kingdom, the definition used for official purposes, in connection with the introduction of new methods of review and control, has changed over time. Some years ago a rather wide definition was in use, comprising all the current and capital expenditures of public authorities – both central and local, and including national insurance funds – together with the investment undertaken by nationalised industries.[2] In the first White Paper on public expenditure programmes, debt interest was excluded from this total on the grounds that 'the forecasting of it is dependent on a number of arbitrary assumptions about the level of expenditure, taxation and interest rates' over the five-year period that was under consideration.[3] In a more recent White Paper [4] separate treatment is given to the investment of nationalised industries and certain other public enterprises, and these together with debt interest are excluded from the main public expenditure total that is used for planning purposes. It is this amended (and reduced) total of public expenditure which has now been made subject to constraint, in the

---

[1] Once again, economic advice which fails to do this is of rather limited value, and unlikely to be given much attention.

[2] Cf. the Plowden Report on the control of government expenditure [12].

[3] White Paper on public expenditure, 1963 [13], p. 2.

[4] 1966 White Paper [14], p. 8.

form of a maximum increase, over the period 1964–5 to 1969–70, of $4\frac{1}{4}$ per cent per annum at constant prices.

One route by which one may arrive at a budgetary constraint on total public expenditure is by imposing strict limitations on the extent to which rates of taxation are permitted to rise. An apparently simple form of limitation would result from a decision that taxation rates must not change in an upward direction. Although it is most unlikely that any government would be so rash as to give an open undertaking to this effect, it is easy to imagine a situation in which ideas of this kind would carry weight. There is evidence that the policies of the early post-war Conservative administration in Britain, following the Conservative return to power at the end of 1951, were influenced by the conviction that taxation was too high. In any case, the implications of this form of derived constraint are of interest in a number of ways.

(a) First, it is apparent that the definition of public expenditure which corresponds to this constraint is a wide one. Debt interest should be included, and so should the investment programmes of public enterprises if these are subject to government authorisation and control.

(b) Second, this may fairly be described as a political constraint with budgetary implications; the distinction between the two forms of constraint becomes blurred. However, the reasons for ruling out any increase in taxation rates need not be exclusively or even primarily political. It may be felt that current levels of taxation are so high as to have a serious effect on economic performance, so that an important object of the constraint may be to improve the prospects for economic growth.

(c) An apparent virtue of the decision that taxation rates should not be increased is its simplicity. But this is deceptive, for three reasons:

(i) There is a problem of deciding what constitutes an increase in rates. In the case of indirect taxes, the yield goes up with rising expenditure with *ad valorem* duties at given rates, but not with specific duties. In the case of progressive direct taxes, the real burden will rise with increases in money incomes even though real income remains constant. There is plenty of scope for argument about how to deal with these situations.

(ii) In some cases, there is a choice between conferring similar benefits through the remission of taxes or through government expenditure.[1] For example, the recent change in Britain in respect of incentives to business investment, from investment allowances to investment

[1] As is pointed out in the 1966 White Paper ([14], p. 13).

grants, implies higher taxation rates and (roughly equivalently) higher expenditure, yet this does not appear to be an economically or politically significant feature of the change. Again, some would argue that government assistance to families with children should take the form of direct cash grants, rather than tax reliefs that reduce liability to pay direct tax. Whatever the merits of such a change, it does not seem that the resulting increase in public expenditure and taxation rates is a serious argument against it.

(iii) In so far as the government can influence the charges that are made by public enterprises, the possibility exists of raising prices and profit margins in this sector, as an alternative to raising taxes.

(d) Subject to the qualification just made, an attractive feature of a strong constraint such as this one is that it reduces the permissible range of alternative choices, and thus simplifies the process of decision-making. The corresponding drawback is that it does so in what is evidently too crude and arbitrary a way. This illustrates a perennial danger that arises from the use of constraints, which is that superior alternatives and possible improvements may be excluded from consideration in the interests of making life simpler.[1] The danger is made all the greater by the fact that simplicity is in itself a virtue.

An alternative form of constraint, which is the one used in the United Kingdom, is to restrict total public expenditure directly, by prescribing a maximum rate of increase over a defined period. This has an important advantage, in that it forces people to look ahead and make projections. Moreover, since the permitted rate of increase is decided in relation to prospective changes in national product, public expenditure decisions are explicitly considered in the context of a general economic model. These features, together with the development of a new classification of government expenditure along functional lines, appear to mark a considerable improvement in British practice. However, relating the budgetary constraint on total public expenditure to the growth of the economy as a whole does not yield any specific limit. Even when the prospective rate of growth of total output is agreed or laid down by higher authority, the problem

---

[1] An important illustration of this point is given in Maass [5] (p. 565), in connection with water resource planning in the U.S. 'In the past water-planners and engineers, in search of constraints to simplify their task of system design, have found it convenient to read inflexibility into governmental institutions and to treat them as immutable, if irrational, restrictions. On the contrary, there is and should be considerable flexibility in legal and administrative forms, which are quite adaptable in the face of demonstrated economic, technologic, social or political need.'

remains of deciding what should be the size of the permitted growth in public expenditure in relation to output.

Here again, the definition of the public expenditure total that is to be constrained depends on what is taken to be the underlying reason for imposing a limit. If the constraining factor is the extent to which taxation rates can be allowed to increase, then (as was noted on page 317 above) a comprehensive definition of public expenditure is appropriate. Thus the change in British practice which has been referred to, from a comprehensive total to one which excludes debt interest and the investment of public enterprises, might be taken as evidence that the nature of the underlying constraint has changed.

Alternatively, the need for an upper limit may result from a decision about the size of the permissible increase in public expenditure as a proportion of total final demand. In this case a more restricted definition of public expenditure may be called for. If the constraint is imposed in the interests of maintaining the share of personal consumption, then all transfers to persons – and not merely debt interest – should be excluded from the total on which a limit is placed: in this case we are concerned only with direct claims on real resources. If, however, the primary object of the constraint is to affect the balance of payments on current account,[1] then all transfers – except those specifically designed to affect the balance of payments – should be included: in this case a fairly comprehensive definition of the total seems to be appropriate.

The current British definition does not correspond to any of the totals that seem to be implied by these reasons for imposing constraints. This is not necessarily a weakness, since administrative considerations may also be relevant in deciding on a definition. There is something to be said for concentrating attention on those expenditure programmes which are most obviously a matter for decision by the central authority, and where in consequence the main problems of choice arise. This implies leaving out the items which can be taken as given. In the case of debt interest, it could be held that these are largely determined by contractual obligations, so that no problem of decision arises.[2] Again, the investment of public corporations might be regarded as a matter which is or should be left to the judgement of the enterprises themselves, subject perhaps to certain

---

[1] In which case the purpose of the budgetary constraint can be described as economic rather than political, especially if the argument referred to at the end of section 2 above is accepted.

[2] As was noted in the first paragraph of section 3 above, this is not the reason that has been given for excluding debt interest.

broad rules imposed by the central authorities, such as the use of a common rate of interest for discounting.[1] Clearly there is scope for debate here,[2] especially since in practice there is a large non-discretionary element in most expenditure programmes even when formally this is not the case.

Despite the difficulties which may thus arise in applying it, the principle of imposing a budgetary constraint of this kind, in terms of a permitted rate of increase in total expenditure, seems to be a useful one. The formal objection to constraints, that they may preclude the adoption of an optimal strategy, can only be taken seriously if the ingredients of that strategy can be clearly specified. In relation to the aggregate of public expenditure, it is obvious that this cannot be done. For public investment, we have the useful rule that all projects should be undertaken for which the present discounted value of prospective social benefits exceeds that of social costs. By applying this test in a consistent way to the cases where benefits and costs are measurable, we can hope to get some idea of the extent to which existing constraints are precluding the adoption of desirable projects, and to work towards a state of affairs in which this no longer happens. But this still leaves a good deal of public expenditure to be accounted for, where theory can give us only limited guidance.

Another argument for a constraint arises from our ignorance of the economic system, and of the future course of demand and output. One reason for imposing a limit on public expenditure is to prevent the level of demand from becoming excessive, given certain agreed assumptions about taxation, interest rates and so on. But the maximum level of expenditure that will be consistent with this aim cannot be precisely determined. Spending departments can generally argue that a little extra will make no difference or is well within the margin of error of the estimates.[3] Thus any limit, however well devised, must have a certain degree of arbitrariness.[4] Someone has to draw a line. The art is to draw the line intelligently.

[1] The reason actually given in the 1966 White Paper for excluding this investment is that 'the nationalised industries are enterprises producing goods and services for sale; and the size and composition of their investment are considered in relation to the industrial needs of the economy and the commercial policy of the undertakings themselves, and have less in common with the generality of central and local government expenditure than with that of the rest of industry' ([14], p. 2).

[2] This is recognised in the 1966 White Paper, which states that 'there may in future be room for changes in the definition and boundaries of the aggregate to which a limit is applied' ([14], p. 13).   [3] I owe this point to Mr M. F. G. Scott.

[4] Though different forms of limit have different degrees. The British type of constraint is much less restrictive than either the one referred to earlier in this section, or an alternative which would consist in setting a maximum permissible ratio of public expenditure (in some sense) to national product.

4 THE ALLOCATION OF PUBLIC EXPENDITURE

Some of the arguments of the previous section are also applicable here. The case for formulating expenditure plans for a period of some years ahead, and for the use of financial guidelines in the planning process, applies to the components of public expenditure as well as the total. But there is one form of broad constraint which is especially relevant to particular programmes, as distinct from the total. Much of the expected increase in expenditure may arise from what is regarded as an obligation to fulfil existing commitments and to put into effect policies which have already been laid down. This is not a very rigid constraint, since at a pinch commitments can be modified or given up and policies can be changed. However, there are obvious reasons why this is difficult and politically embarrassing, so that the scope for manœuvre is limited. Hence the frequently-made distinction between prospective increases in expenditure which are the logical outcome of existing agreed policies, and those which would result from a change in policy.[1] Although this distinction is perhaps difficult to defend on formal grounds, the political constraint which is implied in it is probably unavoidable, and may serve a useful purpose. It is not a bad thing that governments should feel obliged to treat their earlier commitments seriously, and to pay some regard to the hopes and expectations they have aroused.

A stronger form of constraint is involved when a change of policy is carried into effect by imposing what is intended to be a binding and very stringent financial limit on a particular programme. A good recent example of this is the decision of the United Kingdom Government to cut back defence expenditure in the financial year 1969–70, to a figure some 20 per cent below what it could have been expected to be on the basis of the policies which existed when the Labour Party came into office in October 1964. A ceiling has been imposed of £2,000 million at 1964–5 prices in 1969–70. A firm budgetary constraint of this kind raises some interesting issues which, though they also arise in other situations, become more evident in this one.

There are three main objections that might be made to a budgetary constraint of this kind. First, a figure laid down in this way may be held to

[1] Thus the 1966 White Paper, describing the process of allocating public expenditure between departments, tells us that a division was made 'between "basic" programmes, which were to be drawn up within limits laid down in advance and related to the development of the individual services already in train, and "additional" programmes, representing the cost of further improvements which could be undertaken if more resources were made available' ([14], p. 4).

represent an unduly arbitrary decision. In principle, the budgetary limit should be arrived at by looking closely at the costs and utilities of a variety of alternatives: by what may be a fairly lengthy iterative process, the relevant trade-offs can be established, and one can have a reasonably firm basis for thinking that the figure that eventually emerges makes sense. A stronger constraint of the kind illustrated here is essentially a short-cut through this process of iteration, with a corresponding risk that alternatives will not be properly weighed.

Second, the constraint may create or strengthen perverse incentives within the government machine. A target fixed for a particular year may give rise to bogus and inefficient devices to meet it, such as the acceleration or postponement of payments or the arbitrary rephasing of programmes within the total. Ministries of finance are generally aware of these possibilities, but may not be able to prevent them altogether; and by the time the decisive year comes round, the politicians who set the target, who may have staked a fair amount of political prestige on it, may not be entirely averse from resorting to them.

Third, an overall financial constraint of this kind may fail to take account of the possibility that a given money expenditure may have different implications for resource costs, according to the way in which it is made up. In the case of a country with balance of payments difficulties, an obvious example of this is that a given amount spent abroad may be the equivalent in real resources of a larger – on some arguments, a considerably larger – amount spent at home. In such a case, some form of shadow pricing is desirable. This is not compatible with the use of a budgetary constraint defined in traditional terms of what goes into the defence vote.

As against these objections, there is the counter-argument that in dealing with a major and controversial programme of this kind there may be no other way of getting results. As we have seen above, some degree of arbitrariness is unavoidable; and it may not require a lengthy examination of alternatives for a government to decide, quite reasonably, that a change of policy must be firmly laid down, and enforced by a very clear and binding constraint which is well understood by all concerned.

It is therefore possible to argue that even a strong and apparently arbitrary constraint may have good effects despite its limitations and disadvantages. In this case again it may be noted that such a budgetary constraint may be imposed partly in the interests of economic efficiency. For example, if one accepts the view that the rate of growth in Britain has been held down as a direct or indirect result of balance of payments problems, there is a case for reducing the defence effort as part of a programme for growth.[1] If this can best be done by imposing a strong constraint, then any harmful economic effects of the constraint may be small in comparison with the gains that it brings.

It is interesting to note that although no use is made of formal budgetary constraints in deciding on the prospective total of defence expenditure in the United States, a recent analysis has suggested that this may be a weakness rather than a virtue. The decisions that have been reached on the submission made by the services have implied the existence of a constraint which has not been made fully apparent. Thus

> The Department of Defense has operated under a strong implicit budget constraint without making effective use of this constraint as a planning instrument. . . . The military contribution to the force planning process would be greatly improved by reorganising the [Joint Strategic Objectives Plan] to present alternative recommended forces for several mission budgets.[2]

This illustrates both the point that was made on page 313 above, that where constraints are unavoidable it is better to make them formal and explicit, and also the possibility that they may have a positive role in the decision-making process.

In conclusion, we may point to two ways of helping to ensure that political and budgetary constraints on expenditure programmes are well designed.

Within individual programmes, such as health or education or defence, the introduction of programme budgeting and systems analysis can make a very big contribution, as U.S. experience has shown.[3]

As *between* programmes, an important factor is the extent to which the political process generates and provides for informed and reasonably objective discussion, at the highest level, of the problem of expenditure allocation. In the case of the United Kingdom, the report of the Plowden committee recommended that 'there should be an improvement in the arrangements to enable Ministers to discharge their collective responsibility for the oversight of public expenditure as a whole'.[4] An interesting item in the recent White Paper is the information that the financial limits for the main expenditure programmes, in the 1965 review of public expenditure, was made by 'a group of senior Ministers, none of whom had

---

[1] This argument is put in Maddison [15], (p. 9).
[2] Niskanen [16].
[3] Cf. for example Niskanen [16], Enthoven [17 and 18], and Novick [19].
[4] Plowden committee report [12], p. 12.

large Departmental responsibilities for any particular block of expenditure, under the chairmanship of the Chancellor of the Exchequer'.[1] This seems to have been an attempt to meet the Plowden committee's point, which is an important one.[2]

5 POSTSCRIPT

In so far as any conclusions emerge from this rather untidy discussion, they have for the most part been stated above, on page 310. A final conclusion, no more original than the others, is that the life of the (allegedly) practical economist is not easy. In dealing with constraints, we are in the exciting but dangerous territory where political strategy and welfare economics merge into one another; and the economist may well be alarmed, not only by his lack of expertise in the first of these, but also about the degree of usefulness which he can claim in view of the teachings of the second.[3] Further, it is often difficult or impossible in this area to distinguish clearly between ends and means: the two may interact. This point has been well made by Enthoven in relation to defence policy; and his statement of it may serve as the ending to this paper.[4]

> The traditional formulation of operations research problems in terms of ends and means – how can I maximise the achievement of an objective or a set of objectives for a given cost, or alternatively, how can I minimise the cost of achieving a certain set of objectives? – has its place, but its place is limited. At the defense policy level, the major part of systems analysis is the exploration of the interaction of ends and means. By that interaction is meant that what are objectives from one point of view are means from another; that what is worth trying to do depends on what is possible to do, or on how effective the means for doing it are; and that any given objective is likely to be one of a number of alternative ways of achieving a still broader objective.

[1] White Paper on public expenditure [14], p. 5.

[2] Caulcott [20] has argued that 'the American system is potentially more effective, within the executive branch of government, for getting a balanced expenditure policy. While the Budget Bureau must depend on its Director in its high policy dealings with other departments, his strength is that of the support that the President gives him. A strong Presidential interest can ensure a unified expenditure policy. . . .' (p. 287).

[3] There is an excellent concise treatment of this latter point in Baumol [21].

[4] Enthoven [18], pp. 16–17.

REFERENCES

[1] Stephen A. Marglin, 'Objectives of Water Resource Development: A General Statement', ch. 2 of *Design of Water Resource Systems*, by Arthur Maass and others (Macmillan 1962).
[2] Stephen A. Marglin, 'Economic Factors Affecting System Design', ch 4 of Maass, op. cit.
[3] W. Arthur Lewis, *Politics in West Africa* (Allen & Unwin, 1965).
[4] T. Balogh, 'Equity and Efficiency: The Problem of Optimal Investment in a Framework of Underdevelopment', *Oxford Economic Papers*, Feb 1962.
[5] Arthur Maass, 'System Design and the Political Process: A General Statement', ch. 15 of Maass, op. cit.
[6] Report from the Select Committee on Nationalised Industries: The Gas Industry (House of Commons Papers 280, H.M.S.O. 1961).
[7] Otto Eckstein, 'A Survey of the Theory of Public Expenditure Criteria', a contribution to *Public Finances: Needs, Sources and Utilization* (National Bureau of Economic Research, Princeton University Press, 1961).
[8] P. D. Henderson, 'The Use of Economists in British Administration', *Oxford Economic Papers*, Feb 1961.
[9] Hans Heymann, Jr, 'The Objectives of Transportation', ch. ii of *Transport Investment and Economic Development*, ed. Gary Fromm (Brookings Institution, Washington, D.C., 1965).
[10] Dudley Seers, 'Why Visiting Economists Fail', *Journal of Political Economy*, Aug 1962.
[11] Wilfred Beckerman, 'The Determinants of Economic Growth', ch. 3 of *Economic Growth in Britain*, ed. P. D. Henderson (Weidenfeld & Nicolson, 1966).
[12] *Control of Public Expenditure* (Cmnd 1432, H.M.S.O. 1961).
[13] *Public Expenditure in 1963–4 and 1967–8* (Cmnd 2235, H.M.S.O. 1963).
[14] *Public Expenditure: Planning and Control* (Cmnd 2915, H.M.S.O. 1966).
[15] Angus Maddison, 'How Fast Can Britain Grow', *Lloyds Bank Review*, Jan 1966.
[16] W. Niskanen, 'The Defense Resource Allocation Process', a contribution to a forthcoming set of essays on defence management problems, ed. Stephen Enke.
[17] Alain C. Enthoven, 'Economic Analysis in the Department of Defense', American Economic Association, *Papers and Proceedings*, May 1963.
[18] Alain C. Enthoven, 'Decision Theory and Systems Analysis', a lecture delivered in the George Washington University, Washington D.C., Dec 1963.
[19] David Novick (ed.), 'Program Budgeting' (RAND Corporation, 1965).
[20] T. H. Caulcott, 'The Control of Public Expenditure', *Public Administration*, Autumn 1962.
[21] William J. Baumol, 'Informed Judgment, Rigorous Theory and Public Policy', *Southern Economic Journal*, Oct 1965.

14 Management and Financial Constraints in Public Enterprise

S. Wickham

1 INTRODUCTION

Economists have given many definitions of the public enterprise, but in our Western countries no strictly uniform legal specifications exist. In France the State's annual budget and the national accounts contain lists of nationalised companies and public establishments (industrial and commercial), which are accurate enough but not exhaustive.

In accordance with generally accepted economic principle, the term 'public enterprise' will be taken in the following study to mean any undertaking selling its products on the market which the public authorities own in full or in which they hold a majority interest, which has a separate budget and its own management, entrusted by the public authorities with the task of running it as well as possible while complying with instructions received; 'public authorities' is here taken to mean either the State or some local community, international communities being still a thing of the future. The following arguments will be illustrated by means of examples derived from public transport undertakings in France which are listed in Appendix A.

2 AUTONOMY AND CONSTRAINTS

The public enterprise, differing from a civil service department but resembling a private firm, does not have any power to give orders to or impose constraints on its potential suppliers or customers. While it may be granted the sole right to exploit certain techniques or sites the commercial advantages it derives from them do not go beyond the limits of the powers at the disposal of a private enterprise, which are always dependent on the preferences of the public, on technical innovations and on any action taken by third parties.

The authorities nowadays take greater care to see that public enterprises are genuinely subjected to market discipline and do not receive unfair advantages (particularly social, fiscal or financial) as compared to private firms.

While the public enterprise does not exercise any constraint on its environment, it is subject to constraints applied by the public (central) authorities which own and control it.   Not only must the management of the public enterprise observe the laws generally applicable, not only must it comply with the general objectives and operating rules laid down for it by the central authority (annual *a posteriori* checks being made to ensure that it does), but it must obtain express *a priori* agreement from the central authorities for most of its more important decisions (prices, wages, investments).   The discretionary powers actually wielded (directly or indirectly) by the central authorities with regard to the appointment of the managers of public enterprises suffice to consolidate this state of subordination.   While these managers (who are frequently in France civil servants) enjoy personal common-law guarantees concerning their salaries and status, the powers of command entrusted to them within the public enterprise, with the exceptional advantages attached to them, remain decidedly insecure.   The majority of senior civil servants in France (especially those enjoying exceptional status such as magistrates or university professors) are more independent of the government than the managers of public enterprises.

Thus the autonomy of the public enterprise, which is generally said to be a necessary precondition for partial public ownership without state control or excessive centralisation, must be properly understood as follows.   The public enterprise is autonomous in the sense that it forms a single unit for accounting purposes, with advantages stemming from its sub-optimisation procedures.   The Minister in charge of the Soviet railways does not dissociate railway policy from general policy of the U.S.S.R.   The board of directors and the general management of the French railways concentrate, within the limits of the instructions given them, on running the enterprise entrusted to them as well as they possibly can.   But there is no independence of the managers of the public enterprise from the central authorities.

The degree of freedom in the management of public enterprise depends on the number and compatibility of the administrative constraints imposed by the central authority as well as the commercial constraints imposed by the market.   The former are generally considered as capable of replacing the latter to a certain extent; a reduction in administrative control is justified for those public enterprises facing the stiffest competition.   The multiplication of constraints does not necessarily paralyse the public enterprise (they cancel each other out to some extent), but it does mean that the enterprise is faced with an extra short-term deficit through no fault of its own. In the long run its development is distorted by investments chosen on other than logical grounds; in consequence, management efficiency is impaired.

Any additional restrictions imposed by the central authority on the freedom of decision of those in charge of a public enterprise represents a financial cost to the latter which may, to some extent, be expressed in figures, and affects operating results in the first instance and the financing of investments in the second.

The management of a public enterprise, with specific constraints laid down by the owner (public authorities), has certain points of resemblance with the development, in private enterprise, of subsidiaries controlled by an outside group, i.e. autonomous units which are not independent but are nonetheless separate from their parent companies with which they have to negotiate the investments or even the selling prices on which their financial resources depend.

3 OPERATING RESULTS AND FINANCING OF INVESTMENTS

(1) OPERATING BUDGET, OPERATING RULES AND CAPITAL BUDGET

The operating results of a public enterprise are the difference between current revenue and current expenditure $(R - E)$. The former may be subdivided into three sections:

R.1: commercial operating earnings, the product of the quantities sold and the price $(Q \times P)$;

R.2: the reimbursement by the public authorities of the facilities provided or services rendered by the public enterprise (transport of soldiers, school children, civil servants, etc. . . .);

R.3: financial income from subsidiaries of the public enterprise.

Expenditure may be subdivided as follows:

E.1: variable costs dependent on the volume of activity, i.e. on the quantities supplied (in transport there is a substantial and variable difference between the capacity offered at a given time and that actually sold);

E.2: fixed expenditure (administrative and financial charges dependent on the size or total capacity of the public enterprise, whatever its rate of activity);

E.3: calculated charges, designed to bridge the time-gap between successive financial years (sums set aside for amortisation and miscellaneous risks). Some people consider that $D.3$ should also include a return on the public enterprise's own funds at the minimum market rate.

The financial objective (or operating rules) to be assigned to the public enterprise depends mostly on its market position. The status or ownership is also a reference:

—operation at a profit ($R - E$ maximum) for heterogenous competitive public enterprises in which private interests (without holding majority shares), are associated with public interests under a system of state capitalism. This may be observed, in France, in the case of pipeline transport, domestic air services and international shipping;

—balanced budget operation, for enterprises which are entirely publicly owned but more or less competitive; the equilibrium may be broad or narrow, depending on whether the total expenditure to be covered includes $E.3$ or not;

—operation at a deliberate deficit for monopoly public enterprises with the task of providing a public service which must be sold at the marginal cost if optimum operation is to be achieved ($R.1$ approaching $E.1$). The larger public enterprises (particularly in transport) normally work at decreasing costs, so that the expected operating deficit will be covered by a loss-offsetting subsidy which must be included in the public authorities' budget one year in advance.

Moreover, in public enterprises means of financing and investment decisions should in theory be independent of their operating results. Proper business administration (for private and public enterprises alike) implies separate operating and capital budgets. A firm may complete its financial year with a substantial profit, while remaining in debt, its liquidity situation being so difficult that, despite appearances, its investments will have to be cut back at least provisionally. Another firm, on the contrary, may show a deficit at the end of its financial year while having accumulated financial reserves and sufficiently favourable medium-term prospects to justify, again despite appearances, the immediate undertaking of ambitious investments.

This lack of connection between operating results and investment programmes has long been recognised in the fully collectivised economies of Eastern Europe, where operating results have no economic significance and where decisions concerning gross investments are referred to those in charge of a central fund and large enough to cover the Plan. The distinction should be just as carefully marked in the case of our public enterprises in Western Europe (partial collectivisation), the operating results of which do not have much more economic significance, as is explained below.

(2) MANAGEMENT CONSTRAINTS, FIXED PRICES AND REAL LOSS

The public enterprise is generally subjected by the central authorities to three major operating constraints:

—the obligation to provide, in the general interest, facilities on which no profit can be made, known as public service constraints (obligation on a public transport carrier to carry the full peak traffic – daily passenger traffic peak or seasonal peak);
—the obligation to run small branch lines in rural areas, the provision of services for distant overseas territories, etc. . . .;
—the obligation to do all or part of its purchasing, including equipment, from domestic producers, for whom contracting for the public enterprise represents a reserved market;
—a compulsory ceiling on selling prices; there are reduced rates for social reasons (urban passenger transport, current charges for which, in the Paris area, are often, for the S.N.C.F. or the R.A.T.P., scarcely half what would be the most profitable charge); to this must be added, under the conditions of quasi chronic inflation prevalent until recently in France, recurrent intervention to delay rises in the charges of public enterprises with a view to holding back a general price rise.

The operating results of public enterprises would be economically significant:

—if the services rendered to the public authorities (daily transport of school children, long-distance transport of soldiers or civil servants) were invoiced by the public enterprise at the same rates as for private customers, i.e. $R.2$ and $R.1$ would be economically additive;
—if the financial cost of public service burdens (and the possible extra price paid for exclusively home-manufactured equipment) were met by an annual reimbursement ($R.2$) which would be carefully calculated and kept quite separate from the services rendered ($R.2$) and from any subsidy given to offset a deficit;
—if amortisation costs ($E.3$) were freely worked out by the public enterprises on what are accepted as standard bases in industrial accounting.

In such a case the operating deficit would chiefly express the results of the rating policy adopted by the public authorities: marginal rating in the very rare cases where this is in fact adopted, support rates, social rates and miscellaneous rebates in normal practice (voluntary but not systematic deficit).

Actually those three above-mentioned conditions are only rarely met. In the case of present-day transport services in France, the differences remain moderate in the case of public enterprises competing on the international market (shipping lines and Air France). But they are considerable, on the other hand, for inland transport. Furthermore, since public opinion tends spontaneously to apply to public enterprises the criteria on which private capitalist undertakings should be assessed, the public authorities cover up the operating losses resulting from rating constraints by granting an 'annual stabilisation rates indemnity', the method of calculating which is open to some criticism. This is confused within $R.2$ and may lead to the production of a purely fictitious balanced buget for the year (as in the case of the R.A.T.P.).

Moreover the amortisation allowances ($E.3$) are frequently fought over or bargained for between the management of the public enterprise, which would like to see them increased, and the central authority, which wishes to impose a strict ceiling; the result depends on the social conditions of the moment at least as much as on accurate calculations. In the case of the French railways, the annual amortisation allowance for rolling stock is a percentage of the turnover which may vary from one year to another (recently it has been around 8 to 9 per cent). The work of renewing infrastructures and fixed installations is confused with current maintenance expenditures.

4 BUREAUCRATIC BARGAINING ON INVESTMENTS BETWEEN THE TREASURY AND PUBLIC ENTERPRISES

The situation outlined above has the following consequences:

(a) The Treasury bears annual charges for the operation of public enterprises which far exceed the loss-offsetting subsidies indicated in the public accounts of those public enterprises. These are legal obligations for the Treasury which cannot refuse them, since they are the results of the management constraints imposed by the government and specification of the states of the public enterprises.

M

The central authority does at least go on trying to keep the annual accounting deficits of public enterprises down to the minimum (as they are to a great extent involuntary and not systematic), by placing a limit on amortisation allowances, among other methods.

(b) The amount of resources of its own on which a public enterprise may draw to finance its investments is generally lower, comparatively speaking, than that available to private firms engaged in comparable activities, particularly in the case of public enterprises with heavy deficits. The supplementary outside resources on which the enterprise has to call (loans obtained from banks or raised on the market, public investment credits) are the result of bargaining with the Treasury, which attempts to bring its own financial requirements into line, as far as possible, with those of the various public enterprises. While the Treasury is legally bound to pay the public enterprise the reimbursements and operating subsidies laid down in the agreed calculating rules, the amount of additional capital resources (outside financing) allocated to the public enterprise is assessed at the discretion of the Treasury or the central authority (the fact that this assessment is made annually calls in question in France, at intervals, the successful completion of mid-range indicative Plans).

The management of the public enterprise, being anxious to develop and improve its competitivity, therefore finds it to its advantage to minimise its apparent need for supplementary financing and to maximise its apparent operating deficit by means of various expedients (well known, likewise to the managers of subsidiaries in private industry) :

—inflation of amortisation allowances ;
—presenting re-equipment as major maintenance; repairing and manufacturing new equipment as much as possible with the aid of its own staff rather than by paying outside private industry (the S.N.C.F. uses its equipment until it is completely worn out, which deprives private railway equipment builders of the necessary outlets; Air France announced its intention of building a special workshop for repairing and overhauling Caravelles, a service which the builder, Sud Aviation, another public enterprise, offered to provide on very favourable terms, etc. . . .);
—transferring their most profitable activities and the corresponding equipment to subsidiaries, or subsidiaries of subsidiaries, since it is much harder for the central authority to keep a close check on the

latter's activities and resources.[1] R.3 comes out in most cases as the residual surplus income of its subsidiaries which the public enterprise did not want to reinvest on the spot.

The supervisory bodies and commissions maintained by the central administration in order to supervise the public enterprises attempt to discover or prevent these accounting subterfuges, designed to increase the public enterprise's own financial resources without the central authorities' becoming aware of the fact.

(c) The combination of public service and pricing constraints leads paradoxically to the overdevelopment of public enterprises and to an increase in their investment requirements as compared to what would be the situation if the managements of public enterprises were perfectly free to decide on their operating programmes (abandonment of unprofitable services) and to fix their charges (increase in rates).

The constraints imposed by the central authorities increase the public enterprises' financial requirements while at the same time reducing their resources. The managers of French public enterprises, who at present, in most cases, have a capitalist conception of good management, generally resent this situation as irrational; but this is not obvious. Public enterprises have to carry out more or less specific tasks which normally involve financial disadvantages (as compared with private firms). The competitive equilibrium would be endangered by discriminatory facilities in favour of public enterprises (as compared with private business), but not by specific disadvantages to them. The financial result of public enterprise is not by itself a significant criterion of success, but disequilibrium on current accounts makes financing of investment more uneasy.

5 CONCLUSION

The distinction between the monopolist public enterprises and the competitive ones was long felt to be of major importance; the latter were required to run and finance themselves under conditions resembling those of private enterprises as closely as possible.

Nowadays, when frontiers have been thrown open and alternative services have become much more numerous, all public enterprises are

---

[1] Hence the desire periodically expressed by the French National Economic Council – to place limits on, and possibly cut down, the number of subsidiaries of public enterprises.

gradually facing up to a more or less competitive situation with sub-ordination to market rules: their market power (great or small) will have to be ascertained, and may change frequently . But the main differentiation among public enterprises should refer to their financial needs. A less doctrinal approach to partial socialisation of means of production in Western societies seems proper. Deficiency of competition, and mono-polistic power were previously argued. Deficiency of private saving and private financing is of more concern for new ventures which appear rapidly growing or highly capital intensive (atomic power, space ventures, air transport, etc.) Financial autonomy of the public enterprise is possible only under two conditions: that its market power be relatively strong; that its financial needs for investment be relatively small: either for low capital intensity or for slow growth.

APPENDIX A

LIST OF THE MAIN FRENCH PUBLIC ENTERPRISES IN THE TRANSPORT FIELD

Run at broad equilibrium or at slight profit

Name	*Purpose*	*Ownership*
TRAPIL	Transport by pipeline of refined products between Rouen and Paris.	Majority of shares owned by French state. French or foreign petroleum companies also hold an interest.
Cie GÉNÉRALE TRANSATLANTIQUE	Sea Transport, of passengers and goods, mainly on the Atlantic.	State holds majority interest. Some small private shareholders.
Cie MESSAGERIES MARITIMES	do.	do.
AIR FRANCE	International air transport of passengers and goods.	Entirely public ownership.
Cie AIR INTER	Air transport of passengers within French territory.	S.N.C.F. 25%, Air France 25%. Local communities, Private banks.
AÉROPORT DE PARIS	Building and operation of airports in the Paris area.	Entirely public ownership.
Société AUTOROUTE ESTÉREL–CÔTE-D'AZUR	Building and operation of the Nice–Marseilles toll-paying motorway.	French state and local communities.

Run at narrow equilibrium or at a systematic deficit

Name	Purpose	Ownership
SOCIÉTÉ NATIONALE DES CHEMINS DE FER FRANÇAIS (S.N.C.F.)	Rail transport of passengers and goods on French territory (other transport operations by subsidiaries, particularly urban road transport).	French state 51%, Former private railway companies, now financial companies.
RÉGIE AUTONOME DES TRANSPORTS PARISIENS (R.A.T.P.)	Rail and road transport of passengers in the Paris area.	State, City of Paris and nearby communities.
RÉGIE AUTONOME DES TRANSPORTS DÉPARTEMENTAUX (R.A.T.D.)	Urban passenger transport in provincial cities.	
PORTS AUTONOMES		French state.
MOTORWAY COMPANIES (other than Estérel–Côte-d'Azur)	Building and operation of toll-paying motorways.	French state and local communities.
Cie GÉNÉRALE POUR LA NAVIGATION DU RHIN	Operation on the Rhine of merchant fleet, derived mainly from German reparations in 1945.	French state.

15 The Second-Best Case for Marginal Cost Pricing

R. Turvey

1 NATURE OF THE PROBLEM

In practice such factors as precedent, a desire for continuity, accounting conventions, the desire for a quiet life and a variety of political notions about what is fair to this or that body are relevant when the pricing policy of public enterprises is being settled. The questions of income distribution and economic efficiency which interest the economist can never be the sole determinants of policy. But they deserve rigorous examination none the less and can provide a standard of reference even if they alone are insufficient to determine policy.

The following discussion deals exclusively with economic efficiency, and thus does not pretend to cover all aspects of the problem but merely sets out my ideas on the conditions which are necessary for efficient resource allocation. Most economists would agree that economic efficiency would be increased if two changes were made in those parts of the economy where the allocation of resources is determined by market choices. First, all prices should as far as practicable be made equal to the long-run marginal costs of the goods and services in question (with social rather than private costs being taken into account where there are palpable divergences). Second, the rate of interest used in making investment decisions and in annuitising capital costs in the calculation of long-run marginal costs should be uniform throughout the economy and equal to the marginal social rate of discount.

Reality diverges from the optimum set out just above, because, *inter alia*, in the private sector of the economy:

(a) indirect taxes make the ratios of price to marginal factor cost very different from one group of goods and services to another;

(*b*) the interest rates used or (via capital rationing) implicit in some private investment decisions differ from the marginal social discount rate;

(c) partly offsetting this, some private investment attracts fiscal incentives of one sort or another (cash subsidies in the U.K.);

(d) some major divergences of private and social costs are not corrected for;

(e) market imperfections abound.

Some of these obstacles to efficient resource allocation in the private sector may be modifiable, but the assumption of this paper is that by and large they are a permanent feature of the economic landscape.

The problem considered in this paper is what should be done in the *public* enterprise sector, assuming the continued existence of most of the above features of the private sector. Thus the question is one of sub-optimisation. This brings us to the point technically known as 'second-best': that the conditions required in the public enterprise sector to achieve overall optimisation are not necessarily required for sub-optimisation. It no longer follows automatically that public enterprises should price at long-run marginal cost. Nor, in the second-best situation, does it follow that the marginal rate of return before tax on private investment measures the marginal social productivity of private investment, since capital goods, co-operating factors and products are not all priced at marginal cost.

To achieve sub-optimisation of the sort examined here, new rules thus have to be worked out, to meet three issues:

(a) Choice by public enterprises of how they will produce a given set of outputs, in so far as this choice is affected by the relative costs of different methods.

(b) Setting the relative prices of the outputs of public enterprises which are substitutes for each other (or for products of the private sector) so that free choice by their customers will sub-optimise the output mix within the group of substitutes.

(c) Achieving the right distribution of resources in general between public enterprises on the one hand and the private sector on the other, by fixing the price level of each group of substitutes appropriately.

These three issues may be exemplified as: (a) atomic versus coal-fired electricity generating stations, (b) fares of domestic nationalised airlines and railways on competing routes, and (c) the profit-earning requirements imposed on public enterprises.

2 CHOICE OF INPUTS

These issues really solve themselves when the public enterprise is simply one part of an industry which is otherwise privately owned as in the case of British Road Services which competes on equal terms with many private road hauliers. Such public enterprises cannot follow price policies radically different from those current in their respective industries. At the opposite extreme, of low substitutability and price elasticity of demand, there stand post offices and water supply undertakings. The problem is most difficult and most interesting somewhere in between, as with state railways and nationalised airlines competing with private vehicles on internal routes or where the nationalised fuel industries (coal, gas and electricity) compete with a privately owned oil industry. The rest of the discussion relates only to such cases.

Minimising the cost of a given mix and level of outputs is the first problem. The difficulty of this in a second-best situation is that input prices may fail to measure the value of the social marginal product of those inputs in alternative uses. The wages of otherwise unemployable miners or the cost of inputs with a high import content at a time when the currency is under-valued constitute two examples. Such cases of obvious and direct divergence between social and private costs can only be dealt with by some sort of shadow-pricing, albeit rough. In what follows I shall refer to this as the use of 'corrected' market prices. Assuming this to be done, there seems to be no alternative to requiring public enterprises to minimise their costs as measured by corrected market prices, because

(a) no better guide is available;
(b) money costs provide a means for the control of managerial efficiency within each industry;
(c) sub-optimisation requires that the marginal rate of substitution of any pair of inputs be uniform throughout the public enterprise sector, a condition which is secured by cost minimisation and a common set of (corrected) input prices.

This last condition has fairly wide implications owing to input-output relationships within the public sector. As just expressed it relates, for example, to the fact that both the post office and the electricity industry can use copper and aluminium in cables and both use the same kind of labour and machines for digging trenches. But a similar condition is required for sub-optimisation where an input is also an output, as in the use of coal by the public electricity industry and electricity by the nationalised coal industry. Here there are two marginal rates of transformation which must be equated in order to achieve sub-optimisation and if this is to be done in a decentralised way, by the use of the price mechanism, it is necessary that the price paid by each industry for the other's product shall equal its marginal cost. Again, State railways may use publicly generated electricity and carry coal from nationalised mines to power stations. Complications such as this strengthen the case for marginal cost pricing. This case can thus be taken as established for transactions *within* the public enterprise sector.

Another aspect of cost minimisation is the temporal one. All public enterprises face choices between more or less capital expenditure now and less or more current expenditure over a series of years. This involves not only the price ratio between different inputs, capital and current, which is the matter dealt with in the last paragraph, but also the discount rate. Here, sub-optimisation requires that the marginal rate of transformation between present and future inputs be uniform within the public enterprise sector.

The conclusions reached so far concerning the first issue (a) on page 337 are thus that public enterprises should minimise costs calculated with market prices of inputs (roughly corrected for obvious divergencies from social cost), that they should use a common discount rate for comparing less and more remote costs and that their sales to each other should be at marginal costs calculated accordingly.

3 THE OUTPUT MIX

The next issue set out in (b) on page 337 relates to the relative prices of the different outputs of public enterprises (for sales outside the public enterprise sector) and of close substitutes produced by private firms. It brings in, that is to say, not only the relationship between public-sector gas, coal and electricity prices but also private-sector oil prices as well. Similarly it brings in not only the rail fares and (internal) air fares of public enterprises but also the long-distance coach fares of private operators. Here, economic efficiency requires that the price ratios which face purchasers of fuel and of transport services should equal long-term social marginal cost ratios. Once again, the difficulty of a second-best situation is that marginal costs of outputs calculated on the basis of market prices of inputs provide an imperfect message, so that one cannot rigorously prove that marginal cost pricing would be superior to, say, average cost pricing. But is there not a presumption in favour of the former?

(a) As already proposed, rough correction should be made for the more immediate and palpable divergences between social and private cost, at least in the case of the public enterprises.

M 2

(b) To some extent, different public enterprises buy the same inputs and, as already proposed, should all measure the cost of using them at the same prices. In so far as a change in their product mix would involve a re-allocation of these inputs between the enterprises in question proportionality of their product prices to long-run marginal costs is a necessary (though not sufficient condition) for equating product price ratios to marginal rates of transformation between these products.

(c) Where some of the output of one public enterprise is an input of another, the marginal cost pricing already proposed must be matched by a price ratio for sales to the public which reflects long term marginal cost ratios in order to secure that the customers' marginal rate of substitution between them equals their marginal rate of transformation.

(d) The ratio of the prices charged for substitutes to their (corrected) marginal costs by private enterprise can be roughly estimated and used to set the ratio for the public enterprises concerned.

Consideration of this issue thus adds to the earlier conclusion (i) that the prices of public enterprise products should equal their long-term marginal costs for sales *within* the public enterprise sector, the further requirement (ii) that they should be proportional for sales *outside* the public enterprise sector for each group of substitutes such as fuels or transport services. The price/marginal cost ratio should be determined with reference to the cost structure and pricing policy of the private enterprises supplying one of the group of substitutes. This is, be it noted, not entirely an exogenous variable, since it can be altered by taxing the privately produced product – as in the case of the U.K. tax on fuel oil.

If a price/marginal cost ratio in excess of unity is prescribed it must only apply to sales by the respective industry group to the rest of the economy, and not to inter-industry sales *within* the group. To have coal sold to the electricity industry, for example, at the same price ($x\%$ in excess of long-run marginal social cost) as that charged for similar coal sold to the public would make the price of electricity (at $x\%$ above marginal cost to the electricity industry) more than $x\%$ greater than its marginal *social* cost. Thus, in terms of this assumed example, either the electricity industry must pay less than the public for its coal or at least it must act as if the price were less.

4 LONG- AND SHORT-TERM MARGINAL COSTS

It has so far been assumed, rather than argued, that long-term rather than short-term marginal costs are relevant. Given an optimal investment policy the two are equivalent, however, for an optimal investment policy equates the cost of producing more by expanding capacity with the cost of producing more by using existing capacity more intensively. We owe this proposition to the French writers on public utility pricing (see my exposition of it in my note 'Marginal Cost Pricing in Practice' in *Economica*, November 1964) and it has recently been restated by Herbert Mohring in his contribution to *Measuring Benefits of Government Investments* edited by Professor Dorfman.

The calculation of long-term marginal cost involves the annuitisation of the cost of new assets over their anticipated useful life. As with relative input prices, economic efficiency requires that the discount rate used for this purpose should be uniform and the same as the discount rate used for input choices (already discussed at the end of section 2 above).

5 RELATION TO THE REST OF THE ECONOMY

There now remain two main tasks in formulating guidelines for public enterprises. The first is to decide how the ratio between prices (for sales to the public) and long-run marginal costs (calculated on market prices with corrections) should be set. There is freedom of action with respect to this ratio when either the whole group of substitutes is supplied by public enterprise or when the prices charged by private suppliers of one of the group can be altered by taxation. The second task is to consider principles for the choice of discount rate. Both tasks relate to the third issue set out on page 337, because a change in the price level of the products of public enterprises would affect the demand for these products and hence the level of inputs. Thus either an increase in the price/ marginal cost ratio or a rise in the uniform discount rate would raise prices and reduce the volume of resources used in the public enterprise sector. The difference between these two changes is that a rise in the discount rate would

(a) raise prices more in the case of more capital intensive projects;
(b) have an additional long-run downward effect on net investment, by lowering the capital intensity of new investment.

A simple solution, in principle, would be to set the price/marginal cost ratio at unity and put the discount rate equal to an estimate of the average risk-adjusted rate of return before tax expected on private investment projects which are just at the margin between acceptance and rejection. (This, be it noted, has nothing whatsoever to do with accounting rates of return on the book value of existing assets.) But while simple in principle, it is not obviously desirable because of the problem raised at the beginning of section 3. An example may be helpful. Suppose, just for the sake of argument, that, on balance

(a) heavy indirect taxation causes the market price of oil to exceed its marginal social cost;

(b) congestion makes the prices of long-distance private road transport of goods and passengers considerably less than their marginal social costs.

The pricing at long-run marginal cost in the nationalised gas, electricity and coal industries and in the railways would lead to excessive resource use in the former group and too little in the latter. Correction for this by raising the discount rate used in the fuel industries and lowering that applied in the monopoly transport industries would correct this only at the expense of introducing new distortions. Thus if (a) and (b) are assumed not only to be true but also to be unalterable, they should determine the price/marginal cost ratios prescribed for the two groups of public enterprises.

While, if this were done, it should produce the right allocation of resources within each group of industries (issue (b) of page 337) there is no reason to suppose that it will achieve the right allocation between each group taken as a whole and the rest of the economy (issue (c) at the end of section 1 above). One might argue that the price/marginal cost ratio chosen should equal the average ratio ruling in the rest of the economy, but I do not see how one could hope to estimate that average. Nor do I see how to estimate the marginal rate of return on private investment. Thus I have nothing better to suggest than suboptimising within each group of substitutes on the lines discussed above, using

(a) a discount rate that is not obviously unreasonable, say 8 per cent;

(b) a price/marginal cost ratio determined by an estimate of the ratio in respect of privately produced substitutes;

using changes in taxation on the privately produced substitutes to restrain (or encourage) the general level of claims on resources made by each group if this level is judged by the government to be too high (or low).

6 A CONCLUDING POINT: FINANCIAL TARGETS

Given a prescribed ratio of prices to long-run marginal costs, $100 + x\%$, for each group of competing public enterprises and given forecasts of costs and sales, it is possible to forecast the gross annual surplus and the book value of net assets of each enterprise, to divide the one by the other and to call the result a target rate of return. While it is difficult to see that this would serve any useful purpose as regards resource allocation, it will justly be said that some form of financial target does serve a useful purpose in keeping managements on their toes. This requirement could be met by calculating the gross surplus in the manner just indicated (which allows both for any divergence between input prices and their estimated social cost and for the cost of any socially desirable but unremunerative ventures which have been decided upon) and making it a target expressed in terms of an absolute sum of money. If the surplus were calculated on a constant price level assumption in order to avoid the difficulty of forecasting future inflation, the target could be subject to an escalation clause.

It is conceivable that the target may fall short of normal depreciation provisions. If this happens it means that efficient resource allocation is incompatible with book profits. The phenomenon is not uncommon; it happened with canals in the nineteenth century and some railways in this one. So the notion that all public enterprises ought always to show a profit has nothing to recommend it.

16 New Methods of Economic Management in the U.S.S.R.: Some Features of the Recent Economic Reform

V. P. Gloushkov

1 THE PROBLEM

It has become almost axiomatic nowadays for economists that, in circumstances both of 'sustained growth' and of modern technical and scientific progress, changes in planning and management methods at all levels of the economy are a constant necessity in order to secure more rational use of the immense productive resources.

The theme of my paper is 'new methods of economic management in the U.S.S.R.', or: 'the recent economic reform in the U.S.S.R.: its substance, implementation and implications'. This subject matter is, I believe, both important and topical, for three reasons.

First, it covers the main issue of the new economic policy of the Soviet Union, endorsed by the XXIII Congress of the Communist Party of the U.S.S.R.

Second, the economic policy of the Soviet Union, and other socialist countries as well, is based wholly on the public ownership of means of production and distribution. All over the world, the economic activities of the public sector are assuming new significance. This is because the developments in centrally planned socialist economies have shown some of the basic techniques necessary for proper behaviour of the economy, whereas the free operations of the market mechanism have led to a paradox of poverty among plenty.

Third, the economic reform, which is to be implemented throughout the Soviet Five-Year Plan, 1966–70, continues to evoke controversial comment in the West. This can be attributed to the fact that this economic reform is a serious attempt, on a strictly scientific basis, to ensure a skillful combination of centralised planned management with extensive initiative of single enterprises. This problem has not yet been practically solved in the most advanced capitalist countries. The Soviet policy to find ways and means of correct application of the principles of material incentives in the development of production is the true converse of the notorious Western 'prices and incomes policy'.

What is going on now in the national economy of the U.S.S.R. is not just a question of new changes, it is one of a system of profound economic measures of an all-embracing nature aimed at improvement of the style and methods of management and planning. The aim of this measures is the correction of the utilisation of the economic laws of socialism in the interests of the further growth of production and raising the standard of life of the people.

Friends of scientific socialism have assessed changes in the U.S.S.R. correctly and its fees, as usual, have recently said quite a lot about 'a crisis in Soviet economy? Some people even had the illusion that our latest economic measures represented a retreat from socialism.

In an editorial on 5 October 1965, headed 'Soviet Capitalism', the *New York Times* declared that the Soviet Union is 'introducing a measure of capitalism without capitalists'. That same month the London *Daily Telegraph* said, 'The planning mechanism is in large part to be dismantled and a market economy installed in its place.' The French newspaper *Les Eches* put it more sharply, 'Western observers believe the Soviet Union has taken a decisive step towards transition to capitalist methods.' And so on and so forth, most of it in the same vein.

First of all, what could 'capitalism without capitalists mean?' To me it means something like *a sickness without sick people'*. In that case, then, the sickness has been wiped out. Much of this comment is based on misunderstandings and delusions following from a poor knowledge of our economic system. I hope that it is through more detailed information and free exchange of opinions that we can reach out towards a better perception of objective truth. And it would mean much for further development of mutual understanding and friendly relations between the economists of countries with different economic and social systems existing on our planet.

2 WHERE THE U.S.S.R. STANDS TODAY

At this juncture it would be appropriate for me to give a general picture of contemporary Soviet economic reform. But naturally I should like to start with a brief outline of the objective stimulation given to this reform by the aims and nature, by real achievements and difficulties, of the U.S.S.R. economy.

Next year the Soviet Union will celebrate its fiftieth anniversary. For Soviet people this jubilee will be of special importance.

Over a period of fifty years, despite appalling hardships, Russia has been transformed from the poor and backward country into a modern industrial power. It produces now one-fifth of world industrial production whereas on the eve of the Great October Socialist revolution Tsarist Russia's share was less than a thirty-third, 3 per cent. This could only be achieved by the effective implementation of national economic planning on the basis of the socialisation of the means of production, by making them the property of all the people. Only this ensures unity of purpose on the part of all society, or the majority of it and makes production to serve its chief purpose – the constant improvement of the peoples' standard of living.

In the last seven years the Soviet economy developed at a rapid rate. Suffice it to say that during 1959–65 fixed assets of industry doubled, the increase in industrial output was in excess of planned targets (80 per cent) and reached 84 per cent, national income in 1965 had grown by 53 per cent over 1958. Real *per capita* income has increased 20 per cent in the last five years. At the same time important qualitative changes have taken place in the pattern of production – the share of the science-based industries that determine the general technical standards of industry has risen and many new types of machinery, equipment and instruments on a par with the best models in the world have appeared.

The imposing headway that has been made in the fields of national economy, science, culture, education and health in the U.S.S.R. is not the full story. 'When examining economic development', L. I. Brezhnev, the General Secretary of the Communist Party of the S.U., pointed out in his report to the 23rd Congress of the Party – 'we must mention the faults in our work as well as its positive aspects'. In recent years such unfavourable symptoms have been manifested in two problems.

(1) Some industries have not reached the planned level in output and labour productivity.

(2) The emphasis has sometimes been on quantity rather than quality.

Reasons for not reaching planned levels are, of course, many and varied. In some cases there have been mistakes in compiling plan targets, e.g. a plan for a particular branch of industry may have been too optimistic, capital investments have been dispersed, protracted construction schedules and delays in commissioning of new capacity have occurred. Further, shortcomings in the supply of raw materials and semi-finished goods may hold up certain industries. A third group of reasons was connected with the regional system of industrial management which divided the management of branches of industry among numerous areas, prevented uniformity of technological policy and cut off research institutions from production and thus held up the development and introduction of new machinery.

An outcome of the deficiencies listed above is that new industrial capacity is not always being used to its fullest extent and efficiency in the use of fixed assets and investments has lately dropped somewhat.

Actually most of the problems which confronted the Soviet Union make the whole world kin at our age of planning and technical and scientific revolution. It must be emphasised, however, before proceeding to examine just what our new measures are, that the still existing methods of planning and management have served their purpose well in the past, when there were tremendous shortages of all kinds of goods as the country fought to make good the damage of war and to develop the basis of socialism. It is the very success in achieving this aim that has created the new problems. The decisive advantage of our social system is that we have many possible ways to solve these problems, fast and resolutely.

The new Five-Year Plan will secure stable and high rates of growth of national income, production in all branches of the economy and the living standards of Soviet people. By 1970 national income will have risen by 40 per cent, industrial output by 50 per cent, agricultural output by 25 per cent and real incomes per head of population will have risen around 30 per cent in five years. The planned increase of the public consumption fund in the national income the simultaneous growth of the production accumulation fund are feasible only if the efficiency of the socialised production increases.

Thus we see that a growing level of productive forces, increasing speed of development and the increasing complexity of an expanding Soviet economy have the required introduction of new methods and forms of industrial management and planning. These methods were found, tested in practice and put into operation.

3 INTRODUCTION OF THE NEW SYSTEM OF PLANNING AND MANAGEMENT

At the March and September 1965 Plenums of the C.C. C.P.S.U. a new approach to economic management was evolved and the principles of the Communist Party's economic policy at the present stage of development were defined. These principles consist in giving a greater role to economical methods and stimuli in running the economy, radically improving state planning, extending the economic activities and initiative of factories and collective and state farms, and making factory staffs more responsible for and materially more interested in the results of their work.

My special point is that the Soviet economic reform now being carried out cannot be regarded as some isolated measure. It covers all the basic problems of improving economic relations in our society, including the system of economic management, planning and stimulating of production.

Under the new system higher remuneration and improvement in working and living conditions will be ensured by drawing on two sources: the resources concentrated in the hands of the state, and that part of the income (profit) which will remain at the enterprises in ever increasing amounts in the form of an incentive fund and a fund for social and cultural measures and housing construction. From now on, rises in the wages of factory and office workers will largely depend on the results of operation of their respective enterprise, such as an increase in the volume of goods sold, improvement of its quality, rise in labour productivity and level of profitability and growth in the amount of profit. Broad possibilities are opened up before the personnel of each enterprise.

The implementation of this reform will be gradual as it will require considerable change not only in people's attitudes but also great changes within government organisations, in relationships among government departments and between the Central government and regional authorities. It means also great changes: (a) in relationships between State and enterprises; (b) between industrial enterprises and between them and trading organisations; (c) between the enterprise and the collective of its blue and white collared workers.

4 CHANGES WITHIN GOVERNMENT ECONOMIC ORGANISATIONS

On the organisational level, a number of new ministries were set up, to deal with different industrial branches. They include ministries for the automobile industry, for the electrical engineering industry, for the machine-tool and instrument making industry, and so on. They are called upon to insure the comprehensive development of industry, to combine ably centralised guidance by industry with inter-industry regional coordination. Similar ministries were set up in the various republics that make up the U.S.S.R. At the same time the U.S.S.R. Supreme Economic Council, the U.S.S.R. Economic Council, and the Republic Economic Councils and the Economic Councils of the 'economic areas' were abolished, and the State Planning Committee as a Union-Republican organ is now directly subordinated to the U.S.S.R. Council of Ministers.

Thus, while retaining some of the positive features of the existing system of centralised planning, the tendency to regionalism ('parochialism', as Brezhnev called it), was abolished, thereby overcoming the weakness of the 104 regional Economic Councils where there were never enough specialists with a really sound knowledge of techniques of individual branches of the economy. The new ministries will contain leading technical and planning specialists for each important branch. In other words, the men who know the job will be in charge.

The central point of the whole system is the improvement of economic relations between single industrial enterprises and other production combines and the national economy taken as a whole. Perhaps the most important change envisaged in this connection is an increase in the independence of factories and other producing organisations, and a drastic reduction of 'red tape.'

5 THE ENTERPRISE AND SOCIETY IN THE SOVIET UNION

The enterprise is the key unit of a modern economy. Its profitable working is important for both socialist and capitalist economies at any time, but particularly in these days of scientific and technical revolution the prosperity of a national economy ultimately depends on the performance of the individual enterprise. However, I cannot avoid mentioning that a socialist plant, as distinct from a capitalist plant, is public property and this fundamental difference is a decisive one. Socialist and capitalist ownership of means of production are diametrically opposite by nature and for this reason an entirely different relationship exists between society and enterprises under two socio-economic systems – socialism and capitalism. There are two formulae defining this relationship. One of them is Charles E. Wilson's famous aphorism, 'What's good for General Motors is good for the country'. In contrast, Soviet economists clearly state their point of view which is, 'What is good for society must be good for every enterprise. And, conversely, what is bad for society, must be extremely bad for the workers of every enterprise.'

On the face of it, the formulae of Soviet and bourgeois economists may seem to have much in common, but in reality there is a fundamental difference between them. If we look closer at the two formulae, we shall see that they proceed from an entirely different understanding of the relationship between the interests of society and those of the enterprise. The decisions of the 23rd Party Congress are based on the assumption that the interests of society as a whole have priority, while the interests of individual enterprises should play a subordinate role and must be adapted to the interests of the former. Only in the latter case can production be managed in a manner that will satisfy the requirements of the people to the fullest degree and advance all members of the community in every possible way. With this aim in view the State is applying new forms and methods of economic management enabling it to combine centralised planning with a wide economic initiative, and making the interests of enterprises and of every worker identical with and dependent on the interests of the community as a whole. If we proceed from the American businessman's formula, which gives priority to private interests, we shall inevitably arrive at the conclusion that centralised planning is unnecessary and the economic autonomy in socialist enterprises can be extended only if centralisation is rejected.

In reality, the independence of enterprises and centralised socialist planning form a single dialectic unity, which means that they are inseparably linked and reinforce each other.

6   THE PLAN AND INITIATIVE IN THE NEW SYSTEM OF ECONOMIC MANAGEMENT

As a result of the reforms, a number of functions formerly carried out by the central planning and economic bodies, are now being entrusted to enterprises, naturally making for their greater efficiency and manœuvrability. Under the economic reform, factories will be set targets by higher planning organisations only in respect to: 'the volume of goods to be sold, the main assortment of goods, its wages fund, its rate of profitability and the amount of profit, its payments into the State budget and allocations from the State budget.' And, on a more general level: 'the volume of centralised capital investments and the development of production capacities and fixed assets, the main assignments for introducing new technology, indices of material and technical supplies.'

Other indices, notably the productivity of labour, number of workers, and the level of average wages, from now on will be decided by the individual factory or enterprise.

These measures mean that the enterprises will get much more independence, economic stimulation will be increased, and direct links will be formed between suppliers and consumers.

Thus, the running of enterprises, chiefly by administrative means through directives from above, is being replaced more and more by the system of economic levers – prices, profit, premiums and credit.

Will this weaken centralised management? Certainly not. Central planning and economic bodies will now be freed from a mass of routine work and be able to give more time and attention to long-term planning, to key problems in developing different branches of industry, regions and in advancing the whole economy. This will put planning and management on a more scientific basis.

We have shown how mistaken are those authors who declare that the extension of economic autonomy of socialist enterprises is tantamount either to retaining 'rigid' State policy in economic affairs, or, contrary-wise, to the retreat from the principle of democratic centralism both in planning and management of the Soviet Economy.

Such assertions are especially wrong if we turn to the changes in Soviet industrial relations.

The basic wages and salaries of factory and office workers will continue to be raised by central initiative as before. At the same time the enter-prises must have at their disposal, in addition to the wages fund, their own source for stimulating the workers to individual achievements and to high overall results for their enterprises. That is why in a socialist enterprise an increasing role is assigned to the working people and to their organisa-tions (trade unions). The economic reform makes for the wider participa-tion of the masses in production management. The bourgeois press passes in complete silence this aspect of the reform, because in the Western countries such fundamental questions as social relations, systems of pay, new approaches to industrial conflict, control of executives by the repre-sentatives of employers are still hard core problems to be solved.

The idea is to provide such conditions in enterprises that every partici-pant in production – be he the director or rank-and-file worker – shall be materially interested and shall display equal concern for raising the efficiency of production. Soviet people are becoming more and more interested in the most effective use of all the resources of production – working time, equipment and raw materials.

This means that the income of the workers, including the managing personnel, of a Soviet factory will be determined, to a much larger extent, by their fulfilment (mainly) and over-fulfilment (partly) of the targets listed above. And the really important target in that list is the amount of goods sold, which will define the size of profit received by the enterprise.

During the new Five-Year Plan each enterprise will have a Five-Year Plan of its own as well as yearly plans. The trade unions take an active part in elaborating all these plans and in controlling their fulfilment. Such a system is evidence to the fact that the essence of our planning is not formed or implemented in any specifically 'rigid' system. Collective as well as individual discipline, of course, has to be maintained, but the plans are based in equal measure on initiative and a creative approach, on broad democratic principles.

7   THE ROLE OF SOCIALIST MARKET RELATIONS IN THE CURRENT ECONOMIC REFORM

All socialist countries are commodity producing societies, and continue being such at every stage of their development. This also applies to trade. That is why centralised economic management is not the only regulator of all production based on the public ownership of the means of production, though it is the chief one. Centralised planning is an integral part of socialism. It helps Soviet society avoid over-production crises. But it is indivisible from indirect production control, which will remain applicable so long as commodities are exchanged through the medium of money, and so long as a socialist market continues to exist.

The denial of the existence of a socialist market, even if in a less naked form, is typical of bourgeois economists. All of them use practically the same argument: centralised planning excludes a market and vice versa. French economists R. Mossé and S. Voinea try to prove that there is no market under socialism, that 'there are no relations of any sort between sellers and buyers,' and that 'the law of supply and demand, and the market mechanism have completely disappeared in the Soviet Union'.

But trade and money circulation have assumed so large a scale under socialism that one has to be blind not to notice it. The trouble with Western critics of the current economic reform is that they cannot imagine any market other than the capitalist type. Effective centralised planning is really incompatible with a capitalist market, and there is no such market in socialist countries. This, of course, does not mean that there is no market at all. The improvement of the system of market interrelations in socialist economies is the aim of another group of important changes in the economic interrelations in the U.S.S.R., involving the system of relationships among firms. In an advancing economy there is a much greater degree of inter-dependence among enterprises, and, in a planned economy as in any other, the late-arrival of supplies can throw a whole factory out of gear. Now, factories will have to assume direct responsibility for fulfilling their contracts with other factories.

Sometimes enterprises produce low quality goods which the consumer does not want and thus remain unsold. Instead of using an overall volume of production index, the controls of enterprises should, therefore, incorporate assignments for the volume of goods actually sold. Enterprises will then have to pay greater attention to the quality of goods they produce and it will help increase the control of the consumers over the quality of goods. Economic stimuli will now be used extensively in the efforts to improve the quality of production. The enterprises producing above-standard quality goods are now allowed to add surcharges to whole-sale prices, thus increasing their profit. There are plans to provide special credits for the additional expenditures connected with the improvement of the quality of product.

One of the basic aims of the economic reform is the increase of the efficiency of utilisation of fixed and circulating production assets. An important part in the solution of these problems, will be played by the gradual introduction, beginning with 1966, of payments for fixed production assets and circulating assets. These payments will consist of money incorporated by the enterprises in the budget on account of their profit. The payments for assets will help to stimulate, first of all, a better utilisation of the existing production assets and to determine more accurately the requirements for new capital investments. In the new conditions the enterprise itself (and not the state, as formerly out of the budget and the profits of other well-functioning enterprises) will expand as necessary its circulating assets out of the profits additionally received as a result of expanding its activity. In this connection it is necessary to stress once more the important role played in the new system of incentive by the trade unions. The latter directly participate in the distribution of the incentive funds.

Nowadays, one of the key areas of management of the economy in the advanced countries which needs reform is company law. That is why in the U.S.S.R. the new Statute governing a socialist state production enterprise was created. This statute among its other tasks helps and increases the rights of enterprises in planning their activity, and lays down the relations between the state, executives and employees within each enterprise.

All the above-mentioned changes point to the important conclusion that the greatly increased flexibility of planning and management of the Soviet economy is the essential feature of the recent economic reform in the U.S.S.R. The introduction of economically realistic prices is the last but not the least important condition both for ensuring this flexibility and for transferring enterprises to the new system. Prices must to an ever greater degree reflect the socially necessary expenditure of labour, guarantee the recovery of production costs, provide sufficient profit for every normally functioning enterprise to cover payments for assets, build up incentive funds and expand production.

The task of developing basic methods of calculating new wholesale prices of industrial commodities is assigned to the special State Committee for prices created under the U.S.S.R. State Planning Committee and the U.S.S.R. Ministry of Finance.

The wholesale prices of industrial commodities will be more thoroughly worked out. It will be a most essential prerequisite of the new reform because if prices are not made realistic economic calculations lose their dependability, which in turn encourages the adoption of subjectivist decisions. Without this, the loss-and-profit accounting system and economic incentives could not be really effectively applied.

To interest the factory in taking and fulfilling its greater planned assignments, which will now relate as much to quality as to quantity, the 'profit motive' is to be strengthened.

8 WHAT IS THE DIFFERENCE BETWEEN SOCIALIST PROFIT AND CAPITALIST PROFIT?

There is another group of critics of our new reform. They claim that the Soviet Union is compelled to 'whip up' her economy by using 'private interest' and such categories as 'loss and income, profit motive'. And that is the beginning of the process of socialism going capitalistic, they say.

The name of the noted Soviet economics professor, Evsey Liberman, the author of two articles in *Pravda* in 1962 and 1964 (titled 'Plan, profit, premiums') is also used for this purpose. Distorting the ideas expressed in his articles discussing the role of economic levers in tying closely the plan and initiative, some Western commentators invented the myth of 'Libermanism.' This snappy term is used now by the Western press to describe the shift towards private enterprise and the market economy allegedly taking shape in the U.S.S.R. This is wrong because under socialism profit represents not the income of private owners of enterprises but the income of society, used wholly to meet social needs. Profit serves as a source for expanding production, and for providing free social and cultural services. This is a very far cry from capitalism, because in the Soviet Union there are no capitalists, share-holders, stock-brokers, profiteers or any other 'money-makers' and the social soil from which capitalists arise has been also removed for ever.

Professor Liberman addressing himself to 'the easy victims of anti-Soviet propaganda' showed that this fabricated myth of 'Libermanism' has nothing in common with the new system of planning and stimulation. He actually wrote, 'My articles contain nothing to give the slightest reason for such a distorted description of our reform.' The latter, he stated, was not an invention of his own but was 'the well-balanced expression of public opinion in the U.S.S.R. . . . . worked out by a great army of practical workers, scientists and leading managers'. It is well known that the adoption of the decision of the C.P.S.U. on the reform was preceded by a country-wide discussion conducted on the broadest democratic basis.

Now let us examine the role profit plays in the Soviet Union. We define profit as the monetary form of the value of the surplus product. Both under capitalism and socialism the surplus product is expressed in the value form of profit. That is inevitable because socialism does not do away with commodity production. However, socialism excludes antagonistic private commodity producers, each acting on his own in the market with the aim of extracting profits. Under socialism, social community production is organised and planned by the State with the aim of satisfying the common and individual requirements of all members of society with maximum efficiency.

There can be no doubt about the necessity of surplus product in a socialist economy. Production can be expanded only at the expense of surplus product. And if production did not expand then society would languish in poverty.

Anyone who thinks the difference between capitalism and socialism is that the former recognises and hails profit while the latter rejects and condemns it is profoundly mistaken. The crux of the matter lies in *how, and in whose interests, profits are used.* Lenin spoke of profitability of socialist enterprises as a prerequisite for building a communist society. The whole of the Soviet Union's great production machine has been created from our profits. The same applies to our defence potential, and it could therefore be said that people in the West got dividends from Soviet profits because our armed forces were instrumental in saving them from the plague of fascism.

Our current economic reform aims at increasing the profitability of

Soviet enterprises. Under our conditions profit can serve as a good indicator of production efficiency. Our profit is the difference between the economically realistic planned prices of goods and their cost. Since, in principle, prices express the norms of expenditure of socially necessary labour, a rise in profitability means a rise in productivity. Socialist profit arises solely from more efficient production, from less expenditure of raw materials, power and labour per unit of output. We want our factories to turn out high-grade goods of the kinds that are needed at a profit, and we intended to encourage them to do so.

Each enterprise by retaining a larger part of its profit will create three kinds of funds – the fund for boosting production, the fund for material incentives (payment of the current premiums and bonuses at the end of the year) and the fund for social and cultural measures and housing construction.

The important thing to grasp is the designation of profit in the Soviet Union. It cannot fall into any private hands, with the exception of that part of the profit that is paid to deserving workers as a bonus. As mentioned above, bonuses cannot be turned into capital, that is, used to extract further surplus value for the purpose of private enrichment. The main share of profits in the Soviet Union goes to expand production and for social services, such as free education, free medical treatment, pensions, and the advancement of science and the arts.

9 THE PROGRESS OF CURRENT ECONOMIC REFORM IN THE SOVIET UNION

The new economic reform accentuates the decisive role of socialist profit in serving the needs of the people. Forty-three large enterprises have gone over to the new system of planning at the beginning of this year. Thanks to greater economic incentives they look forward to a profit 11,400,000 roubles bigger than originally planned.

Introduction at the enterprises of an economic reform is a most important condition for the fulfilment of the industrial development plan. A number of large enterprises, employing altogether over 300,000 industrial and office workers, have been working under the new system, since the beginning of this year. During the second quarter, another large group of 200 enterprises employing almost 700,000 men was transferred to the system. This will be followed by the introduction of the new system in many branches of engineering, the food industry and the chemical industry. At the turn of 1967, the number of industrial and office workers at enterprises operating under the new system is to be almost one-third of the total labour force in industry.

In introducing the new system, the first two groups of industrial enterprises undertook to make an additional 150 million roubles of profit over and above the planned figure.   Most of the enterprises which began working the new way in the first six months of the year have overfulfilled the enlarged plan for sales and profits.   Revenues to the State budget have increased.   The enterprises now have the appropriate funds for boosting production, material incentives and social and cultural measures and housing construction.   The wages of industrial and office workers have increased.

Take, for example, the Krasny Oktyabr Plant in Volgograd.   Operating under the new system, it expects to produce an additional profit of 800,000 roubles this year.   Of this sum 80,000 roubles (10 per cent) will go into the national budget, 600,000 roubles (75 per cent) will be paid out to the employees as bonuses, and the remaining 120,000 roubles (15 per cent) will go for housing construction.

As a result the enterprises have been able to double their bonus funds and appropriations for housing and the construction of kindergartens, nurseries and children's summer camps.

10 CONCLUSIONS

(1) The new system is the most powerful innovation in the U.S.S.R.'s 1966–70 Five-Year Plan.   It has vital long-term implications.   It is a many-featured, nation-wide move towards giving a more democratic content to economic life.   Producing enterprises and their personnel will have a large scope in deciding what to do and how to do it, will have responsibility for the economic effectiveness of their work, and will be materially rewarded in accordance with their achievements in this respect.

(2) The new system is not a triumph of capitalism, as some in the West believe, but is a triumph of sensible accounting and of socialist economic science.   It brings Soviet society closer to the historical concept of advanced Communist society – the planned, rationally organised co-operation of free and capable people who decide their own objectives and the means of teaching them.

(3) Though there are still many problems to be solved, the facts of life have already shown that the pursuit of the new economic policy will facilitate the creation of the conditions necessary to accelerate technical progress, greater efficiency in social production and in the development of the productive forces.

(4)   Finally, a few words about centralised planning, a fundamental feature and advantage of Socialist system.   The economic reform not only continues centralised planning but strengthens it.   Centralised planning will improve and become more flexible after we trim away the superfluous indicators and give enterprises a free hand to settle many questions on the spot.

The Directives of the 23rd Party Congress for the new Five-Year Plan emphasised that centralised planning should concentrate first and foremost on improving the basic economic proportions and distribution of production, and the all-round development of economic regions.   Centralised planning will promote higher rates of production and deliveries of the main goods.   It will implement an integrated national policy in the spheres of technical progress, investment in capital construction, wages, prices, profits, finance and credits.

We thus see that centralised planning assures optimum utilisation of resources, the criterion being a maximum growth of national income, which means, in the final analysis, a rise in the people's living standard.

REFERENCES

[1] *23rd Congress of the Communist Party of the Soviet Union* (Moscow 1966) pp. 68–71, 208–10.
[2] *New methods of economic management in the U.S.S.R.* (Nevesti Press Agency Publishing House, M. 1965).
[3] *Moscow News*, 14 May 1966.
[4] *Pravda*, 19 July 1966.

17 Economies of Scale and Investment over Time [1]

H. P. Chenery and L. Westphal

1 INTRODUCTORY

The allocation and co-ordination of investment is a central feature of development policy. Half the total investment activity in underdeveloped countries is typically carried out by the government itself; much of the remainder is influenced through licensing, price policies and import controls. When development policies are successful, large changes can be made in the economic structure and the stock of capital doubled in ten or fifteen years.

Problems of investment policy have usually been discussed in terms appropriate to a mature economy in which the growth of the capital stock is slower and economies of scale are relatively unimportant. The framework of partial analysis applied to individual projects that is justifiable under these circumstances breaks down when there are significant economies of scale in related sectors of a developing economy. A more comprehensive economic model is then needed to take account of the multiple limitations on both the composition of output and the supply of factors. Since new investment may produce relatively large changes in the economic structure over a period of a few years, partial analysis based on existing prices can be quite misleading. Not only do marginal rules of allocation break down, but even the possibility of calculating numerical solutions to planning models of any complexity is only now being developed.

In the absence of a general theory of investment allocation for developing countries, a variety of special theories and intuitive suggestions have been put forward.[2] Among the best known are the Rosenstein–Rodan

[1] We are indebted to David Kendrick, Stephen Marglin and Paul Roberts for helpful suggestions on the formulation of the problem and computational possibilities. Andrew Szasz assisted in the computations. Our research has been supported by the Project for Quantitative Research in Economic Development, Center for International Affairs, Harvard University. A technical appendix presenting a mathematical model of the material and more data is available from Hollis Chenery, Economics Department, Harvard University.
[2] For references see p. 387 below.

theory of the Big Push [18, 19], the Nurkse–Lewis theories of Balanced Growth [12, 16, 17], Leibenstein's concept of Critical Minimum Effort [11], Hirschman's theory of Unbalanced Growth [9], and the attempts of authors such as Fleming [7], Lipton [13], Scitovsky [20], Streeten [22] and Sutcliffe [23] to reconcile some of the conflicting conclusions. Among the central issues in this debate are:

(i) the effects of limited export possibilities and economies of scale on the optimal pattern of investment;
(ii) the relations between investments in overhead facilities and in commodity production;
(iii) the importance of utilising external resources to secure an initial spurt in investment and growth.

The discussion has served to clarify the assumptions underlying the several approaches, but it has not yet provided an adequate basis for empirical analysis.

These questions cannot be answered without a more precise description of the economic structure and specification of policy objectives. We therefore propose to reformulate several earlier approaches in such a way that formal optimising procedures can be applied to the resulting model. A series of experiments will then be undertaken to determine the optimal investment patterns that are characteristic of situations involving economies of scale in related sectors.

2 FORMULATION OF THE PROBLEM

In partial analysis, the effects of economies of scale in one sector on investment in related sectors are traditionally discussed under the heading of 'external economies'.[1] However, determination of the optimal choice of investments in inter-related sectors involves a simultaneous allocation among them. This requires a more comprehensive formulation in which welfare is maximised (or cost minimised) subject to constraints on demand and factor use. In general equilibrium analysis, it is not necessary (and often not possible) to allocate welfare gains or cost savings to individual investment decisions. For this reason, the concept of 'external economies' has never acquired much operational value.

With allowance for economies of scale, our formulations of the problem of investment choice will follow the modified input-output approach to development programming that is exemplified in the models of Chenery

---

[1] The clearest formulation of dynamic externalities is that of Scitovsky [20].

and Kretschmer [3], Manne [15], Bruno [1], and Eckaus and Parikh [6].[1] These programming models determine the optimal pattern of investment when the composition of domestic final demand is given and the main choices are between domestic production and imports. The problem of vertical and horizontal interdependence is thus posed in an empirical context and simple form – i.e. with both input coefficients and the composition of demand fixed.

The effects of economies of scale in a single sector on the pattern of investment over time have been analysed in a partial equilibrium framework by Chenery [2] and Manne [14]. The growth of demand and the supply cost of inputs are taken as given; the optimum plant size and the intervals between investments are determined to be a function of the scale economies, the rate of growth of demand, the cost of imports and the interest rate.

Our approach incorporates elements of this single-sector analysis into a simplified dynamic inter-industry programming model. The model has the following structural characteristics:

(i) linear production activities with economies of scale in the use of capital and constant coefficients for other inputs;

(ii) import and export activities for traded commodities;

(iii) two scarce factors – domestic investment resources and imported goods;

(iv) domestic consumption of each commodity as a function of income;

(v) limited access to foreign loans;

(vi) a welfare function which depends on consumption over time, terminal capacity, and the amount of terminal debt.

These structural elements have been chosen to include most of the determinants of the investment patterns described in the literature. The principal patterns previously discussed may be identified as:

(i) *Rodan – Nurkse (Balanced) Growth*, which is characterised by simultaneous investment in many sectors and a large capital inflow (big push) in early periods;

(ii) *Scitovsky – Streeten (Unbalanced) Growth*, in which there is an alternation of investment among sectors with imports filling the gaps between supply and demand.[2]

---

[1] The principal differences among these analyses are in the degree of disaggregation, the treatment of investment and other resource limitations, and the number of time periods considered.

[2] We refer to Streeten's analysis of the effects of economies of scale [22, pp. 176–7], in

(iii) *Specialisation* according to existing comparative advantage, normally in the export of primary products and import of manufactured goods.

Since the arguments for balanced growth are based on the limited possibilities of expanding exports, we have found it useful to define the problem as that of jointly allocating investible resources and foreign exchange over time. The lumpiness of efficient investments makes it necessary to borrow and invest irregularly, so that the balance of payments becomes as important in determining the optimal investment pattern as the balance of savings and investment.

There are several tradeoffs to be considered in a framework of significant scale economies and two scarce factors:

(i) the cost of borrowing vs. the gains from exploiting economies of scale;

(ii) the cost of deferring investment vs. the gains from larger plants;

(iii) the loss of present consumption vs. the creation of greater future capacity;

(iv) the loss of current commodity output vs. the gain from exploiting scale economies in overhead (non-importable) services.

Optimal allocation of investment involves balancing all of these factors. It rarely produces the simple patterns implied by more partial analyses.

3 THE MODEL

Previous studies of Chenery [4] and Haldi [8] have used simple inter-industry models to explore some of the effects of economies of scale on investment patterns. These attempts were severely limited by the lack of an efficient method of solving programming problems including economies of scale short of enumerating all the feasible solutions. The recent development of integer programming algorithms makes it feasible to work with models containing a greater number of activities characterised by economies of scale. To exploit these possibilities, we have designed a four-sector model containing scale economies in two industries which is solved for up to ten time periods. After an extensive process of trial and error, we have developed a computable model which includes most of the significant features assumed in previous studies.

---

which he cites an example taken from Scitovsky. Hirschman's concept of unbalanced growth [9] is based on psychological reactions that cannot readily be included in this type of analysis.

(A) ACTIVITIES IN THE MODEL

The first cycle of investment and production activity and the parameter values for the basic model are represented in activity analysis form in Table 1. The magnitudes of the most important parameters are intended to be realistic although the degree of aggregation makes the results of illustrative value only. Table B-1 of Appendix B gives a list of the symbols used in the paper.

Production and trade activity and consumption levels in period zero (the initial period) are derived from specified initial capital endowments under the assumption of no excess capacity. From these activity levels the initial endowments of savings and foreign exchange available for investment are determined.[1] Consequently, the investment variables of period zero are the first set of activities in the dynamic model.

The four production sectors in the model are intended to represent the manufacturing complex and the export sector of a dual economy. The four sectors include finished, intermediate, and primary goods-producing industries (sectors one through three respectively) as well as a sector providing overhead facilities (sector four). With one exception, the rest of the economy – i.e. handicraft industry and traditional primary production not included in sector three – is excluded from the model.[2] The production of finished and intermediate goods requires inputs from sectors outside the model. The 'auxiliary investment' (AI) activities show the cost of the increased capacity necessary to provide the other inputs required for production in sectors one and two.[3]

The intersection of the production and trade activities with the production and primary resource constraints of period one in Table 1 gives the standard input-output portrayal of economic activity. Due to our hypothetical economy's stage of development, it is assumed that finished and intermediate goods cannot be exported profitably and primary products are not imported. The output of the overhead sector is not traded. Production in sectors one and two also requires non-competitive imports as intermediate inputs, as shown in the 'FE' row for period one.

---

[1] Table 2 below illustrates these calculations.

[2] As an alternative interpretation, the four sectors in the model might be understood to represent a highly integrated set of sectors within an economy. One such set is the complex described by Chenery [4], which includes electric power, coal and iron ore mining, steel and finished metal products.

[3] The importance of 'auxiliary investment' in this model is the role it plays in matching the pattern of investment to the supply of investible resources over time. Over-investment in a sector to realise economies of scale need not be accompanied by over-investment to provide the external inputs.

N

TABLE ONE

TABLEAU OF BASIC ACTIVITY SET

Activities		$T=0$							
					Investment				
Constraints	Equation Number	I_1^0	F_2^0	I_2^0	I_3^0	F_4^0	I_4^0	AI_1^0	AI_2^0
$T=0$									
Primary Resources									
FE	1	-0.20	-19.0	-0.15	-0.60	-57.6	-1.28	-0.10	-0.05
DS	2	-0.53	-42.0	-0.45	-7.00	-108.0	-2.40	-0.27	-0.15
$T=1$									
Capacity									
1. Finished	4-1	1.0							
2. Intermed.	4-2			1.0					
3. Primary	4-3				1.0				
4. Overhead	4-4						1.0		
Auxiliary (1)	5-1							1.0	
Auxiliary (2)	5-2								1.0
Production									
1. Finished	6								
2. Intermed.	7								
3. Primary	8								
4. Overhead	9								
Primary Resources									
FE	12								
DS	13								
Fixed Charge			$+1.0$			$+1.0$			
Constraints			200.0	-1.0		200.0	-1.0		
O									

$$* \; = \Sigma_j f_{1j}F_j^1 + \overset{4}{\underset{i=1}{\Sigma}} f_{2i}I_i^1 + \overset{2}{\underset{i=1}{\Sigma}} f_{3i}AI_i^1 - B^1 + UFE^1 + MS^1.$$

$$\dagger \; = \Sigma_j u_{1j}F_j^1 + \overset{4}{\underset{i=1}{\Sigma}} u_{2i}I_i^1 + \overset{2}{\underset{i=1}{\Sigma}} u_3 AI_{ii}^1 - B^1 - 0.8 MS^1.$$

Notes: Equation numbers refer to formal statement of model in the technical appendix. convenience the following constraints are not shown:

   3: Debt limit.

  10: Production cannot decrease in Sector 3.

  11: Consumption Growth Constraint.

So that a positive entry in the matrix would denote provision and a negative entry use, all equati have been multiplied by minus one.

	T=0				T=1							
	Transfer of Primary Inputs			Production				Trade			CN	RHS
D^0	UFE^0	MS^0	X_1^I	X_2^I	X_3^I	X_4^I	M_1^I	M_2^I	E_3^I	CN^I	
1·0	−1·0	−1·0									$\geq$ −40·0
1·0		0·8									$\geq$ −82·3
			−1·0								$\geq$ −50·0
				−1·0							$\geq$ −75·0
					−1·0						$\geq$ −160·0
						−1·0					$\geq$ −126·7
			−1·0								$\geq$ −50·0
				−1·0							$\geq$ −75·0
			1·0				1·0			−2·4	=90·0
			−0·40	1·0				1·0		−1·7	=75·0
			−0·12	−0·48	1·0				−1·0	−0·2	=11·5
			−0·10	−0·21	−0·35	1·0				−1·0	=50·0
−1·07	1·0		−0·04	−0·06			−1·0	−1·0	1·0		$\geq$ *
−1·07			0·2	0·2	0·2	0·2					$\geq$ †
											= 1 or 0
											$\geq$ 0
											= 1 or 0
											$\geq$ 0
										43·0	

Domestic savings (DS) are generated by production in each sector, a formulation that avoids the necessity of measuring total income separately. We assume that the traditional sector of the economy does not supply net savings and that public and private saving are rigidly linked to production, as specified by the entries in the 'DS' row in the production columns (X_1 through X_4).[1]

The consumption activity (CN), which enters the objective function,

[1] This formulation allows for differences in taxes and savings rates among sectors, but we have not utilised this possibility in our numerical estimates.

assumes rigid complementarity of demand between the four goods.[1] The consumption activity is stated in terms of the growth of consumption above its level in the previous period.

We turn now to the investment variables of period zero. A one-period gestation lag from investment to usable capacity is assumed for each sector, so that investments in period zero come on line in period one (see the capacity constraints). Economies of scale enter the model in the investment cost functions of sectors two and four (activities F_2, I_2 and F_4, I_4). These cost functions are characterised by a 'fixed charge' (F_i) incurred if investment takes place and a 'variable charge' (I_i) which depends on the level of investment. The resulting cost function exhibits constant marginal cost and declining average cost. The fixed charge constraints assure that the fixed charge will be incurred if capacity is built through the operation of the variable charge activity.

Investment in sectors one and three and auxiliary investment take place at constant average cost. Investment in capacity in any sector requires two factors, foreign exchange (FE) and domestic savings (DS). The domestic savings charge associated with an investment activity gives the total resource cost of investment, while the foreign exchange charge expresses its import component separately. The productive mechanism whereby savings are translated into capacity through investment is not detailed in the model.

The block of activities titled 'Transfer of Primary Inputs' provides for the transfer of 'FE' and 'DS' both between periods and within the period. In this model constraints on the transfer of investible resources over time assume vital importance because they limit the extent to which scale economies can be realised through the concentration of investment in one period. Without activities providing for transfer over time of investible resources, investment in a given period would be limited to the investible resources generated in that period. In the real world, such activities include changes in foreign exchange reserves and stocks of commodities, external borrowing and changes in the proportions of income that is saved. We include two such activities, borrowing and changes in reserves. The debt or borrowing activity (D) secures additional resources from outside the economy. In accord with the conceptual framework of national income accounting, it yields a unit of both foreign exchange and domestic savings in the current period at the cost of repaying both

---

[1] Lack of substitution in final consumption is the source of 'horizontal interdependence' assumed by Nurkse and other balanced growth theorists.

resources in a later period. The U.F.E. activity (representing reserve changes) transfers unused foreign exchange from one period to the next. We neglect stockpiling of commodities, so unused domestic savings cannot be similarly transferred without being combined with imports as completed investment projects.

A third transfer activity (MS) converts foreign exchange into domestic resources for investment. The increase in savings from this activity results from reducing accumulated foreign exchange reserves. The additional resources imported may be thought of as investment goods – such as cement – that are normally produced domestically. The latter aspect has led us to assume that 1 unit of foreign exchange can replace only 0.8 units of domestic savings (DS).

The full model consists of ten cycles of activity like that shown in Table 1; it begins with investment in period zero and ends with production, trade and consumption in period ten. In some experiments the model has also been computed for shorter periods, which only necessitates a change in the valuation of terminal capacity.

(B) CONSTRAINTS ON THE SYSTEM

This section gives a brief verbal description of the principal constraints on the system. Appendix B contains a formal algebraic statement of the optimisation model.

In the first period the total use of foreign exchange on investment account and the amount of savings to be invested are limited to the initial endowment of investible resources plus borrowing. Investment in each succeeding period is similarly constrained by the production, trade and the transfer activities of that period. The debt limit is formulated in such a way that the debt of the previous period must be repaid along with the interest charge, either through renewed debt or from savings and foreign exchange generated by current production.

The availability of foreign borrowing to a less developed country is one of the central limitations on the system. Criticisms of the balanced growth theories have stressed its importance in the real world. We show this limit in the form of a ceiling on the allowable debt of each period. The debt limit is varied parametrically to show its effect on the optimal pattern of investment during the plan period.

Since labour is a free good in the model, production is limited only by available capacity. In sectors one and two production is further limited by the auxiliary capacity needed in sectors outside the model to provide intermediate inputs. Since resources devoted to primary production are not readily transferable to other sectors, we require that the production level in sector three does not fall. The consumption of each product, both on final and intermediate account, is equal to production plus imports (less exports) in each period.[1]

The final constraint is a means of incorporating a non-linear element of diminishing marginal utility in the objective function. Consumption growth (i.e. the level of the CN activity) is constrained to be at least two units in each period. Without this constraint, optimisation often leads to a concentration of consumption growth in a short period.

(C) THE WELFARE FUNCTION AND TERMINAL CONDITIONS[2]

Since the operation of the model terminates with production and consumption in the final period, it is necessary to insure sufficient foreign exchange and savings for post-plan growth. The economy is required to provide these resources for post-plan investment in amounts at least equal to their initial endowments. Value is given in the objective function (in terms of the contribution to post-terminal consumption) to the 'excess' of foreign exchange and domestic savings passed over the initial endowments into the post-terminal future.

External debt is allowed in the terminal year, but its level cannot be increased above that of the previous year. The cost of terminal debt in the objective function is the opportunity cost in terms of consumption of the foreign exchange and domestic savings required for repayment. (The optimal solutions to the model as initially specified always involve repayment of debt by the terminal period.)

Since over-investment and excess capacity are expected as a result of scale economies, it is necessary to value terminal excess capacity in the objective function. Excess capacity in a sector in the terminal period reduces the necessity for investment in that sector in the immediate future. Seen in this light, the value of excess capacity in the terminal period is the opportunity cost of investible resources in periods beyond the plan horizon needed to supply the expected demands in these sectors. Transferring excess capacity to post-plan periods is thus similar to providing foreign exchange and domestic savings for post-plan investment. Since capacity

---

[1] Equality is imposed on two accounts: first, to preclude the simultaneous production and disposal of a product to obtain the savings thereby created (excess capacity in sector four would give rise to this kind of behaviour if product disposal were allowed): and second, to avoid problems associated with the valuation of utilised and excess capacity.

[2] Appendix B gives a more detailed discussion of the terminal conditions and their derivation.

is specific to a given sector, some type of optimisation must be utilised to determine the opportunity cost of the future foreign exchange and savings whose use is released by virtue of terminal excess capacity. The procedure adopted is described in the appendix. It should be noted that terminal excess capacity can not be restricted *a priori* to those sectors in which scale economies are present.

Having assessed the value of excess capacity in the terminal period, it is also necessary to value capacity utilised in production in that period. The composite of terminal capacity in each sector necessary to sustain a unit of consumption is therefore given the value of one unit of consumption sustained through an infinite time horizon (ignoring depreciation). Consumption growth in each period is given a value in the objective function equal to the value of a stream of consumption beginning in that period and continued through the terminal period.

In summary, the function to be maximised is the sum of four elements: (1) the discounted value of consumption during the plan period; (2) the value of capacity utilised in the terminal period which was not present at the beginning of the plan period; (3) the value of unused capacity in each sector; (4) the cost of terminal debt. The activities in the welfare function are all valued in terms of composite units of consumption over an infinite time horizon.

(D) SOLUTIONS TO THE MODEL

In solving the model we have used the Land and Doig algorithm [10]. This algorithm is a sophisticated, if time consuming, means of searching among the feasible solutions for the highest value of the objective functions.[1] In this context a feasible solution results from a process of sub-optimisation. Each integer variable (the F_i^T) is set at either zero or one and the optimal values of all other activities are determined by linear programming. In principle there are 2^n such feasible solutions (where 'n' is the number of the integer variables), each of which is optimal for the pattern of fixed charges incurred. The optimal solutions for several model specifications are given in Appendix Tables A-3, A-4 and A-5.

The prices associated with the feasible solutions are similar to shadow prices of linear programming in that they represent the marginal value products of the resources, given the 'basis' and the pattern of fixed

---

[1] Other mixed integer algorithms were tested but were judged inferior because they yielded only one feasible solution in reaching the optimum but took about the same amount of computer time.

charges incurred.[1]   However, the prices cannot be used to judge the profitability of an activity not already in the model.   In general the model must be solved again whenever a new variable is introduced.   The question of whether or not to invest in a sector with scale economies can thus be determined only by comparing the welfare value of the solutions in which that investment does and does not take place.   It is only valid to use prices to test the profitability of other activities for a given pattern of investment in scale economy sectors.

In the process of obtaining the model in its present form, we worked with similarly specified models which were run for three, four and seven periods.   To solve directly the ten period model with its twenty integer variables for the optimal solution would have required days of computer time.   Therefore we relied on knowledge gained from these earlier runs to select solutions for the ten-period model.   The following procedure was used.   A four-period model having the same specifications as the ten-period model (except that terminal valuations differ) was solved for the optimal pattern of fixed charges.[2]   Next a seven-period model with the integer variables of the first four periods set at the values of the optimal four-period solution was solved for the optimal pattern of fixed charges in the last three periods.   This process was then repeated in going on to the ten-period solution.

The best solution to the ten-period model obtained in this iterative fashion is not known to be *the* optimal solution (with respect to the pattern of fixed charges incurred).   However, a number of alternative solutions to the ten-period model were computed using knowledge gained from the shorter planning period models to set the integer variables at different values.[3]   Since little improvement was achieved, we are confident that our 'best' solutions are at least close to optimal.

4   INVESTMENT PATTERNS

In order to derive some broad conclusions from these experiments in optimisation it is first necessary to identify some general properties of the

[1] Two differences should be noted: unlike linear programming, prices associated with one set of activity levels may also be associated with a different set of activity levels (hence the problem with using prices as decision guides in scale-economy models); (ii) the minimum value of the dual associated with any integer solution will exceed the maximum value of the primal.

[2] This process required from three to four hours of time on the I.B.M. 7094 computer for each solution.

[3] The investment patterns and welfare values of 41 experimental solutions are summarised in Table 4 below.

solutions. Since a complete description of a ten-period solution requires several hundred variables, we have sought key elements that determine the dominant features of the pattern of resource allocation. For most purposes a solution is adequately described by the yearly amounts of capacity, production and imports in each sector. The pattern of investment is dominated by the size and timing of capacity increases in the scale-economy sectors. The simplest characterisation of an investment pattern, therefore, is by the number and size of plants built in sectors 2 and 4 during the ten-year period.[1]

Our experiments with the ten-period model lead to the classification of investment patterns shown in Table 2. The original set of parameter specifications is identified as Model I. Its optimal solution involves the

TABLE TWO

INVESTMENT PATTERNS IN THE TEN-YEAR MODEL*

Number of Steel Plants (Sector 2)	Number of Overhead Investments (Sector 4)			Total Solutions
	1	2	3	
0 (A)	A1 (0)	A2 (2)	A3 (1)	(3)
1 (B)	B1 (2)	B2 (15)	B3 (10)	(27)
2 (C)	C1 (2)	C2 (6)	C3 (3)	(11)
Total solutions	(4)	(23)	(14)	(41)
Model I	0	4	11	15
Model II	3	7	2	12
Model III	1	12	1	14

* Based on Table 4. Figures in parentheses show the number of solutions corresponding to each pattern in the first series of experiments. The three Models are distinguished as follows:

Model I: Debt limit 75.
Model II: Debt limit 150.
Model III: Debt limit 150 for years 1–5, 300 thereafter.

construction of one plant in sector 2 (steel) and two in sector 4 (overhead facilities) during the ten year period. This investment pattern is identified as B2 for Model I, or IB2. A number of alternative timings must be examined for each such pattern to determine the optimal time for construction of each plant.

The characteristics of the optimal solution for each model can be

[1] Our cost function implies that capacity is increased only by building new plants.

N 2

brought out by comparison to a number of the more promising alternatives. Two alternative specifications of the model have been made in
which the amount of external resources available was increased to make
possible larger investments. A complete listing of the solutions is given
in Table 4. They cover eight of the nine possible patterns indicated in
Table 2.[1]

(A) THE BASIC PATTERN

The features typical of an optimal investment pattern will be shown by
considering the best solutions to Models I and II. Their assumptions
differ only in the increase in external debt that is allowed during the plan
period, which is 75 units for Model I and 150 units for Model II. Model
II is taken as representative of developing countries in the past decade,
in which the net deficit on current account has typically amounted to about
a quarter of gross investment.[2] The increase in debt of 150 units in Model
II finances about a quarter of investment in the first five years of the
optimal solution. Model III (discussed below) is designed to show the
effects of an equal increase in borrowing in the second five years.

The full detail of these Models cannot be presented in this paper.[3] For
each Model the calculations bring out the relations between increases in
capacity, production, imports and exports in each of the four sectors.
Because capacity is fully utilised in period 0, the cycle starts with investment in overhead facilities (symbolised by electric power), which are
necessary for increased production in all other sectors. A steel plant is
built in period 2 and a second power plant in period 6. These three
plants account for about 40 per cent of total investment in this segment
of the economy.

To adjust to these lumpy investments, positive net borrowing takes
place in periods 0, 2 and 6, and investment in other sectors is curtailed.
In fact the low debt ceiling assumed in Model I causes other investment
to be virtually eliminated in these three periods, as shown below.
The investment and borrowing patterns are dominated by the timing of
the overhead investments, which take up to 30 per cent of the investment
resources and are concentrated in two periods. Scale economies make it
optimal to build plants large enough to take care of the growth of demand

----

[1] These were selected after extensive experimentation with the three-period version
of the model.
[2] This is the median value found by Chenery and Strout [5, p. 684] for a sample of
31 underdeveloped countries.
[3] The values of the main variables in the solutions are given in Appendix B, available
from the authors.

for the following five years even when it is necessary to defer almost all other investment in order to do so.

Investment in intermediate products (which we symbolise by steel) takes place only once; the increase in capacity in both models is equal to about twelve years' growth of total demand. As Manne has shown [14], the availability of imports makes it efficient to postpone construction in order to build a larger plant with lower unit costs.

The inclusion of vertical and horizontal interdependence in our model brings out a further feature not previously noted: it is efficient in Model I (and to a lesser extent in Model II) to *reduce* steel production in periods 5 and 6 in order to postpone the construction of added power capacity so that a more efficient plant can be built in period 6. In this way, the importation of steel indirectly postpones the requirement to expand power production and makes possible a more economical plant. The expansion of primary production and exports during these years provides a more economical alternative to increasing power and steel production, even though long-run comparative advantage favours steel when a larger plant can be built.

As a further reflection of the importance of realising greater economies of scale, consumption increases are held to a minimum until after the second power plant has been built. In period 7 production in all sectors expands, final consumption rises more rapidly, and primary production is diverted from exports to the production of intermediate products and finished goods. Once the bottleneck has been removed, there is a rapid increase in power use.

Because of the evident effects of the power shortage in both models, it might be supposed that advancing the construction of the second power plant by a year or two might be advantageous. This turns out not to be true, as shown in Table 4 below, because the smaller plant that would have to be built would hamper growth and raise costs in later years.

The general pattern of investment revealed by these solutions is much closer to the Scitovsky–Streeten concept of alternating investments in different sectors than it is to any of the versions of balanced growth. Exports are essential to this pattern. In the short run it is efficient to increase investment in primary production even though long-run comparative advantage favours import substitution in the two manufacturing sectors. The latter factor is outweighed by the increased flexibility made possible by imports during the transitional period when capital is relatively scarce.

The effects of alternating scale economy investments on the financing of total investment and imports are shown in the last three figures for each model. Irregular investment requires the repayment of debt (and building up of exchange reserves) in order to finance the bulge in investment and imports of investment goods in period 6 by again increasing debt and reducing reserves.

The need to balance investment over time also leads to investment in finished goods (in Model I) in advance of the increase in demand, even though there are no economies of scale in this sector. Without this further adaptation to the lumpiness of investment in other sectors, the increase in total consumption would have to be deferred even longer.

(B) EFFECTS OF VARYING EXTERNAL RESOURCES

It is apparent from the preceding discussion that external resources are exceedingly important to the realisation of economies of scale because they make possible periodic bulges in total investment considerably in excess of domestic savings. In the first two models, the cost assigned to external debt in the terminal year caused it to be reduced to zero at the end of the period. The marked increase in capacity in all sectors between Models I and II is therefore due entirely to temporary borrowing, which makes it possible to construct larger and more efficient plants.

To explore this phenomenon in greater detail, we have assumed in Model III a further doubling in the availability of external resources. To avoid an unrealistic bulge in investment in the first period, however, the debt limit is raised from 150 to 300 only in period 6. The cost of terminal debt has also been lowered so that it is no longer advantageous to repay debt within the ten-year period.

Model III has the same timing of investment as Models I and II, but there is now a more substantial 'big push' in period 7 after the debt limit is raised.[1] The power plant completed in this period is 50 per cent larger than that in Model II and at the same time there is a big jump in finished goods capacity. These increases permit final consumption to increase much more rapidly than before and the excess steel and power capacity are fully used by the end of the period.

The feasibility of this investment pattern requires that the future spurt in demand for steel be anticipated at the beginning of the period when the steel plant is built. Although all conditions in Models II and III are identical for the first five years, the steel plant constructed in the first

---

[1] A more gradual rise in the debt limit would not greatly affect the result, since this investment pattern is optimal even without the further increase in external capital.

five-year plan under Model III must be 30 per cent larger to satisfy the future demand for steel five or six years later from plants that will be built only when final demand increases.

The direct and indirect effects of increasing the availability of foreign resources on total welfare are summed up in Fig. 17.4 and Table 3. The direct effect is the cost saving resulting from constructing larger plants, which is shown in Fig. 17.4. The total reduction in investment cost for Models II and III (compared with the unit costs of Model I) is shown in Table 3, line 7. The *indirect* effects of external borrowing are even greater, however. The more rapid growth that is produced by more efficient

TABLE THREE

EFFECTS OF EXTERNAL RESOURCES *

	Model I	*Model II*	*Change from I*	*Model III*	*Change from I*
1. Terminal Consumption (ΣCN)	28	40	+ 12	54	+ 26
2. Total Value (W)	3436	4165	+ 729	5538	+ 2102
3. Total Investment (ΣI)	1237	1398	+ 161	1758	+ 521
4. Capital inflow (ΣF)	− 27	− 66	− 39	200	+ 227
5. Total Savings (3 − 4)	1264	1464	+ 200	1558	+ 294
6. Average Productivity of Investment (2 ÷ 3)	2·78	2·98		3·15	
Sources of Improvement over Model I					
7. Reduction in Investment Cost †		102		185	
8. Increased Savings		200		294	
9. Increased Capital Inflow		− 39		227	
10. Total (7 + 8 + 9)		263		706	
11. Productivity [(ΔW ÷ (7 + 8 + 9)]		2·77		2·98	

* Derived from optimal solutions to each model as given in Tables A-3-3, A-4, and A-5 below.

† Difference between actual investment cost and cost of building the same size plants at the average unit costs of Model I.

allocation of resources as well as lower-cost capacity results in a substantial increase in total savings. Table 3 shows that for Model II, where there is no increase in terminal debt compared to Model I, these indirect effects account for over 60 per cent of the substantial welfare gain (21 per cent) that results from increasing the debt limit.

The increase in external borrowing in Model III produces a gain in welfare of 60 per cent above Model I. Cost savings from larger plants and increased savings from more rapid growth again account for the bulk of the total. Comparing Model II and Model III, it can be seen that a net increase in capital inflow amounting to 15 per cent of total investment is highly productive because of these indirect effects. Further increases would be less productive because the size of investment in Model III exploits most of the available economies of scale.

(C) DEVIATIONS FROM THE OPTIMAL PATTERN

Since perfect co-ordination of investment cannot be achieved in either a planned or a market economy, it is important to determine the effects on total welfare of departures from optimality in the size and timing of investments. As these costs have been investigated by Manne and others [14] in a partial equilibrium context, we will concentrate on the adjustments that are necessary in the pattern as a whole. A detailed examination of one alternative solution illustrates the adjustments that can be made and their net cost.

The optimal pattern for all three models requires sufficient foresight to accept periodic power shortages in order to build larger plants. A plausible 'real world' alternative would be to keep up with demand at the cost of building smaller and more expensive plants. Such an investment policy is illustrated in Fig. 17.5, in which the investment cycle in sector 4 is cut from 6 to 3–4 years and 3 plants are built instead of 2. Optimisation for Model I under these restrictions gives the investment and production patterns of Fig. 17.5. Keeping up with the demand for power leads to higher steel and power production over the period and greater power capacity at the end. The cost of this policy is reflected in smaller power plants that cost 15 per cent more per unit of capacity and hence reduce the investment available for sectors 1 and 3. The welfare cost to the economy of this single change in investment policy is 3 per cent of the total value of Model I, as shown in Table 4.[1] This pattern requires less advance planning of investment, however, and is less dependent on steel imports.

Table 4 gives a number of other examples of the cost of changes in the investment pattern or of departures from optimal timing. Timing of investment is more critical in Model I because limited external resources reduce the possibilities for adjustments in other sectors.[2] The investment patterns that are most closely competitive to the optimal (B2) are B3 for

[1] The optimal Model I solution for pattern B3 is No. 24 (shown in Fig. 17.5), which has a value of 3342. Solution No. 11 is optimal for pattern B2 and has a value of 3436.
[2] It is notable that departures from the optimal timing of one or two years do not produce very large welfare losses.

TABLE FOUR
VALUES OF EXPERIMENTAL SOLUTIONS[1]

Investment Pattern	Timing of Invest- ment in Sectors: 2	4	Model I	Model II	Model III
A 2	—	0,5			(1) 3950
	—	0,7		(2) 3266	
A 3	—	0,4,7	(3) 2572		
B 1	2	0		(4) 3553	(5) 4291
B 2	1	0,5			(6) 5068
	1	0,7		(7) 4130	
	2	0,4	(8) 3265		
	2	0,5	(9) 3405		(10) 5512
	2	0,6	(11) 3436 *	(12) 4165 *	(13) 5538 *
	2	0,7	(14) 3382	(15) 4157	(16) 5511
	2	0,8		(17) 4080	(18) 5398
	3	0,5			(19) 5008
	3	0,7		(20) 4117	
B 3	1	0,4,7	(21) 3254		
	2	0,3,7	(22) 3148		
	2	0,4,6	(23) 3234		
	2	0,4,7	(24) 3342 [2]	(25) 3711	
	2	0,5,6			(26) 5034
	2	0,5,7	(27) 3295		
	2	0,7,8		(28) 3746	
	3	0,4,7	(29) 3255		
	5	0,4,7	(30) 3221		
C 1	2,7	0		(31) 3601	
	2,8	0		(32) 3644	
C 2	1,1	0,5			(33) 4912
	2,6	0,7			(34) 5471
	2,7	0,7		(35) 4068	(36) 5474
	2,7	0,8			(37) 5372
	2,8	0,7			(38) 5438
C 3	1,3	1,4,7	(39) 3114		
	2,6	0,4,7	(40) 3179		
	2,7	0,4,7	(41) 3165		

[1] Each value is calculated from the optimal solution for the specified timing of invest-ments in sectors 2 and 4, Solution numbers in parentheses. Best solutions for each Model are starred.

[2] Optimal solution for pattern B3, Model I.

Model I and C2 for Model III. Continued specialisation on primary exports instead of import substitution in steel is quite costly in all models under the given assumptions, although the construction of the steel plant can be postponed 2 or 3 years without great loss (as shown by solution 30).

Apart from the ten-period solutions given in Table 4, we have calculated the effects of a number of different specifications of the parameters in the model for shorter periods. Among the changes tested were higher discount rates, greater returns from exporting, and possible export of manufactured goods. Since the results were essentially those predictable by partial analysis, they will not be reproduced.

(D) IMPLICATION FOR DEVELOPMENT PLANNING

These experiments bring out an aspect of development plans that is only beginning to be adequately appreciated: their function in balancing investment over time. Scitovsky [21, 213–14] reached a very similar conclusion in trying to reconcile the arguments for balanced and unbalanced growth:

> . . . several-year investment plans, of which one hears so much nowadays, may be regarded as plans for unbalanced growth, extending to several years so as to restore balance by the end of the period for which the plans are made. In the interim, imbalance manifests itself by the completion of productive capacity before the demand for its full utilisation has arisen, or by the creation of consumers' or producers' demand before the capacity to fill this demand is completed. The temporary excess capacity may have to be accepted in most cases as an inevitable cost of (temporarily) unbalanced growth for the sake of securing economies of scale; the temporary excess demand may be filled by imports, which is one reason why the availability of foreign loans or foreign exchange is so strategic a factor in investment planning. Such dependence on foreign trade, however, is very different from that which accompanies unbalanced growth concentrated on industries with a comparative advantage. For one thing, this is a temporary dependence, while that is permanent; for another, the dependence here is primarily on foreign import supplies, there on foreign export markets.

The costs of errors in judging plant size that may result from poor forecasts of future demand and of improper timing of interrelated investments are suggested by the solutions in Table 4. The welfare costs shown understate the actual losses likely to be incurred because they assume that the rest of the conomy adjust optimally to the investment pattern in the scale-economy sectors, which is most unlikely.

5 CONCLUSIONS

This study has attempted to give greater precision to the discussion of alternative investment patterns by restating several of the principal hypotheses in programming terms. We have shown that under realistic assumptions as to the nature of horizontal and vertical interdependence, the timing of investment in scale-economy sectors has a substantial effect on the timing in other sectors and hence on the whole investment pattern. The optimal pattern balances gains from larger plants against costs of deferring investment in other sectors and the resulting loss of growth in income and savings. The general characteristics of this pattern include both the type of alternation envisaged by Scitovsky and Streeten and the exploitation of an integrated spurt in investment foreseen by Rodan.

The use of a comprehensive optimising model has also provided some new perspectives on the characteristics of optimal allocation patterns. In a rapidly growing economy the timing of investment is often more important than the choice of sectors along static comparative-advantage lines. In order to exploit economies of scale in some sectors, it is necessary to limit investment in others, if necessary by using small-scale techniques that will prove to be inefficient at a later date. In our model, primary production performs this function; it is expanded whenever necessary to secure imports, even though these imports are periodically replaced with lower cost domestic production.

Although the concept of 'optimal overcapacity' was derived from a partial equilibrium analysis, an explicit consideration of the effects of interdependence leads to an analogous concept of 'optimal shortages'. The gains from building a bigger power plant next year must be weighed against the cost of lost production this year in power-using sectors. These opportunity costs can only be determined in a more comprehensive analysis. Our optimal power cycle consists of 3–4 years of excess capacity and 1–2 years of power shortages.

Even though the choice between domestic production and imports is central to the present model, comparative advantage is hard to define or measure in a system containing economies of scale and limited investment resources. In the scale-economy sectors, the critical question is the plant size and timing at which import substitution becomes profitable. There is no possibility of a timeless ranking of projects along partial equilibrium lines because the need to accommodate the lumpy investments causes relative profitability to vary year by year. While this phenomenon is exaggerated by considering only part of the whole economy as we have done, it is of considerable empirical importance in underdeveloped countries.

The policy significance of these theoretical and illustrative findings can only be evaluated when more realistic models are tested. Our results emphasise the importance of jointly planning the allocation of investment and foreign exchange over time in order to allow for alternating production and imports. The advantages of this broader approach to development planning appear to be substantial as compared to more traditional methods of allocating each scarce factor separately.

APPENDIX

(A) THE METHOD OF SOLUTION

As noted in the text, the formal characteristics of our model place it taxonomically within the class of mixed integer programming problems. Of the several methods of solution we have selected the Land and Doig algorithm for application to our model because it yields global optima.[1],[2] The only drawback of this method is the time consumed in solution. The time needed does not depend in a predictable fashion on the number of integer variables in the problem: the solution of model IA ($p = .05$) required slightly over one hour on an I.B.M. 7094 while the solution to model IA (post-plan $p =$ infinity) represents under ten minutes of computer time. The more complex terminal conditions bring the values of the various integer solutions (solutions in which the integer variables have integer values) closer together and are responsible for the six-fold increase in running time.

The first step of the algorithm is the solution of the linear programming (LP) problem in which the integer variables (F_j^T) are restricted to positive fractional values. This solution is used to select an integer variable which is to be set to both zero and one successively. The LP problems associated

[1] A. H. Land and A. G. Doig, 'An Automatic Method of Solving Discrete Programming Problems', *Econometrica*, July 1960, pp. 500–21.

[2] The authors are grateful to Dr Paul Roberts of the Harvard Transport Research Center for making available to them his computer code for the Land and Doig solution method. They also wish to acknowledge the assistance of Mr Robert Burns of the Center, and the work of Dr Kirit Parikh of M.I.T. Center for International Studies who made some necessary modifications in the code.

with each value of this variable are solved. In the next step, the first integer variable is held at the value giving the best solution and another integer variable is set to zero and one. From the values of the solutions to these two LP problems and to the remaining problem in which the first integer variable was constrained, the algorithm determines the next integer to be set. In this fashion the algorithm maps out a tree whose branches are given by the level of the integer variables. The process of setting integers to zero and one always proceeds from the best of the previous solutions from which branches have not yet been eliminated (and which are feasible). A globally optimum solution is obtained when a feasible all-integer solution exists whose value is 'better' than that of any other solution at the extremities of the tree. Summarising, in the case of a maximisation problem the algorithm reaches the best all-integer solution by obtaining progressively lower upper bounds to that solution.[1]

From the above it is seen that not all of the solutions on the tree need have integer values for the F_j^T. The number of integer solutions on the tree varies depending upon the nature of the problem. It should be stressed that each solution obtained in the branching process yields maximum objective value subject to the constraints of the model and for the particular levels to which the constrained integer variables are set. Consequently, each integer solution gives the unique activity levels necessary for optimum welfare *given the pattern of fixed charges incurred*. The optimal solution has the highest value among the integer solutions.

Because of the additional constraints required to set variables to integer levels, the prices obtained for integer solutions in which not all of the F_j^T are integer-constrained by the programme are not economically meaningful. It is possible to show that when all of the integer variables have been constrained to integer levels by the algorithm the dual decomposes to make the price of constraints within the model economically meaningful as stated in the text.[2] Thus, so long as the F_j^T have been integer constrained by the branching process, the prices associated with the dual are unaffected by the integer constraints (which force the F_j^T to be fractional when not integer constrained).

---

[1] The algorithm is an alternative to a complete enumeration of all the integer solutions to the problem at hand (2^n such solutions exist when n is the number of integer variables): it is an attractive alternative because it generally involves the solutions of far fewer linear programming problems that does complete enumeration.

[2] The '#' symbols appearing for prices in the presentation of the model solutions indicate that the decomposition was incomplete because not all F_j^T were integer constrained.

In general, therefore, the prices obtained from the dual are marginal value products and are similar to shadow prices in linear programming with two exceptions. The correspondence between prices and activity levels in linear programming is unique; this is not the case in fixed charge problems. In brief, prices associated with one set of activity levels may also be associated with a different set of activity levels. However, for one set of activity levels there is one and only one set of prices. Also, the minimum value of the dual associated with any integer solution will exceed the maximum value of the primal. These qualifications need not deter us from using prices corresponding to integer solutions as marginal revenue products (which they most certainly are). They serve only as warnings that the use of prices to determine the global optimum is not possible. Of course, prices are valid only for a particular basis; and prices depend upon the F_j^T incurred in the integer solution.

(B) DERIVATION OF TERMINAL CONDITIONS FOR BASIC MODEL

The specification of terminal conditions is a major difficulty in programming models; our model is certainly no exception to this unfortunate circumstance. The derivation of the terminal conditions is discussed in detail below.

The welfare function values a plan of activity primarily on the basis of its contribution to consumption levels during the plan and in the post-terminal future. The valuation of consumption growth is straightforward and needs no comment beyond noting that the multiplicative factor 5.3 in the ϕ_C component is the sum of the consumption of each good in the consumption vector. With respect to the terminal valuations α_k, β_k, ρ and γ, they are best discussed with reference to Table A-1.

One of the central features of our model is the existence of four distinct patterns of production which are the only possible means of satisfying consumption demands: (I) production of all four goods domestically; (II) import of intermediate goods with domestic production of the remaining products; (III) production at home of goods two, three and four with importation of good one; and (IV) domestic provision of primary goods and overhead facilities with imports of finished and intermediate goods. Within any period the model economy will have a comparative advantage in one of these patterns. Given the consumption vector, the input-output matrix yields, for each pattern, the production levels necessary to sustain one unit of consumption. These production levels are given below. When imports are called for, production in sectors three and four includes that necessary to provide foreign exchange for imports.[1]

Pattern	Production in Sector			
	1	2	3	4
I	2·40	2·66	2·02	2·51
II	2·40	0·00	3·24	2·37
III	0·00	1·70	3·52	2·59
IV	0·00	0·00	4·30	2·51

Using the production data, it is possible to determine the average investment cost per unit of consumption associated with a given level of the consumption vector for each of the production patterns. The second and third columns in Table A-1 give the average investment of foreign exchange and domestic savings associated with each pattern for a consumption level of fifty units. These costs yield the starting point of the valuation procedure.

In the context of the model there are two principal means of providing within the plan period for post-terminal growth. Either investable resources may be passed into the post-terminal future or over-investment within the plan period may provide excess capacity which may be used for future growth. There are two advantages to the latter method: first, over-investment provides a means of smoothing out the use of investable resources over time; and second, where scale economies are present, over-investment is a means of lowering the average cost of providing consumption. The matching of use and supply over time is an important element where there are limits to the transfer of resources available in one period to another period. The welfare value associated with each mode of guaranteeing post-terminal growth is the value of the post-plan consumption which it makes possible.

The value of foreign exchange and domestic savings available for investment in period four is the value of the consumption made possible through the investment of these resources. The value of one unit of consumption sustained from period four through an infinite time horizon is given by V^4. Division of V^4 by the average investment use of foreign exchange by a production pattern gives the average value of foreign exchange invested in that pattern (α_k). 'r_k' gives the investment of domestic savings necessary to yield the value α_k when invested in conjunction with one unit of foreign exchange in pattern 'k'. Thus, the

---

[1] Note that foreign exchange is also required on production account in sectors one and two.

investment of 1 unit of foreign exchange and 3·70 units of domestic savings in pattern I gives rise to 13·33 units of welfare value. Value is given to the provision of terminal foreign exchange and savings only if it exceeds the initial endowments of these resources. Difficulties associated with the use of prices as decision tools in scale economy models require this formulation.

The value of terminal excess capacity is determined in a similar fashion. The existence of excess capacity available for use post-plan represents a reduction in the foreign exchange and domestic savings needed for investment to obtain a given level of post-terminal growth. Excess capacity should be valued in terms of the foreign exchange and domestic savings which it 'releases' from post-plan investment. One assumption is necessary to make the valuation. The consumption value of excess capacity depends upon how quickly it is put to use. We have assumed a post-terminal rate of growth which gives terminal excess capacity the same value as capacity coming on line in the second post-terminal period. The value of a unit of consumption available from period five to infinity is V^5. The value of a unit of foreign exchange and r_k units of domestic savings released from investment in pattern 'k' by the presence of excess capacity is β_k. To ascertain the amount of each investable resource released by excess capacity within a sector we assumed that pattern I is the relevant production mode. The second column in the second half of Table A-1 gives the production level in each sector associated with the operation of the consumption activity at level fifty. The third and fourth columns give the average investment of foreign exchange and savings needed for the level of production in column two in each sector.

Reference to Table 2 of the text and to the formal statement of the model show how the valuation of terminal foreign exchange domestic savings and excess capacity is incorporated into the model. Since it is *a priori* impossible to determine the post-plan pattern of production, it is necessary to consider each pattern as a possible means of achieving post-plan growth. Furthermore, inclusion of all the possible patterns allows the model to determine terminal values within reasonable limits and without their being specified in a more arbitrary fashion than that used here. Finally, explicit statement of the post-plan investment alternatives allows the model to optimise within the plan period with partial knowledge of post-plan alternatives.

The most arbitrary assumptions in the valuation of terminal resources concern the appropriate level of consumption and the rate of post-plan growth. The assumptions are necessary because average investment cost is the relevant cost from which to determine the consumption value of the investable resources. Simply stated, what is required for maximum welfare is the minimisation of the average cost of providing the consumption bundle. The assumption of a consumption level of fifty units yields production levels requiring investment in plants of a size somewhat larger than those built within the plan period in the various solutions. Also it is in keeping with the derivation of terminal values by a means which stresses the long-run alternatives. In the short run, the value of the investable resources of period four may derive only from investment in overhead facilities.

A very long-run view is used in valuing utilised capacity in the terminal period. In the long run, production in the four sectors will take place at the ratios given by the production levels of one of the patterns necessary to provide a unit of consumption. This is so by virtue of the unchanging pattern of consumption demand with growth in total income. The activity VUC_k gives the value $V^4 (=\gamma)$ to the utilised capacity necessary

TABLE A-1

TERMINAL CONDITIONS

Pattern of Investment	Average Use at $CN-50$		Parameters of Model		
			r_k	α_k	β_k
			$\dfrac{average\ DS}{average\ FE}$	$\dfrac{V^4}{average\ FE}$	$\dfrac{V^5}{average\ DS}$
	FE	DS			
I	7·21	26·68	3·70	13·33	12·70
II	6·85	32·45	4·74	14·03	13·37
III	7·30	34·48	4·78	13·17	12·54
IV	6·94	38·28	5·51	13·85	13·91

Variable	Production Level	x_i, y_i average FE	x_i', y_i' average DS
X_1	120·0	0·200	0·530
X_2	133·0	0·293	0·766
X_3	101·0	0·600	7·000
X_4	125·5	1·739	3·261
DI_1	120·0	0·100	0·270
DI_2	133·0	0·050	0·150

$$V^4 = \gamma = \sum_{T=4}^{\infty} \frac{5\cdot3}{(1\cdot05)^T} = 96\cdot14$$

$$V^5 = \sum_{T=5}^{\infty} \frac{5\cdot3}{(1\cdot05)^T} = 91\cdot56$$

to yield a unit of consumption under production pattern '*k*'. Using optimisation to choose the pattern or patterns in which terminal utilised capacity is valued allows the infinitely long run to have some influence upon investment in the plan period.

TABLE A-2

TERMINAL SPECIFICATIONS

Parameter	$CN=20$		$CN=50$	
r_1	3·28		3·70	
r_2	4·16		4·74	
r_3	4·10		4·78	
r_4	4·79		5·51	
x_1	0·200		0·200	
x_2	0·507		0·293	
x_3	0·600		0·600	
x_4	2·427		1·739	
y_1	0·100		0·100	
y_2	0·050		0·050	
x'_1	0·530		0·530	
x'_2	1·239		0·766	
x'_3	7·000		7·000	
x'_4	4·551		3·261	
y'_1	0·270		0·270	
y'_2	0·150		0·150	

	$p=0·05$	$p=0·05$	$p=0·10$	$p=0·20$
α_1	10·11	13·33	6·07	2·55
α_2	11·21	14·03	6·39	2·69
α_3	10·01	13·17	6·00	2·52
α_4	11·09	13·85	6·31	2·65
β_1	9·63	12·70	5·52	2·13
β_2	10·67	13·37	5·81	2·24
β_3	9·54	12·54	5·45	2·10
β_4	10·56	13·19	5·74	2·21
γ	96·14	96·14	43·80	18·40
ρ	8·91	12·93	5·62	2·16

Finally, the cost of terminal borrowing is given by the value of domestic savings and foreign exchange in the post terminal period upon which interest of '*r*' per cent must be paid. The value of foreign exchange and domestic savings used to determine the cost of borrowing represents an educated guess on the basis of the computation in Table A-1. The cost of terminal borrowing in the basic model is 12.93.

To determine the influence of terminal valuations on the optimal solution, several discount rates and a different value for the consumption level from which average costs are calculated were used. Table A-2 presents the terminal valuation parameters for these specifications.

REFERENCES

[1] M. Bruno, 'A Programming Model for Israel', in I. Adelman and E. Thorbecke *The Theory and Practice of Economic Development* (Johns Hopkins, 1966).

[2] H. B. Chenery, 'Overcapacity and the Acceleration Principle', *Econometrica*, Jan 1952.

[3] H. B. Chenery and K. Kretschmer, 'Resource Allocation for Economic Development', *Econometrica*, Oct 1956.

[4] H. B. Chenery, 'The Interdependence of Investment Decisions', in Abramovitz, *et. al.*, *The Allocation of Economic Resources* (Stanford, 1959).

[5] H. B. Chenery and A. M. Strout, 'Foreign Assistance and Economic Development', *American Economic Review*, Sep 1966.

[6] R. Eckaus and K. Parikh, *Planning for Growth* (Draft Copy) (Massachusetts Institute of Technology, 1966).

[7] M. Fleming, 'External Economies and the Doctrine of Balanced Growth', *Economic Journal*, June 1955.

[8] J. Haldi, *Economies of Scale in Economic Development*, Memorandum No. E-7, Stanford Project for Quantitative Research in Economic Development (Stanford, 1960).

[9] A. Hirschman, *The Strategy of Economic Development* (New Haven, 1958).

[10] A. H. Land and A. G. Doig, 'An Automatic Method of Solving Discrete Programming Problems', *Econometrica*, July 1960.

[11] H. Leibenstein, *Economic Backwardness and Economic Growth* (New York, 1957).

[12] W. A. Lewis, *The Theory of Economic Growth* (Homewood, Illinois, 1955).

[13] M. Lipton, 'Balanced and Unbalanced Growth in Under-developed Countries', *Economic Journal*, Sept 1962.

[14] A. Manne, *Investments for Capacity Expansion: Time Location and Time Phasing* (London, 1967).

[15] A. Manne, 'Key Sectors in the Mexican Economy', in A. Manne and H. Markovitz, *Studies in Process Analysis* (New York, 1963).

[16] R. Nurkse, 'Balanced and Unbalanced Growth', in *Equilibrium and Growth in the World Economy* (Harvard, 1962).

[17] R. Nurkse, *Problems of Capital Formation in Undeveloped Countries* (Oxford, 1953).

[18] P. Rosenstein-Rodan, 'Problems of Industrialization in Eastern and South-Eastern Europe', *Economic Journal*, Jun–Sep 1943.

[19] P. Rosenstein-Rodan, 'Notes on the Theory of the "Big Push"', in H. Ellis (ed.), *Economic Development for Latin America* (London, 1961).

[20] T. Scitovsky, "Two Concepts of External Economies", *Journal of Political Economy*, Apr 1954.

[21] T. Scitovsky, 'Growth – Balanced or Unbalanced?' in Abramovitz *et al.*., *The Allocation of Economic Resources* (Stanford, 1959).

[22] P. Streeten, 'Unbalanced Growth', *Oxford Economic Papers*, Jun 1959.

[23] R. B. Sutcliffe, 'Balanced and Unbalanced Growth', *Quarterly Journal of Economics*, Nov 1964.

18 The Effect of Fluctuations in Public Expenditure and Taxation on Economic Growth

J. Sandee and J. H. van de Pas[1]

1 A VERBAL STATEMENT OF THE PROBLEM

Most growing economies run into rising prices, balance-of-payments deficits, or both, and most governments then feel they should deflate demand – only a little, of course, and temporarily. The impression is given that a little bit of deflation will not affect the volume of G.N.P.; the first dose is supposed to act on prices and imports only. This is wishful thinking at best, and wilful deceit at worst, but it helps in introducing a most unpopular policy.[2] In the same vein, the deflationary policy is supposed to be temporary only – just a short respite from an expansion that has got out of hand – but no lasting slackening of the pace. To moderate inflationary measures, such as new expenditure programmes or tax reliefs, rather than discard them altogether, looks politically feasible, and economically sound. No permanent harm is supposed to be done, as only some hot-house growth is killed off which could not survive anyway. In actual fact, G.N.P. is, of course, reduced in volume, productive investment drops off, and the country ends up with less productive capital than it would otherwise have had, so that G.N.P. will forever be lower than it might have been.

The real loss, as compared to a smooth, continuous, optimal growth is in the investment foregone when G.N.P. was below capacity. It would have been better to grow somewhat less fast, but steadily. G.N.P. would always have remained at full capacity level, golden rules would have been observed, and the country would have followed the path prescribed by optimum growth theorems.

---

[1] It is impossible to apportion exactly the shares of responsibilities for this paper. The model is probably mostly van de Pas's work; but it is, of course, based on a model constructed by C. A. van den Beld; H. S. Tjan has perhaps contributed most of the laborious detailed work, together with J. C. Siebrand. The adaption of the model for the purposes of this paper was the idea of Sandee. The paper has been discussed between Sandee, van de Pas, Siebrand and F. A. Nulle.

[2] Deflationary policies are politically more or less acceptable in times of deflation only. Prophets of doom only get a hearing when times are bad.

This is about as far as the verbal treatment will take us. The problem is, how much of all this is true, and how important are the effects discussed.

2 THE IDEAL MODEL

To solve this problem for a given country, we need quite a large model. No such model exists as yet, but we may try to describe its main elements

How many sectors should it distinguish? In any case, a distinction should be made between domestic and international sectors, because the balance of payments looms large in our problem. Of the components of the domestic sector (such as trade, transport, electric power, construction) some are affected by specific items of final demand (construction is the main example), while others vary in the gestation lags of their investment (electricity takes much more time than trade). In the markets for international goods, fluctuations of the volume and the prices of the various commodities are highly correlated, and it may be enough to distinguish only two or three (say, foods, raw materials and manufactures). A model which turns upon the degree of utilisation of productive capacities (such as a Harrod–Domar model) should thus distinguish at least six sectors, each with its own capacity.

The time-unit need not be as short as a quarter of a year, but it is likely that significant detail is lost if the unit is to be longer than a year. Observation lags and political gestation lags together come to something less than a year already, and optimum policies should take these into account.

The minimum distance of the horizon may well be 5 years, but many growth analysts prefer 10 years or so. This hinges on the subjective discount rate – how much is one interested in events in 1976. In certain investments gestation lags of 3 years are common, and to accommodate these, 5 years are a minimum.

The Harrod–Domar model consists of a production function and a saving equation. In a sector model each sector will need its own production function, and in many sectors investment is financed in ways peculiar to that sector.

Prices cannot be overlooked; one needs at least as many prices as there are commodity-producing sectors.

Labour will largely be interchangeable between sectors, but there are exceptions: agriculture may only release surplus labour at a certain maximum rate, other sectors, such as construction, may be able to attract labour at certain maximum rates only.

In Western Europe, migration of labour is important enough to affect unemployment, which in its turn affects wages and prices.

Migration of capital is also quite important, and may strongly contribute to inflationary conditions. So far, no model has satisfactorily incorporated movements of capital.

Taxes, transfers and government expenditure on goods and services are the main instruments of government policy, and need to be explicitly recognised as such.

Some analysts would even like to incorporate liquid assets, bank credits and one or two rates of interest. It is easy enough to add some equations, to satisfy this desire.

Such a model would in theory allow us to determine the optimum strategy at any point of time, given the observations of past events available at the moment considered, the joint probability distribution of exogenous variables in the future, and of such part of the recent past as has not yet been statistically observed, given also a preference function valid at the moment concerned, which includes valuation of volumes and prices of nearby and distant flows of goods and services.

With 6 sectors and 5 years, such a model need not require more than 240 equations, a manageable size with modern computers. It is the administrative effort required rather than computational or statistical limitations that has so far prevented everybody from constructing it. We must use such models as we have, while trying to build bigger and better ones.

3 THE MODEL USED IN THIS PAPER

Among the Netherlands Central Planning Bureau models now in reasonable working condition we have selected a 3-sector, medium-term model of recent construction (end 1965). This model contains nearly all the features of the macro-, medium-term-model, published earlier.[1] It has three sectors. A much larger model of the same type, with many more sectors, was also available, but as less experience had been obtained as yet in its operation, this was not considered further. It should also be remembered that the administrative, and even physical problems of handling such a large model are really formidable. A serious drawback of the model chosen is that it employs only one undivided five-year

---

[1] C. A. van den Beld, J. H. van de Pas, H. S. Tjan: 'A Medium Term Macro Model for the Netherlands', pp. 23–40 in *Modelli econometrici per la programmazione*, edited by the Scuola di Statistica dell' Università, Firenze (1965).

period. To discuss fluctuations with a medium-term model is obviously impossible; below we shall explain what expedients were used to make the most of it.

The Central Planning Bureau has only one annual model; this is a strict macro-model, and it has no production function, as it is used for short-run problems only. This practically excludes the possibility of using it on growth problems.

The model selected for this paper consists of 66 equations listed in Appendix A. The symbols used are explained in Appendix B. Going through the equations, one will recognise the model as a cross between a classical Harrod–Domar and a Leontief model, which has some price effects attached to it. Appendix C discusses some features of the model that are of no direct interest to the subject of this paper (although, of course, all elements of the model contribute to its outcome).

There are, however, three cases in which effects that are cumulative over time are considered, and within the context of this paper these deserve a special discussion.

The first of these is the production function case, of which equation (39) is an example. It reads

$$i_2^b = 1 \cdot 82 \ v_2 - 19 \cdot 65 \ a_2 - 26 \cdot 23$$

where i_2^b = investment in manufacturing in 1970, in billions of guilders at 1965 prices

v_2 = value added in manufacturing in 1970, also in billions of guilders at 1965 prices

a_2 = employment in manufacturing in 1970, in millions of man-years.

In the conventional production function, it is not current investment but the capital stock that, together with employment, determines output. Here, the capital stock is represented by current investment in the following way.

To obtain the capital stock at the beginning of 1970, which is supposed to affect output in 1970 as a whole, one starts at the beginning of 1965, and adds investment in each of the five years 1965 through 1969. This investment is supposed to increase linearly between 1965, when it is $_{65}i_2^b$, and 1970, when it reaches i_2^b. The annual increment in investment may be Δ, so that

$$i_2^b - {}_{65}i_2^b = 5\Delta.$$

Total investment in the five-year period 1965–9 is then equal to

$$5 \, _{65}i_2^b + 10\varDelta = 3 \, _{65}i_2^b + 2 \, i_2^b.$$

Of these terms, the first is consolidated with the constant. The equation now reads, in its customary production function form,

$$v_2 = 0.274 \, (2 \, i_2^b) + 10.80 \, a_2 + 14.40$$

which is equivalent to (39).

The coefficient 0·274 is the gross yield of gross investment in manufacturing; putting it otherwise, the gross incremental capital-output ratio corrected for the contribution of labour, or ICOR (L), equals $\dfrac{1}{0.274} = 3.65$.

The coefficient 10·80 is the marginal product of labour, put at 10,800 guilders per man-year in 1970.

Equation (32) is the second case of cumulative effects being taken into account. It reads

$$P_{imm} = -0.73 \, w + 0.01 \, P_B + 0.11$$

where P_{imm} = immigration in 1970 in millions
$\quad w$ = unemployment in 1970 in millions
$\quad P_B$ = labour force in 1970 in millions.

In spite of this apparently immediate effect of labour market conditions on immigration, the idea behind this equation is that immigration in 1970 is affected by unemployment in relation to the labour force in each of the 5 years 1966–70, with equal weights, i.e.

$$P_{imm} = -0.243 \sum_{1966}^{1970} {}_t w + 0.003 \sum_{1966}^{1970} {}_t P_B + \text{constant}.$$

As in the former case, the assumption is made that $_t w$ and $_t P_B$ increase linearly over time, and we shall again call the increment over time $\varDelta$, so that

$$_{70}w - {}_{65}w = 5\varDelta$$

and

$$\sum_{1966}^{1970} {}_t w = 5 \, _{65}w + 15\varDelta = 2 \, _{65}w + 3 \, _{70}w.$$

Upon substitution, (32) is obtained.

The third instance of cumulative effects is the wage equation which reads

$$p_a = 10.48 \, h - 22.62 \, w + 0.27 \, P_B. \tag{51}$$

Here, wages in 1970 are supposed to vary with the average of the unemployment levels in each of the 6 years 1965–70. This is the usual wage-determination assumption: the *rise* in wages depends on the *level* of unemployment.

4 ENDS AND MEANS IN STEADY GROWTH

The model discussed is primarily constructed to analyse the effect of gradual changes, over the 1965–70 period, *of* exogenous variables (data *and* instruments) *on* such endogenous variables as are interesting to the policy-maker (target variables, or simply 'ends').

The following table lists the effects of certain means on certain ends. It is, of course, an abstract of the 'reduced form' of the model.

TABLE ONE
STEADY GROWTH EFFECTS

Ends	*Means*					
	Government purchases manufactures $-c_2$	Government purchases services $-c_3^g$	Wage tax T_L	Profit tax T_Z	In-direct taxes T_K	Autonomous investment $-I$
Volume of private consumption c	$+0.115$	$+0.225$	-0.643	-0.499	-0.338	-0.446
Price of private consumption p_c	-0.012	-0.021	-0.012	-0.006	$+0.007$	-0.004
Unemployment w	$+0.003$	$+0.005$	$+0.004$	$+0.005$	—	$+0.006$
Volume of productive investment i	-0.254	-0.289	-0.183	-0.748	-0.409	-0.884
Volume of G.N.P. v	-0.219	-0.190	-0.144	-0.443	-0.148	-0.513
Foreign surplus in current prices $B-M$	$+0.460$	$+0.397$	$+0.497$	$+0.708$	$+0.516$	$+0.747$

Most variables in this table are expressed in billions of guilders (prices of 1965 or 1970, as the case may be), but p_c is an index-number (1965 = 100), w is in millions of man-years. Signs of 'means' have been chosen such that all 'means' increase the foreign surplus (all elements in the $B-M$ row are positive). This means that *reductions* of c_2^g, c_3^g, or I are considered, and *increases* of either of the three taxes. To put it otherwise, all 'means' are shown as used in a deflationary direction.

One example may confirm the notions the reader will have formed by now: in the w row the I element is $+\cdot006$. This means that an exogenous reduction of autonomous investment in 1970 by one billion guilders will increase unemployment in 1970 by 6,000 man-years.

As usual, most 'means' work in highly similar directions: there is something to say for using only one measure of 'inflation or deflation', which could be either prices, or the volume of G.N.P., or investment, or the foreign surplus. It will be noted that private consumption strikes a difference in this respect: a reduction of government expenditure on goods or services will *increase* private consumption, simply because more goods and services will be left over for the public to consume. From the welfare point of view, there is no gain, of course, as one billion of government consumption is foregone at the same time.

It should be stressed once more that this table is based throughout on the assumption of steady growth of everything. It is the effect of a gradual exogenous reduction of investment that is shown, reaching one billion by 1970, and the effect on unemployment is such that by 1970, unemployment has gradually become 6,000 higher than it would have been otherwise.

This means, of course, that this table gives only a small part of the information we need.

5   THE TRANSITION TO SHORT-TERM FLUCTUATIONS

If profit taxes are gradually raised so as to reach a 1970 level one billion higher than otherwise, investment will fall gradually so as to be 0·748 billion below its earlier value by 1970. Everything changes gradually, and this means that the total additional tax pressure in the whole 5-year period 1966–70 must have been $0\cdot2+0\cdot4+0\cdot6+0\cdot8+1\cdot0=3\cdot0$ billion. Total investment foregone in all 5 years was $3\times0\cdot748=2\cdot244$ billion.

In this conclusion, the length of the period had no effect on the relationship between means and ends: each billion of tax still causes 0·748 billion of investment reduction.

And this is how we come to a conclusion which is obviously inaccurate: that any billion of profits tax, however distributed over time, will lead to a shortfall of 0·748 billion of investment. The steady-growth table will be used for short-run effects as well.

If we stopped at this point, very little would remain of the verbal conclusions drawn at the beginning of this paper. It would not matter whether deflation would be nicely spread out over a purposefully designed growth-path, or whether it would be introduced *ad hoc*. It will be remembered that the verbal discussion made much of the difference between a growth path where capacity would be fully occupied all the time (moving all along the ceiling) and uneven growth where capacities would sometimes be partly occupied only (somewhere between the ceiling and the floor, if there is a floor).

Some of this idea can be incorporated into the present model. The investment foregone through a one-time increase in profit taxes has already been calculated; it only remains to introduce it into the production function as a reduction in the capital stock available in 1970.

This looks like double-counting, and yet it is not. For if we only used the steady-growth reduced form of the model for short-term fluctuations we would implicitly assume that after the profit tax has been returned to its old level, everything returns to its former level, and this is manifestly untrue. We have to consider separately the impact of investment foregone, through a short-run deflationary impulse, on the capital stock and productive capacity.

This is easily done, as the above discussion of the production functions has explained already how they can be interpreted so as to incorporate the capital stock rather than current investment. The investment shortfall is introduced as a reduction in the capital stock, similar to a reduction caused by fire or inundation, and the effect is again calculated by means of the model.

For immigration, the second cumulatively affected variable in the model, the results are about the same. Here, the idea was that five years of unemployment rates together would determine immigration. If the short-term disturbance discussed would have all run out within one year, only one annual rate would have been affected; if it had taken longer, more rates would have been changed, but the cumulative effect would be the same. The best way to treat immigration is similar to that of investment: first determine the primary effect by means of the steady-growth table, and then introduce it as a disturbance in the immigration equation.

Finally, wage increases cumulate the effects of unemployment levels throughout the 1965–70 period, and thus also react to a temporary change in unemployment. Investment, immigration and wage increases in this way produce secondary, lasting effects of short-term deflationary measures. These have been computed for each of the 'means' defined before, and added up. The following table shows the results.

A short-term increase in profit taxes T_z which would increase tax pressure by 1 billion for as long as it lasted (one year, for instance) would

O

thus afterwards cause consumption to be 0·236 billion lower each year, and forever.

Lasting effects

	$-c_2^g$	$-c_3^g$	T_L	T_Z	T_K	$-I$
c	−0·066	−0·083	−0·056	−0·236	−0·133	−0·280
p_c	−0·001	−0·000	+0·000	+0·002	+0·001	+0·002
w	−0·002	−0·002	−0·001	−0·000	−0·000	−0·000
i	+0·027	+0·030	+0·019	+0·077	+0·042	+0·091
v	+0·009	−0·018	−0·022	−0·119	−0·077	−0·143
B−M	+0·026	+0·025	+0·014	+0·054	+0·027	+0·063

6 COMPARING SHORT-TERM AND LONG-TERM POLICIES

We are now able to compare the effects of short-term and long-term policies. The former will have immediate effects for as long as they last, and lasting effects ever after. The long-term policies will have effects spread out over the 5-year period, and, of course, lasting effects after that as well. To compare immediate and lasting effects we need a horizon, or a discount rate.

These are entirely subjective matters, and we can do no better than guess what policy makers would feel about effects happening 3 or 5 or 7 years hence. One more or less realistic weighting would be to compare

—the immediate effects of the short-term policies, *plus* three years of their lasting effects, and
—the total effect of the gradual policies over a whole 5-year period, i.e. three times the effect in 1970.

To obtain the total effect of short-term policies we must then add the 'steady growth' table (which is used to obtain the immediate effects!) and three times the 'lasting effects' table. The result is shown below.

One more operation is now required to obtain true comparability,

Total effects of short-run policies

	$-c_2^g$	$-c_3^g$	T_L	T_Z	T_K	$-I$
c	−0·083	−0·024	−0·710	−1·207	−0·735	−1·284
p_c	−0·014	−0·021	−0·011	−0·001	+0·011	+0·003
w	−0·002	+0·002	+0·002	+0·004	+0·002	+0·005
i	−0·173	−0·198	−0·126	−0·518	−0·285	−0·612
v	−0·193	−0·245	−0·210	−0·800	−0·379	−0·942
B−M	+0·539	+0·473	+0·540	+0·869	+0·598	+0·936

namely 'standardisation' of either means or ends. As they now stand, the columns in the tables represent the effects of arbitrarily chosen quantities of 'means'. There is no easy way to make the 'means' comparable, but 'ends' can individually be compared from column to column. We shall 'standardise' on the foreign surplus $B-M$. This is the most important 'end' of all deflationary policies in practice, while prices, the other possible 'end', are very little affected by almost all policies, so that they are less suitable as standards.

The results of standardisation are shown below.

Steady growth effects of

	$c_2^g=$ $-2\cdot18$	$c_3^g=$ $-2\cdot52$	$T_L=$ $+2\cdot01$	$T_z=$ $+1\cdot41$	$T_K=$ $+1\cdot94$	$-I=$ $-1\cdot34$
c	$+0\cdot25$	$+0\cdot57$	$-1\cdot29$	$-0\cdot71$	$-0\cdot66$	$-0\cdot60$
p_c	$-0\cdot03$	$-0\cdot05$	$-0\cdot03$	$-0\cdot01$	$+0\cdot01$	$-0\cdot01$
w	$+0\cdot01$	$+0\cdot02$	$+0\cdot01$	$+0\cdot01$	$+0\cdot00$	$+0\cdot00$
i	$-0\cdot55$	$-0\cdot73$	$-0\cdot37$	$-1\cdot06$	$-0\cdot79$	$-1\cdot18$
v	$-0\cdot48$	$-0\cdot48$	$-0\cdot29$	$-0\cdot63$	$-0\cdot29$	$-0\cdot69$
$B-M$	$+1\cdot00$	$+1\cdot00$	$+1\cdot00$	$+1\cdot00$	$+1\cdot00$	$+1\cdot00$

Total effects of short-run measures

	$c_2^g=$ $-1\cdot86$	$c_3^g=$ $-2\cdot11$	$T_L=$ $+1\cdot85$	$T_z=$ $+1\cdot15$	$T_K=$ $+1\cdot67$	$-I=$ $-1\cdot07$
c	$-0\cdot15$	$-0\cdot05$	$-1\cdot32$	$-1\cdot39$	$-1\cdot23$	$-1\cdot37$
p_c	$-0\cdot03$	$-0\cdot05$	$-0\cdot02$	$-0\cdot00$	$+0\cdot02$	$+0\cdot00$
w	$-0\cdot00$	$+0\cdot01$	$+0\cdot00$	$+0\cdot01$	$+0\cdot00$	$+0\cdot01$
i	$-0\cdot32$	$-0\cdot42$	$-0\cdot23$	$-0\cdot60$	$-0\cdot48$	$-0\cdot65$
v	$-0\cdot36$	$-0\cdot52$	$-0\cdot39$	$-0\cdot92$	$-0\cdot63$	$-1\cdot01$
$B-M$	$+1\cdot00$	$+1\cdot00$	$+1\cdot00$	$+1\cdot00$	$+1\cdot00$	$+1\cdot00$

The main criterion for comparison will be private consumption c with some attention being given to prices p_c as well. Unemployment w is so little affected that it offers little opportunity for comparison. Investment i and G.N.P. v are ends rather than means. Private consumption is thus the most important criterion of efficiency.

However, in the first two columns government consumption c^g is also affected. Assuming that the growth pattern is about optimal with respect to the distribution between public and private consumption, both types of consumption effects can be simply added up.

This immediately makes a reduction of government expenditure on goods and services the least attractive way to relieve balance-of-payments troubles, and it is a lucky circumstance that in practice little is ever done in this line for balance-of-payments reasons. The little that is done, however, helps a great deal to reduce price increases, and if prices are the main reason for deflation, these are the most effective instruments.

Increasing taxes, or reducing government-financed productive investment, are less harmful ways of restoring balance-of-payments equilibrium.[1] Wage taxes T_L have rather unfavourable results as compared to the other measures in this range, at least as far as steady growth effects are concerned, and indirect taxes T_K also require a high amount of tax increase for each unit of foreign exchange saved. Profits taxes T_Z and government-financed investment I would thus appear to be the best steady growth regulators. Between these two, there is little to choose.

If short-run adjustments become necessary, greater damage is done to consumption. Taxes, and government finance of productive investment are still better regulators than current government expenditure, however.

7 EPILOGUE

The calculations have amply confirmed the verbal conclusion that good planning is better than waiting with deflationary policies till the very last moment. There is great advantage in growing along the ceiling, even if in the beginning the ceiling is somewhat lower than it might be.

It is rather late now to mention uncertainty. Good planning is all very well, but nature and the rest of the world are so unstable that even with quick-acting compensatory domestic policies quickly applied, growing along the ceiling may be impossible. Intuitively one may perhaps say that the advantages of planned steady growth over last-minute deflationary corrections become smaller if the latter can be combined with adjustments to fluctuations imported from abroad, or caused by nature. It would, however, require a very well-informed government, with strong powers, to make use of this opportunity, and it would require a model at least as refined as the 'ideal' model described above to find out what the optimum planned growth would be.

---

[1] It may be thought odd that it is better to reduce productive investment than government current expenditure. The reason is that government expenditure is an end in itself.

APPENDIX A

No. Description	Equation
Final demand	
1. Exports of industrial sector	$b_2 = 25{\cdot}92b_{c2} - 78{\cdot}43p_b + 77{\cdot}52p_b' - 4{\cdot}74$
2. Exports of services sector	$b_3 = 0{\cdot}09(b_1 + b_2 + m_{good}) + 2{\cdot}58$
3. Sales of industrial sector for capital formation in enterprises	$i_2^h = 0{\cdot}75(i - i_m^h)$
4. Sales of services sector for capital formation in enterprises	$i_3^h = 0{\cdot}25(i - i_m^{hg})$
5. Sales of industrial sector for capital formation by government	$i_2^{hg} = x_{ig} - i_m^{hg}$
6. Material government consumption of industrial products	$c_2 = 0{\cdot}74(x_g - f_g - g - c_m^g)$
7. Material government consumption of services	$c_3 = 0{\cdot}26(x_g - f_g - g - c_m^g)$
8. Private consumption of industrial products	$c_2 = 0{\cdot}31c - 13{\cdot}77p_{c2} + 13{\cdot}40p_c + 4{\cdot}56 + 0{\cdot}42\lambda$
9. Private consumption of services	$c_3 = 0{\cdot}31c - 13{\cdot}81p_{c3} + 14{\cdot}62p_c + 4{\cdot}22 + 0{\cdot}40\lambda$
10. Value of private consumption	$C = 0{\cdot}90L_B + 0{\cdot}20Z_B + 8{\cdot}69$
11. Volume of private consumption	$c = 0{\cdot}88C - 41{\cdot}12p_c + 46{\cdot}88$
12. Distribution of the volume of consumption	$c = c_1 + c_2 + c_3 + c_m$
Gross Output	
13. Gross output of agriculture	$x_1 = 0{\cdot}10x_1 + 0{\cdot}06x_2 + \qquad\qquad\qquad b_1 + \qquad\qquad\quad c_1 + n_1$
14. Gross output of industry	$x_2 = 0{\cdot}30x_1 + 0{\cdot}28x_2 + 0{\cdot}11x_3 + b_2 + i_{2h}^h + c_2 + n_2 + i_2^{hg} + c_2^g + x_{wo}$
15. Gross output of services sector	$x_3 = 0{\cdot}04x_1 + 0{\cdot}06x_2 + 0{\cdot}13x_3 + b_3 + i_3 + c_3 + c_3^g$

Appendix A (*continued*)

No. Description	Equation
Imports	
16. Imports for capital formation in enterprises	$i_m^h = 0.35i - 4.13p_{mi} + 4.09p_i - 0.11$
17. Imports for private consumption	$c_m = 0.21c + 2.27p_c - 2.47p_{mc} + c_m^{EEG} + c_m^{toerisme} - 5.46 + 0.18\lambda$
18. Imports of agricultural sector	$m_1 = 0.04x_1 - 0.05$
19. Imports of industrial sector	$m_2 = 0.27x_2 - 4.52$
20. Imports of services sector	$m_3 = 0.10(x_3 - x_3') - 0.11$
21. Total imports of goods and services	$m = m_1 + m_2 + m_3 + i_m^h + c_m + i_m^{hg} + c^g + b_m + n_m$
22. Total imports of goods	$m_{goed} = m - m_{die}$
23. Total imports of services	$m_{die} = 0.50b_3 + c_m^{toerisme} - 0.31$
Value added	
24. Value added in agriculture	$v_1 = 0.56x_1 - m_1$
25. Value added in industry	$v_2 = 0.60x_2 - m_2$
26. Value added in services sector	$v_3 = 0.76x_3 - m_3$
27. Total value added in enterprises	$v = v_1 + v_2 + v_3$
Labour	
28. Employment in industry	$a_2 = 0.05v_2 - 0.07p_a + 0.82p_i$
29. Employment in services sector	$a_3 = 0.07v_3 - 0.03p_a + 0.35p_i$
30. Employment in enterprises	$a = a_1 + a_2 + a_3$
31. Dependents employed in enterprises	$a_a = a - a_z$
32. Immigration of employable persons	$P_{imm} = -0.73w + 0.01P_B + 0.11$
33. Total supply of labour	$P_S = P_{sau} - 1.00(w - w_{65}) + P_{imm} - P_{em}$
34. Total demand for labour	$P_D = a + a_g$
35. Unemployment	$w = P_S - P_D$

No. Description	Equation

Equation (column header)

| 36. Dependent employable population | $P_B = a_a + w + a_g$ |
| 37. Labour productivity | $h = 0.02v - 0.28a + 1.19$ |

Capital Formation

38. Gross capital formation in agriculture	$i_1^b = 1.77v_1 - 19.10a_1 - 2.93$
39. Gross capital formation in industry	$i_2^b = 1.82v_2 - 19.65a_2 - 26.23$
40. Gross capital formation in services sector	$i_3^b = 4.01(v_3 - v_3') - 43.15a_3 - 16.72$
41. Gross capital formation in enterprises	$i = i_1^b + i_2^b + i_3^b$

Prices

42. Export price (goods and services)	$p_b = 0.03p_a - 0.34h + 0.41p_{mrm} - 0.41p_{mrm}' + 0.99p_b' + 0.43K - 0.36H' + 0.35d$
43. Price of capital formation in enterprises	$p_i = 0.04p_a - 0.45h + 0.29p_{mrm} + 0.34p_{mi} + 0.44 + 0.41d$
44. Price of agricultural products for private consumption	$p_{c1} = 0.13p_a - 0.38h + 0.11p_{mrm} - 0.23v_1 + 4.02a_1 - 0.19 + 1.24d$
45. Price of industrial products for private consumption	$p_{c2} = 0.09p_a - 0.28h + 0.34p_{mrm} - 0.02v_2 + 0.38a_2 + 0.01 + 1.24d$
46. Price of services for private consumption	$p_{c3} = 0.09p_a - 0.31h + 0.37p_{mrm} - 0.03v_3 + 0.43a_3 + 0.03 + 1.24d$
47. Price of private consumption	$p_c = 0.02p_{c1} + 0.42p_{c2} + 0.37p_{c3} + 0.19p_{mc}$
48. Price of dwellings constructed	$p_{wo} = 0.12p_a - 1.30h + 0.18p_{mrm} + 1.02 + 1.64d$
49. Price of capital formation by government	$p_{ig} = 0.12p_a - 1.23h + 0.34p_{mrm} + 0.86 + 1.64d$
50. Price of government consumption	$p_g = 0.06p_a - 0.64h + 0.17p_{mrm} + 0.94 + 1.64d$
51. Wage level in enterprises	$p_a = 10.48h - 22.62w + 0.27P_B$

Taxes

52. Direct taxes on wage income	$T_L = 0.16(L + L_g + L_F) - 1.96$
53. Direct taxes on non-wage income	$T_Z = 0.40(Z + Z_F) - 1.96$
54. Indirect taxes	$T_K = 0.11(C + I + N + X_g + X_{wo} + X_{ig})$

Appendix A (*continued*)

No.	Description	Equation
	Incomes and remaining Equations	
55.	Total wages paid by enterprises	$L = 12\cdot43a_a + 3\cdot53p_a - 43\cdot85$
56.	Total wages paid by government	$L_g = 0\cdot83p_a + 18\cdot89a_g - 10\cdot30$
57.	Disposable wage income	$L_B = 0\cdot99(L + L_g + L_F) - T_L$
58.	Value of gross capital formation in enterprises	$I = 12\cdot81p_i + 1\cdot10i - 14\cdot09$
59.	Value of dwellings constructed	$X_{wo} = 4\cdot28p_{wo} + 1\cdot20x_{wo} - 5\cdot14$
60.	Value of capital formation by government	$X_{ig} = 1\cdot19x_{ig} + 5\cdot19p_{ig} - 6\cdot17$
61.	Value of government consumption	$X_g = 1\cdot10x_g + 4\cdot01p_g - 4\cdot42$
62.	Value of exports	$B = 42\cdot93p_b + 1\cdot02(b_1 + b_2 + b_3 + b_m) - 43\cdot81$
63.	Value of imports	$M = 0\cdot99(m_1 + m_2 + m_3 + i_m^{hg} + c_m^g + b_m + n_m) + 1\cdot09i_m^h + 1\cdot06c_m + 4\cdot37p_{mi} + 8\cdot28p_{mc} + 30\cdot62p_{mrm} - 43\cdot71$
64.	Non-wage income	$Z = I + C + N + B + X_{wo} + X_g + X_{ig} - M - F - T_K - F_g - G - L$
65.	Disposable non-wage income	$Z_B = 0\cdot86(Z + Z_F) - T_Z$
66.	Investment finance	$I = 0\cdot80(Z_B + F) - 2\cdot51$

APPENDIX B

List of symbols used

All symbols concerning employable population refer to millions of man-years. Among the other, the lower-case characters refer to volumes or prices, the capital ones to values.

The wage level (p_a) is measured in '000 of guilders per year; all other prices are indices (1965 $=1\cdot00$). The values are measured in billions of guilders.

The subscript 65 refers to the base year 1965.

In the model the sector variables bear the subscripts 1, 2, 3, for agriculture, industry and services respectively. In this list these subscripts are represented by j.

a	number of persons employed in enterprises
a_j	number of persons employed in sector j
a_a	number of dependents employed in enterprises
a_g	number of government employees
a_z	number of self-employed
B	total exports of goods and services
b_j	exports of sector j
b_{c2}	volume of world imports (index, 1965 $=1\cdot00$)
b_m	re-exports
C, c	private consumption
c_j	private consumption of sector j products
c_j	material government consumption of sector j products
c_m	imports for private consumption
c_m^{EEG}	additional imports of consumption goods from Common Market countries on account of tariff reductions
$c_m^{toerisme}$	consumption by Dutch citizens abroad
c_m^g	imports for government consumption
d	dummy variable
F	depreciation allowances of enterprises
F_g, f_g	depreciation allowances of government
G, g	imputed interest of government buildings
h	labour productivity
H'	labour costs in competing countries (index, 1965 $=1\cdot00$)
K	absolute level of labour costs in the Netherlands, relative to the base year level in competing countries
I, i	gross capital formation in enterprises
i_j^b	gross capital formation in sector j
i_j^h	sales of sector j for capital formation in enterprises
i_j^{hg}	sales of sector j for capital formation by government
i_m^h	imports for capital formation in enterprises
i_m^{hg}	imports for capital formation by government
L	total wages paid by enterprises
L_B	disposable wage income

O 2

L_F	wage income from abroad
L_g	total wages paid by government
M, m	total imports of goods and services
m_j	total imports of goods and services by sector j
m_{die}	total imports of services
m_{goed}	total imports of goods
N, n	total increase in stocks
n_j	sales of sector j for increase in stocks
n_m	imports for increase in stocks
P_B	dependent employable population
P_D	total demand for labour
P_{em}	emigration of employable persons
P_{imm}	immigration of employable persons
P_S	total supply of labour
$P_{S_{au}}$	autonomous supply of labour
p_a	wage level in enterprises
p^b	price of exports (goods and services)
p'_b	price of exports (goods and services) of competing countries
p_c	price of goods and services for private consumption
p_{cj}	price of sector j products for consumption
p_g	price of government consumption
p_i	price of capital formation in enterprises
p_{ig}	price of capital formation by government
p_{mc}	price of imported consumption goods
p_{mi}	price of imported capital goods
p_{mrm}	price of imported raw materials
p'_{mrm}	price of raw materials imported by competing countries
p_n	price of stocks
p_{wo}	price of dwellings construction
T_K	indirect taxes
T_L	direct taxes on wage income
T_Z	direct taxes on non-wage income
v	total value added in enterprises
v_j	total value added in sector j
v'_3	total value added in dwellings
w	unemployment
x_j	gross output of sector j
x'_3	gross output of dwellings
X_g, x_g	total government consumption
X_{ig}, x_{ig}	government capital formation
X_{wo}, x_{wo}	construction of dwellings
Z	non-wage income
Z_B	disposable non-wage income
Z_F	non-wage income from abroad
λ	variable for balancing sales of consumption goods by sectors and the level of total consumption

Endogenous are d, λ, and all the variables in the left-hand sides of the equations.

APPENDIX C

Special features of the model

In equations 8, 9 and 17 the variable λ appears. This distributes two kinds of discrepancies between the three endogenous kinds of consumer expenditure. One discrepancy arises because c_1, consumption of agricultural products, is exogenous, and thus does not automatically fit endogenous consumption c. The other discrepancy is simply the aggregation error that always appears when sector relationships are aggregated (unless their coefficients have been estimated so as to prevent this altogether).

The d variable appearing in equations 42, 43, 44, 45, 46, 48, 49 and 50 is formally of the same type, but it may have a more distinct economic interpretation. In the eight equations, prices of eight flows of goods and services are related to costs, and profit margins are related to the d variable which adjusts itself so that prices and volumes meet. In a way, d measures the amount of inflation in the economy, and distributes its effects over the eight prices distinguished. This feature already occurred in the macro model;[1] in fact, any model using several prices could employ such a device.

The treatment of immigration in equation 32 is discussed in the main text. Equation 33 states that any change in unemployment w affects labour supply to the same amount but negatively or, putting it otherwise, every unemployed person prevents another person from joining the labour force. This 'doubling' effect, which occurs in many other models, is based on observation of actual movements of the labour force.

[1] See footnote on page 390.

19 Performance and Respective Spheres of Public and Private Enterprise

R. Jochimsen

1 SETTING OF THE PROBLEM

Competition between public and private enterprise is a perennial topic for controversy. Though many issues are covered in the debate I am restricting myself to two: the determination of the border-line to the scope of public enterprise and the rules which are to govern the behaviour of public enterprise.

The normative theory of general socio-economic optimum does not offer an answer to the question of the choice between public and private enterprise. In regard to the rules of competition the theory tells to bar every artificial distortion of the competitive conditions. Unfortunately, the general theory of socio-economic optimum is subject to several fundamental objections which obstruct its direct application in practical policy:

(1) the existence of and the supply of public goods are not adequately considered;

(2) distributional problems are either ignored, or optimum distribution of wealth is somehow presupposed; but 'there is no meaning to total output independent of distribution';[1] besides the problem of measuring efficiency there are the productivity aspects of distribution of wealth bearing on the efficiency of the market mechanism (degree of economic integration of the market system, degree to which reproduction of factors is assured by market income);

(3) no standards or mechanisms are provided for the 'total conditions' of an optimum: Who is to decide and to enforce them, and how?

(4) it is not possible, for technological and other reasons, to realise all potential marginal conditions; if certain marginal conditions cannot be put into effect, it cannot be established, according to the theory

[1] K. J. Arrow, *Social Choice and Individual Values* (Cowles Commission Monograph no. 12, New York, 1951) p. 40.

of the second best,[1] that the marginal cost pricing rule should generally be observed;[2]

(5) even if all marginal conditions would be realised, the marginal cost pricing principle cannot be put to use because 'the conditions which have to be met before it is correct . . . are so restrictive that they are unlikely to be satisfied in practice'.[3]

Thus splitting the conditions of socio-economic optimum into allocative problems (which are 'non-controversial') and distributive and structural problems – which are 'controversial' and political – does not provide sufficient ground for deciding on rules of competition. On the contrary, each objection can be used to justify public enterprise while the corresponding behavioural characteristics for public enterprise cannot be fixed.

The economic order provides for the basic approach with which society attempts to realise its conception of socio-economic optimum. The economic order includes the institutions and principles which determine the welfare function of society (subordination), the mechanisms of co-ordinating households and firms (market mechanism, central planning, or collective bargaining) as well as the agents which dispose of the factors of production (e.g. legal framework of property).

The classical market system is based on a very limited list of goals for direct public action, the market mechanism of perfect competition and the extensive use of private enterprise. In most western market economies it is the general policy of most governments that it 'has ordinarily no right to compete in a private enterprise economy',[4] because 'people understand their own business and their own interests better and care for them more, than the government does, or can be expected to do'.[5]

Government 'will not start or carry on any commercial activity to

[1] For an attempt to overcome some of the difficulties of the general theorem of the second-best cf. H. Timm, 'Bemerkungen zu einem fundamentalen Problem der Theorie des Zweitbesten', in E. v. Beckerath, H. Giersch, H. Lampert (eds.), *Probleme der normativen Ökonomik und der wirtschaftspolitischen Beratung*, Schriften des Vereins für Socialpolitik, xxix (Berlin, 1963) 285 ff.

[2] This also provides an argument against the policy of 'as-if'-competition, as proposed – among others – by L. Miksch, *Wettbewerb als Aufgabe*, 2nd ed. (Godesberg, 1947).

[3] J. de V. Graaff, *Theoretical Welfare Economics* (Cambridge, 1957) p. 154. For a list of these assumptions, cf. pp. 142 ff. See also T. Thiemeyer, *Grenzkostenpreise bei öffentlichen Unternehmen* (Köln/Opladen, 1964) pp. 73 ff. Similar objections are to be advanced against the average cost and the marginal cost plus péage pricing rules.

[4] Memorandum of the Director of the Bureau of the Budget, 27 October 1956, quoted in Committee on Government Operations, U.S. Senate, *Government Competition with Private Enterprise* (Washington, D.C., 1963) p. 28.

[5] J. S. Mill, *Principles of Political Economy* ed. W. J. Ashley (reprint New York, 1965) p. 947.

provide a service or product for its own use if such product or service can be procured from private enterprise through ordinary business channels'.[1] Furthermore, 'Government shall not engage in commercial or industrial activities unless it is found to be necessary or advisable to do so in the public interest after considering all pertinent factors'.[2] In competing with private enterprise public enterprise should be granted no special advantages. The burden of proof for any interpretation of these principles lies with government which wants to limit the avenues open to private enterprise.

It is generally admitted today that these formulae are either ideologically determined or empty boxes. They provide no operational yardsticks for deciding on the border-line or the rules at stake.

The classical market mechanism which automatically works towards realising the marginal conditions is frequently not present, or inefficient. Under these conditions private enterprise, seeking to maximise profits, is either unable, unwilling, or not acceptable to government's interpretation of the public interest. Static general equilibrium analysis of the market system acknowledges several cases of market failure: [3]

(1) Failure of existence of market solutions (e.g. public goods).
(2) Failure of incentives and signals (e.g. deficits occur if price is set equal to marginal cost).
(3) Failure of market form (e.g. monopoly and monopsony).
(4) Failure of appropriation of costs and returns (e.g. divergencies between private and social costs or returns).

In dynamic analysis, the possible failures to guarantee full utilisation of factors, to invest optimally with respect to economic growth and to contribute to technological progress must be added. The problem is how to overcome these apparent inefficiencies of the market mechanism, often used to justify public enterprise. Their mere existence sets no rules as to how public enterprise should compete with private enterprise. Furthermore, the nature of the competitive process has changed, and substitute mechanisms for perfect competition have not yet fully developed.

Individual profit maximisation is not controlled effectively by competitors. The vision of the stationary state, with full adjustment of economic plans leading to zero net profits is not borne out by present realities, because the objective as well as the subjective conditions of competition

---

[1] Memorandum of the Director of the Bureau of the Budget, op. cit. p. 24.
[2] Ibid. p. 7.
[3] Cf. F. M. Bator, 'The Anatomy of Market Failure,' *Quarterly Journal of Economics*, LXXII (1958) 353 ff.

have changed very greatly. We have experienced an 'organisational revolution' (Boulding). It has been accompanied by the metamorphosis of competition away from the atomistic struggle between essentially powerless partners [1] into overt or tacit collusion, into parallel behaviour, or into spontaneous 'inter-firm organisation' (Phillips). Small enterprises in atomistic competition, with low price elasticities of supply, confronted with high price elasticities of demand, make up but one segment of the modern market economy. Present-day patterns of co-operative behaviour make it possible, particularly if governments follow full employment policies and trade partners inflate even faster, to influence prices even in markets with near-perfect competition.[2]

This argument holds *a fortiori* for oligopolistic and monopolistic markets proper. Here enterprises command a significant range of discretion in pricing power.

New mechanisms to reinforce the competitive process, though changing its pattern, have arisen through countervailing power among groups (Galbraith), the creative destruction of new industrial (Schumpeter), the predominance of non-price competition as well as the loosening rigidities in the structure of consumer's expenditures as a consequence of rising average incomes.[3] These and other mechanisms and trends provide long-run restraints on reaping large and certain profits. But they are not necessarily effective enough as to the extent and timing desired for optimum utilisation of resources.[4]

For these reasons the decision to adopt a market system, a clearly political one today as always, does not provide the clear-cut, mechanistic solution of how competition is to be organised, what should be publicly or privately provided and how the rules of competition are to be solved. If, on the other hand, the market mechanism, as it operates *de facto*, is considered an absolute value (e.g. it best serves individual freedom), and if the choice of an optimum set of goods for society is considered inadmissable (e.g.) because of interpersonal non-comparability of utilities), public enterprise cannot be justified, as in fact no general economic policy with the sole

---

[1] Cf. A. E. Ott, *Marktform und Verhaltensweise* (Stuttgart, 1959) p. 44 passim.

[2] Cf. the lengthy discussion of the possibilities to shift the incidence of direct taxes to final demand.

[3] Cf. R. Jochimsen, 'Marktform und wirtschaftliche Entwicklung', *Zeitschrift für die gesamte Staatswissenschaft*, CXXII (1966) 35 ff. Remember, however, that this trend is partly offset by other secular trends, such as industrialisation, urbanisation, commercialisation and the 'revolution of rising expectations' (ibid. pp. 36 ff.).

[4] Even systems of collective bargaining, organised and supported by government, cannot guarantee such a result. Cf. the inherent difficulties to institutionalise such countervailing powers as 'the consumers' and 'the savers'.

exception of public goods provision by government. The admission of failures of the market system to realise the optimum may justify public intervention. In that case specific intervention in addition to the basic decision in favour of market economy, can be formulated and enacted.

In order to discuss these issues within a reasonable context it is essential now to analyse the structure and behavioural characteristics of both public and private enterprise in a modern market economy.

2 A CRITIQUE OF PRIVATE ENTERPRISE

The classical concept of competition between public and private enterprise is based on specific images of private and public enterprise, their behavioural characteristics and objectives.[1] Most of economic theory pictures private enterprise as having a sole objective, to maximise net profits by satisfying consumers' demand in competition with other private firms. The process of production today is characterised by division of labour inside the firms, separating the capitalist-entrepreneur from dependent labour, and the capitalist-entrepreneur in turn has become divided among owners and managers. These features demonstrate that the vision of the private firm as an isolated, small one-man enterprise which seeks to maximise profits is a misleading generalisation. In fact, it must be happy to survive.

Managers of big corporations are largely free from effective control by owners. At the same time the area of discretion in pricing and investment policy are not subject to the profit motive. That all targets of managerial behaviour must centre around profit maximisation[2] is false logic: An important aspect of economic behaviour is concerned with the optimal allocation of resources in terms of a given target. This objective may be profit maximisation or the realisation of some target rate of return on capital invested or it may be some other goal. All these targets presuppose the technical maximum problem and the minimisation of costs to be solved for any output.[3]

The scheme in Table 1 pictures some of the most important objectives

---

[1] On the concept of enterprise cf. J. Jewkes, *Public and Private Enterprise* (London, 1965) p. 40.

[2] This popular conception is exposed by A. Schnettler, *Öffentliche Betriebe* (Essen, 1956) p. 21 f.

[3] Usually these preconditions are confused with profit maximization behaviour itself. Literature on the morphology of public enterprise superabounds with such an identification, cf., e.g., A. Schnettler, *Betriebe, öffentliche Haushalte und Staat* (Berlin, 1964) pp. 36 ff.

of private enterprise, the restraints they are subjected to by the competitive process, the net results they realise and their socio-economic performance in terms of prices, production and employment as well as investment and technology.

TABLE ONE

Objective of Firm	Restraints	Net Result for Firm	Socio-economic Performance
1. Profit maximization (profit$=g$)	(a) perfect competition	zero profits ($g=o$)	No pricing power. Investments with positive profits. Production and employment maximum. Technological progress doubtful.
	(b) oligopolistic competition, range for discretionary pricing power large, particularly if co-operative	sizeable profits ($g>o$)	Power to administer prices and output. Investments as long as rate of return exceeds rate of interest on capital market. Technological progress promoted.
	(c) monopoly (natural or practical) *but*: threat of nationalisation or monopoly control by state	large profits ($g>o$)	Prices or output are parameters of action. Investments limited by price elasticities of demand. Technological progress controlled.
2. Target rate of return on capital invested (rate$=r$)	(a) perfect competition	($r=i$) ($i=$ rate of interest on capital market)	Cf. 1(a).
	(b) oligopolistic competition	planned ($r>i$)	Cf. 1(b). In addition: Prices will be minimum compatible with *r*. Investment function strengthened since *r* is accounted in terms of capital invested which may be increased. This effects the choice of technique i.e. enforces substitution of labour by capital.
	(c) monopoly	planned ($r>i$)	Cf. 1(c).

Thus there are three groups of private enterprises in a modern economy: small business, big business and public utilities, corresponding to polypolistic and oligopolistic competition as well as to monopoly (franchise-system or other forms of practical or natural monopoly). Small business, i.e. classical private enterprise proper, whether pursuing profit maximisation or target rates of return by and large is effectively checked by competitors; cartels and collusions are relatively difficult to organise, they are met with antitrust and anticartel policy of government. Big corporations, whether in oligopolistic competition or in practical monopoly, have a choice. The area of choice is largest with 'collective enterprise' (Means) outside the public utilities' sphere (where prices and earnings are regulated). It is big business which has the largest realm for discretionary pricing power. There is a strong argument for a predominantly public character of big business. Most of the decisions of big corporations whether on prices, production, employment, investment and research as well as on location and mergers have far-reaching consequences for the whole economy, significantly affecting general political objectives of government.

We have to ask, as J. S. Mill [1] did in his days, whether this type of private enterprise can still command the classical arguments for undistorted competitive conditions and for maximum reliance on private enterprise throughout the economy. Mill admits, with respect to joint-stock companies, that the argument in favour of private enterprise and against government intervention are turned upside down. It may be argued, however, that managers of large corporations feel a stronger sense of social responsibility than private capital-owners and entrepreneurs of small firms do.[2] It remains open to discussion, however, why corporate management should take on such responsibility,[3] how it knows what is in the social interest [4] and who fixes what goals are to be enforced and by what methods performance is to be tested.

Unrestricted profit maximisation, for a number of reasons, is out of question for most big business, since its political effects may induce political control or even nationalisation. Thus quite often a target rate of return is set which amounts to smaller total profits than would seem possible. This target rate can be reached by means of various programmes of pricing, production and investment policy, each having a different set of side-effects. (For profit maximisation in its strict sense there is only one programme.) These political and social implications are particularly important with respect to pricing; prices are 'administered', minimising

[1] Cf. J. S. Mill, op. cit. pp. 96 ff.

[2] Cf., e.g., the statement of Sen. E. Dirksen of Illinois, quoted by G. C. Means, Statement before the Subcommittee on Antitrust and Monopoly of the Committee of the Judiciary, U.S. Senate, 85th Congress, 2nd Session, Part 9 – *Administered Price Inflation: alternative public policies* (Washington, D.C., 1959) p. 4772.

[3] Cf. G. C. Means, ibid.

[4] Cf. ibid. p. 4773.

the use of pricing power compatible with the target rate of return, relying on costs as parameters of action, quality variations, etc.

Targets and standards of performance, whether of mere profit maximisation or of any other type of targets, necessitate a systematic approach to business planning and evaluation of the accounting system.

The modern techniques of intrafirm planning, with standard or accounting values in the flow and the stock analysis of resource utilisation, are based on methods of rationalisation such as operations research (systems analysis).[1] These techniques, as well as the use of incentive systems along economic and technological criteria of performance, can be used in any type of industrial or commercial organisation, regardless of targets, patterns of behaviour, legal ownership, and type of goods produced.

The meaning of the concepts of private enterprise, property, and interest have changed significantly in the context of the modern economy. The realisation of public interest solely by relying on private interest is becoming increasingly doubtful. Under these circumstances public enterprise, its justification and its potential, look rather different from what it has been traditionally.

3 A CRITIQUE OF PUBLIC ENTERPRISE

Traditional economic thought implies that public enterprise is an element alien to market economic systems. There are several established exceptions to this rule, however, which today are generally accepted. Furthermore, there has been no economic system in history where public enterprise did not play a significant role. Four groups of both private and public enterprises are distinguished (see Table 2).

Three purposes of public enterprise can be distinguished:

(1) Public enterprise supplying the economy with public goods (public enterprise proper, special public corporations); [2]

(2) public enterprise supplying the government with private goods which presumably could be produced by private enterprise, but where procurement is not possible for reasons of national security,

---

[1] This need for non-market organisation of efficient allocation of resources is universal, e.g. governments, public enterprises, centrally planned economies as well as big companies have to deal with it. See, e.g., R. N. McKean, *Efficiency in Government Through Systems Analysis* (New York, 1958). For a model of accounting values for centralised and decentralised systems of intra-firm management cf. W. Buhr, *Dualvariable als Kriterien unternehmerischer Planung* (Meisenheim/Glan, 1966).

[2] Sometimes these are produced by privately owned enterprise. This presupposes either legal monopoly or some form of taxing power to cover deficits.

nonavailability in the market or nonaccessability at the location of demand. Also, procurement from private enterprise may be too expensive.[1]

(3) Public enterprises operated in competition with private enterprise for other reasons
    (a) public utilities: publicly owned and mixed companies.
    (b) public companies.

In the first two cases the quality and the quantity of goods and services to be produced are established by direct political decision. They are concerned with effectuating some of the total conditions of general optimum. Excepting public enterprise proper which produces for government supply

TABLE TWO
TYPES OF PRIVATE AND PUBLIC ENTERPRISE

(I) *Privately-owned Enterprises*	(II) *Publicly-owned Enterprises*
(1) private enterprises proper ('small business')	public enterprises proper (integral part of government)
(2) public utilities ('collective enterprise')	public utilities
(3) big corporation ('collective enterprise')	public companies
(4) non-profit organisations (of persons, unions, churches and other institutions of public life)	public corporations with special statute making them quasi-autonomous

(5) mixed companies
(of persons, private firms, local,
state and central governments)

because private bids [2] are too expensive, the problem is limited to the issue of the border-line to privately-owned enterprise. The question of competitive conditions does not enter in any significant sense.

The third case is different. Here we must ask whether the border-line and the competitive conditions can be weighed against those of private enterprise by means of economic criteria, which have political content no

---

[1] For the difficulties of establishing this need for public enterprise see the Hearings before a Subcommittee of the Select Committee on Small Business, U.S. Senate, *Government Competition with Private Business* – 1957, 85th Congress, 1st Session (Washington, D.C., 1957); and: *Government Competition with Business: Liquid Oxygen Production*, Hearings and Report, 86th Congress, 2nd Session, 2 volumes (Washington, D.C. 1960) as well as Committee on Government Operations, op. cit.

[2] Cf. E. Welter, *Der Staat als Kunde, Öffentliche Aufträge in der Wettbewerbsordnung* (Heidelberg, 1960).

doubt but which can be discussed in terms of economic welfare. Publicly-owned public utilities, mixed companies and public companies are operating in direct competition with private enterprise, mostly big corporations. Here each decision may have significant effects of transforming the economic and socio-political order, one way or the other.

The legal status and set-up of public enterprise is left out of consideration. It raises institutional problems of great interest, but these are only indirectly pertinent to the aims of this paper. Of more relevance are the objectives and the behavioural characteristics of these firms. Quite frequently no difference in behaviour is encountered between public and private enterprise, even if the legal or political purposes of the public companies diverge from profit-maximisation. However, there is one exception: private non-profit organisations, which are founded by groups of citizens, by trade unions, other social movements or political institutions, in order to pursue some specific social goal quite often fitting in with the public interest or at least within the large realm of the social responsibility promoted by the government. In certain countries, like the Federal Republic of Germany, these enterprises assume significant proportions [1] and have for most practical purposes are included in public companies.

Based on the general realisation of minimum cost combinations public enterprises can pursue all kinds of objectives.[2] The most important are:

(1) Profit maximisation
  (a) unrestricted, except by market forces;
  (b) restricted by certain social or political objectives or price policy (profits may be either zero, or positive or negative);
(2) Full cost principle:
  Prices as low as possible and differentiated according to certain targets under the restriction that
  (a) a fair rate of return on capital invested;

---

[1] See, e.g., W. Hesselbach, *Die gemeinwirtschaftlichen Unternehmen, Der Beitrag der Gewerkschaften zu einer verbraucherorientierten Wirtschaftspolitik* (Frankfurt, 1966).

[2] O. Triebenstein, *Die industriellen Staatsunternehmen und die Möglichkeit und Notwendigkeit ihrer instrumentalen Verwendung in marktwirtschaftlich organisierten Volkswirtschaften* (Berlin, 1958) p. 28, extending the classical conceptions of R. Liefmann, *Die Unternehmungsformen mit Einschluss der Genossenschaften und der Sozialisierung*, 2nd ed. (Stuttgart, 1921) pp. 205 ff., distinguishes four types of public enterprise: A. Welfare state orientation: (1) Public institutions (subsidy according to established needs), (2) Public firms (full cost principle), B. Profit motive orientation: (3) Public corporations (restricted by special socio-economic functions), (4) Public companies (unrestricted).

    (b) no return on equity capital;

    (c) a negative rate of return on all capital invested (the costs of production are only partly recovered) is earned;

(3) Sufficient supply of goods and services at fixed fees which recover a small or insignificant portion of total costs.

Objective (2a) formally coincides with the behavioural characteristics of private corporations, seeking to achieve a target rate of return. Targets (1b) with negative profits, (2c) and (3) imply subsidies to the operation of the firm, financed either by capital losses and repeated new stock issues, or by recurrent transfers. Since continuous payments out of the general budget presuppose costly political decisions, it will be passed only rarely. Public utilities, mixed companies and public companies will in all probability operate within the range of targets (1a), (1b) with positive or zero profits, (2a) and (2b) where they remain largely independent. With respect to semi-public or mixed public-private goods, public enterprise sometimes follows a combination of full cost pricing and fee pricing. For instance, public health service is combined with social insurance and publicly subsidised hospitals. The public goods character of the service is 'paid for' by a fee or none at all; the private goods component is, at least partly, paid for by a price related to cost. It is extremely difficult to design efficient allocation systems without pricing elements, but relying solely on the good judgement of the patients and the doctors.

    Management of public enterprises today seems neither inherently more efficient nor less efficient than management of private enterprise when compared by kind of operation, size and market problems. There is a strong danger, however, that a political spoils system develops. Connected with this is the central problem of effective control of public enterprise. It happens quite often that the government imposes acute, but temporary, political targets rather than setting long-range stable objectives and seeking to enforce them. As long as the firms are breaking even or doing better, government may face a difficult job enforcing its objectives and behavioural norms. Public enterprises maximising profits in flourishing markets without effective restraints may exert a tremendous political influence. They may raise the question: who controls whom – government management or management government?[1] These are not unchanging, principal characteristics of public enterprise, but *quaestiones facti* which can be altered.

---

[1] Cf. the author's study on Italian public enterprise in W. Weber (ed.), *Gemeinwirtschaft in Westeuropa* (Göttingen, 1963) pp. 284 ff.

Only if public enterprise is to maximise profits (a political decision which is open to serious objection), if its size and market share is quite small *and* if it is blocked from participation in collusion, etc., no additional standards of performance are needed. In all other cases it is necessary for both public and private enterprise to have additional rules of behaviour besides the mere submission to the market system. Thus rules of competition are an issue for both sides.

4 GOALS AND RULES OF CONDUCT FOR PUBLIC COMPANIES AND BIG PRIVATE CORPORATIONS

We have seen that large segments of private enterprise and much of public enterprise chooses goals and rules of behaviour instead of, or in addition to, mere short-run profit maximisation. However, social responsibility and public interest are empty boxes which need adequate, politically responsible interpretation. This is a duty of government which is responsible under the constitution to maintain the economic system and to serve the goals of political action. With respect to private enterprise the public interest needs to be fixed in legal incentives or disincentives as well as prohibitions; with respect to public enterprise they need direct determination of objectives and rules of conduct.

Public enterprise is one of many instruments at the disposal of government for economic policy. The functions which public enterprise can serve are:

(1) Protection and improvement of economic order: to neutralise economic power concentration and to promote competition.
(2) Progress in economic growth and development: to further technological advances, structural adjustments, housing, locational decisions desired (pioneering and imitating).
(3) Supply of goods and services: the production and distribution of public goods and public utilities.
(4) Stabilisation of economic activity: assistance of monetary and fiscal policy to maintain full utilisation of resources and stability of price level.

The competitive, developmental and supply functions are original tasks assignable to public enterprise; in general, they support one another. The stabilisation function, on the other hand, can only be a derived function which, taken for itself, provides no argument for running a public enterprise; but anticyclical adjustments in prices, investment and employment policy can be made, though only to a limited degree, without interference with the primary tasks.[1]

There are no unique, or typical, or basic behavioural characteristics of public enterprise.[2] The founders or owners of public enterprises should exert their will, right and power of control [3] to bind public enterprise to the desired objectives and rules of conduct. This can best be done by obliging management to follow the specific statute to be set up for public enterprise. Statutes also have the advantage of permitting parliament to participate in the process of goal fixing.[4] The statutes should fix the objectives and rules of conduct with reasonable clarity and precision, leave their execution to management and limit the influence of the executive branch of government to control (including the nomination of members for the board of trustees who, in turn, elect the members of the executive board of directors). It would be possible to delegate the control (in addition to the auditing) to a standing committee of parliament or to a specialised autonomous government agency.

Typically, the choice of objectives for public enterprise is seen as between short-run profit maximisation and other targets, such as to supply the market according to some kind of full cost pricing rule. It is my opinion that profit maximisation is unacceptable as a target for public enterprises, because of the general conflict of profit maximisation with the functions of public enterprise enumerated on page 417. Public enterprise should be subjected directly to a goal of public interest (or to several goals, with an indication of the priorities). These functions, it may be noted, do not include to reap profits to increase public revenue, which is done much better by direct or indirect taxation. Fiscal monopolies can be exercised by indirect taxation which effectively controls net profits. Thus there is no need for government to go into business itself. Self-financing the expansion of public enterprises should also be limited by a target rate of return. As it is not possible, as a general principle, to justify the existence

[1] Cf. B. Molitor, 'Öffentliche Wirtschaft und Privatisierung', *Hamburger Jahrbuch für Wirtschafts- und Gesellschaftspolitik,* v (1960) 83 ff.

[2] Cf. W. Krelle, *Theorie wirtschaftlicher Verhaltensweisen* (Meisenheim a. Gl., 1953) pp. 166, 17c.

[3] The necessity of control is practically rejected in the thesis of the International Office for Research and Information on Collective Economy. Cf. 'Preisbildung bei öffentlichen Unternehmen, Thesenfolge der Internationalen Forschungs- und Informationsstelle für Gemeinwirtschaft', in *Archiv für öffentliche und freigemeinnützige Unternehmen,* vii (1965) 255. (For the English version of this article see: 'Price Setting in Public Undertakings', by the I.C.R.I.C.E. Theory Committee, in *Annals of Collective Economy,* xxxiii (1962) pp. 270–82.

[4] Cf. R. Kelf-Cohen, *Nationalisation in Britain: The End of a Dogma* (London, 1958) p. 161.

of public enterprise by reference to its profit earning capacity,[1] it is not admissable either to do so with reference to objectives of pioneering social policy; this must be left to social legislation, collective bargaining, etc.

Rules of conduct for public enterprises indirectly also set conditions and political targets for private enterprises. There are four different issues at stake:

(1) abolition of distortions of competitive conditions between public and private enterprise;
(2) regulation of private enterprise by government;
(3) direct control of private enterprise by monopoly control or national-isation;
(4) public companies as 'the pike in a fish-pond', i.e. outsiders' competition to supplement market forces.

The plea for abolishing distortions in competition is concerned with the artificial differences in the competitive conditions of public and private enterprise. They can be grouped under these four charges of governments' preferential treatment of public enterprises: [2]

(1) different regulation of taxation;
(2) different treatment of return on capital invested;
(3) other special favours, such as subsidisation (potential or actual, direct or indirect); preferential treatment with state procurements; special treatment under antimonopoly and anticartel legislation; obstacles (put up by government) to private competitors ;
(4) special factors, such as size of enterprise (easy access to capital market); low risks for investment in bonds (lower rate of interest); early notice of planned government actions.

Even if one admits that the obstacles to the marginal cost equals price rule are tremendous, the basic problem of cost calculation to ascertain all relevant costs, remains. As to kind and extent of costs in general, equal

---

[1] See, however, Th. Keller, 'Die Einnahmen aus privatwirtschaftlich betriebenen und öffentlichwirtschaftlichen Unternehmen–Die Eigenwirtschaft öffentlicher Unternehmen', in F. Neumark/W. Gerloff (ed.), *Handbuch der Finanzwissenschaft*, 2nd ed. II (Tübingen, 1956) 182 ff. Keller distinguishes 20 different arguments for public enterprise, among them profit maximisation for revenue purposes.

[2] This list was compiled from W. Hamm, *Kollektiveigentum, Die Rolle öffentlicher Unternehmen in der Marktwirtschaft* (Heidelberg, 1961) pp. 82 ff.; A. Nussbaumer, *Wettbewerb und öffentliche Unternehmungen* (Wien, 1963) pp. 76 ff., 104 ff.; *Commission on Organization of the Executive Branch of the Government, Business Enterprises* (Washington, D.C., 1955) pp. 11 ff.

treatment should be effected, barring favours stemming from legal regulations and government behaviour. These differences in competitive conditions are partly trivial and partly irremovable (as, e.g. heading 4).

As to taxation (charge 1) the case is obvious with respect to cost taxes, like taxes on turnover, on productive capital or net property, mergers, issue of bonds, etc. It is different for the corporate income tax or any other tax on net profits. While cost taxes may be regarded as payments for indirect benefits and services which are, by the intention of parliament, to be shifted to final consumption, profit taxes are based on the net surplus; it is not intended that they shall be shifted.

Different treatment of capital costs (charge 2) includes low pressure for dividends, advance of special credits, leaving dividends with enterprises without charging any or the normal rate of interest. There is no valid argument for not accounting for capital costs equally in both private and public enterprise with respect to all decisions of management. The real difficulty lies in the fact that the costs of risk bearing and of access to the capital market, and to other sources of finance, because of size and public ownership of the firm, cannot be equalised; these are 'natural' differences in competitive conditions which also characterise big business in the private sector. Flexibility with respect to liquidity effects of dividends, interests, etc., is found everywhere in big business, and small business is forced to follow this pattern.

Other charges of special favours (charge 3) are more substantiated, particularly when public companies are striving for profit maximisation, or are serving to foster competition. Here public enterprise should compete on equal footing with private enterprise.

In cases where public enterprise is concerned with developmental and supply functions no such general rule can be found. Deviations as to competitive conditions must be allowed, but the burden of proof for different treatment rests with government.

Here two opposing principles of pricing should be weighed against one another and a political decision be reached which takes into account the existence of 'neighbouring' competitors (e.g. in transportation):

(1) pricing should reflect the 'real' costs which enterprise causes the economy;
(2) pricing should reflect social and political goals such as improvement of distribution of real income, housing, location of industrial activity, and employment, or hygienic, cultural and other values.

Since there are no objective keys to imputing costs [1] and since public companies exercise the power to administer prices (particularly when granted a franchise) there is room for price differentiation by market splitting (discriminating monopoly). The imputational problem gets the more difficult, the larger the firm, the more differentiated the offer, the more complex partial markets. There may also be internal cross-subsidisation.[2] In addition there is the possibility to subsidise externally the operations of public enterprise out of public budgets, if cross-subsidisation is not borne by the market or if it is judged to be unjust or politically infeasible.[3]

Railroad subsidies provide a good example. Though having lost its 'natural' monopoly in long-distance transportation, it still should not be run like a commercial firm which drops those lines which, by one standard of calculation or another, do not cover costs. The existence of a co-ordinated railway system throughout the economy has important dispersion effects on location, particularly if there is a legal obligation to enter into contracts and if equal rates are charged for equal distances.

The case of regulating both private and public enterprise has long been established in public-utility legislation on network monopolies. Here, beyond the general framework of competitive conditions, rates and earnings are regulated by government or special public agencies. However, the rule, 'fair return on the fair value of capital invested', has often turned out to be regulation in favour of owners of public utility firms and against the interests of consumers.[4] The rules – to bind the target rate of return to the interest rate prevailing on the capital market and to the fair value of a reasonable capital investment – are difficult to enforce and have many political side-effects. In particular, this yardstick does not settle the question of investment, expansion and innovation.

Since this conflict cannot be solved without giving up the objectives, and since regulation seems to involve an ever more elaborate and bureaucratic examination without real progress in enforcing the public interest, there is a strong argument in favour of public enterprise taking the place of privately-owned and mixed public utilities.

---

[1] Cf. *Preisbildung bei öffentlichen Unternehmen*, op. cit. pp. 256 ff.

[2] 'Public ownership . . . enables national resources to be redistributed according to different principles from those imposed by the profit motive. . . . Not only can the public corporation allocate its services and products to different classes of customers on the principle of cross-subsidization. . . .' M. Shanks (ed.), *The Lessons of Public Enterprise: A Fabian Society Study* (London, 1963) p. 302.

[3] The Rome Treaty establishing the E.E.C. provides *expressis verbis* for such possibilities, Vide Article 90, para. 2, E.E.C. Treaty.

[4] Cf. V. A. Mund, *Government and Business*, 3rd ed. (New York, 1960) pp. 483 ff., for the principal problems of commission control.

The case for direct control of private and public enterprise rests on two arguments: binding management directly (beyond competitive conditions and fixing rules for rates and earnings) or transfer of ownership. The drafting and execution of detailed rules of behaviour would call for an even more elaborate apparatus of bureaucracy with direct control than with regulation. Thus a shift of ownership does not solve the problem, but puts it only in a different wrapping.

Methods of forced decartelisation and deconcentration of large segments of big business have not been successful either. It appears that neither direct control, nor nationalisation, nor deconcentration is an adequate means; in addition they may be tremendously costly in terms of side-effects such as a lowering of the growth rate and the level of economic activity.

In this situation public enterprise as an outsider in oligopolistic and monopolistic markets may help to come to a solution. Besides free entry of products, as well as firms from abroad, public companies may be used as a yardstick to enforce an acceptable rate of return on capital; at the same time this will induce generally expansion of production (to pioneer technology or to imitate new developments).[1]

Only selected, efficient enterprises which are competing with other public companies should be used for this purpose. The firms should be companies of private legal form. In general, public corporations or private companies with autonomous management should be preferred to government's direct operation of production. Mixed companies (here as elsewhere) have no particular advantages, but only disadvantages: the only exception being enterprises with a developmental function in research, technology, regional or general development policy. The firms should never receive authoritarian support from government using its sovereign powers.

As to pricing and investment, public enterprises in direct competition with private enterprise should be like a pike in a fish-pond. They should normally minimise prices, compatibly with a target rate of return on capital at the level of the interest rate for bonds. While in general the owners or founders of public enterprise should put up the means of finance and, in case of target rates of return at capital market level, the capital market should be used; self-financing via price should be the exception in very rare cases. It is important to realise, however, that

---

[1] This concerns a fundamental problem of economic order: to activate the flow and utilisation of new ideas and inventions in innovations wherever possible. Cf. J. Jewkes, *Public and Private Enterprise*, op. cit. p. 90, passim.

public enterprises in direct competition with private enterprise must be allowed to maintain their market shares and to be flexible in this respect, in order to play their role. Public enterprises exercising the competitive function should be organised in 'straight' combination of firms which centre in the branches selected for checking the pricing power of big business or organised small business.

It seems impossible to fix the border-line between public and private enterprises once and for ever. The burden of proof (for the actual frontier) is with government. Firms which are the property of government should be sold, unless a convincing case can be made for their serving either a competitive or a developmental (or a supply) function. With respect to the need to grant the executive certain powers to purchase and sell stock as the instrumental character requires, parliament should have to be asked if the total value of holdings are to be reduced; the need for their increase, generally in proportion to economic growth, has already been established.

This analysis has presupposed highly developed market economies. Conclusions would be different for developing countries. The developmental function of public enterprise is clearly dominating, while the competitive and the supply functions slowly increase in importance. Here, the infrastructural prerequisites of economic development [1] will command the most interest. Though the public sector takes up a much smaller part of national product, the real danger lies in the temptation for the government and the management of public enterprises to consider the dominant developmental role as lasting and indispensable. It is here that public enterprise may play a significant role it can help to create private initiative and to produce that pattern of competition between different persons, objectives and behavioural characteristics which promotes free society and economic growth at the same time.

[1] Cf. R. Jochimsen, *Theorie der Infrastruktur: Grundlagen der marktwirtschaftlichen Entwicklung* (Tübingen, 1966).

20 Consistency of Action: The Compatability of Decision-taking by Private and Public Enterprises [1]

J. R. Houssiaux

1 THE DEFINITION OF THE PUBLIC SECTOR

Public and private enterprises may coexist under many economic regimes, in a market economy or in a planned economy, and with various degrees of State intervention.[2] In this paper we will select the framework of a market economy with a certain level of indicative planning and of State intervention in the market mechanism and in the preparation and execution of the plan.[3] This is the situation prevalent in most Western European economies.

In such an economic system, the level of planning and of State intervention have an impact on the size of the public enterprise sector. Two criteria may be used to define this sector. The first and traditionally used definition is related to the ownership of the means of production: the public sector is taken to include all publicly owned production units. Under this definition, the public sector will usually be larger in the economies where planning and State intervention are greater. But this relationship is not automatic, for the internal factors leading to growth of the public sector often contribute as much to its extension as do new nationalisation programmes.

But there is a second criterion which may be used to define the public enterprise sector, one according to which the State, to implement its economic policy, delegates certain executive functions to decision-making

[1] This report was prepared during a stay at the Center for International Affairs, Harvard University. I am specially indebted to Professor R. Bowie, Director of the Center.

[2] One may try to distinguish between a planned economy and a controlled economy. If it is assumed that planning Centres are distinct bodies from traditional administrative agencies, it is possible to design a planned economic system which does not involve bureaucratic controls. The weakening of planning tendencies in Europe since 1958 and the progressive return to a market economy have from time to time been accompanied by a strengthening of direct state intervention in the functioning of the economy.

[3] Two different kinds of dirigism can therefore be identified, the first relating to intervention in the market mechanism, the other concerning planning procedures. The second gives the State a preponderant role in the preparation and the execution of the plan, paving the way for a move from indicative to authoritarian planning.

units thus conferring an instrumental function on them. The sector of public enterprise is the total set of the production units, given this 'instrumental function' by the State, either when they are set up, or with the passage of time and in the light of circumstances. Identification of where the instrumental function is discharged leads to classification of the components of the public enterprise sector. Five categories will be considered:

(a) State or local economic agencies or administrations, and public undertakings.[1]
(b) The so-called national enterprises which constitute the industrial public sector independently of their origin and legal statute.
(c) The mixed enterprise, i.e. the firm in which the State or a local administration holds shares.
(d) The direct or indirect, majority or minority, subsidiaries of the two preceding categories, including joint subsidiaries.
(e) Some private enterprises which, apart from general measures of economic policy, are under the control of the State or any of its specialised agencies in such a way that their major decisions are the direct result of state intervention. The importance of these quasi-public enterprises will differ according to the country in which they are located, the government in power, and the traditional relationship between administration and industry.[2]

The most common way of defining the public sector is to list public enterprises by reference to a legal statute which may, moreover, vary in time and over space. This is usually sufficient if all that is required is to draw up an inventory of public enterprises. Placing emphasis, as is done in this paper, on the 'instrumental function' and how it devolves on those who exercise it, brings out the fact that the tasks which the public sector performs are changing, at the same time as the public sector's content is itself undergoing change. For example, the traditional functions of the public enterprises in the defence sector in France may now be discharged jointly by a public agency and private contractors. This development will

---

[1] It is sometimes quite difficult to distinguish between these agencies or administrations and public enterprises as they are traditionally understood. There has, for example, been some discussion recently about the nature of the French fuel monopoly and its management, the question being whether it falls within the dispositions of Articles 37 and 90 of the Treaty of Rome, which deal respectively with national monopolies and public enterprises.

[2] The present French Minister for Economic Affairs, M. Michel Debré, has recently stressed the 'public service' aspect of the activity of private business in certain sectors of the economy, and the duties which are the natural counterpart of the right to operate within national boundaries.

often be found when, as a result of their legal status, public enterprises cease to be the docile executants of economic policy they may have been at one time. During the last few years, public enterprises appear to have become rather more reluctant to apply directives relating to investment, price or wage policy. The State may therefore confer the 'instrumental function' on decision-making units whose legal statute is not that of a public enterprise. These may be either new administrative bodies or more tractable privately controlled firms, the 'quasi-public' enterprises.

The concept of 'public enterprise' is not easily applied for economic analysis. The public sector, which is what it is as the result of particular historical circumstances, is heterogeneous, with different features in different countries. In spite of some progress in the organisation of State participation in productive activity, the growth of the public sector is mainly caused by exceptional circumstances. An explanation may indeed be available for the constitution of a given public enterprise or the development of another one, but there is no satisfying general explanation of the growth of the public sector during a given period. Yet some successive stratification can be found that strengthens the historical character of the public sector in Europe. The desire of the State to expand the energy sector, to improve regional development, to secure national defence, to raise educational standards, or simply, for example, to promote tourism, explains why a specific kind of instrumental function was transferred to a newly created public enterprise and subsequently became the charter from which it takes its mandate for action. Public enterprises often stress their so-called 'specific goal', which may be railroad transportation, or coal mining, or banking, or electricity production, and so on. The list of 'specific goals' proper to given public enterprises and which is supposed to distinguish their activities from those of the private sector tends to reflect the successive stages in the historical growth of the public sector rather than disclose any rational construction. Nevertheless, the following content can be given to the instrumental function:

(1) a function of collective organisation acting on behalf of the entire society; the attributes of this function include the prediction of future developments, improvement of working methods in the sector, and progressive adaptation to the consequences of change; this is exemplified by the function discharged in producing and delivering electricity, or organising a telephone service;

(2) an incentive and regulative function, for instance avoiding cartellisation or private monopolisation of a sector, overcoming the barrier

constituted by high costs of entry to an activity, stimulating new investment, promoting better geographical distribution of production units, etc.; this is especially the case in industries where public and private enterprise are in competition.

2 THE ALLOCATION OF RESPONSIBILITY BETWEEN PUBLIC AND PRIVATE SECTORS

The result of State intervention in the exercise of these two functions is a sharing of activities and tasks between the private and public sectors. This sharing, which constitutes the first level at which it is possible to evaluate the compatibility of the private and public sectors, changes from period to period both as to objectives and activity coverage. To undertake a detailed examination of the aims of the public authorities in setting up a public enterprise would go beyond the scope of this paper, but to facilitate the subsequent discussion, seven categories of arguments which are advanced to justify State intervention may be listed:

—to transfer sectors with increasing returns to public enterprise;
—to impede or counteract the operations of private monopolies;
—to organise an industry where private action is inadequate;
—to protect a national industry threatened by foreign competition;
—to attain a desirable level and distribution of 'collective consumption';
—to ensure an adequate level of social infrastructural investment;
—to obtain better co-ordination of the various activities in a sector run by private enterprise.

Clearly public enterprise is not always essential to correct the imperfections of social and economic organisation which the seven categories of motives listed above purport to remedy. We should ascertain case by case the various alternatives and compute the net social cost of State intervention, i.e. the impact on economic agents considered as a whole of the creation or the extension of an element of public enterprise. For example, the presence of public enterprises in shipbuilding in France or Italy shows that the public element in a sector is not in itself a sufficient condition for the industrial or regional reconversion required; the public sector cannot become 'the hospital for ailing enterprises'.

A list of the main sectors in which public enterprises are developing or are already active can be drawn up rapidly. It includes the eight following:

(1) activities connected with regional investment and development;
(2) agricultural production and trade;

P

(3) energy;
(4) basic industries other than agriculture and energy;
(5) activities related to national defence;
(6) other manufacturing (non-defence);
(7) some service industries, in particular those related to social or cultural needs;
(8) financial services.

During the last decade the growth of the public sector in Europe has mainly been in the first two of the above categories. Attempts have been made to create new types of public enterprise to achieve the aims set by the authorities. It seems likely that once the main framework for regional development and improvement and distribution of farm products has been built, the growth of public enterprise in these two sectors will end; at this stage, it will be possible to define the conditions of coexistence of private and public enterprise on a stable basis. Sector 7, becoming progressively more differentiated, will replace the first two sectors as a main source of public sector development. In sectors 4 and 6, the public sector will grow, as it were, by contagion in the form of public shareholdings and joint ventures or with the help of public-holding corporations. Sector 8 will most likely, at least in Western Europe, become one of the sectors in which State intervention develops most rapidly. New methods of financing, calling for the participation of para-state financial organisms, will appear at the same time as former public enterprises will tend progressively to take on the character of financial institutions, in particular the public enterprises in the energy sector (sector 2).

The balance between public and private enterprises will, therefore, be called into question continually with the passage of time. In many European states, the largest enterprises are public enterprises, whether measured by value added, labour force, or turnover and this has been the position for many years. Some of these enterprises have had a high rate of growth reflecting either a policy of intensive self-financing or recourse, sometimes for all the capital required, to the bond market. These two techniques are less easily employed with falling rates of profit resulting either from state-imposed price freezes or the reappearance on financial markets of competition between public and private would-be borrowers. The relative share of the large public enterprise may not be decreasing, but it can no longer increase as rapidly as in the past to the extent that incentives for growth and the means to finance it are similar for private and public enterprises. It may be added that some large public enterprises have been created during the last decade, either by nationalisation of existing private firms or by the merger of previously scattered public interests. Here and there, also, some formerly large public enterprises have declined in importance with the disappearance of some or all of their *raison d'être*. Nevertheless, the universe of the large public enterprise is not going to shrink; indeed, the likely outlook is a strengthening of the tendency to public concentration as new public holding corporations join the family of existing public enterprises.

Statistical data on public enterprises and their subsidiaries in European countries [1] reveal a high degree of similarity in their past development. Nevertheless, some comments may be presented suggesting a degree of divergence in future developments as between countries:

(1) With the exception of the two first sectors – regional and agricultural activities, the direct creation of new public enterprises by nationalisation or using other techniques seems to be more frequent in France, Italy or the United Kingdom than elsewhere.

(2) In all sectors, decentralisation of public enterprises seems to be a more important policy aim in Germany and the Netherlands than in France, Italy, or Great Britain. In the first two countries district or provincial authorities or, often, existing public enterprises or consortia of public enterprises, are selected to establish new public enterprises as these are felt to be required.

(3) The growth of public enterprise through shareholdings, direct subsidiaries or joint ventures with the private sector is current everywhere in Europe, although apparently on a rather lesser scale in Germany and Great Britain than in France or Italy.

(4) It does not seem as though the much publicised denationalisation ('reprivatisation') movement in Germany, which has resulted in a diminishing share of the equity capital of some public enterprises owned by federal or local authorities, leads to a divergence of German from general European trends; it merely shows a difference in the management of the public sector. Some countries, such as France and Italy and more recently the United Kingdom, try to organise their public sector on a rational basis and to plan its development. The German Government, by contrast, continues to apply an empirical policy of unplanned creation of public enterprises in sectors where this proves necessary.

---

[1] I have been allowed to consult the register of public enterprises recently established by the European Centre for Public Enterprise, Brussels.

3 THE GROWTH OF THE PUBLIC SECTOR

The growth of the public sector results from the association of two historical tendencies : the normal preference of political authorities in Europe for monopoly-type situations, and secondly, the extension of the State's role in the economic sphere.

The first tendency is an old and well-established one in Europe; it explains both the creation of the first public enterprises in the eighteenth century and the reactions of governments to the Great Depression or the aftermath of World War II. The view held is that a monopolistic structure is the only one able to deal efficiently with a depressed market, or inversely, one which is growing too rapidly, providing the monopoly in question is conferred on a public enterprise. State monopoly is thus the logical culmination of the process of capitalist concentration. Such a monopoly, it is felt, will also protect the economy against the entry of foreign competitors and against competition from substitute products, particularly those imported from abroad. Therefore, the decision to move a sector from private to public control has been able to occur independently of any trend to state dirigism; when exceptional circumstances have to be faced, the authorities transfer the right to produce or distribute a good or service to a monopoly, so as to implement a complete change in the structure and organisation of the sector in question. The alternative policy would be the establishment of effective antitrust rules aimed at the improvement of the structure and behaviour of the sector; but the former policy is always preferred to the latter, explicitly or implicitly. Although this attitude still prevails in most European countries, it is being increasingly challenged. Moreover, the sectors in which such reactions may effectively occur are becoming more and more uncommon as a result of greater international market orientation and the development of competition from substitute products.

The extension of the role of the State in the economic sphere has been too often discussed in the literature to be taken up here. However, two brief comments may be made on some of its consequences.

First, this extension has been generated only to a limited extent as the result of an economy or to gain control of docile executive agencies. An inspection of the history of State intervention in the French petroleum industry or the list of the successive acts governing British airline organisation suffices to cause the too frequently held conception of a rationally planned socialisation, applied in stages, to be abandoned. The result of this disorderly growth of public enterprises in modern capitalistic countries is that a phase of rational reconstruction has followed each phase of extension of the public sector. At present, this rational reconstruction follows three major directions:

(a) The constitution of national enterprises whose specific aims are defined in the Nationalisation Act or other legislation setting them up. These 'natural sectoral monopolies' are exemplified by the E.N.E.L. recently created in Italy.

(b) The establishment of large public holding corporations directly controlling many public or mixed enterprises, with an important portfolio of equity shares of private firms, and sometimes managing part or all of the State portfolio. The Italian I.R.I. is the model of this kind of holding corporation, which can be either general or specialised. Some public enterprises of the first kind, for example the French coal board, 'Charbonnages de France', may be progressively transformed to the second sort as they extend their participation in activities more or less closely linked to their natural monopoly and so come to constitute new holding corporations.

(c) The creation of public pilot-enterprises, i.e. public firms which are mandated purposely to operate in an existing competitive market. In certain cases, these firms fall under public ownership because of particular circumstances – war, or a failure of management followed by State, local authority or public enterprise takeover. In others, the enterprise may be constituted to provide a model and guidance for a sector whose performance, for whatever reason, falls short of what is deemed desirable. The management of these pilot-firms will follow the policy line for the sector laid down by the administration so far as competitive conditions allow it sufficient freedom of action. Experience with such enterprises will be analysed below, for it is precisely in these sectors that the most arduous problems of compatibility between private and public firms must be faced, and these problems are independent of those arising from the competitive relations between public and private enterprises in the different markets. Public enterprises of the first two types listed are most often at the origin of the creation of public pilot-enterprises, for example old 'natural monopolies' affected by competition from substitute products; this competition is felt first at the boundaries of the industry, i.e. at successive stages of manufacture of the products of the natural monopoly. To defend its position, the enterprise must penetrate new markets by creating specialised subsidiaries, often, moreover, in collaboration with private enterprise. This is also the case, almost by definition of their function, of public holding corporations which have progressively enlarged their scope of operation since they were first set up in the aftermath of the 1929 crisis. The trend to rationalisation of the public enterprise sector in these three directions will have to be allowed for in our study of the impact of public enterprise on the decisions of the private sector. But this rational reconstruction is itself only provisional, and may well have to be reconsidered in the light of future vicissitudes of international trade relationships and technical progress.

The second of the two comments deals with the philosophy underlying the extension of State intervention. There are two main streams of thought, one of which may be traced back to Sismondi and the 'romantic socialism' of the early nineteenth century, the other to the organicist of dirigist thinking whose roots can be found still earlier in Germany, France and Italy.

Despite the voluminous literature on the nationalisation movement after 1945 in France or in Great Britain, it is all but impossible to distinguish between the two tendencies in the motives expressed in the Nationalisation Acts. The desire gradually to diminish private ownership of the means of production and to transfer the control of public enterprises to the population as a whole appears in the distinction between 'national' and 'state' control of activities. But a little consideration of this distinction, with the ambiguity it long conferred on indicative planning in Europe, shows its illusory nature. Nationalisation, and, in general, the growth of the public sector has been intended to achieve, and sometimes has succeeded in achieving, a stronger control by the State of the working of the key sectors of the economy.

This trend may no longer be quite so clear. The extension of the public sector in the three directions discussed reflects a new philosophy which may be called 'optimalist' or 'paretian'. The authorities are conscious of the imperfections which characterise the operation of markets in our day. This is not the place to analyse the causes of these imperfections, although it is often fair to say that the State itself is responsible for the structure and performance of some industries in the private sector. The essential point is that the State takes notice of the gap between actual and optimal results, and denounces its main causes, excessive advertising, inadequate adjustment to technical progress, inappropriate regional location, price inflexbility, lags or mistakes in the decision-making process, all of which prejudice the achievement of short-term equilibrium, potential growth and the welfare of society as a whole. Some governments deduce from this that public enterprises are the only way to eliminate these drawbacks, and three procedures are usually proposed – first, transfer of all the natural monopolies to State control to obtain 'optimal' management in these industries; secondly, elimination of the imperfections in a given private sector by creation of a public-pilot-enterprise; thirdly, correct allocation and transfer of resources between sector swith the assistance of public-holding corporations.

4 OPTIMALIST AND DIRIGIST APPROACHES

To test how closely the factual development of the public sector respects this theoretical tendency, we shall have to study the principles underlying the management of the three categories of public enterprise. Before doing so, an attempt is made to distinguish the new 'optimalist' approach from the old 'dirigist' one, to see how far these two approaches can in fact be distinguished. Human nature is such that imperfections in the operation of the public sector are likely to be identical in essence to those listed for the private sector: lags and mistakes in the decision-making process, inaccurate demand forecasting, delays in applying new techniques, irrationality and arbitrariness in price setting, inability to convert to new activities in good time, etc. In those countries in which historical circumstances resulted in all productive facilities being State controlled, these imperfections gave birth to a reform known as 'Libermanism'. Even with the help of a simulation model, it is vain to attempt to compare the performance of an economy whose imperfections basically reflect a malfunctioning of private enterprise, with the same economy where the imperfections stem from bad organisation of the public sector. Common sense would suggest that so long as a certain threshold beyond which imperfections are deemed intolerable by the society as a whole has not been reached, the *status quo* should be maintained in favour either of the private or of the public sector. But once this threshold has been crossed – and it will be measured against different standards in different countries – the situation will differ according to the sector in which the imperfections are observed. Transfer of a public enterprise to the private sector is much less likely than the reverse. More usually, reforms are introduced to reduce the imperfections of the public sector. The methods employed for this purpose will be of emulative interest for private enterprise. Against this, the modern management techniques of the private sector may be imposed on the public sector, resulting in a change in the techniques of control implemented by the responsible authorities.

We have mentioned that the State has its share of responsibility for imperfections observed in the operation of the private sector. Observation of recent efforts by the French Authorities, for example, to introduce a quasi-nationalised monopolistic structure in such major sectors as the steel, chemical, non-ferrous metal, and heavy electrical industries, leads to the conclusion that a dirigist policy can tolerate imperfections, so long as it appears that direct corrective intervention will suffice to avoid the most noticeable abuses. The same is true for imperfections in the public sector: defective resource allocation (for instance, energy policy), delay in adjustment to new techniques (subsidies to obsolete industries and then takeover by the State), lags in meeting demand (the housing, education and public health sectors) and so on, may often be considered as decisions voluntarily taken by the government, intent on enforcing a method of operation on the economic system which may run counter to the principles of a Paretian optimum, but has the merit of having been chosen and accepted by the authorities. The State usually considers that it will be able, as time passes, to correct the clearest deficiencies by a political redefinition of priorities. The differences between the optimalist approach of a public sector whose operations are governed by automatic mechanisms (whose components will be examined later for the three types of public enterprise envisaged) and the dirigist approach of intervention by the political authorities have not been sufficiently emphasised by public finance economists. In practice the two are closely interwoven. The combination presently adopted in industrialised countries, particularly in Europe, tends to lay more stress on the first approach under the pressure of the development of international competition; the degree of freedom available to the political authorities is not large enough for considerable imperfections in the public sector to be allowed to subsist; and the same imperfections will, as time passes, seem less easily tolerable. For instance, the price paid by the publicly controlled oil companies for their crude oil can no longer exceed the world price for long without provoking protest by users.

This conclusion leads to two brief comments: first, the pressure of international competition may incite certain political authorities to preserve the 'national' character of their public enterprises, i.e. to maintain their ability to intervene in the economy through the public sector. One of the main obstacles to further trade liberalisation is its restriction of the State's freedom of action in the economic sphere, in particular its own public enterprises. Secondly, the degree of freedom of the State following the recent growth of international competition is considerably less reduced for the larger countries in many sectors of activity than for the smaller ones due to the importance of the domestic market in total sales. A country such as the United States could support a public sector replete with imperfections and still maintain an entire set of political priorities whose consequences would be felt by the rest of the world. This is particularly true of choices in the fields of national defence, space research and nuclear armament. The various public programmes undertaken by the United States Government since 1962 – urban redevelopment, the anti-poverty campaign, the enlarged educational and health service – illustrate a dirigistic policy consisting of an adjustment of political priorities in the light of events. There is no guarantee that modifications of a reactionary type might not be implemented in certain circumstances. Likewise it is possible for a large country such as the U.S.A., whose public sector is growing very rapidly, consciously to impose certain imperfections in its functioning on its own population, as well as on the rest of the world. This will be the case to the extent that the political priorities set by the administration culminate in results which differ from those to be obtained from 'Paretian' management. But it should be recognised that the United States has for many years operated a system of 'regulation' of its public enterprises. This system, for all its deficiencies, greatly reduces the possibility of arbitrary action by subjecting the regulated sector to the ultimate control of the Supreme Court.[1]

5 INSTRUMENTAL FUNCTIONS

Imperfections in the public sector must be limited to the extent possible. This entails the need to define a 'workable' structure and behaviour so that it becomes, for the public sector, parallel to the 'workable competition' which the authorities seek to maintain in the private sector. We have first to study the elements which interfere with the constitution and functioning of a workable public sector, so as to be able to define the boundary between what can be accepted and what may no longer be. In order to see the elements which interfere with the operation of the public sector, we return to the concept of 'instrumental function' introduced

---

[1] See B. W. Lewis, 'Ambivalence on public policy toward regulated industries' in *American Economic Review*, May 1963, p. 38. Mr Lewis concludes that the controlling authorities can adjust themselves to any kind of proposed criteria, Paretian or otherwise.

earlier.   The 'instrumental function' can be divided into three components:

(a) The instrumental function exercised by the State in the act of setting up a public enterprise and in the subsequent decisions to allocate further resources to it.   This will be denoted as the *original* instrumental *function.*

(b) The instrumental function exercised in the current operations of a public enterprise.   Here, the role of the State is not limited to choice of the path to be followed by the public enterprise and checking the results actually obtained.   It also sets the development policy of the public enterprise and its management rules, more or less respecting the conditions of the Paretian optimum.   We shall label this the *permanent instrumental function.*

(c) The instrumental function in which the public enterprise is a medium for achievement of general policy objectives relating to all private economic agents, consumers, savers, workers, private firms.   In this case, the public enterprise is merely an intermediate means to a more general end, and is used for example to limit the rate of wage increase, to stabilise prices, to aid a sector in recession, to guide the export effort, to encourage spending for scientific research, etc.   We shall call this the *indirect instrumental function.*

6 IMPERFECTIONS OF THE PUBLIC SECTOR

We shall classify the imperfections of the public sector that we wish to confine within the boundaries of a 'workable' system into two categories:

First, the correct size of the public enterprise may be under- or overestimated in relation to the tasks the undertaking has to fulfil.   In this case, imperfections are caused by inefficient discharge of the original instrumental function.   An appropriate increase in the size of the public enterprise – for instance by fusion of two public enterprises, or by a merger between a private enterprise and a public unit – may be one method of coping with this first difficulty.   Another is the allocation of fresh financial resources to a public enterprise in deficit.   Still another is to adjust the tasks of the public enterprise to its structural capabilities, for example by changing its product range or its degree of vertical integration.   An extreme remedy is to return the public firm to the private sector.   Indicative planning, national multi-annual programmes for public investment or the creation of special administrative agencies such as the F.D.E.S. in France appear to provide a natural framework for the adaptation of the public sector over time and the elimination of imperfections which can be traced to structural deficiencies of public enterprises. Another technique for elimination of major imperfections and adaptation of the public sector is a periodic reappraisal of its tasks, objectives and methods such as those being conducted at present by the French Government and the E.E.C.

The second kind of imperfection arises not from the scarcity of resources available to the public enterprises, but from their inefficient use. This may be due to poor management of the public enterprises; and appropriate modification of the techniques of control should result in maximum reduction of the imperfections. Efficient control is particularly necessary in sectors of public activity where there is little competition – directly or through substitute products – with private industry. Even in competitive sectors, however, control will avoid emergence of a situation in which private firms follow the defective management pattern of their public competitors. It has been argued that workable competition among private firms may be more difficult to enforce the greater the extension of the public sector.

Poor resource utilisation by a public enterprise may also follow from inopportune State intervention in the public sector. Sometimes the permanent instrumental function is used in such a way as to impose management decisions which run counter to the achievement of its 'specific goal' by the public enterprise; or public enterprises may be used to accomplish tasks beyond their normal scope of activity. In these circumstances the imperfections can be corrected only by intervention of the institutions responsible for control of the public sector, and even then, only if these institutions are independent, and enlightened enough to be able to divert the State from intervening in the day-to-day management of the public enterprises.

7 A WORKABLE PUBLIC SECTOR

After this analysis of the origin of imperfections in the structure and operation of public enterprises, we shall now consider the three main categories of public enterprises listed earlier, so as to define the conditions for 'workable' or acceptable public sector management.

It is difficult to find a clear demarcation line in this context. The content of 'workable competition' for the private enterprise sector is usually defined by the antitrust authorities, progressively developed from an empirical succession of cases. The same is true for the public sector; the existence of conscious and organised institutionalised control is, therefore, a decisive element for the establishment of 'workable' public sector economics. We shall analyse the nature of this control and its relations to the rules pertaining to private enterprises.

(a) *The operating conditions of the natural monopolies.* The following working assumptions will enable the boundaries of the sector of public enterprises considered as natural monopolies to be delineated:

(1) The activity of these enterprises is designed to fulfil an economic objective only, the production of goods and services.
(2) Their operations should be as satisfactory as possible from the viewpoint of the community generally. This may be achieved by fixing the production level so as to minimise average unit cost; by pricing goods and services at marginal cost; by selecting the discriminatory price structure which maximises total profit and, therefore, the rate of self-financed investment; or any intermediate combination of these incompatible aims, i.e. minimum cost of production, marginal cost pricing, and price discrimination to maximise monopoly profits.
(3) They are in a monopolistic position and are not subject to competition from substitute products. They have complete control of supply, present and future, and some influence on the shape of the demand curve.

It must be accepted that there is no sector in which these conditions are completely satisfied. Natural monopolies are in practice never totally able to follow the golden rule of the public monopoly – marginal cost pricing – whose drawbacks in application have often been demonstrated in the literature.[1] They may utilise the technique of internal 'cross-subsidising' which has so often been reproved, for example in the United Kingdom.[2] Finally, 'pure' sectoral monopoly situations are becoming more and more rare. Public enterprises are being exposed to ever-growing competitive pressures from substitute products. At the same time the external economies which they may realise for other activities outside their sector are not taken into account in their own management decisions. These external economies may be sufficiently great for the State to consider them as a

[1] Cf. J. R. Nelson, *Marginal Cost Pricing in Practice* (New York, 1964).
[2] Cf. W. G. Shepherd, *Economic Performance under Public Ownership* (Yale, 1965), ch. 6.

joint product of the enterprise, and, in order to maximise them, to impose management rules which involve running at a loss, or implementing another pattern of activity than the one which would normally have been chosen by the enterprise. In this last case, the function of the natural monopolies is to select the level and techniques of production which yield the greatest net amount of external effects for the whole set of economic agents.

The operation of the natural monopolies therefore seems to be committed to two main principles: the first principle, to which public enterprises attach much weight, is simple. It is that they must behave as if they were engaged in an imperfectly competitive market, somewhere in the region between minimum average cost of production and marginal pricing. Secondly, the public firms are committed to respect a set of external conditions, supposedly a reasonable one, provided by the State – a minimum investment programme to be financed out of profits, minimum social costs, and a minimum of external economies to the benefit of other economic agents. Some public natural monopolies, such as the French Electricity Supply Board or some of the large public undertakings in the United Kingdom, have tried to formulate a management policy, based on these two principles, and yet feasible in practice. The results may well be closer to a theoretical optimum than would be the results to be obtained from an oligopolistic market with imperfect knowledge. We may conclude that the management of the natural monopolies restricts the imperfections of the public sector, imputing a social cost to them at the same time. This last responsibility – social costs, external economies, forced growth – which normally weighs adversely on the cost curve and long-period receipts, is balanced by a joint product which is a public good and therefore cannot receive any direct monetary value – social advantages, external effects, growth impulses. The control institutions have to determine, *ex ante* and *ex post*, the relationship between the extra costs and the estimated overall value of the corresponding non-monetary advantage to the private sector and the rest of the economy.

(b) *The operating conditions of the public holding corporation.* As has been previously stated, the public holding corporation is a form of enterprise which is still in a transitional phase. A list of such enterprises would be very short, even if new rudimentary institutions, such as the Industrial Reorganisation Corporation set up in January 1966 in the United Kingdom, were included.

The public holding corporation performs three main functions which correspond to the activities of a merchant bank, an investment trust, and an investment programming agency:

(1) Management of the State investment portfolio, with the primary aim of maximising its yield. In discharging this function, the holding corporation acts as a public merchant bank. But where the services of a merchant bank in the private sector may be ascertained for its owner in terms of long- or short-term profit, this is not true of the services rendered by a public holding corporation to the State; its activity is far too differentiated. As the intermediary between the State and the management of the natural monopoly, the public holding corporation participates in the administrative negotiations regarding the external burdens or constraints imposed upon the public enterprise. As shareholder in a public pilot-enterprise in the competitive sector, it must of course supervise profitability, as would a merchant bank; but it must also define, together with the enterprise, the particular management rules needed for the latter's pilot role, as they are related to the targets for the sector set by the planning office or the supervising ministry.

(2) Orientation of the coverage and expansion of the State portfolio. The holding corporation is charged by the State to select the sectors and private firms in which State participation is to increase, and to decide on the form in which this expansion will be realised. In this function, the public holding corporation acts as an investment trust administering the State portfolio as would a private company in its customers' best interest. In view of the size of the portfolio, comparison with the German trades union bank is inevitable. The public stake in the firms whose shares it holds tends naturally to grow with time, partly as a result of cyclical interventions in stock markets intended to steady prices. The State may also act through traditional financial intermediaries, through insurance companies having the characteristics of public organisms, or again through institutions analogous to the Bureau of Industrial Development whose creation was once recommended by Professor J. M. Jeanneney. The public holding corporation, or the set of institutions which presently discharge its functions, is thus able to orient or strengthen the position of the State in the sectors in which it is interested in the light of the economic situation or pursuant to the aims of the national plan.

(3) Investment programming by public enterprises. The public holding

corporation may be considered as the despatch centre for public funds to be invested in public sector enterprises or in the economy at large. In this way, the direction of future production, the transfer of investment funds from one budget chapter to another, the distribution in time of the operational phases of an investment programme, can all be considered explicitly in the most rational possible conditions. Here, the public holding corporation plays the role of an investment planning commission, a function which is discharged in some cases by an administrative body proper (e.g. the F.D.E.S. in France), in others by a public financial institution (the I.R.I. in Italy). In allocating investment funds, the public enterprise may occasionally be led to modify the standard system of rules in order to allow for particular State objectives, generally discriminating in favour of a particular element of the public sector. However, there have also been cases in which the proceeds of a State loan have been applied to the benefit of private firms rather than the public sector, a procedure which gave rise to some unease among public enterprises, whose expansion potential was limited by the provisions of the budget.

The funds deployed in the operations of public holding companies are generally supplied in the form of share capital, or out of treasury funds; in the latter case increases are decided by the government or by Parliament, as the case may be. Apart from these initial funds, the holding corporation may borrow in financial markets, or sometimes even accept deposits placed with public savings institutions. At all events, household savings are the source of the best part of the funds available for investment by the holding corporation.

The holding corporation is therefore a necessary intermediary between this saving and the enterprise sector, whatever method is employed to obtain the funds invested. The public holding corporation in Europe is placed somewhere between the public enterprises and the public authorities. It is also a linkage point between public and private enterprises; as a result, its relationships with these three groups tend to become modified as progress is made in freeing financial markets and rendering them more uniform. It follows that competition with other private or public financial institutions, domestic or foreign, limits the scope for intervention by the holding corporation in the affairs of the companies in which it has shareholdings, immediately such intervention has an aim other than the maximisation of the return on its investment. These circumstances

set parallel limits to the external conditions and constraints which
the State can implement to influence the management of public
holding corporations.

(c) *The operation of public pilot-enterprises.*   It has already been pointed
out that the appearance of public enterprises in competitive sectors has
usually been the outcome of the interplay of a particular set of circumstances.   This, however, is an insufficiently convincing explanation inas-
much as the number of sectors in which such enterprises operate is tending
to grow in all countries.   From advertising through tourism and automobile production to distribution of agricultural products, it would be
hard to cite a single commercial or industrial sector in which a public
enterprise is not present in at least one of the advanced countries.   It has
already been mentioned that intervention by the State, or by individual
components of the public sector more often reflects practical considerations than it does ideological motives.   The two fundamental aims of the
public pilot-enterprise are to generate competition in industries which
need this spur to increase productivity, and to implement a rational organisation of the operations and growth of industries in which anarchic conditions have resulted in unacceptably low levels of productivity.   These two
aims may be contradictory in theory, but they can coexist in practice.
Since public pilot-enterprises operate predominantly in oligopolistic
markets, it is even possible occasionally to identify a succession of phases
of tacitly accepted leadership followed by phases in which this leadership
is contested more vigorously, and the public enterprise is forced to deal
with competition.

Although management decisions in public pilot-enterprises may be
taken in the same way as decisions by a private entrepreneur under oligopolistic competition, the State may impose certain external conditions or
constraints, as in the case of natural monopolies.   The only difference is
that the management rules for the natural monopolies are here normally
replaced by the rules of competition, which apply to all the enterprises.
The supplementary constraints imposed by the public authorities – and
they further call for special controls to ensure that they have been respected
– raise the question of how pilot-enterprises can manage to adapt to the
hard conditions of life in oligopolistic markets.   If their investment, price,
wage, locational, labour force training and other policies are settled for
them by the State without adequate allowance for existing competitive
conditions, the danger is that the enterprises with the lowest profits and
productivity will be the pilot-enterprises.   How then can they stand up to

competition? This depends on their competitors' reactions. The weaker the competition, the more the constraints the State may impose in its interventions in the public enterprises; but if competition strengthens, the State's possibilities of intervention fall away correspondingly. The State may, however, endeavour to transfer to the private enterprises a part of the burden carried by the pilot-enterprise, for example by para-fiscal taxation imposed on the sector in question. It may well be that such tax systems will develop further in Europe.

8   INSTITUTIONAL CONTROL

All the elements required to understand the development of the relations between public enterprises and the private sector are now available, save one, namely, the institutional control of the public enterprise, which determines the existence of a 'workable' structure and behaviour for the public enterprise sector.

The purely legal aspect of this problem has been under study for a long time, but it has only recently received attention by economists. Some authors distinguish two phases of public control, *stewardship*, which covers the prerogatives of the government and of the administration in general, and *verification*, the supervision of management operations, and which may be undertaken by various authorities, administrative, juridical or parliamentary. This distinction corresponds quite closely to the distinction in this paper between control over the external conditions or constraints imposed by the State in discharging its permanent and indirect instrumental functions, and control of rational management of public enterprises as it has been described in the preceding section.

It seems preferable, however, to distinguish between three types of control. These are:

—*statutory control* which flows from legal status and is exercised by the organs of the public enterprise;
—*policy control*, the selection of the main lines of development of the public enterprise by reference to the general interest;
—*confirmatory control*, ex post examination of working methods, accounting and financial results, and the extent of implementation of the main objectives.

(a) *Statutory control* tends to divide into two parts, external and internal control. The first is undertaken by agencies outside the public enterprise.

These agencies' activities are a counterpart of the general liberty of management action conferred on the directing organs of the enterprise, which includes the power to set prices, to determine the appropriation of profits, to formulate borrowing policy, and to decide the volume and allocation of the factors of production used in the productive process. These powers may be wholly in the hands of the public enterprise, or as in Italy, for example, they may be shared with such intermediate organisms as the public establishments (I.R.I. and E.N.I.) or the sectoral holding companies (FINSIDER). Nor should the external control neglect the problem of the representation of minority interests. The present tendency is for company law progressively to extend the degree of protection of minority interests in private firms. The same ought to be the case for public enterprises, for mixed enterprises and even more naturally, for subsidiary companies owned jointly with private interests. Turning to internal control, this is realised through the direct participation of the State in the administration of the public enterprise – appointment of the board of directors, replacement of directors, nomination of the managing director and top management.

(b) *Confirmatory control* involves consideration of the general interest to a much greater degree than in the past. The authorities responsible for this control – the Public Accounts Committee, specialised commissions for auditing the accounts of public enterprises, etc. – have gradually tended to extend their verification to include an examination of how far a given public enterprise is operating in line with the general interest. This has led them to request the public authorities to clarify the meaning of 'general interest' in a particular concrete situation, or, if need be, to define the general interest themselves from criteria which have been developed progressively. In this last case, the controlling authorities appear to have an interest which goes beyond the profits of the preceding period. They also seek to assess how far the results were influenced by the external conditions and constraints imposed by the public authorities. In a system of control such as that regulating the public sector in Italy, confirmatory control may be said to be simultaneously governmental (the Ministry of Public Shareholdings), legal (the Public Accounts Committee) and parliamentary (examination of the report on the programme). But it may also be observed that in the last analysis the control relates as much to the State which imposed the constraints as to the enterprise which applied them. Confirmatory control must therefore be subdivided into two distinct categories, control of management and control of the application of the concept of the general interest.   In general, it appears to be undertaken more and more in the framework of 'statutory' control, with State comptrollers or government commissioners taking cognisance of day-to-day management operations.   The authorities which have traditionally been responsible for confirmatory control may tend henceforth to act as an independent court of appeal to pass judgement on a management record which has already been subject to supervision.   They also serve to advise public opinion of the conditions under which the management of the national patrimony by the public enterprises has been undertaken.   Furthermore, the present institutions appear to be developing a sort of 'chamber for evaluation of the general interest' whose functions, however, are still too often dispersed among too many institutions.[1]   An organism of this kind is likely to have its existence confirmed and its role extended in the future, in particular when several divergent interpretations of the general interest can be put forward validly.

(c) *Policy control* is *a priori* control by definition.   It may be implicit, resulting from provisions in the statute of the public enterprise.   This is the case, for example, when procedures are laid down governing increases in capital or borrowing, the acquisition or disposal of industrial assets, depreciation policy, the accumulation and use of reserves, etc.   In point of fact, the existence of a statute cannot prevent the implicit rules being specified in such a general way that the content and methods of implementation of policy control may change over time.   It has been argued that such change would necessitate intervention by the legislative or regulatory authority, and there are countries in which policy control is undertaken primarily by statutory organs or by the administration to which stewardship has been entrusted, in so far as the act setting up the enterprise has so directed.   However, even in those countries whose attitude on this point is the most restrictive, there is also a less formal policy control.   This control may operate on a day-to-day basis within the managerial organs of a public enterprise, or to an ever-increasing degree in specific consultative organisations such as planning commissions, specialised parliamentary committees, or groups of experts specially designated by the responsible administration.

If the term policy control is taken in the general sense of control of general policy concerning the path to be followed by the public enterprise, there are two types to be distinguished, namely short- and long-term

---

[1] One of the most perfected forms of this system is the pre-eminent role played by the Ombudsman in the Scandinavian countries.

control. Short-term control relates essentially to wage and price determination, although in these two fields its application may increase rather
than reduce the amplitude of fluctuations. The arbitrary stabilisation of
wages in the public industrial sector during an inflationary period may
subsequently give rise to catch-up increases when the overheating of the
economy has been moderated, and these may transpire to have been an
adverse factor in generating fresh inflationary pressures. The same is true
of charges for goods and services supplied by administrative bodies
(administrative prices).[1] Some authors have argued that it is preferable
in an inflationary period to use the public sector to mop up excess household purchasing power through high administrative prices rather than to
direct it to other sectors by setting low administrative prices. However,
the opposite policy has regularly been followed in practice, so that short-
term policy control has introduced distortions into the structure of relative
prices, to the detriment of public enterprises. For this reason, it may be
questioned whether short-term policy can really be subject to any control
other than verification of the extent to which current decisions are adequate in terms of the orders of magnitude which are considered as
long-term objectives – target wages, target employment, target prices,
etc.

Long-term policy control is more easily made acceptable to public
enterprises. In most cases, they operate in sectors of activity requiring
what may be called 'heavy' investment; this term relates to slowly amor-
tised indivisible equipment involving massive financing, and whose installation may take several years. It is clear that in these circumstances policy
control based on the short-term economic situation may engender irregular
long-term development, and this in turn leads to higher costs, installation
of a lower quality of equipment, and a lower average rate of growth of the
sector. It can be seen therefore that the two types of policy control, the
first directed to a correct assessment of the long-term needs of the economy,
the second to a rigorous evaluation of financing opportunities for the sector
in the light of the successive phases of the short-term economic situation,
are mutually complementary and reinforcing. For this reason, the bodies
responsible for working out the development programmes of public enterprises must attempt to assess their implications on the assumption of
different cyclical situations at each stage of execution of the programme.
Inversely, governments cannot be refused the right to establish which
sectors of public enterprise activity can be used as a vehicle for a short-

---

[1] Postage rates, rail fares, electricity tariffs etc., to the extent that the services in
question are furnished by public sector bodies, or their prices fixed by them.

term recovery or stabilisation policy, so long as the long-term programmes of these sectors are not affected thereby. Studies of this question in Great Britain[1] show that although the general trend of investment in the public sector is less likely than the private sector to vary in the light of the cyclical situation, the opposite is true of short-term changes in investment expenditures. The statistics of public enterprise investment outlays show that there are marked quarter-to-quarter variations; these create delays in the realisation of long-term programmes. The public enterprises will of course attempt to catch up on the schedule once inflationary pressures have been satisfactorily contained, but the result may nevertheless be some inefficiency in carrying out growth programmes and an increase in costs which is not compensated by the benefit from the minor contribution to anti-cyclical policy.

9 THE INFLUENCE OF MARKETS

Traditionally, the managements of most public enterprises consider that their main contribution to the general welfare is through their function of production. Provision of a public service is understood to mean placing certain goods at the disposition of the public, while organising output and distribution in line with the requirements specified by the public authorities. It is therefore easy to see why public enterprises in the past have been more interested in supply factors and the growth of output than they have been in the nature of demand. This attitude was strengthened still further in Europe by the scarcities and underconsumption of the immediate post-war period. The emphasis placed on the allocative function is clear in the case of natural monopolies, but it is found too in the case of public holding corporations, which also deal with a product of which stocks are limited, to wit, borrowable funds. But even those public enterprises which operate in a competitive sector have often continued to give priority to production and supply problems; until quite recently the basic principles of industrial and commercial management applied by the majority of public enterprises related to such matters as the availability of adqeuate capacity and the organisation of an appropriate allocation of production as between different users. User demand, however, has a major competitor when the conditions of product allocation are being settled, in the form of the public authorities who will quite willingly assume the right to define which consumer needs ought to be satisfied, and the hierarchy of preference scales. Moreover, consumers will be placed, either as individuals or as

[1] See W. G. Shepherd, op. cit. (1965) ch. 8.

representatives of interest groups, on the board of directors of a public enterprise. The belief that the consumer must be represented in the decision-making bodies of the public enterprise, and that he has the democratic right to make his voice heard when important decisions are being taken, is still firmly held in governments and public enterprises at the present time.

Emphasis on the production and distribution of goods has an influence on the view of the market's operation taken by the public enterprise. The fact that the volume of output has been fixed, price scales decided, and distribution techniques selected with the co-operation of all the interested social groups leads to the final result being considered as equivalent to the result emerging from the operation of an ideally functioning competitive market: gone the imperfections resulting from inadequately informed market operators, gone the waste created by cut-throat competition, gone the exploitation of consumer surplus. The public enterprise acts, it is true, as an arbitrary allocator, but as an allocator aiming to maximise the utility derived by customers from his goods or services; the situation is one of a 'quasi-market'. This approach, which is neither very old nor very rare, has in many cases been adopted in the private sector too. Contagion from the public sector has been rendered all the easier to the extent that the private firms were running a sectoral monopoly, that there was a latent product scarcity, and the State or its administrative bodies in a position directly to control the decisions taken. In Europe, however, the concept has crumbled away in the public sector itself with the ending of scarcities and the extension of the public sector. Competition from substitute products and the entry of public enterprises into more competitive sectors have progressively educated both the public enterprises and their private competitors. It is, of course, still possible for public enterprises to limit competition by requesting privileged treatment from the public authorities or by continuing to play an allocative role in an industry which has been cartellised. As a general rule, however, public enterprises have attempted to adjust to the normal operation of the market, although with occasional manipulation in order to accomplish a special task entrusted them by the public authorities. The consequence is that on the supply side, markets in which public enterprises operate have special characteristics which differentiate them from the normal oligopolistic market.

If we consider the labour market, the market for input materials and the product market, we find the public enterprise having a quite different outlook from the private firm, even where the two are in competition:

(a) Public enterprises take no account of the reactions of private employers on the labour market, even if the eventual result is a loss of qualified or competent manpower. The private firms in the French engineering industry have thus reaped considerable benefit from the occupational training given in the apprenticeship centres of the nationalised Renault automobile firm.

(b) No attempt is made by them in collective bargaining to raise issues of factor competition, labour saving investment or potential recourse to immigrant manpower.

(c) Systematic use is made *vis-à-vis* suppliers of formally competitive procedures in the issue of invitations to tender, but in practise there is a preference for guaranteed availability of supplies, for national suppliers, for materials which have been inspected on the premises of sub-contractors, and, in particular, for integrated supplies. This situation is found, for example, in the relations of national munitions factories with their supply network.

(d) Public enterprises have only an incidental interest in the supply techniques used by their competitors.

(e) They may ignore competition from substitutes for a considerable length of time; they may even ignore direct competition: European public enterprises were very late in adopting modern advertising techniques.

(f) They are interested in competitors' production and distribution techniques only in exceptional cases. This results from the fact that public enterprises have often had a technical or administrative advantage in competing with private firms.

The attitude of private firms to public enterprises in these three markets (labour, input, product) is often completely different. To them, the behaviour of the public sector is a fixed datum in the process of selecting their own options:

(1) The wage scales and fringe benefits adopted in the public sector are used as reference standards and upper limits for their operations on the labour market.

(2) Individuals' remuneration may vary more from the average than in the public sector, for example, to allow for a greater level of skill – often with a preference for skills learnt in a centre run by the competing public enterprise.

(3) Private firms are more likely to bargain for better terms from suppliers than their public competitor; they hesitate to bind themselves

to a single supplier over the long term, even when the subcontract provisions allow for control.

(4) Private enterprise pays greater attention to ruling market conditions, and also to competitors' present and probable future behaviour. They make no attempt to modify the decisions of the competing public enterprise, but integrate them into their own decisions as a parameter.

These differences between the behaviour of private and public enterprises find their natural expression in markets, and lead to decisions which have been approached from different viewpoints and have different outcomes, doubtless with greater regularity so far as the public enterprise is concerned, and with greater variability – and therefore flexibility – in private firms. It may readily be deduced that the extra-market relations of public and private enterprises will diverge in similar fashion to their intra-market relations. However, this point calls for further specification: to the extent that there is State intervention in the private sector, either by generalised application of the instrumental function or through the medium of joint bodies such as planning commissions, there will be a certain parallelism between such decisions of the private and public enterprises as are not wholly governed by market considerations; these include questions of the volume of investment, research expenditures, geographical location, staff training etc. By contrast, if the instrumental function is exercised solely in respect of the public sector, any parallelism in decision taking or coherence of action can only follow from acceptance by private enterprise of the distortions imposed by the public sector, as a trade-off for external economies arising from public sector decisions. There is a big difference between coherence of decision taking which stems from the spreading of burdens imposed by the State over all enterprises in a sector, and the coherence which reflects recognition of an inevitable constraint tempered by substantial advantages. It is difficult to specify concretely what the present position is, so closely interwoven are the two forces which which promote parallelism in decision-taking. These forces are countered by others working in favour of restriction of the public sector (section 10). They are reinforced by still others which make for the compartmentalisation of the economy as a result of public sector decisions (section 11), and those which, in the opposite direction, promote changes in the attitudes of public enterprises (section 11).

10 SECTORS SUITABLE FOR PUBLIC ENTERPRISE

The public enterprise sector has long benefited from privileges accorded by the authorities, initially intended to balance the exceptional costs attaching to the nature of the services for which responsibility was taken. In this context, the statute of each enterprise was specifically tailored to its needs, and control procedures served mainly to verify the effectiveness of the trade-off between burdens and privileges. Private enterprises are now in an analogous situation. Each firm has its own particular statute, based on its individual relations with the public authorities. Like a public enterprise, it may receive subsidies, be awarded advantageous contracts, or benefit from privileges connected with the execution of particular projects. At one time there was a marked tendency in European government circles to argue in favour of the 'specialised nature' of action involving public enterprise; particular functions, together with associated special privileges were in principle, it was felt, best discharged by public enterprises. A listing of the main characteristics of the particular burdens carried in connection with the instrumental function has already been given: the acceptance of social costs, the generation of external economies to the benefit of other sectors. It was also assumed during this period that these particular functions could not be evaluated in money terms, and that the services rendered weren it such as could be invoiced to those who benefited from them, sometimes unknowingly. Much stress is often laid on the role of external economies in the growth of global sector productivity, but it has proven impossible to find exact statistical measures of productivity and to allocate it among different sectors. For this reason, proposals were advanced to select sectors of specialisation to be reserved solely for public enterprise, these sectors to include all productive activities responsible for major external economies. A policy of this kind is occasionally envisaged as a way of 'containing' the public sector. At other times, it has represented a full-scale programme of progressive extension of public enterprise, in so far as the majority of sectors produce a greater or lesser volume of external effects to the benefit of economic agents as a whole.

However, the development of planning techniques has caused the policy of 'specialised sectors' to be abandoned. French housing policy may be taken as an example. This sector is clearly capable of supplying a number of external economies to industry: availability throughout the country of sufficient dwellings to promote geographical mobility of labour, and through concomitant shifts in the location of industry, to increase labour productivity in all branches of activity; but they have been late in coming.

Application of planning methods showed that this objective could be reached by co-operation between private and public enterprises. It has even been contended recently that the only specialised sectors to be brought into the ambit of public enterprise in future should be those in which specialisation is capable of producing temporary or permanent external economies, to the extent that the activities in question are the subject of freely discussed political options accepted by the majority. In present-day society, these activities outside the scope of the plan should, however, be reduced as far as possible, and their effects subjected to careful scrutiny.

11 CONSISTENCY OF DECISIONS

The role of public enterprises in the planning process has often been stressed.[1] The various French plans, the recent Italian and British programmes and the first medium-term economic programme of the Common Market all confirm the function of the public enterprise in the development and execution of the plan. In all these cases, a large sector containing the public enterprises, fairly homogeneous as to structure and management techniques, ensuring the presence of the public authority in new activities, controlling the operation of the key sectors for economic development, and, by means of a kind of systematic compartmentalisation, providing a framework for the economy as a whole, is considered as one of the most important institutional conditions for the implementation of long-term growth policies. It follows, by reason of the residual role played by private enterprise, that decisions in the private sector are almost by necessity compatible with the decisions of public enterprise and the recommendations of the plan: private firms have little other choice than to operate within the framework of procedures implemented by the planning authorities. Despite the tendency for public enterprise in Europe to pay greater heed to market factors, the assumption that a public sector is being formed in Europe which is both relatively homogeneous and spread among an increasing number of activities seems reasonable. The so-called 'law of vertical disintegration'[2] has acted in favour of this development. Whereas at one time it was sufficient to control basic industries to ensure that directives reached the whole of the manufacturing sector, the control of final activities, in particular the distribution of final products, now plays an increasingly efficient role in this process. This trend has forced the old

---

[1] See in particular P. Saraceno, 'Planning in Public Undertakings', *Annals of Collective Economy*, xxxiv (1965) 71 ff.

[2] *Loi du 'renversement des intégrations verticales'.*

natural monopolies to diversify to some extent, and progressively to abandon their traditional activities in the basic sectors. The closure of coalmines in Europe, which has been accelerating since 1957 has been accompanied by the entry of the Coal Boards into sectors which are far removed from the raw material which was at one time the touchstone of State intervention. The French National Railway System is closing branch lines with one hand and increasing its stake in air transport with the other.

The public sector is homogeneous in the sense that it promotes its own growth by applying the old principle of cross-subsidisation, financing entry into new markets by using the profits earned in declining activities.[1] Public enterprises usually succeed in setting up a subsidiary, either alone or in collaboration with a competitor, at the end use stage of the extremely competitive manufacturing and distributive sectors. This dispersion may also be explained by the desire to be in a position rapidly to implement a particular aim taken up by the public authorities in any sector and at any time. This compartmentalisation of the economy through public enterprise is in progress in several European countries, including Italy, Austria and France.

In these circumstances, there may be concern that public enterprises will follow a somewhat nationalist policy, unless the national authorities accept rules guaranteeing a kind of internationalisation of the objectives of public enterprises. Private business, subject to the pressures of this frame, would then go in the same direction; and the concept of a national enterprise forms no part of the economist's analytical tool-kit. In practice, however, the decisions of private enterprise are attracted to two opposite poles, whose magnetic properties consist respectively of the existence of a coherent ensemble of national public enterprises, and the development of a nucleus of multinational businesses whose operations are based on the mechanisms of world markets, the international division of labour and the free play of competition. However, the decentralised structure of the great international firms facilitates their adaptation to different local situations. This works in favour of strengthening the attraction of public enterprises. There is a continuing trend for private enterprise to make common cause with public enterprise. At the outset, there is a simple system of market leadership, with domination by the public enterprise. This has been transformed over the past ten years into a simultaneous collaboration-contest process. Collaboration becomes all

---

[1] Unfortunately, cross subsidisation more often works the other way round: the profitable sectors of the public enterprise subsidise those which are in decline.

the more necessary at the national level because the market is small while the projects to be realised in common are large; contest, in that the private firm is continually drawn outside the national orbit by activities which oblige it to slacken the links which bind it to the national public enterprise.

The consistency of decision-taking by private and public enterprises in a planned but open economy is the consequence of a dual acknowledgement. Firstly, there is the acknowledgement by the planners responsible for coordinating the investment decisions of the public enterprise sector, setting prices, or ordering supplies, of the implications of the opening of the economy to foreign competition. Thus the scope for irrational, antieconomic or discriminatory actions is gradually being reduced.[1] Secondly, there is the acknowledgement by private business of the influence of the options accepted by the public enterprises as characteristic elements of the operation of their own markets. It is up to the private firm to balance off the advantages derived from the presence of major public decision-taking centres against the distortions and other handicaps resulting from the economic setting provided by the public enterprise. In France, this compensation is discussed in the modernisation commissions of the plan, sector by sector; and the more marked the influence of the public sector, or the less the extent to which public decisions align with the conditions of foreign competition, the livelier the discussion. It follows that the modernisation commissions ought normally to be the forum for ensuring the coherence of decisions, at least the most important of them, those concerning investment. Experience shows that disagreement has often been registered in these discussions when they have taken place, as for example, in the meetings for the automobile sector in the fourth and fifth plans. But in most cases, these discussions in the vertical commissions have carefully avoided this and many other important subjects, such as industrial structure.

So far as decisions affecting the day to day conduct of affairs are concerned on such questions as wages, credit or prices – private enterprise may contest certain decisions taken by public enterprises either on an individual basis (e.g. when an order is placed by a public enterprise, or the public enterprise raises its rates), or collectively through employer federations. In the latter case, the private firms attempt to have the rules which affect their own decisions modified in their favour, or such questions as

---

[1] This consequence has already been analysed by P. Bauchet, *Propriété publique et planification* (Paris, Cujas, 1962). See also J. Marchal, 'Les Décisions d'investissement dans les entreprises publiques', *Annals of Collective Economy*, XXXV (1964) 264 ff.

price, credit or wage control, geographical location, etc., rather than to constrain the public enterprise to change its policy.

However, dirigist intervention by the stewardship authorities affecting both public and private enterprises is the most frequently used procedure for maintenance of formal coherence between the decisions of the two groups, in the context of the general or sectoral policies adopted by the public authorities. Two specific examples of this procedure, which is intended to set the limits of the field of choice of the private enterprise once the main public decisions have been taken, are provided by stability contracts (*contrats de stabilité*) between the administration and an industry, or by individual exemptions granted following specific applications by private industrialists.

There is a considerable difference between the coherence of decision-taking which results from an automatic adjustment between the two types of decision-taking units, private and public, and the coherence which is imposed from above by the stewardship authorities. Recourse to the second method is generally the outcome of a setback reflecting either bad will or incapability on the part of those concerned. Causes may be, in the case of public enterprise, a refusal to adjust to changed market conditions, the maintenance of declining activities, excessive emphasis on irrational objectives etc., while factors operative in the case of private enterprise may be the inability to meet external competitive conditions, or to use the existing national environment to the best advantage. It is therefore often the case that dirigistic action in the form of authoritative price setting is the best way to impose price scales on private enterprise which will enable it to compete with foreign suppliers, and that judicious government procurement is the best way to induce structural change and increased efficiency.

Attention has already been drawn to the propagation of public enterprise through shareholdings and the creation of new subsidiaries, most often jointly with the private sector but occasionally in association with other public enterprises. Shareholding is not merely a technique for extension of the public sector. Its essential feature is that it provides a means of co-operation between private and public enterprise, a way of injecting private enterprise into sectors which can no longer remain the exclusive preserve of the great public corporations, or, on the contrary, a way of ensuring realisation of major projects to which the state cannot remain indifferent, but which are beyond the scope of private capital acting in isolation. This development will be regretted by some, welcomed by others, it spells the end of the segregation of public enterprise, and the abandonment of the thesis of specialisation. Some authors believe that this infiltration by the public sector prepares the way for a fresh bout of major nationalisation projects. There are others whose view is that growing participation in the activity of the private sector is a dilution of the activities of public enterprises, and a neglect of what ought to be their essential functions as defined in their statute.

One need not necessarily agree with either of these two extreme views. On the one hand, there seems little point in the State undertaking fresh nationalisations in order to vary the existing relationship between public and private enterprise when there exist more flexible ways of introducing public sector participation where technological process calls for modification of the existing structure of production. On the other hand, while it is reasonable to avoid the dilution of authority which follows from State participation in minor industrial activities, this is no reason for failing to undertake new State intervention where this is necessary. In contemporary nations, particularly in Europe, this dilemma can be resolved by distinguishing public activities into two sectors, the first a State-run sector limited to essential activities, a sector into which entry by private enterprise is so onerous as to be difficult if not impossible, and in which there is wider scope for non-economic decision taking, the second a mixed sector containing purely State-owned enterprises, mixed private-public enterprises, and purely privately owned firms. In this second sector coexistence of enterprises with different statutes is not the result of a distribution of activities according to their statute – activities which are unprofitable for public enterprise, new activities calling for joint ventures, activities which can profitably be undertaken by private enterprise – but it can be ensured by closer standardisation of norms of control. A certain degree of similarity can already be recognised in such sectors between the statutory control applied to public enterprises and the control exercised by the relevant organs of limited companies (control by supervisory boards, auditors, general meetings of shareholders). It may of course be argued that the control of public enterprises is generally more severe, and more effective, than is the case for private enterprise, at least in Europe. All this means is that the control mechanisms of private enterprise have not developed efficiently enough in the past. In various countries in Europe, the public authorities are at present attempting to reinforce the frame in which private business operates by reforming company law.

These trends should bring the control rules applied to public and private enterprise in the mixed sector into closer alignment. Thus the return of public enterprises to the private sector, which may result from an improved orientation of controls in these firms as easily as it may reflect the growth of the number of enterprises in which both the public and private sector have holdings, is accompanied by a structural reform of the private sector whose effect is to improve its capacity to adjust to new definitions of the general interest. We are not yet at the stage where the shares of the great public enterprises are quoted on the stock exchange. But if we examine the joint ventures in which public enterprise participates, and draw up a consolidated balance sheet of their activity, the conclusion is that this process is happening in the case of a certain number of European public enterprises, as it happened a long time ago for public utilities in the United States. A return to private ownership in the mixed sector is thus compatible with expansion of the activity of the public sector. This contrasts with the effect of new nationalisation, which increases the degree of segregation at the same time as a considerable volume of fresh capital funds, in the form of compensation for expropriation, is put in the hands of the public.[1]

Given the present outlook for population growth in Western Europe, the mere maintenance of past growth rates depends basically on the increase of productivity per employed person. It would be wrong to minimise the importance of productivity increases resulting from transfer of manpower from less to more productive sectors, and from the flow of productive investment within individual sectors. However, it is the author's view that in many economies, and particularly in France, productivity growth stemming from these two factors has to a large extent been hampered if not stifled, by the absence (or presence in insufficient quantity) of what may be called 'the permissive factor' – the volume of annual infrastructural investment, or the rate at which the collective equipment available to the economy is renewed.

Realisation of the potential economies of scale in productive sectors which technological progress has brought within reach is conditioned by improvements in education, urban organisation, health, and road and air transport infrastructures, to mention only a few. It has often been pointed out in private industry that the same equipment, *caeteris paribus*, produces extremely different results in different countries. This gap, which measures the difference between the external economies transferred by national environments to a given unit of output, can be an important factor in international trade; and it can influence the living standards and collective welfare of whole peoples, as well as their growth.

---

[1] The methods employed to indemnify former shareholders gave rise to considerable protest when E.N.E.L. was set up in Italy, and again when steel was renationalised in Great Britain.

The public authorities must deal with two distinct problems if the organisation and operation of the economy is to confer the maximum benefit in terms of effectively used external economies:

(a) Minimisation of imperfections in the sector responsible for the renewal of collective equipment.
(b) Maximisation of the external economies available to directly productive sectors and minimisation of the imperfections in these industries, which must adapt themselves progressively to the new possibilities opened up by the renewal of collective equipment.

In most cases, the job of renewing collective equipment is entrusted to public enterprises, acting in association with mixed enterprises. Investment decisions in the collective equipment sector should therefore aim to maximise the rate of renewal of collective equipment within the limits of an overall budgetary constraint, taken as given for present purposes. In the second place, pricing and other management decisions of public enterprises should be so taken that the external economies transferred by the collective equipment are the greatest possible. Finally, to ensure renewal of this equipment in satisfactory conditions, the industries responsible for concrete projects – the construction and civil engineering industries, the electrical and machinery industries, the ferrous and non-ferrous metal industries – must all be in a position to adjust in quality and in quantity to the new public demand.

The mechanisms required to realise these objectives are usually those of a planned economy. Different mechanisms may of course be used in different countries. In some cases, the programmes for collective equipment will be presented as an overall package, as is done in France, Great Britain and Italy. By contrast, in other cases they may be presented as separate projects; this is done in Germany, the Netherlands and the United States. The programmes may be open for more or less independent implementation by local and regional authorities, as they are in Germany and in the Vth French Plan. Elsewhere they may remain entirely under the control of the central authorities, or divide up into two categories, federal or central programmes on the one hand, and local or regional programmes on the other.

There are cases in which large private enterprises have a noticeable influence on the generation and transmission of external economies. Where this is so, their attention should be drawn to the effect of alternative investment projects from the standpoint of the general interest.

The objective it is sought to attain by having major investment decisions by the private sector controlled by those responsible for planning is a praiseworthy one. Public enterprises have from time to time been set up in the supplying sectors – construction, civil engineering, construction and engineering materials, etc., and they have an important role to play in sign-posting the way for private firms to adjust to the new demand emanating from the public sector. However, in these mixed sectors, planning mechanisms must be meshed with market mechanisms so as to maintain effective competition in the execution of orders placed by the public sector. The attempt made by the French planners to promote the organisation and adjustment of supplying industries was an almost total failure, both in concentrated activities such as the supply of girders or non-ferrous metals for construction operations, and in predominantly small-firm sectors such as construction materials or industrial construction products. Recourse to authoritarian directives by the stewardship authorities has often had to re-place the adjustments which the planning authorities and the pilot enterprises had hoped the private sector would have been led to undertake voluntarily.

The problem to be solved in the 'directly productive' sectors is not any simpler; it consists of the elimination of the imperfections in the private sector and correction of its inability to adapt to market conditions.

Two types of adjustment procedures may be applied in these sectors. The first involves recourse to the market mechanism, either in the form of competition between pilot enterprises and private business, or by initiating the adjustment process through the award of provisional subsidies which, if they distort competitive conditions for a time, enable the firms in question to operate more efficiently afterwards. This last method was employed in Italy to promote the development of the new industrial growing points at Bari and Taranto. The second adjustment procedure consists of State intervention to offset market deficiencies. Actions under this heading include arbitrary relocation, regrouping of private firms judged to be inefficient, and occasionally even arbitrary specification of price or production levels.

12 SOME CONCLUSIONS

In conclusion, a number of suggestions will be made for measures to be applied in Europe, and more particularly in the E.E.C., to improve the consistency of decisions taken by public and private enterprises.

1 *An attempt to harmonise the statute of public enterprises.* This harmonisation is extremely necessary. It is open to some enterprises to develop

Q

by diversification into new sectors, but in other cases, diversification can only follow a modification of statute. Furthermore, in Europe today, the differences in respect of such questions as the definition and application of control, stewardship, nomination of Board members, direct State intervention, regulation of competition with private enterprise, etc., are still too great. In this field as in others, rapid agreement on a schedule for aligning the legislation of the various E.E.C. countries is called for.

(2) *Improvement of control by the collectivity of public enterprises' policies.* Planning methods have obviously not yet resulted in provision of public enterprises with clear instructions on the relative importance of their different tasks and the direct and indirect effects on the economy which they should have. Better sectoral studies by the planning services, particularly of sectors supplying collective investment goods, are required to specify these aims, both on a national and international (E.E.C., O.E.C.D.) scale.

(3) *Improvement of* ex post *collective control of public enterprises.* It is indispensable for modern states and for the economic agents affected, in particular private enterprises, to be informed of the profits and growth of public enterprises during preceding financial periods. Improvements in information have been made by the public enterprises themselves, but it would be useful to have reports by control authorities such as the public accounts committee or the competent administrative commissions, published with the minimum delay.

(4) *Improvement of conditions of State use of public enterprises to further economic policy.* A first approach is to request governments to limit the fields in which they intervene through the medium of public enterprises. A second is to avoid using certain techniques of direct intervention through public enterprises, in particular where they involve discriminatory actions.

(5) *Application to public enterprises of common law provisions governing competition.* This would be implemented not only in sectors in which public and private enterprise are in competition, but also for development of competitive relations between national monopolies and foreign producers.

(6) *Constitution of a number of multi-national public enterprises.* Most often, such enterprises would have limited aims, e.g. common exploitation

of large-scale equipment, as for the channel tunnel. But in the longer run, it is possible to conceive of public enterprise in a productive sector on a European scale, such, for example as might result from a Renault–Volkswagen merger, or fusion of the Italian E.N.I. and the new French petroleum enterprise, E.R.A.P. Doubtless it would be over-optimistic to expect rapid developments in this direction, to the extent that the accounting of public and private enterprises continues to be verified in terms of national territories rather than with respect to the real markets, which coincide to a progressively diminishing extent with existing national frontiers.

21 The Coherence of Public Enterprises: planning *v.* market forces[1]

P. Bauchet

1 INTRODUCTORY

This paper deals with the coherence only of public enterprises,[2] leaving public administration and the public financial sector to be discussed in other reports. Two sets of questions are involved in the coherence on public enterprises:

(1) The compatibility of budgetary expenditure occasioned by the activity of public enterprises, that is, grants and subsidies, with budgetary expenditure elsewhere in the public sector and with budgetary revenue. This implies the definition of the optimum level and distribution of expenditure as between activities concerned with public health, social purposes, education, transport, etc., and lies outside the scope of this paper, which deals with public enterprises only.

(2) The compatibility of the policies of public enterprises. The best-known aspect of this question is that of co-ordinating investment and production, given that public enterprises, with the help of public funds, often engage in sterile competition. But more generally speaking, there is an obvious case for policy co-ordination in all fields.

Here the further question arises whether coherence is a matter which concerns public enterprises alone and ought to apply only within their sector. If this is to be so, the implication is that public enterprises are to

[1] Translation from the French by Elizabeth Henderson.

[2] Annex I reproduces the full list of public enterprises in France as contained in an Annex of the Finance Act. It includes all firms, excluding subsidiaries, in which more than 30% of the capital is in public hands. However, the figures given in the tables of this report refer, not to the above full list, but only to those enterprises which are considered as such in the French national accounts; they are enumerated in Annex II.

Annex II lists enterprises classified by economic sectors, in three categories: Public services in industry and trade, economic intervention agencies, and nationalised firms. The first are subject to close official control, the second extend the action of public administration, and the third have a management system similar to that of private firms.

be treated apart, that the price policy of the public sector, say, in transport (State Railways, Air France) is different from the price policy of competing private firms.

Are there any special reasons why the sector of public enterprises should thus be withdrawn from the market and its activities governed by the decisions of public authorities? Should we attribute it to the fact that the government should find it easier to intervene in its own sphere? Is it the absence of competition? Or is it because public enterprises need to be assigned purposes of general interest?

The question to be analysed first is: Should government, within the setting of the Common Market, establish a separate policy for the public enterprises under its control and thus make sure of a kind of coherence peculiar to the public sector, or should this be left to the market forces?

A few introductory remarks about the effectiveness of planning in the creation of policy coherence among public enterprises may here be in order; they draw on the example of my own country, France.

2 PLANNING AND THE COHERENCE OF THE PUBLIC SECTOR IN FRANCE

Some of the government decisions affecting the public sector in France have to do with medium-term objectives under the economic plan, others with short-term, cyclical policies.

(A) MEDIUM-TERM DECISIONS

Medium-term decisions relate mostly to production and plant. Such decisions are not taken for all public enterprises, which latter can, from this point of view, be divided into three categories:

(i) those which escape all recurring official decisions regarding the future; this is the case of the nationalised Renault works and of many other nationalised firms, mostly in the third category of national accounting;

(ii) those for which the volume of investment is laid down in the plan and the necessary finance provided from budgetary funds, but without any explicit definition of details; this is the case of firms in the national accounting category of public services in industry and trade (public housing boards, hospitals, etc.);

(iii) those whose investment figures in the plan and for which the manner of financing is laid down in detail; this category includes only firms in the energy and transport sectors, excluding petroleum.

In case (iii), the procedures of decision are as follows:

(a) The amount of investment in plant and equipment for a five-year period is determined as part of planning at the Commissariat Général au Plan, in consultation with the Minister concerned, the Finance Minister, the General Commissioner of Planning and members of the modernisation commissions concerned, namely, those of energy and transport. The government does not stop short of specifying the nature of the equipment to be used, if such a decision is thought to be in the national interest; thus the air companies had to choose certain types of aircraft, and Électricité de France a particular type of process ('filière') for the production of nuclear energy.

(b) The manner in which this investment is to be financed is laid down on the advice of the Conseil de Direction, the Board of Directors of the Economic and Social Development Fund. This is an institution in which the authors of the Plan play a key part; it approves the programmes for fixed investment, and lays down the order of priorities, the expenditure ceiling and the manner of financing each programme. If the traditional resources of the public enterprises prove insufficient, the Fund makes up the shortfall by credits. However, the Conseil de Direction intervenes in public enterprises only if they belong to the energy or transport sector.

To safeguard the progress of investment programmes stretching over several years, other procedures were used in their time, especially the so-called programming laws. But these are of no practical significance any more today.

(c) The programmes for enterprises in the energy and transport sectors are defined once a year. The managers of the companies concerned submit to the government an application for authorisation of new investment. The special committees and the Board of Directors of the Economic and Social Development Fund approve the programme discussions, the representatives of the Commissariat au Plan and officials from the Ministry responsible and the Finance Ministry try to reconcile the planning targets, the cost of the programmes and the national financial imperatives – in other words, they see how they can both implement the plan and meet the demands of short-term policy.

The reason why government takes so much interest in the equipment of nationalised firms in these two sectors is that the relevant investment programmes account for a sizeable part of total investment and, as Table 1 shows, are financed in large part by public funds. Nevertheless, only new expenditure is subject to careful review.

Apart from medium-term decisions of this kind, the public sector is the scene of intervention of a much more short-term nature.

(B) SHORT-TERM INTERVENTION

Short-term intervention is geared to cyclical developments and may be concerned with prices and wages.

TABLE ONE

CONTRIBUTIONS OF VARIOUS SOURCES OF FINANCE TO
TOTAL INVESTMENT OF NATIONALISED ENTERPRISES[1]

(per cent)

Source of Finance	1963 Outturn	1964 Provisional Figures	1965 Initial Estimates
Capital endowment funds	2		
Extraordinary subsidies	10·5	7	8
Investment subsidies	0·5	1	4
Self-financing net of loan repayment [2] and excluding extraordinary subsidies	2	12	12
Long-term loans	80	76	73
of which: public loans	40	31	38
from economic and Social Development Fund	32	28	23
from *Caisse des Dépôts*	8	16	12
miscellaneous		1	
Medium-term loans (prefinancing)	2	4	1
Percentage of investment so financed	97	100	98
Carry-over	3	0	2
Percentage ratio of depreciation and contingency reserves to investment	54	53	51

[1] Enterprises concerned: C.E.A., Charbonnages, E.D.F., G.D.F., Compagnie Nationale du Rhône, S.N.C.F., R.A.T.P., Aéroport de Paris, Air France.
[2] The self-financing share would be much larger if loan repayments were not deducted, namely, 22 per cent in 1963 and 27% in 1964 and 1965.
Source: *10th Report of the Economic and Social Development Fund*, p. 26 or 247.

(a) The prices of goods and services are a matter of close concern to the government which, in its battle against inflation, often does not resist the temptation to freeze first the prices of its own enterprises. The products of these latter, it is true, account for a sizeable part of family budgets (11 per cent, of which 4 per cent for heating alone) and expenditure on producer goods. Beyond containing price rises in general, the government discriminates in favour of certain social groups or regions. For instance, the State potassium mines of Alsace have to sell fertilisers at a fixed price so as to keep down costs in agriculture. Similarly, in the interests of regional development electricity and transport tariffs are often uneconomic. Caught in the dilemma of working toward a true price system, as insistently recommended by the Fifth Plan, or else choosing a price level which fits in with short-term stabilisation policy, the government thought it right to sacrifice the first alternative.

This policy jeopardises the public sector's medium-term growth targets. Consumer choices are not those which would result from a comparison of true prices, and no longer correspond to the projections. These disturbances might lead to imbalance between real investment demand and planned production. Any company, incidentally, whose prices are frozen finds itself faced with a growing internal deficit. In some cases, this had led firms to cut down on planned investment projects, and invariably they turn to the government for help. But government aid depends closely on the cyclical situation, and the development of public enterprises thus becomes subject to chance factors hard to reconcile with medium-term targets.

(b) Wage-fixing, too, is essentially a matter of short-term policy. Incomes policy is still in its infancy in France, is barely defined and is at present of a purely indicative character. The government uses its own public sector to keep down wages, as it does prices, and this sharpens labour unrest. The firms are deprived of all power, since the negotiations are conducted over their heads by trade unions and government authorities, and wages themselves are ruled by short-term considerations. It is hardly surprising, in these circumstances that the various collective procedures for determining wages in a rational and balanced manner have run into discordance and abrupt stoppages which compromise the chances of medium-term development policies.

It cannot be said, therefore, that public decisions have as much coherence as might be wished. Nor is this all. The situation may get worse as the frontiers open up. The Common Market is, at this stage already, responsible for the tightening up of countercyclical policies, for the priority accorded to price stability and for the retrenchment of certain investment projects. With progressively more and more freedom of trade, the markets for the goods and services of public enterprises will no doubt become more subject to cyclical fluctuations and it will become correspondingly more difficult to carry out medium-term projects. In France as in other countries of the European Economic Community, people are beginning to wonder whether the market will supersede government in ruling the public sector. But can the market ensure coherence? And if so, should it be left to do so?

3 COHERENCE THROUGH THE MARKET OR THROUGH PLANNING?

As the trade barriers fall, the first reaction of governments is to protect their public sectors and to rescue them from a market which threatens to upset them. In France, all the authorities need do is to go further in manipulating the variables already under their control, that is, production, investment, sales prices, wages and finance funds. Certainly, it would be well to do away with the present incoherences by allowing for medium-term targets in fixing prices and wages. It would also be well to broaden the field of medium-term programming, for which in France, at present, the Plan and the Economic and Social Development Fund are responsible, and to extend it beyond the energy and transport sectors to other enterprises, especially to state-controlled petroleum companies and to subsidiaries in which public enterprises have a majority interest. Nor does it seem unfeasible to bring the whole public sector within the scope of planning supported by a range of finance facilities for implementation. If, therefore, the government should wish to adopt a policy of this kind, it does not lack the means of intervention to do so.

But in actual fact governments have rather less freedom of action. Loth as they are to leave the coherence of the public sector to the sole play of market forces, governments come up against obstacles to public intervention even on the present scale.

(A) LIMITATIONS OF THE MARKET IN GOVERNING PUBLIC ENTERPRISES

It is not possible here to do more than list the chief arguments put forward to justify public intervention.

(a) The redistribution of income. This fundamental aim of public intervention has for long been one of the motive forces of 'nationalisation'. Governments today are rightly asking themselves how this redistribution can be achieved, and conclude that it is better to proceed directly by means of taxes or subsidies than indirectly through the price policy of the public enterprises – a policy which has too often led to a faulty redistribution.

(b) The danger of regional imbalances. As the market expands, economic activities tend to relocate themselves around the most dynamic centres – in the case of the Common Market, the triangle Paris, Hamburg, Milan. The least favoured regions, for instance western France, are exposed to the danger of rapid decline. The government tries to use its enterprises to help these regions preserve a reasonable level of activity; examples are the location of nuclear power stations in central France and Britanny, or the pressure which is being exercised on the Renault works to put up factories in Normandy. Governments are unwilling to renounce the means by which they can influence the location of their enterprises.

(c) Continuity of supplies. Governments want to be sure of certain basic supplies, especially of energy, not only on the most economic terms but also with guaranteed continuity in the event of cold or hot war. This is something which the market does not provide.

(d) Protection of national producers. Free trade opens up national markets to large foreign concerns incomparably richer in financial resources than European competitors. Rightly or wrongly, governments may wish to protect certain national activities from being crushed and therefore buttress them with the financial power of the budget.

(e) Absence of effective demand. Part of the public sector, that is the enterprises grouped under public services in the French national accounting scheme (see Annex II), such as hospitals, low-cost housing, research centres, etc., furnish services which the market would not furnish because there is no effective demand for them. The government sells goods and services at a low price and keeps a very close watch on their production.

But these arguments are valid only for certain enterprises in the public sector and cannot justify intervention on a comprehensive scale, which comes up against a number of obstacles.

(B) OBSTACLES AGAINST GENERAL INTERVENTION IN THE PUBLIC SECTOR

General intervention goes against the present policy trend and contradicts the market forces.

(a) The present policy trend is for growing liberalisation. The Soviet example is particularly striking. The Soviet government used to work with five target indicators, namely, value of sales, basic commodity composition, profit rate, wage bill, and financial transfers to and from the budget. Now it seems that wages are to be withdrawn altogether from general planning, and in the case of some enterprises the same applies to other indicators. The extreme case is that of road transport depots, for which only one single target is fixed, namely, the amount of tax levied on profits.

In France, it will surely be a logical consequence of the Common Market that the Treasury's discriminatory low-interest loans will have to be discontinued. Even now, the Finance Ministry is moving in this direction. We are witnessing a diminution of the part played by the Economic and Social Development Fund, which is the Treasury's extension and, as we have seen, has a key function in financing and controlling the public sector. The Fund now covers only those requirements which are not met by other sources, namely, self-financing, the capital market and loans from semi-public institutions. Loans from the Fund now cover only 10 per cent of the nationalised firms' investment in plant and equipment, compared with 23 per cent in 1959. As a result, the effectiveness of medium-term planning is impaired, because the authorities can furnish less credit to make sure of the implementation of programmes and these latter are, therefore, less firmly backed by financial guarantees. If this trend should continue, the medium-term investment programmes for the energy and transport sectors will become no more than indicative. All the government would do would be to approve the firms' investment decisions and, if need be, supply them with additional new capital by replenishing their endowment funds. This would also imply leaving the enterprises with far-reaching discretion in fixing their prices, so that they can build up more self-financing funds.

(b) The spontaneous mechanisms of the economy sometimes defeat intervention, or indeed deprive it of all usefulness.

In the labour market, the play of supply and demand has swept away all the barriers which the government had put up against wage rises. The only effect of having unions negotiate with the government instead of employers has been to delay certain wage increases, or rather, in most cases, to induce the management of the firms concerned to camouflage such increases. In an effort to keep their skilled labour, firms are offering all kinds of hidden benefits, such as bonuses, payments in kind or more rapid promotion. In some cases, labour pressure has led to a change in the statute of public enterprises to make room for higher wages; there is no other explanation for the transformation of the former Régie des Tabacs et Allumettes. It follows that it is not merely ineffective, but positively harmful to intervene too strictly in this field, for to do so means disabling the existing institutions and making it impossible to reintroduce order into a wage situation which has become clandestine.

Similarly, market mechanisms react against price controls. We have the telling example of the blocked tariffs for rail transport in the metropolitan and suburban area of Paris. What happened was that demand increased so strongly that it could not be met with the existing equipment, of which there was not enough because it was unprofitable for the firms concerned. The same applies to telephones and to power distribution in rural areas; both are too cheap and new would-be users have to wait a long time before they can be connected up. Sometimes the competing private sector, like road hauliers or private owners of railway carriages, takes advantage of this unsatisfied demand to charge high prices. Soon it will be our European competitors who will take advantage of our controls [1] and will mop up excess traffic maybe even on our own territory.

Competition has indeed infiltrated what used to be considered the public monopolies *par excellence*. Examples are air transport, shipping and land transport in what has become a world market. A whole set of price controls originally intended for the sole purpose of breaking monopolistic power thus loses its point. But is there any use even in rational, and hence not harmful, price controls? To answer that question one would have to be very sure that, left to its own devices, the firm would not follow a price policy which in the end effect was much the same as one imposed upon it by a government determined to be rational. No research has shown so far that, say, a government-enforced marginal price of development is not very close to the spontaneous price.

4 CONCLUSION

In France planning does not, as such, ensure coherence in the behaviour of public enterprises. It intervenes in different degree in neighbouring sectors (electricity and petroleum). It does not align the different variables to the same target. It has failed to adapt itself sufficiently to a free trade situation. The whole rationale of planning in the public sector needs to be redefined.

The first principle which must govern this redefinition is that a distinction has to be made between the different purposes of public enterprises, whose juridical status gives them an entirely artificial and illusory unity. If a firm can sell only at an unprofitable price and needs to be subsidised, then it must form part of a system of controls and interventions which inevitably isolates it from the market. If, by contrast, a firm's activities are competitive and profitable, planning in the setting of the Common Market should merely regulate these activities and not put government in

---

[1] It may be worth recalling, in this connection, that a price stop sometimes works to the benefit of those who are least in need of it and thus leads to a sort of redistribution of income in reverse.

the place of the firm's management.   Coherence in the public sector
implies not uniformity, but diversity of policies.

ANNEX I

LIST OF PUBLIC ENTERPRISES, EXCLUDING SUBSIDIARIES,
CLASSIFIED BY JURIDICAL STATUS; 1964

1. Public establishments of the State, in the field of industry and trade:

Électricité de France
Gaz de France
Charbonnages de France
Comptoir de Vente des charbons sarrois
Régie Autonome des Pétroles
Bureau de Recherche du Pétrole
B.R.G.G.M.
Caisse Nationale de l'Énergie
Office National de Navigation
Ports autonomes
Aéroports de Paris
Régie autonome des transports parisiens
Office National interprofessionnel des Céréales
O.N.E.R.A.
Centre National d'Études spatiales
Centre Scientifique de recherche du bâtiment
Institut National de Recherche chimique appliquée
Fonds d'Orientation et Régularisation des Marchés agricoles
S.E.I.T.A.
O.R.T.F.
Société Nationale des entreprises de Presse
Centre National du Commerce Extérieur

Some public establishments of the State in the field of industry and trade
enjoy not only financial autonomy but are separately incorporated in their
own right:

Régie Nationale des Usines Renault
Mines domaniales des Potasses d'Alsace
O.N.I.A.
Commissariat à l'Énergie atomique

2. National companies and state companies:

State companies exercising their activities in overseas 'départements' and territories;
Companies in French-speaking African countries and in Madagascar.

(*Note:* This would be the place to enumerate nationalised financial institutions; virtually all nationalised credit and insurance firms are joint-stock companies.)

3. Mixed companies in which more than 30 per cent of the equity is in public hands; they are nearly all joint-stock companies:

	Government shareholding per cent
Agence Havas	57·6
Société financière de Radiodiffusion	99·9
Actualités françaises	54
Union générale cinématographique	99·9
Nord-Aviation	99·7
Sud-Aviation	99·8
S.N.E.C.M.A	89
S.N.C.F.	51
Compagnie Nationale du Rhône	50·2
Compagnie Générale Transatlantique	63·7
Cie des Messageries Maritimes	50
Cie Nationale Air France	70
Société Française de Transports Pétroliers	30
Société de transports pétroliers par pipe-line	31
Société Française des pétroles	35
Compagnie Nationale du Rhône	50
Cie française de câbles sous-marins et de radio	99
Sté concessionnaire du tunnel routier sous le Mont-Blanc	100

A few mixed companies are of the private limited liability company type:

COGEP	99·8
SOTELEC	42·8
SOCOTEL	51
SOMEPOST	50·2

ANNEX II

LIST OF THE PRINCIPAL PUBLIC ENTERPRISES IN FRANCE BY
ECONOMIC SECTORS

The following is a list of 'public enterprises' as classified in the national accounts,
in three categories:

> Public services in industry and trade   P.S.
> Economic Intervention Agencies   E.I.
> Nationalised firms   N.F.

Sectors	*Enterprises*	*Category*
Agricultural and food industries	Régie Commerciale des Alcools	E.I.
	Service d'Exploitation industrielle des Tabacs et Allumettes (S.E.I.T.A.)	P.S.
Solid mineral fuels	Charbonnage de France	N.F.
Electricity, gas water . . .	Électricité de France	N.F.
	Cie Nationale du Rhône	N.F.
	Gaz de France	N.F.
	Commissariat à l'Énergie Atomique	P.S.
Petroleum and motor fuel	Bureau de recherche des Pétroles	P.S.
	Régie autonome des Pétroles	N.F.
	Sté Nale des pétroles d'Aquitaine	N.F.
	Sté de Recherche et Prospection des Pétroles d'Alsace	N.F.
	Cie d'Exploration pétrolière	N.F.
	Sté de Transports pétroliers par pipe-line	N.F.
Motor vehicles and bicycles	Régie Nale des Usines Renault	N.F.
Shipyards, aeronautics	Office Nale d'Études et Recherches Aérospatiales	P.S.
	Direction des Études & Fabrications d'Armement	P.S.
	Sté Nale d'Études et construction de moteurs d'avion (S.N.E.C.M.A.)	N.F.
	Sud-Aviation	N.F.
	Nord-Aviation	N.F.
Chemicals and rubber	Mines domaniales de Potasse d'Alsace	P.S.
	Office Nale industriel de l'Azote	P.S.
	Service des Poudres	P.S.
Printing and publishing	Imprimerie Nationale	P.S.

Sectors	*Enterprises*	*Category*
Transport	Aéroport de Paris	P.S.
	Sté Nale des chemins de fer français	N.F.
	Régie autonome des transports parisiens	N.F.
	Régie autonome des transports communaux	N.F.
	Cie Gle Transatlantique	N.F.
	Messageries Maritimes	N.F.
	Air-France	N.F.
Telecommunications	Postes et Télécommunications	P.S.
	France-Câbles	N.F.
Housing	Office public d'habitations à loyer modéré (H.L.M.)	
Miscellaneous services	Office de Radio-Télévision Française	P.S.
	Théâtres nationaux	P.S.
	Hôpitaux	P.S.
	Agence Havas	N.F.
	Union Générale Cinématographique	N.F.
Marketing	Fonds d'Orientation et de régularisation des marchés agricoles (F.O.R.M.A.)	E.I.
	Office Nal. interprofessionnel des Céréales	E.I.

22 Socialist Planning and Capitalist Programming: an analytical comparison of the procedures [1]

A. Pokrovski

1 THE DISTINCTION BETWEEN PLANNING AND PROGRAMMING

Economists today frequently use the term 'planning' without making a distinction between the types of social system in which it is carried out; and this inevitably distorts the meaning of a large number of essential economic terms. Starting with the two most widely recognised approaches to the objective necessity for national economic and social planning mentioned in the title of this paper, it is quite clear that they are considerably different from each other, not only as far as the economic and social systems in which they operate are concerned and in their basic principles and methods of application, but also in the extent of their hold over the national economy and in the degree of their efficacy.

The type of economic planning practised by the socialist countries is a method of managing the national economy which, on the basis of the common ownership of the means of production in at least the principal sector, establishes a direct link between the State plan and the production functions of the individual enterprises, guiding them so that all the requirements of economic growth are met. I hardly need to point out that I am talking here about the theoretical concept of 'planning'; I leave on one side for the moment the possible mistakes that can arise from an incorrect combination of the two principles of centralisation and autonomy of operation, from displays of 'voluntarism' in the choice of the principal objectives or from the inadequacy of the planning calculations.

It will be realised that the plans and the methods of application are by no means identical in the various socialist countries. In particular, the degree of centralisation in the decision-making as to the various objectives of the plan, the concrete tasks of economic policy, the organisation of the stages of planning procedure, the techniques used and so on, differ from country to country; but the theoretical basis of which I have spoken, and which provides the foundations of socialist planning procedure, is the same in every one of these countries.

[1] Translated by Robert Price.

Precisely the same can be said of the programming practised by the capitalist countries. This also has a theoretical basis peculiar to itself, which rests upon objective laws. I in no way share the views expressed by certain Soviet economists in the early 1950s, who claimed that any element of planning was alien to the very nature of capitalism. Such views are themselves opposed to Marxist–Leninist theory. It will no doubt be of interest to the representatives of Western economic thought to recall that, some fifty years ago, Lenin was putting forward an opinion on this matter, diametrically opposed to that mentioned above. He wrote in 1918: 'If trusts exist, planning must also exist' (*Complete Works*, ch. 24, p. 210, Russian edition). But, on the other hand, the founder of the theory of imperialism also stressed that capitalism had never and would never be reconcilable with anything other than a partially planned economy.

The type of economic planning which is gradually emerging in the current state of capitalism possesses clearly defined *social* characteristics which lead me to describe it, not as 'planning', but as 'programming' of national production. As distinct from planning, economic 'programming' can be defined as a policy pursued by the State, which is imposed upon a private monopoly system of production and consists of the *co-ordinated stimulation*, on a macro-economic scale, of certain sectors of the economy, in order to solve the major problems which confront the dominant groups.

It is important to stress here that this policy of programming is not conceived of as providing the means to so manage each sector of the economy that the objective possibilities of harmonious growth are realised, but merely to stimulate the growth of certain so-called 'dynamic' branches which are particularly important for foreign trade or which have military and strategic significance.

It will be realised that programming is further distinguished from planning in that it is of an essentially indicative character: the programmes adopted are, with few exceptions, not of a compulsory nature, backed up by administrative or legal sanctions. In the countries where programming is practised (the U.S., Canada, the Federal Republic of Germany and Austria not being among them at the present time), the organs of the State adopt a planning law and publish a long-term plan that contains the chosen growth objectives of the country, by sector, by branch, or by region. The plan also indicates, on the basis of approximative calculations, the expected increases in private consumption in investment and in public sector requirements, the possible increase in exports and so on. Broadly speaking, there is no administrative or contractual connection between this plan and the operations of each individual firm, with the possible exception of a few 'quasi-contracts' concluded between a government body and a firm, such as are found in the French and Spanish programmes. It can be said that these economic programmes are of decisive significance only for the nationalised enterprises and even they cannot completely avoid the influence of the fluctuations of the market, because of the small part of production which they provide.

In the Soviet Union, the plan has the force of law. The individual enterprises are obliged to carry it out. But one should not conclude from this that the directive element is the main determining characteristic of planning in a socialist economy. A socialist economy merely makes it *possible* to manage production by means of directives. This method was widely used during the initial phases of the country's development, when the need to build up a number of industrial complexes was dictated not only by the desire to obtain an immediate economic result – sometimes, indeed, this was a minor consideration – but also by the need to attain certain long-term social goals and by the need to construct a basis for socialism. Today, the situation is different. The Soviet economy has achieved a high level of maturity, the construction of socialism is complete, and the need for a much higher level of production has now come to the forefront: new tasks must be considered in the formulation of planning theory. We have to discover the best way of combining the methods of planned economic management by directive and the methods of 'stimulation'.

It is a commonplace to point out that the same problem of centralisation and stimulation is found today, in all its acuteness, in those Western countries which make use of programming. What are the solutions to this important dilemma of our time, that are offered by socialist planning and capitalist programming procedures respectively? On which points do they converge so as to permit fruitful collaboration and where are the fundamental differences of principle on which the two systems are based?

2 CENTRALISATION

Let us begin with the concept of centralisation, which clearly constitutes one of the most essential principles of socialist planning. The planning procedure starts 'from above': the planning agency not only determines the *general* directions of economic growth (which is equally characteristic of Western-style programming), but also ensures the mutual consistency of the planned tasks of the individual producing units.

Western economists often believe that the principle of centralisation implies a detailed ordering of the running of every individual enterprise. This type of policy is not consistent with a theory of planning which is based upon the rule of operational autonomy: a rule which results from the objective requirement for firms to be profitable. This requirement implies the widely recognised principle and method of permitting 'operating autonomy'. In fact, an increased emphasis upon this principle of planning and its implications constitute one of the essential elements of the economic reform which is taking place at present in the Soviet Union, after its adoption at the Plenary Session of the Central Committee of the Communist Party of the U.S.S.R. in autumn 1965.

The centralisation principle in the theory of socialist planning implies that the principal aims of the plan, as well as the practical measures for its implementation (whether by directive or by indirect financial stimulants), are established *by the central planning agency and are legally binding*. Thus, the methods of conducting the management of industry and agriculture, decided by Soviet science and sanctioned by the government, have the force of law and acquire from this fact an imperative (i.e. obligatory) character. This is, however, not directly applicable to the question of exactly what methods are to be used, since the principle of centralisation in economic planning supposes that stimulative and incentive measures, calculated to leave as much scope as possible to the initiative of the firms themselves, can be used, as well as methods of a directive character. The socialist mode of production provides very wide opportunities for the application of a highly perfected system of planning.

The current rate of scientific and technical progress obliges the planner to draw up economic plans at the national level; highly composite and highly aggregated. This fact imposes a qualitatively new task upon the individual enterprises: their principal aim must be to increase, not the volume of production, but its efficiency. For the time being, agreement has been reached on the principles of the division of responsibilities between, on the one hand, the central organs of planning control – GOSPLAN, the central ministries and the ministries of the federated republics – and, on the other hand, the individual enterprises. The central organs have to fix the principal objectives for the growth of production at a sufficiently high level of aggregation – at the national level and at the sectoral level – and can only trespass into the affairs of the individual enterprise in cases of justifiable necessity. But how does one define 'justifiable necessity'? This is probably one of the most serious problems for the theory of socialist planning.

The types of question which are to come under the jurisdiction of the central planning agencies at the macro-economic level are very clearly defined. They include the whole range of decisions connected with the establishment of global objectives such as the level of consumption, accumulation, gross national product and the national income. In this sphere of activity the aims of planning coincide, from a formal point of view, with those of programming. These are to establish an optimum relationship between consumption and accumulation on the basis of chosen criteria (which will clearly vary between the different social systems), and on the basis of an optimum inter-sectoral balance. While capitalist programming limits itself to what is generally known as 'final demand', and is consequently unable to go further than establishing very general objectives of sectoral production and implementing the appropriate stimulants, socialist planning, in clear contrast with the advantages provided by State control of production, is able to proceed to a scientific analysis of the mutual production relationships that exist *within* each of the many branches of industry, an analysis without which it is impossible to determine with any precision the co-efficients of productive consumption which constitute the matrix of balanced inter-sectoral relationships.

By virtue of this fact, the opportunities for raising the efficiency of national production are considerably improved. The way is open to the solution of every aspect of the problem of the organised management of the national economy on the basis of well-informed criteria, and leading to the choice of a balanced policy. These criteria may, for example, be maximum *per capita* consumption (at the global level), or maximum labour productivity (at the level of the industrial branch), or full employment of productive capacity, or maximum profitability (at the level of the individual enterprise) and so on. In this last case we come up against the same question again, of the degree of penetration of plan directives into the sphere of the individual enterprise. The growth of productivity requires that the basis upon which the initiative of the enterprises can be exercised should be enlarged. This can be achieved by reducing the proportion of the national income distributed from the centre and increasing the amount at the disposal of the individual enterprises in the form of general finance.

3 THE LIMITS OF AUTONOMY

But how far can the increased autonomy which results from this conception of the role of management actually go? It is clearly not appropriate to this conception, that such questions as, for example, the detailed specifications of all the products to be manufactured (quality of the materials, dimensions, shape, etc.), or the fixing of the rules for the internal organisation of production in the various enterprises and of the detailed contents of agreements made between different establishments, should be included within the decisions to be taken at the highest level. Such questions are better dealt with by the individual enterprises themselves. And in fact, a considerable part of the planning of the types of product produced by each establishment is already carried out by contractual agreements between them. And when individual enterprises plan an important role in the management and control of production, economic stimulants must come to assume considerable importance.

Thus, the principal goal of the decisions adopted at the Plenary Assembly of the Central Committee of the Communist Party of the U.S.S.R. was to reinforce the economic stimulation of the enterprise, while strengthening the *economic* control over the use of finance. It is precisely for this reason that instruments of economic management, such as the payment of a tax to the State calculated on the value of the fixed and working capital held by the individual enterprise, differential rates of turnover tax, long-term credits and so on are gaining in importance.

We regard *the system of taxes on the value of fixed and working capital held by the individual enterprise* as particularly important. This system was adopted, as is well known, at the Plenary Session of the Central Committee of the Communist Party in October 1965. The principal function of these taxes is to stimulate the more efficient use, from an economic point of view, of machinery and equipment. They oblige every manager to calculate the expected result to be obtained from using a particular machine, before it is in fact used. Management has to calculate in advance the profit that can be derived from the use of new machinery (by reducing the costs of production, improving quality or increasing the volume of output) and has to do its best to obtain an optimal result, taking into account the fact that, besides having the funds required to pay the tax on the capital, it will also have to dispose of the necessary means of finance for the 'material stimulation' of the enterprise. Thus, by having to pay a tax on its capital resources, the enterprise is brought to a strict respect of the interests of the national economy as a whole.

By virtue of the new system of autonomous administration the majority of the objectives of the individual enterprise's own plan are established by the management – even such objectives as the costs of production and labour productivity. The enterprise carries out the planned production of goods in the required quantities, settles its accounts with its suppliers, and pays the State a tax, the amount of which is strictly determined on the amount of productive capital at its disposal.

That part of the profit which then remains to the enterprise is considered as the composite criterion of its activity, and is used to finance the 'material stimulus' to the workers of the establishment in question. Depending on its size, the profit goes into one or more of three 'stimulant' funds: (a) the fund for material encouragement; (b) the social, cultural and housing fund; (c) the fund for the development of production.

The equation for the profit of the enterprise is of the following form:

$$B = P - (C + nK).$$

Where B represents the profit of the enterprise (or its economic efficiency) per unit produced or for an annual period.

P—the unit cost of production or the total cost of the annual production for sale on the market.

K—the value of the productive capital of the enterprise per unit of product, or for the annual aggregate volume of production for sale.

n—the rate of tax imposed on productive capital.

$(C + nK)$ = the total outgoings of the enterprise per unit of product or for the total annual production.

The introduction of the tax on capital has three results: first, an increase in return; second, a reduction in the amount of machinery and equipment which are not being put to productive use; and third, it should encourage the use of only those resources that can be assured of some fixed minimum level of efficiency.

Another type of planned stimulus to production is that of *differential rates of turnover tax*. These rates are calculated on the basis of the difference between, on the one hand, the value of goods sold at the fixed retail prices minus the commercial margin, and on the other, total outgoings plus the forecast profit, as assessed by the Ministry of Finance of the U.S.S.R. These tax rates provide a very flexible instrument for the planned management of the economy. By causing them to vary, the production of new products can be stimulated, and enterprises are given a material interest in producing a greater quantity and variety of goods.

It has been the case that the introduction of a tax to be paid to the central Exchequer, proportional to the productive capital utilised by the enterprises, has led to a concurrent progressive reduction in the levels of turnover tax.

But the measures decided upon at the Plenary Session of the Central Committee of the C.P.S.U. in the autumn of 1965, concerning the new relationship to be established between the undivided enterprises and the central organs of the State, are to be brought into operation progressively over a period of several years. In these circumstances the scope for differential rates of turnover tax will remain quite significant for some time to come. Moreover, the need to perfect this method of management of the planned economy is assuming increased importance for the improved application of the principle of autonomous administration of individual enterprises.

In a different way, the application of *price stimuli* can become an effective way of planning increased economic efficiency, both at the level of the individual enterprise and at the level of the national economy. The decisions of last autumn make it clear that prices should, firstly, help to create the stable conditions in which high levels of profitability can be attained and, secondly, should help to distribute the labour force in a more rational manner between the different branches of the economy.

In this connection, the concept of price stimuli that has emerged in Soviet economic theory is of exceptional interest for the application of the economic reforms.[1] In the way it is envisaged, the system of price stimuli will depend directly on the principal objectives of the plan. In addition, the calculations take into account both the objectives of the production programmes and the given data on resources available in limited quantities and the way that these resources are to be utilised. Since the use made of these resources (labour, fixed capital, etc.) differs between the different variants of the plan, the system of price stimuli also varies, not only as a function of the production plan, but also as a function of the planned utilisation of the limited resources which corresponds to it.

The prices in this system are described as 'stimuli', because they are expected to be the economic instrument by means of which harmonisation is achieved between the macro-economic optimum (i.e. the global optimum, as defined by the objectives of the production programme that is established by the central planning agency), and the 'partial' optima (i.e. the individual optima of the different branches of the economy, which are attained by the maximisation of aggregate profits by each productive union of enterprises and by each individual enterprise). The economico-

[1] Cf. V. Dadajan, 'La Direction optimale de l'économie et les tâches de la cybernétique économique', *Messager de l'Université Moscou*, N. 1, 1966.

mathematical model of a system of 'price stimuli' is constructed in the following way:

(1) The central planning agency knows the different variants of the production programme available to the economic agent responsible for carrying out the chosen programme: in addition, it knows the degree of utilisation of the available resources that is entailed by each of these variants (total or partial utilisation).

(2) It chooses a production programme and looks for that price system which will be the most profitable for the economic agency that has to apply the programme. (We assume that this agent, once the list of prices to be applied is known, will himself proceed to calculate his optimum by mathematical programming on the basis of a given criterion of profitability.)

(3) The mathematical procedure by which the price-stimuli are calculated is basically a method of determining the limits between which the profitability of the production of various goods can vary. These limits are determined by the pattern of resource utilisation in the chosen programme variant – which resources should be fully utilised and which only partially? To go on to describe the decision algorithms concerned would be to digress from our subject, so I shall not do so here.

4 THE OPTIMAL COMBINATION OF CENTRALISATION AND AUTONOMY

I have attempted to describe how the problem of finding the optimal combination of centralised measures for the application of the plan and economic incentives is viewed in the Soviet Union. In those Western countries in which programming is practised, research is also being undertaken in this direction; but the impossibility of centralised intervention into the internal affairs of private enterprises hinders effective organisatory action by the State (and even more by private organisations), aimed at producing an optimal national output. It is true that the vast system of incentives, organised by the State (tax concessions, favourable credit terms, preferential tariffs on State provided services, etc.) plays a very active catalytic role in pushing the economy in the direction required by the plan. But these 'flexible' methods of government regulation have proved themselves notwithstanding fairly rigid. They give an initial boost to the growth of certain branches of production, but prove incapable of subsequently halting the movement, once it has gathered momentum; the 'braking distance' has proved itself to be too long, and the social wastage which results from repeated economic crises, called 'recessions' in the West, remains considerable. Thus, we have seen countries which practise programming, like France and Japan, drawing up 'interim' plans when the economic situation deteriorates seriously, the unsuccessful policy of 'stop-go' in England, and other similar measures.

The spontaneous character of technical change and the fluctuations of the market oblige managers, as a general rule, to try to optimise production so as to maximise profits – a micro-economic criterion, which can never coincide with the interests of the nations as a whole, even if the plans are based on dynamic coefficients of inter-sectoral exchange.

The absence of the objective economic conditions for the elaboration of scientific and systematic programmes dealing with the whole economy is compensated to some extent, in the 'programming' countries, by the quality of the technical instruments used to draw up the programmes. In this respect, the work that is being done on the conditions for simultaneous product and finance equilibrium is of particular interest, notably the French model of 'growth at variable prices', the English model of Professor Richard Stone and others. Where these technical instruments of plan-formation are concerned, far from wishing to labour the differences of principle between planning and programming, I would like to stress the convergence of the two systems at many points. It is on these points that common research can be undertaken, with the same practical orientation and the same scientific value for both planners and programmers. Among the common problems of applying the theory of planning, the following can be distinguished as the most important:

—the elaboration of general macro-economic growth models.
—the effectiveness of the economic measures that are deployed at national, regional or sectoral level.
—the study of methods of obtaining the economic information that is necessary for the management of the economy at every level.

It is in the scientific elaboration of the methods of creating State programmes of economic growth that the greatest opportunity lies for collaboration between Soviet and Western economists. In this respect, the papers presented to this conference have without doubt been an important contribution.

Summary Record of the Discussions

By M. V. Posner
and H. Tulkens

Discussion of Professor Papi's Paper

Professor Neumark introduced the paper. He intended to select particular topics in this far-reaching and interesting paper, rather than to attempt to survey the whole of its coverage. Professor Papi had discussed 'the mixed economy'. But there are mixed economies where the relative importance of the two sectors is 90 per cent against 10 per cent, as before World War I, or 75 per cent against 25 per cent, as between 1920 and 1940, and finally 60 per cent against 40 per cent, as is now the case in many western countries. The problems arising in each of these cases might be quite different, and the solution as well. The discussion could perhaps consider whether there could be a common form of analysis appropriate to all these various forms of economic systems.

Professor Papi was concerned to discuss how far an equilibrium could prevail in the relationship between the two sectors. In passing, while Professor Papi had noted the divergences that could occur between planned expectations and actual outcomes, he had concentrated on those cases where outcomes were worse than expectations; the problem of insurance against this risk then arose. But it was equally possible, in principle, that achievements would be greater than expectations – could there be then some form of negative insurance?

Professor Papi had suggested that plans by the state were necessarily inferior to plans formulated by private individuals. While Professor Neumark recognised this possibility, he thought there were ways in which there could be encouraged the harmonised development of the public and private sectors, and modern techniques such as cost-benefit analysis could be used to ensure that state expenditure fitted in with expenditures in the private sector. He agreed with the analysis of the methods of intervention open to the state which Professor Papi had enumerated, but did not agree that the method of taxation was necessarily as negative as Professor Papi had suggested. It might be possible, by deliberate and wise use of taxation, to improve situations rather than worsen them: in this way the activity of the public sector could improve and complement that of the private sector, rather than damaging it.

Professor Neumark distinguished between the way in which a mixed economy had worked in the past and the way in which it worked now: he thought that it would be the importance now attached to the economic planning role of the state authorities that explained the difference.

At the end of his paper, Professor Papi expressed his conviction that the true 'protagonist' of economic development in any country could only be the individual and not the State. Professor Neumark suggested that there were countries where the role of the government in this respect was overestimated; but one should also keep in mind that the 'spirit of sacrifice', which Professor Papi himself invoked in his paper, was in fact often lacking in the real world. To take the author's agricultural example, if his position led him to hold that agriculture should be preserved even when it was not profitable, Professor Neumark could not share such an opinion. Here again, the need was evident for a cost-benefit analysis which could serve to provide a basis for decisions based on an accurate comparison of alternative solutions. Finally, Professor Neumark summed up by agreeing with the author on the need for harmonisation between individualistic free initiative and public activity; there remained, however, the need to analyse what might be the most appropriate means of achieving such co-ordination.

Professor Mossé said that it was important to remember the contribution of Lange and Sir Robert Hall among others in stressing, in opposition to von Mises, the possibility of rational calculation in the public sector. Secondly, Professor Mossé reminded the meeting, (and suggested that it might be a matter for subsequent discussion), that the state need not act 'rationally' in its administration of the public sector. A non-market rationality, or what might better be called, a 'reasonable' standard of behaviour and method of choice, was possibly more appropriate than market decision making as laid down in text-book expositions of a market private sector.

Professor Delivanis thought that it might be possible on occasion for the Treasury (as part of the public sector) to act in a way which would neutralise the policy of the central bank, and that the temptation to behave in this manner might be great for countries faced with balance-of-payments disequilibrium, particularly developing countries. For such countries the desire to ensure the fulfilment of the plan might lead to what Professor Papi would describe as incompatible behaviour of the public sector in its relationships with the private sector.

Mr Kolm thought that the appropriate distinction was not that between the state and private individuals, because after all, the state was made up of private individuals. What we must do is to distinguish between market mechanisms and other ways of achieving certain economic goals. It was this distinction which was most important in analysing the relative behaviours and roles of the public and private sectors.

Professor Zielinski could not agree with Professor Papi's suggestion that there was something instrinsically worse about public planning than about private planning. There are certain functions which only public sector planning can fulfil and in these fields private planning is incompetent. Morevoer, as was demonstrated in Professor Marglin's paper, there were conditions under which the processes by which a market would try to reach an optimal allocative distribution of resources between competing activities would succeed only imperfectly, while a directed solution might succeed more completely. Again Professor Papi had emphasised that there were certain problems of allocation and decision-making that were common to all economic systems, and that therefore it was incorrect to believe that some forms of social organisation made it easier for certain types of economic progress to be achieved. But Professor Zielinski thought that in many cases social change was necessary, for instance in the process of economic development for emerging countries, and where economic improvement could only take place as part of a general attempt to achieve social change. Thus Professor Papi had suggested that regardless of the type of political regime there were necessary stages of economic development through which any economy must pass. Even if it were true that no particular stage could be avoided or bypassed by a developing country, it would still be possible for the public authority to try to expedite the process, and it would in many cases be necessary for the public authority to take decisive action to precipitate the move from one stage of development to another.

Professor James agreed that it was useful to look at the three forms of public intervention in the economy – its processes of taxation, of spending, and of intervening in particular private sector operations. But he could not always fully accept Professor Papi's description of how these processes would work. For instance, it was not necessarily true that state intervention had to be confined to a narrow area of activity – it was now possible and sometimes desirable for the state to intervene in very wide areas. Professor Papi had suggested that when the state levied taxes which reduced the savings of particular individuals these savings were necessarily 'sterilised' – but surely it was possible merely to redirect these savings. Again, there were areas of public expenditure where Professor Papi's rule of 'marginal utility' was surely not wholly applicable. There were non-directly-economic ends such as education, the police force and so on where the State had to spend for reasons not directly connected with the market.

Professor Herschel thought that there were particular reasons why the public authorities in developing countries should not accept the decisions arrived at by the market. How could the market, for instance, arrive at the correct solutions about time preference and willingness to bear risks? Surely the changing and correction of private plans was in fact the function of the public authorities. Why was it generally accepted that double taxation should be avoided? Surely there was nothing particularly wicked in the public authorities removing the same sum of money in two slices rather than deciding to take it all out with one single piece of tax imposition.

Mr. Schmidt-Luders thought that one important point had been omitted by Professor Neumark – the problem of how to translate the national plan into its regional applications. The reality was that, however desirable it might be to produce regional versions of national plans by scientific processes, regional political pressures were such that possible irrationalities were introduced. This was a fact of reality that must be recognised.

Professor Musgrave asked for clarification of Professor Papi's views on the effect of budget surpluses in the public sector on the availability of resources for private sector saving. We had to distinguish between surpluses on current account alone and surpluses on the total of capital and current expenditures.

Professor Papi, replying to the discussion, said that by a mixed economy he meant one in which the public sector comported itself in a manner which would allow the rules of the market to operate in the private sector successfully and did not outrage these rules in its own activities. He adhered to his view that public planning could only occur successfully when there was individual planning first, but that it was important to struggle to ensure the greatest rationality in State expenditures. The important question was to ask what sort of planning should be practiced – should we have indicative planning, should we have compulsive powers in the hands of the authorities, or should we allow private planning to be dominant? He recognised the importance of having some forms of indicative planning but emphasised the importance of achieving a balance between the activities of the public authorities and those of the private sector which were the main producers of wealth.

Discussion of Professor Barrère's Paper

Introducing the paper, *Professor Robinson* said that the main point stressed by Professor Barrère was the importance of maintaining a degree of coherence or consistency between the activities of the public and private sectors and discussed the three ways – market forces, planning, and the state budget – by which such consistency could be brought about. But what was meant by consistency in this context? Was it, as Professor Barrère seemed to suggest, a question of the balance between the different activities in the public sector? Was it a question of the achievement of some optimum size of the public sector relative to the private sector? If internal balance were the definition which Professor Barrère applied, how could one test the achievement of such consistency? In any case, he was not sure whether Professor Barrère's hard distinction between the public and private sectors of the economy could be maintained. Surely it was not wholly correct to suggest that the public sector procedeed necessarily by coercion only without any relationship to the rules of the market. There was shading between public sector and private sector activities with at the one extreme the provision of services by the State on completely non-market criteria, and at the other extreme the activities of public enterprises whose pricing and investment policies were subject to constraints rather similar to those imposed by the private sector. In between these two extremes there were state interventions – for instance the subsidy of agriculture – which were motivated and controlled by a mixture of aims. The essential part of Professor Barrère's contribution was the discussion of the ways in which consistency could be achieved. We could enthrone the market as the ultimate ruler; we could try to impose public criteria of a non-market variety; or we could ask what in particular is the role of the plan and of the market respectively in economic activity. Which seemed the best way to proceed?

Professor Robinson was very interested in Professor Barrère's account of the role of the state budget and the way in which budgetary activities might run counter to the intentions of the plan or the way in which the market operated. There was the extremely complex problem of the extent to which it would be correct for the state to use public sector investment as an instrument for the short-term control of the economy. The British experience had been that this apparently attractive device had the extreme disadvantage of starving the public sector of needed investment funds in the long run. But if one abandoned this instrument of policy, and at the same time was unwilling to use either the control of private investment or deflationary policies, what tools for policy were in fact available?

Professor Sandee took up Professor Robinson's worry about the desirability of using public investment as a short-term policy instrument. He thought that taxation and possibly monetary policy were preferable. He based this view on the experience of the Netherlands in 1958, where an attempt to limit public investment (defined in Holland as largely municipal expenditure on such things as roads and drainage) had led to a general fall in economic activity because the fall in investment had wider consequences than had been expected. The cut in expenditure had been concentrated largely on earth-moving activities and instead of this having the general economic effect desired, there had been a series of induced falls in expenditure in other closely related sectors which managed to achieve the maximum disruption of economic activity with the minimum amount of general freeing of resources which was required.

Professor Musgrave asked whether this weakness of the use of public investment as a regulator was something that was really peculiar to the public sector. Might it not also be true that the control of private investment would lead to the same unpleasant and uncontrollable results? Was Professor Sandee's and Professor Robinson's view based on the fact that certain forms of activity – for instance earth-moving in Professor Sandee's example – concentrated in the public sector? Was the point perhaps that any use of investment as a regulator was mistaken, and that one should regulate private consumption instead?

Mr Kolm thought that the appropriate distinction was between the political and the economic activities of the state – in its economic activities the State was acting as a collection of individuals to achieve certain collective purposes. The budget of the state was not merely a constraint upon the activities of the private sector, it was a way in which those activities could be organised. One important case in which there might emerge a contradiction between the public and private sectors was the French example, where to achieve the purposes of the plan the state encouraged concentration of output; and this concentration in turn destroyed part of the competitive mechanisms on which the market part of the economy relied.

Professor Herschel returned to Professor Musgrave's point and thought that Professor Robinson had put the problem correctly. The difficulty about using public investment as a regulator is that public investment was often concentrated in those sectors which were sufficiently basic to act as constraints upon the growth of the economy as a whole. To starve these sectors of investment funds might create bottlenecks.

Professor Mossé noted a point that had been raised also in the paper of Professor Papi, that there were two functions of public enterprise. One field of activity appropriate to the public sector was the supplementation and indeed the imitation of market activity. But another field was the provision of services and the taking of decisions which the private sector would not take.

Professor Plotnikov was particularly interested in Professor Barrère's discussion of the economic rationality of the state. Can the public sector be rational and can this rationality lead to efficiency? In Professor Barrère's construction where the market was not in balance the plan might play a complementary role in restoring the balance. But could it also be possible that these roles were reversed, and in other economic systems where the plan was not completely in balance the market mechanism could be introduced to achieve the necessary balance? It was quite wrong to suggest that the market mechanism was inconsistent with State planning. In socialist countries there was consideration given to the use of market mechanism, but this did not mean that planning was being abandoned, merely that appropriate measures were being introduced to supplement and execute the intentions of the plan. The State must influence prices

R

and only when the prices had been influenced could the market properly be used. Such a policy would be truly rational.

Professor Wickham said that in France public investment had always exceeded plans and private sector investment had often been below the expectations in the plan. The problem was the relationship between the expectations in the private sector and the achievements in the public sector and the confidence of the private sector in the possibility of achieving the targets set out in the plan. If confidence was high, then 'too much' private investment might ensue. If confidence were 'too low' too little investment would result. Therefore the crucial question in establishing a relationship between the public plan and the private market was in fact a question of confidence.

Professor Barrère replied to the discussion and said that his paper had tried to describe what took place in the French economy and at the same time to analyse it, not to lay down what should take place. His definition of coherence was not one concerned with the size of the public sector but with the question of the degree of internal consistency within the public sector and also of the consistency between the allocation of resources insisted upon within the public sector and the allocation required by market forces. Take the example of population growth and the strains which this throws upon the educational system. When population growth accelerates there are required more schools and universities and at the same time it is necessary to provide more teachers and more buildings for these institutions. Thus the public sector would be required to plan consistently the building of new schools, the building of new establishments to train teachers, the supply of manpower into the teaching profession, and so on. These plans would have to be consistent. At the same time, the private sector would have to provide resources for the building operations, and deprive itself of the skilled manpower which would pass into the teaching profession. The activities of all parts of the economic system must be consistent with each other and this consistency was particularly important in the one where decisions taken by the market and the decisions taken explicitly by the State, because the instruments by which these decisions were arrived at differed in the two cases. This was what was meant by coherence or consistency. Experience had shown that the market had certain weaknesses, particularly in its treatment of long-term problems: the foresight of the market was limited, and the horizon of its vision was unduly short. Nevertheless the market had some strengths which were well known. It followed that both market and planning were needed, and the job of the modern economy was to combine in appropriate proportions market and plan criteria. In the case of the policy exercised by the state in housing, this combination was particularly important. Under some market conditions it would be true that only luxury houses were built: but for political and social reasons the state must insist that a reasonable balance between different forms of house-building was maintained. As regards the question of whether the public sector could really be regarded as a compulsive part of the economy and the private sector as the market part he agreed that obviously the activities of the Renault publicly owned motor car factory were constrained by market forces. But he would regard Renault for these purposes a part of the private sector. He had been most interested in Professor Robinson's remarks on the role of public investment as a regulator. It had so happened in France that public envestment always ended up by taking a larger share of the available resources than had been planned – he agreed with Professor Wickham on this point. Therefore the question of starving the public sector of investment funds by using investment as a regulator did not really arise.

Discussion of Professor Marglin's Paper

Introducing the paper, *Professor Malinvaud* expressed his appreciation of a most original and stimulating piece of work. While he was in agreement with the method used by the author as well as with most of his conclusions, his comments would be concerned only with the scope of the arguments presented.

The problem considered by Professor Marglin was one that concerned the *preparation* of a plan which might be relevant to an entire economy or alternatively to a sector of it. The problem arose because the planner had no direct information on the technological constraints under which the plan was to be established; only the individual firms had complete knowledge of their technology. Hence, an exchange of information needed to be organised between the planner and the firms, in order that the plan might finally possess the desired characteristic. The ways in which such an exchange could be conceived and organised were numerous, and the choice of one of them was a challenging problem for economists.

Professor Marglin's essential result was an unconventional one – namely that planning procedures based on prices did not economise on information as compared with command allocations. Professor Malinvaud commented that economists in the past had tended to emphasise the distinction between the two systems in order to find justification for certain types of economic organisation. There was some dogmatism, he added, in interpreting any advantage granted to price allocations as a justification for the market economy, and in interpreting similarly any useful property of command procedures as a justification of central planning. Even Professor Marglin did not escape completely from this danger, as became evident in the introduction and in various comments in his paper.

As mentioned above, the discussion was only relevant to the preparation of the plan, and not to its implementation. To Professor Malinvaud's thinking, such a discussion should be wholly of a technical character, and essentially deal with a detailed study of the properties of those procedures which were susceptible of being used in practice. Then, perhaps, such procedures could be grouped into categories, and one could start searching for the most valuable aspects of those based on prices on the one hand, of those based on commands on the other. However, such a systematisation seemed to be premature at this stage.

Notwithstanding his basic agreement with Professor Marglin's results, Professor Malinvaud added the following three qualifications: first, he noticed that three specific procedures were studied in the paper; that was a rather slender basis for drawing a general conclusion. It was not even certain that those procedures were the most valuable ones in practice for the iterative preparation of plans. Second, Professor Marglin had not established a rigorous equivalence, but only an approximate one, between the price and command versions of the planning procedure. In order to switch from one version to the other, one needed either to linearise non-linear functions, or to substitute the value of a variable at the $n - 1$st iteration for the value of the same variable at the nth step. Such approximations were unimportant if the iteration process proceeded by very small steps. In practice however, this could not be the case: the preparation of a plan was always limited to a very small number of information exchanges between the firms and the planner. Third, Professor Marglin's model was an oversimplified one: there was only a single output, produced by means of single input, and by various firms using different technologies, but all subject to decreasing returns. Was the analysis of such a model sufficient for drawing a general conclusion? For instance, would not there be further difficulties if many inputs were brought into the picture? With a single input, the demands and supplies successively made by a firm revealed the marginal productivity of that input; but with several inputs, they only revealed a linear combination of the marginal productivities of those inputs. Similarly, constant returns to scale – which are quite frequent in industrial technologies – appear to affect in a very different way price and command procedures, respectively. Indeed, if no special caution is taken, price procedures failed in the case of constant returns because the firms' demands and supplies were in general not uniquely defined.

Mr Kolm asserted that both the price and the command procedures presented were, in fact, methods of central planning; the price procedure did not represent the functioning of a decentralised market. It was only an exception when real markets worked like an auction (the stock markets, and some fish and food markets) as described by Walras; in general, information exchanges occurred between two economic agents, or between one seller (or buyer) and his potential buyers (or suppliers). Hence, the information systems prevailing were much more different from the command system than the 'price system' described in the paper. Moreover, computations were different because there was no central computing agency; this implied that the costs of information and computation, and their effects on the rest of the real market economy, were very different from those of centrally planned (command economy, contrary to what the paper suggested. And indeed, was it true, at least from a Wicksellian point of view, that an economy without information costs would always be in a Pareto-optimal state, without any unemployemnt?

Professor Mossé pointed out that only the relationship between firms, their suppliers and the central agency were considered in the paper. But what about the essential relationships between the firms and the consumers? When those were brought in, it became insufficient to limit the analysis to that of the production function, since one ignored what would be done with the output.

In the same spirit, *Professor Jochimsen* asked the author to make more precise the kind of welfare function he was using to represent the preference pattern he assumed for the outputs, and *Professor Tardos*, calling on his planning experience in Hungary, asked whether other welfare functions than those leading to more Pareto-optimality should not be introduced into the analysis.

Professor Sen followed up this last point by suggesting that such a question actually went somewhat beyond Professor Marglin's framework. Indeed, the author's purpose was to show the equivalence of the adjustment process with the command system and also with the price system in achieving whatever it is that the price system does achieve. Since the price system did achieve Pareto-optimality in the absence of externalities, the discussion implicity concentrated on that. If the price and the command system were to be shown equivalent in the process towards achieving a maximisation of social welfare going beyond Pareto-optimality, we had to examine first whether the price system did at all achieve such a maximisation. A price system did not necessarily achieve a social goal beyond Pareto-optimality, and without further assumptions, the question of the *process* towards this achievement did not arise.

Regarding the paper itself, which Professor Sen considered to be breaking fresh ground, he wanted to make this comment concerning the point that the firm revealed just as much about its production function by letting the central authority directly know about its marginal products as it would if it only sent its orders, given the prices set by the central authority. This result depended on the differentiability of the production function. If there was a lack of smoothness, the orders did not tell us much about the production function as the relevant description at the margin would. The marginal conditions here took the form of a set of inequalities, and the one-to-one correspondence of orders and the marginal conditions disappeared. This was not a serious criticism but it did outline the need for going into the more general formulation which Professor Marglin provided at the beginning, and to recognise that none of the specific results of the paper depended on the more restrictive differentiable model in terms of which most of the analysis was carried out.

Professor Marglin's reply emphasised that his main efforts had concentrated on trying to delineate what the market system did not provide, although it obviously provided something in terms of allocation of commodities. In particular, he wanted to separate the issues of information exchange, and of incentive effects of the price system. He mentioned also that the price system, as it was described in the paper, allowed one to dispense with a central agency. He finally agreed with Professor Malinvaud that the study of just three procedures was insufficient; no doubt one could continue for a long time, analysing a whole series of procedures, but this method would hardly be practical. On the question of how big the steps were in the iterative processes here considered, he thought that all convergence studies made hitherto essentially assumed small steps iterations.

SESSION FOUR

Discussion of Professor Zielinski's Paper

Professor Delivanis, in opening the discussion proposed firstly to make some general remarks. Secondly to analyse the four systems of socialist industry, thirdly to examine very briefly its management mechanism, and finally to suggest some possible conclusions.

One of the aims of the nationalisation had always been the application of economic principles within the national economy with the reservation, however, that not only economic but also political and social considerations would influence both those directly in charge and, even more so, the central planning board. It followed that investment decisions, fixing the types and volumes of production, and last but not least price and wage decisions, would not always be defensible on strictly economic arguments. That meant that in some cases for one of these reasons supply might be smaller than needed. More generally, on the other hand, those in charge of a socialist industry were eager to extend its activity as much as possible by reinvesting profits, by securing additional capital from the government or by reducing payments to their suppliers, to their staff and to the treasury. They tried, moreover, to improve their performance not only in terms of the results achieved but also on the basis of various criteria established, provided than in doing so they shared their main objectives.

With this in mind the reader of Professor J. Zielinski's admirably systematic and lucid paper would be surprised that he stressed the complexities of the system applied by socialistic countries to the control of their industry.

The socialist enterprise had to be constructed as a cybernetic system composed of feeding, information, stimulation and steering systems. The first was concerned with the problem of securing the capital needed either from the profits (dependent sector) or from outside, mainly the government (independent sector). Might he add in fairness that those in charge of a Western firm tried to increase their profits at the expense of consumers, suppliers, staff and labour force by reducing, to a minimum, dividends; and they found capital also by borrowing, which in a period of inflation was the cheapest way of securing capital? As a socialist firm sold at the level of buyer prices, cost was not decisive. In practice with low costs, transfers to the treasury were possible, provided those in charge were willing or under obligation to transfer. With high costs, subsidies had to be paid to the firm concerned, if prices were to be kept down. Inflationary pressures developed when, not infrequently, subsidies were paid with the proceeds of central bank credits, as had been made clear in Professor Oyzanoroski's paper to an earlier I.E.A. conference on inflation. The information system aimed to find out how the economic out-turn compared with certain transformation rules. It used criteria which were appropriate to general or specific tasks. Some of them served more than one function, e.g. profit, which was at the same time a success indicator and a feeding system regulator, since investment was encouraged by high profit. The stimulation system relied on a variety of a factors which were listed and analysed in Professor Zielinski's paper. Lastly the steering system tried to discover why the industry (socialist of course) did not conform to the instructions of the Central Planning Board.

The management mechanism of the Central Planning Board relied on the information transmitting system, on the principles of enterprise functioning (the management formula), and on the macro-economic feeding system. The Board in turn relied on prices, orders, rates of bonus and operational changes in the information and stimulation systems. Professor Zielinski was in favour of the wide use of prices. Because of the form of construction of the success indicators and of the feeding system regulators, there were three types of management formula, of which the simplest was the best. But this was used only in Yugoslavia. When based on prices or bonuses the model of management is parametric. This was favoured by Professor Zielinski. Usually there was a compromise between cipher and open orders, since some of the latter were not fulfilled. The use of a large number of success indicators needed Professor Delivanis thought to be discouraged, quite apart from the fact that it appeared that each of them involved some hidden vested interest. If prices were to be more widely used, the shpere of the enterprise authority had to be broadened.

Professor Delivanis concluded by supporting Professor Zielinski's recommendation that synthetic success indicators with the broadest reception sphere should be used, that ptices should be the principal indicators and that open information should be abandoned, so far as possible. It was necessary, Professor Delivanis emphasised, not to forget the difficulties involved in achieving a noninflationary balance. The problem of inflation in the socialist countries should not be underestimated.

After a number of other participants had intervened or asked questions, *Professor Zielinski* briefly replied.

SESSION FIVE

Discussion of the Papers by Professors Samuelson and Musgrave

It had been decided to discuss the papers of Professors Musgrave and Samuelson together. *Mr Turvey* opened the discussion, introducing primarily the paper of Professor Samuelson. He welcomed Professor Samuelson's paper as being as usual full of many good things. In particular, there were three contributions which should be particularly noted. In the first place, Professor Samuelson concentrated almost completely on the normative aspects of the subject – laying down what should be done rather than describing the state of affairs as it might be at any point of time. His problem was to deal, simultaneously with the questions how much *should* be spent on, for instance, trying to reach the moon by 1970 and how much should be spent on, say, afforestation in the Adironacks. Professor Samuelson was concentrating, it seemed to Mr Turvey, entirely on what should take place, whereas Professor Dorfman was concerned with the factors that influenced the amount spent on these two typical activities at different times in any economy or in different economies at any point of time. Secondly, Professor Samuelson's paper was to be welcomed because it recognised the absurdity of the principle of voluntary agreement about public expenditure: Mr Turvey believed that this was the correct *point de depart*. Thirdly, Professor Samuelson included, as a kind of bonus for those who studied the paper in depth, many interesting points in his appendix on welfare economics. Although the relevance of these contributions to the problems discussed in the main part of Professor Samuelson's paper was not entirely clear, Mr Turvey welcomed in particular the comments on pricing policy and Professor Samuelson's reworking of the original theorem of Boiteux as reported in the article by Drèze in the *American Economic Review*.[1] The general result – that the excess of prices over marginal costs should be proportionate to the elasticity of demand – was of considerable interest in the practical problems of the pricing policies of public enterprises. But Mr Turvey recognised that this problem was essentially one of the second best: one had to recognise that marginal cost pricing policies were not followed in any form, and that there was substantial ignorance about values of the relevant elasticities. In Mr Turvey's own paper it was suggested that, although this ignorance was considerable, it was reasonable to assume that the cross-elasticities of demand between different products of the fuel market was greater than the elasticities between any of these fuels and competing products in other sectors, and that therefore it was right to aim at a correct allocation of resources within the fuel industry neglecting any misallocations which might ensue between the fuel industry and other sectors.

However, despite these three reasons for welcoming Professor Samuelson's paper, Mr Turvey had some reservations. There seemed to be an unfortunate lack of correspondence between the cases of public expenditure which were important in practice, and the definitions of public goods as made by Samuelson and Musgrave. There could be public goods which had nothing to do with public expenditure, and parts of public expenditure which were not public goods. Thus, if Professor Samuelson were to play a trumpet loudly and his neighbour were to be disturbed thereby, Professor Samuelson's trumpet-playing, by his own definition, would be a public good: but it had nothing whatsoever to do with public expenditure. Similarly, there were many public goods which did not enter in any way into the preference patterns of individuals. Mr Turvey therefore offered a new definition, which was as follows: a public good is any good which enters more than once into any utility function; or enters more than once into any production function; or once at least in some utility function and in addition once at least in some production function.

The other doubt or object for which Mr Turvey felt in reading Professor Samuelson's paper was the reference on page 109 to the nibilism which must result if any of the methods put forward by Professor Samuelson was not accepted. Mr Turvey felt strongly that the analysis advanced by Professor Samuelson was, alas, of little practical use: nevertheless Mr Turvey thought that much of economics continued to be of considerable use in public policy. The inapplicability of Samuelson's model to the economic situation as it really existed, stemmed from three causes. First Professor Samuelson had stressed that optimal allocation was possible only if there were possible lump sum redistributions. Mr Turvey knew of no such general method of redistribution, and in these circumstances, unfortunately no doubt, Professor Samuelson's model was inapplicable.

Secondly, we had to face the problem of specifying a social welfare function in order to solve the Samuelson problems. But in many issues of real life ordinary people were concerned not with social welfare in the sense of achieving the optimum distribution of real income between individuals and considering

[1] Drèze, J., 'Some Postwar Contributions of French Economists to Theory and Public Policy, with Special Emphasis on Problems of Resource Allocation', *American Economic Review*, liv, No. 4, Part 2, pp. 1–64 (June 1964).

each problem in the light of the known wealth or income of the individuals concerned, but with alternative concepts – e.g. 'fairness'. This well known common law principle could be supplemented and replaced by many others, none of which had much to do with income distribution in the economic sense.

Thirdly, in many issues of real life, it was common practice for individuals to delegate their responsibilities on the problems of the purchase and paying for public goods to their representatives in Parliament. No individual could have a view on the host of special expenditure or taxation problems, and in order to achieve what he believed would be the best possible result, the individual would elect a representative to decide on his behalf – a representative chosen because of his general qualities. This implied that Professor Samuelson's model was inapplicable.

Professor Sen then introduced Professor Musgrave's paper taking first his definition of a public good, and the two crucial characteristics of 'non-rivalness' in consumption and 'non-excludability' from consumption. One of these things can occur without the other. 'Non-rivalness' without 'non-excludability' curves – curves which would show the preference of different individuals for social goods taking into account the representative individuals' relative share of the cost of these goods. The 'costs' hypothetically incurred reflect the willingness of individuals to pay for the social good, and therefore the system can be used as a pseudo-pricing device. On the basis of the intersection of the respective offer curves it is possible to obtain an equilibrium point which is also Pareto-optimal, and if the individuals reveal their true preferences such a point can in fact be achieved. But game-theory considerations intrude, and sincere reporting of true preferences by individuals may be against their own interest.

In this discussion Professor Musgrave encountered the well known and difficult question of the degree of separation possible between considerations of efficiency and those of distributional equity. Professor Musgrave maintained that it is necessary to deal with the problems one at a time, and concentrated on the questions of efficiency. Professor Sen was inclined to agree with a view expressed later by many others in commenting on Professor Musgrave's paper, that this process was unsatisfactory. The author tried to avoid this problem by appropriate assumptions, but Professor Sen did not believe this escape to be possible. The reason for this impossibility was that our ideas of fairness of distribution were related to the distribution of goods and not to (or not exclusively to – that of means of production. Our ideas of social justice or welfare were not related to the distribution of iron ore, oak trees and margarine between individuals, but rather to the composition and division of the products. We did not in fact form our judgements on income distribution without knowing something more about production and prices.

Professor Sen then turned to a comparison between Professor Samuelson's ideas on public goods and Professor Musgrave's discussion of the taxonomic classifications of social goods and the mixtures of cases. Professor Samuelson's new definition of a public good was one which entered more than one person's utility function. This was of course a general case of consumption externality, and it might not be obvious how all such cases could be subsumed in the framework of public goods. *A* may be annoyed by, or alternatively enjoy *B*, smoking a pipe, but of course the two had different attitudes to *B*'s pipe. It mattered very

R 2

much as to who owned the pipe. A transfer of the pipe from B to A would affect both persons' utilities. How, one might wonder, did this fit into the equal consumption aspect of Professor Samuelson's public goods? The trick lay in not taking a pipe as a public good, but a pipe belonging to A as one public good, and that belonging to B as another. Thus x_{ij} could be taken to be the amount of the i-th good going to the j-th individual. With m goods and n individuals we had $m \times n$ elements x_{ij}. Every x_{ij} need not of course be positive, and might well be zero. In principle any individual j's utility function U^j might depend on any or every item in the vector (x_{ij}):

$$U^j = U^j (x_{1,\,1},\, x_{1,\,2},\, \ldots,\, x_{1,\,n}; \ldots; x_{m,\,1},\, x_{m,\,2},\, \ldots,\, x_{m,\,n}). \tag{1}$$

We could remember the set of x_{ij}, according to some correction, to arrive at the following expression for j's utility, with x_k, when $k = 1, 2, \ldots, m \times n$:

$$U^j = U^j (x_1, x_2 \ldots, x_{m \times n}). \tag{1*}$$

This was exactly like Samuelson's classic model of public good, though this was based on assuming nothing other than externality in consumption. Note that Professor Samuelson's 'equal consumption' assumption was quite harmless. All it meant was that the same variable entered A's utility function which entered B's. Both the individuals enjoyed, as it were, B's pipe, though B might get a lot out of it and A little, or a negative amount, or be quite unaffected by it.

Not only did this model embrace the case of all kinds of public goods; as Samuelson emphasised, it also included all 'private goods'. Assuming, for simplicity, differentiability of the utility functions, the case of a private good y corresponded to the following conditions being fulfilled:

$$\frac{\partial U^j}{\partial x_{y,\,r}} = 0, \text{ for all } j \text{ and } r, \text{ with } j \neq r. \tag{2}$$

Samuelson's crucial condition II for optimal allocation of public goods remained unchanged in this model:

$$\sum_{j=1}^{n} \frac{U^j k}{U^j 1} = -\frac{F_k}{F_1}, \tag{3}$$

where F was the usual production function, the subscripts of U^j and F referred to the respective partial derivatives, and good 1 was a private good for individual j. It was to be noted that it did not matter whether k was a private good or public, and the Samuelson allocation equation held in general for interior solutions. In the case of two pure private goods we got form (3) the familiar neo-classical condition, in terms of the notation of (1) rather than of (1*):

$$\frac{\dfrac{\partial U^j}{\partial x_{i,\,j}}}{\dfrac{\partial U_j}{\partial x_{1,\,j}}} = \frac{-F_i}{F_1}. \tag{3*}$$

So far so good. Professor Samuelson's case covered all cases of public goods as well as private goods; it was even more general than he claimed. But what about Professor Musgrave's claim that there do exist polar cases of private goods, public goods, and mixed goods? The polar case of private goods had already been discussed, in terms of condition (2). Another polar case was one where either (i) x_i, j cannot be distinguished from x_i, r, or (ii) the distinction did not matter. Unlike the obvious distinction between A's pipe and B's there was little possibility of distinguishing what is euphemistically called 'defence' between that for A and that for B. This corresponded to case (i), while case (ii) might be illustrated by a well in an Indian village situated in the compound of a family which all the neighbours could use freely as if it was in their own compound. A transfer of the well from one family's compound to that of another would leave the utilities of all families in the community unchanged. In this case of a 'pure' public good z, we have given the values of the set (x_{ij}):

$$\frac{U^j}{x_z, j} = \frac{U^j}{x_z, r} \text{ for all } j \text{ and } r. \tag{4}$$

So Professor Musgrave was right, according to Professor Sen, in distinguishing between polar cases and mixed ones – this in spite of the perfect generality of Professor Samuelson's optimailty conditions. There was a distinction between cases like defence, or the well freely used by everyone, on the one hand, and the less extreme kinds of externality (A's pleasure from or disgust at B's pipe.) While Professor Samuelson's equations were perfectly general, they contained possibilities of 'pure' public goods just as they also embraced 'pure' private goods. Professor Musgrave's exercises involving specific cases, pure and impure, did seem to make good sense as a supplement to the general picture outlined by Professor Samuelson.

Professor Margolis suggested that there were five different problems arising out of these two rich and important papers. First, the question of what is a public good, and the question as to whether the problems of public goods should be analysed in a global way, as did Professor Samuelson, or in a more specific manner, as did Professor Musgrave. Second, was there some manner in which it was possible to discuss the efficiency of a public finance system separately from its equity? Third, what form should be taken by the social welfare function that we were using for this discussion and the question whether it was necessary to specify a social welfare function at all? Under the same heading, we could discuss the question of whether the 'voluntary exchange' principle was viable or not. Fourth, one could consider the point raised by Mr Turvey about the possibility of measuring the relationships whose form was examined in Professor Samuelson's model, and examine their applicability to problems of the practical policy. Last, one could discuss if we had time the pricing problems raised in the appendix to Professor Samueslon's paper. It was agreed that the problems of choice at a political level should be delayed until the discussion of Professor Dorfman's paper.

The Conference then proceeded to discuss the aspects of the definition of public goods. *Professor Dorfman* suggested that we were far from clarity on the definition of a public good. If, for instance, following Professor Sen, we were to accept the simplest possible formulation, such as 'my utility depends on the happiness of all others', almost every form of income or expenditure was associated in some sense with a public good. For instance, as a *reductio ad absurdum*, my happiness as a shareholder in a tobacco firm depended on my neighbour's consumption of cigarettes. This made cigarettes 'a public good'. Perhaps this definition was absurd, but how could we stop before reaching this absurdity.

Professor Samuelson intervened to suggest that it was in fact possible to stop reaching Professor Dorfman's absurdity. Public goods could be quite additive – separable in mathematical terms – to the ordinary private independent goods and satisfactions, and there was no need to extend the domain of public goods to cover the whole of economic activity.

Mr Terny suggested that we should speak not of public goods but of collective goods, and indeed not of goods but of services: 'collective services' seemed to cover most of these cases that had been discussed. He noted that Professor Samuelson had moved from his original definition of a public good – goods which could be consumed by one individual without reducing the consumption possibilities of another individual – to a definition involving the concept of externalities. On the whole, Mr Terny regretted this shift. The problem in considering externalities was that there seemed no way of stopping before reaching the sort of absurdity to which Professor Dorfman had drawn attention – to take Mr Turvey's case of the trumpets, if Professor Samuelson's neighbour had partaken of a good breakfast he would mind the trumpet noise less: but did this make even breakfasts into public goods?

Professor Marglin suggested that in his reply Professor Samuelson should consider whether the definition of a public good was not in fact closely related to the problem of the theory of capital. Several of the cases of public goods which had been examined seemed to be concerned with indivisibilities and increasing returns: for instance, my ability to enjoy a cinema performance depended on the willingness of others to attend cinemas and so cover between them the major part of the capital cost of providing the performance. There was hence some convenience in confining the definition, as other speakers had suggested, to a public service rather than goods; otherwise all things might become public goods in some ways.

Mr Kolm thought that in terms of Professor Sen's generalisation of the Samuelson system, the theoretically sound way of setting the problem was to consider than any service be described by a set (a vector) of parameters which represented quantities, various qualities etc.... These parameters entered into each individual's utility function, along with the paramenters of other services, of the individual's situation, etc.... For every individual, the parameters of a service might be, between them and with other parameters, substitutable, or complementary, or strictly complementary. We were mostly interested in the link between the various parameters for the various individuals. Of special interest would be the fact that individual values (algebraic marginal willingness to pay) of a parameter, taking into account its indirect effects on other parameters by way of the constraints, had the same or different signs (i.e. Musgrave's non-rivalness or rivalness). These relations were generally not the same for the various parameters of a given service.

An important example was that the benefits from all traditional instances of 'public goods' (lighthouses, TV emissions, roads, theatres, parks, municipal and government services, etc...) were linked to a certain occupation of a certain space during a certain time. While there was non-rivalness for many parameters of the good, there was always rivalness for the space x time volume occupied (this was the most common device for exclusion). But there was also generally a certain substitability between the various possible space x time volumes linked to this consumption.

Although we should practically have to build 'summaries' (index-numbers) to define and measure the service, it was doubtful that this would be done correctly if we did not start from a theoretically thorough view of the problem.

These remarks suggested that a less vague vocabulary was needed. For instance, we might say that h is a *collective consumprion* of (is collectively consumed by) a collectively described by a set of i's containing more than one element, if $v^i \neq 0$ for all $i\epsilon\tau$. We might say that h is a collective *concern* for such a collectivity if $v_h^i \neq 0$ for all $i\epsilon$. We might say that h is a collective consumption or a collective concern without qualification if there exist respectively some such τ's. Of course, a collective consumption is a sepcial case of collective concern (and a collective concern is also a collective consumption if there is at least three i's such that $v_h^i \neq 0$), etc.... We keep the term *public good* for something which is described by a set of parameters one of which, at least, measures a collective consumption. Similarly we call *public concern* something which is described by a set of parameters one of which, at least, measures a collective concern. *Public consumption* might be kept for what is bought by public expenditures. We use the term *externality* to express that an agent endures, whether he likes it or not, the consequences of a decision in which he has taken no part. Finally, it might be useful to find words to specify whether individual concernments are of the same nature or are very different in kind. Doubtless, this vocabulary is perfectible, but it is certainly better than calling everything a 'public good'.

Finally, it might be useful to find words to specify whether individual concernments were of the same nature or were very different in kind.

Professor Guitton noted that as a result of the definitions in Professor Samuelson's paper, one came near to reducing the problems of the public economy to those of the private economy. He, together with many other Frenchmen, was concerned with the relationship between public planning and the private sector. He was not sure, and here he echoed the comments of Mr Turvey, whether the construction in Samuelson's paper in fact made it easier to arrive at proper decisions about the role of public policy.

The conference then moved on to the discussion of the social welfare function.

Professor Sandee suggested that the formulation of Professor Samuelson's equation III seemed neutral, but did it in fact imply that all men were equal? (Professor Samuelson later replied that this was not so in fact, and Professor Sandee accepted the answer.) Secondly, he was interested in the possibility of applying a sort of 'inverse method'. The set of utility and production functions defiine an optimum. One could assume the existence of an optimum in any concrete situation, and then try to define production functions and utility functions which were consistent with such a real situation being optimal. This, of course, would not be a search which could have one unique end, but it might limit the number of functions that would need to be examined. He would welcome a discussion on this possibility.

Professor Delivanis wished to limit himself to a single point at the end of

Professor Musgrave's paper. It was suggested that Western society accepted inequalities in luxury goods provided equality was secured in necessities. He hoped that Professor Musgrave would consider the following possibilities: first, that the category of necessities was expanding in an affluent society; second, that if necessities were supplied free of charge to the poorer people, the latter would be able to use their increasing income exclusively for luxuries and thus reduce the differences of their living conditions from those of the richer people whose tax burden would have increased in order to supply necessities to those who need them.

Mr Kolm was rather surprised and unhappy that Professor Samuelson had purported to destroy completely the principle of voluntary exchange. If everyone in the room were contemplating the possibility and desirability of increasing the amount of light coming from the chandelier, we could go round each person and ask how much they would be prepared to contribute in order to have a little more light. The total sum contributed could then be sent to the electricity company who would then provide the lights. What was there about this process that was impossible?

Widespread throughout Professor Samuelson's paper was a basic confusion between Wicksell's and Lindahl's theories which were in fact very different (and also, secondarily, between Lindahl's theory and Johansen's which was supposed to describe it but was also different). This entailed errors of interpretation and even calumnies towards these authors and some of their commentators. As instances, take:

—page 102's assertion: 'one of my main findings has been the falsity of that theory's replying on voluntary exchange' when applied to Wicksell;
—in the appendix: 'as Wicksell sensed... it pays no one to behave according to the voluntary exchange theory';
—the use of quantities as functions of prices and 'pseudo-tax-prices' as pseudo-demand functions, which do not fit at all in Wicksell's analysis;
—the criticism of Professor Musgrave about the indeterminacy introduced by public goods (footnote on page 102);
—the criticisms of Wicksell's 'approximate unanimity'.

Although the differences between Lindahl and Johansen were much less important than those between them and Wicksell, it was very interesting to notice that Lindahl's determination of the quantity of the public good (a garden) in his second paper was *not* a marginal but an 'all or nothing' process and therefore it did not yield a 'Pareto-optimal point' which was obtained with a lesser quantity; notwithstanding that in his first paper Lindahl gave, in a passage he says he owes to Wicksell, the formula marginal cost = the sum of the marginal willingness to pay, which is the 'Pareto-optimum' condition.[1]

As for Wicksell, one could address to him the reproach of not stating explicitly enough from the beginning that the outcome of his process was not uniquely determined (when nothing was known of the 'bargaining powers'). However,

[1] It is impossible to say if Lindahl's change is a conscious evolution or a mistake. Note, by the way, that Professor Johansen is not immune from mistakes: when income is redistributed his 'Lindahl point' does not move on the same line of 'Pareto-optimal' points, but this whole line is changed.

he acknowledged clearly this indeterminacy when he discussed the wealth distribution problem.

Professor Musgrave was right, notwithstanding Professor Samuelson's and others' criticism, when he explained that the introduction of public goods in a previously purely private economy, with a given wealth distribution, introduced an indeterminacy which generally did not exist before. This was exactly what had to be added to the first part of Wicksell's analysis (before his consideration of the initial distribution of wealth) in order to make it valid.

Professor Samuelson attributed to Wicksell and, although this was less improper to Lindahl, what were Johansen's ideas. It was not necessary to recall here what these authors had written, but it was necessary to emphasise the following fundamental point: Wicksell's process is truly voluntary but its outcome is indeterminate. On the other hand Johansen's Lindahl-optimal state is determinate, with a given initial distribution of wealth, but it entails a revelation problem; people will hide their preferences.

That a Wicksell process yields the formula marginal cost = the sum of the marginal willingness to pay, can be shown by direct reasoning on the 'marginal voluntary contribution'.[1]

This latter process shows that the 'demand functions' for public goods in the true voluntary exchange theory were not quantities as functions of prices and 'pseudo-tax prices' equal to marginal willingness to pay, as was argued in Professor Samueslon's paper. They were marginal willingnesses to pay as functions of the prices of private goods and the quantities of public goods.[2] One had to play the dual game to its end.

In order to make a Wicksell process determinate, one could try: first, to consider the initial distribution of wealth as a separate problem; and second, to establish a rule to allocate the cost of public goods. Any rule which would secure that at the optimum the marginal contribution of everybody was equal to his marginal willingness to pay was acceptable for 'Pareto-optimality'. For instance the rule that everyone should pay for each public good the product of its quantity by his marginal willingness to pay for it, i.e. a Musgrave's allocation branch (or a Johansen's Lindahl's pricing), is acceptable. But then two problems arose: first, the valid rule depends on income distribution and the optimal income distribution depends on the outcome of the application of the rule; however, for small changes and around the optimum the legitimate neglect of terms of order higher than the first disposes of this objection, justifies this dichotomy, and enables each 'branch' to adjust as if the other branch were optimally behaving. But, second, the rule, whatever it is, introduces incentives to lie and revelation problems. Wicksell did not tackle all that.

In order to make the optimum determinate, Professor Samueslon wants a Social Welfare Function, an 'ethical valuation'. But the question: *whose* ethical valuation, *whose* Social Welfare Function? is a relevant one. If you want to have your Social Welfare Function increased rather than mine, I can play the Voluntary Exchange game and ask you: how much are you willing to pay to

[1] See Kolm, *Introduction à la théorie du role économique de l'Etat: fondements de l'économie publique* (I.F.P., Rueil-Malmaison, 1964), Rome I, chapitre iii.

[2] And the demand function for a private good depends upon the quantities, and not the 'pseudo-tax-prices', of public goods.

induce me to accept this? This 'neo-Wicksellian' reasoning yields a unique optimum which can be obtained by successive moves accepted by unanimity or at worst unanimity minus one, which is a good Wicksell-like 'approximate unanimity'.

Finally, when comparing Professor Samuelson's overall maximisation, Professor Wicksell's overall discussion, Professor Musgrave's Branch Functional finance and Professors Lindahl-Johansen Benefit taxation, one must take into account not only determinacy and revelation problems but also costs of contacts, contracts, discussions and decisions, which were thoroughly forgotten in this 'very general' paper.

Professor Jochimsen drew attention to a point which ocurred in both Professor Samuelson's and Professor Musgrave's papers. Professor Samuelson suggested that it was necessary to decide lump sum transfers and taxes simultaneously; Professor Musgrave insisted that there must be proper voting procedure to decide spending and taxation policies. But were these alternative methods of establishing social welfare function really possible? He would like to have some discussion of the political possibilities which were open taking into account modern theories of the state.

Professor Musgrave pointed out that his paper had been available to Professor Samuelson when Professor Samuelson was preparing his contribution, but Professor Samuelson's paper had not been available to Professor Musgrave. Professor Musgrave, however, wished to point out that he had been very glad to profit from Professor Samuelson's advice and comments. Although there were shadings of opinion and methods between his paper and Professor Samuelson's, they had strong similarities and he would be particularly grateful if Professor Barrère could comment on any divergences which still existed between his views on the one hand and those of Professor Musgrave and Professor Samuelson on the other. For Professor Musgrave there was really no alternative to rational calculation in this field – the only possible alternative would be irrational coercion by the state. Personal preferences had to be considered as the basis of the system. Although he was in general agreement with Professor Samuelson's approach, there were differences. Professor Samuelson was more general and in Professor Musgrave's view distinctions between the different types and versions of public goods were most important. In many ways he wished that Professor Samuelson's extremely able chimpanzee had climbed the trees rather than merely surveying the forest. It was most important to establish which were the 'mixed goods' – because otherwise we would have the absurdity that some goods were entirely subsidised and other goods had no subsidy at all. Again we must distinguish between benefits which flow in one direction only and benefits which might flow in two ways. He was very glad that Professor Sen had raised the problems of the distinction between allocation and distribution. This was a public finance problem on which we must have a policy. Indeed, in the whole of this field it was most important to have a policy, because otherwise those interested in distribution would be in favour of the groups they were interested in, and then would swing to the opposite extreme of being in favour of low taxes when taxes seemed to be regressive in their impact. He agreed with Professor Sen and Professor Samuelson that in principle problems of taxation and the distribution of benefits should be decided simultaneously. He agreed that voting procedures were both necessary and possible, and concluded by re-emphasising the points that he had made at the end of his paper.

Professor Samuelson said that he agreed with Professor Marglin that there was an overlap between problems of capital and problems of public goods, but the overlap was not complete: it was possible to have public goods which had nothing whatever to do with capital, for instance the case mentioned by Professor Dorfman of fluoridation of water supplies. He agreed with Mr Turvey that the word public good might be unfortunate, but he insisted that the domain of public good was not co-terminous with the domain of the public sector. He was interested by Mr Kolm's remarks but doubted whether any results could come from the use of game theory in this field and the principle of voluntarism necessarily implied the use of game theory. He could not welcome Mr Turvey's suggestion that his paper was entirely normative – he had emphasised the normative aspect but considered himself as establishing both a descriptive and a normative framework. Neither could he accept Mr Turvey's suggestion that his theory was inapplicable to real cases because this would imply that in fact most real tax and benefit problems were cases of what Professor Musgrave would call merit wants. He insisted that the appendix to his paper, although perhaps making his contribution of excessive length, was relevant to the paper and were practical examples of what his policy would imply. As regards Mr Turvey's example of the trumpets he thought that on reflection Mr Turvey would agree that this problem was covered by Professor Samuelson's own discussion of road transport in the appendix. He was inclined to accept Mr Kolm's use of the term goods and services and public concern rather than 'public goods' and thought this a helpful extension of the language. He would leave one passing thought with Mr Turvey: the whole notion of a 'second best solution' was offensive to his mind, because he thought one should speak instead of the 'domain of feasible first bests'.

Professor Barrère replied to the challenge made by him to Professor Musgrave to consider whether there might be some practicable alternative to the Musgrave-Samuelson approach to public goods. Professor Barrère approached this question in a scientific spirit, and considered that only an ideological prejudice could lead one to insist that all activities of the public power should be subject to the final test of their ability to satisfy private wants. There were both 'biens publics' (collective goods) and goods which satisfied private wants. These were two distinct types of goods produced for two distinct types of reason and was a mistake to elide the two. He agreed that collective needs were not necessarily served by what Samuelson would call public goods, but nevertheless there were a whole collection of public activities paid for by public funds which were decided on quite rational grounds which had little to do with the sort of analysis which Professors Samuelson and Musgrave had so elegantly achieved.

Turning now to the applicability issue, *Professor Sandee* started by questioning Professor Samuelson's use of the term algorithm. Was it perhaps used in its proper sense of a prescription to a computer? Was it a metaphor for a market mechanism working by iteration? Was it an instruction to policy makers who would in turn use computers? He did not think that Professor Samuelson would care to comment. Secondly, he thought the time might be ripe to apply Professor

Samuelson's model to the real world – hence helping to meet some of Mr Turvey's objections. The trouble was the size of the model and the number of equations. The number of equations was equal to $nx + m$, where s was the number of persons involved, n was the number of private goods, and m the number of public goods. The task would be to reduce n or s. He thought this could be done by applying the model say to the city of Boston for a particular year. In this case the m's are three distinct forms of public expenditure; the n's are merely one, because all private goods can be subsumed under one head; and s could perhaps be taken as equal to 4 (distinguishing four types of Bostonians according to income). This gave eight equations and we could then establish the utility functions by a process which he would call vicarious introspection – related to the method which he had referred to in his earlier contribution as the inverse method.

Professor Musgrave replied to Professor Barrère that his method was surely neutral ideologically speaking, because, as Lange and Taylor had shown, even in a socialist economy the ultimate reference to consumer wants was quite consistent with a socialist organisation of society.

Professor Samuelson, in reply to Professor Sandee, accepted that perhaps he should have used the term 'psuedo-algorithm'. He was not sure that he was as eager to apply his model as quickly as Professor Sandee was to see it done, and thought the time was not yet ripe to quantify the relationships in which he was interested.

SESSION SIX

Discussion of Mr. Kolm's Paper

Introducing the paper, *Professor Marglin* dealt with only the first part, which was an attempt to combine and present in an integrated form three different pieces of theory: the theory concerned with the production and demand of public goods; the theory concerned with distribution; and the theory concerned with inter-personal welfare comparisons. The essence of the Kolm system was that each individual entered into the utility function of us all. Partly this was concerned with what had been called in the Samuelson and Musgrave papers public goods, partly it was concerned with the general phenomenon of altruism and jealousy. It was this general phenomenon which was the main point of the Kolm paper. Mr Kolm, after a detailed and demanding analysis, came to the extremely strong result that there was an optimum distribution of a fixed set of consumption goods between individuals – an optimum distribution which was dependent upon the individual utility functions but which was unique. Mr Kolm's point could be illustrated by a simple example. If we allowed utility to depend in a simple way upon consumption so that one extra unit of my consumption gives me one extra unit of utility, my dependence upon your utility in a two-individual world could be illustrated as in equation (1); similarly your dependence upon my utility could be illustrated in equation (2). We could then display these two equations, taking suitable values for the v's on the following diagram:

$$\sigma U_1 = \sigma C_1 + v^1 \sigma U_2 \tag{1}$$

$$\sigma U_2 = \sigma C_2 + v_1^2 \sigma U_1. \tag{2}$$

In the diagram the point of intersection of the two curves (E) was a point of equilibrium – an equilibrium which we could imagine being reached by a process of iteration rather like a multiplier process. The iterative process would be convergent to a single equilibrium point only if the values of the v's were less than unity, and this was provided for in Mr Kolm's model.

So far there was nothing remarkable or unacceptable about the model – it asserted merely that if two persons' utility were interdependent, and they started from an initial distribution of consumption goods between them, there was some redistribution of consumption goods which would make them happier. The point of intersection was an equilibrium, but Mr Kolm wanted it to be a unique equilibrium. Could this be true? If instead of expressing the equations in terms of changes in the amount of goods available to the two individuals, we instead adopted a more general statement, it was possible to establish utility functions which, provided that one allowed for inter-personal comparisons and traditional Pigovian additive utilities, would enable us to arrive at Mr Kolm's result. But if we recognised the difficulties in comparing the utilities of different individuals and followed the mathematics to its conclusions, there did not seem to Professor Marglin to be proof that Mr Kolm had established his point.

Professor Samuelson suggested that if in fact Mr Kolm succeeded in doing what Professor Marglin had suggested was his aim – to establish an objective criterion for the distribution of income between individuals – he would have solved more than the problem of justice, he would have produced little short of a miracle. Pareto optimality can always be defined, but the problem is which Pareto optimum is the best. Professor Samuelson wondered how in fact the rabbit was put into the hat: as far as he could see the only way would be to accept cardinal utility and there were no other alternatives.

There was danger in the use of an ambiguous word like 'optimum'. He could remember, back in 1937 when Abram Bergson was preparing his classic paper on welfare economics, reading over and over with him each word of Pareto that involved the concept of the optimum. What we today call 'Pareto optimality' was not really clearly understood by Pareto himself: thus he speaks of *the* optimum instead of *an* optimum, as if he did not realise that Pareto-optimality alone leaves you with an *infinity* of points on the utility-possibility frontier. The narrow 'new welfare economists' of the 1930's who rediscovered the Pareto-optimality conditions did not sufficiently realise that they are merely 'necessary' conditions, quite insufficient to lead to any conclusions if not supplemented by a Bergson social welfare function; given such a function, we see the Pareto-optimality conditions to be merely those necessary conditions which can be written down *independently* of the nature of the social welfare function, and such independence warns us of their uselessness in isolation.

We had to judge the acceptability of an axiom by its consequences. He proposed to calculate what were the consequences of Mr Kolm's basic axiom about the optimum in the following special case so as to show why he felt obliged to reject it.

Draw up Man 1's indifference contours between his consumption C, and Man 2's; similarly draw up Man 2's. Now suppose that each happens to have convex contours *that are parallel* in the direction of his own C_i. Then, one could write for utilities:

$$U^1 = C_1 + f_1(C_2)$$
$$U^2 = C_2 + f_2(C_2), f_i''(C_j) < 0,$$

and, it could be shown (as Marglin had suggested) that in this case Mr Kolm's axiom leads to accepting the consequence of maximising summed Benthamite utilities:

$$\text{Max } U^1 + U^2 \text{ subject to}$$
$$C_1 C_2 \qquad C_1 + C_2 = \bar{C}.$$

Now what is compelling in 1966 about such a procedure? If we think its *results* arbitrary, we must think Mr Kolm's fundamental axiom to be arbitrary and unacceptable. The riddle of justice remains!

Professor Musgrave wondered which game Mr Kolm was playing: was it one of the following:

1 We start out with a given distribution of resource endowments. Assuming that A derives utility not only from his endowment but also from that of Y and Z, people may agree to rearrange the endowment distribution, with everybody deriving a benefit from the rearrangement.

2 We start out with a given distribution of votes (say equal) and let people determine (by stipulating some voting rule, say, majority) how income is to be distributed. (The Edgeworth case.)

3 We assume strict measurement of utility and comparability between persons, as well as additivity. We now maximise total utility by equating marginal utilities. This is the old Pigou game which can now be amended to allow for A deriving utility from B's income, etc.

None of these games (and there can be others) provided a fundamental solution to the distribution problem. (1) started with an endowment distribution; (2) started with a vote distribution and voting rule; (3) was unacceptable because of additivity, and even if it were acceptable, there was no obvious reason why maximising total utility should be the guiding criterion. It appeared that Mr Kolm felt his formulation to be different from these three models and to provide a more suitable answer. Professor Musgrave wondered whether it did.

Professor Guitton said that he had tried his best to follow Professor Marglin's exposition, and would indeed in other circumstances like to be his pupil. But the purpose of this symposium was to study the basic points and he could not see his way clearly to an understanding of what Mr Kolm was trying to achieve. Was Mr Kolm aiming at computative justice or was there some other end in view? He suspected that a great deal of the confusion and mathematics arose from an unclear definition of what justice was.

Mr Kolm then replied to the discussion. He felt that he should point out that much of Professor Marglin's interesting exposition was not so much derived from Mr Kolm's paper as entirely original work – original work of high quality. He would concentrate his own reply on those points where he disagreed with the comments made by various contributors. He did not agree, to start with, that his method was similar to merely the maximisation of a sum of utilities. The discussion was related to that which had taken place earlier in the day on the nature of public goods: in many ways the distribution of wealth and particularly of income is a public good in its truest sense (in particular, it is a 'collective concern', as defined in the paper). The point he had tried to make in his paper and on which he disagreed with Professor Samuelson in particualr was the possibility of coming to agreement between individuals on the best distribution of income. He thought that there were methods by which agreement could be reached, and could not accept the suggestion that game theory had nothing to offer us in this field.

SESSION SEVEN

Discussion of Professor Sen's Paper

Mr Kolm introduced the paper by pointing out that its basic subject was the analysis of social justice and, more specifically, of distributive justice in particular. Although this has been less studied by economists than the analysis of production, it is no less important a subject, nor must it be expected to be any less complex.

Certain subjects dealt with by Professor Sen, and the authors to whom he refers, had been discussed during the Age of Enlightenment and of the Revolution; thus the consideration of certain aspects of the intensity of preferences (cardinality) as a means of escaping from the impasse created by the fact that rational social choices are not possible due to Arrow's condition of 'independence of irrelevant alternatives', is the exact replica of the introduction by Laplace (after Borda) of the system of 'vote by points' in order to avoid the 'intransitivities' raised by Condorcet in the context of majority votes.

In another context, the search for an index, here called a social welfare function, which could take account of the justice of the distribution of income, has been the object of numerous discussions among Italian economists at the turn of the century.

The analysis of distributive justice made its first written appearance in English with Hugh Dalton's famous article in the *Economic Journal* in 1920. This article plays, for the analysis of distributive justice, the role played by Frank Ramsey's 1928 article in the same journal for the analysis of optimal growth. Professor Sen takes up the story at the next stage, which is the introduction by Abram Bergson in 1938, then by Oscar Lange and Paul Samuelson, of a social welfare function dependent on all the possible parameters of the states of the world. This step perhaps constituted progress of a sort on the plane of logic, but on the plane of economics it was, due to the excessive generality of the proposed tool, a step backward in relation to the more specific proposals that had been made previously. Moreover, it drove economists to demand that they have a social welfare function before they had got down to work, and to consider the determining of it as exogenous to their studies. That is why Kenneth Arrow's destructive criticism in 1951 had such a salutary effect in stimulating studies like the one we were here discussing, which would lead to an effective specification of the social optimum.

Professor Sen rightly observes that for arriving at this result a social welfare function is an unnecessarily powerful tool. It is enough, he states, to be able to define a 'choice set'. Perhaps he might even add that if the possible choices are defined within the limits of the actions to be carried out, then this 'choice set' must contain only one element: the action (standing alone by definition for it excludes all others) that has to be performed.

In addition, Professor Sen explains that Bergson's proposal and Arrow's criticism do not really deal with the same thing. Mr Kolm thought that we can in fact pick out four differences between these concepts. The first, well described in Sen's paper but less fundamental than the others, is that Bergson is talking about an ordinal function while Arrow is considering the more general notion of a social preference ordering. The second is that Bergson's social welfare function, in so far as it is concerned with the sovereignty of the consumers, is an implicit function of the possible states of nature through the intermediary of the corresponding values of the individual indices of welfare, while in Arrow's formulation of the problem the 'social welfare function' (when the ordering can be so described) is at the same time a *function* of these states and a *functional* of the individual welfare functions (when the individual preference orderings can be so described). The third difference is that Bergson's individual utility functions are functions only of the amounts consumed by the individuals concerned, while Arrow's individual preference orderings bear *a priori* on all the characteristic features of the states of the world. To put this in Arrow's terms, Bergson is talking about *personal tastes* and Arrow about individual *values*.

Therefore, from the three points of view put forward, Bergson's function is really one particular case of Arrow's 'function'; as an obvious consequence, Arrow's theorem establishing the impossibility of the existence of his own 'function' is a valid criticism of Bergson's function. The fourth difference is that Bergson considers his functions as representing the ethical or social or political preferences of one person, that is, in Arrow's terms, a part, at least, of the social 'values' of that individual. Why one individual is considered rather than another is outside Bergson's argument; if then Bergson's function were taken as a 'function' of Arrow's social choice, that individual would be a 'dictator' in the last-named writer's view; on the contrary Arrow is trying to find an aggregate of Bergson's function for all individuals.

Arrow has pointed out that there exists no social welfare function which meets a number of conditions. Following a now classic procedure, Professor Sen wonders which of these conditions might be relaxed more or less so as to make the existence of such a function possible. One way of achieving this is to consider that the individual preferences in a society present certain similarities. Making more general use of the result arrived at by Black, Professor Sen shows that some restriction of the possible set of individual orders of preference permits a simple majority vote to perform the required social welfare function; the result, therefore, contributes also to the analysis of that process of arriving at a decision first introduced by Condorcet and developed by the Reverend Dodgson (known in literature as Lewis Carroll).

Another way consists of making a direct attack on the condition of 'irrelevance of independent alternatives'. On this point Professor Sen shows that the consideration of cardinal individual utilities (that is, defined only up to an increasing function) is not the only way to define social welfare; however, in Mr Kolm's opinion, this is to insist insufficiently on the fact that the result depends essentially on keeping the same system of aggregation – the sum of the values of the individual utilities – when the specifications of these utilities change.

Professor Sen goes on to comment on a proposal put forward by Harsanyi consisting of two parts. The first is a summation theorem which states that if at one and the same time all the individual preferences as well as the social preferences were Bernoulian-Neumanian for risked choices (that is that they are homogenous linear functions of the probabilities), and if the sovereignty of the consumers is respected (at least in case of indifference), then the social welfare function is a balanced sum of the individual welfare functions (all these functions being, of course, cardinal). The theorem is evident since, if we call π^j the probability of the eventuality j, and Φ a function having as many variables as there are individuals, the hypotheses amount to saying that

$$\sum_j \pi^j w^j \equiv \Phi(\{\sum_j \pi^j U_i^j\})$$

for all the admissible π^j's, that is taking it that $\sum_j \pi^j = 1$ and $0 \leqslant \pi^j \leqslant 1$ for every j.

The result is that Φ is a homogenous linear function of its variables. Let us note that Fleming[1] arrived at the same result without bringing in risked choices by directly applying to the social welfare function hypotheses like those which lead von Neuman or Marschak or Herstein and Milnor to the linear form of the welfare index for risked choices.

In the second place, Harsanyi along with others proposes the notion of 'impersonality': if a person has equal chances of being in exactly the same physical environment as various individuals belonging to society and of being of exactly the same opinions as those individuals, and if his behaviour in the face of risk is Bernoulian, that person has a social welfare function which is the unweighted sum of the individual utilities. This function is therefore the same for all individuals; it is, by definition, 'Bergsonian' (it is an individual value for Arrow), but a rule of unanimity permits the definition of an identical 'Arrowian' function.

Mr Kolm thought, however, that these authors and Professor Sen ought not to say that this function describes *ethical* preferences; it results, in fact, simply from egoism in the face of risk on the part of various individuals. Above all, the chief weakness of the interpretation is that it is completely unrealistic: any guess I may make (subjective probability) about my situation and still more about my preferences and the opinions I shall hold in the future is quite different from a guess I may make as to the frequency distribution of these situations and

---

[1] 'A Cardinal Concept of Welfare', *Quarterly Journal of Economics*, August 1952.

opinions in society. Nevertheless the principle retains some interest on condition that it abandons its interpretation of 'risked egoism' in favour of an interpretation that we can call 'purely ethical', the planner's preferences – such is indeed, at bottom, the object of the report under discussion – are obtained by him, as a result of his efforts to feel himself both objectively and subjectively in the situation of the various members of society. But in that case risk no longer comes in to act as the base for the principle of aggregation by summation. One could restore linearity with the aid of Harsanyi's or Fleming's hypotheses mentioned in the preceding paragraphs, or seek other methods of aggregation.

Be that as it may, an unweighted sum of individual utilities like that resluting from the principle of impersonality, depends on the specifications of these utilities. Professor Sen properly pointcd this out. Mr Kolm wanted to add in even more precise terms, that in order for it to be an acceptable social welfare function, it demands that each individual utility be defined up to an arbitrary additive constant (the multipliaction by an equivalent positive number of all the indices is also admissable). Therefore these utilities must be more precise than cardinal, and *a fortiori* than ordinal.

Finally Professor Sen directs his interest at another kind of uncertainty: that which springs from the fact that the planner does not know the preferences of the various individuals exactly. Lerner points out (though he does not make his hypotheses precise enough), and Professor Sen demonstrates, that if the chances that individuals have different 'capacities for enjoying income' are equal, if these capacities are measured by utilities which are concave functions of income, if the social welfare function is an unweighted sum of the individual utilities, if the social welfare function in case of uncertainty is Bernoulian (that is, the mathematical expectation of its value in the various eventualities) and finally if the problem consists of distributing a given income, then the optimal distribution consists of having all the incomes equal. Let us note that for Lerner there is, as there must be, only the optimum, while Professor Sen shows only that equal distribution is one of those which maximises the social welfare function; but Professor Sen would have ended up with the same result as Lerner did if he had supposed that the individual utiltiy functions were *strictly* concave.

Friedman and Samuelson have criticised Lerner's analysis and have proposed alternatives. One of the criticisms is that in fact one does have some knowledge of the capacities of different individuals for enjoying income, the result of which is that the probable distribution of these capacities is not the same for each of the individuals concerned . Moreover, Professor Sen observes, the use of Bernoulian preferences in case of risk – and even, might one add, that of probabilities – is open to criticism. In reply to both these objections, Professor Sen demonstrates that one arrives at the same result if, retaining all other hypotheses, one replaces this behaviour in the presence of risk by a 'maximin' behaviour. This choice, we know, consists of turning the worst eventually into the best one possible without being concerned about the rest. It therefore represents a very prudent mode of conduct for which it is possible to find certain moral justifications when dealing with the distribution of income. With this principle of choice, the symmetry between individuals which was previously the identity for each of them of the distribution of the utility functions, reduces to very little: namely that one was never sure that some individual could not have such a utility function. As in the 'probabilist' case, Professor Sen merely ends up with the conclusion that equal distribution is one of the methods of allocation which maximises the social welfare function, but he would have shown that this optimum is the only one if he had imposed strict concavity on the utility functions.

Mr Kolm expressed three sets of reservations about these two developments of Lerner's ideas by Professor Sen.

The first concerned the use as a social welfare function of a sum of individual utility functions, and that of specified individual utility functions (up to an additive constant); reference had already been made to this above. Still more did it seem to him that the maximum could be defined starting from purely ordinal considerations.[1]

The second set of observations concerns the demonstrations which seemed unnecessarily complicated. In both cases, that of probability and that of maximin, the result springs from the fact that the possibility set and the maximand are symmetric with the set of incomes, and that the possibility set is convex and the maximand quasi-concave in these variables (strict quasi-concavity ensures that there is one and only one optimum).

Following Professor Sen's notations, but calling however X (instead of D) the vector of the x_i's, the properties of the possibility set result from its definition: $\sum_i x_i = X$ or perhaps $\sum_i x_i \leqslant X$, with perhaps $x_i \leqslant 0$ for each i.

In the 'probabilist' case, the results given for the maximand are deduced from the formula (2), $P = \sum_i [\sum_j U^j(x_i)]$:

1 P is symmetric in the x_i's since it is a sum of identical functions $\sum p^j U^j(x_i)$ of these variables.

2 If the $U^j(\xi)$ are concave, $\sum p^j U^j(\xi)$ is concave, therefore $\sum_i [\sum_j p^j U^j(x_i)]$ is concave with respect to x, and it is also quasi-concave with respect to x; the same goes for the strict properties.

In the maximin case, if the U^j are concave, $W(C, x)$ is concave with respect to x for each C, because C is a sum of $U^j(x_i)$; $\underset{C}{\mathrm{Min}}\, W(C, x)$ is concave with respect to x, according to a well-known theorem, and this function of x is thus quasi-concave; the same holds for the strict properties. Now, let us call π a permutation of indices i; it transforms C into C^π and x into x^π. We have $W(C, x) = W(C^\pi, x^\pi)$. Let π^{-1} be the inverse permutation of π. Finally let us call C_x a C such that $\underset{C}{\mathrm{Min}}\, W(C, x) = W(C_x, x)$. One gets then successively: $W(C_x\pi, x^\pi)$ $< W(C_x^\pi, x^\pi) = W(C_x, x) < W(C_{x\pi}^{\pi^{-1}}, x) = W(C_{x\pi}, x^\pi)$ and thus $W(C_x\pi, x^\pi)$ $= W(C_x, x)$, which establishes the symmetry of $\underset{C}{\mathrm{Min}}\, W(C, x)$ with respect to x.

To sum, up in both cases the symmetry of the maximand springs from the fact that the problem posed sets up no distinction between the various – i's

---

[1] Cf. Sections II and III of Mr Kolm's paper in this volume. Note, however, that in the last part of his study he is introducing a series of hypotheses certain of which permit the justification of a maximand of the form retained by Professor Sen although the method used for arriving at that result is an entirely different one.

(impartiality), and the quasi-concavity (respectively the strict concavity) arises out of the concavity (respectively out of the strict concavity) of the preferences.

Mr Kolm's third observation sprang from the fact that he had some *a priori* doubts about the economic interest of a study which concluded that incomes have to be equally distributed. Such a result in fact proves that this study glosses over two problems which are among the main problems of economics in general, and the main ones of the analysis of social justice in particular. One is that there are several sorts of assets and that even from a purely ordinal point of view preferences (that is the shape of the indifference maps) vary according to individuals; one can perhaps, however, consider this question apart within the setting of compensatory justice in order to isolate the problem of purely distributive justice in which incomes (or homogenous wealth) would be adequate variables. The other is that in the problems that are of interest to economists the amount to be distributed is not independent of the distribution. It is thus that the problem of choice arises between a less unfair distribution of available income and property on the one hand, and the mainatining of incentives to production on the other, and more generally of the best compromise between justice and the efficient functioning of society. In that case, even if impartiality provides a symmetric social welfare function, the best distribution of wealth is not equality.

Professor Samuelson commented as follows: faced with Arrow's Impossibility Theorem, economists are tempted to relax one or another of his four axioms. As Professor Sen points out, the axiom on independence of irrelevant alternatives is often singled out for rejection. When cardinal intensities of preference are introduced, another of Arrow's axiom's – that the social ordering shall be definable from individual orderings alone – is denied, as Sen says. What I should like to suggest is that cardinality does not provide a way out of the impossibility dilema, but only a way in to another Impossibility Theorem.

Consider Men 1, 2 and 3; situations (A,B,C). Let each of these men have a cardinal rating indicated by the triplet of numbers (P_A^j, P_B^j, P_C^j). [By convention these can be fractions: e.g. if I prefer A to B and B to C, and if I would be indifferent between an even-odds prospect of A or C and between B with certainty, the triplet of numbers could be $(1/8, 2/8, 3/8)$ or $(1^m/n, 2^m/n, 3^m/n)$ indifferently.]

The cardinal ratings of each individual can now be used to define a social cardinal rating, again depictable by a triplet of numbers (P_A^0, P_B^0, P_C^0), which are now to be determinate functions of the nine cardinal numbers of the individuals, namely

$$P_A^o = \pi_A(P_A^1, P_B^1, P^1; \ P^2, P_B^2, P_C^2; \ P_A^3, P_B^3, P^3), \text{ etc.}$$

Now, in the spirit of Arrow's original axiom, let one impose four reasonable axioms on the (Π_a, Π_b, Π_c) functions. It is Professor Samuelson's conjecture, which he cannot claim yet to have proved, that no functions can exist that satisfy four such axioms.

Professor Lundberg wondered whether one were not giving too much attention to the comparison of different states of income distribution instead of considering the transfer between different states. People's capacity to enjoy life is a learning process, and this learning process only takes place in a transition. However we approach equality, intensity of feeling amongst us increases.

Professor Musgrave wanted to take up one point. The argument used by Lerner for assuming equality in the capacity to enjoy utility seemed to deny any knowledge whatsoever about distribution between individuals. But surely it would be plausible to assume, by analogy with the distribution of heights, that there was some sort of normal curve, but that one had to be completely ignorant about location of any individual upon that curve. With this combination of ignorance and knowledge, one could, however, arrive at conclusions not all that dissimilar from Lerner's.

Professor Mossé noted that in Mr Kolm's analysis it was implicitly assumed that the achievement of output maximisation requires a certain amount of inequality. In other words, a psychological sensitivity to pecuniary gains seems to be considered as the essential stimulus in economic activity. But is not such a basis too narrow, from a psychological point of view? Are not there other incentives which are susceptible to lead men to exceptional results, such as religious or pseudo-religious motivations for instance? Maybe that efficiency and equality are not so much remote as it is usually assumed.

In regard with Mr Kolm's introduction of the paper, *Professor Malinvaud* expressed his appreciation for the suggestive graphical presentation of the dilemma between justice and incentives as regards income distribution. However, he wondered whether the fundamental problem was not rather to show how the production possibility frontier is depending upon the possible systems of incentives. To his knowledge little work had been done so far in that essential direction.

Mr Kolm answered that indeed there are several possible incentive systems, among which some are dominating the others. His curve was based only on the dominating ones.

Professor Jochimsen finally asked two questions. First, what meaning does Professor Sen attach to the words 'these postulates are highly appealing'? Secondly, what is the relationship between the choice set and the principle of the irrelevance of independent alternatives?

In his reply, *Professor Sen* first thanked Mr Kolm for his very lucid presentation of some of the contents of his paper. He expressed his agreement with most of the points raised, and then made the following comments:

Mr Kolm points out that equality is the natural result to expect in a model of symmetry. I largely agree with this, and as I have pointed out in my paper, Lerner's result (our Theorem II) follows directly from the properties of a weighted aggregate of a set of concave functions. The result in the case of Maximin decision criterion (Theorem III), while somewhat less intuitive, is by no means counter-intuitive. In fact Kolm's alternative demonstration of the theorems are short partly because of his extensive use of intuitive results, and I would hesitate to call them alternative 'proofs' in the strict sense. However, they throw important light on the nature of the theorems.

Regarding Mr Kolm's point that questions of distribution are closely linked with those of efficiency and for a complete solution of the problem we have to deal with the two together, there is no difference. The question of social welfare function embraces both, and most of my paper was devoted to this general formulation. The last two sections only posed a special problem in this field viz., that of pure distribution. I agree with Professor Mossé that the conflict between efficiency and distributive justice is often over-stated, but nevertheless there *is* a conflict, and Kolm is undoubtedly wise in wanting the two problems to be solved simultaneously. This general problem of social ordering involving both these aspects can, it seems to me, be better treated if we understand each aspect in its purity. That is the sole advantage in discussing the pure problem of distribution, just as it provides the sole argument for the enormous mass of literature that exists today on the pure problem of efficiency, i.e., on Pareto optimality.

An important point made by Mr Kolm is that the ethical relevance of people's attitude to *as if* risk and uncertainty is open to question, and Harsanyi's model in particular is not very interesting. I must confess that I do find Harsanyi's model relevant to ethical discussions. One trouble with the standard debates on political economic questions is the impression one has that people's attitude to alternative systems is strongly influenced by their own vested interests. For example, the classic defences of capitalism have appeared to the socialists to be based on the defender's class back-ground. If so, there is a lack of ethics in this argument, which is related to Harsanyi's conditions of 'impersonality' not being satisfied.

Regarding the question whether in a situation of *as if* uncertainty individuals should be assumed to maximise the mathematical expectation of utility, I think there is a legitimate reason for hesitation. Harsanyi assumes it but only because his utility numbers satisfy the Marschak postulates. It is relevant to ask whether these postulates will in fact be satisfied. My purpose in this section was only to show that even if the maximisation of mathematical expectation is taken to be the basis of individual choice in ethical preferences, we do not necessarily get from it a unique social ordering combining the individual preferences. That is the content of Theorem I.

Coming now to the points raised by the others, once again I am substantially in agreement with what has been said. The chairman (Professor Lundberg) pointed out that in moving from one social state to another the costs of these movements should not be ignored. This indeed is quite correct. In the description of the alternative social states this would be fully taken into account. Thus, the description of alternative social states is not independent of where we start from, and in our social ordering this fact must be reflected.

Professor Lundberg is also right in pointing out that the differences in the capacity to enjoy income often arise from past experience. This provides a stronger argument for equality in the long run than in the short, on the utilitarian ground. This is important, but my own position is somewhat more extreme. Like Lerner I find little reason to expect even today a strong correlation between income distribution and the distribution of pleasure capacities. This provides the motivation of Lerner's theorem (Theorem II), and it appeals to me greatly, even though I have tried to extend Lerner's argument in a non-probabalistic direction (Theorem III). This is not to deny that if there were such a correlation it could substantially be due to differences in past experience, and equality might eventually change such systematic biases.

Professor Musgrave's suggestion about a normal distribution of pleasure capacities being more favourable to equality is worth investigating. However, for Lerner's argument or mine on egalitarianism, the assumption of normal distribution is not necessary. But in a more conventional model of total utility maximisation in a non-stochastic setting, it is possible that normal distribution may be relevant. We have to look into this, but Professor Musgrave's interesting conjecture does not seem to be an obvious one.

I am very grateful to Professor Malinvaud for his kind words on my paper. Regarding his observations on Kolm's statement of the problem of interpersonal distribution, I am substantially in agreement.

On Professor Jochimsen's question regarding our use of the concept of the 'choice set', the purpose is to distinguish between (a) the existence of a best alternative (or some best alternatives) in a given set of choices open to us, and (b) the existence of a complete social ordering. The former is the problem of the existence of a 'choice set', which for a finite set is a less demanding requirement than Arrow's requirement of a complete social ordering. For the purpose of choice, the former may be sufficient, and the latter may not be striclty necessary, even though the difference narrows down if we impose some rationality conditions on the choice function. Sufficiency conditions for the existence of choice sets for, say, the method of majority decisions seem to be much less demanding than those for the existence of a complete social ordering.

I am grateful to Professor Jochimsen for asking what precisely do we mean by a postulate being 'highly appealing'. I wish I knew exactly what 'highly appealing' *should* mean. The methodology of a substantial branch of welfare economics is to take a set of postulates that appear to be acceptable to most people and see their consequences. Works of Arrow, Harsanyi, Koopmans, and others exemplify this methodology. Now, if the postulates are not themselves very interesting or acceptable, the results need not interest us much. So we do need some criterion of acceptability of postulates, and I guess this is where the appeal of the postulates comes in. The criterion is undoubtedly vague, but not entirely devoid of content. For example, the condition of 'non-dictatorship' of Arrow is much more appealing than a condition which would have wanted precisely the opposite.

To take a less obvious example let us take the difference between Harsanyi's 'impersonality' and Samuelson's discussion of interpersonal uncertainty, which I have commented on, and which Kolm has gone into. In Harsanyi's case one considers oneself in the position of others *with* their tastes and preferences; in Samuelson's case one places oneself in the objective position of another *without* their subjective preferences. I believe that Harsanyi's model is more interesting from an ethical point of view. Consider the case when we are distributing some apples and oranges between A and B, and while A loves apples and hates oranges, B loves oranges and hates apples. With Harsanyi's model each will put oneself in the position of the other and respect their preferences. With Samuelson's model, A should argue that each should have some apples, for he will place himself in the position of B with his own preference for apples. But B hates apples. Similarly about oranges for A. The distributional decision reached by the Samuelson exercise will seem to be less appealing than the one arrived at Harsanyi's model. This is, of course, no criticism of Samuelson's model, for it was not meant as an ethical exercise. But it does illustrate why economic analysis might have something to contribute on clarifying the ethical interest of one postulate *vis-a-vis* another.

However, these criteria of appeal, or interest, or reasonableness, are not very precise, and that is my difficulty in dealing with Professor Samuelson's somewhat enigmatic conjecture. One does not quite know which are these 'reasonable' postulates based on cardinal utility that are going to be shown to be irreconcilable. I suspect he is bothered by the fact that mere cardinality does not help if interpersonal comparisons are altogether ruled out. Cardinality does permit the fixation of arbitrary origins and units for different person's utility scales, and without some restriction being imposed on their relative magnitudes by considerations of an interpersonal nature, not much use can be made of the individual utility members for social choice. If this is the point that Samueslon has in mind, there is no difference between us.

SESSION EIGHT

Discussion of Professor Malinvaud's Paper

Introducing the paper, *Professor Dorfman* said that the problem of uncertainty impinged on the discussion of public goods in two ways: first, it was obvious that expenditure or investment in public goods was affected by uncertainty, just as all other economic activities were; secondly, and much more importantly, a market system might, under certain specified assumptions, achieve 'ideal allocation', but if uncertainty were present, imperfections might result, and these imperfections themselves might call for additional public expenditures or public intervention of one sort or another. It was this class of problems which Professor Malinvaud's paper was mainly trying to tackle. The basic trouble arises because there is in paractice no market for 'contingent' claims to goods – the principle of insurance is not in practice sufficiently widely recognised. In actual fact one very often wants more of a commodity or a service where uncertainty is present. Two practical examples might illustrate the principle. First, one could consider the case of electric power transmission, where the more insecure the transmission link might be, the more we needed to double or treble the supply line as an insurance against failure. Secondly, because the production of electronic equipment (e.g. transistors) was a process where it was certain that a number of unsound components would be manufactured, it was necessary to produce a larger quantity so that the required number eventually passed the test: the poorer is the quality control, the more we need to produce. It might be argued that neither of these desired outcomes would be the ones that would be generated by a normal price-guided market such as that composed by Walras – in such markets the greater the degree of uncertainty the lower the level of resources that would be employed.

Professor Dorfman asked two questions. First, were the examples he had just produced 'fair', either to the traditional analysis or to the analysis produced by Malinvaud? Secondly, if this contrast between actual and desired behaviour of existing markets was fair, would it not be possible for these to emerge an institutional arrangement which would enable ordinary markets to produce the desired result? On the first point, there were undoubtedly some markets where the hazardousness of the method of production was recognised in the price that was set in the market: this would be true of the cost-plus method of purchasing for defence contrasts, or the high prices commonly paid for risky agricultural products. Again, there were of course many forward markets for all sorts of commodities, in which risks could be hedged. Risks could be pooled, so that the risk facing any individual was much reduced. Finally, there were already in some markets devices for attracting resources with the intention of changing the probability distribution of the outcomes of particular activities – investment to produce more hardy varieties of plants for instance, investment in inventories to reduce risks of shortages, and so on. Would it be correct to say that these were methods of evading and meeting the dilemmas to which Professor Malinvaud had drawn attention?

Mr Turvey suggested that we apply the analysis of uncertainty to electricity generation, and the problem of stand-by capacity. Estimating the potential peak demand for electricity a number of years hence (because of the time-lag in the building of new generating or transmission of plant) was compounded by uncertainty about the weather, about plant repair time, about the possibility of failure of water supply for hydro-electricity, and so on. A view had to be taken on how much risk the public was willing to bear. This view must be formed, explicitly or implicitly, on a comparison of the marginal cost of an additional kilo-watt of capacity compared with the marginal benefit of an avoided interruption in supply. These calculations were done, one way or another, and a notion was arrived at of the margin of spare capacity to which it was appropriate to aim. One then had to ask the Malinvaud question: would an increase in risk – to be defined as an increase in the dispersion of the frequency distribution of possible outcomes – lead to more or less plant being bought? But to answer this question, either normatively or descriptively, we had to ask about the effects of a policy of investing in more plant on the level of costs, on the level therefore of prices charged by the electricity supply industry, and therefore on the eventual demand for electricity. The greater the elasticity of demand, the more we would have to recognise that an increased plant-margin will lead necessarily to a lower expected sale of electricity. So, in practice, an increase in expected risk (greater fears about a really bad winter, for instance) might lead to a higher plant margin, and therefore a higher investment for any given mean expectation of sales; but this greater hedge against risk would itself lower the mean expectation of sales, and therefore the total of resources going to electricity would be less the greater the risk. It followed that elasticity of demand must be carefully considered in the analysis of Professor Malinvaud.

Professor Musgrave pointed out that in his own analysis he had come to the conclusion that a tax with loss off-set would produce a greater allocation of capital resources to an activity surrounded by uncertainty than a situation without tax at all. On the other hand, a tax without loss off-set might or might not help, depending on the relative weight given to income and substitution effects. Professor Malinvaud seemed to differ on this second point. It was interesting to ask why this might be so.

Mr Kolm wanted to make four remarks. First, he would like to see Frank

Knight's vocabulary abandoned, because it is inconsistent with the usual significance of the terms: indeed, risk is a conjunction of uncertainty and a non-in-
difference among the eventual outcomes; it has nothing to do with the possibility
of assigning probabilities to the latter. Secondly, the 'risk premium' of the
formula in Professor Malinvaud's paper should be written on the other side of
the equality sign (otherwise, it is an insurance premium), under additive rather
than multiplicative for, and bear upon one commodity only (i.e. money). Third,
there might be a danger that the model of page 240 would suggest that
homogenity in conjecturing on future events is more important that improvement
of the knowledge thereabouts, even if the latter is unevenly spread among the
economic agents; now this seems not to be the case Finally, in regard to the
remarks made by Professor Dorfman and Mr Turvey, Mr Kolm mentioned that
risk provides an example of a continuum of intermediate cases between collective
and private consumption, which is quite often met in reality: namely all the
cases of 'collective consumption with negative correlation' of services with
limited capacity. If the correlation between individuals demands at a given time
is equal to <1, consumption is private; if it is -1, consumption *a priori* is collective; and all intermediate cases can be considered.

Professor Delivanis expressed his interest in the very rich paper of Professor
Malinvaud. There were however certain points on which he wanted to comment.
As far as the allocation of resources is concerned, there is no doubt that the
collective utility is the aim, but this cannot be carried out without some very
substantial risks. When the public sector is concerned the only risk involved for
the decision-makers is an unexpected disaster. This may happen when hydro-
electric plants are constructed and there is no water. The cost of building at the
same time thermo-electric plants has to be added. This reduces the danger of
leaving the country without power in an emergency. As far as the private sector
is concerned, risk is always considered when resource is decided provided the
entrepreneurs know about it and act rationally. When Professor Knight says
that they forget risks, he is considering irrational entrepreneurs. It is clear that
the latter are often influenced by prestige considerations and not by the marginal
profit, as was proved in some research carried out by Professor Lundberg in
Sweden. Entrepreneurs have further to face the risk from nationalisations and
from excessive taxation. This explains why despite continuous monetary depreciation some investments are considered too risky even if financed by loans.

Professor Sen started his intervention by commenting on some of the practical
implications of the analytical conclusions of the paper. Typically, the author
did not pronounce on the question whether more risky lines of business should
belong to the public sector, but his analysis did throw light on this question.
First, the non-uniformity of attitudes to uncertainty which Professor Malinvaud
shows to be non-optimal indicated difficulties with atomistic allocation. This
covered both non-uniformity of *attitude* to uncertainty as well as differences in
expectation of the future. Secondly, Malinvaud separated out 'financial risks'
which were real to individuals 'without being real to the community'. Thirdly,
the calculations of risk premium might go wrong if some 'current practices'
were followed. This had implications also for the efficiency of the public *versus*
the private sector. Finally, with a tax system where there was no public participation in losses, Professor Malinvaud showed that private allocation might go

wrong. A public enterprise could, however, do better by taking an objective function different from the one used by the private sector. These considerations did not immediately determine the relative efficiency of the public and private sectors in risky situations. But they threw light on this very practical question.

Next, there was one specific point in the paper which Professor Sen wanted to comment on; Professor Malinvaud quoted Arrow's conclusion in favour of risk-neutrality for public firms based on the assumption of no correlation between the stochastic variables applying to the firm and the contingent price. This lack of correlation was disputed by Professor Malinvaud, when he came to the discussion of private firms, by pointing out the similar impact on different firms of things like technical progress. In the case of the public sector also, the correlation between a_e anf p_{l_e} might be significant. Professor Dorfman had already referred to the case of agriculture and the similar impact of weather conditions. In the uncertain field of primary products, to which many public projects are aimed, there might be a very important relation between the stochastic variable applying to the firm and the contingent price.

There was also a point about the interpretation of the price p_{l_e} that was extremely important for public decision taking. For a public decision taken, p_{l_e} might not be the contingent market price but the one corresponding to the social objectives. If a special weight was attached to the consideration of region-wise distribution in project evaluation, p_{l_e} might include a special extra weight for the regional income, if it were a poor region. With a crop failure in one region, the market price of the commodity concerned might not change much if that region was a relatively small one and transport was highly developed; but the weight that the planners might wish to attach to that region's income might go up considerably. On a broader interpretation of the contingent price, relevant to a public decision-maker, the correlation between that and the variable a_e might be significant even when the contingent *market* price was not strongly correlated to a_e.

Professor Zielenski had three comments to make. First, he disagreed with Arrow's thesis that for most public investments no risk premium should be deducted from their expected value. The argument supporting it was that most of such projects were exposed to specific risks which were not correlated with those affecting the global production, and whose effects on that production were often negligible. But was it really so?

(i) When the share of public investment increased – and in France, for example, this share was about 50 per cent of total investment – the impact of the public investments on the aggregate production was very substantial.

(ii) One could say that public investment was more concentrated in fewer fields than private investment and on average was of bigger size than private investment. In Professor Zielenski's view this indicated the need for including the risk problem, because the consequence of failure of certain public investment projects could be quite serious.

(iii) On practical grounds the government could hardly be expected to disregard the risk associated with its investments. Even if the impact of unsuccessful projects on total production was small, its negative *political* importance

S

might be great. Moreover, many governments tried to avoid – as much as possible – the accusation that they were wasting the taxpayers' money.

His second comment was concerned with the problem of risk aversion at the enterprise level. It was the experience of socialist countries that risk aversion at the enterprise level was intimately connected with the incentives system used. It was found, for example, that if the share of a firm was very high, the risk aversion increased considerably. So the problems of risk aversion at the enterprise level should be analysed in relation to the incentives system used.

His third comment concerned the necessity of taking risks into account in constructing public policy projects. Properly constructed plans or programmes must have built-in flexibility and shock-absorption to cope with uncertainty. And indeed, out of three basic reasons for formulating plan targets in the form of medium term plans, two stemmed from uncertainty. These reasons were the following: (i) the time span of a medium-term plan was long enough for accomplishing most investment projects; (ii) during a 5–7 year period there was a fair chance that some random factors (e.g. bad crops) would cancel out; (iii) there was time during the period for corrective action; since the basic weaknesses in the plan and in the mechanism of its fulfillment usually revealed themselves during the first or second year, they could still be corrected within the planning period.

Professor Sandee recalled the importance of the 'certainty equivalent' concepts which had been developed in the literature in the past ten years: the main advantage of it was that when it could be shown to exist in a given situation, then the optimal policy consisted of ignoring the uncertainty. He expressed the view that in the real world the adoption of the hypothesis of certainty equivalents was usually the right and best solution.

Mr Stoleru supported Mr Kolm's remark on the inappropriateness of Knight's vocabulary in regard to 'risk' and 'uncertainty' – especially when they are used in French where these words have another meaning. He wanted moreover to take up Professor Malinvaud's conception of the role of the state: in the absence of markets for contingent claims to commodities, according to his paper, the state should calculate risk premiums in order to correct the inefficiencies due to this imperfection of the market mechanisms. However, there were at least two other ways for the state to intervene in the system, which perhaps might be better, namely (i) to create such markets for contingent claims, and (ii) to try to reduce the risks by influencing their probability distributions; Mr Pierre Massé had defined the economic plan in this way when he said that the French Plan is a 'reducer of uncertainty'.

Mr Tardos wanted to put a question: We know that all investment decisions are made under uncertainty. The risk of certain decisions cannot be determined in a completely objective way. In most cases you have about the uncertainty different indices, but the reality of these does not differ significantly. That meant on the one hand – according to Mr Tardos' experiments – that the decision-makers in the public sector or in a sector of industry which is heavily monopolistic in the best case have to accept one of the possible indices of the uncertainty and are making their decision on that basis. On the other hand, in industries where we have separate firms and the decision-making is not concentrated, we have a possibility that in different firms different decisions are made according to the same question and results of the given decisions are competing in the market.

On the basis of these two cases we could see that having a public sector or a monopolistic industry it may happen that a lot of risky but often very efficient investment fails to be achieved. The question arose whether the benefit from the concentration or the disadvantages of failing to make valuable experiments were greater for the whole economy. Mr Tardos realised that the answer to that question was different in different cases; but he thought that a deeper analysis of it could give a good solution to the problem of how far we should go with concentration of investment decision-making or with extending the share of the public sector.

Mr Posner contrasted two examples. In the first, two identical commodities were produced by different techniques, and one of these techniques was more uncertain than the other: in this case, it was clearly right to devote less resources to the more uncertain or risky technique. In the second example, there would be two different commodities, and here it might be appropriate to shift more resources into the risky enterprise because the product might be more desirable in some sense. The analysis of this second case was clearly related to elasticity of demand, as Turvey had pointed out. Put in this way, Malinvaud's contribution seemed less revolutionary. If the extra resources were investment resources to replace current ones, investment in the risky technique might not take place because of risk aversion in the private sector. But if the commodities were different (as in the second case) the investment could be done, because the selling price of the commodity could be raised without the severe limitiation of competition. This led to the familiar conclusion that risk taking investment flourished in markets where there was less competition. A high degree of competition might not encourage the optimal amount of risk taking investment. This seemed to be the major message of Malinvaud's analysis.

Professor Guitton made the suggestion that the problem of uncertainty could very well be included in the theory of public goods; indeed, the need for safety has many characteristics of a 'public want'. Hence, the question arises whether safety and escaping from the uncertainties of the world are services to be provided individually or publicly. On the other hand, Professor Guitton raised a fundamental question regarding the effects on the economic incentives of a complete reduction of risks and uncertainties. Would not a universal insurance system, such as the one described in the first part of the paper, put in danger the entrepreneurial spirit of the economic agents, and, hence, the growth mechanism itself of the economy?

Professor Malinvaud, replying to the discussion, thanked all those who had given him the benefit of their advice, and in particular Professor Dorfman who had actually isolated the gaps in his analysis.

His argument was, he admitted, incomplete from several points of view. Notably he had started from the principle that existing price systems did not provide adequate clues for the decisions that have to be taken when facing an uncertain future. (Mr Turvey had in fact produced a fine illustration of this principle.) But, he said, he agreed with Professor Dorfman in recognising that, in certain cases of risk, the system of prices played an effective role. Thus, if our societies were stationary ones, each agriculturist would know, from observation of the past, how the price of his produce should vary in relation to natural conditions. Examples such as this were, however, few in number. He pointed out besides that markets for contingent claims should not be confused with future markets which, moreover, exist solely for a few products and a limited future.

In a comprehensive study of the decisions to be taken in an uncertain future, it would be equally necessary to analyse all the measures aimed at reducing the harmful effects of the risks. On this point it would be necessary to make frequent references to the scientific literature to which operational research and 'management science' have given rise in the course of the last few years. However, these measures were not fundamentally different from productive operations properly speaking. They implied in fact the use of certain resources in order to arrive at a plan of final consumption, which would not be subject to too great risks. As a general theory one could therefore consider these measures as being implicitly treated in the analysis of production.

He claimed that from the very moment one began to question the efficiency of an economy in which markets for contingent claims to commodities did not exist, one was embarking on a search for a lesser evil or a 'second best'. As always happened in such cases, the theory became far less reliable and one was naturally led to advance theses which were not altogether justified. His own analysis evidently did not escape that danger.

Professor Malinvaud had admitted that there would be a certain amount of risk aversion in private undertakings which would be consistent with collective preferences. But this was not strictly accurate as he had moreover pointed out in a footnote to his paper. Even then one could dispute his suggestion to standardise the attitude of enterprises towards risk. He could therefore understand the doubts expressed by Mr Kolm. That question certainly called for deeper investigation than he himself had so far given it.

He went on to add that an analogous observation could be applied to his analysis of the effects of taxation, an analysis which ought moreover to have been developed, as Professor Zielinski suggested, so as to cover all types of incentives. He was taking the opportunity, he said, to specify that the analysis differed little in fact from that which had some time previously been presented by Professor Domar and Musgrave.

Finally he stated that, in his opinion, one could not insist too much on the importance of studying the part played by risk in the management of private undertakings. Professor Delivanis had made a pertinent observation on that subject. He wanted above all, he said, to associate himself with the preoccupation that Professor Guitton had expressed in his question: 'Does not public intervention for the reduction and standardisation of the risks to which undertakings are subject affect the incentive to attempt something new?' He could offer no answer to the question but was not unaware of its importance.

SESSION NINE

Discussion of Professor Dorfman's Paper

Introducing the paper, *Professor Barrère* said that it dealt with an attempt to synthesise the teaching of political and economic science on decsion making. These decisions of course went beyond purely market consideration, but nevertheless it might be useful to formulise the considerations in budgetary debate. The first question raised was that of the basis for centralised decisions. This was the whole question of the definition of public goods. The fundamental point was that there was no market for public goods, and it was therefore necessary to have instruments to analyse centralised decisions on public goods. This was Professor Dorfman's point of departure, and with it Professor Barrère agreed. Secondly, the author considered a group of questions on the decision making process. Professor Barrère had two doubts about this. First, there was adopted a pluralist view of society, in which groups within the nation had preferences for public goods, and each group was homogeneous in its preferences. But given that these groups do exist and that we have to analyse our problems on the basis of their existence, how can the State possibly adopt a weighting of the preferences of the groups, when we bear in mind that some groups are more closely identified with the aims of the over-all State than are other groups. This seemed a great problem. Secondly, we were faced with the terrible problem of assessing the benefit received by different individuals or groups, and if the criterion of consumer surplus was rejected, what did we put in its place? Did we really have to estimate the demand curves of all individuals?

The third group of problems suggested by Professor Dorfman concerned the production programmes for public goods, and Professor Barrère had most trouble with this section. It seemed to be based on a model with general static balance between the public and private sectors. The author proposed to assess public output and public input into the private sector. But how could one conceive of a marginal cost of public goods? How could one conceive of a political weighting applicable to the physical burden? All these problems were raised, and were very interesting, but perhaps they were not fully solved.

Mr Kolm did not think that the paper was as revolutionary as Professor Barrrèe suggested, but nevertheless, he admitted that it provided many improvements on existing models. Thus for instance the way in which Professor Dorfman considered satisfaction levels, or the fact that he used the 'willingness to pay', which were more tangible than ordinal utility indices, or even the use of a political science vocabulary – although calling on a group rather than an individual does not add very much to the theory nor to the analysis of voting procedures since its first English formulation by Bowen in 1943.

But on the other hand, Mr Kolm regretted that the introduction of the parameters w_α amounted to an implicit use of a social welfare function; and also that the allocation of the tax burden by means of constant parameters θ_{g0} did not reflect progressive income taxation, which is of paramount importance in the political choice regarding public goods. Finally, Mr Kolm pointed out to

Professor Barrère that if there are by and large no *markets* for public goods, there are however *bargainings* ('marchandages'), and these are precisely the subject matter of public economies; in other words, the state should not be considered as an agent but rather as a *process*.

Professor Wickham noticed that a basic distinction was being made as regards the production planning of public goods as compared with private goods; he then wondered what should be done in the case of strong complementarity between the two kinds of goods (e.g. highway construction and automobile purchases).

Mr Terny had three comments that he wished to make. The first was concerned with the concept of a public good, which he preferred to call 'a collective service', as already suggested in the discussion of Professor Samuelson's and Musgrave's papers. In view of the multiplicity of definitions and concepts, Mr Terny proposed to unify them by considering (i) that every collective service was a result of a joint production with multiple users, and (ii) that every collective service was in itself a joint product of two elements, one being quantiative, and the other qualitative (e.g. for a highway: the number of vehicles per unit of time would be the former, and the speed the latter). A pure collective service would imply that the quality is the same for all users. His second comment concerned the static character of Professor Dorfman's model. When one was dealing with the state and with government activities, was one not bound to consider intertemporal choices, covering several generations? Hence, his preference function had a time horizon which was necessarily broader than that of the groups he is made of. Thirdly, Professor Dorfman's vision of government was essentially one of a compromising body, aiming to make compatible the preference functions of its constituents. But what about the *leadership* function of government, which was at least as important as the compromising one? It did not appear to fit very well within Professor Dorfman's model.

Professor Herschel asked how provision was made for the future in Professor Dorfman's model? It is appropriate to have another hypothetical group representing posterity?

Mr Posner wondered whether Professor Dorfman's analysis was prescriptive or descriptive. He found it hard to accept that all governments really operated in a way which could sufficiently be described by such an analysis. For instance, when any government tried to allocate resources at the margin to, say, hospital building, it was influenced not by utilities of different individuals, nor really by class or narrow sectarian interests. Doubtless a government would wonder in a vague sort of way how its spending decisions would affect its luck in subsequent elections, but they were seldom precise in this calculation, and indeed from time to time consciously strove after higher motives. Perhaps the State, like the heart, has motives which pure reason cannot fathom. Rationality is not and should not be absent from public decision making, but discussion of private utilities and group interests are not the whole story.

Professor Peston thought that it was important to get the model right rather than to ask about its descriptive reality at this stage. He asked Professor Dorfman to define what he meant by government; there seemed to be several definitions in the paper, and they were not all the same.

Professor Jochimsen wondered about the nature of the political constraint in

Professor Dorfman's paper. The author had said that such constraints might be of equal importance as technological constraints. This seemed to reflect on the role assigned to government – if the government were a mediator or a leader influencing the preference functions of groups in the economy, the political constraints can be changed, and strategies could be available to influence political constraints. This was surely the nature of government.

Professor Guitton was struck by what seemed to him to be a basic ambiguity in Professor Dorfman's paper. Individual preferences were made the basis of public decision making, but the test of whether or not they were satisfied could be made only very imperfectly through the political machine and not through the market mechanism. Personal preferences seem to require a market, and to be analysed by means of the maximisation models of standard economic theory; on the other hand, political decisions were global ones, not susceptible of marginal analysis. And yet, Professor Dorfman tried to re-introduce the economist's maximisation tool in that field. This puzzled Professor Guitton.

Professor Samuelson made the following comment. 'Earlier Mr Turvey made the contrast between my paper as a normative theory and Professor Dorfman's as a descriptive theory. I should like to clarify what may be a misleading view. My paper does present norms; at the same time, as in the pseudo equilibrium, it presents a possible positive description, albeit one that I criticise as being unrealistic. I believe the same critique is in order concerning the Dorfman model.

'To demonstrate this, let me prove the following fact: the Dorfman equations become identical to the Lindahl-Johansen-Musgrave pseudo equilibrium when we make supplementary assumptions that suffice to make them rigorously relateable to conventional theory – e.g. the assumption of constant marginal utility of a private good to each man (so that money does unambiguously measure utility or advantage function $F^{\alpha}(g,p)$; and so that sub-aggregation can be rigorously made on the numbers of a political group to form a collective advantage function). Except for Dorfman's constraints, below which no group can go, maximising Dorfman's

$$\Sigma_{\alpha} W_{\alpha} F^{\alpha}(g, p) = \theta_{\alpha 0} p(y - y^{-0})$$

always brings us to the same g configuration as does the Lindahl intersection of my Appendix and of Musgrave's paper.

'Now why should one believe that the political process described sketchily by Professor Dorfman would lead remotely to, or be importantly guided by, maximisation of such a function? I must record the impression that the argumentation and evidence given does not seem to me persuasive.'

Professor Margolis thought that there was a considerable need for the sort of work illustrated in the paper. It was vital to have understanding of how a government behaves, and the question we had to ask ourselves was whether our analysis of public goods is appropriate to a positive theory of government behaviour. But the government seemed too sketchily described for us to have appreciation of how his model works. It is important to recognise that there are different groups operating in government. In the United States for instance there is the well-known division between the Civil Service, the Elected Chief Executive, and the Legislature. The government acts in some sense as a mediator between the private interests represented in the legislature. All who advise government know that it is this mediating role which cause difficulties. We had to recognise that much of the time of civil servants was spent in pre-occupation with their own careers and interests.

Professor Robinson disagreed strongly with Professor Margolis on his description and analysis of the civil servant. (Professor Margolis and he after some controversy agreed that there seemed to be a difference of experience on the two sides of the Atlantic). Professor Robinson expressed his view that some sort of public good was the aim of the executive branch of government.

In reply to the discussion, *Professor Dorfman* commented that he had his own lists of doubts and uncertainties about his own paper. For instance, why had not Professor Musgrave complained that his theory of taxation was too naive? Of course the paper was complicated enough already but even so it was severely inadequate in this respect. Secondly, the rigid separation between decisions on the distribution of the tax burden and decisions on expenditures was not correct. Thirdly, Professor Lundberg had reminded him that he excluded transfer payments. Fourthly, he agreed with the general criticism that the objective function of the ruling political group was inadequate and incorrect. But he wished to receive advice on how to improve it. There must be some way of writing down objectively what government groups were up to.

As regards the point on which he had been pressed by Mr Posner and others – that government somehow has a vision of good society rather than attempts to maximise something or the other in its choice of public investment decisions – this seemed to him a naive objection, of the same category as the objection to the theory of consumer behaviour that 'housewives do not maximise anything'. Is not the problem mainly that we have not sufficiently defined what the government – or indeed the housewife – is maximising?

SESSION TEN

Discussion of Mr Stoleru's Paper

Mr Tardos introduced the paper by pointing out that it dealt with three main problems. First, the problem of the level, of the degree of aggregation of investment planning – should it be for individual projects, for individual enterprises, or for the economy as a whole? Secondly, what should be the discount rate that should be used, and should it be common to all investment projects? Thirdly, what is the relationship between planning in the French economy and planning in the Socialist countries? Because of the big share in public investment going to the French electricity supply industry, because electricity is very close to the final market and because it is a basic good, it is a very interesting case to consider. Questions of the price elasticity of demand have to be taken into account, but nevertheless the basic problem is one of cost minimisation.

Hence this method of planning is not applicable to other public sector examples. For instance the case of transport cannot be treated as a whole, because it is not possible either to aggregate demand or aggregate benefit from transport activities. The most important question is certainly the discount rate obtained from the money market, rather than the shadow price for investment funds found by exploring the implications of the investment constraints?

Commenting that it was pleasant to find one's feet on the ground after some days in the clouds, *Professor Sandee* suggested that there should be one discount rate applicable to each period of time, in order to take account of the different application of constraints at different times. On transport, he did not quite agree with Mr Tardos that it was not possible to think of the transport system as a whole. Surely there was a network, not a sum of individual separate services.

Professor Sen took up the point of timing investment in roads. Which of a set of projects should be postponed? Mr Stoleru seemed to assume that the cost of construction was constant over time, and that the rate of interest was constant over time. This produced a very neat formula but it perhaps was not entirely right. Problems of the optional choice of timing investment were very complex.

It appeared to *Mr Henderson* that, with great regret, he had to acknowledge that French practice was worse than English practice in investment decisions, although French theory was more elegant than English theory. The importance of financial constraints in the case of electricity; the arbitrariness of the choice between productive and non-productive investment; the constraint imposed by inflationary conditions on the availability of the money market; the reliance on self-finance – all these problems common to the two economies did not seem to be fully solved in the French case. As regards the central issue of the discount rate, it depended on the purpose which the discount rate was meant to serve. If it was an indicator of the opportunity cost of investment funds, then to use it as a rationing device would be sensible; if, on the other hand, it were a measure of social time preference, then there would be no point.

Mr Tulkens raised the problem of the absence of economic management, investment planning and marginal cost pricing in the nationalised telecommunications industry. He wondered why the currently existing techniques of programming and graph theory had not yet been fully applied in this sector, to which they are particularly well suited, and which would be quite helpful in developing more sound management policies.

Mr Kolm pointed out that although it was now fashionable in France to advocate 'true prices' (*la 'vérité des prix'*), a personal short survey of the opinions of the competent people in charge or pricing in the relevant services showed that quite different meanings were attached to this expression. Some people refer to short-term marginal cost pricing, *sensu stricto*; some other people mean long-term marginal cost pricing, in the sense of the 'cost and development'; still other responsible men meant marginal cost pricing of the elements of output which are privately consumed, and pricing 'a lathisgrave' for these elements which are collectively consumed (i.e. – that each customer pays the product of the marginal monetery value of this element times the quantity of such elements consumed). In fact, another fourth group of services were applying on *ad valorem* pricing policy, '*à la* Colson'. At least some co-ordination of ideas among French administrations might be called for.

Concerning the uniqueness of the discount factor in various branches of industry, Mr Kolm thought thatit should not be advocated on the basis of theoretical considerations. Indeed, since (i) interest rates are different according to their terms, (ii) investments have different life times in the various branches, and (iii) such real stocks of capital are for the most part illiquid (i.e. non transferable from one branch to another, or only at a loss), different discount rates in different branches are quite justified from a theoretical point of view.

Mr Posner asked what the relationship was between Professor Marglin's work on the optimal timing of investment decisions and the formula produced in Mr Stoleru's paper? He commented that the variability of discount rates at different dates into the same project was a complication of great importance often forgotten in practice.

Professor Malinvaud replied to Mr Posner that Mr Stoleru's formula was not very different from that of Professor Marglin, in the simple case that had been taken. Abraham had, as a matter of fact, obtained the Marglin result in France independently. Professor Malinvaud also recommended prudence as regards the uniqueness of the discount factor as between various industrial branches: this position assumes that a perfect equilibrium is prevailing at any time on the capital market, implying perfect access to the market for both savings suppliers and capital demanders.

Professor Delivanis remarked that the author had referred to the possibilities of comparing the advantages to be expected from various resource allocations and believed that this was possible only when 'productive results' were to be expected. He thus excluded improvements of education and of social infrastructure. In Professor Delivani's view, the author was too pessimistic. First because such improvements of the results were capable of measurement, at least conceptually, second, because their repercussions were rightly considered so important, he begged Mr Stoleru to re-examine his conclusions in this connection.

In his reply, *Mr Stoleru* commented first on the discount rates issue: if one has three different plans one has three different sets of constraints and therefore three different rates of interest. There was no reason to believe that this was embarassing. Of course the discount rate would actually vary between different dates, and the current market rate of course reflected the rate of inflation, amongst other things. The whole point of planning was not to equalise misery by insuring that marginal cuts in investment hurt all people roughly to the same degree, but rather by the use of scientific method to abandon the concept of bargaining and adopt a more rigorous method in investment planning. As regards the telecommunications industry, Mr Stoleru said it was essentially administrative lack of initiative in starting economic analysis of the sector, but he also mentioned the difficulties of statistical measurement of the time and geographical patterns of demand. Finally, concerning the measurement of the profitability of 'unproductive' investments, he agreed that he had been too pessimistic. Education for instance had been studied by CEDREL which had come up with statistical estimates.

SESSION ELEVEN

Discussion of Professor Peston's Paper

Professor Mossé, opening the discussion, said that at a first reading Professor Peston's paper was very difficult of comprehension to any Frenchman. It seemed to have no central theme or conclusion, but after several re-readings he had come to see what Professor Peston was trying to argue – that a variety of heterogeneous factors were capable of influencing the determination of prices. Some of these issues had already been discussed in relation to earlier papers. Others would arise in relation to Mr Turvey's paper:

Professor Mossé suggested that there were four themes that could usefully be discussed in relation to the present paper:

1 micro-economic analysis in terms of costs, prices and incomes;
2 surpluses and deficits – a subject necessarily linked to the micro-economic analysis, but in turn leading on to macro-economic analysis and the study of social welfare;
3 the meaning and implications of commercial management;
4 inter-sectoral and organisational problems, representing wholly macro-economic and political aspects.

This was not Professor Peston's order of procedure, but the difference was not basic.

In regard to the first theme, the micro-analysis in terms of costs prices and income, Pareto-optimality was the point of departure with measurement of marginal cost and marginal benefit – the latter was assumed to be measured by the demand curve, and welfare to be maximised where there was a price and quantity for which demand was equal to marginal cost. But here Professor Peston introduced a whole series of difficulties and variants, leading one to criticise the marginalist for much. What are the difficulties? A peak-hour kWhr of electricity was not the same thing as a kWhr off-peak. The time horizon circumscribed the calculation. There were questions of joint costs and of how to impute overheads. Professor Peston in relation to these issues seemed to agree basically that one could take one's stand on average cost.

The problem of overheads could, he thought, best be posed in rather different terms. The problem was that of the relative priority of price and quantity in price determination. Did one start from a determined price and seek to determine a quantity? Did one start from a quantity and seek to determine a price? Did one move back and forth? If the path was from price to quantity with the quantity as the variable, was it the quantity that gave a balance at average or at marginal cost? Was it possible to achieve a three-fold balance between marginal cost, average cost and demand? This was doubtful. A balance between average cost and demand would yield a financial balance. But a balance between marginal cost and demand would result in a financial deficit or surplus. If one insisted on a balance between marginal cost and demand one must recognise that a surplus or deficit was probable.

Alternatively, one could follow another line of approach and determine the quantity to be produced in some authoritarian way and then act to fix a price at which the market would be cleared, oblivious of cost. Again there would be surpluses or deficits. This inevitably raised political issues. Should an authority decide that we should all have telephones but none of us have electric lights? One came back in the end to political procedures. Should one or should one not decide the quantities to be supplied democratically on the basis of votes? This led Professor Mossé to the second theme of Professor Peston's paper – the problem of surpluses and deficits which were bound to arise unless one sold at the point of intersection of the average cost and average revenue curve. Professor Peston raised the issue whether one should aim to break even or one should accept the inevitability of surplus deficits. To break even was too simple a solution. In some cases, too great a proportion of the national savings would be devoted to the public sector. In some cases, if one were not prepared to price above average cost and make a surplus, the level of the service was too low. In the case of France had they not fallen into the errors of making too large an investment by accepting too low a required rate of real return on the investment?

If one was concerned with the rate of return on capital, was it the average return on all capital, the return on new capital, or the marginal return on marginal projects? Professor Mossé was worried as to whether some of the methods of calcualtion that had been adopted in France gave a false illusion of profitability.

Professor Peston had suggested an ingenious arrangement for using a fairly low real rate of interest for financial purposes accompanied by a high shadow price of capital for purposes of project appraisal. The whole question here was how one should account for the cost of capital and how one should deal with the burden of financing a deficit or with the distribution of a surplus. Should the user pay? Should the taxpayer pay? If they were to share the burden, how should it be divided? Could one calculate a rational division? Was there such a thing as a rational division? If the principle was that the users should pay, they should surely be entitled to divide the surplus where there was one. The whole question was bound up with the question of an incomes policy. To Professor Mossé's thinking, the whole question was tied up with wider political issues. Were the prices of nationalised enterprises to be used as instruments of economic policy? In his view it was proper to use lower electricity rates, railway rates, telephone charges in depressed areas as instruments of policy and to accept the consequent deficits or surpluses where they might occur. If a country chose to operate a different macro-economic and political order over and above the market economy, these instruments formed part of the general economic policy of the state.

Coming to Professor Peston's third theme, the commercial management of nationalised industries, Professor Mossé saw no reason why the average performance in public sector enterprises should be inferior to that in private sector enterprises. But what were the criteria of good management? To maximise the chance of survival? To minimise the cost? To secure a rapid turnover of capital? All sorts of parameters might be suggested. Professor Peston had shown the great difficulty of choosing any one measurement of what was meant by commercial management. They had the same problems in France. There had to be precise accountancy – not easy to achieve in perfect precision. There had to be financial equilibrium. He would again stress that financial equilibrium at the intersection of the average revenue and average cost curves corresponded precisely to what in private industry one described as the break-even point. But if one deliberately stepped up production beyond that by government decision, one was in fact accepting a deficit of some given order of magnitude. Since nationalised industries were instruments of economic policy, it was inevitable that there should be different criteria of good management between the private industrial and commercial sectors and the public sectors. It was wholly proper to make profits on tobacco and losses on hospitals. It was not right to exclude political and social criteria. The principles of commercial management should not be exclusive of these other considerations.

Professor Peston's fourth theme, the inter-sectoral relations, was bound up with the questions of organisation. From what Professor Peston had said about complementarity and substantiality there emerged a set of relations similar to a Leontief input/output table. Professor Peston posed the problem (but Professor Mossé could not see how one could solve it) of optimising these inter-relation-ships. But how was one to achieve the transition to this optimal situation? At what level should one seek the optimal relationships? What authority should decide this? To produce electricity, there were four possible alternatives: coal, nuclear, oil and hydro-power. If coal and electricity were not under the same authority and coal was priced at a high price, what you gained on coal you lost on electricity. It was better to have a single board running the two and selling coal to itself at the lowest possible price and making profits on the electricity. It might be proper to sell coal outside at a high price and buy oil. But the best decision and the best approach to the optimum was likely to be made by a central decision-making body. In all these organisational problems the optimum solu-tion ought not to depend on the actual form of the organisation.

All these issues led one forward to further political problems, not only con-cerning coherence between nationalised sectors but also the whole general policy of the government, inclusing considerations of national defence. In Professor Mossé's view it was quite impossible to eliminate all appeal to the value judge-ments of the national political authority. Their decisions, based on trial and error, were not irrational since they reflected the general will of the nation.

Mr Kolm said that as a Frenchman and an economist, he was always very embarassed when he discussed the subject of pricing of public utilities with Anglo-Saxon economists, because they praised the French for their mistakes and they blamed them for their qualities. Of course, the mistake was 'marginal cost pricing' in electricity and the quality was the *ad valorem* pricing of the French railways.

On 'marginal cost pricing', his point was not the 'second best' problem since that would be discussed on another paper. It was that this 'marginal cost pricing', when applied in an increasing returns industry, entailed a financial defi-cit which had to be made good by the general public budget, i.e. thanks to general taxation. Now these taxes were not poll taxes and, hence, all of them generally entailed welfare losses. This point was not mentioned by 'marginal cost pricing' theoreticians whose models, although they emphasised *general* equilibrium, were not so general as to include public finance (and public goods), as they should have done. Anyway, even if there were neither second best nor deficit problems it would have been a mistake to say, as it has often been said,[1] that this 'marginal cost pricing' is the only pricing compatible with the optimum. All that the classical theory says is that the marginal unit for the marginal consumer must be sold at marginal cost. It says nothing about the pricing of infra-marginal units and consumers.

The alternative solution was the discriminating monopoly pricing which has been advocated by Jules Dupuit for bridges and railways in his 1844 and 1849 articles,[2] and later deepened and applied to build the French railways pricing system by his successor as professor of economics at the Ecole des Ponts et Chaussées, Clement Colson.[3] Dupuit's pricing was compatible with the optimum and it might cover full costs, notwithstanding 'revelation' difficulties for which Dupuit and Colson proposed (and the latter applied) practical solutions.

Dupuit's ideas were widely misunderstood, even by Walras himself (see his comments in the *Elements*, and his letters to Cournot). As for Colson, the mis-understandings went to the point that nowadays, while his pricing system is *still* the official rule, there is probably nobody living in France who understands how he instituted it. It is particularly revealing to notice that he called his system 'pricing *ad valorem*' meaning at the value of the transportation service for the user, whereas everybody today believed that it meant related to the value of the good transport, i.e. proportional to this value (which was, for Colson, only one of the many sources of indication of the value of the service rendered). One of the reasons for this misunderstanding was that Colson established as a discriminating device the rule of fixing the official price rather high and then allowing specific price reductions to users who could not afford the service at this price but who could pay more than the individual marginal cost; but now econo-mists and engineers currently said that a pricing system which contained so many specific exceptions could obviously not be a good one.

Now, one might wonder why the marginal-cost-priced electricity balanced its budget whereas the *ad valorem* priced railways did not, when it should be the opposite. The reason is, of course, that neither of these two industries actually applied its principles. This was not surprising for railways having regard to what has just been said. As for the marginal cost principle, it should be noticed that one of its basic flaws, which it shared with a Musgrave (Johansen-Lindahl) pricing system was that the price depended on the definition of the 'quantity' of the service rendered. This was well illustrated by Marschak's criticism of Boiteux's paper on the pricing of the guarantee of electric power at the 1951 C.N.R.S. colloquium on risk: for independent demands, variances provided the additive quantities in the classical theory, which resulted in non-discriminating pricing; but marginal cost pricing of variances covered only half of the full cost;

---

[1] For instance this argument is strongly emphasised in Hotelling's article 'On Railway Rates . . .' (*Econometrica*, 1938) which has been especially influential for the French application of marginal cost pricing.

[1] *Annales des Ponts et Chaussées*; English translation in *International Economic Papers*.

[3] For a clear theoretical statement, see the chapter ii ('Considerations economiques sur la determination des prix des transports') of *Transports et tarifs* (J. Rothschild, Paris, 1898), and chapter i of book VI of his *Cours d'économie politique a l'Ecole des Ponts et Chaussées et a l'Ecole Polytechnique* (Gautheir-Villars, Paris).

whereas Electricité de France marginal cost pricing of standard deviation was discriminatory (proportional to the user's standard deviation) but it covered full cost.

Professor Prest commented on commercial principles. He suspected that Peston's account was somewhat too sophisticated. He recalled the history of the Australian post-office which had two sets of accounts – one for the budgetary purposes and the other set called 'commercial'. The budget account showed a loss and the commercial account showed a profit. The budget account included all capital expenditure in the year, and the commercial account showed only the capital charges which had to be borne. This was the sort of trick that could be played.

Mr Henderson commented that profit maximisation must be subject to certain constraints. Because of the complexity of formulating these constraints, and a wish not to be tied to any specific formulation, the subject was always left in a vague and unsatisfactory state.

Mr Glouskov said that it had become almost axiomatic to many economists that most nationalised industries were usually working at a loss or at best on a break-even basis. The argument of the so-called 'inefficiency' of state-owned industries had been often used against the extension of the nationalised sector to cover other leading industries both in developed and in undeveloped countries. But, as the experience of his own country had shown, the great social welfare benefits of the nationalised industries could not be ignored. In this respect, Professor Peston's paper was to his mind a very interesting scientific achievement. It was also very convincing in the wealth of sources quoted, with which he was glad to be thoroughly acquainted.

He agreed with Professor Peston's arguments 'for nationalisation of private industries which are likely to have an important social impact'. He was convinced that this process, never mind how slowly it was currently progressing, was in general irreversible in the present age of planning and of scientific and technological revolution. He would like to add that the new planning policy which was being followed in British nationalised industries had something in common with the planning practice traditional in his own country (for example the efforts to elaborate comprehensive intra-industrial plans for the fuel and transport industries on a national basis). His own comparative studies had led him to the conclusion that the new economic policy adopted for nationalised industries in Great Britain – as outlined in the latest White Paper – with emphasis on decentralisation and adaptation of some kind of free commercial pricing policy reflected the growing economic role of state intervention in industrial policy in the free enterprise economics of Western countries.

He thought that Professor Peston's analysis of the influence of the British Government on the pricing policy of the nationalised industries, might be pushed somewhat further. British practice, as set out in the paper, confirmed that not only the taxation and expenditure policies of the State but also its intervention in the relations between nationalised and private enterprises had been greatly influencing the revenues and costs and the optimum models of price of the former. Take, for example, the transport industries of the United Kingdom which were now almost equally divided between State and private enterprises, as the result of the contraction of the State activities. For that reason he could not agree that the prerequisite now for an objective choice of the best economic problems involved the pretence of 'de-mistifying' them, as some of his Western colleagues had been trying to do.

Professor Peston replying to the discussion, commented that he had deliberately kept his paper free from doctrinaire adoption of positions, because he felt that one had to be agnostic on many of the points raised. On the discount rate, for instance, he recalled with some pride his part in imposing it on the British nationalised industries, but could not be certain that the rate chosen was the right rate.

SESSION TWELVE

Discussion of Mr Henderson's Paper

Professor Lundberg, opening the discussion, began by emphasising the positive functions of constraints. In many respects the choice of constraints was an art in itself. If one was to discuss constraints one needed to classify them. From the policy point of view constraints fell into four categories:

(1) the choice of problems to be handled: such choice implied a constraint in the range of setting of the issue; if one chose as policy for a sovereign State a policy of growth of the income of the State itself rather than the income of the world, that, from a policy point of view, formed a policy constraint;

(2) the choice of targets: if one accepted a target of avoiding inflation, the acceptable price level implied a constraint on growth;

(3) the choice of means: if one is considering ways of helping poorer countries, one might rule out certain possible methods as unacceptable; if one was concerned with regional policies or balanced growth, a clash of regional interests might need to be resolved politically;

(4) the working of the economic system: if one was considering the production possibility curve, did one accept all the constraints of the market itself and the implied flexibility? Or did one need to impose constraints on the market mechanism?

If an economist was to be useful in the role of adviser, he was obliged to accept a number of constraints as to both targets and means. He had to accept the basically capitalist society and the slow pace of its practicable transformation. He had to be realistic as to the practical working of measures discussed regarding physical controls, for example, as against a market price system. He had to evaluate the relative defects of different instruments – for example, interest rates – as against credit controls. In regard to exchange rates if he accepted the normal bankers' views, this implied a constraint. In regard to housing, he had to accept the choice as between waiting lists and high rents.

At the same time economists had their biases, their convictions based on insufficient grounds, their love of a particular analytical model. They were inclined to doubt administration and politicians and to question the necessity of some of existing political constraints.

There might be constraint also as to the choice of a model – implying good or bad economics. If one took a model of production, and applied it to the determination of public expenditure, one would be concerned about constraints of various forms: that tax rates should not be increased; that any solution should be effective and simple, thus simplifying decisions. But here one ran into a dilemma: the interest of making life simpler, meant the exclusion of alternative constraints (at a higher level): that public expenditure should be related to growth of G.N.P. – a national budget model. To illustrate from the Swedish situation, there was an excess demand for public services with tremendous investment demands. A capital investment constraint was needed: how rapidly could it grow? The constraint was set by G.N.P. growth rate together with the impossibility of reducing the growth rate of investment by private concerns in free enterprise economy to less than 3 per cent a year, together also with any balance of payments restrictions. In combination these gave room for government expenditure for goods and services to grow by 5 per cent a year. Economists might criticise this model for the balance of payments constraint (the less exports were to rise, the more room was to be left to stimulate them). Other economists might take a price level constraint more seriously.

Mr Henderson had pointed to our ignorance of the economic system. There were big margins of errors in the estimates. Here there was an educational job for economists – to teach politicians and administrators to take the difficulties of estimating seriously – and to realise expenditures were necessarily subject to margins of error.

When one turned to the allocation of public expenditure, there were financial constraints in the budget, the constraint from year to year of meeting commitments and the consequent limitations on the scope of manouvre. He would add one trivial consideration: the problem of inefficiency, waste of resources, when no constructive pressure was imposed by the market. Stringent financial limits might help but they formed a rather poor substitute. Programme budgeting and systems analysis all contributed in their way.

One had also to consider the common method of cutting down the financial limits, for current policy purposes, often under pressure from the balance of payments. Here there were dangers of insufficient allocation motivated by short-term inflationary considerations. But in total over a period of years this became serious and the gains were problematic. Public expenditure allocation in the longer run was more flexible – and here the welfare economist as an advisor should have more to say. But as Mr Henderson had pointed out, the life of the practical economist was not easy; political strategy and welfare economics merged, and it was difficult to distinguish between means and ends.

Was not one reason for the unsatisfactory state of policy that a good welfare economist was apt to be unpractical and rather unworldly and must be so in terms of his abstract operations? As advisor he had to quantify his measurements of the effects of alternative allocations. Theory was not framed in a way helpful to application. One was never engaged in comparing alternative states of equilibrium conditions but in starting from a state out of equilibrium; for instance, in many cases with excess demand for housing, or with inadequate public services and the need for investment. And one studied a short period during which there had been a policy aiming at improvements of allocation, to be accomplished within a number of constraints and resulting in a new stage of different disequilibria. We neeedd to analyse these states of disequilibria more accurarely and not least the dynamic processes of shifting an economy from one state to the other. To that type of realistic setting of their problems, welfare economists themselves showed constraints. Or was it that we had constraints of our comprehension in the search of the literature, deriving from our own understanding-impossibility curve?

Professor Herschel asked why the investment of nationalised industries had to be included in the budget of the central government, at least to the extent to which they were self-financed? If they did not appear in the budget, they were still somehow treated as part of the general expenditure. Was this correct?

Professor Chenery commented that it was very difficult to do anything about constraints unless a specific model was in mind – for instance, if because of the constraints perhaps the level of taxation must not rise above 25 per cent of G.N.P. The problem could not then be analysed unless the welfare objectives were stated.

Professor Delivanis emphasised the importance of the constraint imposed by the desire not to affect the internal, and even more the external, equilibrium of the country concerned; development was bound to upset both, and it had to be decided what resources could be used without danger, as had already been pointed out in Professor Barrère's paper. Mr Henderson had pointed out that the development of the poorer areas could not be pressed too far since it might affect unfavourably the general economic conditions. This had been seen in the recent Yugoslav economic reform which had cut credits for the industrial development of the poorer areas whilst favouring investments for tourism in them. The importance of the constraint imposed by the limitation of public expenditure depended on the source of finance of the expenditure concerned. If credits of the central bank were used, it was different from the conditions when loans were subscribed by savers or from the proceeds of taxes.

Professor Marglin suggested that one of the reasons why economists were not listened to is that they do not recognise constraints; the costs of constraints can be measured and this is an important job for economists to do.

Replying to the discussion, *Mr Henderson* said that he would prefer not to comment in detail on all the points that had been raised, but to take a few specific points and then to refer to two more general issues.

On specific points, he agreed with Professor Marglin's formulation of the problem at the end of the discussion, and also with the criticism of the paper which had been made by Professor Lundberg, that constraints relating to time were a regrettable omission. On Professor Herschel's point, Mr Henderson suggested that it was reasonable to distinguish between the investment of public enterprises and other forms of public expenditure, and that different forms of constraint might be appropriate. For example, one could adopt the rule of sanctioning all public investments with a positive value at an agreed rate of discount; but such a rule could not be generally applied. The question of how investment was financed did not seem important in relation to constraints:

higher public investment in full employment conditions must imply some action to reduce other forms of final demand *pari passu*, irrespective of the means of financing. However, Professor Herschel was correct in suggesting that a higher taxation was not the only instrument of policy for controlling demand; in this respect the formulating of the problem in the paper was insufficiently general.

As to the first of the broad issues which he wished to raise, Mr Henderson said that he could take as a suitable text a phrase used by Professor Lundberg, when he referred to 'the dubious quality of being realistic'. Several references had been made at the conference to the contrasting roles of (so-called) theorists and practical economists. In his view, this was in some ways a dubious and even distasteful categorisation. Economists in business and government ought to think twice before claiming credit for being practical. They were themselves subject to criticism, within their organisations, for being too theoretical and academic; and such criticism sometimes arose from the fact that the (allegedly) practical men who made them were unthinkingly thinking in terms of very over-simplified models which they would be unable to formalise. It was easy for applied economists to fall into a similar trap. Indeed, much of their specialist knowledge consisted simply in knowing how to operate in a particular institutional setting. This was a useful skill, but a highly specific one of little intellectual interest.

On the second issue, Mr Henderson said that he hoped that from a personal point of view one benefit of the conference would be a continuing exchange of ideas of ways of improving public expenditure planning. The contribution of economists was mostly therapeutic – by criticism of confused formulations of the problem, and oversimplified decision rules – but also positive. The positive contribution could take two main forms: helping to quantify the implication of alternative theories at the margin, so as to throw light on trade-offs between expenditure programmes; and the development of pure and more explicit models, which had been rightly emphasised by Professor Chenery. In relation to British practice, it might be useful to state alternatives more explicitly in relation to possible changes in the level and pattern of taxation, so as to present a somewhat clearer outline of alternatives for decision-makers. He was grateful to Professor Chenery for bringing this point to his attention.

SESSION THIRTEEN

Discussion of Professor Wickham's Paper

Professor Prest, introducing the discussion, said that Professor Wickham had compressed into a small space a great deal of interesting information and commentary on French experience. Obviously 'constraints' were here understood in a narrower sense than in the previous paper. It might also be observed that Professor Wickham's definition of public undertakings, as those which have 'a separate budget', would exclude undertakings such as the British Post Office which has hitherto operated within the general government budget, although it has recently been decided to establish it as a public corporation.

The key passages in Professor Wickham's paper seemed to be his statement of operating rules, of management constraints, and of restrictions on amortisation policy. The net result as stated by Professor Wickham was that 'the constraints imposed by the central authorities increase the public enterprises' financial requirements while at the same time reducing their resources'.

In connection with amortisation policy it was necessary to distinguish between amortisation in the strict sense of repayment of debt, and depreciation allocations to cover the estimated annual deterioration in the value of assets. To the latter could be added allocations from profits to reserves either for new investment or to meet contingencies. Generally speaking the rate of debt repayment was likely to be fairly strictly prescribed either by agreement with bond holders, or by statutory sinking fund provisions or even by constitutional requirements as in Australia (where public debt had to be repaid over a period of 53 years). In respect of allocations to depreciation or reserve funds, however, there might well be a considerable degree of freedom.

Professor Wickham suggested on the basis of French experience that public enterprises would try to raise their depreciation provisions as high as possible in order to provide internal funds for new investment, whereas the Treasury would try to keep depreciation rates low in order to exercise stricter control over new investment. It was doubtful whether either proposition was of general validity. Experience elsewhere suggested that public enterprises so far from charging themselves high rates of depreciation consistently were likely to vary their rates arbitrarily from year to year, charging low rates in poor years (thereby minimising their deficits) and charging high rates only in good years (thereby concealing their profits). Similarly experience elsewhere suggested that Treasury policy might be directed not towards checking reinvestment by public enterprises, but to actually encouraging it, even if this meant higher tariffs, in order to reduce demands on the public loan market. This has happened for example with respect to electricity undertakings in both Britain and Australia.

Professor Wickham's paper also directed attention to the very real practical difficulties of determining whether public enterprises were actually operating at a profit or a loss, and what really was their level of investment. Economists were only too apt to ignore these practical difficulties when formulating abstract rules for pricing policy or investment policy. Perhaps the reason was that there are too few economists who know anything about accounting and too few accountants who know anything about economics. However that might be, it was a difficult and expensive process to obtain even approximately accurate assessments of the comparative performance of various public enterprises. Professor Wickham mentioned that a hundred senior civil servants were engaged in supervising the finances of the French railways. In addition to supervisory ministries there were in many countries independent auditor-generals' offices and parliamentary committees. The difficulties were even greater in federal countries, such as the United States, Australia and perhaps Western Germany, where the federal authorities responsible for general economic policy might have no effective means of checking on the performance of public enterprises operated by the States. Thus the attainment of the optimum allocation of investment might in practice be both approximate and expensive.

Mr Kolm said that the traditional justification of nationalisation by one at least of the French schools of economics was this. The optimal price/output decision requires selling at marginal cost. For any service produced under increasing returns, this resulted in a financial loss. Consequently the State should carry the loss of such enterprises. And as a further consequence such enterprises had no reason to minimise their loss. Thus one could not assume that pursuit of the highest profit (or least loss) was an incentive to optimal decisions in this sector of the economy. It could not be compared in this respect with the private sector. It had also been shown in the papers dealing with price-fixing that insistence on selling at a particular marginal cost was mistaken: that by discriminating an enterprise could simultaneously achieve the necessary conditions for optimal output and escape making a loss. Undoubtedly such a pricing policy posed various problems, particularly as to how to discover what consumers might be prepared to pay. But these problems had to be solved if one was to calculate the optimal investment. But this argument completely destroyed the case for nationalisation. All the other arguments for nationalisa-tion – services rendered to the nation, contributions to social justice by selling below cost, services to large families, depressed areas and the rest – were invalid because the State could, if it wished, obtain all these by purchase and subsidy. Private enterprise, on the other hand, had all sorts of advantages of incentives to efficiency, flexibility that a public sector concern did not enjoy. For these reasons he thought that the French public services would be better provided by private enterprise. There were examples of private enterprise in other countries in the provision of motor roads, canals, telephones, transportation, coal mining and so on. The problems were fewer, it was true, where one was starting from the beginning than where one was faced by existing constraints of every kind. In any case the optimal structure of property rights differed from one activity to another.

Professor Bauchet agreed with Professor Wickham that the financial outcome depended not on the planned use of funds or the regulations governing a public enterprise but on the market situation and especially the objectives of the organisation and the priorities which the State attached to particular objectives. A public enterprise had as its objective and the State authority had as its con-cern to maintain the capital of the enterprise, to produce goods which would satisfy consumers, and at the same time to contribute to general equilibrium. If the government overlooked this last objective, and particularly the stabilisation of input prices, the firms affected would be in financial disequilibrium. This affected all the enterprises which provided the basic services to the whole system of production, such as energy.

Dr Pendleton wished to make a comment and pose a question—both somewhat general. The comment was suggested by the paragraph of Mr Wickham's paper reading, 'The authorities nowadays take greater care to see that public enterprises are genuinely subjected to market discipline and do not receive unfair advant-ages . . . as compared to private firms.' If he were writing a similar statement about the situation in the United States, he would have to be much more cautious. While, strictly speaking, 'authorities' might be taking 'greater care', the United States continued to go to great lengths to devise means of protecting public enterprises from the constraints of the private market. Particularly in public utilities and transportation activities – public production of electricity, roads, airports, and waterways – a variety of devices were used. Perhaps most common was the provision of investment funds at rates substantially below market rates. Tax revenues were frequently used directly and bonds had the taxing power of the State to guarantee them. In addition, the deductability of interest from State and local securities from the personal income tax was another device for keeping borrowing rates low. Another way in which 'unfair advantages' were provided was the immunity of public enterprises from virtually all forms of taxation – of which perhaps the most significant were the local real estate and property taxes. These practices reflected both the relatively small size of the public enterprise sector and the relatively small amount of direct competition with private firms.

His question echoed the frequent exhortation heard from Professor Sandee. He was surprised that during this conference they had been exposed to so little quantitative evidence – that so few papers had contained econometric results. This was particularly surprising in view of the fact that the use of operational rules, well grounded in data, were at the heart of the sort of applied economics that the conference had taken for its theme. While tempted to deplore this situation, it was more prudent for him simply to raise the question, and to invite comments as to why not more than two of the papers presented to the conference could fairly be called empirical. Perhaps the conference planners deliberately chose to concentrate on the theoretical issues of public economics; perhaps the branch of economics is still at a stage when empirical work would be poorly grounded and premature; perhaps, as Professor Peston had suggested, economists in advisory capacities do a great deal of rough-and-ready empirical work, but are reluctant to expose to their colleagues either the resulting calculations or the processes that gave rise to them.

Professor Lundberg said that one problem not dealt with in the paper was the institutional form given to the public enterprise. If it was a joint stock company (with the shares owned by the government or some public institutions), then the undertaking's possibilities of playing the rules of the market under equal conditions with private firms was much greater than if the public undertaking had its 'finances' entered into the budget. The fundamental issue was how investments were financed. If by a joint stock company, then the undertaking could keep its profits (after dividends and taxes) for financing investment and could supplement its financial needs by borrowing on the market. In the other alternative the surpluses of the public enterprises entered into the budget and the government could allocate the resources from a 'common pool' according to some uniform criteria. The joint stock company form gave a decentralised solution; that meant more flexibility and less centralised direction. What was best? This issue was one very much discussed in Sweden.

Professor Delivanis had two points that he wished to raise, first the relation of public companies with the government, second the influence of the results of exploitation on investment in public corporations. Professor Wickham believed on the first point that public companies relied on the government as corporations depending from a holding corporation rely on it. Professor Delivanis did not think that this was really so. As a matter of fact public companies tried to expand as much as possible by investing their profits and by securing supplementary capital from the government. Private 'daughter firms' depending on holding companies were allowed to do so as far as profits were concerned only when increased profits were to be expected, when prestige was involved or when transfer to the holding company was forbidden by foreign exchange restrictions. This had happened with the motor car factories in Australia (both English or American owned in Australia as mentioned by Penrose in an article in the *Economic Journal* a few years previously).

So far as the independence of investment in public corporations from their financial results, as proposed by Professor Wickham, was concerned he did not think that this was very dangerous as it led to inflation when, as usually, the proceeds of central bank credits were involved. If this rule should apply, excess investment could be avoided only by arranging that new investments would be made only when existing plants were fully employed and when consumers or users were satisfied. It would not be easy to discover. Financial results of public corporations should include both full amortisation of plants and material and the difference between prices charged under governmental orders and the prices which a private firm would charge to cover both amortisation and profits.

Mr Henderson said that Professor Wickham had referred to the annual bargaining between French public enterprise and the Treasury, over the amount of capital financing, and had suggested that this called in question the system of medium-term economic planning. He wished to ask this question: Did the Treasury take account in their negotiations of the short-term economic situation? Did it, that is to say, try to use control over public investment as an instrument of stabilisation policy (contrary to the impression given in an earlier session by Monsieur Stoleru)?

Professor Wickham, replying to the discussion, expressed his gratitude to Professor Prest and to the other discussants for their interpretation of what he had been anxious to argue. He thought that various conclusions had emerged from the discussion:

(1) It was necessary to distinguish clearly between the regulations and the theory of choice in regard to public bodies engaged in distributing public goods and the conduct of public enterprises selling private goods on the market. The independent budget of a public enterprise (a thing which did not exist in relation to the posts and telegraphs) guaranteed for it an existence independent of the public authority which controlled it. This duality permitted a certain amount of bargaining between the two bodies.

(2) The conduct of public enterprises would gain greatly in clarity if the constraints to which they were subject were more clearly specified. At the theoretical level, as Professor Lundberg had suggested, it was most desirable to establish classifications and definitions of different types of constraints. That apart, in practice the public authority should make much more clear that it did in France, at least, all the various obligations imposed on the various public enterprises. These constraints could be as numerous as one liked. But they ought to be announced in

advance if one was not going to slip into purely arbitrary empiricism.

(3) The calculation of amortisation payments introduced conflicting considerations (as Professor Prest had mentioned, one was concerned with industrial depreciation rather than inflexible financial payments for amortisation) – conflicts between central authorities and a public enterprise and between considerations of the long and short period. In principle in France the controlling authorities, which were wholly independent of those running the enterprises, were under obligation to establish the true financial position on the basis of economic calculation. In practice the standardisation of public enterprise accounting had scarcely begun. Again in principle the financing of the investment of public enterprises was wholly regulated by medium-term programmes and independent of short-term cyclical and budgetary fluctuations. But this had as yet only been very imperfectly achieved, because the Ministry of Finance did not regard itself as completely and inescapably bound by the Plan. This seemed likely to be improved under the Fifth Plan. Economists could help greatly by encouraging the central authority not to behave towards the public enterprises like a very short-sighted owner.

(4) A clear distinction between voluntary and involuntary losses seemed to him to be essential for effective control of public enterprises. As he and others had suggested, sale at a loss on the basis of marginal cost was one possible form among others of deliberate operation at a loss. A loss made by a public enterprise was not *a priori* evidence of bad administration. But the same was not true of any loss whatsoever when realised *ex-post*. To judge correctly *ex-post*, it was necessary that the intended loss should have been announced *ex-ante*.

(5) In France, as elsewhere, the authorities had tended since the last war to give public enterprises advantages both in matters of credit and tax-liability as compared with private enterprises. During the past ten years, as a consequence of the progress of economic thought, there had been a radical change in this respect. The Régie Renault, for example, seemed to enjoy no advantages over its private competitors. Indeed one of its competitors (Citroën) had recently benefited by access to special funds. Did not the Régie Renault none the less gain when its competitors paid out profits? If that was the counterpart of various constraints imposed, was it justifiable?

(6) The public enterprise of many European countries had to work in a setting of state capitalism. It had more and more interrelations with private undertakings (as between coal and the chemical industries). It could acquire control of further private enterprises (the railways and road haulage). A provision of the statute governing most public enterprises which would enable them to issue shares on the market, as Professor Lundberg has suggested, would in many cases provide a very desirable flexibility. Despite the fact that the public authority has power to acquire, where necessary, the control of certain private enterprises on a purely capitalist basis, the public sector showed evidence today of serious rigidities. The complicated legal procedures necessary for nationalisation or denationalisation, as British experience had shown, were less and less justifiable.

The system adopted with success in Spain and Italy of partial and reversible public holdings of shares in enterprises seemed to be preferable.

(7) The relaxation of certain administrative controls and the more competitive operation of many public enterprises corresponded currently in Europe to some reduction in the powers and prerogatives of nationalist states. A 'denationalisation' of numerous public enterprises, in this limited sense, was currently taking place.

SESSION FOURTEEN

Discussion of Mr Turvey's Paper

Professor Margolis, in opening the discussion, said that Mr Turvey's self-imposed task had been to play the role of economic adviser who is seeking to influence policy. What was the basic principle or dogma of such an adviser? It was to achieve some approximation to Pareto optimality. He addressed himself to the problem of designing indexes or prices which would show the appropriate substitution ratios among the inputs of public enterprises, among the outputs of public enterprises which are used by other public enterprises, and among the outputs of public enterprises as they are placed on the general market.

Professor Margolis was sure that Mr Turvey had not had a uniformly sympathetic audience among his colleagues in the public enterprises and unfortunately his task had been greatly complicated by his colleagues from the universities who had developed arguments about the 'second best'. In essence this argument stated that if some of the conditions of optimality were violated in some sectors it would not be efficient for the remaining sectors to operate according to the usually formulated criteria. And often the stronger statement was made: that there are no general efficiency rules that could be given to the remaining sectors. The second best arguments, like the Arrow impossibility theorems, had been disquieting doctrines to those who had had to confront suspicious public officials.

Mr Turvey sought to establish arguments for some general rules for public enterprise in the context of a private economy which abounded with imperfections. Given these imperfections, how should the enterprise behave, if efficiency were the sole objective? As several of those present had said, this goal was a severe limitation on analysis; some would deny the usefulness of an analysis which accepted this limit, but he would pass over this point, making only one small point. The classification of objectives to efficiency and distribution might be too terse. An efficiency objective in practice was often narrowly restricted to evaluation of marketable possibilities of inputs and outputs. Too often vaguely formulated national objectives, such as the aesthetic levels of community life, regional distribution of population, or 'permanent' conservation of natural or artificial symbols of national pride were pushed aside.

Before examining the arguments he would like to comment on the term 'sub-optimization'. It was very useful, but possibly misleading. He would follow Dr Kolm's lead. We were always doing our best. But we always have constraints. He wished to take two cases:

1   How to produce a given output by alternative means. The rules required that the public enterprise

(a) should minimise costs calculated by *corrected* market price of inputs;
(b) should use a common discount rate;
(c) should observe the rule that all sales within the public enterprise sector should be at marginal cost prices.

On rule (a): Mr Turvey had cited three advantages.

On rule (b): This was true with corrected prices, so that money costs were equal to real costs. With money costs it was no guide. But there still remained Professor Wickham's problem of planned deficits, centrally and possibly politically determined.

On rule (c): He confessed to difficulty on this. Professor Malinvaud had commented on the strange results of second best. One should remember that imperfections are not only in the market, but also in the peculiar administrative rules for different agencies. Thus possibly some adjustments were necessary. This affected the rule (b) of a common discount rate. Different agencies would have different access to the capital market and though they may be forced to share a common view of the future, the opportunity cost of capital might be different.

2   The second problem was output mix and the relative prices of different outputs. The rule was that, if sold within public sector, then the goods should be priced at long-run social marginal cost; if sold outside, then sold with a mark-up over marginal cost, and this mark-up should be the same as for its close substitutes.

Professor Margolis' comments were these: The use of long-term marginal cost for all cases was not persuasive. There was a case for estimated discounted cash flows where because of a grid, indivisibilities were less important. Stable prices could be assigned some special virtue. In a less integrated transportation system they were important. He saw no reason in a more complex analysis for using long-run marginal cost. He assumed there was likely to be significant excess capacity.

If a public sector undertaking was to be independent fiscally then some form of discriminatory pricing might be necessary. This gave rise to distributive effects; but it was best to ignore these.

His second question was concerned with the suggestion of differential prices inside and outside public enterprises. It was not clear to him why the public railroad should discriminate between oil, coal and electricity. Why should coal be transferred at marginal cost to the railroad and electricity; at a mark-up to oil; and oil itself at a mark-up to the railroad and electricity; oil and coal at mark-ups to households and firms?

He would like to make a final point: fiscal independence was often advisable. He would hesitate about abandoning it. On the other hand, it was dangerous to be rigid. They had explored too little the rules suggested by Professor

Zielinski and Professor Gloushkov as to how to exercise control while preserving fiscal independence and how to reduce controls on institutions which remained a part of the budget.

Professor Wickham commented that the writings of the French school of engineer-economists (Allais, Hutter, Boiteux) on marginal cost pricing dated from fifteen years earlier. In the past ten years – since 1955 – many public sector enterprises in France had adopted in whole or part the methods of tariff fixing proposed. He thought that as the result of their experience and the analysis of it that had rollowed, three main conclusions had emerged.

Firstly, short-term marginal cost was an unworkable concept. It was impossible to measure with precision. It was extremely unstable. For a transport enterprise, for example (a shipping line or an airline), if the capacity of its craft was not fully occupied instantaneously – as was normally the case – the marginal cost of transport of an additional passenger or ton of freight was effectively zero. Only long-term marginal cost (corresponding closely to what in France was called *coût de développement*) provided a workable basis. He regarded the whole debate about the supposed alternatives of short- and long-term marginal cost as a waste of time.

Secondly, the use of long-term marginal cost as a basis for fixing tariffs did not necessarily imply operating at a loss. In the first place for various activities, marginal long-term cost was close to average cost, so far as this could be measured. Moreover, the average charge which determined the financial result was in practice a political decision. The relevance of marginal cost was limited to the structure of the tariffs – that is to say to the relative prices of the various services or products sold by the public enterprise. The decisions about relative prices did not pre-judge the global decision as to whether one did or did not wish to cover total costs by total receipts.

Thirdly, as Mr Kolm had said, the marginal theory provided one of a variety of possible bases for fixing relative charges. Marginalism was a form of rationality. But it was not a necessity. There were other forms of rationality. He wondered whether, in the light of his long practical experience in Great Britain, Mr Turvey would agree with these conclusions.

Professor Lundberg suggested that shadow prices had to be used under realistic conditions, not least in order to estimate marginal social costs. One could never apply the prices of today; forecasts of future prices were necessary. To take the investment-choice between thermal or hydro-electric stations, the oil prices of the 1970s would decide the choice. The price-forecast (on the basis of trend analysis) would be a strategic shadow price. Attention had to be paid to the wide uncertainty region around the chosen shadow-price.

The choice of a discount rate (in Turvey's case 8 per cent) also meant taking a shadow price. This interest rate did not exist on the market as such – and the grounds for selecting it were very shaky. In Sweden 7 per cent had been chosen; this was just about a threshold rate for continuing with hydro-electricity; above that limit thermal stations would usually be the best choice.

How about the cost of misallocation? They had been putting so much emphasis on the price-system as providing indicators of optimal allocation. There were a number of numerical calculations which, even if doubtful, tended to demonstrate that the deviations from optimum in plausible cases (for the economy as a whole) meant 'welfare-losses' of not more than ¼ of 1 per cent. Professor Lundberg did not believe much in this type of calculation; but their relevance ought to be considered here. Or did the conference dislike quantifications under all conditions?

Mr Kolm said that as Electricité de France was supposed to be the paragon, the archetype, of marginal cost pricing, it was interesting to see how they dealt with 'second best' considerations. In fact, they got rid of these objections by an argument which was basically Kant's categorical imperative: they must, they say, 'choose the price in such a way that if everybody were pricing in the same manner the economy would be in an optimal state'. This was much worse than Mr Turvey's rules of thumb. However, when they had theoretically looked into second best problems – before the adoption of the term 'second best' by economists – their approach was sounder than Mr Turvey's. It consisted in studying the effect on optimal pricing of specified social, political and institutional constraints which prevent the economy reaching the optimum (i.e. the first best defined with production functions as only constraints). The prices were both within the public sector and for sales and purchases by the public sector to and from the private sector. As instances of the constraints studied, he would mention the requirement of budget equilibrium or of given deficit or benefit by Boiteux in his 1956 *Econometrica* article (although he forgot the collective consumption of capital and the possibility and optimality of a Dupuit discrimination), and monopoly position (for the sale of electricity to the aluminium industry) by another writer. One could regret that Mr Turvey's paper did not clearly single out each imperfection with its effect on optimal pricing. Finally, it should be clearly stated that the use of long-run marginal costs and of a unique rate of discount were at best only second best policies, and they should be justified as such.

Professor Sen could not agree that Mr Turvey had evaded the problem of the second best. All he had done was to assert without empirical evidence, that the divergences from the optimum caused by the following of his rule were smaller than the convergences towards the optimum which would be produced by following his rule. This remained to be demonstrated. The mere fact that there was a group of commodities whose cross elasticities of demand were quite high did not produce a knock-down argument for forgetting the difficulties. For instance, it was not sufficient to show that it would be a good idea if prices were charged proportionally to marginal costs in the gas and electricity industries: the proportionality rule had well-known difficulties, associated with the margin between work and leisure.

Mr Turvey, replying to the discussion, asked how prices were to be fixed if it were not along the lines which he had suggested. Where products were highly substitutable in use, and where one had corrected for the most obvious incorrectness in the prices of inputs into productive processes, it still seemed correct to allow the price mechanism to do some work in the allocation of resources in the world in which we work.

SESSION FIFTEEN

Discussion of Professor Gloushkov's Paper

In opening the discussion, *Professor Zielinski* said that all reforms actually carried on or discussed in socialist countries had one basic common feature. That is to say they represented a move away from the use of open information (administrative order) and towards the more extensive use of cipher information, by which he meant prices and rates of bonuses. Within this uniformity, however, two different approaches could be distinguished. The difference lay in the way that parameters used in the process of plan construction, and then in the process of plan fulfilment, were to be determined. One approach – particularly evident in Czechoslovakian and Hungarian reforms – proposed to install, on quite a broad basis, the market-type competitive mechanism, from which the necessary parameters were to be derived. On the other hand they had the Soviet–Polish reforms in which the role assigned to market mechanism was much less and the central fixing of parameters much greater. All socialist countries were moving from non-parametic to parametic management. Some, however, were moving closer to limited-type market socialism, while others were moving towards 'indirect centralism' if he might use Professor Zauberman's phrase, or towards improved 'democratic centralism' in Professor Gloushkov's terminology.

Professor Zielinski's second comment referred to misinterpretation of certain features of economic policy in socialist countries. One frequently encountered such misinterpretations and Professor Gloushkov discussed them in several places in his paper. He himself had found personally three such misinterpretations especially frequent and irritating:

(i) First, many people thought that where there was a profit success indicator, a socialist country had a universal or synthetic stimulus-system. This was obviously not necessarily the case. He thought it could be easily proved (as was shown in diagram 12 of his own paper) that the universal character of the profit success indicator can be easily maintained if a number of specialised bonus conditions were introduced into the stimulus-system. This special boundary condition acted as an extra constraint and made profit a necessary but not sufficient condition for efficiency bonuses.

(ii) Many people thought that when there was a profit success indicator, prices were playing a significant, if not decisive, role in steering the national economy. The truth of this statement depended, however, on the construction of the information system and to be more specific on the transformation rules used in the information system. The economic policy of socialist countries distinguished between so-called 'dependent profit' and 'independent profit' at the enterprise level. The latter was the profit due to price, wage and tariff changes. These changes were neutralised through special transformation rules and the enterprise profit as a success indicator was completely independent of any price/wage/tariff changes. From what he had said it was clear, he hoped, that from the fact that the profit success indicator was used, one could not judge the role of prices in steering the socialist enterprises.

(iii) Finally many people thought that when prices were used to steer socialist production, one had a case of market socialism. As he had already said, this was not necessarily true. It all depended on how prices were fixed – on the market or by the centre, and by the centre he did not necessarily mean the C.P.B.: it might be some lower organ, say a regional price commission, but acting on the basis of C.P.B. instructions rather than according to market indications.

It was Professor Zielinski's belief that if these and various other over-simplified judgements could be corrected, discussion about the working of planned economies could be substantially improved.

Professor Jochimsen wished to ask two questions regarding the new economic system of planning and management. First, what procedures were used to determine prices and to effect the 'price reform' by gradual implementation? In East Germany there had been three different stages. Hundreds of thousands of persons had been engaged in 'negotiating' or calculating the new prices. As a consequence new prices were introduced in one sector which in turn was 'blocked-off' from the rest, using three different prices. Were there methods besides administrative price-fixing? What role was played by the turnover tax in the price fixing? Second, Professor Gloushkov had stated that only ex-penditures for labour were included in price determination. What provision was made for calculating interest on capital to be included in the price? Even if the planning commission used opportunity costs of capital to determine the allocation of funds centrally, this did not solve the capital allocation problem at the private level. Claims for central funds might be inflated if they did not cost anything, and prices were distorted. This had to be seen in conjunction with Zauberman's point that initial capital output ratios in general were very high in socialist countries. This was tied up with the problem of technological progress. How was one to induce firms to make proper use of capital?

Professor Gloushkov, replying, said that though there were still many problems to be solved in the implementation of this reform, one could reach two main conclusions: First, a new socialist system of optimal planning and management was neither an over-centralised, nor an autonomous, one. It was a new form of management of the national economy that provided for an harmonious inter-action of the central planning (but in a more liberal form) and autonomy of every individual economic cell. Second, this system provided an harmony of centralisation and decentralisation. This harmony would be created by a system of optimal planning implemented with the aid of economic cybernetics, that would integrate the optimality criterion of the economy on the regional scale with the specific tests for the individual industries. It also interrelated the play variables expressed in money with those expressed in terms of kind at all levels of the national economy and would work to the final benefit of all citizens of the country.

SESSION SIXTEEN

Discussion of Professor Chenery's Paper

Mr Stoleru, opening the discussion, said that Professor Chenery's paper had three main themes:

(a) Its main inquiry was into increasing returns to capital expenditure with a growth model of three periods and four sectors (primary, intermediate, manufactures and infrastructure investment). The sectors were linked by a simple input-output model which yielded a structure of demand via a production function in which the relation between capital and output is specified.
(b) The simple model, but with foreign trade introduced and foreign borrowing.
(c) Choice then lay between more investment initially and less. The interesting features lay in the assumption of increasing returns in the intermediate or infrastructure sectors. The reason for having two sectors with this property was the distinction between imports that were impossible (infrastructures) and imports that were possible (intermediate goods). The need for capital arose to increase capacity, but with falling unit costs of capital. There was thus a choice, not merely choices between present and future. These choices included choice between:
  (i) capacity to meet 100 per cent of present demand, and
  (ii) capacity initially in excess of demand but with larger and more efficient plant.

The second alternative of (c) could be achieved in various ways: by borrowing, by sacrificing other sectors, by importing to cover the investment in other sectors. Thus there were a whole new series of choices.

If one looked at the results to be expected, intuitively one would expect different variants: balanced growth; Scitovsky-type growth, with alternating doses of heavy investment in different sectors; the 'big push', which corresponded to initial heavy investments all round; specialisation with foreign trade.

Professor Chenery's model incorporated numbers (the relationships were numerical rather than general). The solution had two principle features:

(i) the optimal solution made maximum use of borrowing; and
(ii) in increasing return sectors investment was put high initially, so as to secure full exploitation of increasing returns (the cost of excess capacity was more than offset by cost reductions).

After establishing certain basic solutions, Professor Chenery had gone on to other variants with other data to study the sensitivity of the solution to rate of capitalisation, rate of discount, size of market, possibility of trade, length of time horizon. As regards rate of discount, a progressive increase from 5 to 10 to 20 per cent had a very considerable effect on the solutions and affected the optimum level of investment, implying less emphasis on increasing returns.

Mr Stoleru had some comments and criticisms to offer.

(i) Employment had not been explicitly introduced. The 'optimum' solution might involve too much or too little unemployment.

(ii) The model seemed to him to mix up several essentially different problems: the decision regarding the 'big push' depended on the consumption/ investment choice as well as on increasing returns. The solution for many strategies would be irrespective of increasing returns. An aversion from the world was thus optimal quite apart from increasing returns. The effect of increasing returns needed to be made more explicitly clear.

(iii) The objective function that the model maximised was inevitably complex. But more serious was that for the optimal value, consumption was a very small percentage of the objective function. Thus with different assumptions about the terminal value different optima would appear. The model was apparently very sensitive to assumptions about the terminal date.

Mr Stoleru, in conclusion, wished, therefore, to ask Professor Chenery three questions:

(i) What had he to add about unemployment?

(ii) What he had to say about solutions in the absence of increasing returns?

(iii) Was the low value of consumption in the objective function a defect?

Professor Tardos asked two questions: Did the algorithm give a solution for bigger models with more variables? Big differences were found in the present value of shadow prices in different periods. Would Professor Chenery comment?

Professor Sandee said that Professor Chenery's study represented a major breakthrough – a successful attack on a major problem. He had four comments to make:

(a) From the privately circulated 'Conclusions', it seemed that there were no general results. Thus for a given country the problem of lumpiness would have to be solved for a real case with an integer programme. Details would have to be filled in later with shadow prices to be supplied by the government of the country.

(b) Lumpiness of infrastructure had worse effects because such investment was a prerequisite for production. This appeared to have been overlooked in the model.

(c) From the results, it appeared that there were great advantages in reducing the effects of lumpiness. Imports were a help (where possible); exports could play a similar role (using excess capacity to export).

(d) Professor Chenery's illustrative diagram reminded one of dynamic programming. What about two-dimensional dynamic programming (with consequentially less restraint on number of time-periods)?

Professor Dorfman commented that dynamic programming involved a choice at each stage between all alternatives. It was much too complicated. *Professor Sandee* thought that the relevant choice was to start or not to start industries. *Professor Dorfman* maintained that *all* choices were involved – algorithm got badly out of hand with more than one dimension – and there were several dimensions here.

Mr Turvey argued that things can sometimes be built in stages (build the dam but install turbines in two stages), with only preparatory work done for total eventual size. Do the civil engineering but not the mechanical engineering. In this way lumpiness could be reduced.

Professor Marglin suggested that shadow prices could play a useful role in 'local' decisions; but even in non-increasing return sectors they were unlikely to guide one to the right path.

Professor Chenery, replying to various questions put to him, said his model was not a realistic or planning model. It was better regarded as a laboratory experiment. For planning purposes the objective function would have to be fully specified. Separation of increasing returns was a good idea. It would probably lead to something like solutions. The present formulation was due to unwillingness to incur costs until the value was proved. In reply to Professor Tardos' question, algorithm could solve any size of problem. As regards Professor Tardos' question relating to shadow prices, it was difficult to answer as these jumped around in early periods. They should become more stable when the model runs for longer periods. He agreed with Professor Marglin that shadow prices were only of local assistance. He agreed also with the first point made by Professor Sandee, that the model provided no real guidance for policy decisions as yet. His point relating to exports was a good one. He agreed finally with Mr Turvey, indeed this was an argument which he himself had used some fifteen years earlier.

SESSION SEVENTEEN

Discussion of Professor Sandee's Paper

Professor Guitton, introducing the discussion, said that although Professor Sandee's paper was not specifically concerned with the subject of the conference, it provided a valuable basis for further analysis. The programme committee had set out to answer the question whether it was possible to reconcile two apparently contradictory requirements – long-term growth and short-term equilibrium.

Nowadays, growth seemed to have become the major objective. And while investment was the principle agent of growth, it was known to exercise a de-stabilising influence on prices in the short period. Was it possible, asked Professor Guitton, to eliminate this conflict by a judicious combination of medium-term indicative planning and short-term demand management?

It was thought that one way of achieving this was through control of public sector investment. Might not appropriate controls over public sector investment permit much that was incapable of being achieved by private sector investment, subject as it was to the sudden fluctuations of the market mechanism? How could we test the validity of this intuitive argument?

The basic difficulty, he thought, was the ambiguity of the concept of 'public'

T

investment itself; merely introducing the word 'public' by no means made it clear what was actually meant. Basically, this concept of 'public investment' ought perhaps to be linked to that of a 'social good' which was central to the theme of the whole conference. Public investment could be defined in several ways: but, in particular, on the basis of the type of project – that is one decided by the public authorities – or on the basis of the intended objective – that is, the satisfaction of an indivisible collective need. But, if it was difficult to make a clear distinction between private goods and social goods, it was even more so to distinguish adequately between private and public investment. In fact since the State now exercised direct influence even over private investment by its planning policies and since investment carried out by the State in its role as an economic agent (as opposed to a political authority) appeared very similar to investment by any private economic agent, particularly when this latter was carried out on a large scale, the greater part of investment in the modern economy could be described neither as public nor as private, but as a mixed type.

This, Professor Guitton went on to argue, was why it was difficult to provide an answer to the question that had been asked earlier. And this was also why Professor Sandee had been well advised not to try to answer it either. However, he thought that it should be kept in mind when considering Professor Sandee's model since this was, in his opinion, a first step towards providing an answer to the problem.

As the title of his paper made clear, Professor Sandee was interested in one question only: What effects did fluctuations in public expenditure and taxation have on economic growth? The term 'public investment' was not even mentioned in the model that he had presented; but the implications for it were quite clear. Professor Sandee's procedure, as had been evident throughout the conference, was not to think through the problem in purely abstract terms, but to *measure* the determining factors and on this basis, actively to seek a political solution. It was, in fact, a model for political decision-making. Professor Sandee belonged to the concrete econometric school for whom there was no science where there was no measurement.

It was not a complete and generalised model. It was a global model, but of a sectoral type. Professor Sandee took his basic data from the Dutch economy in 1965: thus, the model was essentially based on a particular historical case. He distinguished three sectors only (agriculture, manufacturing, services) and used annual data. He chose a medium-term 'horizon' of five years, that is, 1965–70. The model contained 66 equations calculated on the basis of previous Dutch economic experience.

Professor Guitton then went on to indicate the essential characteristics of the model. The aim was to measure the deflationary or anti-deflationary effects of changes in certain intermediate variables ('lever' variables) upon the final variables which constituted the objectives to be attained. In a double-entry table of a reduced form the column heads expressed the five 'lever' variables (exogenous or instrumental): purchases of manufactured goods by the State, purchases of services by the State, taxes on wages, taxes on profits, indirect taxes, autonomous investment (i.e. decided by the State) set against the five final variables considered most important: volume of private consumption, prices at which consumption takes place, unemployment in millions of man-years, volume of productive investment, volume of G.N.P. and the balance of trade surplus at current prices.

Professor Guitton pointed out that productive investment had been considered in the model as an end and not as a means. Operating within this framework, the originality of the Dutch model lay in its isolation of two types of effect exercised by the 'lever' variables: the effects of short-term measures and the total effects of regular growth which occurred cumulatively up to the end of the period. Growth was assumed to be regular and linear with continuous adaptation so as to maintain full capacity output. By comparing the short and long term effects of the original measures it ought to be possible to resolve the problem that had been posed at the beginning of the discussion.

As far as Professor Sandee's own calculations were concerned, it was no surprise that the reulsts he obtained from the model confirmed what might have been intuitively expected: taxes or profits and investment financed by the State appeared to be the best regulators for the achievement of steady, non-inflationary, growth.

Professor Guitton then went on to say that he would like to put five questions to Professor Sandee:

1 How could productive investment be considered as a definite result of decisions made by the State? There was a certain ambiguity on this point that was confirmed by the statement that: 'investment i and G.N.P. (v) are to be considered more as end than as means'. Professor Guitton found this lack of clarity somewhat disconcerting.

2 What was the significance of variable d (p. 405, annexe c)? It was a shadow for the harmonisation of price-levels between sectors and had been described as 'one way of expressing the degree of inflation in the economy'. Professor Guitton said that he would appreciate a more detailed explanation.

3 Could the model be generalised? Would it not be feasible to measure the effects of different types of investment and to incorporate them into the model as differentiated 'lever' variables? This would obviuosly mean indentifying the different types of investment and finding a method of qualifying them in empirical analysis: and if it were done it would provide a procedure for answering the original question.

4 Professor Guitton said that when discussing public investment he considered it difficult or even illusory to attempt to analyse its effects without taking account of how it was financed. In a way, the method of financing (whether by different types of taxation or by borrowing) was more important than the object of the investment itself.

5 It was regrettable, thought Professor Guitton, that the model had not been linked to recent studies on optimal growth (cf. in particular, E. Malinvaud 'Les Croissances Optimales', *Cahiers du Seminaire d'Econometrie*, No. 8, C.N.R.S. 1965). Since the aim was to harmonise short-term demand management and medium-term growth policy, it did not seem over-optimistic to consider the possibility of a policy for optimal regulation of the effects of investment and of the short- and long term-effects of public and private sector investment.

Professor Guitton concluded by congratulating Professor Sandee and his research team from the Dutch Central Planning Bureau on their valuable work. It had opened up a new field of scientific investigation, the need for which had been clearly shown by the conference.

Mr Turvey asked whether quantification of damage done by stop-go did not fail to take account of non-linearities and thus of additional and unconsidered effects. He himself would support the non-linear Phillips-style unemployment – wage relation. Would Professor Sandee comment?

Professor Chenery said that Professor Sandee had posed the question: What was the loss of investment and G.N.P.? But his conclusions seemed to deal with other issues, not this one.

Professor Barrère said that stop-go was a favourite policy instrument of many ministers of finance. Professor Sandee's paper developed alternatives. Did they have the properties of reducing public investment? Professor Sandee had apparently adopted two different treatments, according to whether the means adopted were designed for increases or reductions in expenditure. In his model he did not allow for the effect of government action in response to a rise in tax income. The State might respond by increasing its expenditure; this was far more likely than stabilisation, which would increase liquidity. Allowance for this factor would change the model, which was at present too simple in its treatment of this question.

Mr Tardos said that an econometric model dealing with policy targets was a very important subject of study. But the conclusions seemed open to doubt. Professor Sandee had said that the model was too small. What about the possibility of parameterisation? The conclusions were attractive, but sympathy was not the point: a more elaborate treatment was needed.

Professor Stoleru said that most of the equations were naturally price equations. For purposes of estimating the level of wages, it was necessary to take account of the effects of productivity. But there seemed to be no provision for the effects of prices on productivity: Prices were determined by output. The influence of demand seemed to be missing.

Professor Malinvaud thought that Professor Sandee had adopted an extreme Keynesian thesis: the way of acting on private investment seemed to be ineffective and could therefore be discounted. The equation describing private investment contained no instrumental variable, while public investment was under the control of the authorities. This was open to question. Public investment was not easy to adjust. There were some theories which led one to think that monetary policies operating on private investment might be a useful instrument. An additional point: Did the model of the C.P.B. give a good description of lags in behaviour and reactions? If not the results of the model were open to question.

Professor Sandee replying said that, partly as the result of imperfections in the French translation, there were certain points he would like to clear up. The model, as he had explained was a piece of team work. Misunderstandings had arisen over definition of public and private investments. In the model, there was a variable denoting productive investments (including investment by public enterprises). To handle productive investments, the model used equation 66, relating investment to net profits after tax. Thus the government could control productive investment through changes in Tz. Non-productive investment could be reduced fairly easily. In Dutch experience, fluctuations both in private and public investment had not been great. (Six sectors represented in his view a minimum; on the other hand, adding more greatly increased the work.).

The first table showed the effects of change in a given policy regarding investment. The distribution of time (the length of lags) had no effect on results. Thus the same proportions were used for short-term effects (as well as steady growth). Long-term effects on investment had also been studied. In the reduced form, a lower capital stock could be brought in.

As regards the question asked by Professor Barrère, the fate of the cash supplies of government was unknown, but in his view unimportant. As regards the question asked by Monsieur Stoleru as to whether wages did not depend on prices, Professor Sandee put his trust in the equation included in his paper. Prices in fact depend on the variable d as well as on costs, and this was used to balance accounts at current prices. On non-linearity Professor Sandee concluded that if the economy was non-linear in certain respects, then the use of linear or exponential relations involved inaccuracy. But Phillips-type non-linearity was not in fact apparent in Holland.

His reference to full-capacity utilisation should read 'high and constant degree of capital utilisation'; the results were exactly the same on optimisation, the C.P.B. had used such methods, which however fell outside the immediate scope of the paper.

To Professor Chenery's question, his answer was to be found in the final table: the main conclusions could be read off there, with suitable implications. As regards Professor Malinvaud's question lags were of the order of 1-year, and the effects evened out over a 5-year period. Quite a lot was known about lags, and had been taken into account.

SESSION EIGHTEEN

Discussion of Professor Jochimsen's and Professor Houssiaux's Papers

Mr Henderson, opening the discussion of Professor Jochimsen's paper thought that he had put this important problem in a very broad framework: the paper covered a very wide range of issues in a highly concise way. It took as a point of departure the inadequacy of the purely competitive model as a guide to policy, and made a number of interesting suggestions concerning forcible lines of conduct and rules of behaviour which would help us to deal with this situation. This was related to a broad analysis of the types of market behaviour in the private sector, and of the various forms which public enterprise could take. Although Professor Jochimsen was not primarily concerned with drawing detailed conclusions on questions of policy, there were two points made in the

T 2

concluding section of his paper which might be singled out for special mention, namely:

(a) the suggestion that competitive public enterprises might be established in cases of monopolistic or oligopolistic markets, in order to reduce private monopoly profits and provide a stimulus to efficiency;

(b) the general conclusion at the end of the paper that the bulk of proof that public enterprise would give better results than private rested with the government: only if there was solid evidence of its prospective superiority should the decision go in favour of public rather than private ownership.

Mr Henderson suggested than an important issue, which was perhaps given too little emphasis in the paper, was the question of efficiency, in the sense of productivity rather than allocative efficiency. He wished to refer to three aspects of this in the contexts of remarks made in Professor Jochimesn's paper.

1   Profesor Jochimsen had raised two important problems at different points of his paper, namely (a) ensuring greater social responsibilities on the part of private big business, and (b) making enterprises more effectively accountable. Mr Henderson raised the possibility that both these objectives might be formed by the same means, namely the progressive intervention of a system of efficiency audits for both.

2   Professor Jochimsen had referred to the divide between ownership and control in private industry. In so far as this might be a serious problem, it was surely not irremediable. There was scope in many countries for improvements in company law which might make for more efficient operation of the private capital market. In this connection it was perhaps important to remember that actual and potential stockholders were not necessarily ignorant individuals, but included institutional investors and companies themselves. This raised the very interesting question of the effects of take-overs and mergers in private industry. In connection with this set of problems, he wished to draw attention to the analysis of changes in the United Kingdom capital market, published in 1962 by J. F. Wright.

3   The question of mergers led on to the more general problem of economies of scale – economies of centralised control. The question of such economies might be the main argument for public ownership: it was certainly part of the case for nationalising the U.K. steel industry. When this case was argued, three issues arose:

(a) How important were the potential economies?

(b) If they were important, why were they not realised under private ownership?

(c) If they existed and had remained unrealised under private ownership, how confident could one be that a change of ownership would in itself ensure that they would be realised?

Another and distinct efficiency argument for nationalisation might be formulated in the case of industries for whom the government was the main customer, such as the aircraft industry (which incidentally was an interesting case because of the diversity of ownership patterns and of government practice in the three leading manufacturing countries, the U.S., the U.K. and France). This argument, which had recently been advanced in Britain, was that public ownership would lead to greater identity of interest between customer and supplier, with the result that wasteful and expensive systems of government supervision and control could be abolished. One might call this an economy of policing. Again, however, one had to ask whether

(a) the power of control was serious;
(b) a change of ownership would in fact lead to closer identity of interest; and
(c) whether the conflict of interests might not be inveitable or even fruitful.

French experience perhaps suggested that questions of ownership might be largely irrelevant to the problem of improving efficiency in this sector.

Mr Henderson said that he strongly disagreed with Mr Turvey's suggestion that efficiency audits would be of little value because of a lack of expertise outside the firms or industries subjected to the audit. Mr Turvey was failing to recognise the very important point that disclosure by enterprises, and recording of their activities, itself contributed to creating a new expertise: there was a potential virtuous cycle here, which it should be an object of policy to promote.

In introducing Professor Houssiaux's paper, *Professor Herschel* put six questions. First, how did large scale private enterprise really function? Secondly, how did public enterprises operate – how great were their inefficiencies and what were the possibilities of controlling them? Thirdly, what was the interrelation between public and private industry and what in particular was the difference between setting up public enterprises and subsidising private ones? Fourthly, in what ways and in what manner did the need for public intervention in the private economy arise? Was it possible to use public cash to improve competition in the private market? Lastly, what are the proper fields for public and private enterprise respectively?

Mr Turvey took up the first and second of Professor Herschel's questions, and agreed that it would be possible, through the establishment of efficiency audits and cross-industry investigations, to investigate the efficiency of public and large private enterprises. One would use expert knowledge from outside the industry, and management techniques were now sufficiently advanced to make this a possible and useful activity.

Mr Henderson commented that the supply of experts would be increased continuously by giving them opportunities to exercise their expertise.

Professor Robinson thought it was worth remembering why nationalisation often occurred. There were in many industries economies in specialisation – these economies were perhaps more important than economies of scale in the old-fashioned sense. Achievement of these would require monopoly control and hence the case for public enterprise.

Professor Prest said that Mr Turvey had questioned the value, in the case of public enterprise, of outside investigations as suggested by Mr Henderson. What was in question, however, was not usually the technical competence of the engineers and others responsible for the operation of public entreprises. It was rather the need to test the quality of the management, to assess its understanding of the economic and financial implications of its operations, and to clarify the political constraints under which it operates. Personal experience suggested that these objectives could be achieved with some success even by a committee of laymen with no technical knowledge, but with the power to call for documents and to cross examine the senior staff.

Mr Henderson had referred to Professor Jochimsen's suggestion that a public enterprise might operate as an outsider in oligopolistic-monopolistic markets. There were a number of examples in the world of public enterprises being operated in competition with private enterprises that would otherwise be in a monopolistic situation, e.g. Canadian railways and Australian internal airways. The latter experience suggested that the resulting duopoly situation, as might be expected, was difficult to maintain. Parity must be presented in respect of fares, services and aircraft types, otherwise one undertaking would attract all the traffic from the other. Nevertheless the consensus of opinion in Australia was that the system had resulted in better service to the public than would have been provided by either a public or a private monopoly.

Professor Delivanis thought that Professor Jochimsen was right that in theory maximisation of profit by a public enterprise was unacceptable. In practice, however, it was different when it implied that either the budget deficit was reduced or funds for investment were secured. He wanted to refer to the contention of Professor Houssiaux regarding the influence of external economies on the international competitive power of the private firms. It was perfectly valid but was often forgotten in planning. Whenever long-and short-term objectives implied contrary decisions, it was the short-term objectives which had to be given first consideration, since otherwise various catastrophes might occur in the meantime which might lead to a change of objectives.

Professor Jochimsen, replying briefly, said that self-financing could be achieved without profit maximisation. *Professor Houssiaux* added that he agreed that the clash between long and short term aims in the control of investment was a difficult problem.

SESSION NINETEEN

Discussion of Professor Pokrovski's Paper

Introducing the paper *Mr Tulkens* started by expressing his appreciation for Professor Pokrovski's illuminating analysis of the underlying concepts and elements of 'planning' and 'programming', and of their implementation today in the Eastern and Western countries respectively. He proposed to deal briefly with three topics: (i) detailed *vs.* global planning; (ii) incentives and public goods; (iii) incentive-prices (*prix stimulants* in the French text) and wage rates.

Professor Pokrovski had stressed the fact that Soviet planning was in the course of a fundamental modification. The planning was no longer to be conceived as a detailed listing of all products and resource uses. Instead, there had been in recent years a strong tendency towards a more limited definition of rather general objectives, expressed only in aggregate terms. According to the paper, this was essentially due to the growing pace of technical and scientific progress.

If one turned to Western 'programming', it was interesting to observe that precisely the same phenomenon formed one of the greatest difficulties in the planning process, and that it was probably one of the main reasons why more disaggregated plans could not be elaborated by the authorities. Later in his paper, however, Professor Pokrovski has claimed that the inability of Western programming to go farther than the definition of general objectives for the various branches of industry was due to the fact that it could be done only on the basis of final demand. This argument seemed to Mr Tulkens to be disputable. If the capitalistic type of planning was conducted in such terms, was it not because in principle it left to market forces the role of allocating the production of final goods between competing firms, rather than because of any intrinsic inability to extend the planning that far?

On the question of incentives, a general comment might be made regarding the public good concept which had been one of the focus points of the conference. Professor Pokrovski had pointed out that part of the profit made by the Soviet firms was devoted to a social and cultural fund. Now, many 'social' and 'cultural' goods formed excellent examples of public goods. It was thus of great interest to note that in the U.S.S.R. decisions regarding them were being made, at least in part, at the firm level. If we looked back at the capitalist system as it operated at the time when Karl Marx wrote his criticism of it, was it not obvious that one of its most crucial defects was its inability to provide public goods and public 'concerns' (in Mr Kolm's sense)? In most of the communistic revolutionary programmes, the promise of the benefits from such goods seemed to hold a predominant place. And, indeed, very few private firms had ever been induced to use their profits for the production of public goods.

Professor Pokrovski had also discussed the role of 'incentive-prices' (*prix stimulants* in the French text) for various commodities and for labour in particular. The question naturally arose whether such prices should be assimilated with individual wages and whether they bore any relationship to a measurement of the productivity labour.

A concluding question was concerned with the newly experienced system of price-guided planning in the U.S.S.R., as opposed to the previous methods based on physical quantities. Professor Marglin had argued in his paper that from a theoretical viewpoint price-guided allocations were not more efficient than command allocations. Would it be possible to derive any confirmation or disproof of that conclusion from the practical experience of the U.S.S.R.?

Professor Mossé had three questions to ask. What was the influence of demand on the quantities produced? How were wage rates determined? How far was the enterprise free to determine its own product-mix?

Professor Marglin wished to know more about the relation between optimum prices and incentive prices. Were 'Lange prices' used for purposes of plan formulation?

Professor Gloushkov said, in relation to Professor Mossé's questions, that more account was now taken of demand and that market research played an important part. Wage rates were fixed nationally but incentive payments varied locally. Each enterprise was able to make contracts for various amounts of its products. He could not answer Professor Marglin's question. What was the use of having two clocks telling the same time?

Professor Chenery said that developing countries were very much interested in prices. Firstly it was these that affected trade patterns and not costs. Secondly they were concerned about prices for competing goods, and these were often affected, for example, by the rate of interest.

Mr Kolm said that, just as Professor Pokrovski had found interest for Soviet economists in certain work going on in Western countries, so had some of the work relating to recent economic innovations in the socialist countries great relevance to the conduct of public sector enterprises in Western countries. The discussions in earlier sessions had shown the disagreement between Western economists as to the singularity or multiplicity of rates of discount. It seemed to him that the charges based on fixed productive or circulating funds must enter into the calculations of Soviet enterprises in exactly the same way as did interest rates in the West. The differences caused by interest rates in Western conditions derived principally from considerations of the liquidity and period of amortisation of capital investments. They were therefore most anxious to know whether the charges were identical or different, firstly in respect of fixed and circulating funds, secondly in respect of fixed productive funds in different branches of industry, thirdly in respect of different enterprises. How were any differences justified and explained?

Mr Tardos understood that, while prices were based on average cost, they diverged because of subsidies and taxes. How was it intended to use prices? As success indicators or as determinants of demand? Was it hoped that long-run prices would be used in the same way, but with the elimination of subsidies and taxes? How were prices related to international trade decisions and investment decisions? Was all their pricing based on average cost?

Professor Dorfman thought that the public sectors of Britain, France and the United States were all in a mess. Was it because they relied on public companies? Clearly not; for the British difficulties were equally great and they relied on public ownership. Was it because all these countries had a private sector? But the private sector prices performed a very useful function. What, then, was the explanation?

Mr Turvey was anxious to know whether, in principle, the Socialist countries accepted the concept of equimarginal rates of substitution.

Mr Terny, Professor Malinvaud and *Professor Barrère* all wished to know more in detail about methods of making planning decisions.

Professor Pokrovski, replying to the discussion, said that the social optimum was the central point of the whole scientific discussion. It had been examined from a variety of aspects in all the earlier papers of the conference. The purpose of his own contribution was to pose the problem once again, but this time in the form of a comparison of two systems. Why had he done this? In order to help to understand not only the advantages and the limitations but also the whole economic basis of a centrally planned economy.

If one took the Soviet economy, one found it, in terms of its working until very recently, rather too centralised. The Western system, on the other hand, left a great deal of initiative to private enterprise. It was not difficult to appreciate that there was an optimal combination of central planning and initiative by individual enterprises – 'local initiative' as they called it in the U.S.S.R.

Where was this point of balance? It was not difficult by mathematical calculations to establish the social optimum for a capitalist economy. But that was a paper exercise. One was familiar with countless models, but none of them had been used in practice. Obviously, however, some economic basis other than that of complete freedom of initiative for all industrial enterprises was necessary. He himself was a partisan of the view that the basis should be social ownership of the means of production. Public ownership? Certainly, from the point of view of socialist development and economic transformation. Other forms were equally possible, including the co-operative form. But this was going beyond the subject matter of the conference.

He wanted to use the time available to him to reply to three groups of questions which had been asked. First a group of questions relating to the process of preparation of the plan. One began by establishing on the basis of the current objectives of domestic and external policy the essential targets that should be reached during the following quinquennium – and not, as was typical of Weastern planning by establishing final demand. With these objectives determined, the economic authorities sketched out an outline of a plan on the basis of the system of financial and material balances and of the trends of growth of particular branches. But though the objectives might be achieved according to this plan, it was not necessarily the optimal plan. Thus one prepared not only one but several variations of the plan. The enterprises, on their part, taking account of their own potentials and the directives (control figures) which they have received from the tutelary authorities, sent back to them their proposed levels of activity. Totalled under branches and factors, these plans were compared with the first variant of the general plan. The authorities then proceeded to attempt to reach financial equilibrium. It was on this preliminary basis that the final plan was elaborated and given the force of law.

Might he come next to the second group of questions, which had been concerned with the 'capital' charges that were imposed on enterprises in respect of the productive funds (or fixed funds) which they possessed. These charges reflected the relationship between the State, as collective owner of the means of production, on the one hand, and the enterprise as one element in that collectivity, on the other hand – the latter as the element to which the collectivity had entrusted the use of resources which were social property. The charge in respect of the funds employed was nothing more than an additional stimulus in the form of deduction from the net value added.

In principle the rate of charge which should be applied to the value – final or initial – of all funds, ought to be the same for all branches of the economy. But the imperfections of price determination forced them to vary the rates of charges (on the basis of final value) between 6 and 9 per cent. In many cases variations were made to take account of the special external circumstances of particular enterprises. These charges were, moreover, wholly distinct from any charges for amortisation, even if certain economists seemed to confuse them. Amortisation was a simple element in production and merely represented the replacement of wear and tear (if one disregarded the fact that provision for it was often badly calculated). In order to prevent an enterprise from using amortisation provisions to add to its own welfare funds, they were paid into a special bank account and were available only for planned financial expenditures or major renewals of equipment. The transfer of the funds reflected the relationship between the owners – the State – and the actual producers – the enterprise.

He came now to the question of pricing. The fixing of prices in socialist practice was related to the pattern of total production intended by the plan. The magnitude of the total social product being given, it was possible to calculate the price of a unit of production on the basis of the socially necessary costs. These depended on the pattern of social needs and the assumed rate of growth of productivity of labour. Such a method of calculation of prices made it possible to achieve a balance between money flows and goods produced. Obviously in this case prices were uniquely based on socially necessary costs. No purely market price could be regarded in this sense as providing a true basic price. This was what the Polish economists had pronounced in the discussion they had held on this issue.

At the same time, prices served the purpose of ensuring efficiency in production. That was to say that conditions of profitability (gains) emerged for those products for which costs had not yet reached the level of socially necessary expenses. This provided a very important stimulus to the creation of a pattern of production directly corresponding to the directive of the plan. It was in this sense that it was necessary to regard socialist prices as prices which interpreted the interests and needs of the whole society represented by the state.

None the less, since costs were calculated on the basis of given objective conditions of production, these prices gave an opportunity to enterprises, by reducing their costs, to increase their extra-plan profits, which in the cases of some branches of activity were partially available to raise their own funds to the extent of a fixed or declining share. In this way, the State was freeing enterprises from conjunctural fluctuations which were not the result of their own activities. At the same time, it was not making it possible for enterprises to enrich themselves irrespectively of their own efficiency. This meant that the role of price policy was limited to controlling the levels of socially necessary expenditures by such regulation of prices as would ensure a balance in the domestic market and a rate of growth that was practically possible.

SESSION TWENTY

Discussion of Professor Bauchet's Paper

Professor Zielinski, opening the discussion, said that Professor Bauchet had been primarily concerned with two issues: was there internal consistency? Could it be achieved by planning and prices? What were the causes of inconsistency? In medium- and short-term planning it was due to the fact that public enterprises formed the instrument of government intervention. The same was true of budgetary intervention and wage policy.

Professor Zielinski went on to discuss the reasons and occasions for such intervention. There were occasions when intervention was designed to modify the rate of growth. On other occasions it was designed to improve distributional justice. In some cases such intervention increased economic welfare. In some cases it operated against the trend of growth and did damage. He quoted examples from Soviet experience and Common Market experience of each. Professor Zielinski suggested that discussion might be primarily addressed to two main topics: first, how to identify the trend of growth; second, what the planning authority should do to promote it.

Professor Herschel wanted to distinguish more clearly short-term and long-term reasons for intervention.

Mr Kolm said that, unlike most current writing in France, Professor Bauchet's paper treated the optimal division between public and private activities not as an *a priori* political decision but as a matter for rational analysis. This suggested in many cases that private enterprise would be more efficient but public enterprise could introduce considerations of social justice, since the tariffs which might provide the best theoretical solutions came in conflict with political constraints or would affect the incentives to produce or save or reduce the efficiency of prices or charges. Colson in this context had shown many years before that discriminating monopoly, which under increasing returns gave the best solution of the level of activity, gave the worst solution on the basis of distributive justice. Professor Bauchet's paper provided another concrete example of this in the underground and suburban railways of Paris, the demand for which was even more inelastic than he had suggested, even hour-by-hour and day-by-day. A private concern would profit from this by establishing peak-hour charges, which turn out to be higher charges for those with lower average incomes. Such a tariff had been suggested a few years previously, and its distributive effects had led, as might be expected, to its rejection. One had to escape from the idea of an easily soluble problem or learn to study it in greater depth. For the problem was in fact a mixture of problems of efficiency posed by external factors and collective consumption and problems of distributive justice. The former, even if they implied a phenomenon of a collective economic character, were not necessarily better solved by the State than by some regional authority or by some private syndicate or association, the best choice depending on the costs of contact and securing agreement between those concerned and the members of the latter. The two elements were inextricably linked, as was shown by the problems of rent subsidy for large families. But it was important to distinguish the two conceptually in deciding how particular services should optimally be financed and conducted.

Professor Delivanis said that Professor Zielinski had suggested that the Conference should discuss the trends of Western economic policy in recent years and expressed doubts as to whether it was becoming more liberal. He thought he was mistaken in supposing that that had been the trend of policy in recent years, having regard to the recent nationalisation of electricity in Italy and of steel in the United Kingdom. He hoped Professor Bauchet would comment on this.

Professor Mossé, Mr Stoleru and *Professor Sandee* put further questions to Professor Bauchet regarding his interpretation of issues concerning distributive policy, wages policy and constraints imposed by the Treaty of Rome.

Professor Bauchet, replying, said that he hoped that his paper would not be interpreted as indicating any hostility to public enterprises. It would be truer to describe his attitude as one of affectionate irritation. The establishment of enterprises had been inspired by many illusions. One had hoped that the public enterprises would be sensitive to the guidance of the State and that the State would exercise its guidance in the light of a national interest which could easily be defined. In practice, quite apart from the difficulties of defining the national interest, the State had seemed to prove incapable of execising guidance over the public enterprise.

Index

Entries in the Index in Black Type under the Names of Participants in the conference indicate their Papers or Discussions of their Papers. Entries in Italics indicate Contributions by Participants to the Discussions.